Frommer's®
Vancouver & Victoria

My Vancouver & Victoria

by Donald Olson

I FEEL A FRESH SENSE OF ADVENTURE EVERY TIME I RETURN TO BUSY,

buzzing Vancouver. The backdrop of mountains, forests, and sea adds an unusual perspective to an urban landscape filled with soaring glass towers and an architectural sensibility more European than American. Vancouver—dubbed "Hollywood North" by some—is a new city, with an odd, appealing mixture of pioneer spirit and up-to-the-minute trendiness. Explore its neighborhoods and markets, and you'll pick up a distinct international vibe. But cultures don't clash here, they co-exist—each one contributing to the city's cosmopolitan flavor.

Victoria is another story—once so dowdy and dull that local cynics dubbed it a place for the newly wed and the nearly dead. But in the past few decades, the quaint capital of British Columbia has dusted itself off and rediscovered what has always made it so desirable: nature on a grand scale, and a city whose faded charms were ripe for a makeover. Today, Victoria is cozy and relaxing, a mini-maritime delight. Whether you come to watch whales, paddle a kayak, take tea at the venerable Empress Hotel, or stroll the century-old paths of Butchart Gardens (one of the greatest gardens in North America), you'll find Victoria to be an uncommonly pleasant place to visit. The photos in these pages show Vancouver and the surrounding region at its best.

© Floris Leeuwenberg/The Cover Story/Corbis

VANCOUVER AQUARIUM (left) An up-close and personal glimpse of a beluga whale in the icy-blue Arctic Canada exhibit at the Vancouver Aquarium Marine Science Center thrills landlubbers of all ages. For an extra fee, the aquarium also affords visitors the chance to help trainers feed the giant mammals throughout the day.

GASTOWN STEAM CLOCK (above) A quirky urban timepiece, the Steam Clock in Vancouver's historic Gastown gives a steamy rendition of the Westminster Chimes every 15 minutes, drawing its power from the underground steam-heat system. Vancouver's first neighborhood, established around a saloon, Gastown was razed in an 1886 fire, but now boasts some of the city's most fascinating architecture.

FIRST NATIONS TOTEM POLES (left):
Distinctive First Nations artwork is a living tradition throughout British Columbia. A stunning array of totem poles can be found in Vancouver—this one is in Stanley Park. Originally home to the Musqueam and Squamish nations, the park now boasts one of the city's largest collections of totem poles.

KITSILANO BEACH IN SUMMER (below) On warm, sunny days, Vancouver turns into a beach town, Northwest-style. There are many beaches to choose from, but Kitsilano is one of the grooviest. If you get tired of the beach, the adjacent Boho Kits neighborhood is a joy to explore.

BUTCHART GARDENS IN SUMMER (above)
One of the great landscaping feats in North America, the 20-hectare (50-acre) Butchart Gardens—just north of downtown Victoria—can be visited year-round. Displaying more than a million plants throughout the year, the gardens—still under the care of the Butchart family a century after their creation—are a national treasure.

COFFEE AT CAFFE ARTIGIANO (right) No doubt about it: Vancouver's on a coffee buzz. Cafes, coffeehouses, and caffeine are a way of life here. The art of coffee has been perfected at Caffè Artigiano, where your latte comes with a design in the foam.

LIGHTHOUSE ON VANCOUVER ISLAND
(above) On a rocky bluff overlooking the Strait of Georgia stands the Point Atkinson Lighthouse. This lighthouse, in West Vancouver's Lighthouse Park, is just one of about 40 that still survive along Vancouver Island's rugged and scenic coastline.

GREAT BEAR RAINFOREST (right) Great Bear Rainforest on the western coast of Vancouver Island protects a magnificent swath of old-growth temperate rainforest, one of the last places in North America where several bear species—grizzly, black, and the rare Kermode, or spirit bear—thrive.

THE EMPRESS HOTEL Yes, it's touristy and expensive, but tea at the magnificent Empress is a must for visitors to Victoria. You'll be pleasantly pampered and shamelessly stuffed as an assortment of cakes, sandwiches, and scones with clotted cream appears—and disappears—at your table.

WHISTLER (above) For what many consider the best skiing in North America, take the spectacular scenic Sea-to-Sky highway to Whistler Resort, just 2 hours north of Vancouver. Chosen as the site of the 2010 Winter Olympics, Whistler is a world unto itself. In the winter, you can ski from your hotel right to the slopes; in summer, the ski slopes are converted into a world-class mountain bike course.

SCENE AT STORYEUM (right) History and theater mix at Storyeum, Vancouver's newest and most entertaining attraction. Costumed actors lead you into environments that recreate dramatic highlights from the history of the Pacific Northwest and the founding of Vancouver.

DR. SUN YAT-SEN CLASSICAL CHINESE GARDEN (right) One of Vancouver's hidden treasures, the Dr. Sun Yat-sen Classical Chinese Garden reflects the timeless tranquillity and painstaking artistry found in Taoist-inspired Chinese gardens.

SCIENCE WORLD BRITISH COLUMBIA (below) The big, blinking geodesic dome on the eastern end of False Creek, built for the Expo '86 World's Fair, is the appropriate home to Vancouver's science museum. Hands-on adventures—plus a giant-screen Omnimax theater—give visitors to Science World British Columbia a fresh look at the world around them and how it works.

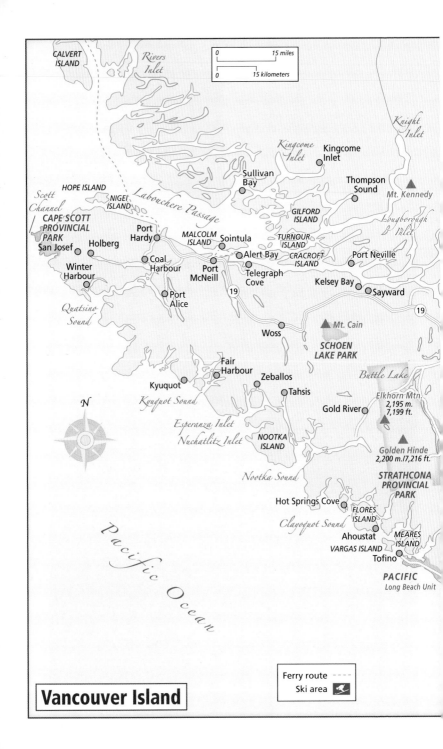

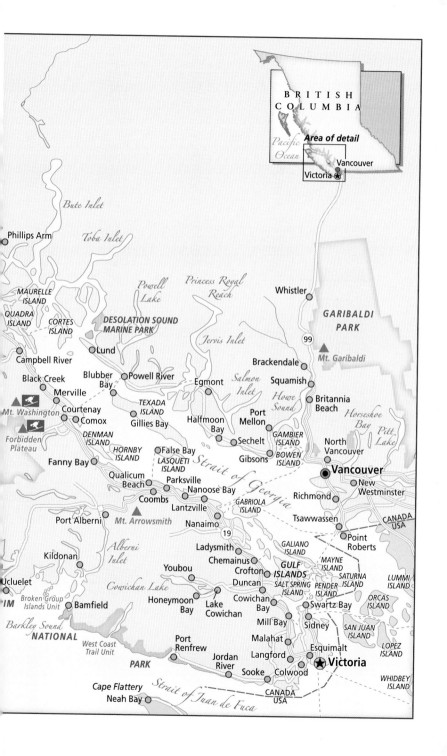

BRITISH COLUMBIA

Pacific Ocean

Area of detail

Vancouver

Victoria ⊛

Bute Inlet

Toba Inlet

Phillips Arm

Powell Lake

Princess Royal Reach

Whistler

MAURELLE ISLAND

QUADRA ISLAND

CORTES ISLAND

DESOLATION SOUND MARINE PARK

Jervis Inlet

GARIBALDI PARK

Mt. Garibaldi

Lund

Campbell River

Black Creek

Blubber Bay

Powell River

Egmont

Salmon Inlet

Brackendale

Squamish

99

Merville

Mt. Washington

Courtenay

Comox

TEXADA ISLAND

Gillies Bay

Halfmoon Bay

Port Mellon

Howe Sound

Britannia Beach

Horseshoe Bay

Pitt Lake

Forbidden Plateau

DENMAN ISLAND

HORNBY ISLAND

False Bay

Sechelt

GAMBIER ISLAND

North Vancouver

Fanny Bay

LASQUETI ISLAND

Gibsons

BOWEN ISLAND

Qualicum Beach

Parksville

Strait of Georgia

Vancouver

New Westminster

Coombs

Nanoose Bay

Richmond

Port Alberni

Mt. Arrowsmith

Lantzville

GABRIOLA ISLAND

Tsawwassen

CANADA USA

Nanaimo

19

Point Roberts

Kildonan

Alberni Inlet

Ladysmith

GALIANO ISLAND

Youbou

Chemainus

MAYNE ISLAND

LUMMI ISLAND

Ucluelet

Crofton

GULF ISLANDS

SATURNA ISLAND

Broken Group Islands Unit

IM

Bamfield

Cowichan Lake

Duncan

SALT SPRING ISLAND

PENDER ISLAND

ORCAS ISLAND

Honeymoon Bay

Lake Cowichan

Cowichan Bay

Swartz Bay

Barkley Sound

NATIONAL

Mill Bay

Sidney

SAN JUAN ISLAND

West Coast Trail Unit

Port Renfrew

Malahat

Esquimalt

LOPEZ ISLAND

PARK

Jordan River

Langford

Victoria ★

Sooke

Colwood

WHIDBEY ISLAND

Cape Flattery

Neah Bay

Strait of Juan de Fuca

CANADA USA

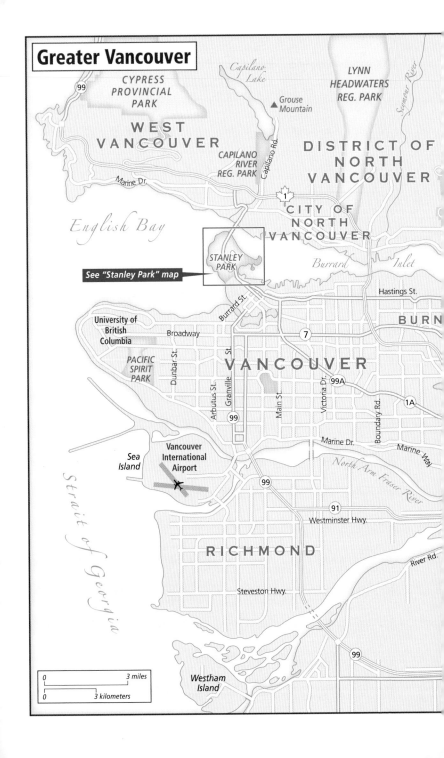

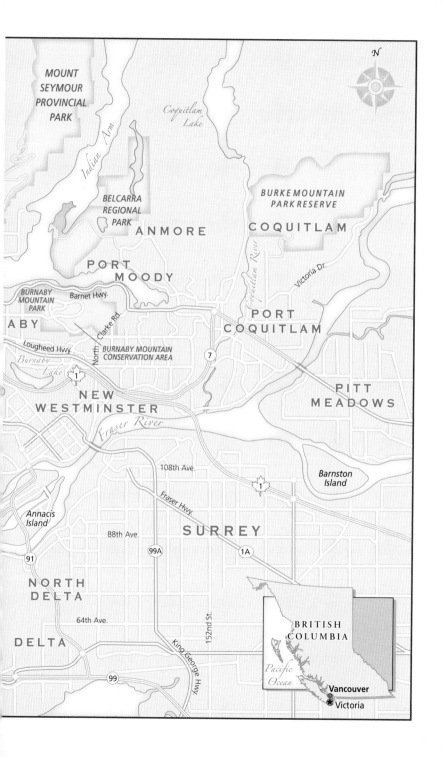

MOUNT
SEYMOUR
PROVINCIAL
PARK

Coquitlam
Lake

Indian Arm

BELCARRA
REGIONAL
PARK

BURKE MOUNTAIN
PARK RESERVE

ANMORE

COQUITLAM

PORT
MOODY

Coquitlam River

Victoria Dr.

BURNABY
MOUNTAIN
PARK

Barnet Hwy.

PORT
COQUITLAM

ABY

Lougheed Hwy.

North Clarke Rd.

BURNABY MOUNTAIN
CONSERVATION AREA

7

Burnaby
Lake

1

NEW
WESTMINSTER

PITT
MEADOWS

Fraser River

108th Ave.

Barnston
Island

Annacis
Island

1

Fraser Hwy.

88th Ave.

99A

SURREY

1A

91

NORTH
DELTA

64th Ave.

152nd St.

BRITISH
COLUMBIA

DELTA

King George Hwy.

Pacific
Ocean

99

Vancouver

Victoria

Stanley Park

Ferguson Point **17**
Fish House Restaurant **20**
Girl in a Wet Suit statue **10**
Hollow Tree/Geographic Tree **15**
Horse-drawn Carriage Rides **4**
Hummingbird Trail/Malkin Bowl **3**
Japanese Monument **6**
Mallard Trail/Brockton Oval **8**
Nature Center **1**
Prospect Point **13**
Ravine Trail/ Beaver Lake **12**
Second Beach **19**
Siwash Rock **14**
Teahouse Restaurant **18**
Third Beach **16**
Totem Poles **9**
Vancouver Aquarium & Marine
  Science Center **7**
Vancouver Children's Zoo/
Variety Kids Farmyard **5**
Vancouver Rowing Club **2**
Variety Kids Water Park **11**

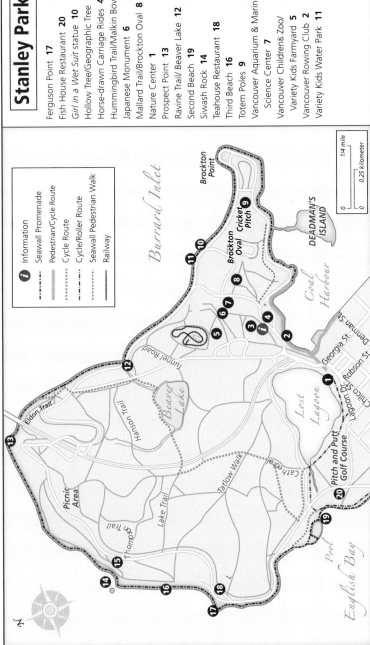

Downtown Victoria

Abkhazi Gardens **20**
Art Gallery of Greater Victoria **18**
British Columbia Aviation Museum **5**
Butchart Gardens **4**
Craigdarroch Castle **19**
Crystal Garden **14**
Dominion Astrophysical Laboratory **5**
Emily Carr House **16**
The Fairmont Empress **11**
Fort Rodd Hill & Fisgard Lighthouse **3**
Hatley Park Castle and Museum **1**
Helmcken House **15**
Maritime Museum of British Columbia **7**
Market Square **6**
Miniature World **10**
Mount Douglas Park **5**
Pacific Undersea Gardens **9**
Parliament Buildings (Provincial Legislature) **12**
Point Ellice House **2**
Ross Bay Cemetery **21**
Royal British Columbia Museum **13**
Royal London Wax Museum **8**
Trans-Canada Highway Mile 0 **17**

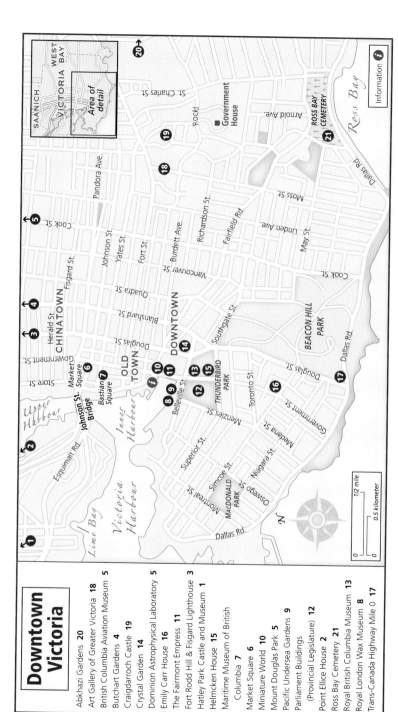

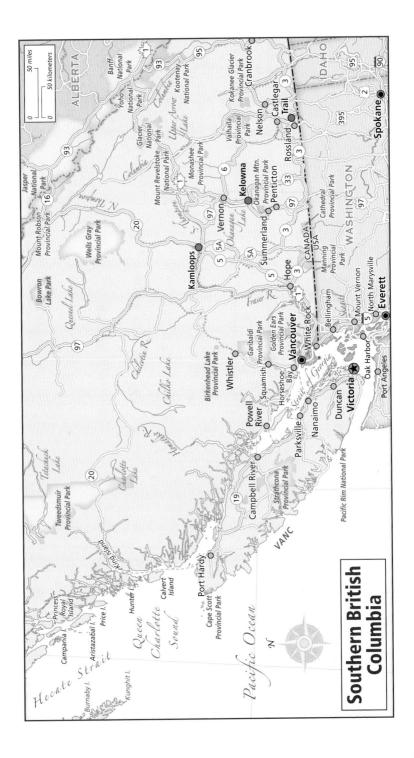

Southern British Columbia

Frommer's®

Vancouver & Victoria

2006

by Donald Olson

with coverage of Whistler

Here's what the critics say about Frommer's:

"Amazingly easy to use. Very portable, very complete."

—*Booklist*

"Detailed, accurate, and easy-to-read information for all price ranges."
—*Glamour Magazine*

"Hotel information is close to encyclopedic."

—*Des Moines Sunday Register*

"Frommer's Guides have a way of giving you a real feel for a place."
—*Knight Ridder Newspapers*

WILEY

Wiley Publishing, Inc.

Published by:

Wiley Publishing, Inc.

111 River St.
Hoboken, NJ 07030-5774

ISBN-13: 978-0-7645-8928-7
ISBN-10: 0-7645-8928-8

Editor: Naomi Black
Production Editor: Katie Robinson
Cartographer: Tim Lohnes
Photo Editor: Richard Fox
Production by Wiley Indianapolis Composition Services

Front cover photo: Vancouver City from aerial perspective
Back cover photo: Victoria: Butchart Gardens on Vancouver Island

For information on our other products and services or to obtain technical support, please contact our Customer Care Department within the U.S. at 800/762-2974, outside the U.S. at 317/572-3993 or fax 317/572-4002.

Wiley also publishes its books in a variety of electronic formats. Some content that appears in print may not be available in electronic formats.

Manufactured in the United States of America

5 4 3 2 1

Contents

List of Maps

An Invitation to the Reader

In researching this book, we discovered many wonderful places—hotels, restaurants, shops, and more. We're sure you'll find others. Please tell us about them, so we can share the information with your fellow travelers in upcoming editions. If you were disappointed with a recommendation, we'd love to know that, too. Please write to:

Frommer's Vancouver & Victoria 2006
Wiley Publishing, Inc. • 111 River St. • Hoboken, NJ 07030-5774

An Additional Note

Please be advised that travel information is subject to change at any time—and this is especially true of prices. We therefore suggest that you write or call ahead for confirmation when making your travel plans. The authors, editors, and publisher cannot be held responsible for the experiences of readers while traveling. Your safety is important to us, however, so we encourage you to stay alert and be aware of your surroundings. Keep a close eye on cameras, purses, and wallets, all favorite targets of thieves and pickpockets.

About the Author

Donald Olson is a novelist, playwright, and travel writer. He has published several novels, most recently *The Confessions of Aubrey Beardsley* and, under the pen name of Swan Adamson, *My Three Husbands* and *Confessions of a Pregnant Princess*. His plays have been staged in the U.S. and Europe. Donald Olson's travel stories have appeared in *The New York Times*, *Travel & Leisure*, *Sunset*, *National Geographic* books, and many other publications. He is the author of *England For Dummies* (winner of the 2002 Lowell Thomas Travel Writing Award for Best Guidebook), *London For Dummies*, *Germany For Dummies*, *Frommer's London from $95 a Day*, *Frommer's Portable London from $95 a Day*, and *Frommer's Irreverent Guide to London*.

Other Great Guides for Your Trip:

Frommer's Irreverent Guide to Vancouver

Frommer's Vancouver with Kids

Frommer's British Columbia & the Canadian Rockies

Frommer's Canada

Vancouver & Victoria For Dummies

The Unofficial Guide to Bed & Breakfasts and Country Inns in the Northwest

Frommer's Star Ratings, Icons & Abbreviations

Every hotel, restaurant, and attraction listing in this guide has been ranked for quality, value, service, amenities, and special features using a **star-rating system.** In country, state, and regional guides, we also rate towns and regions to help you narrow down your choices and budget your time accordingly. Hotels and restaurants are rated on a scale of zero (recommended) to three stars (exceptional). Attractions, shopping, nightlife, towns, and regions are rated according to the following scale: zero stars (recommended), one star (highly recommended), two stars (very highly recommended), and three stars (must-see).

In addition to the star-rating system, we also use **seven feature icons** that point you to the great deals, in-the-know advice, and unique experiences that separate travelers from tourists. Throughout the book, look for:

Finds	Special finds—those places only insiders know about
Fun Fact	Fun facts—details that make travelers more informed and their trips more fun
Kids	Best bets for kids and advice for the whole family
Moments	Special moments—those experiences that memories are made of
Overrated	Places or experiences not worth your time or money
Tips	Insider tips—great ways to save time and money
Value	Great values—where to get the best deals

The following **abbreviations** are used for credit cards:

AE	American Express	DISC	Discover	V	Visa
DC	Diners Club	MC	MasterCard		

Frommers.com

Now that you have the guidebook to a great trip, visit our website at **www.frommers.com** for travel information on more than 3,000 destinations. With features updated regularly, we give you instant access to the most current trip-planning information available. At Frommers.com, you'll also find the best prices on airfares, accommodations, and car rentals—and you can even book travel online through our travel booking partners. At Frommers.com, you'll also find the following:

- Online updates to our most popular guidebooks
- Vacation sweepstakes and contest giveaways
- Newsletter highlighting the hottest travel trends
- Online travel message boards with featured travel discussions

What's New in Vancouver & Victoria

In the summer of 2003, Vancouver was awarded hosting rights to the 2010 Olympic Winter Games. Preparations are already underway, and the excitement in the city (where the skating events will be held) and at Whistler Resort (where the skiing and snow events will take place) is palpable. Prices for restaurants and hotels are sure to go up, but right now, fabulous restaurants and accommodations remain a steal in Vancouver and Victoria, compared to Toronto, Montreal, or any big city in the U.S.

VANCOUVER   Accommodations Always a top choice for cruise-ship passengers who want harbor-front accommodations, the **Pan Pacific Hotel Vancouver** (300–999 Canada Place; ℂ **800/937-1515** or 604/662-8111), conveniently located directly atop the Canada Place cruise ship terminal, now has a new spa featuring a whole range of aesthetic services and a giant new fitness facility in addition to its scenically splendid outdoor pool and hot tub.

Vancouver's newest and coolest boutique hotel, the **Opus Hotel** (322 Davie St.; ℂ **866/642-6787** or 604/642-6787) has also added a small new fitness room with big people-watching windows, and a convenient business center; both facilities are free for guests.

The Beachside Bed & Breakfast on the North Shore, one of the nicest B&Bs in Vancouver, closed in 2004. In 2005, Joan Gibbs, the proprietor, relocated the B&B to a brand-new house in a tony part of West Vancouver and renamed it **Beachside City View Bed & Breakfast** (1180 Renton Place, West Vancouver, B.C. V7S 2K7; ℂ **800/563-3311** or 604/922-7773). The rooms have lovely panoramic views of Burrards Inlet and downtown.

Dining Vancouver's dining scene continues to flourish. In 2005, the always-fabulous **West** (2881 Granville St; ℂ **604/738-8938**) won Vancouver Magazine's prestigious Best Restaurant award. Chef David Hawksworth won top honors as Best Chef.

Winner of Vancouver Magazine's 2005 readers' award for Best New Restaurant, **Chambar** (562 Beatty St.; ℂ **604/879-7119**) is the love child of Michelin-trained chef Nico Scheuerman and his wife Karri. Focusing on Belgian food (and beers), they've crafted a menu that features small and large plates that emphasize fresh local seafood and game.

Coast (1257 Hamilton St.; ℂ **604/685-5010**) is a trendy new hangout where you can find all manner of seafood from exotic coasts around the world, superlatively served up in a loft-style dining room; a dozen lucky diners can request to be seated around the chef's kitchen and receive a special menu prepared inches away.

Everyone's talking about the glamorous new Coal Harbour hot-spot **Lift** (333 Menchions Mews; ℂ **604/689-5438**), built on piers behind the Westin Bayshore Resort and offering the most dramatic views in town, as well as such luxe features as an illuminated onyx bar. The food has yet to impress, but the scene is hot, hot, hot on weekends.

Rob Feenie, chef and proprietor of the legendary **Lumière** (2551 W. Broadway; ✆ **604/739-8185**), considered by many to be Vancouver's top French restaurant, can't seem to sit still, and with so much success coming his way, why should he? Diners will notice a newly renovated dining room and kitchen.

Attractions   Vancouver's newest all-ages attraction, **Storyeum** (165A Water St.; ✆ **800/687-8142** or 604/687-8142), opened in 2004 in the historic Gastown area. This unique underground venue uses a series of theaters, elaborate stage sets, live performers, and state-of-the-art special effects and lighting to tell the history of Vancouver and British Columbia. The show has been revamped to feature more musical numbers and remains a top-notch way to learn about Vancouver's history.

Nightlife   The arty West End boutique hotel **Listel Vancouver** (1300 Robson St.; ✆ 800/663-5491 or 604/684-8461), long a late-night jazz venue, was named the official after-hours jamming headquarters for the Vancouver Jazz Festival. Year-round, top jazz artists perform on weekends in the hotel's intimate bar/lounge.

VICTORIA Accommodations   Just 20 minutes north of downtown Victoria, overlooking a pristine fjord with old-growth forest all around, the **Brentwood Bay Lodge & Spa** (849 Verdier Ave.; ✆ **888/544-2079** or 250/544-2079) opened in 2004 and is gathering kudos. A member of the Small Luxury Hotels of the World group, it features gorgeously styled rooms with handcrafted furniture, First Nations artwork, and spa-like bathrooms

with deep soaker tubs and separate showers. The spa, called Essence of Life, is one of the finest on the West Coast.

Dining Arbutus Grille and Winebar (849 Verdier Ave.; ✆ **888/544-2079** or 250/544-5100), in the gorgeous Brentwood Bay Lodge and Spa, was on Vancouver Magazine's list of "Best New Restaurants" of 2005. The Pacific Northwest cuisine changes daily, that's how fresh it is.

Attractions   Improvements to an old logging road have resulted in the new **Pacific Marine Circle Tour**. The 52-km (32-mile) loop road, which opened in 2005, makes it easier to get to Port Renfrew, Sooke, Jordan River, and Lake Cowichan on a day-long circular tour. For details, check with the **Tourism Victoria Visitor Info Centre** (812 Wharf St.; ✆ **800/663-3883**; www.tourism victoria.com).

SIDE TRIPS Whistler   In June, 2004, a stunning new **Four Seasons Resort Whistler** (4591 Blackcomb Way; ✆ **888/935-2460** or 604/935-3400) opened in the Upper Village and immediately set a new standard for luxury and service. In 2005 the Four Seasons Private Residences opened, giving families an alternative to the traditional hotel guestroom. Visitors can now choose to stay in one of 37 luxury Private Residences that complete the Four Seasons' offerings of 273 guest rooms and suites.

Ucluelet, Tofino & Pacific Rim National Park Reserve of Canada   The fish tacos at Lisa Ahier's lunch truck parked in the Tofino Botanical Gardens are legendary, and the demand was so great that she set up **Sobo** (1184 Pacific Rim Hwy.; ✆ **250/725-4265**), a sit-down restaurant where dinner is served 5 nights a week.

The Best of Vancouver & Victoria

If you really want to understand **Vancouver,** stand at the edge of the Inner Harbour (the Canada Place cruise-ship terminal makes a good vantage point) and look around you. To the west you'll see Stanley Park, one of the world's largest urban parks, jutting out into the waters of Burrard Inlet. To the north, just across the inlet, rise snow-capped mountains. To the east, right along the water, is the low-rise brick-faced Old Town. And almost everything else you see lining the water's edge will be a new glass-and-steel high-rise tower. As giant cruise ships glide in to berth, floatplanes buzz in and out, and your ears catch a medley of foreign tongues, you may wonder just where on earth you are. Vancouver is majestic and intimate, sophisticated and completely laid back, a bustling, prosperous, world-class city that somehow, almost miraculously, manages to combine its contemporary, urban-centered consciousness with the free-spirited magnificence of nature on a grand scale.

Vancouver is probably one of the "newest" cities you'll ever visit, and certainly it's one of the most cosmopolitan. There's a youthfulness, too, a certain Pacific Northwest chic (and cheek) that comes from being used in so many movies that Vancouver is sometimes called "Hollywood North." I can guarantee you that part of your trip will be spent puzzling out what makes it so unique, so livable and lovable, what gives it such a buzz. Nature figures big in that equation, but so does enlightened city planning and the diversity of cultures. Vancouver is a place where people *want* to live. It's a place that awakens dreams and desires.

The city's history is in its topography. Thousands of years ago, a giant glacier sliced along the foot of the coast range, carving out a deep trench and piling up a gigantic moraine of rock and sand. When the ice retreated, water from the Pacific flowed in and the moraine became a peninsula, flanked on one side by a deep natural harbor (today's Inner Harbour) and on the other by a river of glacial meltwater (today called the Fraser River). Vast forests of fir and cedar covered the land and wildlife flourished. The First Nations tribes that settled in the area developed rich cultures based on cedar and salmon.

Some 10,000 years later, a surveyor for the Canadian Pacific Railroad came by, took in the peninsula, the harbor, and the river, and decided he'd found the perfect spot for the CPR's new Pacific terminus. He kept it quiet, as smart railway men tended to do, until the company had bought up most of the land around town. Then the railway moved in, set up shop, and the city of Vancouver was born.

Working indoors, Vancouverites have seemingly all fallen in love with the outdoors. And why shouldn't they? Every terrain needed for every kind of outdoor pursuit—hiking, in-line skating, mountain biking, downhill and cross-country skiing, kayaking, windsurfing, rock climbing, parasailing, snowboarding—is right there in their back-yard: ocean, rivers, mountains, islands, sidewalks. The international resort town of Whistler, which will take center stage during the Winter Olympics in 2010, is just two hours north of downtown Vancouver.

And when they're not skiing or kayaking, they're drinking coffee or eating out. In the past decade or so, Vancouver has become one of the top restaurant cities in the world, bursting with an incredible variety of cuisines and making an international name for itself with its unique Pacific Northwest cooking. The new food mantra here is "buy locally, eat seasonally."

The rest of the world has taken notice of the blessed life people in these parts lead. The World Council of Cities ranked Vancouver second only to Geneva for quality of life (and who wants to live in Geneva?). Surveys generally list it as one of the 10 best cities in the world to live in. It's also one of the 10 best to visit, according to *Condé Nast Traveler.* And in 2003, the International Olympic Committee awarded Vancouver the right to host the 2010 Olympic Winter Games. Heady stuff, particularly for a spot that less than 20 years ago was routinely derided as the world's biggest mill town.

Though some "heritage buildings" still remain in Vancouver, the face of the city you see today is undeniably new. Starting in the 1960s, misguided planners and develop-ers seemed intent on demolishing every last vestige of the city's pioneer past, replac-ing old brick and wood buildings with an array of undistinguished concrete high-rises and blocky eyesores. Citizen outcry finally got the bulldozers to stop their rampage. Luckily, landscaping and gardening was an ingrained part of life in this mild climate, so plants and trees and shrubs were not uprooted for endless parking lots. You may be amazed, in fact, by the amount of green and the number of fountains and the overall lushness of neighborhoods like the West End, which also happens to be one of the most densely populated areas in the world. A building boom preceded Expo '86 and followed it as well, spurred on by enormous amounts of cash pouring in from Hong Kong and Asia. The new towers, made of glass and steel, are much lighter looking and seem more in keeping with the hip, international image that Vancouver is developing for itself.

If you miss the old in Vancouver, you'll find plenty of it in **Victoria,** some 80km (50 miles) across the Strait of Georgia on Vancouver Island. Victoria took the oppo-site approach from Vancouver and preserved nearly all its heritage buildings. As a con-sequence, Victoria, beautifully sited on its own Inner Harbour, is one of the most charming small cities you'll ever find (it has about 325,000 residents in the Greater Victoria area, compared to around 2 million in Vancouver). Since it's on an island, accessible only by ferry (the best way to go) or floatplane, a more leisurely sense of time prevails in Victoria. It's a perfect antidote for stressed-out mainlanders.

For years Victoria marketed itself quite successfully as a little bit of England on the North American continent. So successful was the colonial sales pitch, residents began to believe it themselves. They began growing elaborate rose gardens, which flourished in the mild Pacific climate, and they cultivated a taste for afternoon tea with jam and scones. They were islanders ruled by the mother island from which all culture emanated and was exported.

For decades, this continued, until eventually it was discovered that not many resi-dents of Victoria shared a taste for bad English cooking, so restaurants branched out into seafood, ethnic, and fusion. And lately, as visitors have shown more interest in exploring the natural world, Victoria has added whale-watching and mountain-biking trips to its traditional London-style double-decker bus tours. The result is that Victoria is the only city in the world where you can zoom out on a boat in the morning to see a pod of killer whales, and make it back in time for an expansive afternoon tea. Once the people of Victoria saw the glories all around them instead of those reflected from a dying Empire, the place became a lot more interesting. It's a lot quieter and ten times more laid-back than Vancouver, but that's part of its peculiar charm. And if you add the Butchart Gardens, a truly world-class garden that celebrated its centenary in 2004, and the fabulous First Nations art collection in the Royal B.C. Museum, you've got all you need for a memorable holiday just 90 minutes from the big city.

1 The Most Unforgettable Travel Experiences: Vancouver

- **Taking a Carriage Ride through Stanley Park:** One of the largest urban parks in the world, and certainly one of the most beautiful, Stanley Park is nothing short of magnificent. You can sample the highlights on a delightful 1-hour carriage ride that winds through the forest, along Burrard Inlet, past cricket fields, rose gardens, and the park's superlative collection of First Nations totem poles. See p. 116.
- **Wandering the West End:** Encompassing the *über*-shopping strip known as Robson Street, as well as cafe-lined Denman and a forest of high-rise apartments, the West End is the urban heart of Vancouver. Enjoy the lush trees lining the streets, the range of architecture, the diversity of cultures, the latest fashions and *fashionistas,* and the neat little surprises on every side street. See Walking Tour 1, p. 145.
- **Dining Out on Local Seafood:** Visitors are rightly amazed at the abundance of fresh-that-day seafood available in Vancouver's restaurants. This is a city where an appetizer of raw oysters often precedes a main course of wild salmon or halibut. See chapter 6.
- **Dining Out, Period:** The number of truly outstanding restaurants in Vancouver is astonishing, and the prices are ridiculously low when compared to other food capitals. A meal at one

of Vancouver's top restaurants will wake you up to the glories of the food scene here, and you'll find extraordinary tastes for every budget in chapter 6.
- **Visiting the Vancouver Aquarium:** It's a Jacques Cousteau special, live and right there in front of you. Fittingly enough, the aquarium has an excellent display on the Pacific Northwest, plus sea otters (cuter than they have any right to be), beluga whales, sea lions, and a Pacific white-sided dolphin. See p. 118.
- **Exploring Chinatown:** Fishmongers call out their wares before a shop filled with crabs, eels, geoducks, and bullfrogs, while farther down the street elderly Chinese women haggle over produce as their husbands hunt for deer antler or dried sea horse at a traditional Chinese herbalist. When you're tired of looking and listening, head inside to any one of a dozen restaurants to sample succulent Cantonese cooking. See chapter 6 and Walking Tour 2, p. 150.
- **Marveling at First Nations Artwork in the Museum of Anthropology:** The building—by native son Arthur Erickson—would be worth a visit in itself, but this is also one of the best places in the world to see and learn about West Coast First Nations art and culture. See p. 123.
- **Browsing the Public Market on Granville Island:** Down on False

Southern British Columbia

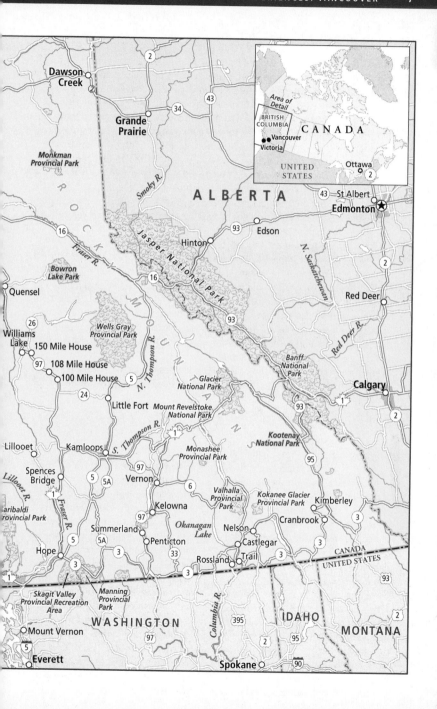

A Short History of First Nations

When Captain Vancouver arrived in English Bay in 1792, there were more than 50 First Nations living in what is now British Columbia, speaking about 30 languages from six distinct language families.

Exactly where each tribe lived, when they arrived, and how many members each had is all now a matter of some controversy, but evidence suggests that the area had been settled for some 9,000 to 10,000 years. One hundred percent of the province's land area is now claimed by one or more First Nations. Negotiations are proceeding slowly: One of the most important aspects of any claim is a band's oral tradition. The stories and legends about where a band came from, what lands it occupied, and how and where it gathered food are thus not just stories and legends; in certain circumstances they are considered the equivalent of legal documents, with their content and ownership a huge issue.

Living in the rainforest, all of these coastal peoples developed an extremely rich and complex culture, using cedar as their primary building material and, for food, harvesting marine resources such as herring, shellfish, and especially salmon. The richness of the local environment allowed these peoples ample surplus; their spare time was devoted to the creation of stories and art. Now undergoing a revival, coastal art, whether in wood or glass or precious metals, usually depicts stylized figures from native mythology, including such universal figures as the Raven, or tribal totems, such as the Bear, Frog, or Killer Whale.

The central ceremony of the coastal First Nations was and is the potlatch, a gathering of tribes held to mark a significant event such as the raising of

Creek, this former industrial site was long ago converted into a truly eye-popping and sense-staggering indoor public market. Hop on the miniferry at the foot of Davie Street in Yaletown and in 10 minutes you'll be there. At the market you'll find incredible food and goodies; put together a picnic and sit outside by the wharf to people- or boat-watch as you nosh. See p. 167.

- **Kayaking on Indian Arm:** Vancouver is one of the few cities on the edge of a great wilderness, and one of the best ways to appreciate its splendor is by kayaking on the gorgeous Indian Arm. Rent a kayak or go with a company—they may even serve you a gourmet meal of barbecued salmon.

See "Outdoor Activities" in chapter 7, p. 134.

- **Discovering the Paintings of Emily Carr at the Vancouver Art Gallery:** It's always a thrill to discover a great artist, and Emily Carr's work hauntingly captures the primal appeal of B.C.'s rugged, rain- and wave-washed forests and shores. See p. 134.
- **Crossing the Capilano Suspension Bridge:** Stretched across a deep forested canyon, high above old trees and a rushing river, this famous pedestrian-only suspension bridge has been daring visitors to look down for over a hundred years. Now you can explore the giant forest trees, too, on a series of artfully constructed treewalks. See p. 125.

a totem pole or the coming of age of a son or daughter. Invited tribes sing and dance traditional songs (which are considered to be their private property), while the host, both to thank his guests and to demonstrate his wealth, gives away presents. At the end of the 19th century, when First Nations culture—supported by a flood of wealth from the sea otter trade—reached unprecedented heights, potlatches could last for days, and chiefs would give away all they had.

The sea otter debacle aside (encouraged by American and British fur traders, coastal natives hunted sea otters to extinction along most of the coast), coastal indigenous peoples were exemplary environmental managers. Pre-contact, First Nations society was divided into a nobility of chiefly families, commoners, and slaves, the latter mostly war captives taken during raids.

In the years post-contact, the coastal First Nations were decimated by diseases such as smallpox (it's estimated that some 10,000 people lived along the coastal waterways and all but 600 of them were killed by smallpox carried by white settlers), by the loss of traditional fishing rights, by the repression of traditional rituals such as the potlatch, and by the forced assimilation into English-Canadian culture. In the decades after World War II, an entire generation of native children was forced into residential schools where speaking native languages and learning native stories were forbidden. The 1980s and 1990s were periods of long and slow recovery. Though still beset by problems, the First Nations communities are on their way back to becoming a powerful and important force on the B.C. coast.

- **Watching the Sunset from a Waterside Patio:** Why else live in a city with such stunning views? Many places on False Creek, English Bay, and Coal Harbour have great waterside patios.

For something different, head to the North Shore, where you don't get to see mountains, but you get stunning city views. See chapter 7.

2 The Most Unforgettable Travel Experiences: Victoria

- **Strolling Victoria's Inner Harbour:** Watch the boats and aquatic wildlife come and go while walking along a paved pathway that winds past manicured flower gardens. The best stretch runs south from the Inner Harbour near the Government Buildings, past Undersea World, the Royal London Wax Museum, and the Seattle ferry dock. See p. 241.

- **Savoring Afternoon Tea:** Yes, it's expensive and incredibly touristy, but it's also a complicated and ritual-laden art form that goes on for at least an hour. Besides, it's good. See p. 216.
- **Catching the Fireworks at Butchart Gardens:** This world-class garden 20 minutes north of downtown Victoria is an absolutely must-see attraction. Gorgeous during the day and subtly illuminated on summer evenings, it

takes on a whole new personality when the famous fireworks begin. Saturday nights in the summertime at Butchart Gardens, you get both. See p. 224.

- **Touring the Royal B.C. Museum:** One of the best small museums in the world, the Royal B.C. does exactly what a good regional museum should do—explain the region and its people. The First Nations galleries are breathtaking reminders of the richness of native culture. See p. 226.

- **Whale-Watching:** Of all the species of orcas (killer whales), those on the Washington and B.C. coasts are the only ones that live in large and complicated extended families. This makes Victoria a particularly good spot to whale-watch because the orcas

travel in large, easy-to-find pods. There's something magical about being out on the water and seeing a pod of 15 animals surface just a few hundred meters away. See "Whale-Watching in chapter 14, p. 240.

- **Touring by Miniferry:** Catch a Victoria Harbour Ferry and take a 45-minute tour around the harbor past the floating neighborhood of West Bay or up the gorge, where tidal waterfalls reverse direction with the changing tide. Moonlight tours depart every evening at sunset. See "Getting Around," in chapter 11, and "Organized Tours," in chapter 14.

- **Biking the Dallas Road to Willows Bay:** Where else can you find a bike path by an ocean with high mountain peaks for a backdrop? See p. 250.

3 The Most Unforgettable Travel Experiences beyond Vancouver & Victoria

- **Skiing and Mountain Biking at Whistler and Blackcomb Resorts:** Why ski anywhere else? The best resorts in North America merged for a total of more than 200 runs on two adjoining mountains, and full-day lift passes are as low as C$59 (US$47) for adults. In the summer, the same slopes become a world-class mountain bike network. See chapter 18.

- **Ziptrekking at Whistler:** Once you're strapped into your safety harness, you're hooked onto cables suspended hundreds of feet above a wild river, leap off, and away you go. Safe for everyone from eight to eighty, Ziptrek is an exhilarating adventure that you'll never forget. See p. 283.

- **Looking for Bald Eagles in Squamish:** The bald eagle is the national symbol of the United States, but in winter, when the salmon are running, you can see more of these huge birds in Squamish than just about anywhere else in the world. See "Wildlife-Watching," in chapter 7, p. 142.

- **Discovering Pacific Rim National Park:** The drive to this rugged maritime park on Vancouver Island's west coast is stunning, and once there, you're in a world of old-growth temperate rainforests and surf-pounded beaches. It's a place where you can experience the primal glories of nature amid the pampering luxuries of a first-class resort. See chapter 18.

4 The Best Splurge Hotels: Vancouver

For a complete description of these and other Vancouver accommodations, see chapter 5.

- **Fairmont Hotel Vancouver** (900 W. Georgia St.; © **800/441-1414** or 604/684-3131): A landmark in the heart of Vancouver, this grand hotel was built by the Canadian Pacific Railway and opened in 1939. The château-style exterior, the lobby, and even the rooms—now thoroughly restored—are built in a style and on a scale reminiscent of the great European railway hotels. See p. 64.

- **Opus Hotel** (322 Davie St.; ☎ **866/ 642-6787** or 604/642-6787): A contemporary boutique hotel that's cool without the attitude, Opus has an offbeat location in Yaletown, an array of room types, luscious room colors and finishes, and a luxurious but nontraditional aesthetic—plus good dining. See p. 68.

- **Pacific Palisades Hotel** (1277 Robson St.; ☎ **800/663-1815** or 604/ 688-0461): Large rooms decorated in apple greens and lemon yellows, a lobby of bold, bright colors, a scene restaurant, and thoughtful freebies

like the use of yoga gear make this West End high-rise one of the top choices for hip hotel aficionados. See p. 74.

- **Pan Pacific Hotel Vancouver** (300–999 Canada Place; ☎ **800/937-1515** or 604/662-8111): Perched atop the Canada Place cruise-ship terminal and convention center, the Pan Pacific features rooms with stunning water, mountain, and city views; a new health club and spa; and first-class service. See p. 68.

- **Wedgewood Hotel** (845 Hornby St.; ☎ **800/663-0666** or 604/689-7777): The only boutique hotel in downtown and the most comfortably luxurious in that European style we love so much, the Wedgewood with its fabulous marble-clad bathrooms and spa invites relaxing and romancing. See p. 69.

5 The Best Moderately Priced Hotels: Vancouver

- **The Aston Rosellen Suites at Stanley Park** (100–2030 Barclay St.; ☎ **888/317-6648** or 604/689-4807): For a West End alternative to a hotel, you can rent a spacious furnished apartment with a fully equipped kitchen, dining area, and living room for the same price as many standard hotel rooms. See p. 75.

- **Coast Plaza Hotel & Suites** (1763 Comox St.; ☎ **800/663-1144** or 604/688-7711): A former high-rise apartment building, the Coast offers

large rooms with walk-out balconies and marvelous English Bay views, right in the heart of the West End. See p. 76.

- **West End Guest House** (1362 Haro St.; ☎ **888/546-3327** or 604/681-2889): Built in 1905 by two Vancouver photographers, this highly regarded B&B in the thick of the West End is filled with the artists' work as well as an impressive collection of Victorian antiques. See p. 77.

6 The Best Splurge Hotels: Victoria

For a full description of these and other Victoria accommodations, see chapter 12.

- **The Aerie** (600 Ebedora Lane, Malahat; ☎ **800/518-1933** or 250/743-7115): A red-tiled villa high atop Mount Malahat, with private terraces

offering views across forested mountains to a long blue coastal fjord, this luxurious splurge features hand-carved king-size beds, massive wood-burning fireplaces, Jacuzzis, and a famed restaurant. See p. 206.

- **Brentwood Bay Lodge and Spa** (849 Verdier Ave.; ℂ **888/544-2079** or 250/544-2079): Every detail in the rooms and bathrooms is perfect and the food is great at this small luxury resort overlooking a pristine fjord 20 minutes north of Vancouver. You can get treatments for two at the fabulous Essence of Life spa. See p. 207.
- **Delta Victoria Ocean Pointe Resort and Spa** (45 Songhees Rd.; ℂ **800/667-4677** or 250/360-2999): The glass-fronted hotel lobby and harbor-facing rooms provide the best vantage point in Victoria for watching the lights on the legislature switch on. This comfortable hotel offers a host of services, including a calm, contemporary, Zen-like spa. See p. 195.
- **Fairmont Empress** (721 Government St.; ℂ **800/441-1414** or 250/384-8111): Architect Francis Rattenbury's masterpiece, the landmark Empress on Victoria's Inner Harbour has charmed princes (and their princesses), potentates, movie stars, and the likes of you and me since

1908. The hotel's Willow Stream spa is a luxurious retreat. See p. 195.
- **Hotel Grand Pacific** (463 Belleville St.; ℂ **800/663-7550** or 250/386-0450): The rooms in this high-rise luxury hotel beside the harbor come with a full array of amenities, and the fully equipped fitness center offers aerobics classes, a 25m (82-ft.) ozonated indoor pool, a separate kids' pool, and a weight room, plus sauna, whirlpool, and massage therapist. See p. 198.
- **Laurel Point Inn** (680 Montreal St.; ℂ **800/663-7667** or 250/386-8721): With panoramic vistas of the harbor and an elegant, Japanese-influenced decor, this is the place for view junkies and design aficionados. See p. 199.
- **Sooke Harbour House** (1528 Whiffen Spit Rd., Sooke; ℂ **800/889-9688** or 250/642-3421): In the little town of Sooke, just west of Victoria, this famed oceanside inn offers quiet West Coast elegance and an exceptional restaurant. See p. 208.

7 The Best Moderately Priced Hotels: Victoria

- **Admiral Inn** (257 Belleville St.; ℂ **888/823-6472** or 250/388-6267): Located on the edge of the Inner Harbour, the Admiral provides friendly service, free bikes, and the most reasonably priced harbor view around. See p. 199.
- **The Boathouse** (746 Sea Dr.; ℂ **866/654-9370** or 250/652-9370): If you're seeking tranquility, privacy, and a memorable location, check out this one-room cottage created from a converted boathouse. Built in a secluded cove on Brentwood Bay, within rowing distance of Butchart Gardens, it features its own private dock and a dinghy. See p. 208.
- **The Magnolia** (623 Courtney St.; ℂ **877/624-6654** or 250/381-0999):

With its central location, elegant lobby, well-designed rooms, and large desks and dataports, the Magnolia is Victoria's best spot for business travelers and those who want understated luxury at a reasonable price. See p. 203.
- **Royal Scot Suite Hotel** (425 Quebec St.; ℂ **800/663-7515** or 250/388-5463): This family-friendly hotel occupies a converted apartment building and offers spacious suites that'll make you and yours feel comfortably at home. The suites come with fully equipped kitchens and there's a video arcade and playroom in the basement. See p. 201.

• **Swans Suite Hotel** (506 Pandora Ave.; *(C)* **800/668-7926** or **250/361-3310**): In the heart of the old town and just a block from the harbor, this newly refurbished hotel is right above Swans Pub, one of the most pleasant restaurant/brewpubs in the city. See p. 205.

8 The Most Unforgettable Dining Experiences: Vancouver

• **Bishop's** (2183 W. Fourth Ave.; *(C)* **604/738-2025**): Owner John Bishop makes every customer feel special, and your palate will tingle when it encounters the sublime delights of his freshest of the fresh Pacific Northwest cuisine. See p. 101.

• **C** (1600 Howe St.; *(C)* **604/681-1164**): The creativity of the chef, the quality of the ingredients, and the freshness of the seafood all combine to make this contemporary restaurant overlooking False Creek the best place in Vancouver for innovative seafood. See p. 87.

• **Cin Cin** (1154 Robson St.; *(C)* **604/688-7338**): For maximum buzz, dine at this Robson Street star on a Friday or Saturday night. It's a lively people-watching spot where the Italian menu is divided into Old World and New, and *tutti* tastes terrific. See p. 97.

• **Coast** (1257 Hamilton St.; *(C)* **604/685-5010**): "Catch it, cook it, eat it" is the motto of this superlative Yaletown restaurant. Fresh fish from around the world are cooked to elegant perfection in a beautiful space created with light wood and a dramatic center-island chef's kitchen. See p. 91.

• **Joe Fortes Seafood and Chop House** (777 Thurlow St.; *(C)* **604/669-1940**): In the heart of the Robson shopping area, Joe Fortes has the best oyster bar in town and prepares its that-day-fresh fish the old-fashioned way, without a lot of culinary intervention. See p. 93.

• **Lumière** (2551 W. Broadway; *(C)* **604/739-8185**): Lumière has often won the top spot in the yearly Vancouver Restaurant Awards. It's expensive but worth it to be pampered by chef Rob Feenie, the darling of the Vancouver food world and an increasingly hot commodity in New York. See p. 101.

• **Raincity Grill** (1193 Denman St.; *(C)* **604/685-7337**): With its low ceiling, crisp linens, windows overlooking English Bay, and fabulous food, Raincity is a place that makes you want to linger—and try everything on the seasonally adjusted menu. See p. 98.

• **Tojo's Restaurant** (202–777 W. Broadway; *(C)* **604/872-8050**): The most sublime sushi in B.C., maybe in all of Canada. Just remember to take out an extra mortgage and practice your so-you're-a-movie-star-I-don't-care look. See p. 102.

• **West** (2881 Granville St.; *(C)* **604/738-8938**): For amazingly fine dining that utilizes the freshest local seasonal ingredients, you can't go wrong with this stellar restaurant in Kitsilano. It's a culinary highpoint of the entire region. See p. 103.

9 The Most Unforgettable Dining Experiences: Victoria

• **The Aerie** (600 Ebedora Lane, Malahat; *(C)* **800/518-1933** or **250/743-7115**): Even if you're not staying at The Aerie, you might want to consider eating there because chef Christophe Letard's cooking is as unmistakably French as his accent, and *tres fantastique*. See p. 220.

- **Arbutus Grille and Winebar** (Brentwood Bay Lodge, 849 Verdier Ave.; ℭ **250/544-5100**): The beautiful dining room of Brentwood Bay Lodge, about 20 minutes north of Victoria, serves a regionally-inspired menu that changes daily according to what is fresh and in season. The wine list is exemplary, and so is the service. See p. 221.

- **Camille's** (45 Bastion Sq.; ℭ **250/381-3433**): Enjoy a glass of fine wine as you savor the fresh, comforting Pacific Northwest cuisine at this quiet, cozy, candlelit restaurant in downtown Victoria. See p. 215.

- **Canoe** (450 Swift St.; ℭ **250/361-1940**): Casual but upscale, Canoe has great beer, good fresh Pacific Northwest food, and the option of dining indoors or out on one of the nicest patios in Victoria. See p. 214.

- **The Fairmont Empress** (721 Government St.; ℭ **250/384-8111**): If you're doing the high tea thing only once, you may as well do it right, and there's no better place than Victoria's crown jewel of a hotel, where the tea is huge and the service impeccable. See p. 216.

- **Il Terrazzo Ristorante** (555 Johnson St., off Waddington Alley; ℭ **250/361-0028**): All you have to do is ask around for Victoria's best Italian restaurant, and people will point you to Il Terrazzo, which features excellent northern-Italian cooking and extra points for the lovely patio. See p. 215.

- **Sooke Harbour House** (1528 Whiffen Spit Rd., Sooke; ℭ **800/889-9688** or 250/642-3421): Quality, freshness, inventiveness, and incredible attention to detail make this fabled inn the most memorable dining experience in (well, near) Victoria. It serves the best gifts from the sea and its own garden, and eating here is always a culinary adventure, well worth the money and the trip. See p. 221.

10 The Best Things to Do for Free (or Almost): Vancouver

You'll find more suggestions for free things to do in "Unforgettable Travel Experiences," earlier.

- **Walk the Stanley Park Seawall:** Or jog, blade, bike, skate, ride—whatever your favorite mode of transport is, use it, but by all means get out to enjoy this superlative and super-exhilarating path at the water's edge. See p. 118.

- **Watch the Fireworks Explode over English Bay:** Every August during the July/August HSBC Celebration of Light, three international fireworks companies compete by launching their best displays over English Bay. As many as 500,000 spectators cram the beaches around English Bay, while those with boats sail out to watch from the water. See p. 24.

- **Stroll the Beach:** It doesn't matter which beach, there's one for every taste. Wreck Beach below UBC is for nudists, Spanish Banks is for dog walkers, Jericho Beach is for volleyballers, Kitsilano Beach is for serious suntanning, and English Bay Beach is for serious people-watching. See p. 134.

- **Picnic at the Lighthouse:** Everyone has their favorite picnic spot—one of the beaches or up on the mountains. One of the prettiest picnic spots is Lighthouse Park on the North Shore. Not only do you get to look back over at Vancouver, but also the walk down to the rocky waterline runs through a pristine, old-growth rainforest. See p. 129.

The Best Websites for Vancouver & Victoria

- **Entertainment Info** (www.ticketstonight.ca): This site is a great place to turn to for half-price night-of tickets and general entertainment information in the Vancouver area.
- **Tourism B.C.** (www.hellobc.com): The official site of the provincial government tourism agency, this site provides good information on attractions, as well as higher-end accommodations.
- **Tourism Vancouver** (www.tourismvancouver.com): The official city tourism agency site provides a great overview of attractions, including an excellent calendar of events, plus a few last-minute deals on accommodations.
- **Tourism Victoria** (www.tourismvictoria.com): Victoria's official tourism site functions much the same as Vancouver's, with up-to-date, comprehensive information about what to do and see around the city.
- **Whistler & Blackcomb Resorts** (www.whistler-blackcomb.com): This site offers a particularly helpful overview of activities and accommodations options available at North America's premier ski resort.

- **Hike the North Shore:** The forests of the North Shore are at the edge of a great wilderness and only 20 minutes from the city. Step into a world of muted light and soaring cathedral-like spaces beneath the tree canopy. See "Hiking" in chapter 7, p. 138.

11 The Best Things to Do for Free (or Almost): Victoria

You'll find more suggestions for free things to do in "Unforgettable Travel Experiences," earlier in this chapter.

- **Climb Mount Douglas:** Actually, you don't even have to climb. Just drive up and walk around. The whole of the Saanich Peninsula lies at your feet. See p. 227.
- **Beachcomb:** Just find a beach, preferably a rocky one, and turn stuff over or poke through the tide pools.

The best beaches are along Highway 14, starting with East Sooke Regional Park, and moving out to French Beach, China Beach, Mystic Beach, and, the very best of all, Botanical Beach Provincial Park, some 60km (37 miles) away by Port Renfrew. Remember to put the rocks back once you've had a peek. See "Beaches," "Especially for Kids," and "Watersports" in chapter 14.

2

Planning Your Trip to Vancouver & Victoria

Whether you're visiting Vancouver and Victoria for business or shopping, dining or dancing, beach walking or backwoods trekking, or all of the above, here are some tips to help you plan your trip.

1 Visitor Information & Entry Requirements

VISITOR INFORMATION

You can get Canadian tourism information at consulate offices in many major cities. The provincial and municipal Canadian tourism boards are also great sources of travel information. Contact **Super Natural British Columbia–Tourism B.C.,** Box 9830 Stn. Prov. Government, Victoria, B.C. V8W 9W5 (© **800/HELLO-BC** or 604/435-5622; www.hellobc.com), for information about travel and accommodations throughout the province.

Tourism Vancouver's Touristinfo Centre, 200 Burrard St., Vancouver, B.C. V6C 3L6 (© **604/682-2222;** www.tourismvancouver.com), and **Tourism Victoria,** 812 Wharf St., Victoria (© **250/953-2033;** for hotel bookings only 800/663-3883 and 250/953-2022; www.tourismvictoria.com), can help you with everything from booking accommodations to making suggestions for what to see and do.

If you're planning to spend time outside the cities, you may also wish to call or write the **Vancouver Coast and Mountains Tourism Region,** 250–1508 W. 2nd Ave., Vancouver, B.C. V6J 1H2 (© **800/667-3306** or 604/739-9011; www.vcmbc.com). For travel information

on Vancouver Island and the Gulf Islands, contact the **Tourism Association of Vancouver Island,** 203–335 Wesley St., Nanaimo, B.C. V9R 2T5 (© **250/754-3500;** www.seetheislands.com).

For cultural information, check out *Vancouver Magazine*'s website at www.vanmag.com. The website www.allianceforarts.com also lists weekly events on the arts in Vancouver.

ENTRY REQUIREMENTS

If you're driving from Seattle, you'll need to clear Customs at the Peace Arch crossing (open 24 hr.; often there's a wait) in Blaine, Washington. You'll pass through **Canadian Customs** (© **800/461-9999** within Canada or 204/983-3500) to enter Canada, and **U.S. Customs** (© **360/332-5771**) on your departure. Duty-free shops are located in Blaine at the last exit before the border going into Canada. On the Canadian side, the shops are a little more difficult to find—they're on the right, just after the speed limit drops to 35kmph (22 mph).

If you fly directly into Vancouver International Airport from another country, you'll go through Customs in the International Terminal. Once you clear passport control, you and your luggage will go through Customs before you leave the terminal. (Even if you don't have anything to declare, Customs officials randomly select a few passengers and search their luggage.)

Visitors arriving by ferry from the U.S. pass through U.S. Customs before boarding and Canadian Customs upon arrival.

For an up-to-date country-by-country listing of passport requirements around the world, go to the "Foreign Entry Requirement" Web page of the U.S. State Department at www.travel.state.gov.

DOCUMENTS FOR U.S. CITIZENS

Bring your passport if you've got one. A passport is the easiest and fastest way to enter Canada and return to the U.S. *Note:* Under the new Western Hemisphere Travel Initiative, as of December 31, 2006, all travelers to and from Canada will be required to have a passport or other accepted document that establishes the bearer's identity and nationality to enter or re-enter the United States. Other documents that the U.S. government anticipates will be acceptable for land and border crossings under this new initiative are SENTRI, NEXUS, and FAST program cards (international frequent traveler programs). This means that you will no longer be able to enter Canada using a driver's license and birth certificate.

For the latest information on passports and entry requirements for U.S. citizens, check the Web page of the U.S. State Department at **www.travel.state.gov**. Naturalized citizens should carry their naturalization certificates. U.S. citizens don't require visas to enter Canada.

Permanent U.S. residents who are not U.S. citizens should carry their passports and Resident Alien Card (U.S. form I-151 or I-551). Foreign students and other noncitizen U.S. residents should carry their passports or a Temporary Resident Card (form 1688) or Employment

Authorization Card (1688A or 1688B), a visitor's visa, I-94 Arrival-Departure Record, a current I-20 copy of IAP-66 indicating student status, proof of sufficient funds for a temporary stay, and evidence of return transportation. *Note:* With changing security regulations, it is advisable for all travelers to check with the Canadian consulate before departure to find out the latest in travel document requirements. You will also find current information on the **Canada Border Services Agency** website, **www.cbsa-asfc.gc. ca**; follow the links under "FAQ."

If you're bringing children into Canada, you must have proof of legal guardianship. Lack of it can cause long delays at the border. Children under 18 not accompanied by a parent or guardian must have a permission letter signed by a parent or legal guardian allowing you to travel to Canada.

Visitors arriving by ferry from the U.S. must fill out International Crossing forms, which are collected before boarding.

DOCUMENTS FOR COMMONWEALTH CITIZENS

Citizens of Great Britain, Australia, and New Zealand don't need visas to enter Canada, but they do need to show proof of commonwealth citizenship (such as a passport), as well as evidence of funds sufficient for a temporary stay (credit cards work well here). Naturalized citizens should carry their naturalization certificates. Permanent residents of commonwealth nations should carry their passports and resident status cards.

Foreign students and other residents should carry their passports or temporary resident cards or employment authorization cards, a visitor's visa, arrival-departure record, a current copy of student status, proof of sufficient funds for a temporary stay, evidence of return transportation, and possibly a visitor's visa. *Note:* With changing security regulations, it is advisable for all travelers to check with the Canadian consulate before departure to find out the latest in travel document requirements. You will also find current information on the **Canada Border Services Agency** website, **www.cbsa-asfc.gc.ca**; follow the links under "FAQ."

CUSTOMS REGULATIONS

Your personal baggage can include the following: boats, motors, snowmobiles, camping and sports equipment, appliances, TV sets, musical instruments, personal computers, cameras, and other items of a personal or household nature. If you are bringing excess luggage, be sure to carry a detailed inventory list that includes the acquisition date, serial number, and cost or replacement value of each item. It sounds tedious, but it can speed things up at the border. Customs will help you fill in the forms that allow you to temporarily bring in your effects. This list will also be used by U.S. Customs to check off what you bring out. You will be charged Customs duties for anything left in Canada.

A few other things to keep in mind:

- If you bring more than US$10,000 (about C$12,500) in cash, you must file a transaction report with U.S. Customs.
- Never joke about carrying explosives, drugs, or other contraband unless you want to have your bags and person searched in detail, plus face arrest for conspiracy. Remember, Canada is a foreign country. The officials don't have to let you in.
- Some prescription medicines may be considered contraband across the border. If you're bringing any, it's best to check with your doctor and bring a copy of your prescription, or contact the **Canadian Customs Office** (© **800/461-9999** within Canada or 204/983-3500).
- If you're over 18, you're allowed to bring in 40 ounces of liquor and wine or 24 12-ounce cans or bottles of beer

and ale, and 50 cigars, 400 cigarettes, or 14 ounces of manufactured tobacco per person. Any excess is subject to duty.

- Gifts not exceeding C$60 (US$48) and not containing tobacco products, alcoholic beverages, or advertising material can be brought in duty-free. Meats, plants, and vegetables are subject to inspection on entry. There are restrictions, so contact the Canadian Consulate for more details if you want to bring produce into the country, or check the Canada Border Services Agency website, www.cbsa-asfc.gc.ca.
- If you plan to bring your dog or cat, you must provide proof of rabies inoculation during the preceding 36-month period. Other types of animals need special clearance and health certification. (Many birds, for instance, require 8 weeks in quarantine.)
- If you need more information concerning items you wish to bring in and out of the country, contact the **Canadian Customs Office** (© **800/461-9999** within Canada or 204/983-3500). You can also find information on the **Canada Border Services Agency** website, **www.cbsa-asfc.gc.ca**.

WHAT YOU CAN TAKE HOME FROM CANADA

Returning **U.S. citizens** who have been away for at least 48 hours are allowed to bring back, once every 30 days, US$800 (about C$1,000) worth of merchandise duty-free. You'll be charged a flat rate of 4% duty on the next US$1,000 (about C$1,250) worth of purchases. Be sure to have your receipts handy. On mailed gifts, the duty-free limit is US$200 (about C$250). With some exceptions, you cannot bring fresh fruits and vegetables into the United States. For specifics on what you can bring back, download the invaluable free pamphlet *Know Before You Go* online at **www.customs.gov**

(click on "Travel," then click on "Know Before You Go Online Brochure"). Or contact the **U.S. Customs Service,** 1300 Pennsylvania Ave., NW, Washington, DC 20229 (© **877/287-8867**) and request the pamphlet.

Citizens of the U.K. returning from a **non-E.U. country** have a Customs allowance of: 200 cigarettes; 50 cigars; 250 grams of smoking tobacco; 2 liters of still table wine; 1 liter of spirits or strong liqueurs (over 22% volume); 2 liters of fortified wine, sparkling wine, or other liqueurs; 60cc (ml) perfume; 250cc (ml) of toilet water; and £145 worth of all other goods, including gifts and souvenirs. People under 17 cannot have the tobacco or alcohol allowance. For more information, contact HM Customs & Excise at © **0845/010-9000** (from outside the U.K., 020/8929-0152), or consult their website at www.hmce.gov.uk.

The duty-free allowance amount in **Australia** is A$900 or, A$450 for those under 18. Citizens 18 and older can bring in 250 cigarettes or 250 grams of loose tobacco, and 1,125 milliliters of alcohol. If you're returning with valuables you already own, such as foreign-made cameras, you should file form B263. A helpful brochure available from Australian consulates or Customs offices is *Know Before You Go.* For more information, call the **Australian Customs Service** at © **1300/363-263,** or log on to www.customs.gov.au.

The duty-free allowance for **New Zealand** is NZ$700. Citizens over 17 can bring in 200 cigarettes, 50 cigars, or 250 grams of tobacco (or a mixture of all three if their combined weight doesn't exceed 250g); plus 4.5 liters of wine and beer, or 1.125 liters of liquor. New Zealand currency does not carry import or export restrictions. Fill out a certificate of export, listing the valuables you are taking out of the country; that way, you can bring them back without paying duty. Most questions are answered in a free pamphlet available at New Zealand consulates and Customs offices: *New Zealand Customs Guide for Travellers, Notice no. 4.* For more information, contact **New Zealand Customs,** The Customhouse, 17–21 Whitmore St., Box 2218, Wellington (© **04/473-6099** or 0800/428-786; www.customs.govt.nz).

2 Money

CURRENCY

The Canadian currency system is decimal and resembles both British and U.S. denominations. Canadian monetary units are dollars and cents, with dollar notes issued in different colors. The standard denominations are C$5 (US$4), C$10 (US$8), C$20 (US$16), C$50 (US$40), and C$100 (US$80). The "loonie" (so named because of the loon on one side) is the C$1 (US80¢) coin that replaced the C$1 bill. A C$2 (US$1.60) coin, called the "toonie" because it's worth two loonies, has replaced the C$2 bill. *Note:* If you're driving, it's a good idea to have a pocketful of toonies and loonies for parking meters.

Banks and other financial institutions offer a standard rate of exchange based on the daily world monetary rate (check **www.xe.com/ucc** for up-to-the-minute currency conversions). Avoid C$100 bills when exchanging money, as many stores refuse to accept these bills. The best exchange rates can be had by withdrawing funds from bank ATMs (automated teller machines). Hotels will also gladly exchange your notes, but they usually give a slightly lower exchange rate. Almost all stores and restaurants accept American currency, and most will exchange amounts in excess of your dinner check or purchase. However, these establishments are allowed to set their

The Canadian Dollar & the U.S. Dollar

The prices cited in this guide are given in both Canadian and U.S. dollars, with all amounts over $10 rounded to the nearest dollar. Note that the Canadian dollar is worth almost 20% less than the U.S. dollar but buys nearly as much. As we go to press, C$1 is worth about US80¢, which means that your C$100-a-night hotel room will cost only US$80 and your C$6 breakfast only US$4.80. The actual exchange rate may fluctuate by a few pennies. Here's a table of equivalents:

C$	US$	US$	C$
1	0.80	1	1.25
5	4.00	5	6.25
10	8.00	10	12.50
20	16.00	20	25.00
50	40.00	50	62.50
80	64.00	80	100.00
100	80.00	100	125.00

own exchange percentages and generally offer the worst rates of all.

The exchange rate between Canadian and U.S. dollars should always be kept in mind. Canada remains a bargain.

TRAVELER'S CHECKS

Traveler's checks in Canadian funds are the safest way to carry money and are universally accepted by banks (which may charge a small fee to cash them), larger stores, and hotels. If you are carrying American Express (© 604/669-2813) or Thomas Cook (© 604/641-1229) traveler's checks, you can cash them at the local offices of those companies free of charge.

ATM NETWORKS

The easiest and best way to get cash away from home is from an ATM. The Cirrus (© 800/424-7787; www.mastercard.com) and PLUS (© 800/843-7587; www.visa.com) networks span the globe; look at the back of your bank card to see which network you're on, then call or check online for ATM locations at your destination. Be sure you know your personal identification number (PIN) before you leave home and be sure to find out your daily withdrawal limit before you depart. Many banks impose a fee every time a card is used at a different bank's ATM, and that fee can be higher for international transactions (up to US$5 or more) than for domestic ones (rarely more than US$1.50). On top of this, the bank from which you withdraw cash may charge its own fee.

The 24-hour PLUS and Cirrus ATM systems are widely available in both Vancouver and Victoria as well as throughout the smaller communities in British Columbia. The systems convert Canadian withdrawals to your account's currency within 24 hours. Cirrus network cards work at ATMs at **BMO Bank of Montreal** (© 800/555-3000), **CIBC** (© 800/465-2422), **HSBC** (© 888/310-4722), **Royal Bank** (© 800/769-2511), **TD Canada Trust** (© 866/567-8888), and at all other ATMs that display the Cirrus logo. None of these ATM systems provides your current balance.

CREDIT & DEBIT CARDS

Major U.S. credit cards are widely accepted in British Columbia, especially American Express, MasterCard, and Visa. British debit cards like Barclay's Visa debit card are also accepted. Diners Club, Carte Blanche, Discover, JCB, and EnRoute are taken by some establishments, but not as many. The amount spent in Canadian dollars will automatically be converted by your issuing company to your currency when you're billed—generally at rates that are better than you'd receive for cash at a currency exchange. However, the bank may add a 3% "adjustment fee" to the converted purchase price. You can also obtain a PIN on your credit card and use it in some ATMs. You usually pay interest from the date of withdrawal and often pay a higher service fee than when using a regular ATM card.

3 When to Go

Tree experts say that a rainforest species like the Western Red Cedar needs at least 30 inches of precipitation a year. Vancouver gets about 47 inches a year, a cause for no small celebration among the local cedar population. *Homo sapiens* simply learn to adjust.

For example, most of that precipitation arrives in the wintertime, when, with a 30-minute drive to the mountains, you can trade the rain for snow. Skiing and snowboarding are popular from mid-December until the mountain snowpack melts away in June. Except in Whistler, hotels in the winter are quiet and the restaurants are uncluttered. This is also the time when Vancouver's cultural scene is at its most active.

Around mid-February, the winds begin to slacken, the sun shines a bit more, and the buds on the cherry trees begin to poke their heads out. By April the azaleas and rhododendrons are in full bloom. The sun comes out, and stays out. From then until the rains close in again in mid-October is prime visiting time for sun junkies. Of course, that's also when most other visitors arrive.

WEATHER

Both Vancouver and Victoria enjoy moderately warm, sunny summers and mild, rainy winters. Above the 49th parallel, you get more sun per summer day than you do down south. There are 16 hours of daylight in mid-June. Only 10% of the annual rainfall occurs during the summer months. Victoria gets half as much rain as Vancouver, thanks to the sheltering Olympic Peninsula to the south and its own southeasterly position on huge Vancouver Island. The average annual rainfall in Vancouver is 47 inches; in Victoria, it's just 23 inches.

Daily Mean Temperature & Total Precipitation for Vancouver, B.C.

	Jan	Feb	Mar	Apr	May	June	July	Aug	Sept	Oct	Nov	Dec
Temp (°F)	38	41	45	40	46	62	66	67	61	42	48	39
Temp (°C)	3	5	7	4	8	17	19	19	16	6	9	4
Precipitation (in.)	5.9	4.9	4.3	3.0	2.4	1.8	1.4	1.5	2.5	4.5	6.7	7.0

HOLIDAYS

The official British Columbian public holidays are as follows: New Year's Day (Jan 1); Good Friday, Easter, Easter Monday (Apr 14–16, 2006); Victoria Day (May 22, 2006); Canada Day (July 1); B.C. Day (Aug 7, 2006); Labour Day (Sept 4, 2006); Thanksgiving (Oct 9, 2006); Remembrance Day (Nov 11); Christmas (Dec 25); and Boxing Day (Dec 26).

VANCOUVER & VICTORIA CALENDAR OF EVENTS

Festivals held in Vancouver and Victoria draw millions of visitors each year and reflect an extraordinary diversity of cultures and events. Things may seem a little quiet in the winter and early spring, but that's because most residents simply head for the ski slopes. Resorts such as **Whistler** and **Blackcomb** (© 866/218-9690; www.whistlerblackcomb.com) have events happening nearly every weekend. If no contact number or location is given for any of the events listed below, **Tourism Vancouver** (© 604/682-2222; www.tourismvancouver.com) can provide further details.

VANCOUVER EVENTS

January

Polar Bear Swim, English Bay Beach. Thousands of hardy citizens show up in elaborate costumes to take a dip in the icy waters of English Bay. Call © **604/665-3418** for more information, or visit www.city.vancouver.bc.ca. January 1.

Dine Out Vancouver. For a limited time every January, Vancouver's hottest restaurants offer three-course dinners for C$15, C$25, or C$35 (US$12, US$20, US$28) per person. For more information contact Tourism Vancouver (© **604/683-2000;** www.tourism vancouver.com).

Annual Bald Eagle Count, Brackendale. Bald eagles gather en masse every winter near Brackendale to feed on salmon. In January 1994, volunteers counted a world-record of 3,700 eagles. The 2005 count wasn't too shabby either with 1,975 raptors tallied. The count starts at the **Brackendale Art Gallery** (© **604/898-3333**). First Sunday in January. Meet at 9am at the Art Gallery for a guided tour.

February

Chinese New Year, Chinatowns in Vancouver and Richmond. This is when the Chinese traditionally pay their debts and forgive old grievances to start the new lunar year with a clean slate. These Chinese communities launch a 2-week celebration, ringing in the new year with firecrackers, dancing dragon parades, and other festivities. Call © **604/415-6322** for information, or visit www.vancouverchinese garden.com. Dates vary yearly.

March

Vancouver Playhouse International Wine Festival. This is a major wine-tasting event featuring the latest international vintages. Each winery sets up a booth where you may try as many varieties as you like. Cheese and pâté are also laid out on strategically placed tables. For more information, call © **604/873-3311** or visit www.play housewinefest.com. Late March or early April.

April

Baisakhi Day Parade. The Sikh Indian New Year is celebrated with a colorful parade around Ross Street near Marine Drive and ends with a vegetarian feast at the temple. Contact **Khalsa Diwan Gurudwara Temple** (© **604/324-2010**) for more information. Mid-April.

Vancouver Sun Run. This is Canada's biggest 10K race, featuring over 40,000 runners, joggers, and walkers who race through 10 scenic kilometers (6.2 miles). The run finishes at B.C. Place Stadium. Call © **604/689-9441** for information or register online at www.sunrun.com. April 17, 2005.

May

Vancouver International Marathon. Runners from all over the world compete here. For information, call © **604/872-2928** or visit www.vanmarathon.com. First Sunday in May.

Cloverdale Rodeo, Cloverdale, Surrey. Professional cowboys from all over North America compete in roping, bull and bronco riding, barrel racing, and many other events. There are pony rides for kids, great food, and a country-fair atmosphere. For information, call ✆ 604/576-9461 or visit www.cloverdalerodeo.com. Third week in May.

International Children's Festival. Activities, plays, music, and crafts for children are featured at this annual event held in Vanier Park on False Creek. For information, call ✆ 604/708-5655 or visit www.vancouverchildrensfestival.com. Late May or early June.

June

VanDusen Flower and Garden Show. Presented at the **VanDusen Botanical Garden,** 5251 Oak St., at 37th Street (✆ 604/878-9274; www.vandusengarden.org), this is Vancouver's premier flora gala. Early June.

Festival d'Eté Francophone de Vancouver/Francophone Summer Festival. This 4-day festival celebrating French music uses various venues and includes a street festival. Performers often include well-known Quebec artists. Call ✆ 604/736-9806 for information or check www.lecentreculturel.com. Mid-June.

Alcan Dragon Boat Festival. Traditional dragon-boat racing is a part of the city's cultural scene. Watch the races from False Creek's north shore, where more than 150 local and international teams compete. Four stages of music, dance, and Chinese acrobatics are presented at the **Plaza of Nations,** 750 Pacific Blvd. For more info, call ✆ 604/683-4707 (www.adbf.com). Third week in June.

National Aboriginal Day Community Celebration. This event offers the public an opportunity to learn about Canada's First Nations cultures. Many events take place at the **Vancouver Aboriginal Friendship Centre,** 1607 E. Hastings at Commercial Street. Call ✆ 604/251-4844 for information. June 21.

Vancouver International Jazz Festival. More than 800 international jazz and blues players perform at 25 venues ranging from the Orpheum Theatre to the Roundhouse. Many are free performances. Call the **Jazz Hot Line** (✆ 604/872-5200) or visit www.jazzvancouver.com for more information. Late June/early July.

Bard on the Beach Shakespeare Festival, Vanier Park. The best backdrop for Shakespeare you will ever see! The Bard's plays are performed in a tent overlooking English Bay. Three different plays are performed every summer. Call the box office (✆ 604/739-0559) or check www.bardonthebeach.org. Mid-June to late September, Tuesday through Sunday.

July

Canada Day. Canada Place Pier hosts an all-day celebration that begins with the induction of new Canadian citizens. Music and dance are performed outdoors throughout the day. A 21-gun salute at noon, precision aerobatics teams in the afternoon, and a nighttime fireworks display on the harbor lead the festivities. Granville Island, Grouse Mountain, and other locations also host Canada Day events. For more information, call ✆ 604/647-7390 or check www.canadadayatcanadaplace.com. July 1.

Steveston Salmon Festival, Steveston. Steveston celebrates Canada Day with a spectacular parade, marching bands, clowns, a carnival, a traditional salmon bake, and more. Call ✆ 604/277-6812 for more info, or visit www.tourismrichmond.com. July 1.

Ecomarine Kayak Marathon. Competitors race sea kayaks in Georgia

Strait. The **Ecomarine Kayak Centre** (© 604/689-7575), at Jericho Beach, hosts the race and can provide details. Mid-July.

Harrison Festival of the Arts, Harrison Hot Springs, lower mainland. This arts festival in the Fraser River valley, just east of Vancouver, attracts performing artists from around the world. Call © 604/796-3664 for more information, or visit www.harrisonfestival.com. Mid-July.

Dancing on the Edge. Canadian and international dance groups perform modern and classic works at the **Firehall Arts Centre** and other venues. For information, call © 604/689-0929 or visit www.dancingontheedge.org. Early to mid-July.

Vancouver Folk Music Festival. International folk music is performed outdoors at Jericho Beach Park. Contact the **Vancouver Folk Music Society** at © 604/602-9798 for more information, or visit www.thefestival.bc.ca. Second or third weekend in July.

Illuminares Lantern Festival, Trout Lake Park. Evening lantern procession circling Trout Lake is a phantasmagoric experience, complete with drums, costumes, fire-breathing apparitions, and lots of elaborate handcrafted lanterns. Various performances start at dusk. For info, call © 604/879-8611 or visit www.publicdreams.org. Third Saturday in July.

Caribbean Days Festival, North Vancouver. The Trinidad and Tobago Cultural Society of B.C. hosts the city's premier Caribbean event at Waterfront Park in North Vancouver, featuring live music, authentic Caribbean food, arts, crafts, and a parade. For info, call © 604/512-2400 or visit www.ttcsbc.com. Third or fourth weekend in July.

HSBC Celebration of Light. Three international fireworks companies compete for a coveted title by launching their best displays accompanied by music over English Bay Beach. Don't miss the big finale on the fourth evening (*Note:* Because of the crowds, some streets are closed to vehicles at night.) Other prime viewing locations include Kitsilano Beach and Jericho Beach. Call © 604/641-1293 for information, or check www.celebration-of-light.com. End of July through first week of August.

Vancouver International Comedy Festival. Comedians from all over Canada and the U.S. around town. Contact **Ticketmaster** for tickets at © 604/683-0883 or check www.comedyfest.com for more information. Last week of July, first week of August.

August

Powell Street Festival. An annual fete of Japanese culture includes music, dance, food, and more. Contact the Powell Street Festival Society (© 604/739-9388; http://powellstfestival.shinnova.com) for info. First weekend of August.

Gay Pride Parade, Vancouver. This colorful gay- and lesbian-pride parade begins at noon. Celebrations at many local gay and lesbian nightclubs take place around town on the same long holiday weekend (B.C. Day weekend). For more info, contact the Pride Society (© 604/687-0955; www.vanpride.bc.ca). First Sunday in August.

Festival Vancouver. National and international artists perform orchestral, choral, opera, world music, chamber music, and jazz concerts in concert halls throughout Vancouver. For information, call © 604/688-1152 or visit www.festivalvancouver.bc.ca. First 2 weeks in August.

Harmony Arts Festival, West Vancouver. This event highlights the talent of North Shore artists, offering free exhibitions, demonstrations, studio tours, theater, concerts, markets, and workshops. Call ℂ **604/925-7268** or visit www.harmonyarts.net for more information. First 2 weeks of August.

Abbottsford International Air Show, Abbottsford. Barnstorming stuntmen and precision military pilots fly everything from Sopwith Camels to Stealth Bombers. This is one of the biggest air shows in the world. Call ℂ **604/852-8511** or visit www.abbotsfordairshow.com for more info. Second weekend in August.

Pacific National Exhibition. The city's favorite fair includes one of North America's best all-wooden roller coasters, many other rides, big-name entertainment, rodeo, and a demolition derby. Special events include livestock demonstrations, logger competitions, fashion shows, and a midway. Call ℂ **604/253-2311** or visit www.pne.bc.ca for more details. Mid-August to Labour Day.

Vancouver Wooden Boat Festival, Granville Island. This free event is a must for wooden-boat aficionados. Call ℂ **604/688-9622** for more info, or visit www.granvilleisland.com. Last weekend of August.

September

Vancouver Fringe Festival. This is the best place to catch new theater. Centered around Granville Island, Commercial Drive, and Yaletown's Roundhouse, the Fringe Festival features more than 500 innovative and original shows performed by over 100 groups from across Canada and around the world. All plays cost under C$15 (US$12). Call ℂ **604/257-0350** or see www.vancouverfringe.com for more info. First and second week of September.

Mid-Autumn Moon Festival, Dr. Sun Yat-sen Garden. This outdoor Chinese celebration includes a lantern festival, storytelling, music, and, of course, moon cakes. For info, call ℂ **604/662-3207** or visit www.vancouverchinesegarden.com. Early to mid-September, according to the lunar cycle (15th day of the 8th month of the Chinese calendar).

October

Vancouver International Film Festival. This highly respected festival features 250 new works, revivals, and retrospectives, representing filmmakers from 40 countries (especially Asia). Call ℂ **604/685-0260** or visit www.viff.org for details. Late September and first 2 weeks of October.

Vancouver International Writers and Readers Festival. Public readings conducted by Canadian and international authors as well as writers' workshops take place on Granville Island and at other locations in the lower mainland. Call ℂ **604/681-6330** or check www.writersfest.bc.ca for details. Mid-October.

Parade of Lost Souls, Grandview Park. A bizarre and intriguing procession takes place around Commercial Drive to honor the dead and chase away bad luck. For more information, call ℂ **604/879-8611.** Last Saturday of October.

November

Remembrance Day. Celebrated throughout Canada, this day commemorates Canadian soldiers who gave their lives in war. Vintage military aircraft fly over Stanley Park and Canada Place, and, at noon, a 21-gun salute is fired from Deadman's Island. November 11.

Christmas Craft and Gift Market, VanDusen Botanical Garden. Popular craft and gift market in a beautiful garden setting. For info, call ⊙ **604/ 878-9274** or check www.vandusen garden.org. November and December.

December

Carol Ship Parade of Lights Festival. Harbor cruise ships decorated with colorful Christmas lights sail around English Bay, while onboard guests sip cider and sing their way through the canon of Christmas carols. For more info, call ⊙ **604/878-8999** or check out www.carolships.org. Throughout December.

Festival of Lights. Throughout December, the VanDusen Botanical Garden is transformed into a magical holiday land with seasonal displays and over 20,000 lights illuminating the garden. Call ⊙ **604/878-9274** for info, or visit www.vandusengaden.org.

First Night. Vancouver closes its downtown streets for revelers in the city's New Year's Eve performing-arts festival and alcohol-free party. Events and venues change from year to year.

VICTORIA & SOUTHERN VANCOUVER ISLAND EVENTS

January

Annual Bald Eagle Count, Goldstream Provincial Park. When the salmon swim up the spawning streams, the tourists aren't the only ones who come to watch. More than 3,000 bald eagles take up residence to feed on the salmon, which begin to run in October. The eagles arrive shortly thereafter. The eagle count usually takes place in mid- to late January when the numbers peak. Throughout December and January, the park offers educational programs, displays, and guest speakers. Call ⊙ **250/478-9414** for exact dates.

Robert Burns's Birthday. Celebrating the birthday of the great Scottish poet, events around Victoria and Vancouver include Scottish dancing, piping, and

feasts of haggis. Most events take place in pubs. January 25.

February

Chinese New Year, Chinatown. See "Vancouver Events," above. Late January or early February.

Trumpeter Swan Festival, Comox Valley. A weeklong festival celebrates these magnificent white birds that gather in the Comox Valley. Check dates with the Vancouver Island tourist office (⊙ **250/754-3500**).

Flower Count. So many flowers bloom in Victoria and the surrounding area that the city holds an annual flower count. The third week in February is a great time to see the city as it comes alive in vibrant color. Call ⊙ **250/383-7191** for more info.

March

Pacific Rim Whale Festival, Tofino, Ucluelet, and Pacific Rim National Park. Every spring, more than 20,000 gray whales migrate past this coastline, attracting visitors to Vancouver Island's west coast beaches. In celebration of the gray, orca, humpback, and other whales in the area, the event features live crab races, storytelling, parades, art shows, guided whale-spotting hikes, and whale-watching boat excursions. Call ⊙ **250/726-4641** for more information. Mid-March to early April.

April

Annual Brant Wildlife Festival, Qualicum Beach. (www.brantfestival. bc.ca). This 3-day celebration of the annual black brant migration to the area (20,000 birds) includes guided walks through old-growth forest and salt- and freshwater marshes that are home to hundreds of bird species. Art, photography, and carving exhibitions as well as birding competitions highlight the event. Call ⊙ **250/752-9171** for info. Early April.

May

Harbour Festival. This 10-day festival takes place in Victoria's downtown district and features heritage walks, entertainment, music, and more. For information, call ☏ **250/953-2033** or visit www.tourismvictoria.com. Last week of May.

Swiftsure Weekend. International sailing races make quite a spectacular sight on the waters around Victoria. For information, call ☏ **250/953-2033.** End of May.

June

Jazz Fest International. Jazz, swing, bebop, fusion, and improv artists from around the world perform at various venues around Victoria during this 10-day festival (☏ **250/388-4423;** www.vicjazz.bc.ca). Late June/early July.

Folkfest. This 8-day world-beat music festival presents daily performances from 11:30am to 11:30pm. Main venues are the Inner Harbour and Market Square in downtown Victoria (☏ **250/388-4728;** www.icafolkfest.com). End of June or early July.

July

Canada Day. Victoria, the provincial capital, celebrates this national holiday with events centered on the Inner Harbour, including music, food, and fireworks. Every city on Vancouver Island has similar festivities, though not as grand as those in Victoria itself. July 1.

Victoria Shakespeare Festival. (☏ **250/360-0234**) Performances of the Bard's works take place around the Inner Harbour from the second week in July to the third week in August.

August

First Peoples Festival. This free event highlights the heritage of the Pacific Northwest First Nations with performances, carving demonstrations, and cultural displays at the Royal British Columbia Museum (☏ **250/384-3211** or 250/953-3557). First weekend in August.

Canadian International Dragon Boat Festival. Traditional dragon-boat races take place in the Inner Harbour, where 120 local and international teams compete. Mid-August.

September

Malahat Challenge (Vintage Car Rally). Competitors race from Victoria to Nanaimo in an amazing array of classic chassis. An end-of-summer jazz festival picks up at the finish line. For info, call the Nanaimo Tourism Association at ☏ **800/663-7337.** Early September.

October

Royal Victoria Marathon. This annual race attracts runners from around the world (half-marathon course available, too). The air is fresh, the temperature is usually just cool enough, and the course consists of gentle ups and downs. Call ☏ **250/658-4520** or go to www.royalvictoria marathon.com for more info. Early October (Canadian Thanksgiving weekend).

November

The Great Canadian Beer Festival. Featuring samples from the province's best microbreweries, this event is held at the Victoria Conference Centre, 720 Douglas St. (☏ **250/952-0360**). Second week in November.

Remembrance Day. See "Vancouver Events," above. November 11.

December

Merrython Fun Run. An annual event (☏ **250/953-2033**) for nearly 20 years, this 10km (6¼-mile) race loops through downtown Victoria. Mid-December.

First Night. See "Vancouver Events," above. Call **Tourism Victoria** at ☏ **250/953-2033** for more details. December 31.

4 Insurance, Health & Safety

INSURANCE

American travelers should review their **health insurance** coverage for travel outside the United States. If you are not adequately covered, take advantage of one of the many health and accident plans that charge a daily rate for the term of your trip. They include the ones offered by Thomas Cook, the American Automobile Association (AAA), and Mutual of Omaha. Canada has health care comparable in quality to that of the United States, but it is also comparably priced, and even for emergency services, insurance or other payment information will be required.

Auto insurance is compulsory in British Columbia. Basic coverage consists of "no-fault" accident and C$200,000 (US$160,000) third-party legal liability coverage. If you plan to drive in Canada, check with your insurance company to make sure that your policy meets this requirement. Always carry your insurance card, your vehicle registration, and your driver's license in case you have an accident. AAA also offers low-cost travel and auto insurance for its members. If you are a member and don't have adequate insurance, take advantage of this benefit.

Note: If you rent a car in British Columbia and plan to take it across the border into the U.S., let your rental agency know for insurance purposes.

Wallach & Company, 107 W. Federal St., P.O. Box 480, Middleburg, VA 20118 (© **800/237-6615;** www.wallach. com), offers a comprehensive travel policy that includes trip-cancellation coverage and emergency assistance in the event of illness, accident, or loss.

For **lost luggage,** on domestic flights, checked baggage is covered up to $2,500 per ticketed passenger. On international flights (including U.S. portions of international trips), baggage is limited to approximately $9.10 per pound, up to approximately $635 per checked bag. If

you plan to check items more valuable than the standard liability, see if your valuables are covered by your homeowner's policy, get baggage insurance as part of your comprehensive travel-insurance package, or consider the "Property Protect" product offered by **Travel Guard,** 1145 Clark St., Stevens Point, WI 54481 (© **800/826-1919;** www. travelguard.com). Don't buy insurance at the airport; it's usually overpriced. Pack in your carry-on luggage all valuables (including books, money, and electronics) that aren't covered by airline policies.

If your luggage is lost, immediately file a lost-luggage claim at the airport, detailing the luggage contents. For most airlines, you must report delayed, damaged, or lost baggage within 4 hours of arrival. The airlines are required to deliver luggage, once found, directly to your destination free of charge.

WHAT TO DO IF YOU GET SICK AWAY FROM HOME

In most cases, your existing health plan will provide the coverage you need. But double-check; you may want to buy **travel medical insurance** instead. (See the section on insurance, above.) Bring your insurance ID card with you when you travel.

If you suffer from a chronic illness, consult your doctor before your departure. For conditions like epilepsy, diabetes, or heart problems, wear a **Medic Alert Identification Tag** (© **800/825-3785;** www.medicalert.org), which will immediately alert doctors to your condition and give them access to your records through Medic Alert's 24-hour hotline.

Pack **prescription medications** in your carry-on luggage, and carry prescription medications in their original containers, with pharmacy labels—otherwise they won't make it through airport security. Also bring along copies of your prescriptions in case you lose your medicine or run out.

If you get seriously sick, ask your hotel concierge to recommend a local doctor—even his or her own. You can also try the emergency room at a local hospital; many have walk-in clinics for emergency cases that are not life-threatening. You may not get immediate attention, but you won't pay the high price of an emergency room visit.

5 Specialized Travel Resources

TRAVELERS WITH DISABILITIES

According to *We're Accessible,* a newsletter for travelers with disabilities, Vancouver is "the most accessible city in the world." There are more than 14,000 sidewalk wheelchair ramps, and motorized wheelchairs are a common sight in the downtown area. The stairs along Robson Square have built-in ramps, and most major attractions and venues have ramps or level walkways for easy access. Most Vancouver hotels have at least partial wheelchair accessibility; many have specially equipped rooms for travelers with disabilities. Most SkyTrain stations and the SeaBus are wheelchair accessible, and most bus routes are lift-equipped. For more information about accessible public transportation, contact **Translink** (© **604/953-3333**; www.translink.bc.ca) for the brochure, *Rider's Guide to Accessible Transit.*

Many Vancouver hotels are also equipping rooms with visual smoke alarms and other facilities for hearing-impaired guests. Some downtown crosswalks have beeping alert signs to guide visually impaired pedestrians.

Victoria is similarly accessible. Nearly all Victoria hotels have rooms equipped to accommodate travelers with disabilities, and downtown sidewalks are equipped with ramps, though few intersections have beeping crosswalk signals for the visually impaired. The **Victoria Regional Transit System** (© **250/382-6161**; www.transitbc.com) publishes the *Rider's Guide,* which includes complete information on which bus routes are equipped with lifts and/or low floors. The most notable spot in Victoria that isn't readily wheelchair accessible is the promenade along the water's edge in the Inner Harbour, which has only one rather challenging ramp near the Pacific Undersea Gardens.

The government of Canada hosts a comprehensive **Persons with Disabilities website** (www.accesstotravel.gc.ca) with resources for travelers with disabilities. In addition to information on public transit in cities across Canada, the site also lists accessible campsites, parks, coach lines, and a number of links to other services and associations of interest to travelers with disabilities. If you can't find what you need online, call © **800/465-7735.**

FOR GAY & LESBIAN TRAVELERS

Since 2003, when the Province of British Columbia announced the legalization of same-sex marriage, Vancouver and Victoria have become favored sites for **gay and lesbian weddings.** Information about the process is listed on the invaluable **www.gayvan.com** website.

What San Francisco is to the United States, **Vancouver** is to Canada—a hip, laid-back town with a large, thriving gay community. In fact, the largest gay population in Western Canada lives here, primarily in the **West End** and **Commercial Drive.** The club, bar, and party scene is chronicled in the biweekly gay and lesbian tabloid, *Xtra! West,* available at cafes, bars, and businesses throughout the West End. The **Gay Lesbian Transgendered Bisexual Community Centre,** 2–1170

Bute St. (© **604/684-5307;** www.lgtb centrevancouver.com), has all kinds of information on events and the current hot spots. Also check out the **Vancouver Pride Society** website (**www.vanpride. bc.ca**) for upcoming special events, including the annual Vancouver Pride Parade. The **Out on Screen Film Festival** is held at the beginning of August; check **www.outonscreen.com** for more details. You'll find hotels and restaurants in Vancouver to be generally very gay-friendly. For nightlife options, see "Gay & Lesbian Bars," in chapter 10.

Also check out **Gay & Lesbian Ski Week** at Whistler, located 121km (75 miles) north of Vancouver; for information, go to **www.outontheslopes.com**.

The gay and lesbian scene in **Victoria** (pop. 345,000 in the Greater Victoria area) is small but active. Explore the gay and lesbian link under "Things to Do" at **www.tourismvictoria.com** or go to the **www.gayvictoria.ca** website. At both sites you'll find information about special places to stay, to dine, and things to do. The **Victoria Pride Parade** and Festival is held every summer in early July; for information, go to www.victoriapride. com. For nightlife options, see chapter 17.

FOR SENIORS

Because B.C. has the mildest weather in all of Canada, Vancouver and Victoria have become havens for older and retired Canadians. Senior travelers often qualify for discounts at hotels and attractions throughout the area. Always ask; you'll be pleasantly surprised at the number of discounts available. **Discount transit passes** for persons over 65 (with proof of age) may be purchased at shops in Vancouver and Victoria that display a FAREDEALER sign (Safeway, 7-Eleven, and most newsstands). To locate a **FareDealer vendor,** contact B.C. Transit (© **604/521-0400**). If you're over 50, consider joining **AARP** (3200 E. Carson, Lakewood, CA 90712;

© **800/424-3410;** www.aarp.org);their card offers additional restaurant and travel bargains throughout North America.

FOR FAMILIES

Vancouver and Victoria are two of the most child-friendly, cosmopolitan cities in the world. Where else would you find a kids market that's filled with children's stores and is located next to a free water park that's equipped with water guns and changing rooms? In addition to the standard attractions and sights, you'll find a lot of adventurous outdoor and free stuff that both you and your kids will enjoy (see "Especially for Kids," in chapters 7 and 14). In both cities you'll find restaurants that aren't cafeteria-style or fast-food establishments, but are decidedly kid-friendly. Some hotels even offer milk and cookies to kids for evening snacks, plus special menus and child-size terry robes.

You may also want to get a copy of *Frommer's Vancouver with Kids* (Wiley Publishing, Inc.).

FOR STUDENTS

The southwestern corner of B.C. is definitely student-oriented territory. The University of British Columbia (UBC, with over 30,000 students) in the Point Grey area, Burnaby's Simon Fraser University, and a number of smaller schools contribute to the enormous student population in **Vancouver.** Student travelers have a lot of free and inexpensive entertainment options, both day and night. The nightlife scene centers on **Yaletown, Granville Street,** the **West End,** and **Kitsilano.** Pick up a copy of *The Georgia Straight* to find out what's happening. Many attractions and theaters offer discounts if you have your student ID with you. While many establishments will accept a school ID, the surest way to obtain student discounts is with an International Student Identity Card (ISIC), which is available to any full-time high-school or college student from **STA Travel** (© 800/781-4040; www.statravel.com), the biggest student travel agency in the world, or from your local campus student society.

In **Victoria,** the University of Victoria (referred to locally as "U. Vic.") has a sprawling campus just east of downtown. The student population accounts for most, if not all, of Victoria's nightlife. Student discounts abound. Pick up a copy of Victoria's weekly paper, *Monday Magazine* (which comes out on Thurs), for current nightclub listings.

6 Getting to Vancouver

BY PLANE

The Open Skies agreement between the United States and Canada has made flying to Vancouver easier than ever. Daily direct flights between major U.S. cities and Vancouver are offered by **Air Canada** (© 888/247-2262; www.aircanada.com), **Alaska Airlines** (© 800/252-7522; www.alaskaair.com), **American Airlines** (© 800/433-7300; www.aa.com), **Continental** (© 800/231-0856; www.continental.com), **Northwest Airlines** (© 800/447-4747; www.nwa.com), and **United Airlines** (© 800/241-6522; www.united.com). Direct flights on major carriers serve 33 cities in North America, including Phoenix, Dallas, New York, Houston, Minneapolis, Reno, and San Francisco; 12 cities in Asia; and 3 cities in Europe.

For domestic travelers within Canada there are fewer options. **Air Canada** (© 888/247-2262) operates flights to Vancouver and Victoria from all major Canadian cities, connecting with some of the regional airlines. Cheaper and reaching farther all the time is the no-frills airline **WestJet** (© 888/WEST-JET or 800/538-5696; www.westjet.com), which operates regular flights from Vancouver and Victoria to Prince George, Kelowna, Edmonton, Calgary, Toronto, Montreal, Ottawa, Halifax, and farther afield.

GETTING THROUGH THE AIRPORT

With the federalization of airport security, security procedures at U.S. airports have become more stable and consistent. Generally, you'll be fine if you arrive at the airport 1½ hours before a domestic flight and 2 hours before an international flight.

To pick up your ticket at the counter, you'll need to show a **current, government-issued photo ID** such as a driver's license or passport (for necessary entry documents, see "Visitor Information & Entry Requirements" earlier in this chapter). If you've got an e-ticket, print out the **official confirmation page**—you'll need to show it at the security checkpoint and your ID at the ticket counter or the gate. (Children under 18 do not need photo IDs for domestic flights, but the adults with them do.)

Security lines are moving faster, but some doozies remain. If you have trouble standing for long periods of time, tell an airline employee; the airline will provide a wheelchair. Speed up security by **not wearing metal objects** such as big belt buckles or metal earrings. If you've got metallic body parts, a note from your doctor can prevent a long chat with the security screeners. Only **ticketed passengers** are allowed past security, except for folks escorting passengers with disabilities or children.

Federalization has stabilized **what you can and can't carry on.** Sharp things are out; nail clippers are okay. The Transportation Security Administration (TSA) has issued a **list of restricted items;** check its website (**www.tsa.gov/public/index.jsp**) for details.

At press time, the TSA is recommending that you **not lock your checked luggage** so screeners can search it by hand if necessary. Instead of locks, the agency says to use plastic "zip ties" instead, which can be bought at hardware stores and can be easily cut off.

For information on getting into the city from the airport, see chapter 4, "Getting to Know Vancouver."

FLYING FOR LESS: TIPS FOR GETTING THE BEST AIRFARE

Passengers sharing the same airplane cabin rarely pay the same fare. A few ways to keep your airfare expenses down follow:

- **Book your tickets long in advance,** stay over Saturday night, or fly midweek or at less-trafficked hours.
- In local newspapers, look for **promotional specials** or **fare wars,** when airlines lower prices on some popular routes, usually in off-season.
- Search **the Internet** for cheap fares (see "Planning Your Trip Online," below).
- Join **frequent-flier clubs.** It's free.

BY TRAIN

VIA Rail Canada, 1150 Station St., Vancouver (© **888/842-7245;** www.viarail. com), connects with Amtrak at Winnipeg, Manitoba. From there, you can transfer to The Canadian, the western transcontinental train that travels between Vancouver and Toronto, with stops in Kamloops, Jasper, Edmonton, Saskatoon, Winnipeg, and Sudbury Junction. Lake Louise's beautiful alpine scenery is just part of this scenically spectacular journey through the Canadian Rockies. Canadians, U.S. residents, and international travelers can purchase a 30-day, two-country **North America Railpass** for US$637 to US$809 at peak season and use it for rail connections to Vancouver. For travel within Canada only, the 12-day **Canrailpass** (C$475/US$380 off-peak; C$763/US$610 peak) is available. Visit www.viarail.com for more information.

Amtrak (© **800/872-7245;** www. amtrak.com) offers daily service from Seattle, though there's currently only one train in the morning; otherwise, the Seattle–Vancouver route is covered by an Amtrak bus. Amtrak also has a route from San Diego to Vancouver. It stops at all major U.S. West Coast cities and takes a little under 2 days to complete the entire journey. All trains arrive and depart from Pacific Central Station, 1150 Station St., just east of the downtown core. The station is close to a SkyTrain (lightrail) station and several city bus routes that travel along Main Street. For information on getting into the city from the train station, see chapter 4, "Getting to Know Vancouver."

BY BUS

Greyhound Bus Lines (© **800/231-2222** or 604/482-8747; www.greyhound. com) offers daily bus service between Vancouver and all major Canadian cities, and between Vancouver and Seattle (at the border crossing, passengers disembark the bus and take their luggage through Customs). For information on Greyhound's cost-cutting **Canada Pass,** which allows for unlimited travel within Canada, and **Discovery Pass,** which allows for unlimited travel in the U.S. and Canada, see the Web site. **Pacific Coach Lines** (© **604/662-8074;** www. pacificcoach.com) provides service between Vancouver and Victoria. The cost is C$39 (US$31) one-way per adult and includes the ferry; daily departures are between 5:45am and 7:45pm. Pacific Coach Lines will pick up passengers from the Vancouver cruise-ship terminal and from most downtown hotels. Call © **604/662-8074** to reserve.

Both bus companies have their terminals at the same station as Amtrak: Pacific

Central Station, 1150 Station St., just east of the downtown core. The station is close to a SkyTrain (light-rail) station and several city bus routes that travel along Main Street.

For information on getting into the city from the train and bus terminal, see chapter 4, "Getting to Know Vancouver."

BY CAR

There are no major freeways within Vancouver, which makes it unique for a major North American city. You'll probably be driving into Vancouver along one of two routes. **U.S. Interstate 5** from Seattle becomes **Highway 99** when you cross the border at the Peace Arch. The 210km (130-mile) drive from Seattle takes about 2½ hours. On the Canadian side of the border you'll drive through the cities of White Rock, Delta, and Richmond, pass under the Fraser River through the George Massey Tunnel, and cross the Oak Street Bridge. The highway ends there and becomes Oak Street, a busy urban thoroughfare heading toward downtown. Turn left at the first convenient major arterial (70th, 57th, 49th, 41st, 33rd, 16th, and 12th aves. will all serve) and proceed until you hit the next major street, which will be Granville Street. Turn right on Granville Street. This street heads directly into downtown Vancouver on the Granville Street Bridge.

Trans-Canada Highway 1 is a limited-access freeway that runs to Vancouver's eastern boundary, where it crosses the Second Narrows Bridge to North Vancouver. When traveling on Highway 1 from the east, exit at Cassiar Street and turn left at the first light onto Hastings Street (Hwy. 7A), which is adjacent to Exhibition Park. Follow Hastings Street 6.4km (4 miles) into downtown. When coming to Vancouver from parts north, take Exit 13 (the sign says TAYLOR WAY, BRIDGE TO VANCOUVER) and cross the Lions Gate Bridge into Vancouver's West End.

BY SHIP & FERRY

Vancouver is the major embarkation point for cruises going up British Columbia's Inland Passage to Alaska. The ships carry more than 1 million passengers annually on their nearly 350 Vancouver–Alaska cruises. In the summer, up to five cruise ships a day berth at **Canada Place** cruise-ship terminal (© **604/ 665-9085;** www.portvancouver.com). A city landmark shaped like a cruise ship and topped by five eye-catching white Teflon sails, Canada Place Pier juts out into the Burrard Inlet at the base of Burrard Street right at the edge of the downtown financial district. **Princess Cruises** (© 800/PRINCESS; www.princess.com), **Holland America Line** (© 800/724-5425; www.hollandamerica.com), **Royal Caribbean** (© 800/398-9819; www.royalcaribbean.com), **Crystal Cruises** (© 866/446-6625; www.crystalcruises.com), **Norwegian Cruise Line** (© 800/625-5306; www.norwegiancruiselines.com), **World Explorer Cruises** (© 650/637-8831; www.wecruise.com), **Radisson Seven Seas Cruises** (© 877/505-5370; www.rssc.com), and **Carnival** (© 866/386-7447; www.carnivalcruise.com) all dock at Canada Place or the nearby Ballantyne Pier. Public-transit buses and taxis greet new arrivals, but you can also easily walk to many major hotels (the Pan Pacific Hotel Vancouver, perched directly atop the cruise ship terminal, is the most convenient; see p. 68).

B.C. Ferries (© **888/223-3779** in B.C. only or 250/386-3431; www.bcferries.com) has three Victoria–Vancouver routes. Its large ferries offer onboard facilities such as restaurants, snack bars, gift shops, business-center desks with modem connections, and indoor lounges. The one-way fare in peak season is C$11 (US$8.40) for adults, C$5.25 (US$4.20) for students and children 5 to 11, and C$37 (US$29) per car. Children under 5 ride free. In the summer, if you're driving, it's a good idea to reserve a space beforehand, especially on long weekends. Call B.C. Ferries reservations at © **888/724-5223** (in B.C. only) or 604/444-2890.

The most direct route is the **Tsawwassen–Swartz Bay ferry,** which operates daily between 7am and 9pm (10pm on Sun). Ferries run every hour with extra sailings on holidays and in peak travel season. The crossing takes 95 minutes, but schedule an extra 2 hours for travel to and from both ferry terminals, including waiting time at the docks. Driving distance from Tsawwassen to Vancouver is about 20km (12 miles). Take Highway 17 from Tsawwassen until it merges with Highway 99 just before the George Massey Tunnel; then follow the driving directions to Vancouver given in "By Car," above. Alternatively, B.C. Transit has regular bus service to both

terminals. From Swartz Bay, there's regular bus service to Victoria.

The **Vancouver–Nanaimo ferry** operates between Tsawwassen and Duke Point, just south of Nanaimo. The 2-hour crossing runs eight times daily between 5:15am and 10:45pm.

The **Horseshoe Bay–Nanaimo ferry** has nine daily sailings, leaving Horseshoe Bay near West Vancouver and arriving 95 minutes later in Nanaimo. From there, passengers bound for Victoria board the E&N Railiner (see "By Train," under "Getting to Victoria," below) or drive south to Victoria via the Island Highway (Hwy. 1).

To reach Vancouver from Horseshoe Bay, take the Trans-Canada Highway (Hwy. 1 and Hwy. 99) east, and then take Exit 13 (Taylor Way) to the Lions Gate Bridge.

7 Getting to Victoria

BY PLANE

For more on air travel security and tips on getting reduced airfare, please see section 6, "Getting to Vancouver," above.

Air Canada (© **888/247-2262** or 800/661-3936; www.aircanada.com) and **Horizon Air** (© **800/547-9308;** www.horizonair.com) offer direct connections from Seattle, Vancouver, Portland, Calgary, Edmonton, Saskatoon, Winnipeg, and Toronto. Canada's low-cost airline **WestJet** (© **888/WEST-JET;** www.westjet.com) offers flights to Victoria from Kelowna, Calgary, Edmonton, and other destinations; WestJet service now extends to a few U.S. cities as well.

Commuter airlines, including floatplanes that land in Victoria's Inner Harbour, provide service to Victoria from Vancouver and destinations within B.C. They include **Air B.C.** (can be reached through Air Canada at © 888/247-2262); **Harbour Air Sea Planes** (© 604/274-1277 in Vancouver, or 250/384-2215 in Victoria; www.harbour-air.com);

Pacific Spirit Air (also known as Tofino Air; © 800/665-2359; www.tofinoair.ca), which serves Victoria in addition to the south and north Gulf Islands from Vancouver Airport and Tofino; **Pacific Coastal Airlines** (© 604/273-8666; www.pacific-coastal.com); and **West Coast Air** (© 800/347-2222; www.westcoastair.com).

In addition to serving B.C. destinations, **Kenmore Air** (© 800/543-9595; www.kenmoreair.com) and **Helijet Airways** (© 800/665-4354; www.helijet.com) offer 35-minute flights between Seattle and Victoria.

For more information on getting into Victoria, see "Arriving," in chapter 11.

BY TRAIN

Travelers on the **Horseshoe Bay–Nanaimo ferry** (see "By Ship & Ferry," under section 6, above) can board a train that winds down Vancouver Island's Cowichan River Valley through Goldstream Provincial Park into Victoria. VIA

Rail's **E&N Railiner** leaves from Nanaimo at 3:37pm Monday through Saturday and arrives in Victoria at 6pm. On Sunday, it departs Nanaimo at 7:07pm and arrives in Victoria at 9:40pm. The Victoria **E&N Station,** 450 Pandora Ave. (© **800/561-8630** in Canada), is near the Johnson Street Bridge. For more information, contact **Via Rail Canada** (© **888/842-7245;** www.viarail.com). For more information, see "Arriving," in chapter 11.

BY BUS
See "By Bus," under "Getting to Vancouver," above, for information about Pacific Coast Lines bus service between Victoria and Vancouver.

BY SHIP & FERRY
See "By Ship & Ferry," under "Getting to Vancouver," above, for information about B.C. Ferries service between Victoria and Vancouver.

Three different ferry services offer daily, year-round connections between Port Angeles, Bellingham, or Seattle, Washington, and Victoria. **Black Ball Transport** (© **250/386-2202** in Victoria, or 360/457-4491 in Port Angeles; www.cohoferry.com) operates between Port Angeles and Victoria. One-way fares are C$9.50 (US$7.50) for foot-passenger

adults, C$38 (US$30) for a car and driver. The crossing takes 1½ hours and there are four crossings per day in the summer (mid-June to Sept), and usually two sailings a day throughout the rest of the year (with a short 2-week closure in Jan).

Victoria Clipper (© **800/288-2535;** www.victoriaclipper.com), operates a high-speed catamaran between Seattle and Victoria, with some sailings stopping in the San Juan Islands. It's a passenger-only service; sailing time is approximately 3 hours with daily runs from downtown Seattle and Victoria. Round-trip adult fares are C$66 to C$133 (US$53–US$106).

May 7 through September, the *MV Victoria Star* operated by **Victoria San Juan Cruises** (© **800/443-4552** or 360/738-8099; www.whales.com) departs the Fairhaven Terminal in Bellingham, Washington, at 9am and arrives in Victoria at 2pm. It departs Victoria at 5pm, arriving in Bellingham at 8pm. Round-trip fares are US$79 to US$89 for adults, with special onboard salmon lunches and Victoria city tour add-ons and overnights available.

Note: If you're riding the ferry between the U.S. and Canada, remember to bring your passport or appropriate photo ID and resident documentation as all passengers go through Customs on international ferry trips.

8 Planning Your Trip Online

SURFING FOR AIRFARES
The "big three" online travel agencies, **Expedia.com, Travelocity.com,** and **Orbitz.com** sell most of the air tickets bought on the Internet. (Canadian travelers should try expedia.ca and Travelocity.ca; U.K. residents can check expedia.co.uk and opodo.co.uk.) Each online agency has different business deals with the airlines and may offer different fares for the same flights, so it's wise to shop around. Expedia and Travelocity will also send you **e-mail notification** when a cheap

fare becomes available to your favorite destination. Of the smaller travel agency websites, **SideStep** (www.sidestep.com) has gotten the best reviews from Frommer's authors. It's a browser add-on that purports to "search 140 sites at once," but only beats competitors' fares as often as other sites do.

Also check **airline websites,** whose fares may be misreported or missing from travel agency websites. Most airlines now offer online-only fares that even their phone agents know nothing about.

Great **last-minute deals** are available through free weekly e-mail services provided directly by the airlines. Most of these must be purchased online and are only valid for travel that weekend, but some can be booked in advance. Also, mega-sites such as **Smarter Living** (www. smarterliving.com) compile comprehensive lists of last-minute specials. For last-minute trips, **site59.com** in the U.S. and **lastminute.com** in Europe often have better deals than the major-label sites.

If you're willing to give up some control over your flight details, use an **opaque fare service** like **Priceline** (www.priceline.com; www.priceline.co. uk for Europeans) or **Hotwire** (www. hotwire.com). Both offer rock-bottom prices in exchange for travel on a "mystery airline" at a possibly not great time of day, often with a change of planes en route. The mystery airlines are all major, well-known carriers—and the possibility of being sent from Philadelphia to Vancouver via Tampa is remote. But your chances of getting a 6am or 11pm flight are pretty high. Hotwire tells you flight prices before you buy; Priceline usually has better deals than Hotwire, but you have to play their "name our price" game. If you're new at this, the helpful folks at **BiddingForTravel** (www.biddingfor travel.com) do a good job of demystifying Priceline's prices. Priceline and Hotwire are great for flights within North America and between the U.S. and Europe. But for flights to other parts of the world, consolidators will almost always beat their fares.

SURFING FOR HOTELS

Of the "big three" sites, **Expedia.com** may be the best choice, thanks to its long list of special deals. **Travelocity.com** runs a close second. Hotel specialist sites **hotels.com** and **hoteldiscounts.com** are also reliable. An excellent free program, **TravelAxe** (www.travelaxe.net), can help you search multiple hotel sites.

Priceline and Hotwire are even better for hotels than for airfares; with both, you're allowed to pick the neighborhood and quality level of your hotel before offering up your money. *Note:* Hotwire overrates its hotels by one star—a four-star is a three-star anywhere else.

You should also see the websites listed in chapters 5 and 12 for bed-and-breakfast info.

SURFING FOR RENTAL CARS

For booking rental cars online, the best deals are usually found at rental-car

---

Frommers.com: The Complete Travel Resource

For an excellent travel-planning resource, we highly recommend **Frommers. com** (www.frommers.com). We're a little biased, of course, but we guarantee that you'll find the travel tips, reviews, monthly vacation giveaways, and online-booking capabilities thoroughly indispensable. Among the special features are our popular **Message Boards,** where Frommer's readers post queries and share advice (sometimes even our authors show up to answer questions); **Frommers.com Newsletter,** for the latest travel bargains and insider secrets; and **Frommer's Destinations Section,** where you'll get expert travel tips, hotel and dining recommendations, and advice on the sights to see for more than 3,000 destinations. When your research is done, the **Online Reservations System** (www.frommers.com/book_a_trip) takes you to Frommer's preferred online partners for booking your vacation at affordable prices.

company websites. Priceline and Hotwire work well for rental cars, too; the only "mystery" is which major rental company you get, and for most travelers the difference between Hertz, Avis, and Budget is negligible.

BY AIR: TRANSPORTATION SITES

Below are the websites for the major airlines operating throughout North America and flying into Vancouver and Victoria. These sites offer schedules and booking, and most of the airlines have E-saver alerts for weekend deals and late-breaking bargains.

- **Air Canada:** www.aircanada.com
- **Alaska Airlines:** www.alaskaair.com
- **America West:** www.americawest. com
- **American Airlines:** www.aa.com
- **Continental Airlines:** www. continental.com
- **Delta:** www.delta.com
- **Horizon Air:** www.horizonair.com
- **Northwest Airlines:** www.nwa.com
- **United Airlines:** www.united.com
- **WestJet:** www.westjet.com

9 Tips on Accommodations

SAVING ON YOUR HOTEL ROOM

The **rack rate** is the maximum rate that a hotel charges for a room. Hardly anybody pays this price, however. To lower the cost of your room:

- **Ask about special rates.** Always ask whether a less expensive room might be available (corporate, student, military, senior, frequent-flier) and whether kids stay free.
- **Dial direct.** When booking a room in a chain hotel, you'll often get a better deal by calling the individual hotel's reservation desk than the chain's main toll-free number.
- **Book online.** Many hotels offer Internet-only discounts, or supply rooms to Priceline, Hotwire, or Expedia at lower rates.
- **Remember the law of supply and demand.** Resort hotels are most crowded and therefore most expensive on weekends, so discounts are usually available for midweek stays. Business hotels in downtown locations are busiest during the week, so you can expect big discounts over the weekend. Many hotels in Vancouver and Victoria have high-season (generally, mid-May through September)

and low-season prices; try booking the day after "high season" ends.

- **Look into group or long-stay discounts.** As a general rule, expect 1 night free after a 7-night stay.
- **Avoid excess charges and hidden costs.** When you book, ask about parking and phone costs. Use your own cell phone, pay phones, or prepaid phone cards instead of dialing direct from hotel phones, which usually have exorbitant rates. Finally, ask if local taxes and service charges are included in your quoted room rate; hotel rooms in B.C. are taxed 17%.
- **Book an efficiency.** A room with a kitchenette allows you to shop for groceries and cook your own meals. This is a big money saver, especially for families on long stays.

LANDING THE BEST ROOM

Somebody has to get the best room in the house—it might as well be you. You can start by joining the hotel's frequent-guest program, which may make you eligible for upgrades. A hotel-branded credit card usually gives its owner "silver" or "gold" status in frequent-guest programs for free. Always ask for a corner room (usually sunnier and larger) or a recently renovated room. If the hotel is renovating, request a room away from the construction. Ask about nonsmoking and views, if that matters to you.

If you aren't happy with your room when you arrive, say so. If another room is available, most lodgings will be willing to accommodate you.

In resort areas like Whistler or Tofino (see chapter 18), ask the following questions before you book a room:

- **What's the view like?** You may pay less for a room that faces the parking lot.
- **Do the windows open?** If they do, and there's alfresco nighttime entertainment nearby, you may want to find out when show time is over.
- **How far is the room from the skiing/beaches and other amenities?** If it's far, is there transportation to and from the skiing or beaches?

3

Suggested Vancouver & Victoria Itineraries

Vancouver and Victoria are pre-emi-
nently maritime cities and the visitor is
always aware of water and the closeness of
the immense Pacific. Vibrant Vancouver
is (mostly) on the mainland, but charming Victoria occupies the southern tip of
Vancouver Island, about 24 nautical
miles to the west. To get the most out of
this glorious part of Canada, you'll need a
car and you'll have to take a ferry to reach
Victoria. In both Vancouver and Victoria
you can ditch your car and use public
transportation or walk, but to enjoy the
almost limitless sightseeing opportunities
outside the cities, a car is essential.

1 The Best of Vancouver in 1 Day

This tour is meant to show off the city as a whole, giving you an overview of what
makes it so uniquely appealing. There are some places where you'll be exploring on
foot, others where you'll drive to reach your destination. Nature, art, culture, and coffee are all part of today's itinerary. Start: Tourism Vancouver Touristinfo Centre, Burrard and Cordova streets.

❶ Canada Place 🎭🎭
Start your day outside, on the upper
(deck) level of the city's giant convention
center and cruise-ship terminal, which
juts out into Burrard Inlet across from the
Touristinfo Centre. From here you'll get a
good sense of Vancouver's natural and
urban topography, with the North Coast
Mountains rising up before you; low-rise,
historic Gastown to the east; Stanley Park
to the west; and a forest of glass residential towers in between. Canada Place is
busiest in summer, when up to four giant
cruise ships may dock in one day. For
more on Canada Place, see Walking Tour
2, chapter 8, p. 150.

❷ Stanley Park 🎭🎭🎭
You can't really appreciate Stanley Park by
driving through it in a car, so park your

vehicle and head in on foot via Lagoon
Drive. Surrounded by a famed pedestrian
seawall, this giant peninsular park invites
hours of exploration. A 1-hour **carriage
ride** (see "Specialty Tours," p. 133) is the
perfect way to see the highlights, including
an amazing collection of **totem poles,** giant
trees, and landscaped areas. See p. 116.

❸ Vancouver Aquarium Marine Science Centre 🎭🎭
One of the best aquariums in North
America is located right in Stanley Park.
Have a look especially at the Arctic
Canada exhibit with its beluga whales,
and the Marine Mammal Deck, where
you can see Pacific white-sided dolphins,
sea otters, and other denizens of Pacific
Northwest waters. See p. 118.

The Best of Vancouver in 1 & 2 Days

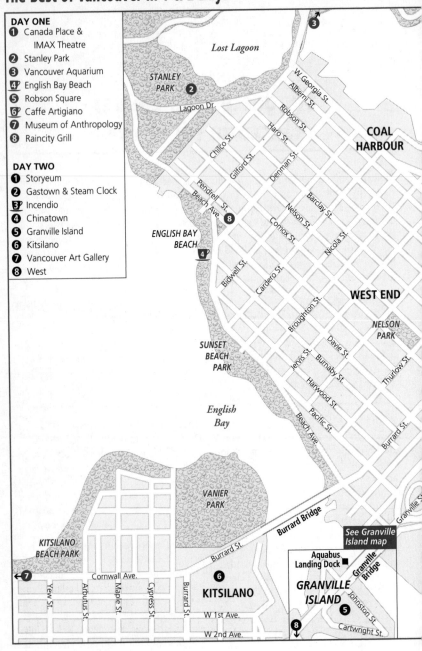

DAY ONE
1. Canada Place & IMAX Theatre
2. Stanley Park
3. Vancouver Aquarium
4. English Bay Beach
5. Robson Square
6. Caffe Artigiano
7. Museum of Anthropology
8. Raincity Grill

DAY TWO
1. Storyeum
2. Gastown & Steam Clock
3. Incendio
4. Chinatown
5. Granville Island
6. Kitsilano
7. Vancouver Art Gallery
8. West

Lost Lagoon

STANLEY PARK

COAL HARBOUR

W Georgia St.
Alberni St.
Robson St.
Haro St.
Chilco St.
Gilford St.
Denman St.
Barclay St.
Nelson St.
Nicola St.
Pendrell St.
Beach Ave.
Cardero St.
Cornox St.
Bidwell St.
Broughton St.

WEST END

NELSON PARK

Davie St.
Jervis St.
Burnaby St.
Thurlow St.
Harwood St.
Pacific St.
Beach Ave.
Burrard St.

ENGLISH BAY BEACH

SUNSET BEACH PARK

English Bay

VANIER PARK

Burrard Bridge

Granville St.

See Granville Island map

KITSILANO BEACH PARK

Aquabus Landing Dock

Cornwall Ave.

GRANVILLE ISLAND

Granville Bridge

Yew St.
Arbutus St.
Maple St.
Cypress St.
Burrard St.

KITSILANO

Johnston St.

W 1st Ave.

Cartwright St.

W 2nd Ave.

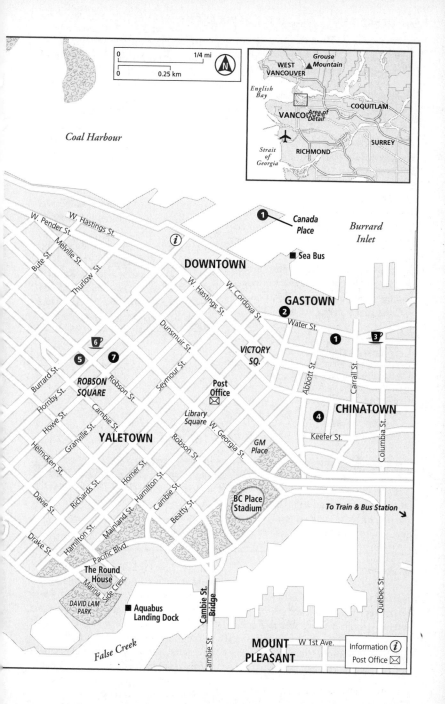

0   1/4 mi
0   0.25 km

N

Coal Harbour

Burrard Inlet

WEST VANCOUVER
Grouse ▲ Mountain

English Bay

VANCOUVER
Area of Detail

COQUITLAM

Strait of Georgia

✈

RICHMOND

SURREY

W. Hastings St.

W. Pender St.

Melville St.

Bute St.

Thurlow St.

ⓘ

1 Canada Place

■ Sea Bus

DOWNTOWN

W. Hastings St.

W. Cordova St.

GASTOWN

2   Water St.

1   **3**

Dunsmuir St.

Seymour St.

6

5   **7**

ROBSON SQUARE

Robson St.

Burrard St.

Hornby St.

Howe St.

Granville St.

Cambie St.

Helmcken St.

YALETOWN

Robson St.

Homer St.

Hamilton St.

Cambie St.

Richards St.

Davie St.

Mainland St.

Hamilton St.

Beatty St.

Drake St.

Pacific Blvd.

The Round House

Marina Side Cresc.

DAVID LAM PARK

■ Aquabus Landing Dock

VICTORY SQ.

Post Office ⊠

Library Square   W. Georgia St.

GM Place

BC Place Stadium

Abbott St.

Carrall St.

CHINATOWN

4   Keefer St.

Columbia St.

Québec St.

To Train & Bus Station →

False Creek

Cambie St. Bridge

Cambie St.

MOUNT PLEASANT   W. 1st Ave.

Information ⓘ
Post Office ⊠

4 ENGLISH BAY BEACH ✦
If the weather is warm, take off your shoes and enjoy the grass, sand, and sunshine at **English Bay Beach**, an all-season gathering spot on the south side of Stanley Park.

You can pick up picnic eats or find take-out food on nearby Denman Street.

5 Robson Street & the West End
How you explore the West End is up to you. You can walk from English Bay Beach down Denman Street and then turn south on Robson, taking in as much of the throbbing shopping and cafe scene as you want. It's also fun to explore the West End as a living neighborhood—the most densely populated in North America! For extra suggestions on exploring the West End, see Walking Tour 1 in chapter 8, p. 145.

6 CAFFÈ ARTIGIANO ✦✦
For the best latte in town, as well as grilled Italian sandwiches and snacks, stop in at this busy café right across from the Vancouver Art Gallery. There's a perfect people-watching patio in front. 763 Hornby St. ✆ 604/685-5333.

7 UBC Anthropology Museum ✦✦✦
Hop in your car for the 20-minute drive to the outstanding Anthropology Museum at the University of British Columbia. Here, in one of North America's pre-eminent collections of First Nations Art, you'll encounter powerful totem poles, spirit masks, and totemic objects, all richly carved and profoundly mysterious. See p. 123.

8 Dinner
In the last decade, Vancouver has become one of the top dining cities in the world, filled with superb restaurants of all kinds. For a romantic dinner that will introduce you to the best of Vancouver's "eat local" food philosophy, reserve a table at **Rain-city Grill** ✦✦✦, 1193 Denman St. (✆ **604/685-7337**), where the windows overlook English Bay, and the regional cuisine is a perfect excuse to linger. See p. 98.

2 The Best of Vancouver in 2 Days

If you've already made your way through "The Best of Vancouver in One Day," you'll find that your second full-day tour takes in a roster of new sights and adventures. Today's itinerary will give you an entertaining handle on Vancouver's past and introduce you to some of Vancouver's most appealing neighborhoods.

1 Storyeum ✦✦✦
Located in Gastown, Storyeum is a new and highly entertaining way to learn more about Vancouver's past. Actors lead visitors into a series of specially designed theatres for time-capsule enactments of key epochs and events, complete with special effects. See p. 120.

2 Gastown & the Steam Clock
Gastown is the oldest part of Vancouver, a low-rise brick district from the late 19th century, now making a comeback after years of neglect. Stroll down Water Street, timing your visit so you'll be in front of the famous steam clock when it steams and chimes at noon. You might also want to shop for a piece of First Nations art at one of Gastown's specialty galleries (see "First Nations Art & Crafts" in chapter 9, p. 164). For a complete tour of Gastown, see Walking Tour 2, chapter 8, p. 150.

❸ INCENDIO ☆

If it's lunchtime and you're in the mood for pizza, head over to **Incendio**, 103 Columbia St. (© **604/688-8694**). Crispy, delicious pizzas at moderate prices make this a local Gastown fave.

❹ Chinatown

Vancouver's vibrant, fascinating Chinatown lies just east of Gastown, and you can walk there or drive. Though parts of Chinatown are touristy, the street markets are lively and authentic. Poke around the district and you'll be surprised at what you discover, including the Dr. Sun Yat-sen Classical Chinese Garden ☆☆. For a complete tour of Chinatown, see Walking Tour 2, chapter 8, p. 150.

❺ Granville Island ☆☆☆

You can easily drive to Granville Island via the Granville Bridge, but it's lots more fun to hop on one of the miniferries from Yaletown Landing and take a 10-minute trip across False Creek. The **public market** ☆☆☆ is pure sensory overload, crammed with every kind of produce, seafood, and food product imaginable, while the area around it is a browser's heaven of shops, galleries, and outdoor-adventure outfitters. See p. 120. For a complete tour of Granville Island, see Walking Tour 3, chapter 8, p. 154.

❻ Kitsilano

You can drive or walk to Kitsilano, the funkily upbeat neighborhood west of Granville Island. Check out the buffed beach scene at scenic **Kitsilano Beach** ☆, facing English Bay. One of the world's largest freshwater pools is there, if you want a summertime swim. Then stroll through the neighborhood to appreciate its appealing charm. For a complete walking tour of Kitsilano, see Walking Tour 3, chapter 8, p. 154.

❼ Vancouver Art Gallery ☆☆

You can drive or you can hop on a no. 4 or 7 bus on 4th Avenue for the 15-minute ride back to downtown Vancouver. Head for the Vancouver Art Gallery, and make your way specifically to the museum's collection of hauntingly atmospheric paintings by B.C. native Emily Carr. Her moodily expressive works sum up all that is grand and glorious in the Pacific Northwest landscape. See p. 119.

❽ Dinner

Cap off your day with a memorable meal at **West** ☆☆☆, 2881 Granville St. (© **604/738-8938**), a culinary highpoint of the city and winner of Vancouver Magazine's Best Restaurant award in 2005. See p. 103.

3 The Best of Victoria in 1 Day

Victoria is less than a quarter of the size of Vancouver, and you can easily hit the highlights in one day if you arrive on an early ferry. The scenic ferry ride—from Vancouver, Seattle, Anacortes, or Port Angeles—is part of the fun. Although it's easy to experience Victoria on foot, by bike, and using public transportation, having a car will help to maximize your sightseeing. For all the transportation options to Victoria, see "Getting to Victoria" in chapter 2, p. 34.

❶ Inner Harbour

Victoria's official facade, epitomized by a pair of landmark buildings designed by Francis Rattenbury, is reminiscent of an era that promoted the idea of a British Empire. A stroll along the Inner Harbour takes you past the **Provincial Legislature** ☆, a massive stone edifice completed in 1898, and the famous Fairmont Empress Hotel, which dates from 1908.

The Best of Victoria in 1 Day

Gladstone Ave.
Vining St.
Begbie St.
St. Charles St.
Rockland Ave.
Arnold Ave.
■ Government House
ROSS BAY CEMETERY
Ross Bay
Pandora Ave.
Dallas Rd.
Moss St.
Cook St.
Johnson St.
Yates St.
Fort St.
Burdett Ave.
Richardson St.
Fairfield Rd.
Linden Ave.
May St.
Cook St.
Fisgard St.
Quadra St.
Vancouver St.
Herald St.
Blanshard St.
CHINATOWN
Douglas St.
DOWNTOWN
Southgate St.
BEACON HILL PARK
Government St.
OLD TOWN
Market Square
Store St.
Bastion Square
Wharf St.
Belleville St.
THUNDERBIRD PARK
Toronto St.
Dallas Rd.
Douglas St.
Government St.
Johnson St. Bridge
Upper Harbour
Inner Harbour
Menzies St.
Medana St.
Equimalt Rd.
Superior St.
Simcoe St.
Oswego St.
MACDONALD PARK
Niagara St.
Lime Bay
Victoria Harbour
Montreal St.
Dallas Rd.

1/2 mi
0.5 km
0
0

Information (i)

SAANICH
WEST BAY
VICTORIA
Area of Detail

1 Inner Harbour
2 Royal B.C. Museum
3 Fairmont Empress
4 Butchart Gardens
5 Il Terrazzo Ristorante

44

Along the busy waterfront you'll also find information on whale-watching excursions, a popular Victoria pastime. For a complete walking tour of the Inner Harbour, see Walking Tour 1 in chapter 15, p. 241.

❷ Royal B.C. Museum ✿✿✿

The highlight of this excellent museum is the First Peoples Gallery, an absorbing and thought-provoking showplace of First Nations art and culture. The other exhibits pale by comparison, but do have a look at the life-sized woolly mastodon if he's on display. See p. 226.

---

❸ FAIRMONT EMPRESS ✿✿

Tea at the Empress is a traditional affair that has remained a real treat despite its fame. Make it your main meal of the day (seatings at 12:30, 2, 2:30, and 5pm), and be sure to reserve in advance. 721 Government St. ✆ **250/384-8111**. See "Taking Afternoon Tea" in chapter 13, p. 216.

---

❹ Butchart Gardens ✿✿✿

This century-old garden is one of the gardening wonders of the world, meticulously planned and impeccably maintained. Though hordes of tourists can jam the paths in the summer months, time your visit for late afternoon and you'll have more room, plus you can stay for the fabulous summer fireworks display. See p. 224.

❺ Dinner

If there's time, have dinner at **Il Terrazzo Ristorante** ✿ (555 Johnson St., ✆ **250/ 361-0028**). Victoria's best Italian restaurant serves delicious, northern-Italian dishes and has a lovely patio for outdoor, summertime dining. See p. 215.

4 The Best of Vancouver, Victoria & Whistler in 1 Week

Lucky the traveler who gets to spend a whole week exploring this ruggedly beautiful and highly civilized part of the Pacific Northwest. If you don't arrive with a car, you can rent one in either Vancouver (see "Rental Cars" in chapter 4, p. 55) or Victoria (see "Arriving" in chapter 11, p. 186). Most visitors travel to Victoria by car ferry, so it's important to know about ferry schedules and reservations (see "Getting to Victoria," chapter 2, p. 34). A week will allow you to savor the delights of both cities and go farther afield to explore Whistler, a year-round resort in the mountains north of Vancouver. The assumption here is that your week begins and ends in Vancouver, the major travel hub.

Day ❶: Vancouver ✿✿✿

Start your week in Vancouver, following "The Best of Vancouver in 1 Day," above.

Day ❷: Exploring Vancouver

Your second day's itinerary in Vancouver is outlined in "The Best of Vancouver in 2 Days," above.

Day ❸: North Vancouver

Now that you've seen Vancouver's West End and West Side, use your third day to get out of the city. At **Capilano Suspension Bridge & Park** ✿✿ (p. 125), you can test your love-hate relationship with heights on the narrow, bouncy suspension footbridge that spans a scenic ravine, or you can hike under the canopies of the tallest trees on a series of tree bridges. Afterwards, drive to the nearby **SkyRide gondola** and be transported to the summit of **Grouse Mountain Resort** 👁, where you'll enjoy panoramic views of the entire region and can choose from different places to dine atop the mountain (p. 126). There are casual dining rooms and picnic areas at Capilano and Grouse Mountain, or you can enjoy fine Pacific Northwest cuisine and a panoramic waterfront view at **The Beach House at Dundarave Pier** 👁 (📞 604/922-1414), a restored 1912 teahouse located on the water's edge.

Day ❹: Vancouver to Whistler 👁👁👁

Take Georgia Street from downtown Vancouver and head west through Stanley Park, across the scenic Three Lions Bridge, and hook up with the spectacular **Sea-to-Sky Highway**, which winds along the edge of Howe Sound and climbs into the mountains. It should take you about 2 hours to reach **Whistler Village**. And once you get to Whistler, ski (it is one of North America's greatest ski resorts, after all). . . or mountainbike, or hike, or Ziptrek, or shop, or pamper yourself with a spa treatment. A casual and delicious lunch or dinner at **Chef Bernard's Chow Thyme Bistro** 👁 (📞 604/932-9795) will set you up for whatever activities are on your agenda. You'll find a complete rundown of Whistler possibilities in chapter 18.

Day ❺: Whistler to Vancouver

Spend the night at Whistler. Before leaving the area, drive to **Nairn Falls**

Provincial Park 👁👁, where the Green River shoots through basaltic rock formations and forms a series of thundering waterfalls (p. 281). The road back to Vancouver along the Sea-to-Sky Highway is just as spectacular in the reverse direction. Once back in Vancouver, enjoy fresh oysters and caught-that-day fish at **Joe Fortes Seafood and Chop House** 👁👁👁 (📞 604/669-1940).

Day ❻: Vancouver to Victoria 👁👁👁

Spend Day Six of your week-long Northwest adventure in civilized Victoria, preferably taking an early morning ferry through the Gulf Islands. For your day in Victoria, see "The Best of Victoria in One Day," above.

Day ❼: Victoria to Vancouver

If time allows and you're eager to see more of the region, make a trip from Victoria to **Pacific Rim National Park** 👁👁👁 on the west coast of Vancouver Island (a 4½ hour drive or 45-minute flight). A temperate rainforest with old-growth trees and a wildly magnificent coastline, it is a place you'll never forget. For a complete summary of what's there, including famous lodges and dining choices, see chapter 18, p. 285. Otherwise, this is the day you return to Vancouver by ferry. Back on the mainland, the Tsawassen ferry terminal is the closest to the Vancouver airport and hooks up with Interstate 5 south to Seattle or north to Vancouver, or you can travel back via Port Angeles, a gateway to Washington's Olympic National Park, or Anacortes.

4

Getting to Know Vancouver

Getting lost as you wander around a fascinating new neighborhood is part of the fun of traveling. And getting lost in Vancouver, or at least losing your directional bearings, is possible, mostly because the main grid of streets doesn't run strictly north-south but rather northwest to southeast, like a parallelogram. If you do become directionally challenged, all you have to do is look for the mountains. They are to the north, across a body of water called Burrard Inlet. If you're facing the mountains, east is to your right, west is to your left, and the back of your head is pointing south. That one tip will generally keep you pointed in the right direction, no matter where you are. You'll also find that Vancouverites are incredibly friendly: If you're scratching your head over a map, almost inevitably someone will ask if they can help. This chapter offers more detailed information on how to find your way around this scenic city. For the best overall introduction to Vancouver, consider taking one of the walking tours in chapter 8.

1 Orientation

ARRIVING
BY PLANE

Vancouver International Airport (© **604/207-7077;** www.yvr.ca) is 13km (8 miles) south of downtown Vancouver on uninhabited Sea Island, bordered on three sides by Richmond and the Fraser River delta. It's the largest airport on Canada's west coast and one of the world's major airports, handling some 15 million passengers annually. The International Terminal features an extensive collection of First Nations sculptures and paintings set amid grand expanses of glass under soaring ceilings. Turn around and look up just before you leave the International Terminal to catch a glimpse of Bill Reid's huge jade canoe sculpture, *The Spirit of Haida Gwaii.*

Tourist information kiosks on Level 2 of the Main and International arrival terminals are open daily from 8am to 11pm. **Parking** is available at the airport for both loading passengers and long-term stays. A **shuttle bus** links the Main and International terminals to the South Terminal, where smaller and private aircraft are docked.

Travelers heading into Vancouver from the airport take the Arthur Laing Bridge, which leads directly to Granville Street, the most direct route to downtown.

There is an international departure surcharge of C$15 (US$12) per person for international air travelers leaving North America, C$10 (US$8) for passengers traveling within North America (including Hawaii and Mexico), and C$5 (US$4) for passengers on flights within British Columbia or the Yukon.

Getting into Town from the Airport & Vice Versa

The **YVR Airporter** (© **604/946-8866;** www.yvrairporter.com) provides **airport bus service** to downtown Vancouver's major hotels and cruise-ship terminal. It leaves from

Level 2 of the Main Terminal every 15 minutes daily from 6:30am until midnight. A one-way fare for the 30-minute ride across the Granville Street Bridge into downtown Vancouver is C$12 (US$9.50) for adults, C$9 (US$7.20) for seniors, and C$5 (US$4) for children. Bus service back to the airport leaves from selected downtown hotels every half-hour between 5:35am and 10:55pm. Scheduled pickups serve the Bus Station, cruise-ship terminal, Four Seasons, Hotel Vancouver, Waterfront Centre Hotel, Georgian Court, Sutton Place, Landmark, and others. Ask the bus driver on the way in or ask your hotel concierge for the nearest pickup stop and time.

Getting to and from the airport with **public transit** is much slower and requires at least one transfer, but it costs less. Public buses are operated by **Translink** (📞 604/953-3333; www.translink.bc.ca). If you wish to travel into town this way, catch bus no. 424 at Ground Level of the Domestic Terminal; it will take you to Airport Station. From there, bus no. 98B will take you into downtown Vancouver. B.C. Transit fares are C$3.25 (US$2.60) during peak hours and C$2.25 (US$1.80) on weekends and after 6:30pm. You must have the exact fare because drivers do not make change. Transfers are free in any direction within a 90-minute period.

The average **taxi** fare from the airport to a downtown Vancouver hotel is approximately C$25 (US$20) plus tip, but the fare can run up to C$40 (US$32) if the cab gets stuck in traffic. **LimoJet** (📞 604/273-1331; www.limojetgold.com) offers flat-rate stretch-limousine service at C$39 (US$31) per trip (not per person) to the airport from any downtown location, plus tip, and can easily accommodate six people. The drivers accept all major credit cards.

Most major **car-rental firms** have airport counters and shuttles.

BY TRAIN & BUS

VIA Rail Canada and Amtrak trains arrive at **Pacific Central Station,** 1150 Station St. (at Main St. and Terminal Ave.; 📞 800/872-7245), the main Vancouver railway station, located just south of Chinatown. You can reach downtown Vancouver from there by cab for about C$10 (US$8). There are plenty of taxis at the station entrance. One block from the station is the SkyTrain's Main Street Station (p. 54); within minutes, you'll be downtown. The Granville and Waterfront SkyTrain stations are two and four stops away, respectively.

Greyhound Bus Lines (📞 604/482-8747; www.greyhound.ca) and **Pacific Coach Lines** (📞 604/662-8074; www.pacificcoach.com) also have their terminals at the Pacific Central Station.

For information on arriving **by ferry,** see "Getting to Vancouver," in chapter 2, beginning on p. 34.

VISITOR INFORMATION

TOURIST OFFICES & PUBLICATIONS   **The Vancouver Tourist Info Centre,** 200 Burrard St. (📞 604/683-2000; www.tourismvancouver.com), is your single best travel information source about Vancouver and the North Shore. An incredibly helpful and well-trained staff provides information, maps, and brochures, and can help you with all your travel needs, including hotel, cruise-ship, ferry, bus, and train reservations. There's also a **half-price ticket office** (Tickets Tonight) for same-day shows and events in Vancouver. The Info Centre is open from May to Labour Day daily from 8am to 6pm; the rest of the year, it's open Monday through Saturday from 8:30am to 5pm.

Tourism Richmond, George Massey Tunnel (📞 604/271-8280), has information about the Richmond and Delta areas, including the heritage fishing village of Steveston.

It's open daily from 9am to 7pm in July and August and daily from 9:30am to 5pm September through June. The office is located north of the George Massey Tunnel and is easily accessible when driving in from the U.S. border through the farm community of Delta.

If you plan to see more of this beautiful province, **Super Natural British Columbia** (© **800/663-6000** or 604/663-6000; www.hellobc.com) can help you. If you're driving from Seattle, there's a **Tourist Information Centre,** 356 Hwy. 99, Surrey (no phone; walk-in service only), located just north of the Customs border crossing at Blaine, Washington.

The free weekly tabloid *The Georgia Straight* (© **604/730-7000**; www.straight. com), found all over the city in cafes, bookshops, and restaurants, provides up-to-date schedules of concerts, lectures, art exhibits, plays, recitals, and other happenings. Not free but equally good—and with more attitude—is the glossy city magazine *Vancouver* (© **604/877-7732**; www.vanmag.com), available on newsstands. The free guide called *Where Vancouver* is (© **604/736-5586**; www.where.ca), available in many hotels, lists attractions, entertainment, upscale shopping, fine dining, and has good maps.

Two free monthly tabloids, *B.C. Parent* (© **604/221-0366**; www.bcparent.com) and *West Coast Families* (© **604/689-1331**), available at grocery stores and cafes around the city, are geared for families with young children, listing many kid-friendly current events. Gay and lesbian travelers will want to pick up a copy of *Xtra! West* (© **604/684-9696**), a free biweekly tabloid available in cafes, bars, shops, and restaurants throughout the West End.

CITY LAYOUT

With four different bodies of water lapping at its edges and mile after mile of shoreline, Vancouver's geography can seem a bit complicated. That's part of the city's maritime charm, of course, and visitors usually don't find it too difficult to get their bearings. **Downtown Vancouver** is on a peninsula: think of it as an upraised thumb on the mitten-shaped Vancouver mainland. **Stanley Park,** the **West End, Yaletown,** and Vancouver's business and financial center (Downtown) are located on this thumb of land bordered to the north by Burrard Inlet, the city's main deep-water harbor and port, to the west by English Bay, and to the south by False Creek. Farther west beyond English Bay is the Pacific Ocean. Just south across False Creek is **Granville Island,** famous for its public market, and the beach community of **Kitsilano.** This part of the city, called the **West Side,** covers the mainland, or the hand of the mitten. Its western shoreline looks out on the Strait of Georgia with the Pacific beyond, and the North Arm of the Fraser River demarcates it to the south. Pacific Spirit Park and the University of British Columbia (UBC), a locus for visitors because of its outstanding Museum of Anthropology, take up most of the western tip of the West Side; the rest is mostly residential, with a sprinkling of businesses along main arterial streets. Both mainland and peninsula are covered by a simple rectilinear street pattern. North Vancouver is the mountain-backed area directly across Burrard Inlet from downtown Vancouver.

MAIN ARTERIES & STREETS

On the downtown peninsula, there are four key **east–west streets** (to be more directionally exact, the streets run southeast to northwest). **Robson Street** starts at B.C. Place Stadium on Beatty Street, flows through the West End's more touristed shopping district, and ends at Stanley Park's Lost Lagoon on Lagoon Drive. **Georgia Street**—far more efficient for drivers than the pedestrian-oriented Robson—runs

Greater Vancouver

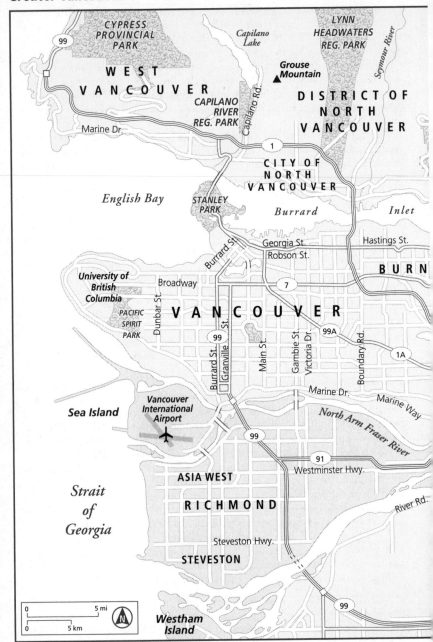

CYPRESS PROVINCIAL PARK

99

Capilano Lake

LYNN HEADWATERS REG. PARK

Seymour River

WEST VANCOUVER

CAPILANO RIVER REG. PARK

Capilano Rd.

Grouse Mountain ▲

DISTRICT OF NORTH VANCOUVER

Marine Dr.

1

CITY OF NORTH VANCOUVER

English Bay

STANLEY PARK

Burrard

Inlet

Hastings St.

BURN

Georgia St.

Robson St.

Burrard St.

University of British Columbia

Broadway

7

PACIFIC SPIRIT PARK

Dunbar St.

VANCOUVER

99

Burrard St.

Granville St.

Main St.

Gambie St.

Victoria Dr.

99A

Boundary Rd.

1A

Sea Island

Vancouver International Airport

✈

Marine Dr.

Marine Way

North Arm Fraser River

99

Strait of Georgia

ASIA WEST

91

Westminster Hwy.

RICHMOND

River Rd.

Steveston Hwy.

STEVESTON

0   5 mi
0   5 km

Westham Island

99

50

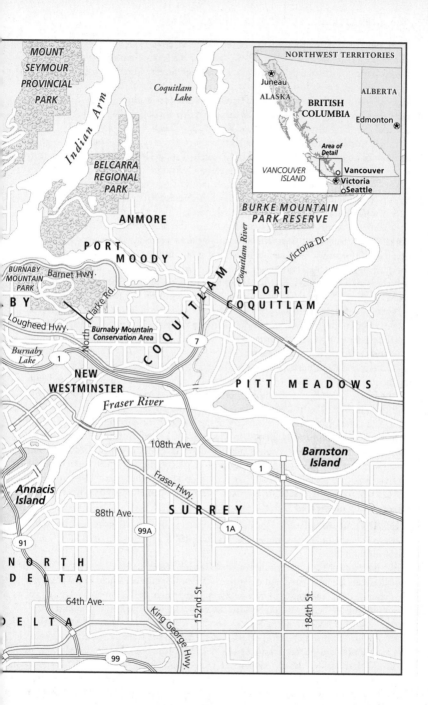

MOUNT
SEYMOUR
PROVINCIAL
PARK

Coquitlam Lake

Indian Arm

BELCARRA
REGIONAL
PARK

ANMORE

BURKE MOUNTAIN
PARK RESERVE

PORT
MOODY

Coquitlam River

Victoria Dr.

BURNABY
MOUNTAIN
PARK

Barnet Hwy.

PORT
COQUITLAM

B Y

North Clarke Rd.

Lougheed Hwy.

Burnaby Mountain
Conservation Area

COQUITLAM

7

Burnaby Lake

1

NEW
WESTMINSTER

PITT MEADOWS

Fraser River

108th Ave.

Barnston Island

1

Annacis Island

Fraser Hwy.

91

88th Ave.

SURREY

99A

1A

NORTH
DELTA

64th Ave.

King George Hwy.

152nd St.

184th St.

DELTA

99

NORTHWEST TERRITORIES

Juneau

ALASKA

ALBERTA

BRITISH
COLUMBIA

Edmonton

Area of
Detail

VANCOUVER
ISLAND

Vancouver

Victoria
Seattle

from the Georgia Viaduct on the eastern edge of downtown through Vancouver's commercial core, through Stanley Park, and over the Lions Gate Bridge to the North Shore. Three blocks north of Georgia is **Hastings Street,** which begins in the West End, runs east through downtown, and then skirts Gastown's southern border as it runs eastward to the Trans-Canada Highway. **Davie Street** starts at Pacific Boulevard near the Cambie Street Bridge, travels through Yaletown into the West End's more residential shopping district, and ends at English Bay Beach.

Three **north–south downtown streets** will get you everywhere you want to go in and out of downtown. Two blocks east of Stanley Park is **Denman Street,** which runs from W. Georgia Street at Coal Harbour to Beach Avenue at English Bay Beach. This main West End thoroughfare is where locals dine out. It's also the shortest north–south route between the two ends of the Stanley Park Seawall.

Eight blocks east of Denman is **Burrard Street,** which starts near the Canada Place Pier and runs south through downtown, crosses the Burrard Street Bridge, and then forks. One branch, still **Burrard Street,** continues south and intersects W. Fourth Avenue and Broadway Avenue before ending at W. 16th Avenue on the borders of the ritzy Shaughnessy neighborhood. The other branch becomes **Cornwall Avenue,** which heads west through Kitsilano, changing its name to **Point Grey Road** and then **N.W. Marine Drive** before entering the University of British Columbia campus.

Granville Street starts near the Waterfront Station on Burrard Inlet and runs the entire length of downtown, crosses the Granville Bridge to Vancouver's West Side, and carries on south across the breadth of the city before crossing the Arthur-Laing Bridge to Vancouver International Airport.

On the mainland portion of Vancouver, the city's east–west roads are successively numbered from First Avenue at the downtown bridges to 77th Avenue by the banks of the Fraser River. By far, the most important east–west route is **Broadway** (formerly Ninth Ave.), which starts a few blocks from the University of British Columbia (UBC) and extends across the length of the city to the border of neighboring Burnaby, where it becomes the **Lougheed Highway.** In Kitsilano, **W. Fourth Avenue** is also an important east–west shopping and commercial corridor. Intersecting with Broadway at various points are a number of important north–south commercial streets, each of which defines a particular neighborhood. The most significant of these streets are (from west to east) **Macdonald Street** in Kitsilano, **Granville Street, Cambie Street, Main Street,** and **Commercial Drive.**

FINDING AN ADDRESS   In many Vancouver addresses, the suite or room number precedes the building number. For instance, 100–1250 Robson St. is Suite 100 at 1250 Robson St.

In downtown Vancouver, Chinatown's **Carrall Street** is the east–west axis from which streets are numbered and designated. Westward, numbers increase progressively to Stanley Park; eastward, numbers increase approaching Commercial Drive. For example, 400 W. Pender would be 4 blocks from Carrall Street heading toward downtown; 400 E. Pender would be 4 blocks on the opposite side of Carrall Street. Similarly, the low numbers on north–south streets start on the Canada Place Pier side and increase southward in increments of 100 per block (the 600 block of Thurlow St. is 2 blocks from the 800 block) toward False Creek and Granville Island.

Off the peninsula the system works the same, but **Ontario Street** is the east–west axis. Also, all east–west roads are avenues (for example, Fourth Ave.), while streets (for example, Main St.) run exclusively north–south.

> **Tips What's West**
>
> The thing to keep in mind, when figuring out what's where in Vancouver, is that this is a city where property is king, and the word "west" has such positive connotations that folks have always gone to great lengths to associate it with their particular patch of real estate. Thus we have the **West End** and the **West Side** and **West Vancouver,** which improbably enough is located immediately beside **North Vancouver.** It can be a bit confusing for newcomers, but fortunately each west has its own distinct character. The West End is a high-rise residential neighborhood located on the downtown peninsula. The West Side is one whole half of Vancouver, from Ontario Street west to the University of British Columbia. (The more working-class **East Side** covers the mainland portion of the city, from Ontario St. east to Boundary Rd.) Very tony West Vancouver is a city unto itself on the far side of Burrard Inlet. Together with its more middle-class neighbor, North Vancouver, it forms an area called the **North Shore.**

STREET MAPS   The Travel Info Centres (see "Visitor Information," above) and most hotels can provide you with a detailed downtown map. *Where Vancouver* (© **604/736-5586;** www.where.ca), a free guide available at most hotels, has good maps. A good all-around metropolitan area map is the Rand McNally Vancouver city map, which is available for C$3 (US$2.40) at the Vancouver Airport Tourism Centre kiosk. If you're an auto-club member, the Canadian Automobile Association (CAA) map is also good. It's not for sale, but is free to both AAA and CAA members and is available at AAA offices across North America. **International Travel Maps and Books,** 539 West Pender St. (© **604/687-3320**), has the city's most extensive selection of Vancouver and British Columbia maps and specialty guidebooks.

VANCOUVER'S NEIGHBORHOODS

Exploring Vancouver's fascinating and distinct neighborhoods is a key part of enjoying the city. For short profiles of the city's most interesting enclaves, see "Neighborhoods to Explore," in chapter 7, beginning on p. 111. For detailed walks through some of Vancouver's neighborhoods, turn to "Vancouver Strolls" in chapter 8.

2 Getting Around

BY PUBLIC TRANSPORTATION

Vancouver's public transportation system is the most extensive in Canada and includes service to all major tourist attractions, so it's not really necessary to have a car (especially if you're staying in the downtown area).

The **Translink** (otherwise known as B.C. Transit; © **604/521-0400;** www. translink.bc.ca) system includes electric buses, the SeaBus catamaran ferry, and the light-rail SkyTrain. It's an ecologically friendly, highly reliable, and inexpensive system that allows you to get everywhere, including the beaches and ski slopes. Regular service runs from 5am to 2am.

Schedules and routes are available online, at the Travel Info Centres, at many major hotels, and on buses. Pick up a copy of *Discover Vancouver on Transit* at one of the Travel Info Centres (see "Visitor Information," earlier in this chapter). This publication gives transit routes for many city neighborhoods, landmarks, and attractions. There is a Downtown Vancouver transit map on the back cover of this guide.

FARES Fares are based on the number of zones traveled, and are the same for buses, SeaBus, and SkyTrain. One ticket allows you to transfer from one mode of transportation to another, in any direction, for 90 minutes. A one-way, one-zone fare (which includes everything in central Vancouver) costs C$2.25 (US$1.80). A two-zone fare—C$3.25 (US$2.60)—is required to travel to nearby suburbs such as Richmond or North Vancouver, and a three-zone fare—C$4.50 (US$3.60)—is required for travel to the far-off edge city of Surrey. After 6:30pm on weekdays and all day on weekends and holidays, you can travel anywhere in all three zones for C$2.25 (US$1.80). **DayPasses,** good on all public transit, cost C$8 (US$6.40) for adults and C$6 (US$4.80) for seniors, students, and children. They can be used for unlimited travel on weekdays or weekends and holidays.

Tip: Keep in mind that drivers do not make change, so you need the exact fare, or a valid transit pass. Pay with cash or buy tickets and passes from ticket machines at stations, Travel Info Centres, both SeaBus terminals, convenience stores, drugstores, and outlets displaying the FAREDEALER sign; most of these outlets also sell a transit map showing all routes for C$1.95 (US$1.50).

BY BUS Both diesel and electric-trolley buses service the city. Regular service on the busiest routes is every 12 minutes through the day to 2am, with service beginning at 5am. Wheelchair-accessible buses and bus stops are identified by the international wheelchair symbol. Some key routes to keep in mind if you're touring the city by bus: **no. 5** (Robson St.), **no. 2** (Kitsilano Beach to downtown), **no. 50** (Granville Island), **no. 35** or **135** (to the Stanley Park bus loop), **no. 240** (North Vancouver), **no. 250** (West Vancouver–Horseshoe Bay), and buses **no. 4** or **10** (UBC to Exhibition Park via Granville St. downtown). From June until the end of September, the **Vancouver Parks Board** operates a bus route through Stanley Park stopping at 14 points of interest. Call © **604/257-8400** for details on this free service or contact © **604/953-3333** for general public transportation information.

BY SKYTRAIN The SkyTrain is a fast, light-rail service between downtown Vancouver and the suburbs. There are two services. The **Expo Line** trains operate from Waterfront to King George station, running along a scenic 27km (17-mile) route from downtown Vancouver east to Surrey through Burnaby and New Westminster in 39 minutes. There are 20 stations along this route; four downtown stations are underground and marked at street level. The **Millennium Line,** which opened in the fall of 2002, makes the same stops from Waterfront to Columbia then branches to Sapperton, Braid, Lougheed town centre, and beyond to Commercial Drive. All stations except Granville are wheelchair accessible; trains arrive every 2 to 5 minutes.

BY SEABUS The SS *Beaver* and SS *Otter* catamaran ferries annually take more than 700,000 passengers, cyclists, and wheelchair riders on a scenic 12-minute commute between downtown's Waterfront Station and North Vancouver's Lonsdale Quay. On weekdays, a SeaBus leaves each stop every 15 minutes from 6:15am to 6:30pm, then every 30 minutes until 1am. SeaBuses depart on Saturdays every half-hour from 6:30am to 12:30pm, then every 15 minutes until 7:15pm, then every half-hour until 1am. On Sundays and holidays, runs depart every half-hour from 8:30am to 11pm. Note that the crossing is a two-zone fare on weekdays until 6:30pm.

BY TAXI

Cab fares start at C$2.30 (US$1.80) and increase at a rate of C$1.25 (US$1) per kilometer, plus C30¢ (US25¢) per minute at stoplights or in stalled traffic. In the downtown area, you can expect to travel for less than C$10 (US$8) plus tip. The typical fare for the 13km (8-mile) drive from downtown to the airport is C$25 (US$20).

Taxis are easy to find in front of major hotels, but flagging one down can be tricky. Most drivers are usually on radio calls. But thanks to built-in satellite positioning systems, if you call for a taxi, it usually arrives faster than if you go out and hail one. Call for a pickup from **Black Top** (© **604/731-1111**), **Yellow Cab** (© **604/681-1111**), or **MacLure's** (© **604/731-9211**).

BY CAR

Vancouver's road system and traffic are easier to handle than those in many other cities, in large part because there are no freeways within the city. Traffic thus tends to move more slowly. If you're just sightseeing around town or heading up to Whistler (a car is unnecessary in Whistler), public transit and cabs will easily see you through. However, if you're planning to visit the North Shore mountains or pursue other out-of-town activities, then a car is necessary. Gas is sold by the liter, averaging around C90¢ (US72¢) per liter; a gallon of gas costs approximately C$3.40 (US$2.72). *Note:* In Canada, speeds and distances are posted in kilometers. The speed limit in Vancouver is 50kmph (31 mph); highway speed limits vary from 90 to 110kmph (56–68 mph).

RENTAL CARS   Rates vary widely depending on demand, style of car, and special offers. If you're over 25 and have a major credit card, you can rent a vehicle from **Avis,** 757 Hornby St. (© **800/879-2847** or 604/606-2868); **Budget,** 501 W. Georgia St. (© **800/472-3325** or 604/668-7000); **Enterprise,** 585 Smithe St. (© **800/736-8222** or 604/688-5500); **Hertz Canada,** 1128 Seymour St. (© **800/263-0600** or 604/606-4711); **National/Tilden,** 1130 W. Georgia St. (© **800/387-4747** or 604/685-6111); or **Thrifty,** 1015 Burrard St. or 1400 Robson St. (© **800/847-4389** or 604/606-1666). These firms all have counters and shuttle service at the airport as well. To rent a recreational vehicle, contact **Go West Campers,** 1577 Lloyd Ave., North Vancouver (© **800/661-8813** or 604/987-5288; www.go-west.com).

PARKING   All major downtown hotels have guest parking, either in-house or at nearby lots. Rates vary from free to C$28 (US$22) per day. There's public parking at **Robson Square** (enter at Smithe and Howe sts.), the **Pacific Centre** (Howe and Dunsmuir sts.), and **The Bay** department store (Richards near Dunsmuir St.). You'll also find larger **parking lots** at the intersections of Thurlow and Georgia, Thurlow and Alberni, and Robson and Seymour streets.

Metered **street parking** may take a trip or three around the block to find a spot; the meters accept C$2 (US$1.50) and C$1 (US75¢) coins. Rules are posted on the street and are strictly enforced; generally, downtown and in the West End, metered parking is in effect 7 days a week. (*Note:* Drivers are given about a 2-min. grace period before their cars are towed away when the 3pm no-parking rule goes into effect on many major thoroughfares.) Unmetered parking on side streets is often subject to neighborhood residency requirements: Check the signs. If you park in such an area without the appropriate sticker on your windshield, you'll get ticketed and towed. If your car is towed away or you need a towing service and aren't a CAA or an AAA member, call **Unitow** (© **604/251-1255**) or **Busters** (© **604/685-8181**). If you are parking on the street, remove all valuables from your car; break-ins are not uncommon.

SPECIAL DRIVING RULES   Canadian driving rules are similar to those in the United States. Stopping for pedestrians is required even outside crosswalks. Seat belts are required. Children 4 and under must be in a child seat. Motorcyclists must wear helmets. It's legal to turn right at a red light after coming to a full stop unless posted otherwise. Though photo radar is no longer used in B.C. (the new government got elected partially on its pledge to eliminate the hated system), photo-monitored intersections are alive and well. If you're caught racing through a red light, fines start at C$100 (US$80). Unlike in the United States, however, daytime headlights (dimmers) are mandatory.

AUTO CLUB   Members of the American Automobile Association (AAA) can get assistance from the **Canadian Automobile Association (CAA)**, 999 W. Broadway, Vancouver (© **604/268-5600**, or for road service 604/293-2222; www.caa.ca).

BY BIKE

Vancouver is a biker's paradise. There are plenty of places to rent a bike along Robson and Denman streets near Stanley Park. (For specifics, see p. 135.) Paved paths crisscross through parks and along beaches, and new routes are constantly being added. Helmets are mandatory and riding on sidewalks is illegal except on designated bike paths.

You can take your bike on the SeaBus anytime at no extra charge. Bikes are not allowed in the George Massey Tunnel, but a tunnel shuttle operates four times daily from mid-May to September to transport you across the Fraser River. From May 1 to Victoria Day (the third weekend of May), the service operates on weekends only. All of the West Vancouver blue buses (including the bus to the Horseshoe Bay ferry terminal) can carry two bikes, first-come, first-served, free of charge. In Vancouver, only a limited number of suburban routes allow bikes on the bus: bus no. 351 to White Rock, bus no. 601 to South Delta, bus no. 404 to the airport, and the 99 Express to UBC.

BY MINIFERRY

Crossing False Creek to Granville Island or beautiful Vanier Park on one of the zippy little miniferries is cheap and fun. These small covered boats act like the *vaporetti* in Venice, connecting various points of interest; they are privately operated, so your public transit pass or ticket is not valid. It's well worth the extra money, though!

The **Aquabus** (© **604/689-5858;** www.aquabus.bc.ca) docks at David Lam Park, the south foot of Hornby Street, the Arts Club on Granville Island, Yaletown at Davie Street, Science World, and Stamp's Landing. Ferries operate daily from 7am to 10:30pm (8:30pm in winter). Ferries operate every 15 minutes to half an hour from 10am to 5pm (later in May and June). One-way fares vary from C$2.50 to C$5 (US$2–US$4) for adults and C$1.25 to C$3 (US$1–US$2.40) for seniors and children. A day pass costs C$12 (US$10) for adults, C$11 (US$9) for seniors, and C$8 (US$6.40) for children. You can take a scenic 40-minute harbor tour for C$8 (US$6.40) adults, C$6 (US$4.80) seniors, and C$5 (US$4) children.

FAST FACTS: **Vancouver**

American Express   The office is at 666 Burrard St. (© **604/669-2813**). It's open Monday through Friday from 8:30am to 5:30pm and Saturday from 10am to 4pm.

Area Codes The telephone area code for the lower mainland, including greater Vancouver and Whistler, is **604**; you need to dial the area code even when calling within Vancouver or Whistler. The area code for Vancouver Island, the Gulf Islands, and the interior of the province is **250**; you do not need to dial the area code within Victoria, but need to use it when calling other places on Vancouver Island.

Business Hours Vancouver **banks** are open Monday through Thursday from 10am to 5pm and Friday from 10am to 6pm. Some banks, like Canadian Trust, are also open on Saturdays. **Stores** are generally open Monday through Saturday from 10am to 6pm. Last call at the city's **restaurant bars** and **cocktail lounges** is 2am.

Child Care If you need to rent cribs, car seats, play pens, or other baby accessories, **Cribs and Carriages** (☎ **604/988-2742**; www.cribsandcarriages.com) delivers them right to your hotel.

Consulates The **U.S. Consulate** is at 1075–1095 W. Pender St. (☎ **604/685-4311**). The **British Consulate** is at 800–1111 Melville St. (☎ **604/683-4421**). The **Australian Consulate** is at 1225–888 Dunsmuir St. (☎ **604/684-1177**). Check the Yellow Pages for other countries' consulates.

Currency Exchange Banks and ATMs have a better exchange rate than most foreign exchange bureaus. See "Money," in chapter 2 for more information.

Dentists Most major hotels have a dentist on call. **Vancouver Centre Dental Clinic,** Vancouver Centre Mall, 11–650 W. Georgia St. (☎ **604/682-1601**), is another option. You must make an appointment. The clinic is open Monday through Wednesday 8:30am to 6pm, Thursday 8:30am to 7pm, and Friday 9am to 6pm.

Doctors Hotels usually have a doctor on call. **Vancouver Medical Clinics,** Bentall Centre, 1055 Dunsmuir St. (☎ **604/683-8138**), is a drop-in clinic open Monday through Friday 8am to 4:45pm. Another drop-in medical center, **Carepoint Medical Centre,** 1175 Denman St. (☎ **604/681-5338**), is open daily from 9am to 9pm. See also "Emergencies," below.

Electricity As in the United States, electric current is 110 volts AC (60 cycles).

Emergencies Dial ☎ **911** for fire, police, ambulance, and poison control. This is a free call.

Hospitals **St. Paul's Hospital,** 1081 Burrard St. (☎ **604/682-2344**), is the closest facility to downtown and the West End. West Side Vancouver hospitals include **Vancouver General Hospital Health and Sciences Centre,** 855 W. 12th Ave. (☎ **604/875-4111**), and **British Columbia's Children's Hospital,** 4480 Oak St. (☎ **604/875-2345**). In North Vancouver, there's **Lions Gate Hospital,** 231 E. 15th St. (☎ **604/988-3131**).

Hotlines Emergency numbers include **Crisis Centre** (☎ 604/872-3311), **Rape Crisis Centre** (☎ 604/255-6344), **Rape Relief** (☎ 604/872-8212), **Poison Control Centre** (☎ 604/682-5050), **Crime Stoppers** (☎ 604/669-8477), **SPCA** animal emergency (☎ 604/879-7343), **Vancouver Police** (☎ 604/717-3535), **Fire** (☎ 604/665-6000), and **Ambulance** (☎ 604/872-5151). See also "Emergencies," above.

Internet Access Free Internet access is available at the Vancouver **public library** Central Branch, 350 W. Georgia St. (© **604/331-3600**). Just across the street, **Webster's Internet Cafe,** 340 Robson St. (© **604/915-9327**), charges for access but generally has a computer available. At the other end of Robson Street there's **Cyber Space Internet Café** (© **604/684-6004**). Or, for some late-night surfing, try **Internet Coffee,** 1104 Davie St. (© **604/682-6668**).

Laundry & Dry Cleaning **Davie Laundromat,** 1061 Davie St. (© **604/682-2717**), offers self-service, drop-off service, and dry cleaning. **Laundry & Suntanning,** 781 Denman St. (© **604/689-9598**), doesn't have dry-cleaning services, but you can work on your tan while you wait. Also, almost all hotels have laundry service.

Liquor Laws The legal drinking age in British Columbia is 19. Spirits are sold only in government liquor stores, but beer and wine can be purchased from specially licensed, privately owned stores and pubs. Most LCBC (Liquor Control of British Columbia) stores are open Monday through Saturday from 10am to 6pm, but some are open to 11pm.

Lost Property The **Vancouver Police** have a lost-property room (© **604/717-2726**), open 8:30am to 5pm Monday through Saturday. If you think you may have lost something on public transportation, call **Translink** (B.C. Transit) 8:30am to 5pm at © **604/682-7887**.

Luggage Storage & Lockers Most downtown hotels will gladly hold your luggage before or after your stay. Just ask at the front desk. Lockers are available at the main Vancouver railway station (which is also the main bus depot), **Pacific Central Station,** 1150 Station St., near Main Street and Terminal Avenue south of Chinatown (© **604/661-0328**), for C$2 (US$1.50) per day.

Mail Letters and postcards up to 30 grams cost C85¢ (US70¢) to mail to the U.S. and C$1.45 (US$1.20) for overseas airmail service; C50¢ (US40¢) within Canada. You can buy stamps and mail parcels at the main post office (see "Post Office," below) or at any of the postal outlets inside drugstores and convenience stores. Look for a POSTAL SERVICES sign.

Maps See "City Layout," earlier in this chapter, on p. 49.

Newspapers & Magazines The two local papers are the *Vancouver Sun* (www.vancouversun.com), published Monday through Saturday, and *The Province* (www.canada.com/vancouver/theprovince), published Sunday through Friday mornings. The free weekly entertainment paper, *The Georgia Straight,* comes out on Thursday. Other papers are the national *Globe and Mail* and the *National Post,* the *Chinese Oriental Star,* the Southeast Asian *Indo-Canadian Voice,* and the *Jewish Western Daily. Where Vancouver,* a shopping/tourist guide, can be found in your hotel room or at Tourism Vancouver. See "Visitor Information," earlier in this chapter, on p. 48, for more visitor-oriented publications.

Pharmacies **Shopper's Drug Mart,** 1125 Davie St. (© **604/685-6445**), is open 24 hours. Several Safeway supermarket pharmacies are open late; the one on Robson and Denman is open until midnight.

Police For emergencies, dial © **911**. This is a free call. Otherwise, the **Vancouver City Police** can be reached at © **604/717-3535**.

Post Office The **main post office** (© 800/267-1177) is at West Georgia and Homer streets (349 W. Georgia St.). It's open Monday through Friday from 8am to 5:30pm. You'll also find post office outlets in Shopper's Drug Mart and 7-Eleven stores with longer opening hours.

Radio CBC Radio One, a public news and information broadcaster akin to National Public Radio or the BBC, is located at 690 AM in Vancouver, 90.5 FM in Victoria, 100.1 FM in Whistler, and 91.5 FM in Tofino.

Restrooms Hotel lobbies are your best bet for downtown facilities. The shopping centers like Pacific Centre and Sinclair Centre, as well as the large department stores like the Bay, also have restrooms.

Safety Overall, Vancouver is a safe city; violent-crime rates are quite low. However, property crimes and crimes of opportunity (such as items being stolen from unlocked cars) occur pretty frequently, particularly downtown. Vancouver's Downtown East Side, between Gastown and Chinatown, is a troubled neighborhood and should be avoided at night.

Taxes Hotel rooms are subject to a 10% tax. The **provincial sales tax (PST)** is 7% (excluding food, restaurant meals, and children's clothing). For specific questions, call the **B.C. Consumer Taxation Branch** (© 604/660-4524; www.rev. gov.bc.ca).

Most goods and services are subject to a 7% **federal goods and services tax (GST).** Save your receipts: You can get a refund on short-stay (less than a couple months) accommodations and all shopping purchases. Each purchase must be greater than C$50 (US$40), and you must have a total of at least C$200 (US$160) to file a claim. (This refund doesn't apply to car rentals, parking, restaurant meals, room service, tobacco, or alcohol.) Hotels and the Info Centres can give you application forms, which you then mail to Revenue Canada on your return home. After processing, the government sends a check to your home address. For details on the GST, call © 800/668-4748 in Canada or 902/432-5608 outside Canada, or visit www.ccra-adrc.gc.ca/visitors. PDF files of the refund forms are on the site for you to print out. If you want your refund right away, **Maple Leaf Tax Refund** (© 800/993-4313 or 604/893-8478) in the Fairmont Hotel Vancouver, 900 W. Georgia St. (in the lower lobby), will process your application and provide a refund on the spot, less an 18% processing fee. You'll have to bring your receipts, two pieces of ID (one of which shows your home address), your plane ticket, and the items you purchased to show to the processing agent. *Note:* If you arrived in Canada by car, Maple Leaf can only give you a refund on your accommodations bills. You can still get a refund on other items, but only by sending in forms by mail, and only if you have your receipts stamped by Canada Customs or a participating duty-free store when you drive out of the country.

Telephone Phones in British Columbia are identical to U.S. phones. The country code is the same as the U.S. code **(1).** Local calls normally cost C25¢ (US20¢). Many hotels charge up to C$1 (US80¢) per local call and much more for long-distance calls. You can save considerably by using your calling card or cellphone. You can also buy prepaid phone cards in various denominations at grocery and convenience stores.

Time Zone   Vancouver is in the Pacific time zone, as are Seattle, Portland, and San Francisco. Daylight saving time applies April through October.

Tipping   Tipping etiquette is the same as in the United States: 15% to 20% in restaurants, C$1 (US80¢) per bag for bellboys and porters, and C$1 to C$4 (US80¢–US$3.20) per day for the hotel housekeeper. Taxi drivers get a sliding-scale tip—fares under C$4 (US$3.20) deserve a C$1 (US80¢) tip; for fares over C$5 (US$4), tip 15%.

Weather   Call (✆) **604/664-9010** or 604/664-9032 for weather updates; dial (✆) **604/666-3655** for marine forecasts. Each local ski resort has its own snow report line. Cypress Ski area's is (✆) **604/419-7669.** Whistler/Blackcomb's is (✆) **604/ 687-7507;** in the summer, the line also provides events listings for the village.

5

Where to Stay in Vancouver

The past few years have seen a lot of activity in the Vancouver hotel business. The building boom associated with Expo '86 was followed by a flush of new hotel construction and renovation in the late 1990s, right up to 2003, when the trendy Opus opened in Yaletown. There are lots of rooms and lots of choices, from world-class luxury hotels to moderately priced hotels and budget B&Bs and hostels.

Most of the hotels are in the downtown area or in the West End. Central Vancouver is small and easily walkable, so in both these neighborhoods you'll be close to major sights, services, and nightlife. Downtown, which includes Vancouver's financial district, the area around Canada Place convention center and cruise-ship terminal, and the central shopping-business area around Robson Square, is buzzing during the day but pretty quiet at night.

One thing to keep in mind when booking a room is that downtown hotels on south Granville Street (the Best Western Downtown Vancouver, Howard Johnson Hotel, and the Ramada Inn and Suites) offer central location without the high price tag, but the area they're in is not very attractive and it's a prime hang-out for panhandlers. It's not dangerous,

but you shouldn't book there unless you have a reasonable tolerance for the tattooed and the pierced.

The West End is green, leafy, and residential, a neighborhood of high-rise apartment houses, beautifully landscaped streets, and close proximity to Coal Harbour, Stanley Park, and the best beaches. When downtown gets quiet at night, the West End starts hopping. There are dozens of restaurants, cafes, and bars along Robson and Denman streets.

You'll also find a couple of hotels and some lovely B&Bs in great old houses on the West Side of Vancouver—that is, the area south of False Creek on Granville Island and in the Kitsilano neighborhood. Staying in "Kits" can be fun because it's a complete neighborhood unto itself and has its own hang-out spots on 4th Avenue and around Kits Beach.

On the upper end of the hotel scale, you'll find that many luxury hotels now have spas or spa services attached to them. Most mid- to upper-range hotels offer a gym of some kind, and many have pools.

Remember that quoted prices don't include the 10% **provincial accommodations tax** or the 7% **goods and services tax (GST).** Non-Canadian residents

---

Tips Fido-Friendly Hotels

Vancouver is one of the dog-friendliest cities in the world. Nearly all downtown and West End hotels allow you to check in your canine companion, usually for an added daily charge of C$15 to C$20 (US$12–US$16).

Bed & Breakfast Registries

If you prefer to stay in a B&B, the following agencies specialize in matching guests with establishments that best suit their needs:

- **Vancouver Bed & Breakfast,** 4390 Frances St., Burnaby, B.C. V5C ZR3 (✆ **604/298-8815;** fax 604/298-5917; www.vancouverbandb.bc.ca).
- **Canada-West Accommodations,** P.O. Box 86607, North Vancouver, B.C. V7L 4L2 (✆ **800/561-3223** or 604/990-6730; www.b-b.com).
- **Town and Country Bed & Breakfast Reservation Service,** 2803 W. Fourth Ave. (P.O. Box 74542), Vancouver, B.C. V6K IK2 (✆/fax **604/731-5942;** www.townandcountrybedandbreakfast.com).

can get a GST rebate on short-stay (less than a couple months) accommodations by filling out the Tax Refund Application (see "Taxes," under "Fast Facts," in chapter 4). And remember, too, that we list the rack rates; these are the rates you would receive if you walked in off the street and requested a room. By checking the hotel's website you'll almost always be able to find lower rates, including special "romance packages" and weekend getaway specials.

RESERVATIONS Reservations are highly recommended June through September and during holidays. If you arrive without a reservation or have trouble finding a room, call the **Hello B.C.** hotline at ✆ **800/663-6000** or **Tourism Vancouver**'s hotline at ✆ **604/683-2000.** Specializing in last-minute bookings, either organization can make arrangements using its large daily listing of hotels, hostels, and B&Bs.

1 Best Vancouver Hotel Bets

For a quick overview of the city's best splurge and moderately priced hotels, see chapter 1, p. 10.

- **Best Historic Hotel:** The **Fairmont Hotel Vancouver** (900 W. Georgia St.; ✆ **800/441-1414** or 604/684-3131) was built by the Canadian Pacific Railway on the site of two previous hotels. It opened in 1939 as Vancouver's grandest hotel. The château-style exterior, the lobby, and even the rooms—now thoroughly restored—are built in a style and on a scale reminiscent of the great European railway hotels. See p. 64.
- **Best for Business Travelers: The Westin Grand** (433 Robson St.; ✆ **888/680-9393** or 604/602-1999), in addition to having some of the nicest modern interior decor and marvelous day- and nighttime views from rooms on its high floors, offers big work spaces, dataports, wi-fi, and lots of electrical plugs, plus—in the 40 Guest Office suites—speakerphones, cordless phones, and combo fax/laser printer/photocopiers. See p. 70.
- **Best Boutique Hotel:** In trendy Yaletown, the new **Opus Hotel,** (322 Davie St.; ✆ **866/642-6787** or 604/642-6787), a member of the Small Luxury Hotels of the World group, has an array of room types, luscious room colors, superb beds, and an overall contemporary aesthetic that sets it apart. See p. 68.

- **Best for a Romantic Getaway:** The **Wedgewood Hotel,** (845 Hornby St.; ℂ **800/ 663-0666** or 604/689-7777), the only boutique hotel in downtown, has a comfy, romantic, European elegance that brings out the romance in everyone. See p. 69.

- **Best West End Hotel:** Rooms decorated in funky apple greens and lemon yellows and a lobby of bold, bright colors with whimsically shaped glass chandeliers make **Pacific Palisades Hotel,** (1277 Robson St.; ℂ **800/663-1815** or 604/688-0461), one of the top choices in the hip West End. See p. 74.

- **Best for Families:** The **Rosedale on Robson Suite Hotel** (838 Hamilton at Robson St; ℂ **800/661-8870** or 604/689-8033), offers two-bedroom family suites that come furnished with bunk beds, decorated in either a sports or Barbie theme and equipped with a large toy chest and blackboard with crayons. On Saturday night, the Rosedale staff puts on a movie or craft night to take the little ones off their parent's hands for a while. See p. 71.

- **Best Inexpensive Hotel:** With all the facilities of a convention center plus cheap, comfortable rooms, **The University of British Columbia Conference Centre** (5961 Student Union Blvd.; ℂ **604/822-1000**), is the best inexpensive choice in the city. See p. 80.

- **Best B&B:** Built in 1905 by two Vancouver photographers, the **West End Guest House** (1362 Haro St.; ℂ **888/546-3327** or 604/681-2889), is filled with the artists' work as well as an impressive collection of Victorian antiques. Fresh-baked brownies or cookies accompany evening turndown service, and the staff is thoroughly professional. See p. 77.

- **Best Alternative Accommodations: The Aston Rosellen Suites at Stanley Park** (100-2030 Barclay St.; ℂ **888/317-6648** or 604/689-4807), has spacious furnished apartments with fully equipped kitchens, dining areas, and living rooms for the same price as many standard hotel rooms. See p. 75.

- **Best Location:** Everyone's definition of a great location is different, but the **Westin Bayshore Resort & Marina** (1601 Bayshore Dr.; ℂ **800/937-8461** or 604/682-3377), is just steps from Stanley Park and Denman Street, with easy access to the seawall and only 10 blocks from downtown. See p. 75.

- **Best Views:** So many Vancouver hotels have outstanding views that it's difficult to choose just one. Still, there's something special about the upper floors of the **Pan Pacific Hotel Vancouver,** (300–999 Canada Place; ℂ **800/937-1515** in the U.S. or 604/662-8111), where the harborside rooms have unimpeded views of Coal Harbour, Stanley Park, the Lions Gate Bridge, and the North Shore's mountains. See p. 68.

- **Best Health Club:** There's a rooftop indoor/outdoor pool, fitness center, weight-and-exercise room, aerobics classes, whirlpool, and saunas at the **Four Seasons Hotel** (791 W. Georgia St.; ℂ **800/332-3442** in the U.S. or 604/689-9333). See p. 65.

- **Best for Sports Fans:** The **Georgian Court Hotel** (773 Beatty St.; ℂ **800/663-1155** or 604/682-5555) is as close to the action as you can get with a bed in the room. B.C. Place Stadium is right across the street, and GM Place is just a few blocks away. See p. 71.

- **Best Bathrooms:** No doubt about it, it's the **Wedgewood Hotel** (845 Hornby St.; ℂ **800/663-0666** or 604/689-7777). Every large, marble-clad bathroom has a deep soaker tub and a separate, marble, walk-in Roman shower.

- **Best Spa:** It's the **Pan Pacific Hotel Vancouver**, 300–999 Canada Place (© **800/ 937-1515** in the U.S. or 604/662-8111), which opened its new, luxurious Spa Utopia in 2005. See p. 68.

2 Downtown & Yaletown

All downtown hotels are within 5 to 10 minutes' walking distance of shops, restaurants, and attractions. Hotels in this area lean more toward luxurious than modest, a state of affairs reflected in their prices.

VERY EXPENSIVE

Delta Vancouver Suites *Kids*   The Delta Vancouver Suites is a full-service, all-suites, high-rise hotel with a special appeal to business travelers. Built in 1995 in the heart of Vancouver's business and financial district, it sits across the street from the Lookout observation tower (p. 120), just minutes from Canada Place, Gastown, Chinatown, and Robson Square. The look throughout is upscale and high-end, with an attractive lobby connecting to a state-of-the-art conference facility. Each suite has a nicely designed desk and mini-office/living area separated from the bed. The corner 09 rooms are long and narrow with a full wall of floor-to-ceiling glass. Room decor is neutral and non-threatening. Consider paying C$20 (US$15) more and upgrading to the Signature Club. This gets you a room on the top three floors, a down duvet, CD player, and access to the Signature Lounge, which puts out a good continental breakfast and afternoon hors d'oeuvres (both included in the upgrade); you can eat outside on the open balcony and enjoy a view of the mountains. All guests can use the large, heated indoor pool and good-size fitness room. Kids are given a welcome pack on arrival, and the Delta is the only downtown hotel where pets can stay for free. Rooms for travelers with disabilities are available. Check their website for special rates and promotions.

550 W. Hastings St., Vancouver, B.C. V6B 1L6. © **877/814-7706** or 604/689-8188. Fax 604/605-8881. www.delta hotels.com. 226 units. Oct 15–Apr C$349 (US$279) double; May–Oct 14 C$409 (US$327) double. Children under 18 stay free in parent's room. AE, DC, DISC, MC, V. Valet parking C$20 (US$16). **Amenities:** Restaurant; bar; indoor pool; health club; spa services; concierge; business center; 24-hr. room service; massage; babysitting; laundry service; dry cleaning; nonsmoking rooms; executive-level rooms. *In room:* A/C, TV w/pay movies and games, dataport w/high-speed Internet, minibar, coffeemaker, hair dryer, iron, safe, bathrobes.

The Fairmont Hotel Vancouver   Thanks to a recent C$75-million (US$63-million) renovation, the grande dame of Vancouver's hotels has been restored to her former glory. A landmark in the city since it first opened in 1939, and located directly across from busy Robson Square and the Vancouver Art Gallery, the hotel has been completely brought up to 21st-century standards but retains its very old-fashioned, traditional elegance. The rooms are spacious, quiet, and comfortable, if not particularly dynamic in layout or finish. The bathrooms gleam with marble floors and sinks and have the kind of solid tubs that you just don't find anywhere anymore. The courtyard suites feature a large luxuriously furnished living room, separated from the bedroom by French glass doors. A state-of-the-art spa features day packages and a la carte treatments including body scrubs and wraps.

900 W. Georgia St., Vancouver, B.C. V6C 2W6. © **800/441-1414** or 604/684-3131. Fax 604/662-1929. www. fairmont.com. 556 units. High season C$339–C$519 (US$271–US$415) double; low season C$289–C$429 (US$231–US$343) double. Children under 18 stay free in parent's room. AE, DC, DISC, MC, V. Parking C$25 (US$20). **Amenities:** 2 restaurants; bar; indoor pool; health club; excellent spa; Jacuzzi; sauna; concierge; tour desk; car rental; business center; shopping arcade; salon; 24-hr. room service; massage; babysitting; laundry service; same-day dry

cleaning; nonsmoking rooms; Fairmont Gold executive-level rooms; rooms for those w/limited mobility; rooms for hearing-impaired guests. *In room:* A/C, TV w/pay movies, dataport, minibar, coffeemaker, hair dryer, iron.

Four Seasons Hotel 🏵🏵🏵 (Kids)   For nearly 30 years now, the Four Seasons has reigned as one of Vancouver's top hotels. The hotel is favored by international business travelers who expect impeccable service and a full array of services—everything from complimentary shoe shines to a car service. From the outside, this huge high-rise hotel across from the Vancouver Art Gallery is rather unappealing. But the elegant lobby opens up into a spacious garden terrace, and the appealingly large, light-filled rooms offer interesting views of downtown with glimpses of the mountains. The marble bathrooms are particularly well done. For a slightly larger room, reserve a deluxe corner room with wraparound floor-to-ceiling windows. One of the glories of this hotel is its health club with an enormous heated pool, half indoors and half outdoors, on a terrace right in the heart of downtown. In 2004, *Travel & Leisure* magazine voted the Four Seasons one of the top 10 highest-ranking hotels for value in Canada.

791 W. Georgia St., Vancouver, B.C. V6C 2T4. ℂ 800/332-3442 in the U.S., or 604/689-9333. Fax 604/844-6744. www.fourseasons.com/vancouver. 376 units. C$340–C$400 (US$272–US$320) double; C$420–C$440 (US$336–US$352) suite. AE, DC, MC, V. Parking C$26 (US$21). **Amenities:** 2 restaurants; bar; indoor and heated outdoor pool; outstanding exercise room; sauna; concierge; car rental; business center; shopping arcade; 24-hr. room service; massage; babysitting; laundry service; same-day dry cleaning; nonsmoking rooms; rooms for those w/limited mobility. *In room:* A/C, TV/VCR, wi-fi, minibar, hair dryer, iron, safe.

Le Soleil Hotel & Suites 🏵   This 5-year-old boutique hotel midway between Robson Square and the financial district tries hard to look like a glamorous French country manor but succeeds only in looking rather fussily overdecorated. The lobby, done with crystal chandeliers, plush carpeting, and gilded, vaulted ceilings, is meant to dazzle. Except for 10 doubles, all the units are suites; for maximum space, the corner suites are best. The problem with some of the units is that the sitting areas have no windows and consequently feel gloomy and confined, despite the Biedermeier-style furniture and richly colored wallpapers and fabrics. Where Le Soleil shines is in its personal service. The hotel made it onto *Condé Nast*'s 2004 Gold List of the world's best places to stay, but if you're looking for a luxury boutique hotel, the Wedgewood or the Opus (see below) are far more appealing.

567 Hornby St., Vancouver, B.C. V6C 2E8. ℂ 877/632-3030 or 604/632-3000. Fax 604/632-3001. www.lesoleilhotel. com. 119 units. May 1–Oct 15 C$400 (US$320) double, C$430 (US$344) suite; Oct 16–Apr 30 C$300 (US$225) double, C$330 (US$248) suite, C$1,000 (US$750) penthouse. AE, DC, MC, V. Valet parking C$20 (US$15). **Amenities:** Restaurant; access to YWCA fitness facilities next door; concierge; business center; 24-hr. room service; laundry service; same-day dry cleaning; nonsmoking rooms. *In room:* A/C, TV w/pay movies, dataport, minibar, coffeemaker, hair dryer, iron, safe.

Metropolitan Hotel Vancouver 🏵   This is a hotel for people who want traditional luxury, full service, and security without any of the hip, friendly trendiness of the Pacific Palisades or Opus (both reviewed below). Centrally situated between the financial district and downtown shopping areas, the Metropolitan mostly caters to upscale business travelers. The rooms are quiet, well-built, and luxurious, with dark-wood furnishings and comfortable beds with fine Italian linens. Beautiful bathrooms feature marble floors, sizable countertops, and separate shower and bath. Many units in the 18-story hotel have small balconies, but the views here are not the hotel's selling point because the building is dwarfed by the Four Seasons across the street. The hotel's restaurant, Diva (p. 87), is regarded as one of Vancouver's top restaurants.

Where to Stay in Downtown Vancouver

The Aston Rosellen Suites
  at Stanley Park **7**
Barclay House in the West End **13**
Beachside City View
  Bed & Breakfast **41**
Best Western
  Downtown Vancouver **20**
Blue Horizon **37**
Buchan Hotel **8**
Camelot Inn **5**
Coast Plaza Suites & Hotel
  at Stanley Park **10**
Days Inn Downtown **36**
Delta Vancouver Suites **33**
Fairmont Hotel Vancouver **31**
Four Seasons Hotel **32**
Georgian Court Hotel **25**
Granville Island Hotel **18**
Hostelling International
  Vancouver Downtown Hostel **16**
Hostelling International
  Vancouver Jericho Beach Hostel **1**
Howard Johnson Hotel **22**
Johnson Heritage House
  Bed & Breakfast **6**
Kenya Court Ocean Front
  Guest House **2**
The Kingston Hotel **28**
Le Soleil Hotel & Suites **35**
Listel Vancouver **14**
Lonsdale Quay Hotel **42**
Metropolitan Hotel Vancouver **34**
Opus Hotel **19**
Pacific Palisades Hotel **38**
Pan Pacific Hotel Vancouver **40**
Penny Farthing Inn **4**
Quality Hotel Downtown/
  The Inn at False Creek **17**
Ramada Inn and Suites **21**
Rosedale on Robson Suite Hotel **24**
Sheraton Vancouver Wall
  Centre Hotel **23**
Sunset Inn Suites **15**
The Sutton Place Hotel **30**
Sylvia Hotel **9**
The University of British Columbia
  Conference Centre **3**
Vancouver Marriott Pinnacle
  Hotel **39**
Wedgewood Hotel **29**
West End Guest House **12**
Westin Bayshore
  Resort & Marina **11**
The Westin Grand **27**
YWCA Hotel/Residence **26**

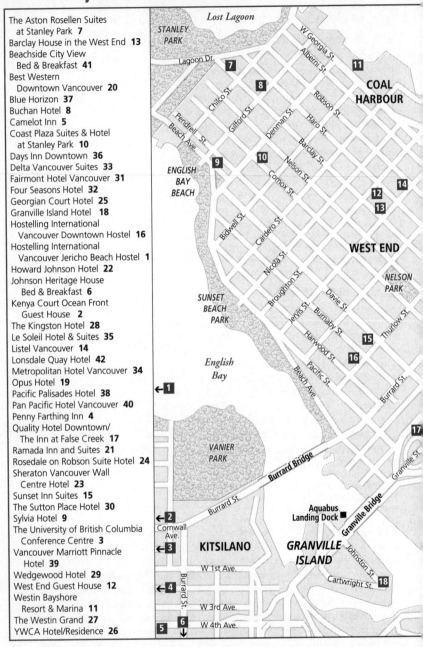

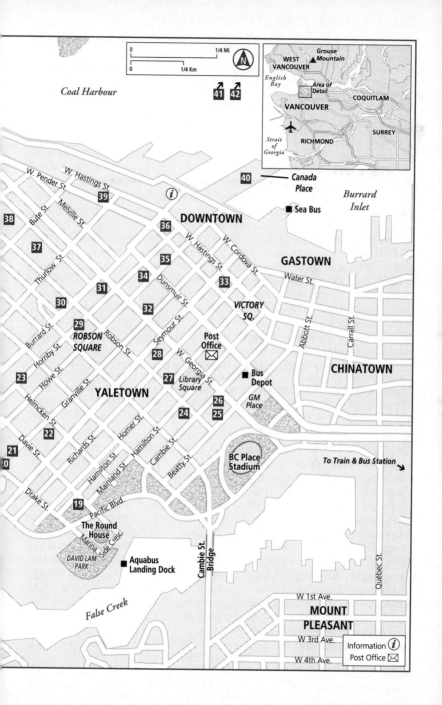

Coal Harbour

41 42

Grouse Mountain ▲
WEST VANCOUVER
English Bay
Area of Detail
COQUITLAM
VANCOUVER
Strait of Georgia
RICHMOND
SURREY

40

Canada Place

Sea Bus

Burrard Inlet

W. Pender St.
W. Hastings St.
39
38
Bute St.
Melville St.
37
Thurlow St.
31
30
Burrard St.
29
ROBSON SQUARE
Robson St.
Hornby St.
23
Howe St.
Helmcken St.
22
Granville St.
21
0
Davie St.
Drake St.
19
The Round House
Marina Side Cresc.
DAVID LAM PARK
Aquabus Landing Dock
False Creek

DOWNTOWN
36
W. Hastings St.
35
Dunsmuir St.
34
32
Seymour St.
28
W. Georgia St.
27
Library Square
24
26
25
Richards St.
Homer St.
Hamilton St.
Hamilton St.
Mainland St.
Cambie St.
Beatty St.
Pacific Blvd.

GASTOWN
W. Cordova St.
Water St.
Abbott St.
Carrall St.
CHINATOWN

VICTORY SQ.
33
Post Office ✉
Bus Depot
GM Place
BC Place Stadium

To Train & Bus Station ↘

Cambie St. Bridge

Québec St.
W 1st Ave.
MOUNT PLEASANT
W 3rd Ave.
Information ⓘ
Post Office ✉
W 4th Ave.

0   1/4 Mi
0   1/4 Km

67

645 Howe St., Vancouver, B.C. V6C 2Y9. © 800/667-2300 or 604/687-1122. Fax 604/643-7267. www.metropolitan. com. 197 units. May–Sept C$399 (US$319) double; Oct–Apr C$319 (US$255) double. Children under 18 stay free in parent's room. AE, DC, MC, V. Underground parking C$23 (US$18). **Amenities:** Restaurant; bar; indoor pool; health club; Jacuzzi; concierge; business center; 24-hr. room service; in-room massage; babysitting; laundry service; same-day dry cleaning; nonsmoking rooms; squash courts; wi-fi in lobby and restaurant. *In room:* A/C, TV w/pay movies, minibar, coffeemaker, hair dryer, iron, safe, bathrobes, CD player, wi-fi.

Opus Hotel ★★★   If you want to stay in a hip, happening, luxury hotel without the attitude sometimes found at trendy stylesetters, try the Opus. Opened in 2002, and now a member of the Small Luxury Hotels of the World group, it's Vancouver's newest hotel and the only hotel in Yaletown, the trendiest area in the city for shopping, nightlife, and dining. Each room is furnished according to one of five "personalities," with its own lay-out, color, and flavor. Everything is done well here, and the luscious room colors are an eye-treat if you're tired of blah hotel interiors. The beds are wonderfully firm with feather duvets and top-quality linens. Bathrooms are fitted out with high-design sinks, soaker tubs or roomy showers (or both), and feature L'Occitane toiletries. For the best views, book one of the corner suites on the seventh floor. Two rooms on the second floor open onto a pretty interior garden terrace. The small but well-equipped exercise room has big windows that let you people-watch on the street while working out on the latest equip-ment, and there's also a business center free for guests' use. The cool Opus Bar serves an international tapas menu and on summer weekends becomes one of Yaletown's late-night see-and-be-scenes. Opus's top-notch restaurant, Elixir (p. 91), serves French brasserie food; if you just want a latte and a croissant, pop into the cute little cafe. A hotel car is available to take you around the city.

322 Davie St., Vancouver, B.C. V6B 5Z6. © 866/642-6787 or 604/642-6787. Fax 604/642-6780. www.opushotel. com. 96 units. May–Oct C$399–C$549 (US$319–US$439) double, C$800 (US$640) suite; Nov–Apr C$319–C$469 (US$255–US$375) double, C$650 (US$520) suite. Children 17 and under stay free in parent's room. AE, DC, MC, V. Valet parking C$20 (US$16). **Amenities:** Restaurant; bar; fitness center; concierge; complimentary car service, 24-hr. room service; laundry service; dry cleaning; nonsmoking rooms. *In room:* A/C, TV w/pay movies, wi-fi, minibar, coffee-maker, hair dryer, iron, safe, bathrobes.

Pan Pacific Hotel Vancouver ★★★   Since its completion in 1986, this 23-story luxury hotel atop Canada Place, with its cruise-ship terminal and convention center, has become a key landmark on the Vancouver waterfront. Guest rooms begin on the ninth floor, above a huge lobby with a wall of glass overlooking the mountains and the harbor. Despite its size, the hotel excels in comfort and service, and it provides the most spectacular views of any hotel in the city. Book a deluxe Harbor and Mountain room and you can wake to see the sun glinting on the mountains of the North Shore, floatplanes taking off from Burrard Inlet, and cruise ships arriving and departing just below your window. The rooms are spacious and comfortable, with large picture win-dows, contemporary furnishings, and a soothing palette of colors. Bathrooms are large and luxurious. Guests have free use of a heated outdoor pool and Jacuzzi overlooking the harbor. In 2005, the hotel opened its new health club (daily use fee), an out-standing facility. Spa Utopia, which opened in 2004, offers men and women a full array of pampering treatments. Café Pacifica puts on one of the best breakfast buffets in Vancouver and is open for casual meals all day; the Five Sails Restaurant (p. 87), open for dinner only, is the hotel's fine-dining option.

300–999 Canada Place, Vancouver, B.C. V6C 3B5. © 800/937-1515 in the U.S., or 604/662-8111. Fax 604/685-8690. www.panpacific.com. 504 units. May–Oct C$490–C$640 (US$392–US$512) double, C$640–C$2,200 (US$512–US$1,760) suite; Nov–Apr C$390–C$480 (US$312–US$384) double; C$480–C$2,000 (US$384–US$1,600) suite. AE, DC, DISC, MC, V. Valet parking C$27 (US$22). **Amenities:** 2 restaurants; bar; outdoor heated pool; health club; spa; Jacuzzi; sauna; concierge; tour desk; business center; shopping arcade; 24-hr. room service; massage; babysitting; laundry service; same-day dry cleaning; nonsmoking floors; squash court. *In room:* A/C, TV w/pay movies, dataport w/high-speed Internet, minibar, coffeemaker, hair dryer, iron, safe.

Sheraton Vancouver Wall Centre Hotel 𝒜

The tallest—and at 736 rooms the largest—hotel in the city, the Wall Centre is hard to miss. Completed in 2001, the hotel occupies a curved spire of black glass and a second, earlier tower with a fountain-filled urban garden between. It may remind you of a futuristic corporate office park, a feeling that's unfortunately reinforced in the rooms, which have floor-to-ceiling polarized glass windows that look out onto great views but can't be opened, so it's like you're always wearing sunglasses. This is upscale Sheraton at its best (or worst, if you hate huge hotels), and because of its size it caters to a lot of tour groups. The hotel features a vast lobby with some nice touches such as a gold-leaf staircase, custom-designed furniture, and hand-blown glass chandeliers. The guest rooms have a clean, contemporary look with blond-wood furnishings and nice bathrooms. Guests have the use of a 12,000-square-foot state-of-the-art health club with an indoor pool; an ayurvedic wellness spa is attached.

1088 Burrard St., Vancouver, B.C. V6Z 2R9. ℂ 800/325-3535 or 604/331-1000. Fax 604/893-7200. www.sheraton wallcentre.com. 733 units. C$299 (US$239) double (average cost; call for additional rates). AE, DC, MC, V. Valet parking C$20 (US$16). **Amenities:** 2 restaurants; 2 bars; indoor pool; health club; spa; Jacuzzi; sauna; concierge; tour desk; business center; salon; 24-hr. room service; same-day laundry and dry cleaning; nonsmoking rooms; executive-level rooms. *In room:* A/C, TV w/pay movies, high-speed Internet, minibar, coffeemaker, hair dryer, iron, safe, bathrobes.

The Sutton Place Hotel 𝒜𝒜

Don't let the bland corporate-looking exterior fool you. Once you enter the lobby of this centrally located hotel, it's pure luxury, comparable to the Four Seasons (reviewed above). The lobby is elegantly decorated with marble, fresh flowers, chandeliers, and French-leaning European furnishings. The rooms here don't skimp on size or comfort and are tastefully decorated in a traditional European style. The one- or two-bedroom junior suites have a small parlor. In larger suites, French doors separate the bedroom from the large sitting area. There's a European-style health club and spa with a big heated pool and sundeck. The Fleuri restaurant serves French Continental cuisine. The hotel has won many awards and made it onto *Condé Nast's* 2004 Gold List of the best places to stay in the world.

845 Burrard St., Vancouver, B.C. V6Z 2K6. ℂ 800/961-7555 or 604/682-5511. Fax 604/682-5513. www.suttonplace. com. 397 units. May–Oct C$487 (US$390) double, C$567 (US$454) suite; Nov–Apr C$327 (US$262) double, C$407 (US$326) suite. AE, DC, DISC, MC, V. Underground self- or valet parking C$22 (US$18). Bus: 22. **Amenities:** Restaurant; lounge (with bistro fare); bakery-cafe; indoor pool; health club; full-service spa; Jacuzzi; sauna; complimentary bikes; children's program; concierge; business center; 24-hr. room service; laundry service; same-day-dry-cleaning service; nonsmoking rooms. *In room:* A/C, TV w/pay movies, high-speed Internet, dataport, minibar, hair dryer, iron, safe.

Wedgewood Hotel 𝒜𝒜𝒜

If you're searching for a romantic, sophisticated hotel with superb service, spacious rooms, fine detailing, a good restaurant, a full-service spa, and a central downtown location, you can't do any better than the Wedgewood. One of the things that makes the award-winning Wedgewood so distinctive is that it's independently owned (by Greek-born Eleni Skalbania), and the owner's elegant personal touch is evident throughout. All 83 units are spacious and have balconies (the best views are those facing the Vancouver Art Gallery and Law Court; avoid the rooms that look out over the back of the hotel). Furnishings and antiques are of the highest quality, and the marble-clad bathrooms with deep soaker tubs and separate walk-in Roman showers are simply the best. The penthouse suite on the 12th floor comes with a fireplace, a large patio, and a luxurious master bedroom. The Wedgewood attracts celebrities, business travelers, visiting dignitaries, and lawyers and judges from the Law Courts; many patrons come for the luxurious spa services. Bacchus, the cozy and inviting hotel restaurant, serves a fairly traditional menu of fish, pasta, and meat. In 2004, *Travel & Leisure* readers ranked the Wedgewood fifth in the world and the best in Canada for value.

845 Hornby St., Vancouver, B.C. V6Z 1V1. © 800/663-0666 or 604/689-7777. Fax 604/608-5349. www.wedgewood hotel.com. 83 units. May–Oct C$500–C$600 (US$400–US$480) double, C$700–C$850 (US$560–US$680) suite; Nov–Apr C$400–C$500 (US$320–US$400) double, C$700–C$850 (US$560–US$680) suite. AE, DC, MC, V. Valet parking C$19 (US$15). **Amenities:** Restaurant; small weight room; spa; concierge; business center; 24-hr. room service; laundry service; dry cleaning; executive-level rooms. *In room:* A/C, TV/VCR w/pay movies, dataport w/high-speed Internet, minibar, coffeemaker, hair dryer, iron, safe, CD player.

The Westin Grand ✦✦✦ *Kids*   It's such a pleasure to find a new luxury-level hotel that's elegant instead of garish, and understated rather than pompous. Completed in 1999 and located across from the new public library and next to the Centre for the Performing Arts, the Westin Grand offers high-end all-suite accommodations within easy walking distance of Yaletown, GM Place, and Robson shopping. The spacious suites are brightened by the natural light pouring in through the floor-to-ceiling windows; if you can, spring for one of the deluxe 09 or 03 units, which have balconies. Sitting rooms come with a sleekly designed concealed kitchenette, and bedrooms feature Westin's trademark *Heavenly* beds. The furnishings throughout are clean-lined and contemporary; the deluxe-level marble-clad bathrooms have separate tub and shower. Rooms for travelers with disabilities are also available. There's a great 24-hour on-site gym with an outdoor lap pool. Kids get a special welcome kit and there are special kids' menus in Aria restaurant.

433 Robson St., Vancouver, B.C. V6B 6L9. © 888/680-9393 or 604/602-1999. Fax 604/647-2502. www.westingrand vancouver.com. 207 suites. May–Sept C$189–C$429 (US$151–US$343) suite; Oct–Apr C$158–C$329 (US$126–US$263) suite. Up to 2 children under 17 stay free in parent's room. Additional person C$30 (US$24) extra. AE, DC, DISC, MC, V. Self-parking C$15 (US$12); valet parking C$19 (US$15). **Amenities:** Restaurant; outdoor pool; excellent health club; Jacuzzi; sauna; children's welcome bag; concierge; business center; 24-hr. room service; in-room massage; babysitting; laundry service; same-day dry cleaning; nonsmoking rooms; executive-level rooms. *In room:* A/C, TV w/pay movies, dataport, kitchenette, minibar, coffeemaker, hair dryer, iron, safe.

MODERATE
Best Western Downtown Vancouver   The 12-story Best Western is just a 5-block walk from the theater area on Granville Street at the south end of downtown. All rooms are comfortable, and some have harbor views. The corner rooms are a bit smaller than the rest, but they do have more light. This hotel is not overflowing with facilities, but the rooms are well furnished and the location is convenient. Accommodations with a full kitchen are available for an additional C$20 to C$25 (US$15–US$19). Bear in mind, however, that while quite safe, this is still a very bohemian, nightlife-oriented, downtown neighborhood. You shouldn't book here unless you have a reasonable tolerance for the realities of street life. You'll save by booking on the website.

718 Drake St. (at Granville St.), Vancouver, B.C. V6Z 2W6. © 888/669-9888 or 604/669-9888. Fax 604/669-3440. www.bestwesterndowntown.com. 143 units, 32 with full kitchen. C$189–C$209 (US$151–US$167) double; C$250–C$350 (US$200–US$280) penthouse. Rates include deluxe continental breakfast. AE, DC, DISC, MC, V. Parking C$6 (US$4.80). **Amenities:** Restaurant; rooftop exercise room; Jacuzzi; sauna; game room; tour desk; shuttle service to downtown; babysitting; laundry service; nonsmoking rooms; corporate rooms. *In room:* A/C, TV/VCR, dataport, coffeemaker, hair dryer, iron, safe.

Days Inn Downtown   Situated in a heritage building dating back to 1910, the well-maintained Days Inn Downtown is conveniently located in the heart of Vancouver's financial district and within easy walking distance to just about everything. All the rooms were refurbished in 1998, and the lobby underwent complete renovations in 1999. For travelers who don't need all the amenities of a large hotel, these small, simply furnished, motel-like rooms are comfortable. Ten of the rooms have showers only. Request a water view or consider a harbor-facing suite; rooms facing east stare directly at the concrete walls of the building next door. You will always get a rate lower than the rack rate below.

921 W. Pender St., Vancouver, B.C. V6C 1M2. ℭ **800/329-7466** or 604/681-4335. Fax 604/681-7808. www.daysinn vancouver.com. 85 units, 10 with shower only. C$219 (US$175) double. AE, DC, V. Valet parking C$10 (US$8). **Amenities:** Restaurant; bar; concierge; laundry service; same-day dry cleaning; nonsmoking rooms. *In room:* A/C, TV w/pay movies, dataport w/high-speed Internet, fridge, coffeemaker, hair dryer, iron, safe, complimentary newspaper.

Georgian Court Hotel ⓕ ⓥ*alue*   This modern, 14-story brick hotel dating from 1984 is extremely well located, just a block or two from B.C. Place Stadium, GM Place Stadium, the Queen Elizabeth Theatre, the Playhouse, and the Vancouver Public Library. You can walk to Robson Square in about 10 minutes. The guest rooms are relatively large, nicely decorated, and have good-size bathrooms. And while the big-time celebs are usually whisked off to the glamorous top hotels, their entourages often stay at the Georgian Court, as it provides all the amenities and business-friendly extras such as two phones in every room, brightly lit desks, and complimentary high-speed Internet access, a service that other hotels almost always charge for.

773 Beatty St., Vancouver, B.C. V6B 2M4. ℭ **800/663-1155** or 604/682-5555. Fax 604/682-8830. www.georgian court.com. 180 units. May 1–Oct 15 C$165–C$215 (US$132–US$172) double; Oct 16–Apr 30 C$115–C$160 (US$92–US$128) double. AE, DC, MC, V. Parking C$9 (US$7). **Amenities:** Restaurant; bar; health club; Jacuzzi; sauna; concierge; business center; limited room service; babysitting; laundry service; dry cleaning; nonsmoking rooms. *In room:* A/C, TV, dataport w/high-speed Internet, minibar, hair dryer, iron.

Quality Hotel Downtown/The Inn at False Creek ⓚ*ids*   The Mexican theme may seem out of place in Vancouver, but it works at this hotel. The Inn at False Creek is a boutique hotel decorated with Mexican art, pottery, and rugs, in a kind of Santa Fe style. Room decor consists of dark green, terra-cotta, and earth tones, and brick for a touch of authenticity. The spacious suites are great for families—15 have full kitchens, and a number of others have glassed-in balconies, which double as enclosed play areas (the hotel staff keeps a supply of board games and puzzles behind the front desk). Rooms on the back side are preferable because the hotel is situated beside the Granville Bridge on-ramp. The traffic noise is minimized in the front, however, by double-pane windows and blackout curtains.

1335 Howe St. (at Drake St.), Vancouver, B.C. V6Z 1R7. ℭ **800/663-8474** or 604/682-0229. Fax 604/662-7566. www.qualityhotel.ca. 157 units. C$79–C$199 (US$63–US$159) double. AE, DC, DISC, MC, V. Parking C$10 (US$8). **Amenities:** Restaurant; bar; outdoor pool; access to nearby health club; Jacuzzi; sauna; concierge; tour desk; car rental; limited room service; babysitting; dry cleaning; nonsmoking rooms; executive-level rooms. *In room:* A/C, TV, dataport, coffeemaker, hair dryer, iron, safe.

Rosedale on Robson Suite Hotel ⓕ ⓥ*alue* ⓚ*ids*   Directly across the street from Library Square, the Rosedale provides good value for the money, particularly when it comes to amenities. All rooms are one- or two-bedroom suites and feature separate living rooms with a pullout couch and full kitchenettes. Very family friendly, the Rosedale offers designated two-bedroom family suites: the kids' bedrooms are furnished with bunk beds and contain a large toy chest. The lobby is oddly laid out and starting to look dated, even though the hotel is less than 10 years old. There's a small gym with an indoor pool. The hotel does a lot of business with tour groups, particularly Australians. Internet rates are considerably lower than the rack rates listed below.

838 Hamilton (at Robson St.), Vancouver, B.C. V6B 6A2. ℂ 800/661-8870 or 604/689-8033. Fax 604/689-4426. www.rosedaleonrobson.com. 275 units. C$270–C$345 (US$216–US$276) suite. Additional adult C$20 (US$16). Rates include continental breakfast. AE, DC, DISC, MC, V. Parking C$8 (US$6.50). **Amenities:** Restaurant; indoor lap pool; exercise room; Jacuzzi; sauna; steam room; children's programs; concierge; business center; limited room service; babysitting; laundry service; dry cleaning; nonsmoking rooms; executive-level rooms. In room: A/C, TV w/pay movies, fax, dataport, kitchenette, coffeemaker, hair dryer, iron.

INEXPENSIVE

Hostelling International Vancouver Downtown Hostel   Located in a converted nunnery, this modern curfew-free hostel offers a convenient base of operations for exploring downtown. The beach is a few blocks south; downtown is a 10-minute walk north. Most beds are in quad dorms, with a limited number of doubles and triples available. Except for two rooms with a private bathroom, all bathroom facilities are shared. Rooms and facilities are accessible for travelers with disabilities. There are common cooking facilities, as well as a rooftop patio and game room. The hostel is extremely busy in the summertime, so book ahead. Many organized activities such as ski packages and tours can be booked at the hostel. There's also free shuttle service to the bus/train station and Jericho Beach.

1114 Burnaby St. (at Thurlow St.), Vancouver, B.C. V6E 1P1. ℂ 888/203-4302 or 604/684-4565. Fax 604/684-4540. www.hihostels.ca. 68 rooms, 44 4-person shared dorm rooms, 24 double or triple private rooms. C$20–C$24 (US$16–US$19) dorm IYHA members, C$24–C$28 (US$19–US$22) dorm nonmembers; C$55–C$57 (US$44–US$46) double members, C$64–C$66 (US$51–US$53) double nonmembers. Annual adult membership C$35 (US$28). MC, V. Limited free parking. **Amenities:** Bike rental; game room; activities desk; coin laundry; wi-fi. In room: No phone.

Howard Johnson Hotel (Value)   As yet another example of south Granville's ongoing gentrification, this formerly down-at-the-heels hotel was bought, gutted, renovated, and reopened in 1998 with an eye to the budget-conscious traveler. Hallways are decorated with photographs of Vancouver's early days, while the rooms are simply and adequately furnished; to get any kind of view, request a unit facing onto Granville. The rooms here are moderately larger than at the Ramada across the street, and more comfortable. The suites have kitchenettes and sofa beds, convenient for families. Bear in mind, however, that while quite safe, this is still a fringy downtown neighborhood where you'll see panhandlers and street kids.

1176 Granville St., Vancouver, B.C. V6Z 1L8. ℂ 888/654-6336 or 604/688-8701. Fax 604/688-8335. www.hojo vancouver.com. 110 units. June–Sept C$149–C$179 (US$119–US$143) double, C$189–C$219 (US$151–US$175) suite; Oct–May C$79–C$159 (US$63–US$127) double, C$129–C$179 (US$103–US$143) suite. Children under 16 stay free in parent's room. In low season, rates include full breakfast. AE, DC, MC, V. Parking C$14 (US$11). **Amenities:** Restaurant; bar; access to nearby health club; concierge; tour desk; laundry service; same-day dry cleaning; nonsmoking rooms. In room: A/C, TV w/pay movies, dataport, coffeemaker, hair dryer, iron, safe.

The Kingston Hotel (Finds) (Value)   An affordable downtown hotel is a rarity for Vancouver; but if you can do without the frills, the Kingston offers a clean, safe, inexpensive place to sleep and a complimentary continental breakfast to start your day. You won't find a better deal anywhere, and the premises have far more character than you'll find in a cookie-cutter motel. The Kingston is a Vancouver version of the kind of small budget B&B hotels found all over Europe. Just 9 of the 55 rooms have private bathrooms and TVs. The rest have hand basins and the use of shared showers and toilets on each floor. In 2004, the hotel added a new lobby, breakfast room, pub-restaurant, and

garden patio. The premises are well kept, the location so central you can walk everywhere, the staff is friendly and helpful, and if you're just looking for a place to sleep and stow your bags, you'll be glad you found this find.

757 Richards St., Vancouver, B.C. V6B 3A6. ✆ **888/713-3304** or 604/684-9024. Fax 604/684-9917. www.kingston hotelvancouver.com. 55 units, 9 with private bathroom. C$58–C$78 (US$46–US$62) double with shared bathroom, C$98–C$135 (US$78–US$108) double with bathroom. Extra person C$10 (US$8). Rates include continental breakfast. AE, MC, V. Parking C$15 (US$12) across the street. **Amenities:** Restaurant; bar; sauna; coin laundry; nonsmoking rooms. *In room:* TV (in units with private bathrooms), no phone.

Ramada Inn and Suites   The Ramada, like the Howard Johnson's across the street from it (reviewed above), was recently converted from a rooming house into a tourist hotel. The motel-like rooms have dark-wood furniture and small desks; for any kind of view, you need to ask for a room facing Granville; otherwise, you may be looking out at a wall. Suites feature a sofa bed, kitchenette, and small dining area, making them useful for families. The location is convenient for exploring downtown and Yaletown, as well as hopping over to Granville Island or Kitsilano. Guests have full access to a nearby sports club. Bear in mind that South Granville, though safe, is not a scenic or shopping area; if urban grit is not your thing, don't book here.

1221 Granville St., Vancouver, B.C. V6Z 1M6. ✆ **888/835-0078** or 604/685-1111. Fax 604/685-0707. www.ramada vancouver.com. 116 units. C$77–C$169 (US$62–US$135) double. Children under 17 stay free in parent's room. AE, DC, DISC, MC, V. Valet parking C$10 (US$8). **Amenities:** Restaurant; bar/lounge; access to nearby sports club; laundry service; nonsmoking rooms. *In room:* A/C, TV w/pay movies, dataport, kitchenette (in suites), coffeemaker, hair dryer, iron.

YWCA Hotel/Residence ✦ *Value*   Built in 1995, this attractive 12-story residence next door to the Georgian Court Hotel is an excellent choice for travelers (male, female, families) on limited budgets. Bedrooms are simply furnished; some have TVs. There are quite a few reasonably priced restaurants nearby (but none in-house). Three communal kitchens are available for guests' use and all guest rooms have mini-fridges. (There are a number of grocery stores nearby.) The Y has three TV lounges and free access to the best gym in town at the nearby co-ed YWCA Fitness Centre.

733 Beatty St., Vancouver, B.C. V6B 2M4. ✆ **800/663-1424** or 604/895-5830. Fax 604/681-2550. www.ywcahotel. com. 155 units, 53 with private bathroom. C$51–C$88 (US$41–US$70) double with shared bathroom; C$75–C$115 (US$60–US$92) double with bathroom. Weekly, monthly, group, and off-season discounts available. AE, MC, V. Parking C$6 (US$4.80). **Amenities:** Access to YWCA facility; coin laundry; nonsmoking rooms. *In room:* A/C, TV in some rooms, dataport, fridge, hair dryer.

3 The West End

About a 10-minute walk from the downtown area, the West End's hotels are nestled amid the tree-lined, garden-filled residential streets bordering Stanley Park. Have no fear: You will not be out of the loop if you stay in the West End, though the area's relaxed, beachy ambience is very different from downtown. Within minutes you can be on Robson or Denman Street, both of them chockablock with shops and restaurants, at beautiful English Bay or Second Beach, or in Stanley Park. Though there are fewer hotels here than downtown, the choices in the West End are more diverse—and so are the people who live in this densely populated section of Vancouver.

EXPENSIVE
Listel Vancouver ✦✦ *Finds*   What makes the Listel unique is its artwork. Hallways and suites on the top two floors are decorated with original artworks from the Buschlen Mowatt Gallery (Vancouver's pre-eminent international gallery), or with

artifacts from the UBC Anthropology Museum. In addition, this Listel has a killer location, right at the western end of the Robson Street shopping and restaurant strip. The interior of this boutique hotel much favored by business travelers is luxurious without being flashy. Rooms feature top-quality bedding and handsome furnishings. The roomy upper-floor suites facing Robson Street, with glimpses of the harbor and the mountains beyond, are the best bets here. Each is individually decorated with handsome, hand-picked pieces of furniture, and some have cozy window banquettes. (Rooms at the back face the alley and nearby apartment buildings.) Some bathrooms are larger than others, with separate soaker tub and shower. In the evenings, you can hear live jazz at O'Doul's, the hotel's restaurant and bar; during the Vancouver International Jazz Festival in late June, it's the scene of late-night jam sessions with world-renowned musicians.

1300 Robson St., Vancouver, B.C. V6E 1C5. © **800/663-5491** or 604/684-8461. Fax 604/684-7092. www.listel-vancouver.com. 129 units. May–Sept C$260 (US$195) standard double, C$320 (US$240) gallery room double, C$600 (US$450) suite; Oct–Apr C$220 (US$165) standard double, C$260 (US$195) gallery room double, C$350 (US$263) suite. AE, DC, DISC, MC, V. Parking C$19 (US$14). **Amenities:** Restaurant; bar; exercise room; Jacuzzi; concierge; limited room service; same-day laundry/dry cleaning; executive-level rooms. *In room:* A/C, TV w/pay movies, dataport w/high-speed Internet, minibar, coffeemaker, hair dryer, iron.

Pacific Palisades Hotel ✸✸✸ *Kids* *Finds* Walk into the Pacific Palisades lobby and you know right away that this is not just another standard-issue hotel. The designer's theme throughout this Kimpton Group property was "South Park (Florida, not the TV series) meets Stanley Park." Sherbet yellows and apple greens with pastel-colored fabrics, bright splashes of color, and whimsical touches make the hotel bright and welcoming to the young and the young at heart (the ubiquitous rock music playing in the lobby can be upbeat or annoying, depending on your mood and musical tastes). Guest rooms, spread out over two towers dating from 1969, are spacious, airy, and equipped with kitchenettes (with minibar items priced at corner-store prices). The one-bedroom suites boast large living/dining rooms and balconies. A few other perks that make this hotel a worthwhile choice are the complimentary afternoon wine tasting in the attached art gallery, the complimentary yoga program (free mat, strap, block, and instruction video), the kid-friendly atmosphere (you can buy yo-yos in the minibar), the large indoor pool and fitness rooms, and the fact that pets stay free (a rarity in Vancouver, where there's usually a cleaning charge). Plus, you're right on trendsetting Robson Street, minutes from beaches, shopping, cafes, and restaurants. Zin (p. 100) is a cool spot for a drink and dinner; the hotel staff is warm, friendly, and helpful. All in all, it's really hard not to like this place.

1277 Robson St., Vancouver, B.C. V6E 1C4. © **800/663-1815** or 604/688-0461. Fax 604/688-4374. www.pacific palisadeshotel.com. 233 units. May 1–Oct 15 C$245 (US$196) double, C$275 (US$220) suite; Oct 16–Apr 30 C$185 (US$148) double, C$275 (US$220) suite. AE, DC, DISC, MC, V. Valet parking C$26 (US$21). **Amenities:** Restaurant; bar; indoor lap pool; excellent health club; spa services; Jacuzzi; sauna; bike rentals; concierge; tour desk; business center; 24-hr. room service; massage; babysitting; coin laundry and laundry service; same-day dry cleaning; non-smoking rooms; basketball court; yoga program. *In room:* A/C, TV, dataport w/high-speed Internet, kitchenette, mini-bar, fridge, coffeemaker, hair dryer, iron, bathrobes.

Vancouver Marriott Pinnacle Hotel ✸ Open since 2000, the high-rise Pinnacle gleams and glows between the West End and Coal Harbour, close to Stanley Park, the waterfront, and the cruise-ship terminal. The rooms are designed to maximize the light and the views, though the views are often partially obstructed by surrounding high-rises (you can pay C$35/US$28 and upgrade to a better view). The rooms in general are fine, fitted up with all the things business travelers expect, but the decor is remarkably bland for a new hotel. Bathrooms are fairly large and well designed with a tub and separate shower. If you can, score one of the -19 rooms (2019, 2119, 2219, and so on); these oval-shaped units max out the window space and offer endless views; plus they're the largest rooms. Upgrade to the concierge level for C$10 (US$8) and you get a nice lounge with complimentary Continental breakfast and evening hors d'oeuvres.

1128 W. Hastings St., Vancouver, B.C. V6E 4R5. © 800/268-1133 or 604/684-1128. Fax 604/298-1128. www. vancouvermarriottpinnacle.com. 434 units. Off-peak season C$199 (US$159) double, peak season C$289 (US$231) double. Children 18 and under stay free in parent's room. AE, DC, MC, V. Self-parking C$23 (US$18); valet parking C$27 (US$22). SkyTrain to Burrard Station. **Amenities:** Restaurant; bar; indoor lap pool; health club; Jacuzzi; sauna; concierge; business center; 24-hr. room service; laundry; same-day dry cleaning service; nonsmoking rooms; executive-level rooms. *In room:* A/C, TV w/pay movies, dataport, minibar, coffeemaker, hair dryer, iron, safe.

Westin Bayshore Resort & Marina 🏨🏨🏨 *Kids*   This is the only resort hotel in Vancouver and has its own marina in case you want to arrive by boat. The enormous lobby with its acres of marble and huge fireplace makes for an impressive entry to this venerable hotel which recently underwent a C$55-million (US$41-million) renovation. Perched on the water's edge overlooking Stanley Park on one side and the city and Coal Harbour marina on the other, the Bayshore is just a short stroll from Canada Place Pier and downtown. The finishes throughout are top quality, and the size of the hotel (which includes a new conference center) makes it like a small city. Rooms in the original 1961 building have been completely refurbished with classic-looking decor, high-tech amenities, comfortable lighting, and floor-to-ceiling windows that open wide. In the newer tower, the rooms are spacious and bright with balconies and large windows. The circular outdoor pool is reputedly the largest in North America; there's a second indoor pool plus a full gym; all manner of spa treatments are available. This family-friendly hotel provides children with their own welcome package and organizes Super Saturdays, a behind-the-scenes tour of the hotel's operations and movie night for the young ones, giving the parents the night off.

1601 Bayshore Dr., Vancouver, B.C. V6G 2V4. © 800/937-8461 or 604/682-3377. Fax 604/687-3102. www.westin bayshore.com. 510 units. C$360–C$470 (US$286–US$376) double; C$550–C$695 (US$440–US$556) suite. Children under 19 stay free in parent's room. AE, DC, MC, V. Self-parking C$18 (US$14); valet parking C$20 (US$16). **Amenities:** 2 restaurants; bar; indoor and outdoor pool; health club; full-service spa; Jacuzzi; sauna; watersports rental; children's programs; concierge; tour desk; business center; shopping arcade; 24-hr. room service; massage; babysitting; laundry service; same-day dry cleaning; nonsmoking rooms. *In room:* A/C, TV w/pay movies, dataport w/high-speed Internet, minibar, coffeemaker, hair dryer, iron.

MODERATE

The Aston Rosellen Suites at Stanley Park 🏨 *Finds* *Kids*   Staying at The Aston Rosellen is like having your own apartment in the West End. Stanley Park and the seawall are just a few blocks away, and busy Denman Street, with its many restaurants and shops, is just 3 blocks east. Converted into a hotel to meet the demand for rooms during the 1986 Expo, the Rosellen has remained a favorite among travelers, with a high rate of repeat guests. The hotel offers a no-frills stay; the lobby is open only during office hours, and guests receive their own key. The largest apartment—1,150 square feet—is known as the director's suite, with two bedrooms, a large dining room, and a spacious kitchen. The remaining apartments are smaller, but none of them really skimps on size. The one-bedroom suites sleep four comfortably, and all units come with fully equipped kitchens, making them a great option for families. A 3-night minimum stay is required; rates drop for longer stays.

100–2030 Barclay St., Vancouver, B.C. V6G 1L5. ℂ **888/317-6648** or 604/689-4807. Fax 604/684-3327. www.rosellen suites.com. 31 units. May–Sept C$199 (US$159) 1-bedroom apt, C$249–C$299 (US$199–US$239) 2-bedroom apt, C$399 (US$319) penthouse; Oct–Apr C$139 (US$111) 1-bedroom apt, C$169–C$229 (US$135–US$183) 2-bedroom apt, C$299 (US$239) penthouse. Minimum 3-night stay. Rates include up to 4 people in a 1-bedroom apt and 6 in a 2-bedroom apt. Cots and cribs free. AE, DC, DISC, MC, V. Limited parking C$5 (US$4); reserve when booking room. **Amenities:** Access to nearby health club and tennis courts; coin laundry; nonsmoking rooms. *In room:* TV, dataport, kitchen, coffeemaker, hair dryer, iron.

Barclay House in the West End *Finds*

The Barclay House, located on one of the West End's quiet maple-lined streets just a block from historic Barclay Square, opened as a bed-and-breakfast in 1999. Built in 1904 by a local developer, this beautiful house can be a destination on its own. The elegant parlors and dining rooms are perfect for lounging on a rainy afternoon or sipping a glass of complimentary sherry before venturing out for dinner in the trendy West End. On a summer day, the front porch with its wooden Adirondack chairs makes a cozy place to read. All rooms are beautifully furnished in Victorian style; a number of the pieces are family heirlooms. Modern conveniences such as CD players, TV/VCRs, and luxurious bathrooms blend in perfectly. The Penthouse offers skylights, a fireplace, and a claw-foot tub; the South Room contains a queen-size brass bed and an elegant sitting room.

1351 Barclay St., Vancouver, B.C. V6E 1H6. ℂ **800/971-1351** or 604/605-1351. Fax 604/605-1382. www.barclay house.com. 5 units. C$125–C$245 (US$100–US$196) double. MC, V. Free parking. **Amenities:** Access to nearby fitness center; concierge; massage; nonsmoking rooms. *In room:* TV/VCR w/pay movies, wi-fi, fridge, hair dryer, iron, video library.

Blue Horizon *Value*

This 31-story high-rise built in the 1960s has a great location on Robson Street, just a block from the trendier Pacific Palisades and the tonier Listel Vancouver (see above for both). It's cheaper than those places, and has views that are just as good if not better, but it lacks their class and feels a bit like a high-rise motel. The rooms are fairly spacious, though, and every room is on a corner with wraparound windows, which maximizes the light and the view; every room has a small balcony, too. In 2000, the hotel renovated all its guest rooms, giving them a clean, contemporary look. Bathrooms are on the small side and have tubs with showers. Upgrade to a Superior room on the 15th floor or higher and you'll get the most breathtaking views looking north towards the mountains or west towards English Bay. If you're super-ecology-minded, book a room on the "Green Floor," which features energy-efficient lighting, low-flow showerheads, and recycling bins. If you're a nonsmoker, make sure you ask for a nonsmoking room, or be prepared for the lingering smell of smoke.

1225 Robson St., Vancouver, B.C. V6E 1C3. ℂ **800/663-1333** or 604/688-1411. Fax 604/688-4461. www.bluehorizon hotel.com. 214 units. C$109–C$179 (US$87–US$143) double; C$119-C$199 (US$95–US$159) Superior double. Children under 16 stay free in parent's room. AE, DC, MC, V. Self-parking C$10 (US$8). **Amenities:** Restaurant; indoor pool; exercise room; Jacuzzi; sauna; concierge; same-day dry cleaning; nonsmoking rooms. *In room:* A/C, TV w/pay movies, dataport, minibar, fridge, coffeemaker, hair dryer, iron, safe.

Coast Plaza Hotel & Suites *Finds*

Built originally as an apartment building, this 35-story hotel atop Denman Place Mall attracts a wide variety of guests, from business travelers and bus tours to film and TV actors. They come for the large rooms, affordable one- or two-bedroom suites, and fabulous views of English Bay. The two-bedroom corner suites are bigger than most West End apartments and boast spectacular panoramas. The spacious one-bedroom suites and standard rooms feature floor-to-ceiling windows and walk-out balconies; about half the units have full kitchens. Furnishings are plain and comfortable, if a little dated. Though there's a good-size heated pool, it's in a basement room that is not particularly appealing.

1763 Comox St., Vancouver, B.C. V6G 1P6. (C) **800/663-1144** or 604/688-7711. Fax 604/688-5934. www.coast hotels.com. 269 units. C$179–C$219 (US$143–US$175) double; C$219–C$299 (US$175–US$239) suite. AE, DC, DISC, MC, V. Valet parking C$8 (US$6.40). **Amenities:** Restaurant; bar; indoor pool; complimentary access to Denman Fitness Centre in mall below; Jacuzzi; sauna; concierge; free downtown shuttle service; business center; shopping arcade; 24-hr. room service; babysitting; coin laundry; same-day dry cleaning; nonsmoking rooms. *In room:* A/C, TV, dataport w/high-speed Internet, minibar, fridge, coffeemaker, hair dryer, iron, complimentary newspaper.

Sunset Inn & Suites *Value* *Kids*

Just a couple of blocks from English Bay on the edge of the residential West End, the Sunset Inn offers spacious accommodations in a great location for a very reasonable price. Units are either studios or one-bedroom apartments and come with fully equipped kitchens and dining areas. Like many other hotels in this part of town, the Sunset Inn started life as an apartment building, which means that the rooms are larger than your average hotel room, and all have balconies. The view gets better on the higher floors, but the price remains the same, so book early and request an upper floor. For those traveling with children, the one-bedroom suites have a separate bedroom and a pullout couch (two in the larger one-bedrooms) in the living room. The rooms on the top two floors have been redone with crisp forest-green walls and hardwood furnishings. Lower floors retain a kind of early 1980s pastel look, but are slowly being upgraded. If style matters, request a refurnished unit when making your reservation.

1111 Burnaby St., Vancouver, B.C. V6E 1P4. (C) **800/786-1997** or 604/688-2474. Fax 604/669-3340. www.sunsetinn. com. 50 units. C$89–C$219 (US$71–US$175) studio; C$99–C$289 (US$79–US$231) 1-bedroom suite. Extra person C$10 (US$8). Children under 12 stay free in parent's room. Weekly rates available. AE, DC, MC, V. Free parking. **Amenities:** Exercise room; coin laundry; nonsmoking rooms. *In room:* TV, free wi-fi, kitchen, coffeemaker, iron.

West End Guest House *Finds*

A heritage home built in 1906, the West End Guest House is a handsome example of what the neighborhood looked like before concrete towers and condos replaced the original Edwardian homes in the early 1950s. Decorated with early-20th-century antiques and a serious collection of vintage photographs of Vancouver taken by the original owners, this is a calm respite from the hustle and bustle of the West End. The seven guest rooms feature feather mattresses, down duvets, and your very own resident stuffed animal. The Grand Queen Suite, an attic-level bedroom with skylights, brass bed, fireplace, sitting area, and claw-foot bathtub, is the best and most spacious room; number 7 is quite small. Owner Evan Penner pampers his guests with a scrumptious breakfast and serves iced tea and sherry in the afternoon (on the back second-floor balcony in the summer). Throughout the day, guests have access to a pantry stocked with home-baked munchies and refreshments.

1362 Haro St., Vancouver, B.C. V6E 1G2. (C) **888/546-3327** or 604/681-2889. Fax 604/688-8812. www.westend guesthouse.com. 7 units. C$95–C$255 (US$76–US$204) double. Rates include full breakfast. AE, DISC, MC, V. Free off-street parking. **Amenities:** Complimentary bikes; business center; laundry service. *In room:* TV/VCR, dataport, hair dryer.

INEXPENSIVE

Buchan Hotel *Value*

Built in 1926, this three-story building is tucked away on a quiet tree-lined residential street in the West End, less than 2 blocks from Stanley Park and Denman Street and 15 minutes by foot from the business district. Like the Kingston (reviewed earlier in this chapter) downtown, this is a small European-style budget hotel which doesn't bother with frills or charming decor; unlike the Kingston, it isn't a B&B, so you won't get breakfast. The standard rooms are quite plain; be prepared for cramped quarters and tiny bathrooms, half of which are shared. The best rooms in the house are the executive rooms. These four front-corner rooms are nicely furnished and have private bathrooms. The hotel also offers in-house bike and ski storage as well as a reading lounge.

1906 Haro St., Vancouver, B.C. V6G 1H7. ✆ 800/668-6654 or 604/685-5354. Fax 604/685-5367. www.buchanhotel. com. 60 units, 30 with private bathroom. C$45–C$75 (US$36–US$60) double with shared bath; C$70–C$95 (US$56–US$76) double with private bath; C$110–C$135 (US$88–US$108) executive room. Children 12 and under stay free in parent's room. Weekly rates available. AE, DC, MC, V. Limited street parking available. **Amenities:** Lounge; coin laundry. *In room:* TV, hair dryer, and iron available on request, no phone.

Sylvia Hotel *Overrated*   If the Sylvia were being built today, all its rooms facing onto English Bay would have balconies and probably be outfitted with luxurious appointments. But balconies were rarities back in 1912, when this venerable and much-used hotel appeared in the relatively unpopulated West End, so all you can do is stare out the windows at what is one of the loveliest views in town. Lots of folks love the Sylvia, mostly for its fabulous location, and many are eager to recommend it, but pretty as the old girl is from the outside, inside she's a bit of a wreck: Tatty carpeting lines the corridors, rooms sometimes smell musty, and in some rooms the mismatched furniture hasn't been updated in decades. The public spaces are the ugliest you're likely to encounter in any Vancouver hotel, lost in a kind of garish 1950s lounge style that is so awful it isn't even camp. That said, you're not going to find waterfront accommodations anywhere else at Sylvia's prices. If you do stay, the best rooms are located on the higher floors facing English Bay. The suites have fully equipped kitchens and are large enough for families. The 14-year-old low-rise annex rooms are no better, and offer less atmosphere.

1154 Gilford St., Vancouver, B.C. V6G 2P6. ✆ 604/681-9321. Fax 604/682-3551. www.sylviahotel.com. 118 units. May–Sept C$95–C$155 (US$76–US$124) double; Oct–Apr C$75–C$105 (US$60–US$84) double. Children under 18 stay free in parent's room. AE, DC, MC, V. Parking C$7 (US$5.60). **Amenities:** Restaurant; bar; concierge; limited room service; dry cleaning; nonsmoking rooms. *In room:* TV, dataport, hair dryer.

4 The West Side

Right across False Creek from downtown and the West End is Vancouver's West Side. If your agenda includes a Granville Island shopping spree, exploration of the laid-back Kitsilano neighborhood, time at Kits Beach, visiting the fabulous Museum of Anthropology and famed gardens on the University of British Columbia campus, strolls through the sunken garden at Queen Elizabeth Park, or if you require close proximity to the airport without staying in an "airport hotel," you'll find cozy B&Bs and hotels in this area of Vancouver.

EXPENSIVE

Granville Island Hotel *Finds*   One of Vancouver's best-kept hotel secrets, this hotel is tucked away on the edge of Granville Island in a unique waterfront setting that's just a short stroll from theaters, galleries, and the fabulous Granville Island public market. Rooms in the original wing are definitely fancier, so book these if you can, but the new wing is fine, too. Rooms are fairly spacious with traditional, unsurprising decor and large bathrooms with soaker tubs; some units have balconies and great views out over False Creek. The best rooms and views are in the Penthouse suites, located in the new wing. If you don't have a car, the only potential drawback to a stay here is the location. During the daytime when the False Creek ferries are running, it's a quick ferry ride to Yaletown. After 10pm, however, you're looking at a C$10 to C$15 (US$8–US$12) cab ride or an hour walk. That said, there's a reasonable amount happening on the Island after dark, and the hotel's waterside restaurant and brewpub are wonderful hang-out spots with outdoor seating.

1253 Johnston St., Vancouver, B.C. V6H 3R9. ℂ 800/663-1840 or 604/683-7373. Fax 604/683-3061. www.granville islandhotel.com. 85 units. Oct–Apr C$170 (US$136) double, C$360 (US$288) penthouse; May–Sept C$270 (US$216) double, C$460 (US$368) penthouse. AE, DC, DISC, MC, V. Parking C$7 (US$5.60). **Amenities:** Restaurant; brewpub; access to nearby health club and tennis courts; small exercise room; Jacuzzi; bike rental; concierge; tour desk; car-rental desk; business center; limited room service; massage; babysitting; laundry; same-day dry cleaning; nonsmoking rooms. *In room:* A/C, TV w/pay movies, dataport w/high-speed Internet, minibar, coffeemaker, hair dryer, iron.

MODERATE

Camelot Inn ⽊ *Finds*   This handsome 1906 house is one of the nicest and most romantic B&Bs in Vancouver. Surrounded by old trees and located just 2 blocks from the nicest stretch of 4th Avenue in Kitsilano, and a 10-minute walk from Kits Beach, the Edwardian-era house is full of gorgeous period details (lots of wood) and decorated in an age-appropriate style. Three guest rooms are located on the second floor and two lovely studios with separate entrances are tucked away in the back. The Camelot Room features a huge sleigh bed and large Jacuzzi tub beneath a leaded bay window. The somewhat smaller Eden Room sports a queen bed, antiques, and a bathroom with large soaker tub. The Camay Room, the smallest, is nice and bright and features a queen bed but only a large shower. The Latvian-born innkeepers serve a very good breakfast. Unusual attention to detail is a hallmark of this find.

2212 Larch St., Vancouver, B.C. V6K 3P7. ℂ **604/739-6941.** www.camelotinnvancouver.com. 5 units. May–Sept C$145–C$189 (US$116–US$162) double; Oct–Apr C$135–C$154 (US$108–US$123) double. Rates include full breakfast. MC, V. Street parking. *In room:* TV, small fridge, no phone.

Johnson Heritage House Bed & Breakfast *Finds*   Innkeepers Ron and Sandy Johnson's eclectic collection of antiques and collectibles is displayed in the nooks and crannies of this 1920 Craftsman home in Vancouver's quiet Kerrisdale neighborhood, a 15-minute drive from the Vancouver airport and about a 10-minute drive to downtown. The Garden room downstairs is quiet and self-contained, with big bright windows overlooking a garden brimming with raspberries and blueberries. Upstairs, the small, cozy Sunshine room (shower only) offers a balcony with a view of the back garden, while the larger Mountain View room offers an excellent view of the Lions and the other peaks of the North Shore. And though the private bathroom for the Mountain View is across the hall, it comes with a giant two-person claw-foot tub. Best of all is the Carousel room: It's large and bright, with a big four-poster brass bed; a working, gas, slate fireplace; and a generously sized bathroom. A full breakfast is served in the spacious dining room that looks out onto the tree-shaded garden.

2278 W. 34th Ave., Vancouver, B.C. V6M 1G6. ℂ **604/266-4175.** Fax 604/266-4175. www.johnsons-inn-vancouver. com. 4 units, 1 with shower only. C$115–C$165 (US$92–US$132) double. Rates include full breakfast. No credit cards. Free parking. *In room:* TV/VCR, dataport w/high-speed Internet, hair dryer, iron.

Kenya Court Ocean Front Guest House *Finds*   There's no sign outside, so from the street this unusual B&B simply looks like the three-story 1926 apartment house that it is. But press button no. 5 as directed, and your hosts will welcome you into their unusual and surprisingly pleasant establishment. There are, in fact, some permanent tenants in the building, but there are also five furnished apartments rented on a B&B basis. Not only is the house in a fantastic location, directly across the street from Kits Beach, one of the most popular spots in Vancouver, but every unit has a view of English Bay, downtown Vancouver, and the Coast Mountains. On the ground floor there's a newly refurbished and very nice little studio with a Murphy bed; the other suites are much larger, with a living room, bathroom, separate bedroom (or two), and full kitchen. In the mornings, you climb up a spiral staircase and are served breakfast in a glass-walled solarium on the roof. One thing to keep in mind: In the summer, Kits Beach and Cornwall Avenue running past it are very busy; this can be either a plus or a minus, depending on your point of view.

2230 Cornwall Ave., Vancouver, B.C. V6K 1B5. © 604/738-7085. h&dwilliams@telus.net. 5 units. C$155–C$175 (US$124–US$140) double. No credit cards. Garage or street parking. **Amenities:** Outdoor pool; tennis court and jogging trails nearby. *In room:* TV, fax, kitchenette, fridge, coffeemaker, hair dryer, iron.

Penny Farthing Inn   Built in 1912, this house on a quiet residential street is filled with antiques and stained glass. There's a common room with a fireplace and in summer, breakfast is served in the English-country-style garden filled with trees and fragrant flowers. All the guest rooms are decorated with attractive pine furniture. On the top floor, Abigail's Suite is bright and self-contained with nice views from both front and back. Bettina's Room features a fireplace and a balcony with lounge chairs. Sophie's Room, though smaller, has a nice porch with two wicker chairs overlooking the front garden. Lucinda's Room—with a private bathroom across the hall—offers the best value of the four. Coffee and a selection of teas, hot chocolate, and freshly baked cookies are always on hand for guests. Fix a cuppa and watch the friendly resident cats at play while you relax.

2855 W. Sixth Ave., Vancouver, B.C. V6K 1X2. © 866/739-9002 or 604/739-9002. Fax 604/739-9004. www.penny farthinginn.com. 4 units. C$100–C$180 (US$80–US$144) suite. Rates include full breakfast. No credit cards. Street parking. **Amenities:** Free use of bikes; business center; nonsmoking rooms; Internet access in common area. *In room:* TV/VCR, fridge, coffeemaker, hair dryer, CD player (in suites only).

INEXPENSIVE
Hostelling International Vancouver Jericho Beach Hostel   Located in a former military barracks, this hostel is surrounded by an expansive lawn adjacent to Jericho Beach. Individuals, families with children over age 5, and groups are welcome. The 10 private rooms can accommodate up to six people. These particular accommodations go fast; so if you want one, call far in advance. The dormitory-style arrangements are well maintained and supervised. Linens are provided. Basic, inexpensive food is served in the cafe or you have the option of cooking for yourself in the hostel's kitchen. The hostel's program director operates tours and activities. This hostel is open May through September only.

1515 Discovery St., Vancouver, B.C. V6R 4K5. © 888/203-4303 or 604/224-3208. Fax 604/224-4852. www.hihostels. ca. 286 beds in 14 dorms; 10 private family rooms. No private bathrooms. C$19 (US$15) dorm IYHA members, C$23 (US$18) dorm nonmembers; C$59 (US$47) double members, C$68 (US$54) double nonmembers. Annual adult membership C$35 (US$28). MC, V. Parking C$3 (US$2.40). Children under 5 not allowed. **Amenities:** Cafe; bike rental; activities desk; coin laundry; nonsmoking rooms.

The University of British Columbia Conference Centre *(Value*   The University of British Columbia is in a pretty, forested setting on the tip of Point Grey—a convenient location if you plan to spend a lot of time in Kitsilano or at the university itself. If you don't have a car, it's a half-hour bus ride from downtown. Although these

are student dorms most of the year, rooms are usually available. The rooms are very nice, but don't expect luxury. The 17-story Walter Gage Residence offers new and comfortable accommodations; many are located on the upper floors with sweeping views of the city and ocean. One- and six-bedroom suites here come equipped with private bathrooms, kitchenettes, TVs, and phones. Each studio suite has a twin bed; each one-bedroom suite features a queen bed; the six-bedroom Tower suites—a particularly good deal for families—feature one double bed and five twin beds. Located next door, the year-round Gage Court suites have two twin beds in one bedroom and a queen-size Murphy bed in the sitting room.

5961 Student Union Blvd., Vancouver, B.C. V6T 2C9. ☎ 604/822-1000. Fax 604/822-1001. www.ubcaccommodation. com. About 1,900 units. Gage Towers units available May 10–Aug 26; Pacific Spirit Hostel units available May 15–Aug 19. Gage Towers: C$42–C$71 (US$34–US$57) single with shared bathroom; C$100–C$200 (US$80–US$160) studio, 1-, or 6-bedroom suites. Pacific Spirit Hostel: C$26 (US$21) single; C$50 (US$40) double; C$61 (US$49) studio suite with private bathroom. Located adjacent to the Gage Residence, the 47 West Coast Suites are available year-round: C$129–C$170 (US$103–US$136) suite. AE, MC, V. Parking C$5 (US$4). Bus: 4, 10, or 99. **Amenities** (nearby on campus): Restaurant; cafeteria; pub; Olympic-size swimming pool; public golf course; tennis courts; weight room; sauna for C$5 (US$3.75) per person; video arcade; laundry. *In room:* A/C, TV, hair dryer.

5 The North Shore (North Vancouver & West Vancouver)

The North Shore cities of North and West Vancouver are pleasant, lush, and much less hurried than Vancouver. Staying here also offers easy access to the North Shore mountains and area attractions, including hiking trails, the Capilano Suspension Bridge, and the ski slopes on Mount Seymour, Grouse Mountain, and Cypress Bowl. Staying here is also often cheaper than staying in Vancouver. The disadvantage is that if you want to take your car into Vancouver, there are only two bridges, and during rush hours they're painfully slow. The passenger-only SeaBus, however, is quick and fairly scenic.

EXPENSIVE

Lonsdale Quay Hotel   Directly across the Burrard Inlet from the Canada Place Pier, the Lonsdale Quay Hotel sits at the water's edge above the Lonsdale Quay Market at the SeaBus terminal. An escalator rises from the midst of the market's food, crafts, and souvenir stalls to the hotel's front desk on the third floor. This hotel calls itself a boutique hotel but suffers from its 1980s design and some strangely chintzy-looking interior room decor (mostly new as of 2004) that may remind you of a motel. Some rooms have unique harbor and city views, but others have weird wedge-shaped concrete balconies and feel closed in. Lonsdale Quay is not particularly appealing after nightfall, when all the shops have closed. This is a good location, however, if you're exploring North Vancouver: The hotel is only 15 minutes by bus or car from Grouse Mountain Ski Resort and Capilano Regional Park.

123 Carrie Cates Court, North Vancouver, B.C. V7M 3K7. ☎ 800/836-6111 or 604/986-6111. Fax 604/986-8782. www.lonsdalequayhotel.com. 70 units. High season C$125–C$225 (US$100–US$180) double or twin, C$350 (US$280) suite; low season C$90–C$165 (US$72–US$132) double or twin, C$250 (US$200) suite. Extra person C$25 (US$20). Senior discount available. AE, DC, DISC, MC, V. Parking C$7 (US$5.50); free on weekends and holidays. SeaBus: Lonsdale Quay. **Amenities:** 2 restaurants; small exercise room; spa; bike rental; concierge; limited room service; babysitting; laundry service; same-day dry cleaning. *In room:* A/C, TV, dataport, minibar, coffeemaker, hair dryer, iron.

MODERATE

Beachside City View Bed & Breakfast 🏆 *Finds*   Joan Gibbs' B&B is in a new and comfortably grand house located in the upscale West Vancouver area known as "The

British Properties," a 10-minute drive from downtown. There are three choices of accommodations: two bedrooms with bathroom between are rented as one unit; the enormous Honeymoon Suite has its own balcony and a luxurious bathroom with Jacuzzi and separate shower; and the family-friendly ground-floor Garden Suite has a bedroom, full-sized kitchen, two bathrooms and glass doors out to the garden. The upper-floor rooms enjoy sweeping views of Burrard Inlet, the Lion's Gate Bridge, Stanley Park, and the skyline of downtown Vancouver. The house is beautifully furnished and full of fine detailing; guests also have use of the private swimming pool. A full breakfast is served in a lovely, light-filled dining room.

1180 Renton Place, West Vancouver, B.C. V7S 2K7. ⓒ **800/563-3311** or 604/922-7773. Fax 604/926-8073. www. beach.bc.ca. 3 units. C$200–C$250 (US$160–US$200) double. Rates include breakfast tray. MC, V. Free parking. Bus: 254. **Amenities:** Outdoor heated pool. *In room:* TV/VCR w/free videos, wi-fi, fridge, coffeemaker, hair dryer, iron, microwave.

6

Where to Dine in Vancouver

Foodies, take note: Vancouver is one of North America's top dining cities, right up there with New York, San Francisco, and any other food capital you can think of. Estimates are that the city has anywhere from *two* to *five thousand* restaurants. What's undeniably true is that Vancouverites dine out more than residents of any other Canadian city. Outstanding meals are available in all price ranges and in many different cuisines, with a preponderance of informal Chinese, Japanese, Vietnamese, and Thai restaurants. There are also top restaurants that for preparation, taste, and presentation of Pacific Northwest cuisine can compete with the best anywhere. Sushi lovers are in heaven here because superlative sushi is available all over for a fraction of what you'd pay south of the Canadian border.

Over the past few years Vancouverites have come to expect top quality, and yet they absolutely refuse to pay the kind of stratospheric prices restaurant-goers pay in New York or London. For discerning travelers who love to dine out and dine well, Vancouver is a steal. There's a cadre of top dining places where Vancouver's trendy, glamour-seeking food acolytes gather to see and be seen; I review them all below.

Most of the top restaurants offer tasting menus, and if you're into food, I recommend that you try them. In particular, the tasting menus at West, C, Raincity Grill, and Cin Cin will give you a brilliant sampling of the best, freshest, and most creative cooking in Vancouver. Keep

in mind, too, that Vancouver is perhaps the West Coast's pre-eminent city for seafood. You can dine on fresh oysters and superbly prepared local fish for much less than you'd pay in any other city.

"Buy local, eat seasonal" is the mantra of all the best restaurateurs in Vancouver, and they take justifiable pride in the bounty of local produce, game, and seafood available to them. More restaurants in Vancouver are shifting to seasonal, even monthly, menus, giving their chefs greater freedom. The trend to tapas or sharing small plates also remains alive and well.

Once less than palatable, British Columbian wines are now winning international acclaim to rival vintages from California, Australia, France, and Germany. The big wine-producing areas are in the Okanagan Valley (in southern British Columbia's dry interior) and on southern Vancouver Island. (If you have a few extra days, both areas are worth a visit.) These wines have received far less publicity than they deserve, so some great bargains can still be had. The sommeliers at the top restaurants will gladly introduce you to British Columbia wines.

There's no provincial tax on restaurant meals in British Columbia, but venues add the **7% federal goods and services tax (GST).** Restaurant hours vary. Lunch is typically served from noon to 1 or 2pm; Vancouverites begin dining around 6:30pm, later in summer. Reservations are recommended at most restaurants and are essential at the city's top tables.

1 Best Vancouver Dining Bets

For a quick overview of the city's top restaurants, see "The Most Unforgettable Dining Experiences: Vancouver" in chapter 1, p. 13.

- **Best Spot for a Romantic Dinner: Raincity Grill,** 1193 Denman St. (© 604/685-7337), with its low ceiling, crisp linens, windows overlooking English Bay, and fabulous food, is a place that makes you want to linger. See p. 98.
- **Best Pacific Northwest Cuisine:** For amazingly fine dining that utilizes absolutely fresh local seasonal ingredients, you can't go wrong with **West,** 2881 Granville St. (© 604/738-8938), a culinary highpoint of the city and winner of Vancouver Magazine's Best Restaurant award in 2005. See p. 103.
- **Best Spot for a Celebration: Cin Cin,** 1154 Robson St. (© 604/688-7338), serves superlative Italian cuisine in one of the city's loveliest and most comfortable dining rooms; the covered, heated patio is wonderful, too. See p. 97.
- **Best View:** For a combination of top-notch food and a killer view, try **The Five Sails** in the Pan Pacific Hotel, 999 Canada Place Way (© 604/891-2892). See p. 87.
- **Best for Kids: Romano's Macaroni Grill at the Mansion,** 1523 Davie St. (© 604/689-4334), has a huge kids' menu, high chairs, and a great old mansion to explore—kids will love it. See p. 99.
- **Best Chinese Cuisine:** The best Vancouver Chinese at the moment remains **Sun Sui Wah,** 3888 Main St. (© 604/872-8822). It's definitely worth the trip. See p. 107.
- **Best French Cuisine:** For several years, **Lumière,** 2551 W. Broadway (© 604/739-8185), won the top spot in the yearly Vancouver Restaurant Awards. You won't be disappointed. See p. 101.
- **Best Service:** Owner John Bishop of the eponymous **Bishop's,** 2183 W. Fourth Ave. (© 604/738-2025), makes every customer feel special. See p. 101.
- **Best Seafood:** The creativity of the chef, the quality of the ingredients, and the freshness of the seafood all combine to make **C,** 1600 Howe St. (© 604/681-1164), the best seafood restaurant in Vancouver. See p. 87.
- **Best Tapas: La Bodega,** 1277 Howe St. (© 604/684-8815), was serving tapas when chefs at all the new tapas upstarts were saving their nickels for a night at McDonald's. La Bodega still does it best. See p. 94.
- **Best Newcomer:** Head to Yaletown, where **Coast,** 1257 Hamilton St. (© 604/685-5010) offers an extensive variety of seafood from exotic coasts around the world, wonderfully cooked and served in a contemporary Zen-inspired dining room. See p. 91.
- **Best Italian:** At the wonderful **Cin Cin,** 1154 Robson St. (© 604/688-7338), the menu is divided into Old World and New World and everything tastes divine. See p. 97.
- **Best Japanese:** The most sublime of sushi is at **Tojo's Restaurant,** 202–777 W. Broadway (© 604/872-8050). Just remember to take out an extra mortgage beforehand. See p. 102.
- **Best Late-Night Dining: Glowbal Grill and Satay Bar,** 1079 Mainland St. (© 604/602-0835), in trendy Yaletown, is the place to be seen sipping and snacking late into the evening. See p. 92.

- **Best Outdoor Dining:** For unsurpassed ocean views, reserve a table under the trees at **Sequoia Grill at the Teahouse in Stanley Park,** Ferguson Point (close to Third Beach; © **604/669-3281**). This patio also doubles as **best sunset spot.** See p. 98.
- **Best Oysters:** In the heart of the Robson shopping area, **Joe Fortes Seafood and Chop House,** 777 Thurlow St. (© **604/669-1940**), has the best raw oyster bar in town, plus fresh seafood served without a lot of culinary intervention. See p. 93.
- **Best Vegetarian: Annapurna,** 1812 W. Fourth Ave. (© **604/736-5959**), has flavorful food; a cozy little room; and the most reasonable wines in town. Who says you have to sacrifice when you're a veggie eater? See p. 105.

2 Restaurants by Cuisine

AMERICAN
Hot Dog Jonny's (West End, $, p. 100)
Sophie's Cosmic Café (West Side, $, p. 106)
The Tomahawk Restaurant (North Shore, $, p. 109)

BARBECUE
Memphis Blues Barbeque House ⊕ (West Side, $$, p. 104)

BELGIAN
Chambar Belgian Restaurant ⊕ (Yaletown, $$$, p. 91)

CARIBBEAN
The Reef (East Side, $$, p. 108)

CASUAL
Bin 941 Tapas Parlour ⊕ (Downtown, $$, p. 93)
Bukowski's (East Side, $$, p. 107)
Café Zen (West Side, $$, p. 104)
The Locus Café (East Side, $$, p. 107)
Mark's Fiasco (West Side, $$, p. 104)
The SandBar (Granville Island, $$, p. 105)

CHINESE/DIM SUM
Park Lock Seafood Restaurant (Chinatown, $$, p. 95)
Pink Pearl ⊕ (Chinatown, $$, p. 95)
Sha-Lin Noodle House (West Side, $, p. 106)

Sun Sui Wah ⊕⊕ (East Side, $$$, p. 107)

COFFEE/AFTERNOON TEA
Caffè Artigiano ⊕⊕ (Downtown, West End, $, p. 109)
Epicurean Delicatessen Caffè (Kitsilano, $, p. 109)
The Fish House in Stanley Park ⊕ (West End, $$$, p. 97)

CONTINENTAL
Delilah's (West End, $$$, p. 97)

DESSERTS
Death by Chocolate (many locations, $, p. 109)
La Casa Gelato ⊕ (East Side, $, p. 110)
Senses Bakery ⊕ (Downtown, $, p. 110)

FAMILY STYLE
Old Spaghetti Factory (Gastown, $, p. 96)
Romano's Macaroni Grill at the Mansion (West End, $$, p. 99)
Sophie's Cosmic Café (West Side, $, p. 106)
The Tomahawk Restaurant (North Shore, $, p. 109)

FISH & CHIPS
Olympia Oyster & Fish Co. Ltd. (Downtown, $, p. 94)

FRENCH

Elixir 🕏🕏 (Yaletown, $$$, p. 91)
Le Gavroche 🕏🕏🕏 (West End, $$$, p. 97)
Lumière 🕏🕏🕏 (West Side, $$$$, p. 107)
The Smoking Dog 🕏 (Kitsilano, $$, p. 105)
West 🕏🕏🕏 (West Side, $$$, p. 103)

FUSION

Fiddlehead Joe's (Yaletown, $$$, p. 92)
Glowbal Grill and Satay Bar 🕏🕏 (Yaletown, $$$, p. 92)
Zin 🕏 (West End, $$, p. 100)

GREEK

Stephos (West End, $, p. 100)

INDIAN

Annapurna 🕏 (West Side, $, p. 105)
Rangoli (West Side, $, p. 106)
Vij's 🕏🕏🕏 (West Side, $$, p. 105)

INTERNATIONAL

Coast 🕏🕏🕏 (Yaletown, $$$, p. 91)

ITALIAN

Amarcord 🕏 (Yaletown, $$$, p. 90)
Bis Moreno 🕏🕏 (Yaletown, $$$, p. 90)
Cin Cin 🕏🕏🕏🕏 (West End, $$$, p. 97)
Circolo 🕏🕏 (Yaletown, $$$, p. 91)
Gusto 🕏 (North Shore, $$$, p. 108)
Il Giardino di Umberto Ristorante 🕏🕏 (Yaletown, $$$, p. 93)
Old Spaghetti Factory (Gastown, $, p. 96)
Romano's Macaroni Grill at the Mansion (West End, $$, p. 99)

JAPANESE

Gyoza King (West End, $, p. 100)
Hapa Izakaya 🕏 (West End, $$, p. 99)
Ichibankan (West End, $$, p. 99)
Tanpopo (West End, $$, p. 99)
Tojo's Restaurant 🕏🕏🕏 (West Side, $$$$, p. 102)

MALAYSIAN

Banana Leaf 🕏 (West End, $, p. 100)

PACIFIC NORTHWEST

The Beach House at Dundarave Pier 🕏 (North Shore, $$$, p. 108)
Bishop's 🕏🕏🕏 (West Side, $$$$, p. 101)
C 🕏🕏🕏 (Yaletown, $$$$, p. 87)
Diva at the Met 🕏 (Downtown, $$$$, p. 87)
Feenie's 🕏 ($$$$, West Side, p. 101)
The Fish House in Stanley Park 🕏 (West End, $$$, p. 97)
The Five Sails 🕏 (Downtown, $$$$, p. 87)
Lift (West End, $$$$, p. 96)
Raincity Grill 🕏🕏🕏 (West End, $$$, p. 98)
The Salmon House on the Hill 🕏 (North Shore, $$$, p. 108)
Sequoia Grill at the Teahouse in Stanley Park (West End, $$$, p. 98)
West 🕏🕏🕏 (West Side, $$$, p. 103)

PIZZA

Incendio 🕏 (Gastown, $, p. 95)

SEAFOOD

Blue Water Café and Raw Bar 🕏🕏 (Yaletown, $$$, p. 90)
C 🕏🕏🕏 (Yaletown, $$$$, p. 87)
The Cannery 🕏 (Gastown, $$$, p. 94)
Coast 🕏🕏🕏 (Yaletown, $$$, p. 91)
The Fish House in Stanley Park 🕏 (West End, $$$, p. 97)
The Five Sails 🕏 (Downtown, $$$$, p. 87)
Joe Fortes Seafood and Chop House 🕏🕏🕏 (Downtown, $$$, p. 93)
The Salmon House on the Hill 🕏 (North Shore, $$$, p. 108)
Sun Sui Wah 🕏🕏 (East Side, $$$, p. 107)

SOUTHWESTERN

The Locus Café (East Side, $$, p. 107)

TAPAS

Bin 941 Tapas Parlour ⭐
(Downtown, $$, p. 93)
La Bodega ⭐ (Downtown, $$, p. 94)
Zin ⭐ (West End, $$, p. 100)

THAI

Simply Thai ⭐ (Yaletown, $$, p. 94)

VEGETARIAN

Annapurna ⭐ (West Side, $, p. 105)
The Naam Restaurant ⭐ (West Side, $, p. 106)

VIETNAMESE

Phnom Penh Restaurant ⭐
(Chinatown, $, p. 96)

3 Downtown & Yaletown

VERY EXPENSIVE

C ⭐⭐⭐ SEAFOOD/PACIFIC NORTHWEST   Eating at C, Vancouver's most creative seafood restaurant, is really an experience equivalent to going to the theater or an opera. Since opening in 1997, the popularity of this trendsetter hasn't flagged for a moment. The waterside location on False Creek is sublime, opening out to a passing parade of boats and people on the seawall; the dining room is a cool white space with painted steel and lots of glass. Ingredients make all the difference here: The chef and his highly knowledgeable staff can tell you not only where every product comes from, but also the name of the boat or farm. Expect exquisite surprises and imaginative preparations: For appetizers, fresh Kushi oysters with a tongue-tickling mignonette fizz, or "virtual smoked" salmon sitting atop a glass vial that releases beechwood smoke essence when the fish is removed, so your nose is included in the show. A piece of hibiscus mousse sits atop fresh sweet Dungeness crab lightly infused with chipotle. And so it goes, each course created like a work of art. For a really memorable dining experience, give Chef Robert Clark a chance to show off and order the seven-course sampling menu. Savor the exquisite cuisine and paired wines as you watch the sun go down over the marina. Fabulous!

1600 Howe St. ② 604/681-1164. www.crestaurant.com. Reservations recommended. Main courses C$28–C$49 (US$22–US$39), taster box C$35 (US$28), sampling menu C$90 (US$72). AE, DC, MC, V. Dinner daily 5:30–11pm; lunch Mon–Fri 11:30am–2:30pm (from May until Labour Day). Valet parking C$7 (US$5.75). Bus: 1 or 2.

Diva at the Met ⭐ PACIFIC NORTHWEST   Diva's revamped triple-tiered dining room with a giant wall of glass brick in the rear makes for an elegant dining experience, but I wish they'd remove those awful paintings. This is a tony, big-money-hotel restaurant that has to satisfy rich, persnickety customers (divas). The menu draws from the best of local fresh seasonal ingredients and takes a light, international approach to spices and seasonings. Seafood is perhaps the best option. If you arrive in the right season, don't pass on the Queen Charlotte scallops, the wild sockeye salmon, or the Pacific halibut with artichoke fennel ravioli. Diva's high-end main courses include meat, fowl, and seafood. You may find cinnamon-smoked duck with white asparagus and morel mushroom risotto, butter poached Nova Scotia lobster tail, or roasted beef tenderloin and glazed short ribs. Ingredients are top-notch. Diva's wine list is regularly rated one of the best in town.

645 Howe St. ② 604/602-7788. www.metropolitan.com. Reservations recommended. Dinner main courses C$26–C$39 (US$21–US$31); lunch C$12–C$23 (US$10–US$18). AE, DC, DISC, MC, V. Daily 6:30am–1am. Bus: 4 or 7.

The Five Sails ⭐ PACIFIC NORTHWEST/SEAFOOD   The view of Coal Harbour, Stanley Park, and the Coast Mountains is utterly magic. And somewhat

Where to Dine in Downtown Vancouver

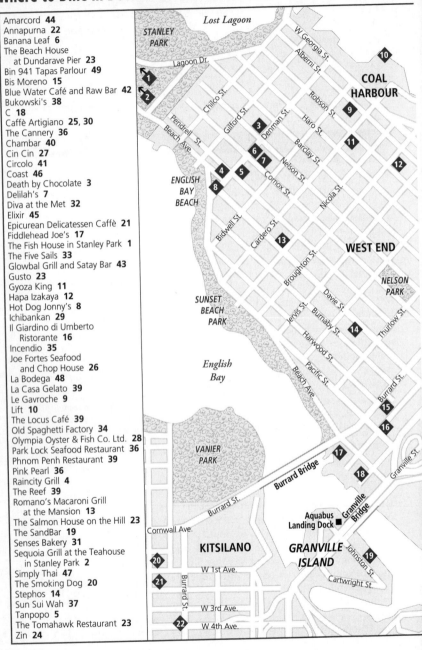

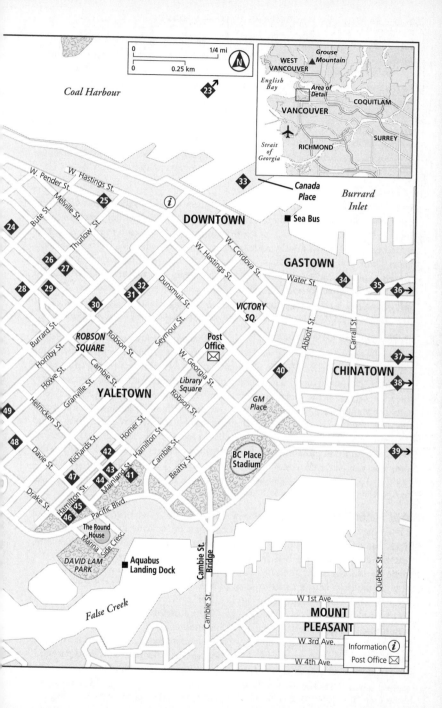

Coal Harbour

23

0 _____ 1/4 mi
0 _____ 0.25 km

Inset map:
Grouse Mountain
WEST VANCOUVER
English Bay
Area of Detail
VANCOUVER
COQUITLAM
Strait of Georgia
RICHMOND
SURREY

33

Canada Place

Burrard Inlet

■ Sea Bus

W. Pender St.
W. Hastings St.
Melville St.
Bute St.
Thurlow St.
25
ⓘ

DOWNTOWN

24

W. Cordova St.

26
27

W. Hastings St.

GASTOWN

Water St.
34
35
36→

28
29

Dunsmuir St.
Seymour St.

31 **32**
30

Burrard St.
Hornby St.
Howe St.
Cambie St.
Robson St.

ROBSON SQUARE

VICTORY SQ.

Abbot St.
Carrall St.

Post Office ✉

40

37→

CHINATOWN

38→

Granville St.
Helmcken St.

YALETOWN

W. Georgia St.

Library Square
Robson St.

GM Place

49

48

Davie St.
Richards St.
Homer St.
Hamilton St.
Cambie St.
Beatty St.

42

BC Place Stadium

39→

47
43
44 Mainland St. **41**

Hamilton St.
Drake St.

45
46

Pacific Blvd.

The Round House
Marina
Side Cresc.

DAVID LAM PARK

■ Aquabus Landing Dock

Cambie St. Bridge
Cambie St.

Québec St.

False Creek

MOUNT PLEASANT

W 1st Ave.
W 3rd Ave.
W 4th Ave.

Information ⓘ
Post Office ✉

surprisingly, given that this restaurant serves the enormous Pan Pacific Hotel atop Canada Place Convention Centre, the food at Five Sails is very good, too—inventive without being too clever. Seafood is where the menu really shines. Try the Voyage of Discovery, a fresh seafood platter featuring Pacific prawns, Dungeness crab, clams, and sushi. Other inventive appetizers include an ahi tuna carpaccio and smoked B.C. salmon. Main courses feature pan-seared halibut, oven-roasted lobster, crispy sea bass, and a slow-roasted B.C. sockeye. Duck, beef, and lamb are also on the menu. The cellar offers a substantial list of wines from B.C. and around the world.

999 Canada Place Way, in the Pan Pacific Hotel. © **604/891-2892.** Reservations recommended. Main courses C$26–C$45 (US$21–US$36). AE, DC, MC, V. Mon–Thurs 6–9:30pm (Fri–Sat until 10pm). SkyTrain: Waterfront.

EXPENSIVE

Amarcord ⚑ NORTHERN ITALIAN Traditional Northern Italian cuisine (in this case, from Emilia Romagna) doesn't get much respect these days, but that's just what Amarcord does, and so well that it's worth swearing off mango-corn chutney sauté and rediscovering the joys of freshly made pasta or risotto teamed with a lovingly prepared sauce. Think gnocchi with Italian sausage, fresh tomato, and basil, or linguini with mussels, scallops, and tiger prawns. Wines hail from Tuscany and California. The atmosphere is formal without being fussy. Service is knowledgeable and very friendly.

104–1168 Hamilton St. © **604/681-6500.** www.amarcord.ca. Reservations recommended. Main courses C$16–C$30 (US$13–US$24). AE, DC, MC, V. Mon–Fri 11:30am–2:30pm; daily 5–10pm. Closed on holidays. Bus: 2.

Bis Moreno ⚑⚑ MODERN ITALIAN This memorable restaurant opened in 2003 and by the end of the year had won *Vancouver Magazine*'s Readers' Choice Award for Best New Restaurant. Bis Moreno offers tasting menus from three to seven courses and encourages patrons to linger. The cooking is modern Italian that utilizes local products and some French techniques; sauces are clean, never more than two or three ingredients. For an appetizer you might choose foie gras with sweet onions, caponata, and chocolate, followed by a superlative handmade ravioli stuffed with lobster in a tomato and basil sauce. The freeform lasagna in a basil pesto sauce is delectable; so is the halibut filet wrapped in prosciutto in a fresh porcini mushroom sauce. The knowledgeable sommelier can pair every course with a delicious B.C. or Italian wine.

1355 Hornby St. (between Pacific and Drake). © **604/669-2812.** Reservations recommended. Tasting menus C$42–C$95 (US$30–US$71) per person. AE, DC, MC, V. Mon–Sat 6–11pm. Bus: 1 or 22.

Blue Water Café and Raw Bar ⚑⚑ SEAFOOD Since opening in the fall of 2000, Blue Water Café in Yaletown has become one of Vancouver's hottest restaurants. If you had to describe this busy, buzzy place in one word it would be *fresh,* as in fresh, seasonal seafood; only the best from sustainable and wild fisheries makes it onto the menu. If you love sushi, the raw bar under the direction of Yoshihio Tabo offers up some of the city's best Japanese-style sushi and sashimi. Frank Pabst, the restaurant's executive chef, creates his dishes in another large open kitchen. For starters, try a medley of Kushi oysters with various toppings. Main courses depend on whatever is in season: It might be spring salmon, halibut, Dungeness crab, or, my favorite dish, smoked B.C. black cod served with ricotta gnocchi, green asparagus, potato, and fresh horseradish cream. The desserts are fabulous, too, especially the frozen espresso parfait. A masterful wine list and an experienced sommelier assures fine wine pairings.

1095 Hamilton St. (at Helmcken) © **604/688-8078.** www.bluewatercafe.net. Reservations recommended. Main courses C$23–C$35 (US$18–US$28). AE, DC, MC, V. Daily 5pm–midnight. Valet parking: C$6.50 ($5.25). Bus: 2.

Chambar Belgian Restaurant ✦ *Finds* BELGIAN   Vancouver's favorite new restaurant (it opened in 2004) occupies an intriguing space in a kind of no-man's-land on lower Beatty Street between Yaletown and Gastown. Michelin-trained chef Nico Scheuerman and his wife Karri have worked hard to make the place a success, and in its first year plenty of plaudits have come its way. The menu features small plates and large plates. Smalls might be mussels cooked in white wine, roasted beets, smoked chicken, and venison tartar or carpaccio. Main courses include market-fresh options such as bouillabaisse with prawns, scallops, mussels, and halibut, or a pork chop with cherry beer compote. For dessert, try the classic Belgian chocolate mousse or the hot mocha soufflé. Chambar specializes in Belgian beers, some 25 varieties in bottles and on tap.

562 Beatty St. ✆ **604/879-7119**. www.chambar.com. Reservations recommended. Small plates C$9–C$17 (US$7.50–US$14); main courses C$17–C$20 (US$14–US$16). AE, MC, V. Mon–Sat 5:30am–11pm. Bus: 5, 17.

Circolo ✦✦ ITALIAN   Umberto Menghi was a pioneer in Vancouver's dining scene, starting some 28 years ago with Il Giardino di Umberto Ristorante (p. 93) and going on to open restaurants in Whistler and a cooking school in Tuscany. Now, with Circolo, he's moved into trendy Yaletown with a strategy that melds together a restaurant, bar, and bistro with a menu influenced by Florence, Paris, and New York. The result is a kind of international eclecticism that mixes traditional northern Italian and local seafood and utilizes some French techniques. My appetizer of Kushi oysters on the half-shell was sea-fresh and sublime, and a pasta course of *risotto ai funghi* (risotto with mushrooms) was perfectly done. The prime veal chop that followed was delicious but almost too large to eat. I think this may be the only restaurant in Vancouver that serves *tagliata alla fiorentina*. The restaurant has a great wine list and offers many wines by the glass. On warm days Circolo's patio is one of the city's finest.

1116 Mainland St. ✆ **604/687-1116**. www.umberto.com/circolo.htm. Reservations required. Main courses C$13–C$36 (US$10–US$29). AE, DC, MC, V. Mon–Sat 5pm–1am. Closed holidays. Bus: 2.

Coast ✦✦✦ *Finds* SEAFOOD/INTERNATIONAL   This dashing new Yaletown restaurant opened in May 2004 and quickly became a culinary and people-watching spot of note. The dining room is a handsomely designed affair with two levels, lots of light wood, and a special "community table" around an induction cooking surface so some lucky diners can watch Chef Sean Riley prepare their culinary teasers. The concept at Coast is to offer an extensive variety of fresh seafood from coasts around the world. So for starters you might have ahi tuna sashimi and avocado salad or a wild, white sea tiger prawn cocktail. Then, from the grill, you could order Pacific cod, wild B.C. salmon, South Pacific John Dory, Indian Ocean tiger prawns, or hand-harvested scallops. "Off-shore" temptations might include Alaskan king crab gnocchi, Louisiana blackened snapper, North Carolina rainbow trout, or Liverpool-style fish and chips. For those who aren't inclined towards fish, there are a few land-based dishes, such as chicken breast stuffed with wild mushroom and goat cheese, beef tenderloin, a veal chop, and Moroccan spiced Australian lamb sirloin. The cooking is just right for every dish, never overdone or underdone, never overwhelming the fish, and a joy for the taste buds. Accompany your meal with a recommended wine from Coast's large cellar.

1257 Hamilton St. ✆ **604/685-5010**. www.coastrestaurant.ca. Reservations recommended. Main courses C$24–C$35 (US$19–US$28). AE, DC, MC, V. Daily 4:30–11pm. Bus: 1 or 22.

Elixir ✦✦ FRENCH   A traditional French brasserie just sort of fits in naturally with the culinary internationalism of Yaletown. There are actually three different parts to

Elixir, located in the hip Opus Hotel: the velvet room, an enclosed space with dark-wood paneling and red velvet banquettes; the brighter, lighter garden room, more appropriate for an informal breakfast or brunch; and an adjacent dining area that looks like a Left Bank bistro. A horseshoe-shaped bar unites and overlooks all three domains. The menu is the same in all three—traditional brasserie food prepared with excellent local ingredients and utilizing a medley of spices culled from former French colonies the world over. For appetizers, think spiced beef tartare with gaufrette potatoes. For salads, think watercress and endives with rich blue cheese, red-wine poached pears, and candied ginger. For soups, think French onion. For main courses, think entrecote with mushroom fricassee, confit of duck with lentils, or braised veal cheeks with celeriac puree. The wine list covers a wide swath of the world, not just French vintages. The pastry chef, as you would expect, excels.

350 Davie St. (in the Opus Hotel). ⓒ 604/642-0577. www.elixir-opusbar.com. Reservations recommended. Main courses C$16–C$34 (US$13–US$27). AE, DC, MC, V. Daily 6:30–11:30am and 5–11pm (Thurs–Sat until 12:30am); Mon–Fri 11:30am–2:30pm; Sat–Sun brunch 10:30am–2:30pm. Closed holidays. Bus: 1 or 22.

Fiddlehead Joe's FUSION Overlooking a marina and the busy entrance to False Creek, just east of the Burrard Bridge, this casual eatery has one of the few outdoor dining patios on the Vancouver seawall. The patio is heated, and that's where you want to sit, enjoying a casual lunch or the busy brunch on Saturday and Sunday. The scene is as much a part of this place as the fusion-style food. During the day, when Fiddle-head Joe's is a cafe, you can sit and people-watch with a coffee, a sandwich, dessert, or a glass of wine. More serious dining begins in the evening. Stick to the simpler dishes here. Tapas offerings include pan-fried soft-shell crabs, pizza, duck confit, and spicy Chinese-style beef tenderloin. For entrees, you can choose dishes such as veal ribs with a cinnamon paprika rub or pepper-crusted ahi tuna. The fusion spice elements work better on some dishes than others. The popular brunch includes skillet frittatas, corned beef hash with poached eggs and hollandaise sauce, and puff pastries filled with scallops, shrimp, and portobello mushrooms.

#1A–1012 Beach Ave. (on the Seawall). ⓒ 604/688-1980. www.fiddleheadjoeseatery.com. Reservations recommended for brunch. Tapas C$7–C$19 (US$6–US$15); main courses C$16–C$26 (US$13–US$21). AE, MC, V. Mon–Fri 11am–10pm; Sat 9am–10pm; Sun 9am–9pm; Sat–Sun brunch 9am–2pm. Bus: 1 or 22.

Glowbal Grill and Satay Bar 🎌🎌 FUSION Glowbal occupies a top spot in the trendy Yaletown dining scene, so if you're looking for an evening of good food served in a bright, buzzy atmosphere, this is a great place to try. The dining room, divvied up into a long elevated bar, a rank of semi-secluded dining tables, a file of glowing dining cubes, and an open kitchen, maximizes the drama all around. Have one of their famous martinis as you peruse the menu, and sample as an appetizer some of the delicious satays. Glowbal started the Vancouver craze for these succulent skewers of grilled meat or fish served with a dipping sauce. The main menu is delicious proof that fusion—the mixing of tastes and flavors from around the world—is alive and well. Maybe start with some tempura artichokes with fresh crabmeat, or Creole marinated fried soft shell crabs. Then, if you're in the mood for seafood, go with whatever is fresh: It may be wild salmon served with Dungeness crab gnocchi, or crusted sea bass with braised tomatoes and red pepper gratin. Service is fun and friendly, the wine list exemplary. There is a guaranteed 45-minute lunch from Monday to Friday featuring a daily special. After hours of dining, the truly in-crowd heads to Afterglow, the small lounge behind the dining room.

1079 Mainland St. © 604/602-0835. www.glowbalgrill.com. Reservations recommended. Main courses C$19–C$29 (US$15–US$23). AE, DC, MC, V. Sun–Thurs 11am–midnight; Fri–Sat 11am–1am. Bus: 2.

Il Giardino di Umberto Ristorante ★★ ITALIAN

Twenty-seven years ago, restaurant magnate Umberto Menghi started this small restaurant tucked away in a yellow heritage house at the bottom of Hornby Street. His Vancouver empire now includes Circolo in Yaletown (see above), but Il Giardino still serves some of the best Italian fare in town. A larger restaurant now adjoins the original house, opening up into a spacious and bright dining room that re-creates the ambience of an Italian villa. The menu leans towards Tuscany, with dishes that emphasize pasta and game. Entrees include classics such as osso buco with saffron risotto, and that Roman favorite, spaghetti carbonara. A daily list of specials makes the most of seasonal fresh ingredients, often offering outstanding seafood dishes. For dessert try the mandarin orange/blood orange panna cotta or lemon mascarpone gelato with hazelnut poundcake. The wine list is comprehensive and well chosen, with many excellent vintages reasonably priced at under C$40 (US$32) a bottle.

1382 Hornby St. (between Pacific and Drake). © 604/669-2422. Fax 604/669-9723. www.umberto.com. Reservations required. Main courses C$14–C$33 (US$11–US$26). AE, DC, MC, V. Mon–Fri 11:30am–3pm; Mon–Sat 6–11pm. Closed holidays. Bus: 1 or 22.

Joe Fortes Seafood and Chop House ★★★ SEAFOOD

Named after the burly Caribbean seaman who became English Bay's first lifeguard, Joe Fortes is the best place to come if you're hankering for top-of-the-line fresh seafood served the "old-fashioned" way, without a lot of modern culinary intrusions. The downstairs dining room evokes a kind of turn-of-the-20th-century saloon elegance, but if the weather's fine, try instead for a table on the rooftop patio. Stick with the seafood because it's absolutely the freshest in town; no farmed fish allowed. The waiters will inform you what's just come in and where it's from. Depending on the season you might find skate, marlin, ling cod, mahimahi, snapper, and sablefish as well as salmon, halibut, and tuna. Each selection arrives simply grilled or sautéed and is served with freshly grilled vegetables. My personal recommendation is that you sample the seasonal oysters because Joe Fortes has the best oyster bar in Vancouver, and/or order the famous seafood tower, which comes with an iced assortment of marinated mussels, poached shrimp, grilled and chilled scallops, marinated calamari, tuna sashimi, Manila clams, Dungeness crab, and local beach oysters. Heavy on the white, the wine list is gargantuan and includes some wonderful pinots from the Okanagan Valley. The desserts here are sumptuous as well.

777 Thurlow St. (at Robson). © 604/669-1940. www.joefortes.ca. Reservations recommended. Main courses C$20–C$32 (US$16–US$26). AE, DC, DISC, MC, V. Daily 11am–10:30pm (brunch Sat–Sun 11am–4pm). Bus: 5.

MODERATE

Bin 941 Tapas Parlour ★ TAPAS/CASUAL

Still booming 6 years on, Bin 941 remains the place for trendy tapas dining. In fact, it pretty much started the small-plate-sharing craze. True, the music's too loud and the room's too small, but the food that alights on the bar or the eight tiny tables is delicious and fun to eat. Look especially for local seafood offerings like scallops and tiger prawns in bonito butter sauce. Sharing is unavoidable in this sliver of a bistro, so come prepared for socializing. So successful was the original model that a second Bin, dubbed Bin 942, opened at 1521 West Broadway (© 604/673-1246). And thanks to the "loose" liquor laws, both Bins are now open until 2am. At both, the tables start to fill up at 6:30pm and by 8pm, there's a long line of the hip and the hungry.

941 Davie St. ⓒ **604/683-1246.** www.bin941.com. Reservations not accepted. All plates are C$10–C$14 (US$8–US$11). MC, V. Daily 5pm–2am. Bus: 4, 5, or 8.

La Bodega ✿ *Value* TAPAS   On a cold and rainy winter evening there is no better retreat than this warm, dark Spanish bar. Grab one of the tables or sneak into a romantic corner and order some soul-warming Mediterranean comfort food. Expect authentic Spanish tapas—garlic prawns, ceviche, marinated mushrooms, pan-fried squid, and good black olives. Specials on the blackboard regularly include *conejo* (rabbit with tomatoes and peppers), quail, and B.C. scallops. All of it comes with lots of crusty bread for soaking up the wonderful garlicky sauces. La Bodega also has a good selection of Portuguese and Spanish wines and the best sangria in town.

1277 Howe St. ⓒ **604/684-8815.** Reservations recommended. Tapas C$3.95–C$7.95 (US$3–US$6); main courses C$11–C$18 (US$8.75–US$14). AE, DC, MC, V. Mon–Fri 4:30pm–midnight; Sat 5pm–midnight; Sun 5–11pm. Bus: 4 or 7.

Simply Thai ✿ THAI   Finally, an authentic Thai restaurant in the trendy heart of Yaletown. The small restaurant, decorated with light wood, terra-cotta tiles, and pale yellow walls, brightens up the dreariest of winter evenings. Watch chef and owner Siriwan in the open kitchen as he cooks up a combination of northern and southern Thai dishes, always using the freshest ingredients. The appetizers are perfect finger foods: *gai satay* features succulent pieces of grilled chicken breast marinated in coconut milk and spices and covered in a peanut sauce, while the strange looking but delicious *cho muang* consists of violet colored dumplings stuffed with minced chicken. Main courses run the gamut of Thai cuisine: noodle dishes and coconut curries with beef, chicken, or pork, as well as a good number of vegetarian options. Don't miss the *tom kha gai*, a deceptively simple-looking coconut soup with chicken, mushrooms, and lemon grass. Siriwan creates a richly fragrant broth that balances the delicate flavors of the lemon grass and other spices with the thick coconut milk.

1211 Hamilton St. ⓒ **604/642-0123.** Reservations recommended on weekends. Main courses C$9–C$17 (US$7.25–US$14). AE, DC, MC, V. Mon–Fri 11:30am–3pm; daily 5–10pm. Bus: 2.

INEXPENSIVE

Olympia Oyster & Fish Co. Ltd. *Value* FISH & CHIPS   This little hole in the wall, just off Robson, Vancouver's trendiest shopping street, serves up the city's best fish and chips. On any given day you'll find West End residents, German tourists, and well-heeled shoppers vying for counter space. There are only a few tables and a window-seat counter, plus three sidewalk tables (weather permitting), but the fish is always fresh and flaky and can be grilled if you prefer. Choose from sole, halibut, or cod, which may be combined with oysters or prawns, too. If you want to take home smoked salmon, the staff will wrap it up or ship it if you prefer.

820 Thurlow St. ⓒ **604/685-0716.** Main courses C$6–C$10 (US$4.75–US$8). AE, MC, V. Mon–Sat 11am–8pm; Sun 11:30am–7pm. Bus: 5.

4 Gastown & Chinatown

EXPENSIVE

The Cannery ✿ SEAFOOD   At least some of the pleasure of eating at The Cannery comes from the adventure of finding the place. Hop over the railway tracks and thread your way past container terminals and fish-packing plants and there it is—a great ex-warehouse of a building hanging out over the waters of Burrard Inlet. The interior, with its exposed beams, fishing nets, and seafaring memorabilia adds to The Cannery's charm, but many come here for the stunning view, one of the best in Vancouver. You'll find good, solid, traditional seafood here, often alder-grilled, with ever-changing specials to complement the salmon and halibut basics. One classic dish is salmon Wellington—salmon, shrimp, and mushrooms baked in a puff pastry. Meat lovers can get a grilled New York steak or Alberta beef tenderloin. Chef Frederic Couton has been getting more inventive of late, but when an institution founded in 1971 is still going strong, no one's ever *too* keen to rock the boat. The wine list is stellar, and the desserts are wonderfully inventive.

2205 Commissioner St., near Victoria Dr. ℭ **604/254-9606.** www.canneryseafood.com. Reservations recommended. Main courses C$16–C$28 (US$12–US$21). AE, DC, DISC, MC, V. Mon–Fri 11:30am–2:30pm; Mon–Sat 5:30–10:30pm; Sun 5:30–9:30pm. Closed Dec 24–26. Bus: 7 to Victoria Dr. From downtown, head east on Hastings St., turn left on Victoria Dr. (2 blocks past Commercial Dr.), then right on Commissioner St.

MODERATE

Park Lock Seafood Restaurant *(Kids* CHINESE/DIM SUM   If you've never done dim sum, this large, second-floor dining room in the heart of Chinatown is a good place to give it a try, even though you'll have to listen to shlocky Western music while you dine. From 8am to 3pm daily, waitresses wheel little carts loaded with Chinese delicacies past the tables. When you see something you like, you point and ask for it. The final bill is based upon how many little dishes are left on your table. Dishes include spring rolls, *hargow* (shrimp dumplings) and *shumai* (steamed shrimp, beef, or pork dumplings), prawns wrapped in fresh white noodles, small steamed buns, sticky rice cooked in banana leaves, curried squid, and lots more. Parties of four or more are best—that way you get to try each other's food.

544 Main St. (at E. Pender St., on the 2nd floor). ℭ **604/688-1581.** Reservations recommended. Main courses C$10–C$25 (US$8–US$20); dim sum dishes C$2.50–C$6 (US$2–US$4.80). AE, MC, V. Daily 7:30am–4pm; dinner Fri–Sun 5–9:30pm. Bus: 19 or 22.

Pink Pearl *⋆ (Kids* CHINESE/DIM SUM   After 25 years in the business, this is still Vancouver's best spot for dim sum. The sheer volume and bustle here are astonishing, and at peak times you may have to wait a few minutes for a table. Dozens of waiters parade a cavalcade of little trolleys stacked high with baskets and steamers and bowls filled with dumplings, spring rolls, shrimp balls, chicken feet, and even more obscure and delightful offerings. At the tables, extended Chinese families banter, joke, and feast. Towers of empty plates and bowls pile up in the middle, a tribute to the appetites of hungry brunchers, as well as the growing bill; fortunately, dim sum is still a steal, perhaps the best and most fun way to sample Cantonese cooking.

1132 E. Hastings St. ℭ **604/253-4316.** www.pinkpearl.com. Main courses C$11–C$24 (US$8.50–US$19); dim sum C$2.95–C$6 (US$2.40–US$4.80). AE, DC, MC, V. Sun–Thurs 11am–9pm; Fri–Sat 11am–10pm (dim sum served 11am–2:30pm). Bus: 10.

INEXPENSIVE

Incendio *⋆ (Finds* PIZZA   If you're looking for something casual and local that won't be full of other tourists reading downtown maps, this little Gastown hideaway is great. The 22 pizza combinations are served on fresh, crispy crusts baked in an old wood-fired oven. Pastas are homemade, and you're encouraged to mix and match—try the mussels with spinach fettuccine, capers, and tomatoes in lime butter. The wine list is

decent; the beer list is inspired. And there's a patio. Much to the delight of Kitsilano residents, a second location with a slightly larger menu has opened next to the 5th Avenue movie theater at 2118 Burrard (© **604/736-2220**).

103 Columbia St. © **604/688-8694.** Main courses C$8–C$12 (US$6.50–US$10). AE, MC, V. Mon–Thurs 11:30am–3pm and 5–10pm; Fri 11:30am–3pm and 5–11pm; Sat 5–11pm; Sun 4:30–10pm. Closed Dec 23–Jan 3. Bus: 1 or 8.

Old Spaghetti Factory *(Kids)* FAMILY STYLE/ITALIAN   Chains are usually disqualified from a listing in this book, but a few extenuating circumstances speak out in favor of the Factory: It's a smallish, Canadian chain; it has a great location in the Gastown heritage district; and it's a great place to take kids, with a selection of half-size, half-price pasta dishes, including spaghetti with meatballs. For the older and more adventurous, there are more complicated pastas with clam sauce or Alfredo sauce as well as non-pasta dishes including veal and steak. A small list of wines is on offer, as well as beer and chocolate milk.

53 Water St. © **604/684-1288.** www.oldspaghettifactory.ca. Main courses C$8–C$14 (US$6.50–US$11). AE, MC, V. Daily 10am–10pm. Bus: 50.

Phnom Penh Restaurant ✦ VIETNAMESE   This family-run restaurant, serving a mixture of Vietnamese and slightly spicier Cambodian cuisine, is a perennial contender for, and occasional winner of, *Vancouver Magazine*'s award for the city's best Asian restaurant. The walls are adorned with artistic renderings of ancient Cambodia's capital, Angkor. Khmer dolls are suspended in glass cases, and the subdued lighting is a welcome departure from the harsh glare often found in inexpensive Chinatown restaurants. Try the outstanding hot-and-sour soup, loaded with prawns and lemon grass. The deep-fried garlic squid served with rice is also delicious. For dessert, the fruit-and-rice pudding is an exotic treat.

244 E. Georgia St., near Main St. © **604/682-5777.** Dishes C$5.15–C$9.25 (US$4.10–US$7.50). AE, MC. Daily 10am–10pm. Bus: 8 or 19.

5 The West End

VERY EXPENSIVE

Lift *(Finds)* PACIFIC NORTHWEST   Time will tell how Lift holds up as a restaurant, but for now it's the hottest new place in town and weekends are jammed. Built on pilings right on Coal Harbour, and with an outdoor roof patio, it offers gorgeous mountain, water, and city views. The interior is luxe, with an illuminated onyx bar and different seating areas for drinking or eating or both. As for the contemporary West Coast cuisine—well, the kitchen hasn't really smoothed out yet, so dishes can be hit or miss. In the evening, the restaurant serves "whet plates," larger than an appetizer but smaller than an entree, so you can dine on dishes such as mussels with prosciutto, basil and white wine or fig braised beef short ribs. Or you can order main courses such as ahi tuna, spiced paella, or roast free-range chicken breast with warm honey and truffle-infused potato salad. The Sunday brunch is hopping, too, and is reasonably priced. The wine list here is good, but with a 300% markup, don't expect to find any bargain delights to accompany your meal.

333 Menchions Mews (behind Westin Bayshore Resort). © **604/689-5438.** www.liftbarandgrill.com. Reservations recommended. Whet plates C$12–C$21 (US$10–US$17); main courses C$24–C$38 (US$19–US$30). AE, DC, MC, V. Mon–Fri 11:30am–2:30pm, daily from 5:30pm, Sun brunch 11am–2:30pm. Bus: 240.

EXPENSIVE

Cin Cin *✿✿✿* MODERN ITALIAN   Celebrities, models, politicians, and Vancouverites in need of great Italian food all frequent this wonderful second-story restaurant on Fashion Central Robson Street. The spacious dining room, done in a rustic Italian-villa style, surrounds an open kitchen built around a huge wood–fired oven; the heated terrace is an equally pleasant dining and people-watching spot. The food at Cin Cin is exemplary, and it's divided into "Old World" (classic) and "New World" (modern) dishes; if you're in the mood to sample a bit of everything, order one of the fabulous five-course tasting menus. Pasta offerings include spaghetti with boar bacon carbonara and melt-in-the-mouth ravioli stuffed with fresh salmon and black cod. From the wood-fired grill and oven come savory dishes such as panko-crusted halibut, veal chops, free-range chicken, and buffalo striploin. You really can't go wrong with any of the dishes; even pizza is done perfectly and comes with a variety of delicious toppings, such as Parma prosciutto with rosemary, asparagus, roasted garlic, and fontina cheese. The award-winning wine list is extensive, as is the selection of wines by the glass. The service is exemplary, the desserts divine. What's not to like?

1154 Robson St. ⓒ **604/688-7338.** www.cincin.net. Reservations recommended. Main courses C$18–C$38 (US$14–US$30); tasting menus C$69 (US$55). AE, DC, MC, V. Mon–Fri 11:30am–2:30pm; dinner daily 5–11pm. Bus: 5 or 22.

Delilah's CONTINENTAL   Walk down the steps from the Denman Place Mall and you've entered Delilah's, a somewhat Victorian-looking place with private corner rooms, cherubim cavorting on the ceiling, wall-mounted lamps with glass shades, and a nicely old-fashioned menu brought up to date by the addition of tapas. First order of business is a martini—Delilah's forte, and the fuel firing the laughter and conversation all around. The tapas menu includes some trendy treats such as house-cured elk carpaccio. Main courses such as the grilled beef tenderloin on roast potatoes with veal stock, stilton, foie gras butter, and fresh horseradish are also worth trying.

1789 Comox St. ⓒ **604/687-3424.** Reservations recommended. Tapas C$8–C$13 (US$6.50–US$10); main courses C$28 (US$22). AE, DC, MC, V. Daily 5:30pm–midnight. Bus: 5 to Denman St.

The Fish House in Stanley Park *✿* SEAFOOD/PACIFIC NORTHWEST/ AFTERNOON TEA   Reminiscent of a more genteel era, this green clapboard clubhouse is surrounded by public tennis courts, bowling greens, and ancient cedar trees. Three rooms decorated in hunter green with dark wood and whitewashed accents reinforce the clubhouse atmosphere. You can enjoy a traditional afternoon tea here every day from 2 to 4pm, or come for lunch or dinner. The dinner menu features well-prepared dishes such as maple-glazed salmon, flaming prawns (done at your table with ouzo), and a seafood cornucopia. The oyster bar has at least a half-dozen fresh varieties daily. Desserts are sumptuous. The restaurant/bar draws a mix of golfers, strollers, tourists, and local execs.

8901 Stanley Park Dr. ⓒ **877/681-7275** or 604/681-7275. www.fishhousestanleypark.com. Reservations recommended. Main courses C$20–C$33 (US$16–US$26); afternoon tea C$24 (US$19). AE, DC, DISC, MC, V. Mon–Sat 11:30am–10pm; Sun 11am–10pm; afternoon tea daily 2–4pm. Closed Dec 24–26. Bus: 1, 35, or 135.

Le Gavroche *✿✿✿* FRENCH   This charmingly intimate French restaurant located in a century-old house celebrated its 25th anniversary in 2004. It has always been a place for special occasions and celebrations, and with food and wine of this caliber, there's a lot to celebrate. We went for the Les Deux Compagnons menu, a five-course menu with wine samplings for two specially designed by Chef Roger Leblanc. It was heaven from first to last bite. We started with tranche of foie gras with orange confit. There followed a trio of albacore tuna smoked, seared, and tartar. After that, owner and host Manuel Ferreira mixed up a classic Caesar salad tableside (Le Gavroche is known for special personal touches like that). Then came lamb sweetbreads with wild mushroom risotto, pancetta, and truffle sauce, followed by a venison chop with Madeira lingonberry sauce. The final bit of perfection was a perfect Grand Marnier soufflé. You can also order a la carte, of course, or choose three- or four-course menus from the daily offerings. The award-winning wine list at Le Gav spans the globe. All in all, you can't go wrong here.

1616 Alberni St. ⓒ 604/685-3924. www.legavroche.com. Reservations recommended. Main courses C$25–C$32 (US$20–US$26); set menus C$50–C$60 (US$40–US$48); Les Compagnons menu for 2 with wine C$150 (US$120). AE, DC, MC, V. Daily from 5:30pm. Bus: 5.

Raincity Grill 𝓕𝓕𝓕 PACIFIC NORTHWEST   This top-starred restaurant, which opened on English Bay in 1990, is a gem—painstaking in preparation, arty in presentation, and yet completely unfussy in atmosphere. Raincity Grill was one of the very first restaurants in Vancouver to embrace the "buy locally, eat seasonally" concept. The menu focuses on seafood, game, and poultry, and organic vegetables from British Columbia and the Pacific Northwest. The room is long and low and intimate, perfect for romantic dining. To sample a bit of everything, I recommend the seasonal tasting menu, an incredible bargain at C$50 (US$40), or C$80 (US$64) with wine pairings. Recent tasting menu highlights included wasabi leaf wrapped beef, grilled Coho salmon with oyster mushroom, pea tip salad and rhubarb broth, Fraser Valley duck breast, a creamily delicious selection of artisan cheeses from Vancouver Island, and a rose and buttermilk panna cotta. The award-winning wine list is huge and, in keeping with the restaurant's philosophy, sticks pretty close to home. From May through Labour Day, Raincity opens a takeout window on Denham Street where you can get delicious gourmet dishes to go, priced at C$4.95 to C$9.95 (US$4 to US$8).

1193 Denman St. ⓒ 604/685-7337. www.raincitygrill.com. Reservations recommended. Main courses C$21–C$32 (US$17–US$26). AE, DC, MC, V. Daily 5–10:30pm; Sat–Sun brunch 10:30am–2:30pm. Bus: 1 or 5.

Sequoia Grill at the Teahouse in Stanley Park PACIFIC NORTHWEST   One of Vancouver's most venerable seaside landmarks, The Teahouse Restaurant, perched on Ferguson Point in Stanley Park overlooking English Bay, was taken over and redone in 2004 to make it more contemporary in cuisine and ambiance. This is a place for sunset-watching and romantic relaxation on the outdoor patio (in good weather) or at a window-side table in the conservatory. The new menu is in keeping with safe tourist choices and a selection of what trendy Vancouverites are eating these days. Small-plate appetizers include wok-fried squid with Thai chiles and oyster sauce and mushrooms stuffed with crab, shrimp, and cream cheese. Main courses are evenly divided between seafood and meat with pasta and risotto thrown in for good measure. Look for B.C. salmon, grilled ahi tuna, mushroom risotto, classic coq au vin, and New York steak. The view here is perhaps more memorable than the food, and after the sun fades, the lights cast a magical glow on the trees and garden.

Ferguson Point, Stanley Park. ⓒ 604/669-3281. www.vancouverdine.com. Reservations recommended. Small plates C$8–C$11 (US$6.50–US$9), main courses C$11–C$28 (US$9–US$22). AE, DC, MC, V. Mon–Fri 11:30am–2:30pm, small plates daily 2:30–5:30pm, dinner daily 5:30–9:45pm; Sat brunch 11:30am–2:30pm, Sun brunch 10:30am–2:30pm.

MODERATE

Hapa Izakaya ⚘ JAPANESE   Dinner comes at almost disco decibels in Robson Street's hottest Japanese "eat-drink place" (the literal meaning of Izakaya), where chefs call out orders, servers shout acknowledgements, and the maitre d' and owner keeps up a running volley to staff about the (often sizable) wait at the door. The menu features inventive nontraditional dishes such as bacon-wrapped asparagus or *negitori* (spicy tuna roll) and fresh tuna belly chopped with spring onions served with munchsize bits of garlic bread. For non-raw fish eaters, there are inventive appetizers and meat dishes and a scrumptious Korean hot pot. The wine list is short and not especially special, but in compensation, the martini and sake lists are both sophisticated and lengthy. The crowd is about a third expat Japanese, a third Chinese (both local and expat), and a third well-informed Westerners. The service is fast and obliging, and the price per dish at this most entertaining of eating spots is very reasonable.

1479 Robson St. ⓒ 604/689-4272. No reservations accepted 6–8pm. Dinner main courses C$8–C$12 (US$6.50–US$9.50). AE, MC, V. Sun–Thurs 5:30pm–midnight; Fri–Sat 5:30pm–1am. Bus: 5.

Ichibankan JAPANESE   In contrast to Hapa (see above) further down Robson, this small basement sushi bar (with a new and rather dramatic red and black interior) has served old-fashioned, straight-up sushi for over two decades. The quality is high and the salmon, tuna, halibut, and other diverse sea creatures come nice and fresh. Prices are extremely reasonable; visitors from the East both near (such as New York) and far (such as Tokyo) are often astounded as to just how cheap and good Vancouver sushi is. There are options for non-sushiphiles, too, including tempura and teriyaki, but if raw fish ain't your thing, you'd be better off directing those dining instincts elsewhere.

770 Thurlow St. ⓒ 604/682-6262. Reservations accepted. Main courses C$6–C$13 (US$4.80–US$10). AE, DC, MC, V. Daily 11:30am–midnight. Bus: 5.

Romano's Macaroni Grill at the Mansion ⓚ*ids* FAMILY STYLE/ITALIAN Housed in a huge stone mansion built in the early 20th century by sugar baron B. T. Rogers, Romano's is a fun and casual chain restaurant with a mostly Southern Italian menu. This isn't high-concept Italian; the food is simple, understandable, and consistently good. The pastas are definitely favorites. Your kids will love the children's menu, which features lasagna and meatloaf as well as tasty pizzas. It's more fun to dine outside on the patio (with heat lamps), which is one of the best in town.

1523 Davie St. ⓒ 604/689-4334. Reservations recommended. Main courses C$8–C$16 (US$6.50–US$13); children's courses C$4.95–C$7 (US$4–US$5.50). AE, DC, MC, V. Mon–Thurs noon–10pm; Fri–Sat noon–11pm. Bus: 5.

Tanpopo ⓥ*alue* JAPANESE   Occupying the second floor of a corner building on Denman Street, Tanpopo has a partial view of English Bay, a large patio, and a huge menu of hot and cold Japanese dishes. But the line of people waiting 30 minutes or more every night for a table are here for the all-you-can-eat sushi. The unlimited fare includes the standards—makis, tuna and salmon sashimi, California and B.C. rolls— as well as cooked items such as tonkatsu, tempura, chicken kara-age, and broiled oysters. There are a couple of secrets to getting seated. You might try to call ahead, but they take only an arbitrary percentage of reservations for dinner each day. Otherwise, you can ask to sit at the sushi bar.

1122 Denman St. ⓒ 604/681-7777. Reservations recommended for groups. Main courses C$7–C$19 (US$5.50–US$15); all-you-can-eat sushi C$22 (US$17) for dinner, C$12 (US$10) for lunch. AE, DC, MC, V. Daily 11:30am–10pm. Bus: 5.

Zin 𝒢 FUSION/TAPAS   Zin's interior was redone in 2004 and now glows with deep reddish hues offset by comfy loungeable sofas and chairs on one side and dining booths on the other with flickering candlelight all around. The restaurant is in the Pacific Palisades Hotel (see chapter 5) but managed separately. Come here for a restaurant meal (breakfast, lunch, or dinner) or tapas made with fresh local ingredients and a global accent. There are lots of small plates priced in the C$8 to C$16 (US$6.50–US$13) range. Dishes include classic steamed mussels and Asian-inspired specialties like coconut crab, shrimp, and rice cakes. You can get a steak and fries, smoked wild salmon with horseradish butter sauce, butter curry scallops, or vegetarian linguine. The result, whether you're dining on entrees or sharing small plates, is a fun, casual experience with cuisine that's more varied and less expensive than any of the glorified pub-food outlets on Robson. Best of all, Zin's martinis still delight, the selection of wines-by-the-glass still is large, and if you're hankering for a Zinfandel, Zin's has the best selection in town.

1277 Robson St. ℂ 604/408-1700. www.zin-restaurant.com. Main courses C$15–C$24 (US$12–US$19). AE, DC, MC, V. Tues–Fri 7am–2pm and 4pm–midnight; Sat 8am–1am, Sun 8am–11pm.

INEXPENSIVE

Banana Leaf 𝒢 MALAYSIAN   One of the city's best spots for Malaysian, Banana Leaf is just a hop and a skip from English Bay. The menu includes inventive specials such as mango and okra salad, delicious south-Asian mainstays such as *gado gado* (a salad with hot peanut sauce) or *mee goreng* (fried noodles with vegetables topped by a fried egg) and occasional variations such as an assam curry (seafood in hot and sour curry sauce) that comes with okra and tomato. For dessert, don't pass up on *pisang goring*—fried banana with ice cream. The small room is tastefully decorated in dark tropical woods; the rather unadventurous wine list features a small selection of inexpensive reds and whites. Service is very friendly.

1096 Denman St. ℂ 604/683-3333. (also 820 W. Broadway; ℂ 604/731-6333). www.bananaleaf-vancouver.com. Main courses C$7–C$15 (US$5.50–US$12). AE, MC, V. Sun–Thurs 11:30am–10pm; Fri–Sat 11:30am–11pm. Bus: 5.

Gyoza King JAPANESE   Gyoza King features an entire menu of *gyoza*—succulent Japanese dumplings filled with prawns, pork, vegetables, and other combinations—as well as Japanese noodles and staples like *katsu-don* (pork cutlet over rice) and *o-den* (a rich, hearty soup). This is the gathering spot for hordes of young Japanese visitors looking for cheap eats that approximate home cooking. Seating is divided among Western-style tables, the bar (where you can watch the chef in action), and the Japanese-style low table, which is reserved for larger groups if the restaurant is busy. The staff is very courteous and happy to explain the dishes.

1508 Robson St. ℂ 604/669-8278. Main courses C$6–C$13 (US$4.80–US$10). AE, MC, V. Mon–Thurs 5:30pm–1am; Fri 5:30pm–1:30am; Sat 6pm–1:30am; Sun 6pm–11:30pm. Bus: 5.

Hot Dog Jonny's AMERICAN   Where do you go when you're craving a venison-and-fennel or duck-and-apple hot dog? To Hot Dog Jonny's, a little gourmet hot dog joint near English Bay. You can get a classic kosher dog from Chicago or a foot-long weenie or a veggie edition. It's the best hot-dog meat you'll ever find, and there are about 40 condiments to choose from.

1061 Denman St. (near Beach). ℂ 604/696-DOGS. Hot dogs C$3.80–C$7 (US$3–US$5.50). MC, V. Sun–Thurs 8am–10pm; Fri–Sat 8am–11pm. Bus: 6.

Stephos *Value* GREEK   A fixture on the Davie Street dining scene, Stephos has been packing them in since Zorba was a boy. The cuisine is simple Greek fare at its finest and cheapest. Customers line up outside for a seat amid Greek travel posters, potted ivy, and whitewashed walls (the average wait is about 10–15 min., but it could be as long as 30 min., as once you're inside, the staff will never rush you out the door). Order some pita and dip (hummus, spicy eggplant, or garlic spread) while you peruse the menu. An interesting appetizer is the *avgolemono* soup, a delicately flavored chicken broth with egg and lemon, accompanied by a plate of piping hot pita bread. When choosing a main course, keep in mind that portions are huge. The roasted lamb, lamb chops, fried calamari, and a variety of souvlakia are served with rice, roast potatoes, and Greek salad. The beef, lamb, or chicken pita come in slightly smaller portions served with fries and *tzatziki* (a sauce made from yogurt, cucumber, and garlic).

1124 Davie St. ✆ 604/683-2555. Reservations accepted for parties of 5 or more. Main courses C$4.25–C$10 (US$3.40–US$8). AE, MC, V. Daily 11am–11:30pm. Bus: 5.

6 The West Side

VERY EXPENSIVE

Bishop's ✸✸✸ PACIFIC NORTHWEST   Whether you arrive on foot or by limousine (there are guests in both categories), owner John Bishop will greet you at the door and lead you to a table in his elegant dining room hung with fine paintings and wood sculpture from the Pacific Northwest. Dining here is an expensive proposition, but among food worshippers Bishop's is considered one of the top five restaurants in Vancouver. All ingredients are locally grown and organic. Everything is seasonal, and the menu changes weekly, but at any given time, Bishop's will have a small collection of the best Pacific Northwest dishes available anywhere. Appetizers might include Dungeness crab with pear-cranberry chutney or grilled Pacific squid with lemon-ginger *aioli* (garlic sauce). Entrees could include roasted wild spring salmon with rhubarb compote, grilled spot prawns and smoked salmon risotto, or rack of lamb with garlic mashed potatoes. The wine selection isn't huge but it's exceptionally well chosen with vintages from along the Pacific Coast. Best to dress "casually elegant" or "smart business" if you're going to splurge here.

2183 W. Fourth Ave. ✆ 604/738-2025. www.bishopsonline.com. Reservations required. Main courses C$30–C$38 (US$24–US$30). AE, DC, MC, V. Mon–Sat 5:30–11pm; Sun 5:30–10pm. Closed Jan 1–15. Bus: 4 or 7.

Feenie's ✸ PACIFIC NORTHWEST   For all the hoopla on Rob Feenie, of Lumière fame, see the next review. Feenie's, his newest creation, opened in 2003, right next door, and became an instant hit with those who wanted to feel close to the celebrated chef but did not have to buy an eight-course meal. In this bright, relentlessly hip dining room you can order something as simple as a gourmet hamburger or hot dog or more upscale choices such as pastas, fresh fish, and various meat dishes. The bar, painted a glowing magenta-red, serves up special martinis and drinks du jour. The fixed-price lunch and dinner menus are a good value for good food.

2563 W. Broadway. ✆ 604/739-7115. www.feenies.com. Reservations recommended. Main courses C$9–C$19 (US$7.50–US$15), 3-course menu lunch C$25 (US$20), dinner C$35 (US$28). AE, DC, MC, V. Mon–Fri 11:30am–2:30pm; daily 5:30–10pm, Sat–Sun brunch 10am–2pm. Closed Jan 1–15. Bus: 4 or 7.

Lumière ✸✸✸ FRENCH   The success of this French dining experiment in the heart of Kitsilano has turned chef Rob Feenie into a hot commodity. What's his secret? Preparation and presentation are immaculately French, while ingredients are resolutely local, which makes for interesting surprises—fresh local ginger with the veal, or raspberries in the foie gras. Lumière's tasting menus are a series of 8 or 10 delightful plates that

Where to Dine in Kitsilano & the West Side

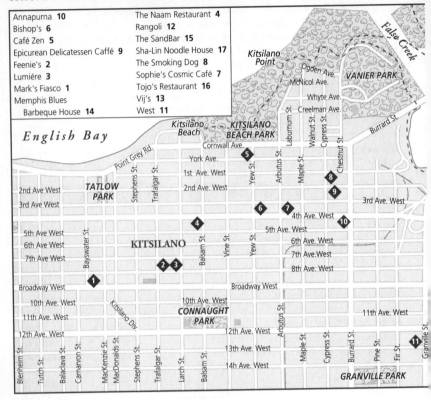

Annapurna **10**	The Naam Restaurant **4**
Bishop's **6**	Rangoli **12**
Café Zen **5**	The SandBar **15**
Epicurean Delicatessen Caffé **9**	Sha-Lin Noodle House **17**
Feenie's **2**	The Smoking Dog **8**
Lumiére **3**	Sophie's Cosmic Café **7**
Mark's Fiasco **1**	Tojo's Restaurant **16**
Memphis Blues	Vij's **13**
Barbeque House **14**	West **11**

change with the season, perfectly matched to a local wine (not included in the fixed price) and gorgeously presented. Diners can choose an all-vegetarian tasting menu (C$120/US$96); a meat-and-seafood kitchen menu (C$130/US$104); or an a la carte menu (3 courses for C$100/US$80). Whatever your choice, sit back and let the pilots in Lumière's kitchen take you on a culinary journey you won't forget. At the adjoining **Lumière Tasting Bar,** patrons can sample just smaller dishes instead of committing to the full eight-course meal. Chef Rob Feenie serves these tasty little treats for C$14 (US$11) a plate. The intrepid Feenie is also the force behind the more casual **Feenie's,** right next door (see review above).

2551 W. Broadway. ⓒ **604/739-8185.** www.lumiere.ca. Reservations required for restaurant, not accepted for bar. Tasting menus C$100–C$130 (US$80–US$104). AE, DC, MC, V. Restaurant Tues–Sun 5:30–9:30pm; tasting bar Tues–Sun 5:30–11pm. Bus: 9 or 10.

Tojo's Restaurant ✺✺✺ JAPANESE Tojo's is considered Vancouver's top Japanese restaurant, the place where celebs come to dine on the best sushi in town. It's expensive, but the food is absolutely fresh, inventive, and boy is it good. The dining room is on the second floor of an office building and opens up to fabulous views of False Creek and beyond (if it's nice, reserve a place on the patio). Tojo's ever-changing menu offers such specialties as sea urchin on the half shell, herring roe, lobster claws,

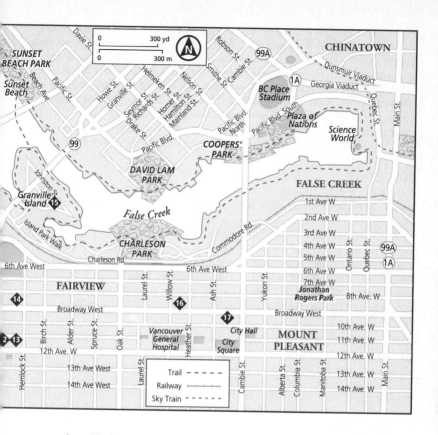

tuna, crab, and barbecue eel. The best thing to do is go for the Chef's Arrangement—tell them how much you're willing to spend (per person) and let the good times roll.

202–777 W. Broadway. ⓒ **604/872-8050.** www.tojos.com. Reservations required 1 week in advance. Main courses C$16–C$30 (US$13–US$24), sushi/sashimi C$8–C$28 (US$6.50–US$22), Chef's Arrangement set meals C$50–C$100 (US$40–US$80). AE, DC, MC, V. Mon–Sat 5–10pm. Closed Christmas week. Bus: 9.

EXPENSIVE

West 𝕬𝕬𝕬 FRENCH/PACIFIC NORTHWEST   I'm just going to come out and say it: I had one of the best meals of my life at West, and I wasn't surprised when it won the 2005 Best Restaurant and Best Chef award from *Vancouver* Magazine. This is a restaurant where details matter, high standards reign, and cooking is a fine art. And yet it's not stuffy or stiff. You'll want to dress up, though, and you'll want to linger over your food, prepared by executive chef David Hawksworth. The credo at this award-winning restaurant is deceptively simple: "True to our region, true to the seasons." What that means is that fresh, organic, locally harvested seafood, game, and produce are transformed into extraordinary creations. Small plates—like steak tartare with quail's egg—can be snacked on at the bar or ordered as an appetizer. The menu changes three to four times a week, but first courses might include house-made ravioli with spot prawns and basil or sweet pea soup with bacon and crostini; for a second course you might find roasted halibut fillet with wild mushrooms, braised pork belly with warm celery and salsify salad, or cider-braised veal cheeks with roasted tongue. For the ultimate dining experience, try one of the seasonal tasting menus—a multi-course progression through the best the restaurant has to offer; there's also an early prix-fixe menu served until 6pm. A carefully chosen wine list includes a selection of affordable wines; wines by the glass and half-bottles. If you're really into cooking, reserve one of the two "chef tables" directly adjacent to the kitchen.

2881 Granville St. ⒸⒸ 604/738-8938. www.westrestaurant.com. Reservations recommended. Main courses C$16–C$41 (US$12–US$33), tasting menus C$71–C$94 (US$57–US$75), early prix-fixe menu until 6pm C$35 (US$28). AE, DC, MC, V. Mon–Fri 11:30am–2:30pm; daily 5:30–11pm. Bus: 8.

MODERATE

Café Zen CASUAL   Sandal-clad traffic from next-door Kits Beach has turned the stretch of Yew Street between Cornwall and 2nd avenues into something of a casual dining mecca. There are numerous pasta options, a couple of pubs, and several neighborhood restaurants, one of the more popular of which is Café Zen. A great breakfast and lunch spot anytime of the week, on weekends this little cafe develops positively un-Zenlike bustle. By 10am the dining room is packed and waiting guests spill out the doorway and up the long steep sidewalk. What's the attraction? A huge brunch menu, fast and efficient service, reasonable prices, and great eggs Benedict.

1631 Yew St. (at York). ⒸⒸ 604/731-4018. Main courses C$6–C$12 (US$4.80–US$9.50). MC, V. Daily 7am–5pm. Bus: 2, 4, 7, or 22.

Mark's Fiasco *Kids* CASUAL   Mark's is the casual pub of choice for the Kitsilano jock-boy crowd, with a brass bar, 15 microbrews on tap, and at least four channels of sports on strategically placed TVs. On the restaurant side, Mark's offers a well-rounded menu of pastas, pizzas, seafood, and pubby dishes. There's a new emphasis on healthy eating here, with an Italian emphasis and some nicely innovative dishes, including low-carb and high-protein options. With a burger and fries starting at C$9 (US$7.25), crayons on every paper-covered table, and a congenial staff, Mark's is also kid friendly.

2468 Bayswater St. (at W. Broadway). ⒸⒸ 604/734-1325. www.markjamesgroup.com. Reservations recommended. Main courses C$9–C$22 (US$7.25–US$18). AE, MC, V. Sun–Wed 11:45am–midnight, Thurs–Sat 11:45am–1:30am. Bus: 9.

Memphis Blues Barbeque House *Finds* BARBECUE   In the busy section of Granville and Broadway, this hole-in-the-wall barbecue pit has made a name for itself with corn-pone, southern-boy barbecue. With *real* southern barbecue—as the owners will endlessly remind you—the meat has to be smoked for hours over a low-heat hardwood fire. Ribs come out tender enough to pull apart with your fingers (which is how food is eaten here—the cutlery is mostly for show) yet still sweet and firm. The beef brisket is cooked long enough that the fat is all rendered out, while the lean flesh remains juicy and tender. The pork butt is slow cooked until you can pull it apart with a fork. Those three meats (plus catfish and Cornish game hen) are essentially what's offered here. Put that meat on greens and you've got a southern salad. Put it on bread and it becomes a sandwich. Serve it on a plate with beans and a potato and it becomes an entree. There are wines by the glass and bottle, but what you want is the ice-cold home-brewed beer. There's now a second location at 1342 Commercial Drive (ⒸⒸ 604/215-2565); same hours apply.

1465 W. Broadway. ⒸⒸ 604/738-6806. Main courses C$7–C$9 (US$5.50–US$7.25); complete meals C$13–C$31 (US$10–US$25). AE, DC, MC, V. Mon–Thurs 11am–10pm; Fri 11am–midnight; Sat noon–midnight; Sun noon–10pm. Bus: 4, 7, or 10.

The SandBar CASUAL   On Fridays and Saturdays, the bar and patio here fill up with 20-something singles and an assortment of baby boomers and beyond, and a DJ starts spinning at 9pm. Those who aren't ready to tear into the pickup scene can actually sink their teeth into a number of fairly decent appetizers and entrees. Shrimp and pork dumplings provide the Asian component of a menu that spans the globe. Mexican-inspired fishcakes are served with a pineapple salsa, while fish taquitos come with a chipotle dip sauce. The menu also offers main courses such as cedar-planked grilled salmon and daily pasta and pizza specials. In summer, the patio on the third floor is fabulous for lazing about in the warm sunshine.

1535 Johnston St., Granville Island. ✆ 604/669-9030. www.mysandbar.com. Reservations not accepted for patio. Main courses C$11–C$21 (US$9–US$17). AE, MC, V. Sun–Thurs 11:30am–10pm, Fri–Sat 11:30am–11pm. Bus: 50 to Granville Island.

The Smoking Dog ✿ FRENCH   To date, the little Kitsilano neighborhood of Yorkville Mews has remained a local secret, perhaps because the few tourists who do venture into this delightful 1-block stretch are immediately confronted with a confusing variety of choices. Should one stop at one of the three cafes, the tapas bar, the sushi spot, the vegan cafe, or this traditional Parisian bistro, complete with patio umbrellas, waiters dressed in black, and a friendly bear of an owner who greets everyone at the door? Food-wise, the Dog is undoubtedly the best of the lot, featuring New York pepper steak, grilled halibut with Pernod sauce, scallops with beurre blanc, omelets, and crepes. If the weather allows, take a seat on the heated patio and enjoy the bustling street life.

1889 W. First Ave. ✆ 604/732-8811. Main courses C$14–C$15 (US$11–US$12). AE, DC, MC, V. Mon–Sat 11:30am–midnight; Sun 5:30–9:30pm. Bus: 2 or 22.

Vij's ✿✿✿ INDIAN   Vij doesn't take reservations and there's a line outside his door every single night. Patrons huddled under Vij's violet neon sign are treated to complimentary tea and *papadums* (a thin bread made from lentils). Inside, the decor is as warm and subtle as the seasonings, which are all roasted and ground by hand, then used with studied delicacy. The menu changes monthly, though some of the more popular entrees remain constants. Recent offerings included coconut curried chicken and saffron rice and marinated pork medallions with garlic-yogurt curry and *nan* (flatbread). Vegetarian selections abound, including curried vegetable rice pilaf with cilantro cream sauce and Indian lentils with *nan* and *raita* (yogurt-mint sauce). The wine and beer list is short but carefully selected. And for teetotalers, Vij has developed a souped-up version of the traditional Indian chai, the chaiuccino. Vij recently opened Rangoli (see below), right next door, for lunch and take-away.

1480 W. 11th Ave. ✆ 604/736-6664. Reservations not accepted. Main courses C$14–C$24 (US$11–US$19). AE, DC, MC, V. Daily 5:30–10pm. Closed Dec 24–Jan 8. Bus: 8 or 10.

INEXPENSIVE

Annapurna ✿ *Value* INDIAN/VEGETARIAN   A Kitsilano favorite, Annapurna's small dining room is hung with dozens of rice-paper lamps in whites, yellows, oranges, and reds that bask the room in a soft, warm glow. The menu is all vegetarian, but with the amazing combinations of Indian spices, herbs, and local vegetables, the dishes are rich and satisfying. Appetizers include samosas, pakoras, and lentil dumplings soaked in tangy yogurt with chutney. A variety of breads, such as paratha, nan, and chapatis, are served piping hot. Entrees such as *aloo-ghobi* (potato curry with cauliflower, onions, and cilantro) or *navrattan korma* (seasonal vegetables simmered in poppy-seed paste, flavored with saffron, aniseed, and sliced almonds) can be prepared from mild to screaming hot. The wine list is small but very reasonably priced.

1812 W. Fourth Ave. ✆ 604/736-5959. www.annapurnavegetarian.com. Main courses C$11–C$13 (US$9–US$10). AE, MC, V. Daily 11:30am–10pm. Bus: 4 or 7.

The Naam Restaurant 🐾 *Kids* VEGETARIAN   Back in the sixties, when Kitsilano was Canada's hippie haven, the Naam was tie-dye central. Things have changed since then, but Vancouver's oldest vegetarian and natural-food restaurant still retains a pleasant granola feel. The decor is simple, earnest, and welcoming: well-worn wooden tables and chairs, plants, an assortment of local art, and a nice garden patio. The brazenly healthy fare ranges from all-vegetarian burgers, enchiladas, and burritos to tofu teriyaki, Thai noodles, and a variety of pita pizzas. The sesame spice fries are a Vancouver institution. And though the Naam is not quite vegan, they do cater to the anti-egg-and-cheese crowd with specialties like the macrobiotic Dragon Bowl of brown rice, tofu, peanut sauce, sprouts, and steamed vegetables.

2724 W. Fourth Ave. ✆ 604/738-7151. www.thenaam.com. Reservations accepted on weekdays only. Main courses C$5–C$11 (US$4–US$9). AE, MC, V. Daily 24-hr. Live music every night 7–10pm. Bus: 4 or 22.

Rangoli INDIAN   Vij's, reviewed above, takes Indian cuisine to inventive new heights and tastes. But Vij's is only open for dinner, so right next door you can get lunch and takeout versions of Vij's curries and other specialties. Try tamarind and yogurt marinated grilled chicken, or mother-in-law's pork curry with mixed greens, naan, and rice. A sweet and savory snacks menu is offered from 4 to 8pm: rice and paneer cakes with fresh mango salsa, vegetable samosas, and warm mango custard are some of the offerings. Rangoli is a hip, simple-looking interior with just a few tables and a lot of stainless steel.

1488 W. 11th Ave. ✆ 604/736-5711. www.vijsrangoli.com. Reservations not accepted. Main courses C$9–C$11 (US$7.25–US$9). AE, DC, MC, V. Daily 11am–8pm. Bus: 8 or 10.

Sha-Lin Noodle House *Kids* CHINESE/DIM SUM   Ever wonder how fresh your noodles really are? At Sha-Lin, you can watch the noodle chef make them right before your eyes. Unique for Vancouver, Sha-Lin is one of the few places where each order of noodles is made from scratch. The chefs mix, knead, toss, stretch, and compress the dough until it almost magically gives way to thin strands. After a quick boil, the noodles are added to the dish of your choice. Two or three dishes make a satisfying meal for two; choose from a wide variety of meat and vegetable dishes. Want more entertainment at your table? Order the special tea and watch the server pour it from a meter-long (3 ft.) pot originally designed to allow male servants to maintain a polite distance from an 18th-century Chinese empress. Watch the server's steady hand as he aims the spout of boiling liquid in the center of your tiny cup—just don't make any sudden movements.

548 W. Broadway. ✆ 604/873-1816. Main courses C$5–C$10 (US$4–US$8). No credit cards. Lunch Wed–Mon 11:30am–3:30pm; dinner daily 5–9:30pm. Bus: 9.

Sophie's Cosmic Café *Kids* FAMILY STYLE/AMERICAN   Sophie's is easily identifiable by the giant silver knife and fork bolted to the storefront. Inside, every available space has been crammed with toys and knickknacks from the 1950s and 1960s. So, understandably, children are inordinately fond of Sophie's. Crayons and coloring paper are always on hand. The menu is simple: pastas, burgers and fries, great milkshakes, and a few classic Mexican dishes. The slightly spicy breakfast menu is hugely popular with Kitsilano locals; lines can stretch to half an hour or more on Sunday mornings.

2095 W. Fourth Ave. ℰ **604/732-6810**. www.sophiescosmiccafe.com. Main courses C$5–C$17 (US$4–US$14). MC, V. Daily 8am–9:30pm. Bus: 4 or 7.

7 The East Side

Many of these "east side" restaurants are on Main Street, which is on the borderlands between upscale west and working-class east. Main thus has some funky urban authenticity to go with its ever-increasing trendiness.

EXPENSIVE

Sun Sui Wah ✿✿ (Kids) CHINESE/DIM SUM/SEAFOOD   One of the most elegant and sophisticated Chinese restaurants in town, the award-winning Sun Sui Wah is well known for its seafood. Fresh and varied, the catch of the day can include fresh crab, rock cod, geoduck, scallops, abalone, oyster, prawns, and more. Pick your own from the tank or order from the menu if you'd rather not meet your food eye-to-eye before it's cooked. Dim sum is a treat, with the emphasis on seafood. Just point and choose. There are plenty of other choices for meat lovers and vegetarians, though they will miss out on one of the best seafood feasts in town.

3888 Main St. ℰ **604/872-8822**. www.sunsuiwah.com. Also in Richmond: 102 Alderbridge Place, 4940 No. 3 Rd. (ℰ **604/273-8208**). Main courses C$11–C$50 (US$9–US$40). AE, DC, MC, V. Daily dim sum 10:30am–3pm and dinner 5–10:30pm. Bus: 3.

MODERATE

Bukowski's CASUAL   The last and booziest of the American Beat poets gets what he always wanted, a bistro named in his honor. So what if he never made it to Vancouver, much less the Bohemian-and-becoming-more-so strip on Commercial Drive. The cuisine is not Polish, but instead a fusiony kind of comfort food perfectly suited to casual dining. Think beef satay, charbroiled chicken on focaccia bread, catfish with black-bean salsa, or steak with peppercorn garlic jus. And beer. Or any one of several wines featured on a daily blackboard. Even more attractive than the food is the friendly, buzzing atmosphere and a clientele too rich to be artists, but hip enough to dress the part. Service is wonderfully unhurried. Dawdle for hours if you want, reading the snippets of Sylvia Plath inscribed on your table, or listening to the live jazz, which plays at Bukowski's most nights after 7pm.

1447 Commercial Dr. ℰ **604/253-4770**. Main courses C$8–C$15 (US$6.50–US$12). MC, V. Mon–Thurs 5pm–1am; Fri–Sat noon–1am; Sun noon–midnight. Live Jazz Mon–Thurs. Bus: 20.

The Locus Café CASUAL/SOUTHWESTERN   Even if you arrive by your lonesome, you'll soon have plenty of friends because the Locus is a cheek-by-jowl kind of place, filled with a friendly, funky crowd of artsy Mount Pleasant types. A big bar dominates the room, overhung with "swamp-gothic" lacquer trees and surrounded by a tier of stools with booths and tiny tables. Cuisine originated in the American Southwest but picked up an edge somewhere along the way, as demonstrated in the roasted half-chicken with a cumin-coriander crust and sambuca citrus demi-glace. Keep an eye out for fish specials, such as grilled tomba tuna with a grapefruit and mango glaze. The pan-seared calamari makes a perfect appetizer. Bowen Island brewery provides the beer, so quality's high. Your only real problem is catching the eye of the hyper-busy bartender.

4121 Main St. ℰ **604/708-4121**. Reservations recommended. Main courses C$9–C$15 (US$7.25–US$12). MC, V. Daily 10am–midnight. Bus: 3.

The Reef *Value* CARIBBEAN   The "JERK" in the phone number refers to a spicy marinade of bay leaves, scotch bonnets, allspice, garlic, soya, green onions, vinegar, and cloves. The Reef serves up a number of jerk dishes, including their signature quarter jerk chicken breast. Other dishes are equally delightful, including a tropical salad of fresh mango, red onions, and tomatoes; shrimp with coconut milk and lime juice; grilled blue marlin; and Trenton spiced ribs. Choose a glass of wine from the thoughtfully selected list, and you have good dining at a bargain price. Afternoons, the tiny patio is drenched in sunlight, while in the evenings a DJ spins the sounds of the Islands.

4172 Main St. © 604/874-JERK. www.thereefrestaurant.com. Main courses C$9–C$15 (US$7.25–US$12). AE, DC, MC, V. Sun–Wed 11am–midnight; Thurs–Sat 11am–1am. Bus: 3.

8 The North Shore

EXPENSIVE

The Beach House at Dundarave Pier *&* PACIFIC NORTHWEST   With its waterfront location, the Beach House offers a panoramic view of English Bay. Diners on the heated patio get more sunshine, but they miss out on the rich interior of this restored 1912 teahouse. The food is consistently good—innovative, but not so experimental that it leaves the staid West Van burghers gasping for breath. Appetizers include soft-shell crab with salt-and-fire jelly; black tiger prawns sautéed in vermouth; and grilled portobello mushroom with Okanagan Valley goat cheese. Entrees have included herb-marinated chicken breast, flat-iron steak atop a potato and leek cake, and baked striped sea bass with basil mousse and rock prawns. The wine list is award winning.

150 25th St., West Vancouver. © 604/922-1414. www.atthebeachhouse.com. Reservations recommended. Main courses C$16–C$36 (US$13–US$29); tasting menus C$30 (US$24). AE, DC, MC, V. Daily 11am–10pm. Bus: 255 to Ambleside Pier.

Gusto *&* ITALIAN   West Vancouverites have always had numerous fine dining options, but for folks in more working-class North Vancouver (to the east of the Lion's Gate Bridge), times were always tougher. That is until the father-and-son Corsi team opened Gusto just steps from the Lonsdale Quay SeaBus Terminal. The comfortable and pleasant dining room is bathed in warm earth tones and has a rustic decor. The menu focuses on the cuisine of Central Italy. To start, try the fresh mozzarella wrapped in prosciutto and radicchio and drizzled with cherry vinaigrette, or the grilled calamari in a tomato coulis. Signature main courses include pistachio-crusted sea bass; duck breast with Frangelico, toasted pine nuts, and grilled orange; and the outstanding spaghetti quattro, a spicy concoction of minced chicken, black beans, garlic, and chile. The wine list leans heavily towards Italy, offering a good selection of reasonably priced Chianti and other table wines.

1 Lonsdale Ave., North Vancouver. © 604/924-4444. www.quattrorestaurants.com. Reservations recommended. Main courses C$10–C$32 (US$8–US$26). AE, DC, MC, V. Mon–Fri 11:30am–2pm; daily 5-10pm. SeaBus to Lonsdale Quay.

The Salmon House on the Hill *&* PACIFIC NORTHWEST/SEAFOOD   High above West Vancouver, the Salmon House offers a spectacular view of the city and Burrard Inlet. The rough-hewn cedar walls are adorned with a growing collection of indigenous West Coast art. An alder wood-fired grill dominates the kitchen, lending a delicious flavor to many of the dishes. Start with the Salmon House Sampler, featuring smoked and candied salmon accompanied by fresh salsas, chutneys, and relishes. Entrees include a seared ahi tuna with a tomato, soy, and cumin barbecue sauce, and alder-grilled B.C. salmon with leeks and rémoulade sauce. Desserts bear little resemblance to early First Nations cuisine: Belgian chocolate mousse and orange crème caramel. The wine list earned an award of excellence from *Wine Spectator*.

2229 Folkstone Way, West Vancouver. (*C*) 604/926-3212. www.salmonhouse.com. Reservations recommended for dinner. Main courses C$13–C$31 (US$10–US$25). AE, DC, MC, V. Mon–Sat 11:30am–2:30pm; Sun brunch 11am–2:30pm; daily 5–10pm. Bus: 251 to Queens St.

INEXPENSIVE

The Tomahawk Restaurant *(finds)* FAMILY STYLE/AMERICAN   Just a typical American-style diner, but with one critical difference that makes it worth a visit: The Tomahawk is packed with Native knickknacks and gewgaws and some truly first-class First Nations art. It all started back in the 1930s when proprietor Chick Chamberlain began accepting carvings from Burrard Band Natives in lieu of payment. Over the years, the collection just kept growing. So how's the food? Good, in a burgers-and-fries kind of way. Portions are large, burgers are tasty, and milkshakes come so thick the spoon stands up straight like a totem pole.

1550 Philip Ave., North Vancouver. (*C*) 604/988-2612. Reservations not accepted. Main courses C$4.50–C$17 (US$3.60–US$14). AE, DC, MC, V. Sun–Thurs 8am–9pm; Fri–Sat 8am–10pm. Bus: 239 to Philip Ave.

9 Coffee, Sweets & Ice Cream

Caffè Artigiano *(★★ (finds)*   Absolutely the best lattes in town, in my opinion. The trick is to start with the perfect beans, brew the coffee to an exact temperature, give the steamed milk the respect it deserves, and pour it out ever so slowly forming a leaf- or heart-shaped pattern in your cup. This is latte-making elevated to an art form. Pop in for a light lunch or pastry, too: The grilled sandwiches and pasta specials are great. The original location on West Pender and Thurlow in the financial district is less intimate than the newer digs on Hornby, right across from the Vancouver Art Gallery; the Hornby location has a little outdoor patio that is perfect for people-watching.

763 Hornby St. (*C*) 604/685-5333. www.caffeartigiano.com. Sweets and sandwiches under C$8 (US$6.50). Sun–Thurs 6:30am–5pm; Fri–Sat 6:30am–6pm (West Pender location not open Sun). Bus: 22.

Death by Chocolate   If your idea of heaven includes rich desserts, then Death by Chocolate is the place to be dispatched. The large menu comes with photographs, but beware: Objects on the page may appear smaller than they are; sharing is encouraged. Some of the tested favorites include: Simply Irresistible, chocolate pudding with fudge center, covered in chocolate sauce; and Devil in Disguise, mocha fudge ice cream in Kahlúa chocolate sauce. Guilt-prone types can salve their consciences with more wholesome, fruitier desserts. Hell-bent ultra-chocoholics, on the other hand, should order up a Multitude of Sins: chocolate cake, chocolate mousse, chocolate crepes stuffed with fruit, chocolate sauce, and, well, you get the idea.

Various locations, including 1001 Denman St., (*C*) 604/899-CHOC, and 1598 W. Broadway, (*C*) 604/730-CHOC. www.deathbychocolate.ca. Items C$4.95–C$11 (US$4–US$9). AE, MC, V. Denman Street location open daily 8am–midnight; hours vary at each location.

Epicurean Delicatessen Caffè *(finds)*   A real Italian *caffè* in Kitsilano, the Epicurean brews a mean espresso. Locals and visitors flock to this tiny neighborhood deli, packing the sidewalk spots on nice days or the cozy small tables inside when the weather turns gray. Italian sweets, biscotti, and sorbet go well with any of the coffees, but for a savory treat, have a peek at the glass display case in the back. Freshly made antipasti,

Caffeine Nation

"I've never seen so much coffee in all my life. The whole town is on a caffeine jag," said Bette Midler, when she performed in Vancouver.

Though the population had been softened up to the idea by a generation of Italian immigrants, the recent fine-coffee explosion started first in Vancouver's sister city to the south. There are now more than 60 of the Seattle-based **Starbucks** shops in the city, as well as Blenz, Roastmasters, and other chain cafes. The Starbucks franchises facing each other on Robson and Thurlow are famed for the movie stars who drop in and the regular crowd of bikers who sit sipping lattes on their hogs. The city's best java joint—fittingly enough—is **Vancouver's Best Coffee**, 2959 W. Fourth Ave. (✆ **604/739-2136**), on a slightly funky section of West Fourth Avenue at Bayswater.

Nearly as good and far more politically correct is **Joe's Cafe**, 1150 Commercial Dr. (✆ **604/255-1046**), in the heart of the immigrant- and activist-laden Commercial Drive area, where lesbian activists, Marxist intellectuals, Guatemalan immigrants, and little old Portuguese men all sit and sip their cappuccinos together peacefully.

For the best lattes, see the review for Caffè Artigiano.

cold cuts, salads, panini sandwiches, and risotto are just some of the delectables available for lunch or takeout. Eat-in guests can sip a glass of wine with the fab food. The menu changes regularly, as the owners try out new recipes.

1898 West First Ave. ✆ **604/731-5370**. Fax 604/731-5369. Everything under C$10 (US$8). Daily 8am–9pm. Bus: 22 to Cornwall and Cypress.

La Casa Gelato ✫ *Finds*   No self-respecting ice-cream fiend could possibly pass up a visit to La Casa Gelato. Trust me; it's worth the trek out to this obscure industrial area near Commercial Drive, where ice-cream lovers gather for a taste of one or more of the 198 flavors in store. Of course you don't get that many flavors by simply serving up chocolate, vanilla, and strawberry. How about garlic, lavender, durian-fruit, basil, or hot chile ice cream? Or the pear with Gorgonzola sorbet. You're entitled to at least several samples before committing to one or two flavors, so go ahead and be adventurous.

1033 Venables St. ✆ **604/251-3211**. Everything under C$6.50 (US$5.25). Daily 10am–11pm. Bus: 10 to Commercial and Venables.

Senses Bakery ✫ *Finds*   This is a new, upscale patisserie with exquisite chocolates handmade by Thomas Haas. It's located downtown, opposite the Vancouver Art Gallery, at Georgia and Howe. Some extremely tempting high-end desserts are offered, including a famous chocolate sparkle cookie with the texture of a cookie but the taste of a truffle.

801 W. Georgia St. (at Howe). ✆ **604/633-0138**. Chocolates and desserts C$1.50–C$8 (US$1.20–US$6.50). Mon–Sat 10am–6pm. Bus: Any bus on Georgia St.

Exploring Vancouver

A city perched on the edge of a great wilderness, Vancouver offers unmatched opportunities for exploring the outdoors. Paradoxically, within the city limits, Vancouver is intensely urban. There are sidewalk cafes to match those in Paris and shopping streets that rival London's. The forest of high-rises ringing the central part of the city reminds some visitors of New York, while the buzz and movement of Chinatown is reminiscent of San Francisco. Comparisons with other places soon begin to pall, however, as you come to realize that Vancouver is entirely its own creation: a young, self-confident, sparklingly beautiful city, like no place else on earth.

1 Neighborhoods to Explore

The best way to get to know a city is to explore its different neighborhoods. Here's a quick guide on where to go and what to look for in Vancouver. For more in-depth explorations, turn to the neighborhood walking tours in chapter 8.

DOWNTOWN

Most of Vancouver's commercial and office space is found in a squarish patch starting at Nelson Street and heading north to the harbor, with Homer Street and Burrard Street forming the east and west boundaries respectively. Many of the city's best hotels are also found in this area, clustering near Robson Square and the water's edge. **Canada Place,** on the waterfront facing Burrard Inlet, is the city's huge convention center and cruise-ship terminal. The most interesting avenues for visitors are Georgia, Robson, and Granville streets. **Georgia Street**—in addition to being the prime address for class-A commercial property—is where you'll find the Vancouver Art Gallery (p. 119), the Coliseum-shaped Vancouver Public Library (p. 155), and the Pacific Centre regional shopping mall. **Robson Street** is Trend Central, crammed with designer boutiques, restaurants, and cafes. Vancouver's recently revived great white way, **Granville Street,** is the home of bars and clubs and theaters and pubs and restaurants (along with one or two remaining porn shops to add that touch of seedy authenticity).

THE WEST END

This was Vancouver's first upscale neighborhood, settled in the 1890s by the city's budding class of merchant princes. By the 1930s, most of the grand Edwardian homes had become rooming houses, and in the late 1950s some of the Edwardians came down and high-rise apartments went up. The resulting neighborhood owes more to the verticality of Manhattan than to the sprawling cities of the west, though the lush landscaping and gardens and gorgeous beaches along English Bay and Stanley Park are pure Northwest. All the necessities of life are contained within the West End's border, especially on **Denman** and **Robson streets:** great cafes, good nightclubs, many and

Downtown Vancouver Attractions

Canada Place & IMAX
  Theatre **8**
Dr. Sun Yat-sen Classical
  Chinese Garden **15**
Fairmont Hotel Vancouver **7**
H.R. MacMillan Space Centre **3**
Lookout! Harbour Centre
  Tower **9**
Museum of Anthropology **4**
Provincial Law Courts **5**
Science World British
  Columbia **16**
Steam Clock **11**
Storyeum **12**
Sun Tower **13**
UBC Botanical Garden &
  Nitobe Japanese Garden **4**
Vancouver Aquarium **1**
Vancouver Art Gallery **6**
Vancouver Centennial
  Police Museum **15**
Vancouver Maritime Museum **2**
Vancouver Museum **3**
Vancouver Public Library **14**
Waterfront Station/SeaBus
  & SkyTrain **10**

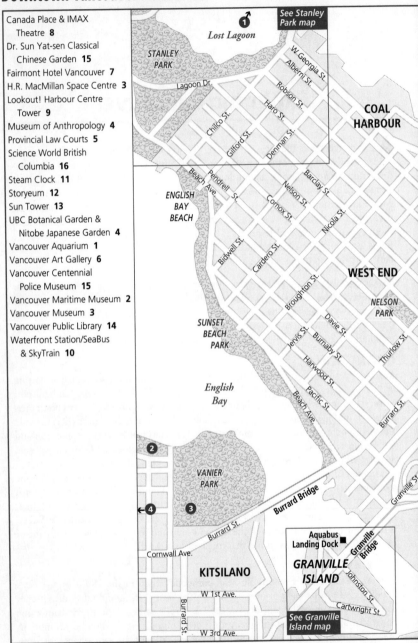

Coal Harbour

0 ——— 1/4 mi
0 ——— 0.25 km
N

Inset map:
WEST VANCOUVER
Grouse Mountain
English Bay
Area of Detail
COQUITLAM
VANCOUVER
Strait of Georgia
RICHMOND
SURREY

W. Hastings St.
W. Pender St.
Melville St.
Bute St.
Thurlow St.

(i)

8 Canada Place

■ Sea Bus

DOWNTOWN

Burrard Inlet

W. Hastings St.
W. Cordova St.
10
9
11 **GASTOWN**
Water St.
12

Dunsmuir St.
Seymour St.

7
6

ROBSON SQUARE
Robson St.
Burrard St.
Hornby St.
Cambie St.
Granville St.

VICTORY SQ.
13

Post Office ⊠

Abbott St.
Carrall St.

CHINATOWN

5
Howe St.
Helmcken St.

YALETOWN

Library Square
14
Robson St.
W. Georgia St.

GM Place

15 →

Richards St.
Davie St.

Homer St.
Hamilton St.
Cambie St.
Beatty St.

BC Place Stadium

To Train & Bus Station ↘

Drake St.
Hamilton St.
Mainland St.
Pacific Blvd.

Marina Side Cresc.

The Round House

DAVID LAM PARK

■ Aquabus Landing Dock

Cambie St. Bridge

16

Quebec St.

False Creek

Cambie St.

W 1st Ave.

MOUNT PLEASANT

W 3rd Ave.

Information *(i)*
Post Office ⊠

varied bookshops, and some of the best restaurants in the city. That's part of what makes it such a sought-after address, but it's also the little things, like the street trees, the mix of high-rise condos and old Edwardians, and the way that, in the midst of such an urban setting, you now and again stumble on a view of the ocean or the mountains.

GASTOWN

The oldest section of Vancouver, Gastown's charm shines through the souvenir shops and panhandlers. For one thing, it's the only section of the city that has the feel of an old Victorian town—the buildings stand shoulder to shoulder and cobblestones line the streets. The current Gastown was built from scratch just a few months after an 1886 fire wiped out the entire city. (There are photographs of proper-looking men in black coats selling real estate out of tents erected on the still-smoking ashes.) Also, rents in Gastown have stayed low, so it's still the place to look for a new and experimental art gallery, or a young fashion designer setting up shop, or a piece of beautiful, hand-carved First Nations art in one of the galleries along **Water** and **Hastings streets.** It's also the setting for the famous Steam Clock on Water Street (see "Gastown & Chinatown" walking tour in chapter 8).

Alcohol has always been a big part of Gastown's history. The neighborhood is named for a saloonkeeper—Gassy Jack Deighton—who, according to local legend, talked the local mill hands into building a saloon as Vancouver's first structure in return for all the whisky they could drink. Nowadays, Gastown is still liberally endowed with pubs and clubs—it's one of two or three areas where Vancouverites congregate when the sun goes down.

CHINATOWN

Even though much of Vancouver's huge Asian population has moved out to Richmond, Chinatown remains a lively kick because it still hasn't become overtly touristy. The low-rise buildings in this lively community are painted in bright colors and sidewalk markets abound. For the tens of thousands of Cantonese-speaking Canadians who live in the surrounding neighborhoods, Chinatown is simply the place they go to shop. And for many others who have moved to more outlying neighborhoods, it's still one of the best places to come and eat. One of North America's more populous Chinatowns, the area was settled about the same time as the rest of Vancouver, by migrant laborers brought in to build the Canadian Pacific Railway. Many white settlers resented the Chinese labor, and race riots periodically broke out. At one point Vancouver's Chinatown was surrounded with Belfast-like security walls. By the 1940s and 1950s, however, the area was mostly threatened with neglect. In the 1970s, there was a serious plan to tear the whole neighborhood down and put in a freeway. A huge protest stopped that, and now the area's future seems secure. For visitors, the fun is to simply wander, look, and taste.

YALETOWN & FALSE CREEK NORTH

Vancouver's former meat-packing and warehouse district, Yaletown has long since been converted to an area of apartment lofts, nightclubs, restaurants, high-end furniture shops, and a fledgling multimedia biz. It's a relatively tiny area and the main streets of interest are **Mainland, Hamilton,** and **Davie.** For visitors, it features some interesting cafes and patios, some high-end shops, and a kind of gritty urban feel that you won't find elsewhere in Vancouver. This old-time authenticity provides an essential anchor to the brand spanking new bevy of towers that has arisen in the past 10 years on **Pacific Boulevard** along the north edge of False Creek. Officially (and unimaginatively) called False Creek North, the area is more often referred to as "the Concorde lands" after the developer, or "the Expo lands" after the world's fair held in 1986 on the land where the towers now stand. Where the shiny newness of Concorde can prove a little disconcerting, gritty Yaletown provides the antidote. And vice versa. The two neighborhoods are slowly melding into one wonderful whole.

GRANVILLE ISLAND

Part crafts fair, part farmers market, part artist's workshop, part mall, and part industrial site, Granville Island seems to have it all. Some 20 years ago, the federal government decided to try its hand at a bit of urban renewal, so they took this piece of industrial waterfront and redeveloped it into . . . well, it's hard to describe. But everything you could name is here: theaters, pubs, restaurants, artists' studios, bookstores, crafts shops, an art school, a hotel, a cement plant, and lots and lots of people. One of the most enjoyable ways to experience the Granville Island atmosphere is to head down to the **Granville Island Public Market,** grab a latte (and perhaps a piece of cake or pie to boot), then wander outside to enjoy the view of the boats, the buskers, and the children endlessly chasing flocks of squawking seagulls.

KITSILANO

Hard to believe, but in the 1960s Kitsilano was a neighborhood that had fallen on hard times. Nobody respectable wanted to live there—the 1920s homes had all been converted to cheap rooming houses—so hippies moved in. The neighborhood became Canada's Haight-Ashbury, with coffeehouses, head shops, and lots of incense and long hair. Once the boom generation stopped raging against the machine, they realized that Kitsilano—right next to the beach, but not quite downtown—was a very groovy place to live and a fine place to own property. Real estate began an upward trend that has never stopped, and "Kits" became thoroughly yuppified. Nowadays, it's a fun place to wander. There are great bookstores and trendy furniture and housewares shops, lots of consignment clothing stores, snowboard shops, coffee everywhere, and lots of places to eat (every third storefront is a restaurant). The best parts of Kitsilano are the stretch of **W. 4th Avenue** between Burrard and Balsam streets, and **W. Broadway** between Macdonald and Alma streets. Oh, and **Kits Beach,** of course, with that fabulous heated saltwater swimming pool.

COMMERCIAL DRIVE

Known as "The Drive" to Vancouverites, it's the 12-block section from Venables Street to E. 6th Avenue. The Drive has a counterculture feel to it. There are posters for ¡*Cuba Libre!* rallies and bits of graffiti reading "Smash Capitalism!" But The Drive also has an immigrant feel to it. The first wave of Italians left cafes such as **Calabria,** 1745 Commercial Dr. (© **604/253-7017**) and **Caffe Amici,** 1344 Commercial Dr. (© **604/255-2611**). More recent waves of Portuguese, Hondurans, and Guatemalans have also left their mark. And lately, lesbians and vegans and artists have moved in—the kind of trendy moneyed folks who love to live in this kind of milieu. Shops and restaurants reflect the mix. Think Italian cafe next to the Marxist bookstore across from the vegan deli selling yeast-free Tuscan bread.

SHAUGHNESSY

Shaughnessy's a terrible place to wander around, but it's a great place to drive. (Distances within the neighborhood are a little too great for a comfortable stroll.)

Designed in the 1920s as an enclave for Vancouver's budding elite, this is Vancouver's Westmount or Nob Hill. Thanks to the stranglehold Shaughnessy exerts on local politics—every second mayor hails from this neighborhood—traffic flow is carefully diverted away from the area, and it takes a little bit of driving around to find your way in. It's an effort worth making, however, if only to see the stately homes and monstrous mansions, many of which are now featured in film shoots. To find the neighborhood, look on the map for the area of curvy and convoluted streets between Cypress and Oak streets and 12th and 32nd avenues. The center of opulence is the Crescent, an elliptical street to the southwest of Granville and 16th Avenue.

RICHMOND

Twenty years ago, Richmond was mostly farmland, with a bit of sleepy suburb. Now it's Asia West, an agglomeration of shopping malls geared to the new—read: rich, educated, and successful—Chinese immigrant. The residential areas of the city are not worth visiting (unless tract homes are your thing), but malls like the **Aberdeen Mall** or the **Yao Han Centre** are something else. It's like getting into your car in Vancouver and getting out in Singapore.

STEVESTON

Steveston, located at the southwest corner of Richmond by the mouth of the Fraser River, once existed for nothing but salmon. Fishermen set out from its port to catch the migrating sockeye, and returned to have the catch cleaned and canned. Huge processing plants covered its waterfront, where thousands of workers gutted millions of fish. Much of that history is reprised in the **Gulf of Georgia Cannery National Historic Site,** near the wharf at Bayview Street and Fourth Avenue (© **604/664-9009**). Since the fishery was automated long ago, Steveston's waterfront has been fixed up. There are public fish sales, charter trips up the river or out to the Fraser delta, and, above all, a laid-back, small-town atmosphere.

PUNJABI MARKET

India imported. Most of the businesses on this 4-block stretch of Main Street, from 48th up to 52nd avenue, are run by and cater to Indo-Canadians, primarily Punjabis. The area is best seen during business hours, when the fragrant scent of spices wafts out from food stalls, while the sound of Hindi pop songs blares from hidden speakers. Young brides hunt through sari shops or seek out suitable material in discount textile outlets. **Memsaab Boutique,** 6647 Main St. (© **604/322-0250**), and **Frontier Cloth House,** 6695 Main St. (© **604/325-4424**), specialize in richly colored silk saris, shawls, fabrics, and costume jewelry. A good place to eat is **Nirvana,** 2313 Main St. (© **604/872-8779**), which offers a medley of Indian favorites.

2 The Top Attractions

DOWNTOWN & THE WEST END

Stanley Park 🅛🅛🅛 *Kids*   The jewel of Vancouver, Stanley Park is a 400-hectare (988-acre) rainforest jutting out into the ocean from the edge of the busy West End. The second-largest urban forest in North America, it's named after the same Lord Stanley who gave his name to professional hockey's top trophy, though truth be told, His Lordship had little to do with the creation of the park. That was due to a cabal of West End landowners who worried that if the vast, beautiful peninsula ever came on the real estate market it would wreck the value of their own holdings. So they convinced the

Stanley Park

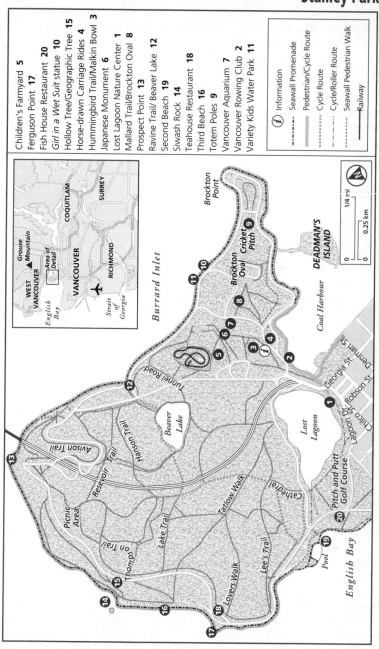

Children's Farmyard **5**
Ferguson Point **17**
Fish House Restaurant **20**
Girl in a Wet Suit statue **10**
Hollow Tree/Geographic Tree **15**
Horse-drawn Carriage Rides **4**
Hummingbird Trail/Malkin Bowl **3**
Japanese Monument **6**
Lost Lagoon Nature Center **1**
Mallard Trail/Brockton Oval **8**
Prospect Point **13**
Ravine Trail/ Beaver Lake **12**
Second Beach **19**
Siwash Rock **14**
Teahouse Restaurant **18**
Third Beach **16**
Totem Poles **9**
Vancouver Aquarium **7**
Vancouver Rowing Club **2**
Variety Kids Water Park **11**

(i) Information
·-·-·-· Seawall Promenade
Pedestrian/Cycle Route
Cycle Route
·········· Cycle/Roller Route
Seawall Pedestrian Walk
++++++ Railway

federal government—which held the land as a military reserve—to gift it to the young city as a park. It turned out to be a wise investment, since exploring the park is one of Vancouver's quintessential experiences.

The park is filled with towering western red cedar and Douglas fir, manicured lawns, flower gardens, placid lagoons, and countless shaded walking trails that meander through it all. The famed **seawall** &&& runs along the waterside edge of the park, allowing cyclists and pedestrians to experience the magical interface of forest, sea, and sky. One of the most popular free attractions in the park is the **collection of totem poles** &&& at Brockton Point, most of them carved in the 1980s to replace the original ones that were placed in the park in the 1920s and 1930s. The area around the totem poles features open-air displays on the Coast Salish First Nations and a small gift shop/visitor information center.

The park is home to lots of wildlife, including beavers, coyotes, bald eagles, raccoons, trumpeter swans, brant geese, ducks, and skunks. For directions and maps, brochures, and exhibits on the nature and ecology of Stanley Park, visit the **Lost Lagoon Nature House** (© **604/257-8544;** open 10am–7pm July 1–Labour Day; weekends only outside this period; free admission). On Sundays they offer Discovery Walks of the park. Equally nature-focused but with way more wow is the **Vancouver Aquarium** && (see below). There's also the **Stanley Park's Children's Farm** (© **604/ 257-8530**), a petting zoo with peacocks, rabbits, calves, donkeys, and Shetland ponies. Next to the petting zoo is **Stanley Park's Miniature Railway** & (© **604/257-8531**), a diminutive steam locomotive that pulls passenger cars on a circuit through the woods.

The park's trio of restaurants includes the excellent **Teahouse** (p. 98) and **Fish House** (p. 97); the third isn't worth patronizing. For swimmers, there's **Third Beach** and **Second Beach** (p. 135), the latter with an outdoor pool beside English Bay. For kids there's a free **Spray Park** near Lumberman's Arch. Perhaps the best way to explore the park is to rent a bike (p. 135) or in-line skates and set off along the seawall. If you decide to walk, remember there's a free shuttle bus that circles the park every 15 minutes, allowing passengers to alight and descend at most of the park's many attractions. There's also a wonderful **horse-drawn carriage ride** (see "Specialty Tours," later in this chapter) that begins near Lost Lagoon.

Stanley Park. © **604/257-8400.** www.city.vancouver.bc.ca/parks. Cost (for whole day) is C$5 (US$3.75) summer, C$3 (US$2.25) winter. Park does not close. Park attractions open late June to Labour Day daily 9:30am–7pm; Labour Day to late June daily 10am–5:30pm. Bus: 23, 35, or 135; free "Around the Park" shuttle bus circles the park at 15-min. intervals from June 13–Sept 28 (visitors can get off and on at 14 points of interest). Parking inside the park often full; leave your car if possible.

Vancouver Aquarium Marine Science Centre && *Kids*   One of North America's largest and best, the Vancouver Aquarium houses more than 8,000 marine species, most in meticulously re-created environments.

In the icy-blue Arctic Canada exhibit, you can see beluga whales whistling and blowing water at unwary onlookers. Human-size freshwater fish inhabit the Amazon rainforest gallery, while overhead, an hourly rainstorm is unleashed in an atrium that houses three-toed sloths, brilliant blue and green poison tree frogs, and piranhas. Regal angelfish glide through a re-creation of Indonesia's Bunaken National Park coral reef, and blacktip reef sharks menacingly scour the Tropical Gallery's waters. (Call for the shark and sea otter feeding times.) The Pacific Canada exhibit is dedicated to sea life indigenous to B.C. waters, including the Pacific salmon and the giant Pacific octopus.

On the Marine Mammal Deck, there are sea otters, Steller sea lions, beluga whales, and a Pacific white-sided dolphin. During regularly scheduled shows, the aquarium staff explains marine mammal behavior while working with these impressive creatures.

For a substantial extra fee (C$150/US$112 per person, C$210/US$157 adult and 1 child age 8–12), you can have an up-close encounter with the belugas. Participants in the Beluga Encounter go behind the scenes to help feed these lovely white cetaceans, then head up to the Marine Mammal deck to take part in the belugas' regular training session. Beluga encounters are available daily from 9 to 10:30am with extra encounters on weekends between 2 and 4pm. On the more reasonably priced Trainer Tours (C$20/US$15 adults, C$15/US$11 children 8–12), you go on a 45-minute behind-the-scenes tour, helping an aquarium trainer prepare the daily rations for and then feeding the sea otters or harbor seals; feeding the sea lions costs C$35/US$26 adults, C$15/US$11 children. Trainer tours are available daily but times vary. Call ✆ **800/931-1186** to reserve all of these programs ahead of time. Children must be 8 or older to participate. *Note:* If you have smaller children, I recommend the sea otters; Steller sea lions are enormous and sometimes a little cranky.

Stanley Park. ✆ **604/659-FISH.** www.vanaqua.org. Admission C$17 (US$12) adults; C$13 (US$9) seniors, students, and youths 13–18; C$9.50 (US$6.75) children 4–12; free for children under 4. Late June to Sept 1 daily 9:30am–7pm; Sept 2 to late June daily 10am–5:30pm. Bus: 135; "Around the Park" shuttle bus June–Sept only. Parking C$5 (US$3.75) summer, C$3 (US$2.25) winter.

Vancouver Art Gallery 𝕲𝕲   Designed as a courthouse by B.C.'s leading early-20th-century architect Francis Rattenbury (the architect of Victoria's Empress hotel and the Parliament buildings), and renovated into an art gallery by B.C.'s leading late-20th-century architect Arthur Erickson, the VAG is an excellent stop to see what sets Canadian and West Coast art apart from the rest of the world. There is an impressive collection of paintings by B.C. native **Emily Carr,** as well as examples of a unique Canadian art style created during the 1920s by members of the "Group of Seven," which included Vancouver painter Fred Varley. The VAG also hosts rotating exhibits of contemporary sculpture, graphics, photography, and video art, from around the world. Geared to younger audiences, the Annex Gallery offers rotating presentations of visually exciting educational exhibits.

750 Hornby St. ✆ **604/662-4719** or 604/662-4700. www.vanartgallery.bc.ca. Admission C$13(US$9.50) adults, C$9 (US$6.75) seniors, C$8 (US$6) students, C$30 (US$23) family; free for children 12 and under. Thurs 5–9pm by donation. Mon–Wed and Fri–Sun 10am–5:30pm; Thurs 10am–9pm. Closed Mon in fall and winter. SkyTrain: Granville. Bus: 3.

GASTOWN & CHINATOWN

Dr. Sun Yat-sen Classical Chinese Garden 𝕲𝕲   This small reproduction of a Classical Chinese Scholar's garden truly is a remarkable place, but to get the full effect it's best to take the free guided tour. Untrained eyes will only see a pretty pond surrounded by bamboo and funny-shaped rocks. The engaging guides, however, can explain this unique urban garden's Taoist yin-yang design principle, in which harmony is achieved through dynamic opposition. To foster opposition (and thus harmony) in the garden, Chinese designers place contrasting elements in juxtaposition: Soft moving water flows across solid stone; smooth swaying bamboo grows around gnarled immovable rocks; dark pebbles are placed next to light pebbles in the floor. Moving with the guide, you discover the symbolism of intricate carvings and marvel at the subtle, ever-changing views from covered serpentine corridors. This is one of two Classical Chinese gardens in North America (the other is in Portland, Oregon) created by master artisans from Suzhou, the garden city of China.

578 Carrall St. ℂ **604/689-7133.** www.vancouverchinesegarden.com. C$8.25 (US$6.25) adults; C$6.75 (US$5) seniors; C$5.75 (US$4.30) children 6–18 and students; free children 5 and under; family pass C$18 (US$14). Free guided tour included. Daily May 1–June 14 10am–6pm; June 15–Aug 9:30am–7pm; Sept 10am–6pm; Oct–Apr 10am–4:30pm. Bus: 19 or 22.

Storyeum 𝕒𝕒𝕒 *Kids*   *Storyeum* means "a place of stories." And that's what you'll get in this appealing new attraction in historic Gastown: an earful and eyeful of stories, all relating to British Columbia. This 70-minute show is so well performed and so well written that you can't help but enjoy it. Visitors are taken down below street level in enormous circular elevators, then led through a series of underground theaters where professional actors portray dramatized events in B.C.'s history and development, from ancient First Nations cultures up through the coming of the railroad and World War II. Each vignette is enhanced by special effects and lighting, and clever songs. It's a kind of unique musical storytelling theater that manages to be clever, upbeat, and optimistic without ignoring the darker side of white European settlement.

165A Water St. ℂ **800/687-8142** or 604/687-8142. www.storyeum.com. C$22 (US$18) adults; C$19 (US$15) seniors and youth 13–18; C$16 (US$13) children 6–12; free children 5 and under. Daily summer 9am–7pm (shows every 30 min.); daily winter 10am–6pm (shows every 60 min.). Bus: 1 or 50.

Vancouver Centennial Police Museum   A macabre and morbidly delightful little place, the Police Museum is dedicated to memorializing some of the worst crimes and crime-stoppers in the city's short but colorful history. Housed in the old Vancouver Coroner's Court—where actor Errol Flynn was autopsied after dropping dead in the arms of a 17-year-old girl—the museum features photos, text, and vintage equipment from files and evidence rooms of Vancouver's finest. The confiscated illegal-weapons display looks like the props department for the film *Road Warrior*. There's also a morgue with pieces of damaged body parts in specimen bottles, a simulated autopsy room, a forensics lab, and a police radio room. The museum also houses an immense collection of matchbox-size toy police cars from around the world.

240 E. Cordova St. ℂ **604/665-3346.** www.city.vancouver.bc.ca/police/museum. Admission C$6 (US$4.50) adults; C$4 (US$3) seniors, students, youths 7–13; free for children 6 and under. Year-round Mon–Fri 9am–3pm; May–Aug also Sat 10am–3pm. Bus: 4 or 7.

THE WEST SIDE

Granville Island 𝕒𝕒𝕒 *Kids*   Almost a city within a city, Granville Island has so much to offer that a day may not be enough to experience it all. Browse for crafts, pick up some fresh seafood, enjoy a great dinner, watch some Shakespeare in the park or

---

360 Degrees of Vancouver

The most popular (and most touristed) spot from which to view Vancouver's skyline is high atop the space needle observation deck at the **Lookout!, Harbour Centre Tower** ⍟, 555 W. Hastings St. (ℂ **604/689-0421**). It's a great place for first-time visitors who want a panorama of the city. The glass-encased Skylift whisks you up 166m (545 ft.) to the rooftop deck in less than a minute. The 360-degree view is remarkable. (Yes, that is Mt. Baker looming above the southeastern horizon.) Skylift admission is C$10 (US$7.50) for adults, C$9 (US$6.75) for seniors, C$7 (US$5.25) for students and youth 11 to 17, C$4 (US$3) children 4 to 10, free for children under 4. It's open daily in summer from 8:30am to 10:30pm and in winter from 9am to 9pm.

My, what an inefficient way to fish.

Ring toss, good. Horseshoes, bad.

Faster! Faster! Faster!

We take care of the fiddly bits, from providing over 43,000 customer reviews of hotels, to helping you find our best fares, to giving you 24/7 customer service. So you can focus on the only thing that matters. Goofing off.

* travelocity
You'll never roam alone.

Granville Island

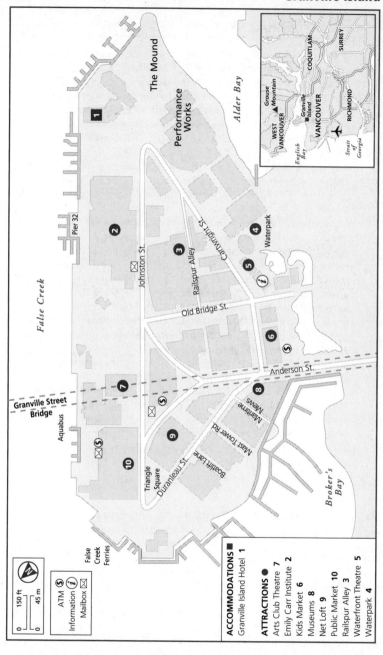

The Mound

Performance Works

Alder Bay

Grouse Mountain
COQUITLAM
WEST VANCOUVER
SURREY
Granville Island
VANCOUVER
RICHMOND
English Bay
Strait of Georgia

Pier 32

False Creek

Johnston St.

Railspur Alley

Cartwright St.

Waterpark

Old Bridge St.

Anderson St.

Granville Street Bridge

Aquabus

Maritime Mews

Mast Tower Rd.

Boathit Lane

Duranleau St.

Triangle Square

Broker's Bay

False Creek Ferries

150 ft
45 m
0

ATM $
Information i
Mailbox ✉

ACCOMMODATIONS ■
Granville Island Hotel **1**

ATTRACTIONS ●
Arts Club Theatre **7**
Emily Carr Institute **2**
Kids Market **6**
Museums **8**
Net Loft **9**
Public Market **10**
Railspur Alley **3**
Waterfront Theatre **5**
Waterpark **4**

Granville's Greatest Hits

Even though the bustling **Public Market** ✦✦✦ makes a fine destination in itself, Granville Island offers much more. To really get a feel for this neighborhood, stroll along the side streets and explore the alleys and lanes away from the main entrance. Check out the recommended attractions below.

- RailSpur Alley's 12 artist studios are perfect for browsing; stop in at the **Al'Arte Silk** to see some of the beautifully hand-painted wearable silk art (RailSpur Alley 1369) or pause at the excellent **Kharma Café** for a latte and pastry (RailSpur Alley 1363; ✆ 604/647-1363).
- Art exhibits at the **Emily Carr Institute** (1399 Johnston St.; ✆ 604/844-3800) showcase the works of the institute's grads and students. You may be looking at the next Andy Warhol. Open daily 9am to 6pm; admission is free.
- In summer, check the **Performance Works** (✆ 604/687-3020) schedule for free outdoor Shakespearean plays or see what's at the **Arts Club Theatre** (✆ 604/687-1644) or **Waterfront Theatre** (✆ 604/685-1731).
- Paddle off into the sunset by renting a kayak from one of the marinas on the west side of the island. Beginners can take lessons or head out on a guided tour. **Ecomarine Ocean Kayak Centre** (✆ 604/689-7575) has everything to get you started. A 3-hour kayak lesson for C$65 (US$49) teaches you the basic strokes. Or, explore the waters around Stanley Park with a guide (C$89/US$67). Experienced paddlers may rent equipment (starting at C$32/US$24 per day for a single kayak).
- Granville Island is one big playground. On a rainy day, duck into the Kids Only Market (daily 10am–6pm) to check out toys, kites, clothes, art supplies, and an indoor play area, or visit the **Granville Island Museum** (✆ 604/683-1939) to admire its collection of model boats and trains. The museum is open daily from 10am to 5:30pm; admission is C$3.50–C$6.50 (US$2.65–US$4.90), free for children 4 and under. On warm days, the free Waterpark is the place to be. Open daily (weather permitting) from 10am to 6pm, late May until Labour Day.

attend the latest theater performance, rent a yacht, stroll along the waterfront, or simply run through the sprinkler on a hot summer day; it's all there and more. If you only have a short period of time, make sure you spend at least part of it in the **Granville Island Public Market,** one of the best all-around markets in the world.

Once a declining industrial site, Granville Island's transformation started in the late 1970s when the government encouraged new, people-friendly developments. Maintaining its original industrial look, the former warehouses and factories now house galleries, artist studios, restaurants, and theaters; the cement plant on the waterfront is the only industrial tenant left. Access to Granville Island is by Aquabus from the West End, Yaletown, or Kitsilano (see "By Miniferry," in chapter 4; the Aquabus drops you at the public market) or across the bridge at Anderson Street (access from W. 2nd Ave.). Avoid driving over on weekends and holidays—you will spend more time in your car, trying to find a parking place, than in the galleries. Check the website (www.granville-island.net) for upcoming events or stop by the information center, behind the Kids Market. *Note:* Also, see Walking Tour 3 in chapter 8 (p. 154).

Located on the south shore of False Creek, under the Granville Street Bridge. For studio and gallery hours and other information about Granville Island, contact the information center at (C) 604/666-5784. www.granville-island.net. The market is open daily 9am–6pm. For information on getting to Granville Island, see "By Miniferry," in chapter 4.

H.R. MacMillan Space Centre (Kids)

In the same building as the Vancouver Museum, the space center and observatory has hands-on displays and exhibits that will delight budding astronomy buffs and their parents (or older space buffs and their children). Displays are highly interactive: In the Cosmic Courtyard you can try designing a spacecraft or maneuvering a lunar robot. Or, punch a button and get a video explanation of the Apollo 17 manned-satellite engine that stands before you. The exciting Virtual Voyages Simulator takes you on a voyage to Mars—or a collision course with an oncoming comet. In the GroundStation Canada Theatre, video presentations explore Canada's contributions to the space program and space in general. The StarTheatre shows movies—many of them for children—on an overhead dome. And on selected nights, you can shoot the moon through a half-meter telescope for C$10 (US$7.50) per camera ((C) **604/736-2655**).

1100 Chestnut St., in Vanier Park. (C) **604/738-STAR**. www.hrmacmillanspacecentre.com. Admission C$14 (US$10) adults; C$11 (US$8) seniors, students, youths 11–18; C$9.50 (US$7) children 5–10; C$6 (US$4.50) children under 5; C$40 (US$30) families (up to 5, maximum 2 adults). Additional Virtual Voyages experiences C$6 (US$4.50) each. Tues–Sun 10am–5pm. Closed Dec 25. Bus: 22.

Museum of Anthropology ✦✦✦

This isn't just any old museum. In 1976, architect Arthur Erickson re-created a classic Native post-and-beam structure out of poured concrete and glass to house one of the world's finest collections of West Coast Native art.

Enter through doors that resemble a huge, carved, bent-cedar box. Artifacts from different coastal communities flank the ramp leading to the Great Hall's **collection of totem poles.** Haida artist Bill Reid's touchable cedar bear and sea wolf sculptures sit at the Cross Roads; Reid's masterpiece, *The Raven and the First Men,* is worth the price of admission all by itself. The huge carving in glowing yellow cedar depicts a Haida creation myth, in which Raven—the trickster—coaxes humanity out into the world from its birthplace in a clamshell. Some of Reid's fabulous jewelry creations in gold and silver are also on display. Intriguingly, curators have recently begun salting contemporary Native artworks in among the old masterpieces—a sign that West Coast artistic traditions are alive and well.

The **Masterpiece Gallery**'s argillite sculptures, beaded jewelry, and hand-carved ceremonial masks lead the way to the Visible Storage Galleries, where more than 15,000 artifacts are arranged by culture. You can open the glass-topped drawers to

---

(Tips) More Time to Explore

If you can't bear to leave the island, consider staying at the Granville Island Hotel (p. 78). One of the best-kept secrets in town, this hotel is reasonably priced, has a fabulous waterfront location, and is located steps from all the island has to offer. Even if you don't stay, it's worth stopping by the hotel's brewpub restaurant, The Dockside Brewery Company, for a brew with a view.

view small treasures and stroll past larger pieces housed in tall glass cases. (For more detailed information, read the conveniently placed reference catalogs.)

Also at the museum is the somewhat incongruous Koerner Ceramics Gallery, a collection of European ceramics that—while interesting—is really only there because old man Koerner had the money to endow the wing to hold his collection.

Don't forget to take a walk around the grounds behind the museum. Overlooking Point Grey are two **longhouses** built according to the Haida tribal style, resting on the traditional north–south axis. Ten hand-carved totem poles stand in attendance along with contemporary carvings on the longhouse facades. *Note:* You might want to combine your visit to the Museum of Anthropology with the nearby UBC Botanical Garden and Nitobe Japanese Garden (see below).

6393 NW Marine Dr. (at Gate 4). © 604/822-5087. www.moa.ubc.ca. Admission C$9 (US$6.75) adults; C$7 (US$5.25) seniors, students, children 6–18; free for children under 6; free Tues 5–9pm. May 21–Aug Wed–Mon 10am–5pm, Tues 10am–9pm; Sept–May 20 Wed–Sun 11am–5pm, Tues 11am–9pm. Closed Dec 25–26. Bus: 4, 10, or 99 (10-min. walk from UBC bus loop).

Science World British Columbia 🕏 (Kids)   Science World is impossible to miss. It's in the big blinking geodesic dome on the eastern end of False Creek. Inside, it's a hands-on scientific discovery center where you and your kids can light up a plasma ball, walk through a 160-sq.-m (1,722-sq.-ft.) maze, wander through the interior of a camera, create a cyclone, watch a zucchini explode as it's charged with 80,000 volts, stand inside a beaver lodge, play in wrist-deep magnetic liquids, create music with a giant synthesizer, and watch mind-blowing three-dimensional slide and laser shows as well as other optical effects. In the OMNIMAX Theatre—a huge projecting screen equipped with Surround-Sound—you can take a stunning trip through a coral reef. Science World also hosts many spectacular traveling exhibitions.

1455 Quebec St. © 604/443-7443. www.scienceworld.bc.ca. Admission C$13 (US$9.55) adults; C$8.50 (US$6.40) seniors, students, children 4–17; free for children under 4; C$43 (US$32) family pass, including 2 adults and 4 children. Combination tickets available for OMNIMAX film. Mon–Fri 10am–5pm; Sat–Sun and holidays 10am–6pm. Sky-Train: Main Street–Science World.

UBC Botanical Garden & Nitobe Japanese Garden 🕏🕏   Serious plant lovers will love the University of British Columbia. The prime attraction on campus, besides the fabulous Museum of Anthropology (see above), is the 28-hectare (69-acre) **UBC Botanical Garden,** home to over 10,000 species of trees, shrubs, and flowers grouped into a B.C. Native garden, a physic (or medicinal) garden, a food garden, and several others. There's also an excellent plant and seed store. Give yourself at least an hour if you want to explore this garden. Nearby is the **Nitobe Memorial Garden,** an exquisitely beautiful traditional Japanese garden considered among the top five Japanese gardens in North America and one of the most authentic Tea and Stroll Gardens outside of Japan. Give yourself about an hour here, too. Cherry blossoms peak in April and May, the iris bloom in June, and autumn brings colorful leaf displays.

Botanical Garden: 6804 S.W. Marine Dr., Gate 8. © 604/822-4208. www.ubcbotanicalgarden.org. Admission C$5 (US$3.75) adults; C$3 (US$2.25) seniors, students, and youth; children under 6 admitted free. Nitobe Japanese Garden: 6565 NW Marine Dr., Gate 4. © 604/822-6038. www.nitobe.org. Admission C$3 (US$2.25) adults; C$2 (US$1.50) seniors; C$1.50 (US$1.10) students. Dual pass for both gardens C$6 (US$4.50). Mar to mid-Oct, both gardens open daily 10am–6pm; otherwise daily 10am–5pm.

Vancouver Maritime Museum (Kids)   The 1920s RCMP Arctic patrol vessel *St. Roch* rests here. From the time Chris Columbus proved that the continent directly west of Europe was not Cathay, every European explorer's overriding quest was to find

the Northwest Passage, the seagoing shortcut to the riches of the east. This little ship is the one that finally did it. The boat, preserved in a large atrium, still has most of its original stores and equipment onboard. Tours of the *St. Roch* are particularly popular with children—they get to clamber around the boat poking and prodding stuff.

The other half of the museum holds intricate ship models, maps, prints, and a number of permanent exhibits. If the weather is pleasant, walk across the expansive front lawn at the edge of False Creek to Heritage Harbour, where the museum keeps a collection of beautiful vintage boats. You can also catch the miniferry to Granville Island or the West End there.

1905 Ogden Ave., in Vanier Park. ℂ **604/257-8300.** www.vmm.bc.ca. Admission C$8 (US$6) adults; C$5.50 (US$4.15) seniors and youths 6–19; C$18 (US$14) families; free for children under 6. Daily 10am–5pm. Closed Labour Day to Victoria Day (1st Mon in Sept to 4th Mon in May). Bus: 22, then walk 4 blocks north on Cypress St. Boat: False Creek Ferries dock at Heritage Harbour.

Vancouver Museum   Established in 1894, the Vancouver Museum is dedicated to amassing evidence of the city's history, from its days as a Native settlement and European outpost to the city's early-20th-century maturation into a modern urban center. The exhibits allow visitors to walk through the steerage deck of a 19th-century passenger ship, peek into a Hudson's Bay Company frontier trading post, or take a seat in an 1880s Canadian Pacific Railway passenger car. Re-creations of Victorian and Edwardian rooms show how early Vancouverites decorated their homes. Rotating exhibits include a display of the museum's collection of neon signage from Vancouver's former glory days as the West Coast's glitziest neon-sign-filled metropolis during the 1940s and 1950s.

1100 Chestnut St. ℂ **604/736-4431.** www.vanmuseum.bc.ca. Admission C$10 (US$7.50) adults; C$8 (US$6) seniors; C$6 (US$4.50) youths 4–19. Fri–Wed 10am–5pm; Thurs 10am–9pm. Bus: 22, then walk 3 blocks south on Cornwall Ave. Boat: Granville Island Ferry to Heritage Harbour.

NORTH VANCOUVER & WEST VANCOUVER

Capilano Suspension Bridge & Park ⟲   Vancouver's first and oldest tourist trap (built in 1889), this attraction still works—mostly because there's still something inherently thrilling about walking across a narrow, shaky walkway, 69m (226 ft.) above a canyon floor, held up by nothing but a pair of tiny cables. Set in a beautiful 8-hectare (20-acre) park about 15 minutes from downtown, the suspension bridge itself is a 135m-long (443-ft.) cedar-plank and steel-cable footbridge, which sways gently above the Capilano River. Visitors nervously cross above kayakers and salmon shooting the rapids far below. A new attraction called **"Treetops Adventure"** features more bridges and walkways, only these are attached to giant tree trunks 24m (79 ft.) above the rainforest floor.

In addition to the bridge, there's a **carving centre** where Native carvers demonstrate their skill; an exhibit describing the region's natural history; guides in period costume who recount Vancouver's frontier days; and a pair of overpriced and poorly serviced restaurants. Though it's quite well done, it's hard to justify the exorbitant entrance fee, and the summer crowds can be offputting. If the admission price is a roadblock, you can have a similar experience at the nearby Lynn Canyon suspension bridge, which is almost as high, set in a far larger forest, almost untouristed, and absolutely free. (See "The *Other* Suspension Bridge," below.)

3735 Capilano Rd., North Vancouver. ℂ **604/985-7474.** www.capbridge.com. Admission C$25 (US$20) adults; C$19 (US$15) seniors and students; C$13 (US$10) youths 13–16; C$6.25 (US$5) children 6–12; free for children under 6.

May–Sept daily 8:30am–dusk; Oct–Apr daily 9am–5pm. Closed Dec 25. Bus: 246 from downtown Vancouver, 236 from Lonsdale Quay SeaBus terminal. Car: Hwy. 99 north across Lions Gate Bridge to Exit #14 on Capilano Rd.

Grouse Mountain Resort ✿   Once a small local ski hill, Grouse has developed into a year-round mountain recreation park. Located only a 15-minute drive from downtown, the **SkyRide gondola** ✿ transports you to the mountain's 1,110m (3,642-ft.) summit in 8 minutes. (Hikers can take a near vertical trail called the Grouse Grind. The best of them can do it in 28 min.) The view from the top is one of the best around: the city and the entire lower mainland, from far up the Fraser Valley east across the Gulf of Georgia to Vancouver Island. You'll also find a restaurant, large-screen theater with wildlife features, an endangered wildlife refuge, ski and snowboard area, hiking and snowshoeing trails, skating pond, children's snow park, interpretive forest trails, a fun lumberjack show, helicopter tours, mountain bike trails, sleigh rides, and a Native feast house. Many of these activities are free with your SkyRide ticket, and they should be, since there's no other way to justify the exorbitant admission fee.

⟨Finds⟩ The *Other* Suspension Bridge

Lynn Canyon Park, in North Vancouver between Grouse Mountain and Mount Seymour Provincial Park on Lynn Valley Road, offers a free alternative to the Capilano Suspension Bridge. True, the **Lynn Canyon Suspension Bridge** ✿ is both shorter and a little lower than Capilano (p. 125), but the waterfall and swirling whirlpools in the canyon below add both beauty and a certain fear-inducing fascination. Plus, it's free.

The park in which the bridge is located is a gorgeous 247-hectare (610-acre) rainforest of cedar and Douglas fir, laced throughout with walking trails. It's also home to an **Ecology Centre** (3663 Park Rd.; ℂ **604/981-3103**), which presents natural history films, tours, and displays that explain the local ecology. Staff members lead frequent walking tours. The center is open Monday through Friday from 10am to 5pm and Saturday and Sunday from noon to 4pm. The park itself is open from 7am to 7pm in spring and fall, 7am to 9pm in summer, and 7am to dusk in winter; it's closed December 25 and 26 and January 1. There is a cafe in the park that serves sit-down and takeout meals. To get there, take the SeaBus to Lonsdale Quay, then transfer to bus no. 229; by car, take the Trans-Canada Highway (Hwy. 1) to the Lynn Valley Road exit (about a 20-min. drive from downtown) and follow Lynn Valley Road to Peters Road, where you turn right.

Six kilometers (3¾ miles) up Lynn Valley Road from the highway is the **Lynn Headwaters Regional Park** (ℂ **604/985-1690** for trail conditions), one of the best places close to the city to experience the breathtaking nature of the Northwest. Until the mid-1980s, this was inaccessible wilderness and bear habitat. The park and the bears are now managed by the Greater Vancouver Regional Parks Department. There are 12 marked trails of various levels of difficulty. Some meander by the riverbank, others climb steeply up to various North Shore peaks, and one leads to a series of cascading waterfalls.

6400 Nancy Greene Way, North Vancouver. ℂ 604/984-0661. www.grousemountain.com. SkyRide C$30 (US$24) adults; C$28 (US$22) seniors; C$17 (US$14) youths 13–18; C$11 (US$9) children 5–12; free children 4 and under. SkyRide free with advance Observatory Restaurant reservation. Daily 9am–10pm. Bus: 232, then transfer to bus no. 236. SeaBus: Lonsdale Quay, then transfer to bus no. 236. Car: Hwy. 99 north across Lions Gate Bridge, take North Vancouver exit to Marine Drive, then up Capilano Road for 5km (3 miles).

3 Vancouver's Plazas & Parks

OUTDOOR PLAZA

Unlike many cities, Vancouver's great urban gathering places stand not at the center but on the periphery, on two opposite sides of the **seawall** that runs around Stanley Park: **English Bay,** on the south side of Denman Street, and **Coal Harbour,** on the northern, Burrard Inlet side, are where Vancouverites go to stroll and be seen. On warm sunny days, these two areas are packed. Another waterside gathering spot is **Canada Place,** built for Expo '86. Built in the shape of a cruise ship, and serving as the city's cruise-ship terminal (as well as a giant convention center, with a giant hotel on top for good measure), it has wide walkways all around it that are super for strolling and offer fabulous views of the mountains.

Designed by architect Arthur Erickson to be Vancouver's central plaza, **Robson Square**—downtown, between Hornby and Howe streets from Robson to Smithe streets—has never really worked. The square, which anchors the north end of the Provincial Law Courts complex designed by Erickson in 1972, suffers from a basic design flaw: It's sunk one story below street level and is next to impossible to access. The Law Courts complex, which sits on a higher level, raised above the street, is beautifully executed with shrubbery, cherry trees, sculptures, and a triple-tiered waterfall, but Robson Square below is about as appealing as a drained swimming pool. Just opposite Robson square, however, the steps of the **Vancouver Art Gallery** are a great people-place, filled with loungers, political agitators, and old men playing chess. It just goes to show you that grandiose urban theory and urban design, especially back in the 1970s, didn't always take the human element into account.

Library Square—a few blocks east from Robson Square at the corner of Robson and Homer streets—is an example of a new urban space that really works. It's immensely popular with locals and has been since it opened in 1995. People sit on the steps, bask in the sunshine, read, harangue passersby with half-baked political ideas, and generally seem to enjoy themselves.

PARKS & GARDENS

Park and garden lovers are in heaven in Vancouver. The wet, mild climate is ideal for gardening, and come spring the city blazes with blossoming cherry trees, rhododendrons, camellias, azaleas, and spring bulbs. And roses in summer. Gardens are everywhere. For general information about Vancouver's parks, call ℂ **604/257-8400** or try www.parks.vancouver.bc.ca. For information on **Stanley Park** ✸✸✸, the queen of them all, see p. 116.

On the West Side you'll find the magnificent **UBC Botanical Garden,** one of the largest living botany collections on the West Coast, and the sublime **Nitobe Japanese Garden** ✸✸; for descriptions of both, see p. 124.

In Chinatown, the **Dr. Sun Yat-sen Classical Chinese Garden** ✸✸ (p. 119) is a small, tranquil oasis in the heart of the city, built by artisans from Suzhou, China; right next to it, accessed via the Chinese Cultural Centre on Pender Street, is the pretty (and free) **Dr. Sun Yat-sen Park,** with a pond, walkways, and plantings.

On the West Side, **Queen Elizabeth Park** ☆—at Cambie Street and W. 33rd Avenue—sits atop a 150m-high (492-ft.) extinct volcano and is the highest urban vantage point south of downtown, offering panoramic views in all directions (although leafy deciduous trees now block some of the best views). Along with the rose Garden in Stanley Park, it's Vancouver's most popular location for wedding-photo sessions, with well-manicured gardens and a profusion of colorful flora. There are areas for lawn bowling, tennis, pitch-and-putt golf, and picnicking. The **Bloedel Conservatory** (🕾 **604/257-8584**) stands next to the park's huge sunken garden, an amazing reclamation of an abandoned rock quarry. A 42m-high (138-ft.) domed structure, the conservatory houses a tropical rainforest with more than 100 plant species as well as free-flying tropical birds. Admission to the conservatory is C$4.25 (US$3.40) for adults, with discounts for seniors and children. Take bus no. 15 to reach the park.

VanDusen Botanical Gardens ☆ (5251 Oak St., at W. 37th Ave.; 🕾 **604/878-9274**; www.vandusengarden.org) is located just a few blocks from Queen Elizabeth Park and the Bloedel Conservatory. In contrast to the flower fetish displayed by Victoria's famous Butchart Gardens (see "Exploring Victoria," chapter 14), Vancouver's 22-hectare (54-acre) botanical garden concentrates on whole ecosystems. From trees hundreds of feet high down to the little lichens on the smallest of damp stones, the gardeners at VanDusen attempt to re-create the plant life of a number of different environments. Depending on which trail you take, you may find yourself wandering through the Southern Hemisphere section, the Sino-Himalayan garden, or the northern California sequoia garden. Should all this tree gazing finally pall, head for the farthest corner of the garden where you'll find a devilishly difficult Elizabethan garden maze. Admission April through September C$7.75 (US$6.20) adults, C$5.50 (US$4.40) seniors, C$5.75 (US$4.60) youth 13 to 18, C$4 (US$3.20) children 6 to 12, C$18 (US$14) families, free for children under 6. Admission is about C$2 less from October through March. Open daily 10am to dusk. Take bus 17.

Adjoining UBC on the city's west side at Point Grey, **Pacific Spirit Regional Park,** called the **Endowment Lands** by long-time Vancouver residents, is the largest green space in Vancouver. Comprising 754 hectares (1,863 acres) of temperate rainforest, marshes, and beaches, the park includes nearly 35km (22 miles) of trails ideal for hiking, riding, mountain biking, and beachcombing.

Across the Lions Gate Bridge, six provincial parks delight outdoor enthusiasts year-round. Good in winter or for those averse to strenuous climbing is the publicly maintained **Capilano River Regional Park,** 4500 Capilano Rd. (🕾 **604/666-1790**), surrounding the Capilano Suspension Bridge & Park (p. 125). Hikers can follow a gentle trail by the river for 7km (4.3 miles) down the well-maintained **Capilano trails** to the Burrard Inlet and the Lions Gate Bridge, or about a mile upstream to **Cleveland Dam,** a launching point for white-water kayakers and canoeists.

The **Capilano Salmon Hatchery,** on Capilano Road (🕾 **604/666-1790**), is on the river's east bank about a half a kilometer (⅓ mile) below the Cleveland Dam. Approximately 2 million Coho and Chinook salmon are hatched annually in glass-fronted tanks connected to the river by a series of channels. You can observe the hatching fry (baby fish) before they depart for open waters, as well as the mature salmon that return to the Capilano River to spawn. Admission is free, and the hatchery is open daily from 8am to 7pm (until 4pm in the winter). Drive across the Lions Gate Bridge and follow the signs to North Vancouver and the Capilano Suspension Bridge. Or take the SeaBus to Lonsdale Quay and transfer to bus no. 236; the trip takes less than 45 minutes.

Eight kilometers (5 miles) west of the Lions Gate Bridge on Marine Drive West, West Vancouver, is **Lighthouse Park** 🎔🎔. This 74-hectare (183-acre) rugged-terrain forest has 13km (8 miles) of groomed trails and—because it has never been clear-cut—some of the largest and oldest trees in the Vancouver area. One of the paths leads to the 18m (59-ft.) **Point Atkinson Lighthouse,** on a rocky bluff overlooking the Strait of Georgia and a fabulous view of Vancouver. It's an easy trip on bus no. 250. For information about other West Vancouver parks, call 🕿 **604/925-7200** weekdays.

Driving up-up-up the mountain from **Lighthouse Park** will eventually get you to the top of **Cypress Provincial Park.** Stop halfway at the scenic viewpoint for a sweeping vista of the Vancouver skyline, the harbor, the Gulf Islands, and Washington State's Mount Baker, which peers above the eastern horizon. The park is 12km (7½ miles) north of Cypress Bowl Road and the Highway 99 junction in West Vancouver. Cypress Provincial Park has an intricate network of trails maintained for hiking during the summer and autumn and for downhill and cross-country skiing during the winter (see the "Skiing and Snowboarding" and "Hiking" sections under "Outdoor Activities" later in this chapter).

Rising 1,430m (4,692 ft.) above Indian Arm, **Mount Seymour Provincial Park,** 1700 Mt. Seymour Rd., North Vancouver (🕿 **604/986-2261**), offers another view of the area's Coast Mountains range. The road to this park roams through stands of Douglas fir, red cedar, and hemlock. Higher than Grouse Mountain, Mount Seymour has a spectacular view of Washington State's Mount Baker on clear days. It has challenging hiking trails that go straight to the summit, where you can see Indian Arm, Vancouver's bustling commercial port, the city skyline, the Strait of Georgia, and Vancouver Island. The trails are open all summer for hiking; during the winter, the paths are maintained for skiing, snowboarding, and snowshoeing (see "Skiing and Snowboarding" and "Hiking" sections under "Outdoor Activities" later in this chapter). Mount Seymour is open daily from 7am to 10pm.

For more suggestions on outdoor activities, see "Wildlife-Watching," p. 142.

4 Especially for Kids

Pick up copies of the free monthly newspapers *B.C. Parent,* 4479 W. 10th Ave., Vancouver, B.C. V6R 4P2 (🕿 **604/221-0366;** www.bcparent.com); and *West Coast Families,* 8–1551 Johnston St., Vancouver, B.C. V6H 3R9 (🕿 **604/689-1331**). *West Coast Families'* centerfold, "Fun in the City," and event calendar, list everything currently going on, including **CN IMAX** shows at Canada Place Pier, **OMNIMAX** (🕿 **604/443-7443**) shows at Science World British Columbia (p. 124), and free children's programs. Both publications are available at Granville Island's Kids Market and at neighborhood community centers throughout the city. For a description of Vancouver's newest kid-friendly attraction, called **Storyeum** 🎔🎔🎔, see p. 120.

To give kids an overview of the city, take the fun trolley tour offered by **Vancouver Trolley Company** (🕿 **888/451-5581** or 604/801-5515; www.vancouvertrolley.com). Gas-powered trolleys run through Downtown, Chinatown, the West End, and Stanley Park (for more info, see "Organized Tours," below).

Stanley Park 🎔🎔🎔 (p. 116) offers a number of attractions for children, including a fabulous and free **Spray Park** near Lumberman's Arch. **Stanley Park's Children's Farm** (🕿 **604/257-8531**) has peacocks, rabbits, calves, donkeys, and Shetland ponies. Next to the petting zoo is Stanley Park's **Miniature Railway** 🎔 (🕿 **604/257-8531**), a diminutive steam locomotive with passenger cars that runs on a circuit through the woods. The zoo and railway are open from 11am to 4pm daily June through early September, plus Christmas week and on weekends October through March depending on weather. Admission for the petting zoo or the miniature railroad is C$5 (US$4) for adults, C$3.50 (US$2.80) for seniors, C$3.75 (US$3) for youths 13 to 18, and C$2.50 (US$2) for kids 2 to 12. **Second Beach** on the park's western rim has a playground, a snack bar, and an immense heated oceanside **pool** ⭐ (✆ **604/257-8371**), open from May through September. Admission is C$4.50 (US$3.60) for adults, C$3.20 (US$2.60) for seniors, C$3.40 (US$2.70) for youths 13 to 18, and C$2.25 (US$1.80) for children 6 to 12. Kids will also be impressed with the collection of giant **totem poles** ⭐⭐⭐ in Stanley Park, and the entire family will enjoy the **horse-drawn carriage rides** ⭐⭐⭐ that begin near Lost Lagoon (see "Specialty Tours," below).

Also in Stanley Park, the **Vancouver Aquarium Marine Science Centre** ⭐⭐ (p. 118) has sea otters, sea lions, whales, and numerous other marine creatures, as well as many exhibits geared toward children.

Right in town, **Science World British Columbia** (p. 124) is a terrific hands-on kids' museum where budding scientists can get their hands into everything. At the **Vancouver Maritime Museum** (p. 124), kids can dress up like a pirate or a naval captain and board the RCMP ice-breaker *St. Roch.*

A trip to **Granville Island** ⭐⭐⭐ by Aquabus or Granville Island Ferry (p. 56) will delight kids, and there are a couple of specific kids' places they'll really enjoy. Granville Island's **Kids Market,** 1496 Cartwright St. (✆ **604/689-8447**), is open daily from 10am to 6pm. Playrooms and 28 shops filled with toys, books, records, clothes, and food are all child-oriented. At **Granville Island's Water Park and Adventure Playground,** 1496 Cartwright St., kids can really let loose with movable water guns and sprinklers. They can also have fun on the water slides or in the wading pool. The facilities are open during the summer daily (weather permitting) from 10am to 6pm. Admission is free; changing facilities are nearby at the False Creek Community Centre (✆ **604/257-8195**).

Across Burrard Inlet on the North Shore, **Maplewood Farm,** 405 Seymour River Place, North Vancouver (✆ **604/929-5610;** www.maplewoodfarm.bc.ca), has more than 200 barnyard animals (from cows to chickens) living on its 2-hectare (5-acre) farm, which is open daily year-round. A few working farms once operated in the area but were put out of business by competition from the huge agricultural concerns in Fraser River valley. The parks department rescued this one and converted it into an attraction. The ticket booth (a former breeding kennel) sells birdseed for feeding the ducks and other fowl. The farm also offers pony rides. Special events include the summertime Sheep Fair, the mid-September Farm Fair, 101 Pumpkins Day in late October, and the Country Christmas weekend. The farm is open Tuesday through Sunday from 10am to 4pm, and on designated holiday Mondays during the same hours. Admission is C$3.50 (US$2.80) for adults, C$2 (US$1.60) for seniors and children. Take bus no. 210 and transfer to the no. 211 or 212.

Greater Vancouver Zoo, 5048 264th St., Aldergrove (✆ **604/856-6825;** www.greatervancouverzoo.com), located 48km (30 miles) east of downtown Vancouver (about a 45-min. drive), is a lush 48-hectare (119-acre) reserve filled with lions, tigers, jaguars, ostriches, elephants, buffalo, elk, antelope, zebras, giraffes, a rhino, hippos, and camels. In all, 124 species roam in spacious enclosures on the grounds. The zoo also has food service and a playground. It's open daily 9:30am to 4pm from October through March, 9:30am to 7pm from April through September. Admission is C$13

(US$11) for adults, C$10 (US$8) for seniors and children 3 to 15, and is free for children under 3. Take the Trans-Canada Highway to Aldergrove, exit 73; parking is C$3 (US$2.25) per day.

The **Burnaby Village Museum,** 6501 Deer Lake Ave., Burnaby (© **604/293-6501**), is a 3.5-hectare (8¾-acre) re-creation of the town as it might have appeared in the 1920s. You can walk along boardwalk streets among costumed townspeople, shop in a general store, ride a vintage carousel, peek into an authentic one-room schoolhouse, and visit a vintage ice-cream parlor that's been at the same location since the turn of the 20th century. At Christmastime, the whole village is aglow in Christmas lights and Victorian decorations. Admission is C$8.15 (US$6.50) for adults; C$5.85 (US$4.70) for seniors, students, and youths 13 to 18; C$4.95 (US$4) for children 6 to 12; and free for children under 6. It's open daily May through September 6 from noon to 4pm, November 20 through December 10 daily noon to 5pm., December 11 through 20 from noon to 8pm, and on holidays noon to 8pm throughout the year. From the Metrotown Skystation take bus no. 110 to Deer Lake. *Tip:* Time your trip to the Burnaby Village Museum to include a visit to the **Hart House Restaurant,** located at Deer Lake (6664 Deer Lake Ave.; © **604/298-4278**). This elegant Tudor-style mansion houses an excellent restaurant, which is a perfect brunch or lunch spot, especially in summer when guests can stroll the lovely gardens. It's open Tuesday through Sunday for lunch from 11:30am to 2:30pm and for dinner from 5:30 to 10pm.

Give your kids some old-fashioned low-tech fun at **Playland Family Fun Park,** Exhibition Park, East Hastings and Cassiar Streets (© **604/255-5161**), an amusement park with an ornate carousel, wooden roller coaster, and miniature golf. Admission for unlimited rides is C$23 (US$18) for those 1.2m (4 ft.) and taller and C$10 (US$8) for those under 1.2m (4 ft.) tall for limited rides. Admission for an adult with a paying child under 12 is C$10 (US$8). There's also a Nintendo Pavilion, Electric City Arcade, and petting zoo. The park is open weekends and holidays from late April to mid-June and Labour Day to the end of September from 11am to 7pm; mid-June to Labour Day daily from 11am to 9pm. Take bus no. 14 or 16.

The **Fort Langley National Historic Site,** 23433 Mavis Ave., Fort Langley (© **604/513-4777**), is the birthplace of British Columbia. In 1827, the Hudson's Bay Company established this settlement to supply its provincial posts. Costumed craftspeople demonstrate blacksmithing, coppering, and woodworking skills, bringing this landmark back to life. It's open daily from 10am to 5pm March through October, and weekdays only 10am to 5pm from November through February. Admission is C$5.75 (US$4.80) for adults, C$5 (US$4) for seniors, C$3 (US$2.40) for children 6 to 16, and is free for children under 6; a family pass is C$15 (US$12). To get there, take the SkyTrain to Surrey Central Station and transfer to bus no. 501. *Note:* The main street of Fort Langley Village, Glover Road, is packed with antiques shops, a bookstore, and cafes (lunch!), and it's only a 2-minute stroll away.

Walk high above the rushing waters at the **Capilano Suspension Bridge & Park** (p. 125) and the **Lynn Canyon Suspension Bridge** (see "The *Other* Suspension Bridge," on p. 126). In winter, **Mount Seymour Provincial Park** (see "Skiing & Snowboarding," on p. 140) and **Grouse Mountain Resort** (p. 126) offer ski programs for kids and adults; in summer, both are great for hikes.

A 45-minute drive north of Vancouver, the **B.C. Museum of Mining,** Highway 99, Britannia Beach (© **800/896-4044;** www.bcmuseumofmining.org), is impossible to miss. Located at the head of Howe Sound, it's marked by a 235-ton truck parked in front. During the summer it offers guided tours of the old copper mine, demonstrations of mining techniques, and includes an underground mine tour and even a gold-panning area where anyone can try straining gravel for the precious metal. It's open daily from the first Sunday in May to Thanksgiving from 9am to 5:30pm; the rest of the year it's closed on weekends. Call ahead for tour schedule; allow about 1½ to 2 hours. Admission is C$15 (US$12) for adults, C$12 (US$9.40) for seniors, students, and youths; and C$45 (US$34) for families; it's free for children under 5.

A whale-watching excursion is one of the most exciting adventures you can give a kid. See "Wildlife-Watching" later in this chapter for information.

5 Organized Tours

If you don't have the time to arrange your own sightseeing tour, let the experts take you around Vancouver. They will escort you in a bus, trolley, double-decker bus, seaplane, helicopter, boat, ferry, taxi, vintage car, or horse-driven carriage.

BUS TOURS

Gray Line of Vancouver, 255 E. First Ave. (© **800/667-0882** or 604/879-3363; www.grayline.ca), offers a wide array of tour options. The "Deluxe Grand City Tour" is a 3½-hour excursion through Stanley Park, Gastown, Chinatown, Canada Place, Queen Elizabeth Park, Robson Street, Shaughnessy, and English Bay Beach. Offered year-round, it costs C$55 (US$44) for adults, C$53 (US$42) for seniors and students, and C$37 (US$30) for children 3 to 11. Departing at 9:15am and 2pm, the bus picks you up from downtown hotels approximately 30 minutes before departure. The daily "Mountains and Sea Tour" takes you up to Grouse Mountain and the Capilano Suspension Bridge. Departing daily at 2pm, it costs C$99 (US$79) for adults, C$91 (US$73) for seniors and students, and C$75 (US$60) for children 3 to 11, including admission and the SkyRide funicular up to Grouse Mountain Resort. Other offerings include day, overnight, and multinight package tours of Vancouver, Victoria, and Whistler, plus helicopter tours and dinner cruises. Gray Line also runs a fleet of double-decker buses on a "hop-on, hop-off" sightseeing loop around the city (C$16/US$13 adults, C$9/US$7 children); buses depart hourly from Canada Place.

Vancouver Trolley Company, 875 Terminal Ave., Vancouver (© **888/451-5581** or 604/801-5515; www.vancouvertrolley.com), operates gas-powered trolleys along a route through Downtown, Chinatown, the West End, and Stanley Park. Between 9am and 6pm in summer (4:30pm in winter), passengers can get on and off at any of the 23 stops, explore, and catch another scheduled trolley. Onboard, drivers provide detailed commentary. Purchase tickets from the driver for C$28 (US$22) for adults and C$14 (US$11) for children 4 to 12 (or at the ticket booth in Gastown at 157 Water St.).

BOAT TOURS

Harbour Cruises, Harbour Ferries, no. 1, north foot of Denman Street (© **604/688-7246;** www.boatcruises.com), will take you on a 3-hour Sunset Dinner Cruise, including a catered gourmet meal and onboard entertainment; cost for adults, seniors, and students is C$70 (US$56); C$60 (US$48) for children 2 to 11. The cruise leaves at 7pm May through October. The 4-hour Indian Arm Luncheon Cruise (May–Sept) includes a salmon lunch, with departure at 11am. Cost for adults, seniors, and children is C$55 (US$49).

Harbour Cruises also conducts a 75-minute narrated Harbour Tour aboard the MPV *Constitution,* an authentic 19th-century stern-wheeler with a smokestack. Tours depart at 11:30am, 1pm, and 2:30pm daily from May 8 to September 20 and once a day at 2:30pm April through May 7 and September 21 through October. Fares are C$19 (US$15) for adults, C$16 (US$13) for seniors and youths (12–17), C$7 (US$5.60) for children 5 to 11, and free for children under 5.

Accent Cruises, 1676 Duranleau St. (© **604/688-6625;** www.champagnecruises. com), offers a 2½-hour Sunset Cruise departing Granville Island weekends May through October at 5:45pm. Cost for adults is C$60 (US$48) with dinner.

Paddlewheeler River Adventures, New Westminster Quay, New Westminster (© **604/525-4465;** www.vancouverpaddlewheeler.com), operates Fraser River tours from New Westminster aboard the 19th-century vessel SS *Native.* The company offers a 3-hour entertainment cruise Wednesday through Saturday evenings with live music, departing at 7pm. Ticket prices are C$20 (US$16) for adults, C$12 (US$9.50) for children 6–12; food and beverages can be purchased on board. More interesting but not regularly scheduled are the lunch cruises and day trips up to historic Fort Langley; call or visit the website for dates.

AIR TOURS

Baxter Aviation Adventure Tours ✿✿✿ (© **800/661-5599** or 604/683-6525; www. baxterair.com), operates daily floatplane flights from its downtown Vancouver terminal next to Canada Place cruise-ship terminal. Floatplanes are single-prop, six-seater planes that take off and land on water. The 20-minute "Vancouver Scenic" tour (C$79/US$63 per person for groups of four) flies over Stanley Park and all around the metro region, giving you an unparalleled bird's-eye view of the magnificent terrain; the 5-hour "Whistler Mountain Resort" tour (C$319/US$255 per person for groups of four) includes a 3-hour stopover. Other tours will take you to Victoria, glacial lakes, and prime fly-fishing and whale-watching spots.

Harbour Air (© **800/665-0212** or 604/274-1277; www.harbour-air.com) is on Coal Harbour just steps west of the Canada Place Pier. Thirty-minute seaplane flights over downtown Vancouver, Stanley Park, and the North Shore are C$99 (US$79) per person; C$79 (US$63) if your party includes four or more people. Many longer tours to alpine lakes and glaciers and nearby islands, as well as regularly scheduled flights to Victoria, Nanaimo, and Prince Rupert, are also available.

From April through September, **Helijet Charters** (© **800/987-4354** or 604/273-4688; www.helijet.com), offers a variety of daily tours that depart from their terminal next to Canada Place and their helipad on top of Grouse Mountain. The "West Coast Spectacular" is a 20-minute tour of the city, Stanley Park, and North Shore mountains for C$143 (US$114) per person.

SPECIALTY TOURS

Early Motion Tours, 1–1380 Thurlow St. (© **604/687-5088**), offers private sightseeing tours around Vancouver aboard a restored 1930 Model A Ford Phaeton convertible that holds up to four passengers plus the driver. Reservations are required. Limousine rates apply: C$100 (US$80) per hour for up to four people with a 1-hour minimum. The office is open daily from 7:30am to 8pm.

AAA Horse & Carriage Ltd., Stanley Park (© **604/681-5115;** www.stanleyparktours.com), carries on a century-old tradition of **horse-drawn carriage rides through Stanley Park** ✿✿✿. Tours depart every 30 minutes mid-March through October from the lower aquarium parking lot on Park Drive near the Georgia Street park entrance. Tours last an hour and cover portions of the park that many locals have never seen. Rates are C$23 (US$18) for adults, C$20 (US$16) for seniors and students, C$14 (US$11) for children 3 to 12.

Yes, the truth is out there and so are the *X-Files* fans. Even though the series has ended, die-hards can still depart on the guided **X Tour** (© **604/609-2770;** www. x-tour.com) to see *X-Files* shooting locations around Vancouver. Costs are from C$25 (US$20) per adult for a 1-hour walking tour to C$150 (US$120) per person (minimum of two) for a 3-hour limo tour.

FIRST NATIONS TOURS

The Tsleil-Waututh Nation of North Vancouver offers a number of cultural and eco-tours that provide an introduction to both First Nations culture and the stunning Indian Arm fjord. Their company, **Takaya Tours,** 3093 Ghum-Lye Dr., North Vancouver (© **604/940-7410;** www.takayatours.com), offers canoe tours in traditional northwest canoes, plant nature walks, full moon paddles, and other tours, at prices running from C$40 to C$75 (US$32–US$60).

WALKING TOURS

Walkabout Historic Vancouver (© **604/720-0006;** www.walkabouthistoric vancouver.com) offers 2-hour walking tours through Vancouver and Granville Island historic sites, complete with guides dressed as 19th-century schoolmarms. Tours depart daily at 10am and 2pm February through November, and by request during other months. Tours are wheelchair accessible. The cost is C$25 (US$20) per person.

During the summer months (June–Aug), the **Architectural Institute of B.C.** (© **604/638-8588,** ext. 306; www.aibc.ca) offers a number of **architectural walking tours** ⊛ of downtown Vancouver neighborhoods, including Chinatown, for only C$5 (US$4) per person. The 2-hour tours run Tuesday through Saturday and depart at 1pm from different locations in the city. Call or visit the website for details and to book.

Or, devise your own walking tour with brochures from the **Vancouver Tourist Info Centre** at 200 Burrard St. (p. 48).

6 Outdoor Activities

Vancouver is definitely an outdoors-oriented city and just about every imaginable sport has a world-class outlet within the city limits. Downhill and cross-country skiing, snowshoeing, sea kayaking, fly-fishing, hiking, paragliding, and mountain biking are just a few of the options. Activities that can be enjoyed in the vicinity include rock climbing, river rafting, and heli-skiing. If you don't find your favorite sport listed here, take a look at chapter 18.

An excellent resource for outdoor enthusiasts is **Mountain Equipment Co-op,** 130 W. Broadway (© **604/872-7858;** www.mec.ca). The MEC's retail store has a knowledgeable staff, the co-op publishes an annual mail-order catalog, and you can find useful outdoor activities information on the website.

BEACHES

Only 10% of Vancouver's annual rainfall occurs during June, July, and August; 60 days of summer sunshine is not uncommon. **English Bay Beach** ⊛⊛, at the end of Davie Street off Denman Street and Beach Avenue, is a great place to see sunsets. The bathhouse dates to the turn of the 20th century, and a huge playground slide is mounted on a raft just off the beach every summer.

On **Stanley Park**'s western rim, **Second Beach** is a quick stroll north from English Bay Beach. A playground, a snack bar, and an immense heated oceanside **pool** 🏊 (✆ **604/257-8370**), open from May through September, makes this a convenient and fun spot for families. Admission to the pool is C$4.50 (US$3.60) for adults, C$3.25 (US$2.60) for seniors, C$3.50 (US$2.80) for youth 13 to 18, and C$2.50 (US$2) for children 6 to 12. Farther along the seawall, due north of Stanley Park Drive, lies secluded **Third Beach.** Locals tote along grills and coolers to this spot, a popular place for summer-evening barbecues and sunset watching. The hollow tree, Geographic Tree, and Siwash Rock are neighboring points of interest.

South of English Bay Beach, near the Burrard Street Bridge, is **Sunset Beach.** Running along False Creek, it's actually a picturesque strip of sandy beaches filled with enormous driftwood logs that serve as windbreaks and provide a little privacy for sunbathers and picnickers. There's a snack bar, a soccer field, and a long, gently sloping grassy hill for people who prefer lawn to sand.

On the West Side, **Kitsilano Beach** 🏊, along Arbutus Drive near Ogden Street, is affectionately called Kits Beach. It's an easy walk from the Maritime Museum and the False Creek ferry dock. If you want to do a saltwater swim but can't handle the cold, head to the huge (135m/443-ft.-long) heated (77°F/25°C) **Kitsilano Pool** 🏊. Admission is the same as for Second Beach Pool, above. The summertime amateur theater, **Kitsilano Showboat,** attracts a local crowd looking for evening fun.

Farther west on the other side of Pioneer Park is **Jericho Beach** (Alma St. off Point Grey Rd.). This is another local after-work and weekend social spot. **Locarno Beach,** off Discovery Street and NW Marine Drive, and **Spanish Banks,** NW Marine Drive, wrap around the northern point of the UBC campus and University Hill. (Be forewarned that beachside restrooms and concessions on the promontory end abruptly at Locarno Beach.) Below UBC's Museum of Anthropology is **Point Grey Beach,** a restored harbor defense site. The next beach is **Wreck Beach** 🏊—Canada's largest nude beach. You get down to Wreck Beach by taking the very steep Trail 6 on the UBC campus near Gate 6 down to the water's edge. Extremely popular with locals, and maintained by The Wreck Beach Preservation Society, Wreck Beach is also the city's most pristine and least-developed sandy stretch. It's bordered on three sides by towering trees.

At the northern foot of the Lions Gate Bridge, **Ambleside Park** is a popular North Shore spot. The quarter-mile beach faces the Burrard Inlet.

For information on any of Vancouver's many beaches, call ✆ **604/738-8535** (summer only).

BICYCLING & MOUNTAIN BIKING

Cycling in Vancouver is fun, amazingly scenic, and very popular. Cycling maps are available at most bicycle retailers and rental outlets. Some West End hotels offer guests bike storage and rentals. Hourly rentals run around C$5 (US$4) for a one-speed "Cruiser" to C$9 (US$7.20) for a top-of-the-line mountain bike; C$15 to C$40 (US$12–US$32) for a day, helmets and locks included. Popular shops that rent city and mountain bikes, child trailers, child seats, and in-line skates (protective gear included) include **Spokes Bicycle Rentals & Espresso Bar,** 1798 W. Georgia St. (✆ **604/688-5141;** www.spokesbicyclerentals.com); **Alley Cat Rentals,** 1779 Robson St., in the alley (✆ **604/684-5117**); and **Bayshore Bicycle and Rollerblade**

Rentals, 745 Denman St. (© **604/688-2453;** www.bayshorebikerentals.ca). *Note:* Be advised that helmets are mandatory and will be included in your bike rental.

The most popular cycling path in the city runs along the **Seawall** ✿✿✿ around the perimeter of Stanley Park. Offering stunning views of the city, the Burrard Inlet, the mountains, and English Bay, this flat, 10km (6¼-mile) pathway attracts year-round bicyclists, in-line skaters, and pedestrians. (*Note:* Runners and cyclists have separate lanes on developed park and beach paths.) Another popular route is the **seaside bicycle route,** a 15km (9½-mile) ride that begins at English Bay and continues around False Creek to the University of British Columbia. Some of this route follows city streets that are well marked with cycle-path signs; the sights include: The Plaza of Nations, Science World, Granville Island, the Pacific Space Centre, the Kitsilano Pool and the Jericho Sailing Centre, and the University of British Columbia, home to the UBC Botanical Garden and Nitobe Japanese Garden (p. 124) and the lush Pacific Spirit Park (see "Parks & Gardens," earlier in this chapter).

Serious mountain bikers also have a wealth of world-class options within a short drive from downtown Vancouver. The trails on **Grouse Mountain** (p. 126) are some of the lower mainland's best. The very steep **Good Samaritan Trail** on **Mount Seymour** connects to the Baden-Powell Trail and the Bridle Path near Mount Seymour Road. Local mountain bikers love the cross-country ski trails on **Hollyburn Mountain** in **Cypress Provincial Park,** just northeast of Vancouver on the road to Whistler on Highway 99. Closer to downtown, both **Pacific Spirit Park** and **Burnaby Mountain** offer excellent beginner and intermediate off-road trails.

BOATING

With thousands of miles of protected shoreline along British Columbia's West Coast, boaters enjoy some of the finest cruising grounds in the world. Explore the many inlets, passages, and islands. You can rent 4.5- to 5m-long (15–16 ft.) powerboats for a few hours or up to several weeks at **Bonnie Lee Boat Rentals,** 1676 Duranleau St., Granville Island (© **866/933-7447** or 604/290-7441; www.bonnielee.com). Rates for a 5m (16-ft.) sport boat that holds four begin at C$50 (US$40) per hour or C$300 (US$240) for an 8-hour package. **Jerry's Boat Rentals,** Granville Island (© **604/644-3256**), is just steps away and offers similar deals. **Delta Charters,** 3500 Cessna Dr., Richmond (© **800/661-7762** or 604/273-4211; www.deltacharters.com), offers weekly and monthly rates for skippered boats that sleep 4.

CANOEING & KAYAKING

Both placid, urban False Creek and the incredibly beautiful 30km (19-mile) North Vancouver fjord known as Indian Arm have launching points that can be reached by car or bus. Prices range from about C$35 (US$28) per 2-hour minimum rental to C$65 (US$52) per 5-hour day for single kayaks and about C$60 (US$48) for canoe rentals. Customized tours range from C$75 to C$125 (US$60–US$100) per person.

Ecomarine Ocean Kayak Centre, 1668 Duranleau St., Granville Island (© **888/425-2925** or 604/689-7575; www.ecomarine.com), has 2-hour, daily, and weekly kayak rentals, as well as courses and organized tours. The company also has an office at the **Jericho Sailing Centre,** 1300 Discovery St., at Jericho Beach (© **604/222-3565**). In North Vancouver, **Deep Cove Canoe and Kayak Rentals,** 2156 Banbury Rd. (at the foot of Gallant St.), Deep Cove (© **604/929-2268;** www.deepcovekayak.com) is an easy starting point for anyone planning an Indian Arm run. It offers hourly and daily rentals of canoes and kayaks as well as lessons and customized tours.

Lotus Land Tours, 2005–1251 Cardero St. (© **800/528-3531** or 604/684-4922; www.lotuslandtours.com), runs guided kayak tours on Indian Arm that come with transportation, a barbecue salmon lunch, and incredible scenery. Operator Peter Loppe uses very wide, stable kayaks, perfect for first-time paddlers. One-day tours cost C$149 (US$119) for adults, C$75 (US$60) for children.

ECOTOURS

Lotus Land Tours, 2005–1251 Cardero St. (© **800/528-3531** or 604/684-4922; www.lotuslandtours.com), runs guided kayak tours on Indian Arm (see "Canoeing & Kayaking," above). From late November to the end of January, this small local company also offers unique float trips on the Squamish River to see the large concentration of bald eagles up close. **Rockwood Adventures** (© **888/236-6606** or 604/980-7749; www.rockwoodadventures.com) has guided walks of the North Shore rainforest, complete with a trained naturalist, stops in Capilano Canyon and at the Lynn Suspension Bridge (p. 126), and a gourmet lunch, for C$75 (US$60).

FISHING

With the Pacific Ocean to the west, and an intricate river and lake system throughout the province, British Columbia has long been one of North America's best fishing destinations. Five species of salmon, rainbow and Dolly Varden trout, steelhead, and sturgeon abound in the local waters around Vancouver. To fish, anglers over the age of 16 need a nonresident saltwater or freshwater license. Licenses are available province-wide from more than 500 vendors, including tackle shops, sporting goods stores, resorts, service stations, marinas, charter boat operators, and department stores. Saltwater (tidal waters) fishing licenses cost C$7.50 (US$6) for 1 day, C$20 (US$16) for 3 days, and C$35 (US$28) for 5 days. Fly-fishing in national and provincial parks requires special permits, which you can get at any park site for a nominal fee. Permits are valid at all Canadian parks.

The B.C. *Tidal Waters Sport Fishing Guide* and *B.C. Sport Fishing Regulations Synopsis for Non-tidal Waters,* and the *B.C. Fishing Directory and Atlas,* available at many tackle shops, are good sources of information. The *Vancouver Sun* prints a daily **fishing report** in the B section that details which fish are in season and where they can be found. You can also check the **Fisheries and Ocean Canada** website at www.pac.dfo-mpo.gc.ca.

Hanson's Fishing Outfitters, 102–580 Hornby St. (© **604/684-8988;** www.hansons-outfitters.com), and **Granville Island Boat Rentals,** 1696 Duranleau St. (© **604/682-6287;** www.boatrentalsvancouver.com), are outstanding outfitters. **Bonnie Lee Fishing Charters Ltd.,** 1676 Duranleau St., Granville Island © **604/290-7447;** www.bonnielee.com), is another reputable outfitter and also sells fishing licenses.

GOLF

Golf is a year-round Vancouver sport. With five public 18-hole courses and half a dozen pitch-and-putt courses in the city and dozens more nearby, golfers are never far from their love. For substantial discounts and short-notice tee times at more than 30 Vancouver-area courses, try calling **A-1 Last Minute Golf Hot Line** (© **800/684-6344** or 604/878-1833).

The public **University Golf Club,** 5185 University Blvd. (© **604/224-1818**), is a great 6,560-yard, par-71 course with a clubhouse, pro shop, locker rooms, bar and grill, and sports lounge. A number of excellent public golf courses, maintained by the

Vancouver Board of Parks and Recreation (© **604/257-8400;** www.city.vancouver. bc.ca/parks), can be found throughout the city. **Langara Golf Course,** 6706 Alberta St., around 49th Avenue and Cambie Street (© **604/713-1816**), built in 1926 and recently renovated and redesigned, is one of the most popular golf courses in the province. Depending on the course, weekend greens fees range from C$25 to C$52 (US$20–US$42) for an adult, with discounts for seniors, youths, and weekday tee times. To reserve, call © **604/280-1818** up to 5 days in advance.

Leading private clubs are situated on the North Shore and in Vancouver. Check with your club at home to see if you have reciprocal visiting memberships with one of the following: **Capilano Golf and Country Club,** 420 Southborough Dr., West Vancouver (© **604/922-9331**); **Marine Drive Golf Club,** W. 57th Avenue and S.W. Marine Drive (© **604/261-8111**); **Seymour Golf and Country Club,** 3723 Mt. Seymour Pkwy., North Vancouver (© **604/929-2611**); **Point Grey Golf and Country Club,** 3350 SW Marine Dr. (© **604/261-3108**); and **Shaughnessy Golf and Country Club,** 4300 SW Marine Dr. (© **604/266-4141**). Greens fees range from C$42 to C$72 (US$34–US$58).

HIKING

Great trails for hikers of all levels run through Vancouver's dramatic environs. Good trail maps are available from **International Travel Maps and Books,** 539 Pender St. (© **604/687-3320;** www.itmb.com), which also stocks guidebooks and topographical maps. You can pick up a local trail guide at any bookstore.

If you're looking for a challenge without a longtime commitment, hike the aptly named **Grouse Grind** from the bottom of **Grouse Mountain** (p. 126) to the top; then buy a one-way ticket down on the Grouse Mountain SkyRide gondola.

If you're looking for a bit more scenery with a bit less effort, take the Grouse Mountain SkyRide up to the **Grouse chalet** and start your hike at an altitude of 1,100m (3,609 ft.). The trail north to **Goat Mountain** is well marked and takes approximately 6 hours round-trip, though you may want to build in some extra time to linger on the top of Goat and take in the spectacular 360-degree views of Vancouver, Vancouver Island, and the snow-capped peaks of the Coast Mountains.

Lynn Canyon Park, Lynn Headwaters Regional Park, Capilano River Regional Park, Mount Seymour Provincial Park, Pacific Spirit Park, and **Cypress Provincial Park** (see "The Top Attractions" and "Parks & Gardens," earlier in this chapter) have good, easy to challenging trails that wind up through stands of Douglas fir and cedar and contain a few serious switchbacks. Pay attention to the trail warnings posted at the parks; some have bear habitats. And always remember to sign in with the park service at the start of your chosen trail.

You can do all the above hiking trails on your own, but should you desire some guidance and company, **Eco Trail Escapes** (© **604/929-5751;** www.ecotrailescapes. com) provides transportation to and from the trailheads, water and snacks, and a guide trained in wilderness first aid. The cost is C$85 (US$68) per person, less if there are others in the party.

A little farther outside the city, the 6- to 10-hour hike to **Black Tusk** is one of the finest day hikes in North America. The trailhead is located in **Garibaldi Provincial Park** (© **604/898-3678**), located 13km (8 miles) north of Squamish, 97km (60 miles) north of Vancouver along Highway 99 on the road to Whistler. The park has five access points; Black Tusk/Garibaldi Lake is the second marked turnoff; it takes about an hour to get there. The trail switchbacks up 1,000m (3,281 ft.) in about 6km

(3.7 miles), then levels onto a rolling alpine plateau with fabulous views. The best times to make this climb are from July to October.

ICE-SKATING

Robson Square has free skating on a covered ice rink on Robson Street between Howe and Hornby streets. It's open from November to early April. Rentals are available in the adjacent concourse. The **West End Community Centre,** 870 Denman St. (✆ **604/ 257-8333**), also rents skates at its enclosed rink, which is open October through March. The enormous Burnaby 8 Rinks **Ice Sports Centre,** 6501 Sprott, Burnaby (✆ **604/291-0626**), is the Vancouver Canucks' official practice facility. It has eight rinks, is open year-round, and offers lessons and rentals. Call ahead to check hours for public skating.

IN-LINE SKATING

You'll find locals rolling along beach paths, streets, park paths, and promenades. If you didn't bring a pair of blades, try **Bayshore Bicycle and Rollerblade Rentals,** 745 Denman St. (✆ **604/688-2453;** www.bayshorebikerentals.com). Rentals run C$5 (US$4) per hour or C$19 (US$15) for 8 hours. For information on in-line skating lessons and group events, visit www.rollerbladevancouver.com.

JOGGING

You'll find fellow runners traversing the **Stanley Park Seawall** ✯✯✯ and the paths around **Lost Lagoon** and **Beaver Lake.** If you're a dawn or dusk runner, take note that this is one of the world's safer city parks. However, if you're alone, don't tempt fate—stick to open and lighted areas. Other prime jogging areas in the city are **Kitsilano Beach, Jericho Beach,** and **Spanish Banks** (for more information, see "Beaches," above); all of them offer flat, well-maintained running paths along the ocean. You can also take the seawall path from English Bay Beach south along **False Creek.** If you feel like doing a little racing, competitions take place throughout the year; ask for information at any runners' outfitters, such as **Forerunners,** 3504 W. Fourth Ave. (✆ **604/732-4535**), or **Running Room,** 679 Denman St. (corner of Georgia; ✆ **604/684-9771**). Check www.runningroom.com for information on clinics and running events around Vancouver and British Columbia.

PARAGLIDING

Summertime paragliding may be the ultimate flying experience. Most of the areas in British Columbia where it's offered are outside Vancouver. Open from April 15 to September 15, **Whistler Paragliding,** in Whistler (✆ **604/938-8830;** www.whistler paragliding.com), offers an introductory tandem flight at C$149 (US$114) or a 2-day course for C$299 (US$239) where you will learn ground handling, complete short hops, and fly with an instructor. In North Vancouver, **First Flight Paragliding** (✆ **604/988-1111;** www.first-flight.ca) offers tandem flights June through September from the peak of Grouse Mountain, at C$150 (US$120) for 1 hour. The actual flight takes approximately 20 minutes.

SAILING

Trying to navigate a sailboat in the unfamiliar straits around Vancouver is unwise and unsafe unless you enroll in a local sailing course before attempting it. Knowing the tides, currents, and channels is essential. Multiday instruction packages sometimes include guided Gulf Island cruises.

If all you want is to get out for a day of sailing, you can charter a 3-hour yacht cruise with **Cooper Boating Centre,** 1620 Duranleau St. (© **604/687-4110;** www.cooper boating.com), which offers chartered cruises, boat rentals, and sail-instruction packages on 6 to 13m (20–43-ft.) boats. Boat rentals start at about C$160 (US$128) for a full-day rental in the off season and go as high as C$500 (US$400) for a full-day rental in the peak season, depending on the size of the boat.

SKIING & SNOWBOARDING

Top-notch skiing lies outside the city at the **Whistler** and **Blackcomb Resorts,** 110km (68 miles) north of Vancouver (see chapter 18). However, you don't have to leave the city to get in a few runs. It seldom snows in the city's downtown and central areas, but Vancouverites can ski before work and after dinner at the three ski resorts in the North Shore mountains. In 2010, these local mountains will play host to the Freestyle and Snowboard events in the Winter Olympics.

Grouse Mountain Resort, 6400 Nancy Greene Way, North Vancouver (© **604/984-0661;** snow report 604/986-6262; www.grousemountain.com), is about 3km (1¾ miles) from the Lions Gate Bridge, overlooking the Burrard Inlet and Vancouver's skyline. Four chairs, two beginner tows, and two T-bars take you to 24 alpine runs. The resort has night skiing, special events, instruction, and a spectacular view, as well as a 90m (295-ft.) half pipe for snowboarders. Though the area is small, all skill levels are covered, with two beginner trails, three blue trails, and five black-diamond runs, including Coffin and Inferno, which follow the east slopes down from 1,230 to 750m (4,035–2,461 ft.). Rental packages and a full range of facilities are available. Lift tickets good for all-day skiing are C$42 (US$34) for adults, C$32 (US$26) for seniors and youths, and C$18 (US$14) for children 5 through 12; children under 4 go free.

Mount Seymour Provincial Park, 1700 Mt. Seymour Rd., North Vancouver (© **604/986-2261;** snow report 604/986-3999; www.mountseymour.com), has the area's highest base elevation; it's accessible via four chairs and a tow. Lift tickets are C$36 (US$29) all day for adults, C$25 (US$20) for seniors, C$29 (US$23) for youths 12 to 19, C$19 (US$15) for children 6 to 11. Nighttime skiing from 4 to 10pm costs less. In addition to day and night skiing, the facility offers snowboarding, snowshoeing, and tobogganing along its 22 runs. There are also 26km (16 miles) of cross-country trails. The resort specializes in teaching first-timers. Camps for children and teenagers, and adult clinics, are available throughout the winter. Mount Seymour has one of Western Canada's largest equipment rental shops, which will keep your measurements on file for return visits. Shuttle service is available during ski season from various locations on the North Shore, including the Lonsdale Quay SeaBus. For more information, call © **604/953-3333.**

Cypress Bowl, 1610 Mt. Seymour Rd. (© **604/926-5612;** snow report 604/419-7669; www.cypressmountain.com), has the area's longest vertical drop (525m/1,722 ft.), challenging ski and snowboard runs, and 16km (10 miles) of track-set cross-country ski trails (including 5km/3.1 miles set aside for night skiing). Full-day lift tickets are C$42 (US$34) for adults, with reduced rates for youths, seniors, and children. Cross-country full-day passes are C$15 (US$12) for adults, with reduced rates for youths, seniors, and children. Snowshoe trail tickets are available for C$7.50 (US$6). Discounts for half-day, nighttime, and multiday tickets are available. Cypress also offers excellent 1-day and 5-day lesson packages for skiing or riding as well as an intro class to cross-country skiing (classic and skate).

Cypress Mountain Sports, 510 and 518 Park Royal S., West Vancouver (© **604/ 878-9229**), offers shuttle service to and from the ski area. Round-trip tickets are C$9 (US$6.75). Cypress Mountain Sports stocks a complete selection of downhill, cross-country (including backcountry, skating, racing, and touring), and snowboarding equipment and accessories. The rental and repair department, staffed by avid skiers, offers a broad selection of equipment. Rental and repair prices are quite reasonable. The store also offers guided hikes in summer and snowshoe treks in winter.

SWIMMING & WATERSPORTS

Vancouver's midsummer saltwater temperature rarely exceeds 65°F (18°C). If you've really got a hankering to have a saltwater swim, there are **heated outdoor pools** at both **Kitsilano Beach** and **Second Beach.** (see "Beaches," earlier in this chapter). You can also take to the water at public aquatic centers.

The **Vancouver Aquatic Centre,** 1050 Beach Ave. at the foot of Thurlow Street (© **604/665-3424**), has a heated, 50m (164-ft.) Olympic pool, saunas, whirlpools, weight rooms, diving tanks, locker rooms, showers, childcare, and a tot pool. Adult admission is C$4.25 (US$3.40). The new, coed **YWCA Fitness Centre,** 535 Hornby St. (© **604/895-5777;** www.ywcavan.org), in the heart of downtown, has a 6-lane, 25m (82-ft.) ozonated (much milder than chlorinated) pool, steam room, whirlpool, conditioning gym, and aerobic studios. A day pass is C$14 (US$11) for adults. UBC's **Aquatic Centre,** 6121 University Blvd. (© **604/822-4522;** www.aquatics.ubc.ca), located next door to the Student Union Building and the bus loop, sets aside time for public use. Adult admission is C$4.25 (US$3.40), C$3.25 (US$2.60) for youths and students, and C$2.50 (US$2) for seniors and children 3 to 12.

TENNIS

The city maintains 180 outdoor hard courts that have a 1-hour limit and accommodate patrons on a first-come, first-served basis from 8am until dusk. Local courtesy dictates that if people are waiting, you surrender the court on the hour. (Heavy usage times are evenings and weekends.) With the exception of the Beach Avenue courts, which charge a nominal fee in summer, all city courts are free.

Stanley Park has four courts near Lost Lagoon and 17 courts near the Beach Avenue entrance, next to the Fish House Restaurant. During the summer season (May–Sept) six courts are taken over for pay tennis and can be pre-booked by calling © **604/605-8224. Queen Elizabeth Park**'s 18 courts service the central Vancouver area, and **Kitsilano Beach Park**'s ✐ 10 courts service the beach area between Vanier Park and the UBC campus.

You can play at night at the **Langara Campus** of Vancouver Community College, on W. 49th Avenue between Main and Cambie streets. The **UBC Coast Club,** on Thunderbird Boulevard (© **604/822-2505;** www.tennis-ubc.ca), has 10 outdoor and four indoor courts. Indoor courts are C$10 (US$8) per hour; outdoor courts are C$6 (US$4.80) per person.

Bayshore Bicycle and Rollerblade Rentals, 745 Denman St. (© **604/688-2453;** www.bayshorebikerentals.com), rents tennis rackets for C$10 (US$8) per day.

WHITE-WATER RAFTING

A 2½-hour drive from Vancouver, on the wild Nahatlatch River, **Reo Rafting,** 845 Spence Way, Anmore (© **800/736-7238** or 604/461-7238; www.reorafting.com), offers some of the best guided white-water trips in the province, at a very reasonable price. One-day packages—including lunch, all your gear, and 4 to 5 hours on the river—start at C$125 (US$100) for adults. Multiday trips and group packages are also available.

Only a 1½-hour drive from the city is **Chilliwack River Rafting** (© **800/410-7238;** www.dowco.com/chilliwackrafting), which offers half-day trips on the Chilliwack River and in the even hairier Chilliwack Canyon. The cost is C$89 (US$71) for adults and C$69 (US$55) for children.

Whistler also offers excellent rafting on the Green River; see "Rafting," in chapter 18, for more information.

WILDLIFE-WATCHING

Vancouver is an internationally famous stop for naturalists, ecotourists, pods of orca whales, and thousands of migratory birds; so bring your camera, binoculars, and bird-spotting books. Salmon, bald eagles, herons, beavers, and numerous rare, indigenous marine and waterfowl species live in the metropolitan area.

Orcas, or killer whales, are the largest mammals to be seen in the waters around Vancouver. Three orca pods (families), numbering about 80 whales, return to this area every year to feed on the salmon returning to spawn in the Fraser River starting in May and continuing into October. The eldest female leads the group; the head of one pod is thought to have been born in 1911. From April through October, daily excursions offered by **Vancouver Whale Watch,** 12240 2nd Ave., Richmond (© **604/274-9565;** www.vancouverwhalewatch.com), focus on the majestic killer whales plus Dall's porpoises, sea lions, seals, eagles, herons, and other wildlife. The cost is C$99 (US$79) per person. The same adult rates apply at **Steveston Seabreeze Adventures,** 12551 No. 1 Rd., Richmond (© **604/272-7200;** www.seabreezeadventures.ca), but the price for seniors is C$89 (US$71) and for children it's C$59 (US$47). Both companies offer a shuttle service from downtown Vancouver. Whale-watching is a great adventure for kids and adults alike.

Thousands of migratory birds following the Pacific flyway rest and feed in the Fraser River delta south of Vancouver, especially at the 340-hectare (840-acre) **George C. Reifel Bird Sanctuary,** 5191 Robertson Rd., Westham Island (© **604/946-6980;** www.reifelbirdsanctuary.com), which was created by a former bootlegger and wetland-bird lover. Many other waterfowl species have made this a permanent habitat. More than 263 species have been spotted, including a Temminck's stint, a spotted redshank, bald eagles, Siberian (trumpeter) swans, peregrine falcons, blue herons, owls, and coots. The **Snow Goose Festival,** celebrating the annual arrival of the huge, snowy white flocks, is held here during the first weekend of November. The snow geese stay in the area until mid-December. (High tide, when the birds are less concealed by the marsh grasses, is the best time to visit.) An observation tower, 3km (1.9 miles) of paths, free birdseed, and picnic tables make this wetland reserve an ideal outing spot from October to April, when the birds are wintering in abundance. The sanctuary is wheelchair accessible and open daily from 9am to 4pm. Admission is C$4 (US$3.20) for adults and C$2 (US$1.60) for seniors and children.

The **Richmond Nature Park,** 1185 Westminster Hwy. (© **604/718-6188**), was established to preserve the Lulu Island wetlands bog. It features a Nature House with educational displays and a boardwalk-encircled duck pond. On Sunday afternoons, knowledgeable guides give free tours and acquaint visitors with this unique environment. Admission is by donation.

To hook up with local Vancouver birders, try the **Vancouver Natural History Society** (© 604/737-3074; www.naturalhistory.bc.ca/VNHS). This all-volunteer organization runs birding field trips most weekends; many are free.

During the winter, thousands of bald eagles line the banks of the **Squamish, Cheakamus,** and **Mamquam** rivers to feed on spawning salmon. The official January 1994 eagle count in Brackendale, a small community near Squamish, recorded 3,700—the largest number ever seen in North America. To get there by car, take the scenic **Sea-to-Sky Highway** (Hwy. 99) from downtown Vancouver to Squamish and Brackendale; the trip takes about an hour. The route winds along the craggy tree-lined coast of Howe Sound through the town of Britannia Beach and past two beautiful natural monuments: Shannon Falls and the continent's tallest monolithic rock face, the Stawamus Chief. Alternatively, you can take a **Greyhound** bus from Vancouver's Pacific Central Station, 1150 Station St. (© **604/482-8747;** www.greyhound.ca); trip time is 1¼ hr. Contact **Squamish & Howe Sound Visitor Info Centre** (© **604/892-9244;** www.squamishchamber.bc.ca) for more information.

The annual summer salmon runs attract more than bald eagles. Tourists also flock to coastal streams and rivers to watch the waters turn red with leaping coho and sockeye. The salmon are plentiful at the **Capilano Salmon Hatchery** (p. 128), **Goldstream Provincial Park** (p. 230), and numerous other fresh waters.

Along the Fraser River delta, more than 250 bird species migrate to or perennially inhabit the **George C. Reifel Sanctuary**'s wetland reserve. Nearby, **Richmond Nature Park** has educational displays for young and first-time birders plus a boardwalk-encircled duck pond. See "Wildlife-Watching," earlier in this chapter for detailed descriptions of both.

Stanley Park and **Pacific Spirit Park** are both home to heron rookeries. You can see these large birds nesting just outside the Vancouver Aquarium. Ravens, dozens of species of waterfowl, raccoons, skunks, beavers, and even coyotes are also full-time residents. The **Stanley Park Ecological Society** (© 604/257-8544) runs regular nature walks in the park. Call or see their website for more information, or drop by the **Lost Lagoon Nature House** in Stanley Park (p. 118).

WINDSURFING

Windsurfing is not allowed at the mouth of False Creek near Granville Island, but you can bring a board to **Jericho** and **English Bay beaches** 🎐 or rent one there. Equipment sales, rentals (including wet suits), and instruction can be found at **Windsure Windsurfing School,** 1300 Discovery St., at Jericho Beach (© **604/224-0615;** www.windsure.com). Rentals start at about C$18 (US$15) per hour, wet suit and life jacket included.

7 Spectator Sports

Spectators and participants will find plenty of activities in Vancouver. You can get schedule information on all major events at Tourism Vancouver's **Travel Info Centre,** 200 Burrard St. (© 604/683-2000; www.tourismvancouver.com). You can also get information and purchase tickets from Ticketmaster at the **Vancouver Ticket Centre,** 1304 Hornby St. (© **604/280-4444;** www.ticketmaster.ca), which has 40 outlets in the Greater Vancouver area, though like every other Ticketmaster, they do charge a fee. Popular events such as Canucks games and the Vancouver Indy can sell out weeks or months in advance, so it's a good idea to book ahead.

AUTO RACING

In late July, the CART Indy Series mounts its biggest annual event, the **Molson Indy,** 750 Pacific Blvd. (✆ **604/684-4639** for information; 604/280-4639 for tickets; www.molsonindy.com). General admission starts at C$20 (US$16), depending on the race day. A 3-day general admission ticket costs C$60 (US$48). The race roars through Vancouver's streets around B.C. Place Stadium and the north and south shores of False Creek, attracting more than 350,000 spectators.

FOOTBALL

The Canadian Football League's **B.C. Lions** (✆ **604/580-7627;** www.bclions.com) play their home and Grey Cup championship games (in good seasons) in the 60,000-seat **B.C. Place Stadium,** 777 Pacific Blvd. S. (at Beatty and Robson sts.). Canadian football differs from its American cousin: It's a three-down offense game on a field that's 10 yards longer and wider. Some of the plays you see will have NFL fans leaping out of their seats in surprise. Tickets run C$20 to C$60 (US$16–US$48).

HOCKEY

The National Hockey League's **Vancouver Canucks** play at **General Motors Place** (otherwise known as the Garage), 800 Griffith's Way (✆ **604/899-4600;** event hotline 604/899-7444; www.canucks.com). Tickets are C$28 to C$100 (US$22–US$80).

HORSE RACING

Thoroughbreds run at **Hastings Park Racecourse,** Exhibition Park, East Hastings and Cassiar streets (✆ **604/254-1631;** www.hastingspark.com), from mid-April to October. Post time varies; call ahead or check the website for the latest schedule if you want to place a wager. There is a decent restaurant there, so you can make a full evening or afternoon of dining and racing.

RUNNING

The **Sun Run** in April and the **Vancouver International Marathon** in May attract many runners from around the world (4,411 runners finished the marathon in 2004) and even more spectators. Contact the **Vancouver International Marathon Society,** 1601 Bayshore Dr., in the Westin Bayshore Hotel (✆ **604/872-2928;** www.vanmarathon.bc.ca), or the **Vancouver Sun Run,** 655 Burrard St. (✆ **604/689-9441;** www.sunrun.com), for information.

SOCCER

The American Professional Soccer League's **Vancouver Whitecaps** (✆ **604/899-9283**) play at Swangard Stadium (✆ **604/435-7121;** www.whitecapssoccer.com) in Burnaby. Admission is normally C$15 to C$25 (US$12–US$20).

8

Vancouver Strolls

Down below's Stanley Park. On the side of the trees there's a beach. You can't see it [points over to left]. Steveston's over there. [points to left] Coast Guard station. There's the Yacht Club, and beyond it, the docks. Then over on the other side of the inlet, there's Grouse Mountain. It's about 4,000 feet high. There's a restaurant on top of it. Nice restaurant.

—from the screenplay for *Playback,* by Raymond Chandler

Chandler's detective Philip Marlow was one of Hollywood's most popular creations, but studio executives so hated his set-in-Vancouver screenplay that it never made it into celluloid. That was back in the days before Vancouver came to be called "Hollywood North" because of all the films that are shot here. Chandler's geography in the above excerpt was a bit off, but that's quite understandable because it can be a little difficult to orient yourself in this city surrounded by water. If you have directional problems, just remember that the grid of streets basically runs northwest to southeast rather than straight north-south, and that the mountains (which you can't always see) are north. The best way to get acquainted with this unique city is to explore its various neighborhoods on foot. The tours below provide a good overall introduction.

WALKING TOUR 1   DOWNTOWN & THE WEST END

Start:	The Fairmont Hotel Vancouver.
Finish:	Cathedral Place.
Time:	2 to 3 hours, not including museum, shopping, and eating stops.
Best Time:	Daytime, particularly during the week when the Law Courts building is open.
Worst Time:	Late in the evening when the shops and offices have closed.

Vancouver's West End is said to be the densest residential district west of Manhattan. I don't know if that's true or not, but what I do know is that urban density has never been more beautifully planned or landscaped than in Vancouver. Every Edwardian house and every high-rise residential tower in the West End is surrounded by lush, beautiful plantings of trees, shrubs, and flowers. This appealingly green idea of the urban working *with* nature instead of against it carries over into Vancouver's commercial downtown, where the placement and orientation of buildings has been carefully controlled to preserve view corridors to the mountains and bodies of water that everywhere form a backdrop to the city. Remember to look up as you wander downtown—often as not, you'll be rewarded with a peekaboo view of a North Shore peak.

Walking Tour 1: Downtown & the West End

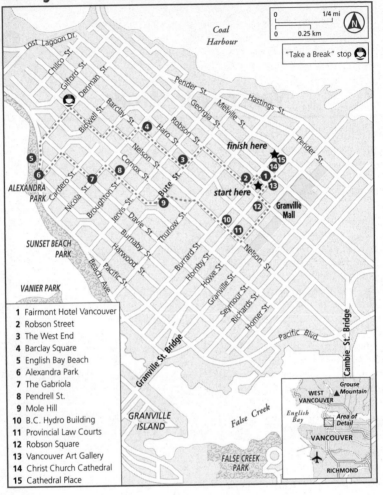

0 — 1/4 mi
0 — 0.25 km

"Take a Break" stop 🍵

Coal Harbour

Lost Lagoon Dr.
Chilco St.
Gifford St.
Denman St.
Pender St.
Georgia St.
Melville St.
Hastings St.
Robson St.
Bidwell St.
Barclay St.
Haro St.
finish here
Pender St.
Nelson St.
Comox St.
Cardero St.
Nicola St.
Broughton St.
Jervis St.
Bute St.
Davie St.
Thurlow St.
start here
Granville Mall
ALEXANDRA PARK
SUNSET BEACH PARK
Burnaby St.
Harwood St.
Pacific St.
Beach Ave.
VANIER PARK
Burrard St.
Hornby St.
Howe St.
Granville St.
Seymour St.
Richards St.
Homer St.
Nelson St.
Granville St. Bridge
GRANVILLE ISLAND
Pacific Blvd.
Cambie St. Bridge
False Creek
FALSE CREEK PARK

1 Fairmont Hotel Vancouver
2 Robson Street
3 The West End
4 Barclay Square
5 English Bay Beach
6 Alexandra Park
7 The Gabriola
8 Pendrell St.
9 Mole Hill
10 B.C. Hydro Building
11 Provincial Law Courts
12 Robson Square
13 Vancouver Art Gallery
14 Christ Church Cathedral
15 Cathedral Place

WEST VANCOUVER
Grouse Mountain
English Bay
Area of Detail
VANCOUVER
RICHMOND

An appropriate place to begin this tour is:
❶ The Fairmont Hotel Vancouver
At 900 W. Georgia St. (℗ **604/684-3131**) and dating to 1939, this hotel is owned by the Canadian Pacific Railway (CPR), just as the city itself was for many, many years. In return for agreeing in 1885 to make Vancouver its western terminus, the CPR was given 2,400 hectares (5,930 acres) of prime real estate—nearly the whole of today's downtown. The Hotel Vancouver is built in the CPR's signature château

style, with a verdigris-green copper roof. It's worth stepping inside to see the grand, old-fashioned ambience of the lobby.

Leaving by the Burrard Street exit, turn left. When you reach the corner, turn right, cross Burrard Street, and you're on:
❷ Robson Street
The shops on this corner get more foot traffic than any others in Canada. Things were different back in the 1950s, when so many German delis and restaurants

opened up that for a time the street was nicknamed "Robsonstrasse." Beginning in the 1980s, the older businesses were replaced with high-end clothiers and new restaurants and gift shops with signs in Japanese. Whether you're into shopping or not, Robson Street is a great place to walk and people-watch. The street has an international cosmopolitan feel to it, and chances are you'll hear Cantonese, Croatian, Japanese, and other tongues as you stroll.

Two blocks farther down Robson at Bute Street, turn left and walk 1 block through a minipark to Barclay Street and you've entered:

❸ The West End

Beginning in about 1959, this down-at-its-heels neighborhood of once-grand Edwardian houses was transformed by the advent of the concrete high-rise. By 1970, most of the Edwardian houses had been replaced by apartment towers, and the West End was on its way to becoming one of the densest—and simultaneously one of the most livable—inner cities on the continent. The minipark at Bute and Barclay is one of the things that makes the neighborhood so successful: Traffic is kept to a minimum on the tree-lined West End streets, so that residents—though they live in the city center—can enjoy a neighborhood almost as quiet as that in a small town. Beautiful landscaping, and plenty of it, adds to the area's appealing allure.

Turn right and walk 3 blocks down Barclay Street to Nicola Street. Along the way you'll see some of the elements that make the West End such a sought-after enclave: the gardens and street trees and the range and variety of buildings—including a few surviving Edwardians, like the Arts and Crafts house at 1351 Barclay, and the pair of houses at the corner of Barclay and Nicola streets, otherwise known as:

❹ Barclay Square

This beautifully preserved bit of 19th-century Vancouver consists of Barclay Manor, built in the Queen Anne style in 1890, and Roedde House, a rare domestic design by British Columbia's leading 19th-century institutional architect, Francis Rattenbury. **Roedde House,** 1415 Barclay St. (© **604/684-7040;** www. roeddehouse.org) is now a museum, open for guided tours Wednesday through Friday at 2pm; C\$4 (US\$3) admission, C\$3 (US\$2.25) seniors, students, and children. Every Sunday, tea is served in the parlor from 2 to 4pm for C\$5 (US\$3.75) per person.

Turn left and walk south down Nicola Street for 1 block—past Fire Station No. 6, then turn right and go 1 block on Nelson, then left again onto Cardero Street, passing by the tiny Cardero Grocery at 1078 Cardero St. All the grocery needs of the West End were once supplied by little corner stores like this one. Turn right and walk 2 blocks on Comox Street to reach Denman Street, the perfect place to:

TAKE A BREAK
If Robson Street is the place Vancouverites go for hyperactive shopping sprees, Denman is where they go to sit back, sip a latte, and watch their fellow citizens stroll past. The **Bread Garden,** 1040 Denman St. (© **604/685-2996**), is a fine spot for coffee and baked goods, particularly if you can nab a table on their outdoor terrace. One block down on the opposite side of the street, **Delany's on Denman,** 1105 Denman St. (© **604/662-3344**), is a favorite man-watching spot for members of the West End's sizable gay community. Straights are more than welcome too, of course, and the pies and cakes at this little cafe are to die for.

When you're ready to continue the walking tour, go 2 blocks farther down Denman Street and you're at:

❺ English Bay Beach

This is the place to be when the sun is setting, or on one of those crystal-clear days when the mountains of Vancouver Island can be seen looming in the distance—or any day at all, really, so long as the sun is shining. Every January 1, shivering Vancouverites in fancy costumes surround the bathhouse here at the very foot of Denman Street (entrance at beach level) to take part in the annual Polar Bear Swim.

Walk southeastward (left, as you're facing the water) on Beach Avenue and you come to a tiny green space with a bandshell known as:

❻ Alexandra Park

Back around the turn of the 20th century, a big Bahamian immigrant named Joe Fortes used to make his home in a cottage near this spot, that is, when he wasn't down on the beach teaching local kids to swim. In recognition of his many years of free service, the city finally appointed Fortes its first lifeguard. Later, a marble water fountain was erected in his memory by the Beach Avenue entrance to the park.

When you're finished looking around the park, head up Bidwell Street 2 blocks to Davie Street, cross the street, turn right, walk 2 blocks farther on Davie Street, and on your left at no. 1531 you'll see:

❼ The Gabriola

This was the finest mansion in the West End when it was built in 1900 for sugar magnate B. T. Rogers. Its name comes from the rough sandstone cladding, quarried on Gabriola Island in the Strait of Georgia. Unfortunately for Rogers, the Shaughnessy neighborhood soon opened up across False Creek, and the West End just wasn't a place a millionaire could afford to be seen anymore. By 1925, the mansion had been sold off and subdivided into apartments. Since 1975, it's been a restaurant of one sort or another—currently Romano's Macaroni Grill (reviewed in chapter 6). The wrought-iron tables in the garden are nice spots to sit on a summer day.

Cut through the garden and walk up through the Nicola Street minipark, turning right on:

❽ Pendrell Street

A few interesting bits of architecture reside on this street. One block farther on, at the corner of Broughton Street, is the Thomas Fee house (1119 Broughton St.),

where one of the city's leading turn-of-the-20th-century developer-architects made his home. Farther along, at the southeast corner of Pendrell and Jervis streets, is St. Paul's Episcopal Church, a 1905 Gothic Revival church built entirely of wood. One block farther along at 1254 Pendrell is the Pendrellis—a piece of architecture so unbelievably awful, one gets a perverse delight just looking at it. Built as a seniors' home at the height of the 1970s craze for concrete, the multi-story tower is one great concrete block, with nary a window in sight.

At Bute Street, turn left and walk 1 block to Comox Street, and you're at:

❾ Mole Hill

These 11 preserved Edwardian homes provide a rare view of what the West End looked like in, say, 1925. That they exist at all is more or less a fluke. The city bought the buildings in the 1970s but continued renting them out, thinking one day to tear them down for a park. By the 1990s, however, heritage had become important. The residents of the houses waged a sophisticated political campaign, renaming the area Mole Hill and bringing in nationally known architectural experts to plead the case for preservation. The city soon gave in.

Cut across the park to Nelson Street and continue down Nelson Street past Thurlow Street to 970 Burrard St., where stands:

❿ The B.C. Hydro Building

Built in 1958 by architect Ned Pratt, it was one of the first modernist structures erected in Canada, and has since become a beloved Vancouver landmark, thanks in no small part to its elegant shape and attention to detail. Note how the windows, the doors, even the tiles in the lobby and forecourt echo the six-sided lozenge shape of the original structure. In the mid-90s, the building was converted to condominiums and rechristened The Electra.

From here, continue on Nelson Street, crossing
Burrard Street and Hornby Street to:

⓫ The Provincial Law Courts

Internationally recognized architect
Arthur Erickson has had an undeniable
impact on his native city of Vancouver.
His 1973 Law Courts complex covers 3
full city blocks, including the Erickson-
renovated Vancouver Art Gallery at its
north end. Linking the two is Robson
Square, which Erickson—and everyone
else—envisioned as the city's main civic
plaza. As with so many Erickson designs,
this one has elements of brilliance—the
boldness of the vision itself, the tiered
fountains (behind them are the offices of
the Crown Attorney—the Canadian
equivalent of a district attorney), the
cathedral-like space of the courthouse
atrium—but, raised above street level, the
entire ensemble is removed from all the
life around it. To reach the courthouse,
take the concrete stairway up and follow
the elevated pedestrian concourse. The
courthouse, with its giant glass-covered
atrium, is worth a visit.

When you've seen the Law Courts, backtrack
along the concourse, and you'll end up at:

⓬ Robson Square

As a civic plaza, Robson Square should be
grand, but in fact it's pretty underwhelm-
ing. Its basic problem is that it has been
sunk 6m (20 ft.) below street grade, so it's
never exactly appealing or inviting to
passersby. Although there's a pleasant cafe
in the square, a UBC bookstore, and an
outdoor ice rink in the wintertime, Robson square lacks the throngs of people
that add the essential ingredient—life—
to a civic plaza. But just look across the
street and you'll see all the life that Robson Square lacks.

Directly across from Robson Square at 750
Hornby St. is the:

⓭ Vancouver Art Gallery

On sunny days, people bask like seals on
the steps of the old courthouse-turned-
art-gallery, a great gathering place and the

perfect spot to see jugglers and buskers,
pick up a game of outdoor speed chess, or
listen to an activist haranguing the world
at large about the topic du jour.

Designed as a courthouse by Francis
Rattenbury, and renovated into an art
gallery by Arthur Erickson, the Vancouver Art Gallery (p. 119) is home to a
tremendous collection of works by iconic
West Coast painter Emily Carr, as well as
rotating exhibits ranging from Native
masks to video installations. Film buffs
may remember the entrance steps and
inside lobby from the movie *The Accused.*

To continue the tour, go around the
gallery and proceed down Hornby Street.
Note the fountain on the Art Gallery's
front lawn. It was installed by a very
unpopular provincial government as a
way—according to some—of forever
blocking protesters from gathering on
what was then the courthouse lawn.
Cross Georgia Street and have a glance
inside the Hong Kong Bank building
(885 W. Georgia St.) at the massive pen-
dulum designed by artist Alan Storey:
The lobby doubles as an art gallery and
frequently hosts interesting exhibits.

Cross Hornby and continue west on Georgia
Street to 690 Burrard, where stands:

⓮ Christ Church Cathedral

A Gothic Revival sandstone church with
a steep gabled roof, buttresses, and arched
stained-glass windows, the Anglican
Christ Church Cathedral was completed
in 1895. It was nearly demolished in the
1930s, when developers offered a lot of
money to the church for the land. A local
reporter uncovered the clergy's plot to
raze the landmark in exchange for a big
profit, and publicized it while negotiations were in the final stages. The public
outcry marked the first shift in local sen-
timent toward the preservation of heritage sites.

Backtrack east to Hornby, turn left, walk half a
block, and climb the few steps into:

⑮ Cathedral Place

Often overlooked by Vancouverites, peaceful Cathedral Place is a charming example of an urban park. The building behind it, at 639 Hornby, is a postmodern structure with small Art Deco parts melded onto a basically Gothic edifice. Some of the panels on its front were salvaged from the Georgia Medical-Dental building, a much-loved skyscraper that used to stand on this site. As for the Cathedral place courtyard itself, it has the formality and calm of a formal French garden, the perfect spot to sit and enjoy a bit of peace.

WALKING TOUR 2   GASTOWN & CHINATOWN

Start:	Canada Place.
Finish:	Maple Tree Square.
Time:	2 to 4 hours, not including shopping, eating, and sightseeing stops.
Best Time:	Any day during business hours, but Chinatown is particularly active in the mornings. If you arrive between noon and 2pm, you can enjoy dim sum at many of the restaurants.
Worst Time:	Chinatown's dead after 6pm, except on weekends in the summer, when they close a few streets to traffic and hold a traditional Asian night market from 6:30 to 11pm.

Chinatown and Gastown are two of Vancouver's most fascinating neighborhoods. Gastown has history and the kind of old-fashioned architecture that no longer exists downtown or in the West End. Chinatown has brightly colored facades, street markets, and the buzz of modern-day Cantonese commerce. One small travel advisory, however: The two neighborhoods border on Vancouver's Downtown Eastside, a Skid Row area troubled by alcoholism and drug use. While there's actually little danger for outsiders, there is a good chance you'll cross paths with a down-and-outer here and there, particularly around Pigeon Park at the corner of Carrall and Hastings streets. The tour route has been designed to avoid these areas.

Begin the tour at:

❶ Canada Place

With its five tall Teflon sails and bowsprit jutting out into Burrard Inlet, Canada Place is meant to resemble a giant sailing ship. Inside it's a giant hotel, giant cruise-ship terminal, and giant convention center. Around the perimeter there's a promenade with plaques at regular intervals explaining the sights or providing historical tidbits. During the summer months this area is jammed with tourists and passengers arriving and departing from Alaskan cruises; the rest of the year you'll have it pretty much to yourself.

To follow the promenade, start by the fountain flying the flags of Canada's provinces and territories and head north along the walkway. On the roof at the far end of the pier a pair of leaping bronze lions point up and out toward a pair of peaks on the North Shore called the Lions (supposedly for their resemblance to the Landseer Lions in Trafalgar Square, but mostly because the local morality squad wanted to eliminate forever the name given the peaks by the rough-minded early settlers—Sheila's Paps). Continue around the promenade and you'll turn and look back towards the city: The line of low-rise older buildings just beyond the railway tracks is Gastown.

Walking Tour 2: Gastown & Chinatown

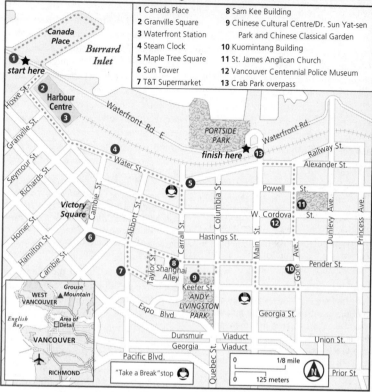

1 Canada Place
2 Granville Square
3 Waterfront Station
4 Steam Clock
5 Maple Tree Square
6 Sun Tower
7 T&T Supermarket
8 Sam Kee Building
9 Chinese Cultural Centre/Dr. Sun Yat-sen Park and Chinese Classical Garden
10 Kuomintang Building
11 St. James Anglican Church
12 Vancouver Centennial Police Museum
13 Crab Park overpass

"Take a Break" stop

To continue the tour, walk back toward shore along the promenade, go down the steps, turn left, and curve along the sidewalk until you pass the Aqua Riva restaurant. Then turn left and go up the steps to an elevated plaza. You're now at:

❷ Granville Square

Had some forward-looking politicians and developers had their way, all of Gastown and Chinatown would have been replaced by towers like the one you see here at 200 Granville. In 1970, the plans were drawn up and the bulldozers were set to move when a coalition of hippies, heritage lovers, and Chinatown merchants took to the barricades in revolt. This undistinguished building was the only one ever built, and the plan was abandoned soon afterwards.

At the east end of the plaza a doorway leads into:

❸ Waterfront Station

Though this Beaux Arts edifice at 601 W. Cordova St. was converted to the SeaBus terminal in the 1970s (SkyTrain was added in 1986), the building was originally the CPR's Vancouver passenger-rail terminal. Look up high on the walls and you'll see oil paintings depicting scenes you might encounter if you took the train across Canada (much easier then than now). On the main floor there's a Starbucks and some tourist shops. This is also where you can catch the SeaBus over to Lonsdale Quay in North Vancouver.

Leave by the front doors, turn left, and proceed to cobblestoned Water Street, Gastown's main thoroughfare. **The Landing,** at 375 Water St., is home to some high-end retail stores and offices. Like most of Gastown's buildings, the Landing was built in the boom years between the Great Fire of 1886 and World War I. Klondike gold fueled much of the construction. As you walk along, note the **Magasin Building** at 322 Water St. Each of the column capitals bears the bronze head of a Gastown notable, among them Ray Saunders, the man who designed the:

❹ Steam Clock

A quirky urban timepiece, the Steam Clock at Water and Cambie streets gives a steamy rendition of the Westminster Chimes every 15 minutes, drawing its power from the city's underground steam-heat system. A plaque on the base of the clock explains the mechanics of it all.

Continue down Water Street, past Hills Indian Crafts (165 Water St.), where Bill Clinton picked up a little bear statuette as a gift for you-know-who. At Abbot Street, cross over to the south side and continue on Water Street until you come to the Gaoler's Mews building (12 Water St.). Duck in through the passageway and:

TAKE A BREAK
The name **Gaoler's Mews** refers to Vancouver's very first jail, which was built on this site. When that burned to the ground in the 1886 fire, the jail was replaced by a fire hall. The current structure was built as a parking garage but was renovated in the 1970s into a remarkably pleasant complex joined to a common courtyard/atrium. You can check your e-mails and have a coffee at the **Internet Café** or enjoy excellent beer and good food at the **Irish Heather**, 217 Carrall St. (© 604/688-9779), accessible either via its back solarium—facing onto the mews—or by going out through the far passageway onto Carrall Street. You have to go this way eventually in order to reach:

❺ Maple Tree Square

A historic spot, Maple Tree Square is where Vancouver first began. The statue by the maple tree (not the original tree, but a

replacement planted in the same spot) is of Gassy Jack Deighton, a riverboat captain and innkeeper who erected Vancouver's first significant structure—a saloon—in 1867. Deighton got the nickname Gassy because of his windy propensity to jaw on at length (gassing, as it was known) about whatever topic happened to spring to mind. In 1870, when the town was officially incorporated as Granville, it was home to exactly six businesses: a hotel, two stores, and three saloons. Most folks called it Gastown, after Jack.

Continue south on Carrall Street to W. Cordova, turn right, and walk 1 block to Abbot Street. Turn left and walk 2 blocks down Abbot, crossing W. Hastings Street and stopping at W. Pender Street, where you get a great view of the:

❻ Sun Tower

At 500 Beatty St., it was the tallest building in the British Empire when it was built in 1911 to house the publishing empire of Louis D. Taylor, publisher of *Vancouver World*. Not only was the building tall, it was also slightly scandalous, thanks to the nine half-nude caryatids that gracefully support the cornice halfway up the building. Three years after the building opened, Louis D. was forced to sell it.

Cross W. Pender Street and continue on Abbot Street until you come to the entrance at 179 Keefer Place of:

❼ T&T Supermarket

So you've seen supermarkets? Unless your hometown is Hong Kong or Singapore, you haven't seen one like this. Just have a gander at the seafood display inside the doors: king crab, scallops, three different kinds of oysters, lobster, and geoducks. Farther in is a host of other wondrous products, including strange Asian fruits like rambutan, lychee, and the pungent durian. Browse, maybe pick up something you don't recognize, and have an impromptu picnic in nearby Andy Livingstone Park.

Outside, walk 1 block east on Keefer Street to Taylor Street. Andy Livingstone Park is farther ahead to your right, but to continue the tour turn left on Taylor Street and walk 1 block north to Pender Street. Turn right on Pender and walk 1 block. Now you're in one of North America's most populous Chinatowns. Our first Chinatown stop, at 8 W. Pender St., is the:

❽ Sam Kee Building

The world's thinnest office building—just shy of 1.5m deep (4 ft. 11 in. to be exact)—was Sam Kee's way of thumbing his nose at both the city and his greedy next-door neighbor. In 1912, the city expropriated most of Kee's land in order to widen Pender Street but refused to compensate him for the tiny leftover strip. Kee's neighbor, meanwhile, hoped to pick up the leftover sliver dirt-cheap. The building was Kee's response. Huge bay windows helped maximize the available space, as did the extension of the basement well out underneath the sidewalk (note the glass blocks in the pavement).

Just behind the Sam Kee Building is the forlorn-looking **Shanghai Alley,** which just 40 years ago was jam-packed with stores, restaurants, a pawnshop, a theater, rooming houses, and a public bath. (**Canton Alley,** on your right between E. Pender and E. Hastings sts., still gives an idea of what these teeming alleyways looked like a few decades ago, but it's now an unsavory hangout for drug users.) More interesting is the **Chinese Freemason's building,** just across the street at 1 W. Pender. The building could be a metaphor for the Chinese experience in Canada. On predominantly Anglo Carrall Street, the building is the picture of Victorian conformity. On the Pender Street side, on the other hand, the structure is exuberantly Chinese.

Walk 1 block farther (east) on Pender Street and you'll come to the:

❾ Chinese Cultural Centre/Dr. Sun Yat-sen Park & Chinese Classical Garden

A modern building with an impressive traditional gate, the cultural center provides services and programs for the neighborhood's thousands of Chinese-speaking residents. Straight ahead as you enter the courtyard, a door set within a wall leads into the **Dr. Sun Yat-sen Park,** a small urban park with a pond, walkways, and a nice gift shop, **Silk Road Art Trading Co.** (561 Columbia St.; ☎ **604/683-8707**), which sells scaled-down replicas of the ancient terra-cotta warriors unearthed in the tomb of Chinese Emperor Qon Shi Huang. Admission to the park is free.

Adjoining the park, and accessible through another small doorway to the right of it, is the **Dr. Sun Yat-sen Classical Chinese Garden** (p. 119). Modeled after a Ming Period (1368–1644) scholar's retreat in the Chinese city of Suzhou, this garden is definitely worth a visit. Dr. Sun Yat-sen (1866–1925), for whom the park and garden are named, is known as the father of modern China.

Exit the Chinese Classical Garden by the gate on the east side, turn left on Columbia Street, and you'll find the **Chinese Cultural Centre Museum and Archives** at 555 Columbia St.

From here, continue on Columbia Street up to Pender, turn right and continue east, peeking in here and there to explore Chinese herbalist shops like Vitality Enterprises at 126 E. Pender. At Main Street, turn right and walk south 1 block to Keefer Street and:

TAKE A BREAK
Though it's Canada's largest Chinese restaurant, **Floata Seafood Restaurant,** 180 Keefer St. (☎ **604/602-0368**), isn't easy to find. In classic Hong Kong restaurant style, it's on the third floor of a bright red shopping plaza/parking garage. Time your arrival for mid-morning dim sum (a kind of moving Chinese smorgasbord) if you can. Alternatively, you might want to check out the recommended Chinatown restaurants in chapter 6.

To continue the tour, stroll east on Keefer Street, lined with sidewalk markets selling fresh fish, fruit, and vegetables. Turn left on Gore Street and walk 1 block north to Pender Street. On your left, at 296 E. Pender St., is the:

⑩ Kuomintang Building

Though often a mystery to outsiders, politics was and remains an important part of life in Chinatown. Vancouver was long a stronghold of the Chinese Nationalist Party or Kuomintang (KMT), whose founder, Dr. Sun Yat-sen, stayed in Vancouver for a time raising funds. In 1920, the party erected this building to serve as its Western Canadian headquarters. When the rival Chinese Communist party emerged victorious from the Chinese civil war in 1949, KMT leader Chiang Kai-shek retreated to Taiwan. Note the Taiwanese flags on the roof.

Return to Gore Street and turn left (north) for 2 blocks. At the corner of Gore and Cordova streets (303 E. Cordova St.) stands:

⑪ St. James Anglican Church

Just before getting this commission, architect Adrian Gilbert Scott had designed a cathedral in Cairo—and it shows.

One block west on Cordova brings you to the:

⑫ Vancouver Centennial Police Museum

Located in the former Coroner's Court at 240 E. Cordova, the **Vancouver**

Centennial Police Museum (p. 120) is worth a visit if you're in a macabre mood. Among other displays, the museum has the autopsy pictures of Errol Flynn, who died in Vancouver in 1959 in the arms of his 17-year-old girlfriend.

Back on Gore Street, walk north 2 blocks to Alexander Street. Turn left and walk 1 block west on Alexander to the:

⑬ Crab Park Overpass

City Hall calls it Portside Park, and that's how it appears on the map, but to everyone else it's Crab Park. It was created after long and vigorous lobbying by eastside activists, who reasoned that poor downtown residents had as much right to beach access as anyone else. The park is pleasant enough, though not worth the trouble of walking all the way up and over the overpass. What is worthwhile, however, is walking halfway up to where two stone Chinese lions stand guard. From here, you can look back at Canada Place—where the tour started—or at the container port and fish plant to your right.

To bring the tour to an end, return to Alexander Street and walk 2 blocks west back to Maple Tree Square (stop 5).

| WALKING TOUR 3 | YALETOWN, GRANVILLE ISLAND & KITSILANO |

Start:	The Vancouver Public Library Central Branch at Horner and Georgia streets.
Finish:	The Capers Building, 285 W. 4th Ave. (at Vine), in Kitsilano.
Time:	2 to 4 hours, not including shopping, eating, and sightseeing stops.
Best Time:	Any time during business hours.
Worst Time:	After 6pm, when Granville Island's shops have closed.

This tour takes you through three of Vancouver's most interesting neighborhoods: the trendy warehouse-turned-retail district of Yaletown, the industrial-area-turned-public-market called Granville Island, and the laid-back enclave of Kitsilano. The tour includes a brief ferry ride and a stroll along the waterfront and beach.

We begin at:

❶ Vancouver Public Library

Designed by architect Moshe Safdie, the library (350 W. Georgia St.; ✆ **604/331-3600**) was enormously controversial when it opened in 1995. Though Safdie denied that the ancient Roman coliseum served as inspiration, the coliseum is exactly what comes to mind when you first see the exterior of this postmodern building. Architectural critics pooh-poohed it as derivative and ignorant of West Coast architectural traditions, but for the public it was love at first sight. The steps out front have become a popular public gathering place, the lofty atrium inside a favored hangout spot and "study-date" locale. Go inside the atrium and then into the high-tech library itself: It's light, airy, and wonderfully accessible.

From the library, walk south down Homer Street and turn left on Nelson Street. At Hamilton Street you're in:

❷ Yaletown

Vancouver's former meat-packing warehouse district, Yaletown was where roughneck miners from Yale (up the Fraser Valley) used to come to drink and brawl. The city considered leveling the area in the 1970s until someone noticed that the raised loading docks would make great outdoor terraces and the low brick buildings themselves could be renovated into commercial space. Though it's taken 20 years for the neighborhood to really catch on, the result is a funky upscale district of furniture shops, restaurants, multimedia companies, and "New York–style" lofts. Hamilton Street and Mainland Street are the trendiest arteries in Yaletown. Note the metal canopies over the loading docks on many buildings—they used to keep shipping goods dry; now they do the same for tourists and latte-sipping Web programmers. Walk down Mainland and turn left at Davie.

Continue southeast down Davie Street, turn right on Pacific Boulevard, and across the street you'll see:

❸ The Roundhouse

The Roundhouse is so named because that's exactly what this brick and timber frame building was, back when this land was the CPR's switching yard. The structure has since been converted into a community center. It's worth ducking inside to have a look at the locomotive that pulled the first passenger train into Vancouver, way back in 1887; you can also see the locomotive from the street, through a giant glass window.

Follow Davie Street south to the False Creek waterfront and the:

❹ Yaletown Landing (at the Foot of Davie St.)

The small forest of high-rises ringing the north shore of False Creek, where you're now standing, is the creation of one company—Concorde Pacific, owned by Hong Kong billionaire Li Ka Shing. Formerly a railway switching yard, the area was transformed for the Expo '86 World's Fair. When the fair came to an end, the provincial government sold the land to Li Ka Shing for a song on the understanding he would build condominiums. And did he ever. The towers have been rising at the rate of three or four a year ever since.

At the landing site, note the large art piece, *Street Light,* designed by Bernie Miller and Alan Tregebov and installed in 1997. The large panels, each of which depicts a seminal event in False Creek's history, have been arranged so that on the anniversary of that event, the sun will shine directly through the panel, casting a shadowed image on the street.

From here, at the end of the dock, catch the **Aquabus miniferry** (✆ **604/689-5858**) for Granville Island, right across False Creek. The little boats leave about every 15 minutes through the day; the fare is C$3 (US$2.25) for adults.

The Aquabus will scoot you across False Creek harbor in about 5 minutes and let you off at:

⑤ Granville Island Aquabus Ferry Dock

To be topographically honest, Granville Island is not really an island; it's more of a protuberance. But it contains a fascinating collection of shops and restaurants, theaters, a hotel, artists' workshops, housing, and still-functioning heavy industry—one of the few successful examples of 1970s urban renewal. The **Granville Island Information Centre,** 1592 Johnston St. (© **604/666-5784**), near the Public Market, has excellent free maps, but they're not really necessary—the place is so compact, the best thing to do is simply wander and explore.

Right at the top of the Aquabus dock there's an entrance into the:

⑥ Granville Island Public Market

This is an amazing place and sells just about anything and everything that's edible. The market is a wonderful place to stop and:

TAKE A BREAK
If it's edible, the **Granville Island Public Market** probably has it, from chocolate to fresh salmon to fresh bread to marinated mushrooms to strawberries picked that morning out in the Fraser Valley. Those with an immediate hunger gravitate to the far side of the market, where **A La Mode** (© **604/685-8335**) sells lattes and fabulous rhubarb-strawberry pie. The most fun way to feed yourself, however, is to roam the market stalls for sandwiches, sausages, or picnic supplies—artichoke hearts, Danish cheese, cold smoked salmon, Indian candy, pepper pâté, freshly baked bread—then head outside for an alfresco feast at one of the tables on the dock overlooking False Creek. The views are great, the fresh air invigorating, and, if you've brought small children along, it's the perfect place to play that endlessly fascinating (to kids) game of Catch the Seagull.

From Triangle Square, the small plaza in front of the public market, head south (left) on Duranleau Street, where you'll pass enticing shops and marine charter services. At Anderson Street turn right and right again on waterside Island Park Walk, following it north to the:

⑦ Government Fish Dock

Want to buy fresh from the boat? This is the place to do it. Find fresh salmon in season (summer and early fall), prawns, scallops, and other shellfish much of the rest of the year. Sales take place every day in high season and on weekend mornings the rest of the year. Hours and availability, of course, depend on the catch.

Continue on the seaside walkway, and eventually you pass beneath the:

⑧ Burrard Bridge

In 1927, the city fathers commissioned noted urban planner Harland Bartholomew to provide some guidance on how to expand their rather raw seaport city. One of Bartholomew's first injunctions: Build beautiful bridges! The Burrard Bridge is the result, an elegant steel span with two castles guarding the approaches at either end.

Walk beneath the bridge and continue along the waterside pedestrian path in Vanier Park to:

⑨ Heritage Harbour

Many older wooden boats find shelter here, including the seiner BCP45 shown on the back of the old Canadian $5 bill. Those interested in a shortcut can pick up a ferry **(False Creek Ferries;** © **604/684-7781)** at this point and ride back to Granville Island (stop 5). On weekdays and in the off season, the ferries run less frequently. Hours and fares are posted on the sign at the end of the dock.

If you're continuing the walk, proceed west along the shoreline. To your left stands artist Chung Hung's massive iron sculpture *Gate to the Northwest Passage.* Just beyond that, the conical building is the **Vancouver Museum,** 1100 Chestnut St. (© **604/736-4431;** p. 125) and **H.R. MacMillan Space Centre** (© **604/738-STAR;** p. 123). The

Walking Tour 3: Yaletown, Granville Island & Kitsilano

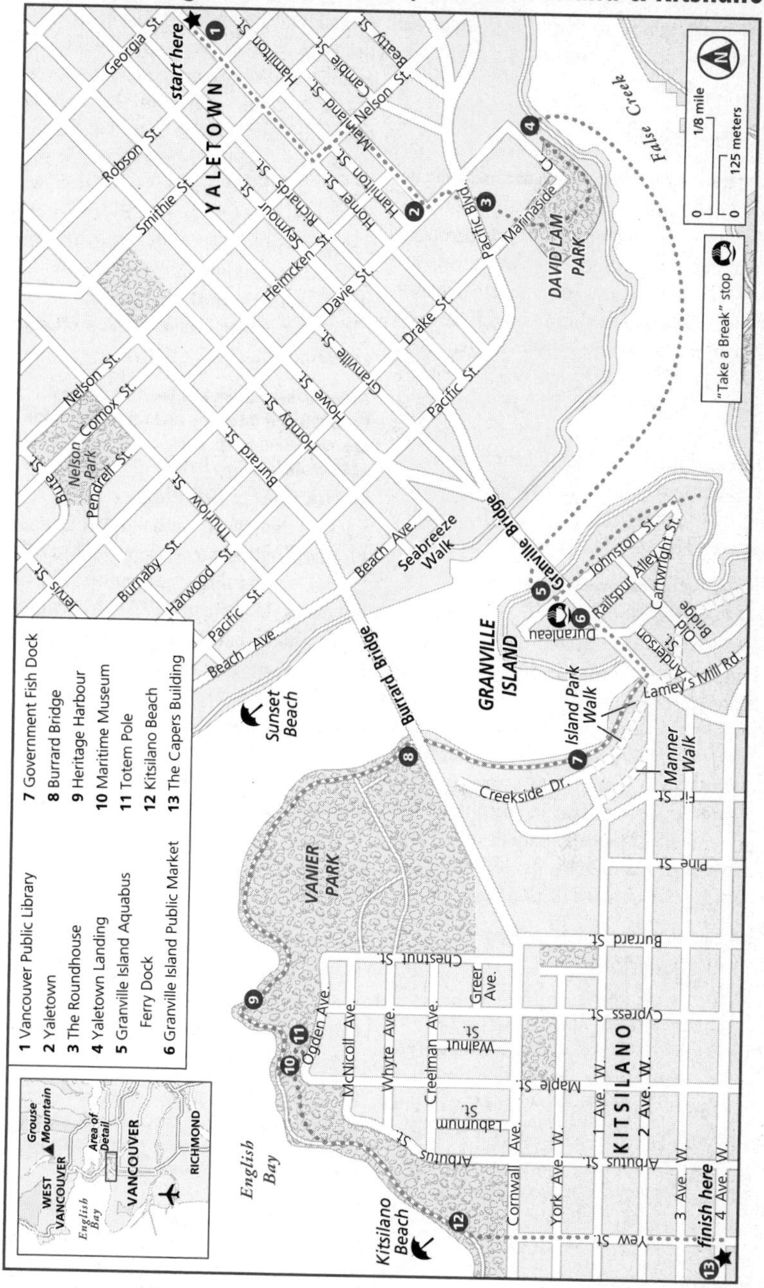
1 Vancouver Public Library
2 Yaletown
3 The Roundhouse
4 Yaletown Landing
5 Granville Island Aquabus Ferry Dock
6 Granville Island Public Market
7 Government Fish Dock
8 Burrard Bridge
9 Heritage Harbour
10 Maritime Museum
11 Totem Pole
12 Kitsilano Beach
13 The Capers Building
"Take a Break" stop
0 1/8 mile
0 125 meters
start here
finish here
YALETOWN
GRANVILLE ISLAND
KITSILANO
VANIER PARK
DAVID LAM PARK
Nelson Park
False Creek
English Bay
Sunset Beach
Kitsilano Beach
Burrard Bridge
Granville Bridge
Old Bridge
Georgia St.
Robson St.
Smithie St.
Nelson St.
Comox St.
Pendrell St.
Hamilton St.
Cambie St.
Beatty St.
Mainland St.
Homer St.
Richards St.
Seymour St.
Heimcken St.
Davie St.
Drake St.
Granville St.
Howe St.
Hornby St.
Burrard St.
Thurlow St.
Bute St.
Jervis St.
Burnaby St.
Harwood St.
Pacific St.
Beach Ave.
Seabreeze Walk
Pacific Blvd.
Marinaside Cr.
Johnston St.
Railspur Alley
Cartwright St.
Duranleau
Anderson St.
Lamey's Mill Rd.
Island Park Walk
Manner Walk
Creekside Dr.
Fir St.
Pine St.
Chestnut St.
Greer Ave.
Cypress St.
Ogden Ave.
McNicoll Ave.
Whyte Ave.
Creelman Ave.
Walnut St.
Maple St.
Laburnum St.
Arbutus St.
Cornwall Ave.
York Ave. W.
1 Ave. W.
2 Ave. W.
3 Ave. W.
4 Ave. W.
Yew St.
WEST VANCOUVER
Grouse Mountain
Area of Detail
VANCOUVER
RICHMOND

low building next to that is the **Vancouver Archives,** 1150 Chestnut (© **604/736-8561**), home to some truly fascinating panoramic photographs of Vancouver back in the early days.

Continue on the waterside path until you come to:

❿ Maritime Museum

For centuries, the quest of every European explorer was to find the Northwest Passage, the seagoing shortcut to the riches of the East. The little ship housed inside the Maritime Museum, 1905 Ogden Ave. (© **604/257-8300**) is the one that finally did it. Tours of the RCMP vessel, the *St. Roch,* are available at regular intervals through the day (p. 124). Out back of the museum, the junk on the lawn by the north side all comes from various ships wrecked on the B.C. coast.

In front of the museum you'll see the:

⓫ Totem Pole

Carved by the exceptional Kwakiutl carver Mungo Martin (who also did many of the poles displayed in the Museum of Anthropology and in Stanley Park), the 10 figures on this 30m (98-ft.) tall pole each represent an ancestor of the 10 Kwakiutl clans. An identical pole was presented to Queen Elizabeth in 1958 to mark B.C.'s centenary. It now stands in Windsor Great Park in England.

Continue on the waterside pathway to:

⓬ Kitsilano Beach

Vancouver is blessed with beaches. From here, they stretch almost unbroken to the University of British Columbia, 10km (6¼ miles) west on the tip of the Point Grey peninsula. Each beach has its own distinct personality. Below UBC, Wreck Beach is a semi-wild strand for nudists and nature lovers. Beaches in between cater to dogs,

picnicking families, and hikers. Kitsilano Beach (Kits Beach for short) is home to a spandex-and-testosterone set that loves a fast and furious game on the volleyball courts. But relaxers love Kits, too. The logs lined up on the beach make it a fine place to lay out a blanket and laze the day away. Small children love to play on the nearby swings, while older kids favor the life-guarded swimming area or the world's largest outdoor saltwater swimming pool. On a clear day, the views of the mountains are tremendous.

About midway down Kits Beach, a sidewalk veers left and takes you up to Yew Street. Follow Yew uphill to 4th Avenue and turn right. At 2285 W. 4th Ave. you'll find:

⓭ The Capers Building

Back in the 1960s, Kitsilano was Canada's Hippie Central, a Haight-Ashbury-like enclave of head shops, communes, and cof-feehouses. In the early 1970s, Vancouver's super-square mayor, Tom Campbell, went so far as to propose rounding up all the tie-dyed long-hairs and shipping them off to a detention center. As the years passed, the hippies' waistlines and wallets got thicker, run-down communes and boarding houses were renovated or replaced with new apartments and condos, and the shops came to reflect Kitsilano's new affluence, though still with a touch of counterculture.

The retail/office/apartment building at 2285 W. 4th Ave. was built according to an innovative energy-efficient design and now serves as home to an excellent book-store called **Duthie's,** and to **Capers,** an organic supermarket.

The walk ends here. You may want to explore the shopping opportunities along 4th Avenue. Or, you can catch a no. 4 or 7 bus to take you back to downtown Vancouver.

9

Vancouver Shopping

Blessed with a climate that seems semi-tropical in comparison to the rest of Canada, Vancouverites never really developed a taste for indoor malls. Instead, most residents shop on the street. Below are a few thoughts on where to start exploring.

1 The Shopping Scene

Outside of malls, stores in Vancouver are generally open Monday through Saturday from 9am to 6pm. A few exceptions: Stores on Robson Street stay open later (usually until 9pm), while stores in Kitsilano open later (around 10am). On Sunday most stores are open 11am to 6pm, but a few remain closed all day. Malls such as the Pacific Centre are open from 9am to 7pm Monday through Wednesday, 9am to 9pm Thursday through Saturday, and 10am to 6pm on Sunday. Come Christmas shopping season, stores extend their hours from 9am to 9pm 7 days a week.

ROBSON STREET   It's been said that the corner of Robson and Burrard gets more foot traffic than any other corner in Canada. Urban myth? Who knows. Anyway, it's a busy, colorful parade of humanity, many individuals from Asia (hence the sushi bars and shops with Japanese signs), most with money. Over the past few years rents have risen so much that Robson Street now mostly offers upscale chain shops and international designer boutiques, though here and there a few local stores survive. Look for high-end fashions, with a focus on young designer fashions. See Walking Tour 1 in chapter 8.

SOUTH GRANVILLE   The 10-block stretch of Granville Street—from 6th Avenue up to 16th Avenue—is where Vancouver's old-money enclave of Shaughnessy comes to shop. Classic and expensive men's and women's clothiers and housewares and furniture boutiques predominate. This area is also the heart of the city's gallery district.

WATER STREET   Though a little too heavy on the souvenir shops, Water Street and Gastown are by no means just a tacky tourist enclave. Look for antique and cutting-edge furniture, galleries of First Nations art, and funky basement retro shops. See Walking Tour 2 in chapter 8.

MAIN STREET   Antiques, and lots of 'em. From about 19th up to 27th, Main Street is chockablock with antiques shops. Rather than outbid each other, the stores have evolved so that each covers a particular niche, from Art Deco to country kitchen to fine Second Empire. It's a fun place to browse, and if your eyes start to glaze over at the thought of yet another divan, the area also has cafes, bookshops, and clothing stores.

GRANVILLE ISLAND   A rehabilitated industrial site beneath the Granville Street Bridge, the Public Market is one of the best places to pick up salmon and other seafood. It's also a great place to browse for crafts and gifts. Particularly interesting is

Kids Market, a kind of mini-mall for children, complete with a Lilliputian entrance-way; toy, craft, and book stores; and play areas and services for the not-yet-10 demographic. See Walking Tour 3 in chapter 8.

ASIA WEST   If you've never been to Hong Kong, or are just itching to get back, this new commercial area on Richmond's No. 3 Road between Capstan and Alderbridge roads is the place to shop. Stores in four new malls—the Yaohan Centre, President Plaza, Aberdeen Centre, and Parker Place—cater to Vancouver's newly arrived Asian community by bringing in goods direct from Asia. If the prices seem a bit high, a simple inquiry is often enough to bring them plummeting down as much as 80%.

PUNJABI MARKET   Just like an imported India, the 4 blocks of Main Street, on either side of 49th Avenue, contain the whole of the subcontinent, shrunk down to a manageable parcel. Look for fragrant spice stalls and sari shops and textile outlets selling luxurious fabrics—at bargain-basement prices.

2 Shopping A to Z

ANTIQUES
Bakers Dozen Antiques   This charming shop specializes in antique toys, model ships and boats, folk art, and unusual 19th- and early-20th-century furniture. 3520 Main St. ℂ 604/879-3348.

Mihrab *(Finds*   Part museum, part subcontinental yard sale, Mihrab specializes in one-of-a-kind Indian antiques for the house and garden. Think intricately carved teak archways or tiny jewel-like door pulls, all selected by partners Lou Johnson and Kerry Lane on frequent trips to the subcontinent. 2229 Granville St. ℂ 604/879-6105. www.mihrab antiques.com.

Uno Langmann Limited   Catering to upscale shoppers, Uno Langmann specializes in European and North American paintings, furniture, silver, and objets d'art from the 18th through early 20th centuries. 2117 Granville St. ℂ 604/736-8825. www.langmann.com.

Vancouver Antique Centre   Housed in a heritage commercial building, this maze contains 15 separate shops on two levels, specializing in everything from china, glass, and jewelry to military objects, sports, toys, retro, '50s and '60s collectibles, home furnishings, and watches. There are even more shops in the neighboring buildings. 422 Richards St. ℂ 604/669-7444.

BOOKS
Blackberry Books   Although this small Granville Island store tends toward general interest, they have a healthy selection of books about art, architecture, and cuisine. They're right across from the public market. 1663 Duranleau St. ℂ 604/685-4113 or 604/685-6188. www.bbooks.ca.

Chapters   Chapters chain bookstores are pleasant and well planned, with little nooks, comfy benches, and a huge stock of titles. It's like the Borders of Canada. 788 Robson St. ℂ 604/682-4066. www.chapters.ca. Also at 2505 Granville St. (ℂ 604/731-7822).

Duthie Books 4th Ave.   This well-known local bookstore on Granville Island, in business since 1957, is a good place to find local authors and stocks an excellent inventory of Canadian and international titles. 2239 W. 4th Ave., Kitsilano. ℂ 604/732-5344. www. duthiebooks.com.

International Travel Maps and Books (Finds)   This store has the best selection of travel books, maps, charts, and globes in town, plus an impressive selection of special-interest British Columbia guides. This is the hiker's best source for detailed topographic charts of the entire province. 539 West Pender St. © 604/687-3320. Also at 530 W. Broadway (© 604/879-3621). www.itmb.com.

Kidsbooks (Kids)   The largest and most interesting selection of children's literature in the city also has an amazing collection of puppets and has regular readings. 3083 W. Broadway. © 604/738-5335. Also 3040 Edgemont Blvd., North Vancouver (© 604/986-6190). www.kidsbooks.ca.

CAMERAS

Dunne & Rundle foto source   Dunne & Rundle is conveniently located downtown and can handle repairs for most major brands and sells parts, accessories, and film. 891 Granville St. © 604/681-9254. www.dunneandrundle.com.

Lens & Shutter   Located near the food court of the downtown Pacific Centre Mall, Lens & Shutter provides film and camera advice, sells and repairs cameras, and develops photos. 8700 W. Georgia St. (in Pacific Centre) © 604/684-4422. Also 2912 W. Broadway (© 604/736-3461). www.lensandshutter.com.

CERAMICS, CHINA, SILVER & CRYSTAL

You can find a great array of sophisticated international china and crystal in the downtown stores. On Granville Island, you can observe potters, silversmiths, and glassblowers as they work their magic.

Gallery of B.C. Ceramics   This Granville Island gallery loft is owned and operated by the Potters Guild of British Columbia and features a collection of sculptural and functional ceramic works from 100 different B.C. potters. Closed on Mondays in January and February. Gallery hours change seasonally, so phone ahead to confirm hours of operation. 1359 Cartwright St. © 604/669-5645. www.bcpotters.com.

Martha Sturdy Originals (Finds)   Local designer Martha Sturdy—once best known for her collectible, usable, hand-blown glassware trimmed in gold leaf—is now creating a critically acclaimed line of cast-resin housewares, as well as limited-edition couches and chairs. Expensive, but, if you've got the dough, the furniture is well worth it. 3039 Granville St. © 604/737-0037. www.marthasturdy.com.

CHINESE GOODS

Silk Road Art Trading Co. (Finds)   This store with an entrance on Columbia Street and another within Dr. Sun Yat-sen Park in the Chinese Cultural Centre sells attractive reproductions of Chinese art objects, including the ancient terra-cotta warriors unearthed in a Chinese emperor's tomb. 561 Columbia St. © 604/683-8707.

T&T Supermarket (Finds)   This store has racks and racks of goods you won't find at home (unless your home is China), but the real entertainment is the seafood bins and the produce section, where strange and ungainly comestibles lurk: fire-dragon fruit, lily root, and enoki mushrooms. 181 Keefer St. © 604/899-8836.

Ten Ren Tea & Ginseng Co.   Whether you prefer the pungent aroma of Chinese black or the exotic fragrance of chrysanthemum, jasmine, or ginger flower, you must try the numerous varieties of drinking and medicinal teas in this Chinatown shop. It also carries Korean, American, and Siberian ginseng for a lot less than you might pay elsewhere. 550 Main St. © 604/684-1566.

Tung Fong Hung Foods Co. *(Finds)*   If you've never been to a Chinese herbalist, this is the one to try: jars, bins, and boxes full of such things as dried sea horse, thinly sliced deer antler, and bird's nest. It's fun to explore and potentially good for what ails you. Chinese remedies can have side effects, however, so before ingesting anything unfamiliar, it's wise to consult the on-site herbalist. 536 Main St. ✆ **604/688-0883**.

CIGARS & TOBACCO

Just remember: if they're Cuban, you'll have to light up on this side of the border.

La Casa del Habano   Directly across from Planet Hollywood on Robson Street, Casa del Habano has Vancouver's largest walk-in humidor. Cigars range in price from a few dollars to over a hundred. 980 Robson St. ✆ **604/609-0511**.

Vancouver Cigar Company   The selection here is reputed to be the city's most extensive, featuring brands such as Cohiba, Monte Cristo, Macanudo, Hoyo de Monterrey, Romeo y Julieta, Partagas, Ashton, and A. Fuente. The shop also carries a complete line of accessories. 1093 Hamilton St. ✆ **604/685-0445**. www.vancouvercigar.com.

DEPARTMENT STORES

The Bay (Hudson's Bay Company)   From the establishment of its early trading posts during the 1670s to its modern coast-to-coast department-store chain, the Bay has built its reputation on quality goods. You can still buy a Hudson's Bay woolen "point" blanket (the colorful stripes originally represented how many beaver pelts each blanket was worth in trade), but you'll also find Tommy Hilfiger, Polo, DKNY, and more. 674 Granville St. ✆ **604/681-6211**. www.hbc.com.

Hills of Kerrisdale *(Value)*   This neighborhood department store in central Vancouver is a city landmark. Carrying full lines of quality men's, women's, and children's clothes, as well as furnishings and sporting goods, it's a destination for locals because the prices are often lower than those in the downtown core. 2125 W. 41st Ave. ✆ **604/266-9177**.

DISCOUNT SHOPPING

The strip of West 4th Avenue between Cypress and Yew streets has recently emerged as consignment-clothing central. New shops open regularly.

In-Again Clothing *(Value)*   This shop has a good variety of seasonal consignment clothing, and the selection keeps up with fashion trends. Don't miss the collection of purses, scarves, and belts. 1962 W. 4th Ave. ✆ **604/738-2782**.

Second Suit for Men & Women *(Value)*   This resale- and sample-clothing store has the best in men's and women's fashions, including Hugo Boss, Armani, Donna Karan,

---

(Finds) **Facials to Go**

If you're looking for someplace to go for a great facial, head over to **Skoah**, 1011 Hamilton St. (✆ **877/642-0200** or 604/642-0200; www.skoah.com). This cool co-ed spa in Yaletown, open 7 days a week, specializes in facials for men and women and sells its own line of organic, locally made skin-care products. The 75-minute "Facialicious" signature treatment (C$90/US$72) includes deep cleansing, exfoliating, delicate extractions, detoxifying, stimulating masks and a soothing foot and hand massage as well.

Nautica, Calvin Klein, and Alfred Sung. The inventory changes rapidly. 2036 W. 4th Ave. ✆ **604/732-0338.**

FASHIONS
FOR CHILDREN

Isola Bella *(Kids)*   This store imports an exclusive collection of rather expensive, high-fashion newborn and children's clothing from designers like Babar, Babymini, Milou, Petit Bateau, and Paul Smith. 5692 Yew St. ✆ **604/266-8808.**

Please Mum *(Kids)*   This Kitsilano store sells attractive Canadian-made toddler's and children's cotton clothing. 2951 W. Broadway. ✆ **604/732-4574.** www.pleasemum.com.

FOR MEN & WOMEN

Vancouver has the Pacific Northwest's best collection of clothes from Paris, London, Milan, and Rome, in addition to a great assortment of locally made, cutting-edge fashions. It seems that almost every week a new designer boutique opens in Yaletown, Kitsilano, or Kerrisdale. International designer outlets include **Chanel Boutique,** 900 W. Hastings St. (✆ 604/682-0522); **Salvatore Ferragamo,** 918 Robson St. (✆ 604/669-4495); **Gianni Versace Boutique,** 757 W. Hastings St. (✆ 604/683-1131); **Polo/Ralph Lauren,** the Landing, 375 Water St. (✆ 604/682-7656); and **Plaza Escada,** Sinclair Centre, 757 W. Hastings St. (✆ 604/688-8558).

Dorothy Grant *(Finds)*   Designed to look like a Pacific Northwest longhouse, this shop is where First Nations designer Dorothy Grant exhibits her unique designs as well as her husband's (acclaimed artist Robert Davidson) collection of exquisitely detailed Haida motifs, which she appliqués on coats, leather vests, jackets, caps, and accessories. The clothes are gorgeous and collectible. She also carries contemporary Haida art and jewelry. Check the website for some samples of the collection. 1656 W. 75th St. (corner of Granville St., near Vancouver's International Airport). ✆ **604/681-0201.** www.dorothygrant.com.

Dream 311   Big-name designs can be found anywhere, but this little shop is one of the few places to show early collections—clothing and jewelry—of local designers. 311 W. Cordova. ✆ **604/683-7326.**

Leone   Shop where the stars shop. Versace, Donna Karan, Byblos, Armani, and fabulous Italian and French accessories are sold in this very elegant building; valet parking provided and private after-hours shopping by appointment for VIPs. Sinclair Centre, 757 W. Hastings St. ✆ **604/683-1133.** www.leone.ca.

Roots Canada   Proudly Canadian, this chain features sturdy casual clothing, where you'll find leather jackets, leather bags, footwear, outerwear, and athletic wear for the whole family. 1001 Robson (corner of Burrard). ✆ **604/683-4305.** www.roots.ca.

Swimco   Located near Kitsilano Beach, this store caters to swimmers and sunbathers, where you'll find a large variety of bikinis and bathing suits in the latest prints and colors for men, women, and children. 2166 W. 4th Ave. ✆ **604/732-7946.** www.swimco.com.

Venus & Mars *(Finds)*   Add some drama to your life. This Gastown boutique features Vancouver designer Sanné Lambert's work, specializing in one-of-a-kind handmade gowns and velvet robes. Some plus sizes also available. 315 Cambie St. ✆ **604/687-1908.** www.venusandmars.nu.

Zonda Nellis Design Ltd. *(Finds)*   Rich colors and intricate patterns highlight this Vancouver designer's imaginative hand-woven separates, pleated silks, sweaters, vests, and soft knits. Nellis has also introduced a new line of hand-painted silks and sumptuous, sheer hand-painted velvet eveningwear. 2203 Granville St. ☎ 604/736-5668. www.zondanellis.com.

VINTAGE CLOTHING

Deluxe Junk Co. The name fits—there's tons of junk here. Amid the polyester jackets and worn-out dress shirts, however, are some truly great finds. Some real bargains have been known to pop up. 310 W. Cordova St. ☎ 604/685-4871. www.deluxejunk.com.

Legends Retro-Fashion Specializing in unique retro clothing, Legends is well known among vintage purists for its cache of one-of-a-kind pieces. Most of the clothes, such as evening dresses, shoes, kid gloves, and other accessories, are in immaculate condition. 4366 Main St. ☎ 604/875-0621.

True Value Vintage Clothing This underground shop has a collection of funky fashions from the 1930s through the 1990s, including tons of fake furs, leather jackets, denim, soccer jerseys, vintage bathing suits, formal wear, smoking jackets, sweaters, and accessories. 710 Robson St. ☎ 604/685-5403.

FIRST NATIONS ART & CRAFTS

You'll find First Nations art all over the city. You don't have to purchase a pricey antique to acquire original Coast Salish or Haida work. As the experts at the **Museum of Anthropology** explain, if an item is crafted by any of the indigenous Pacific Northwest artisans, it's a real First Nations piece of art. The culture is ancient yet still very much alive. Pick up a copy of *Publication No. 10: A Guide to Buying Contemporary Northwest Coast Art* by Karen Duffel (available at the Museum of Anthropology), which details how to identify and care for these beautifully carved, worked, and woven pieces. Bold, traditional, and innovative geometric designs; intricate carvings; strong primary colors; and rich wood tones are just a few of the elements you'll find in First Nations crafts.

Even if you're not in the market, go gallery-hopping to see works by Haida artists **Bill Reid** (the province's best-known Native artist) and **Richard Davidson,** and by Kwakwaka'wakw artist and photographer **David Neel.**

Coastal Peoples Fine Arts Gallery This Yaletown boutique offers an extensive collection of fine First Nations jewelry. The motifs—Bear, Salmon, Whale, Raven, and others—are drawn from local myths and translated into 14-karat or 18-karat gold and sterling silver creations. Inuit sculptures and items made of glass or wood are also worth a look. Custom orders can be filled quickly and shipped worldwide. 1024 Mainland St. ☎ 604/685-9298. www.coastalpeoples.com.

Hill's Native Art ⊛ In a re-creation of a trading post interior, this shop, established in 1946 and claiming to be North America's largest Northwest coast Native art gallery, sells moccasins, ceremonial masks, Cowichan sweaters, wood sculptures, totem poles (priced up to C$35,000/US$26,250), silk-screen prints, soapstone sculptures, and gold, silver, and argillite jewelry. 165 Water St. ☎ 604/685-4249. www.hillsnativeart.com.

Images for a Canadian Heritage ⊛ *Finds* This store and the Inuit Gallery of Vancouver (see below) are government-licensed First Nations art galleries, featuring traditional and contemporary works such as Native designs on glass totems and copper plates. With a museum-worthy collection, this shop deserves a visit whether you're buying or not. 164 Water St. (at Cambie St.) ☎ 604/685-7046. www.imagesforcanada.com.

Inuit Gallery of Vancouver   This store is home to one of Canada's foremost collections of Inuit and First Nations art. Prices are for serious buyers, but it's worth a visit. 206 Cambie St. © **604/688-7323.** www.inuit.com.

Khot-La-Cha Salish Handicrafts *(Finds)*   Hand-tanned moose-hide crafts, wood carvings, Cowichan sweaters, porcupine-quill jewelry, and bone, silver, gold, and turquoise accessories are just a few of the selections at this Coast Salish crafts shop. 270 Whonoak St., North Vancouver. © **604/987-3339.** Turn South on Capilano Rd. (off Marine Dr.) and turn first left (Whonoak is parallel to Capilano Rd.). www.khot-la-cha.com.

Lattimer Gallery *(Finds)*   This beautiful gallery showcases museum-quality Pacific Northwest First Nations Art, including ceremonial masks, totem poles, limited-edition silkscreen prints, argillite sculptures, and expensive gold and silver jewelry. 1590 2nd Ave. © **604/732-4556.** www.lattimergallery.com.

Marion Scott Gallery   For 30 years, this gallery has been well regarded for its Inuit and First Nations art collections. 481 Howe St. © **604/685-1934.** www.marionscottgallery.com.

Museum of Anthropology   Works by contemporary First Nations artisans as well as books about the culture and publications on identifying and caring for Pacific Northwest crafts. University of British Columbia, 6393 NW Marine Dr. © **604/822-5087.** www.moa.ubc.ca.

FOOD

You'll find **salmon** everywhere in Vancouver. Many shops package whole, fresh salmon with ice packs for visitors to take home. Shops also carry delectable smoked salmon in travel-safe, vacuum-packed containers. Some offer decorative cedar gift boxes; most offer overnight air transport. Try other salmon treats such as salmon jerky and Indian candy (chunks of marinated smoked salmon), which are available at public markets such as **Granville Island Public Market** and **Lonsdale Quay Market.**

And even though salmon is the most popular item to buy in Vancouver, coffee flows like water—as does Belgian chocolate.

Chocolate Arts *(Finds)*   The works at this West 4th Avenue chocolatier are made with exquisite craftsmanship. Seasonal treats include pumpkin truffles around Halloween or eggnog truffles for Christmas. They even make chocolate toolboxes filled with tiny chocolate tools. Look for the all-chocolate diorama in the window—it changes every month or so. Native masks of thick dark chocolate make great gifts. 2037 W. 4th Ave. © **604/739-0475.**

The Lobsterman   Live lobsters, Dungeness crabs, oysters, mussels, clams, geoducks, and scallops are just a few of the varieties of seafood swimming in the saltwater tanks at this Granville Island fish store. The staff steams the food fresh on the spot, free. Salmon and other seafood can also be packed for air travel. 1807 Mast Tower Rd. © **604/687-4531.** www.lobsterman.com.

Murchie's Tea & Coffee   This Vancouver institution has been the city's main tea and coffee purveyor for more than a century. You'll find everything from Jamaican Blue Mountain and Kona coffees to Lapsang Souchong and Kemun teas. The knowledgeable staff will help you decide which flavors and blends fit your taste. There's also a fine selection of bone china and crystal serving ware as well as coffeemakers and teapots. 970 Robson St. © **604/669-0783.** www.murchies.com.

Salmon Village   If you want some salmon to take home, Salmon Village has a good selection to choose from. Smoked salmon or jerky are vacuum sealed for travel, and fresh salmon can be packed in an icebox or (for a price) shipped to you anywhere on the planet. 779 Thurlow St. ⓒ 604/685-3378. www.salmonvillage.com.

South China Seas Trading Company   The South Seas have always been a source of intrigue. This shop re-creates a bit of that wonder, with a remarkable collection of rare spices and hard-to-find sauces. Look for fresh Kaffir lime leaves, Thai basil, young ginger, sweet Thai chile sauce, and occasional exotic produce like mangosteens and rambutans. Pick up recipes and ideas from the knowledgeable staff. Granville Island Public Market. ⓒ 604/681-5402.

GALLERIES

On the first Thursday of every month, many galleries host free openings from 5 to 8pm. Check the *Georgia Straight* or *Vancouver Magazine* for listings or **www.art-bc.com** for more details on Vancouver's art scene.

Buschlen Mowatt   This is the city's leading "establishment" gallery. Look for paintings, sculptures, and prints from well-known Canadian and international artists. 111–1445 W. Georgia St. ⓒ 604/682-1234. www.buschlenmowatt.com.

Diane Farris Gallery   Contemporary painting and sculpture, from up-and-coming artists and those who already have arrived. 1590 W. 7th Ave. ⓒ 604/737-2629. www.dianefarris gallery.com.

Monte Clark Gallery *(Value)*   This cutting-edge gallery—in the otherwise slightly staid confines of south Granville's gallery row—is one of the best spots to look for that rising superstar without the rising prices. 2339 Granville St. ⓒ 604/730-5000. www.monte clarkgallery.com.

GIFTS & SOUVENIRS

Buddha Supply Centre *(Finds)*   Want money to burn? At Chinese funerals people burn *joss*—paper replicas of earthly belongings—to help make the afterlife for the deceased more comfortable. This shop has more than 500 combustible products to choose from, including $1-million notes (drawn on the bank of hell), luxury penthouse condos, and that all-important cellphone. 4158 Main St. ⓒ 604/873-8169.

Escents   Beautifully displayed, the large collection of soaps, bath oils, shampoos, and other body products here come in a variety of scents, such as the fresh ginger-citrus twist or the relaxing lavender sea. Locally produced and made with minimal packaging, the all-natural, environmentally friendly products come in convenient sizes and prices. 1172 Robson St. ⓒ 604/682-0041. www.escentsaromatherapy.com.

The Ocean Floor   If you want to bring home a few gifts from the sea, then select from this Granville Island shop's collection of seashells, ship models, lamps, chimes, coral, shell jewelry, stained glass, and marine brass. 1522 Duranleau St., Granville Island. ⓒ 604/681-5014.

JEWELRY

Costen Catbalue *(Finds)*   One-of-a-kind pieces in platinum and gold are made on the premises here by a team of four goldsmiths and artists Mary Ann Buis and Andrew Costen. The two artists' styles complement each other; Buis favors contemporary and clean lines, and Costen's designs tend toward a more ornate Renaissance style. 1832 West 1st Ave. ⓒ 604/734-3259. www.costencatbalue.com.

Forge & Form   Master Granville Island metal designers Dietje Hagedoorn and Jürgen Schönheit specialize in customized gold and silver jewelry. Renowned for their gold and silver bow ties, they also create unique pieces like "tension set" rings, which hold a stone in place without a setting. Their studio is located just past the False Creek Community Centre. 1334 Cartwright St. ✆ **604/684-6298.**

Karl Stittgen and Goldsmiths *Finds*   Stittgen's gold pins, pendants, rings, and other accessories demonstrate his eye for clean, crisp design and fine craftsmanship. Each work is a miniature architectural wonder. 2203 Granville St. ✆ **604/737-0029.**

The Raven and the Bear   If you've never seen West Coast Native jewelry, it's worth making a trip here. Deeply inscribed with stylized creatures from Northwest mythology, these rings, bangles, and earrings are unforgettable. (See also "First Nations Art & Crafts," above.) 1528 Duranleau St. ✆ **604/669-3990.**

MALLS & SHOPPING CENTERS

Pacific Centre Mall   This 3-block complex contains 200 shops and services, including Godiva, Benetton, Crabtree & Evelyn, and Eddie Bauer. 700 W. Georgia St. (at Howe). ✆ **604/688-7236.** www.pacificcentre.ca.

Park Royal Shopping Centre   Park Royal consists of two malls that face each other on Marine Drive, just west of the Lions Gate Bridge. GAP, Coast Mountain Sports, Cypress Mountain Sports, Future Shop, Marks & Spencer, Disney, Eaton's, the Bay, Eddie Bauer, and a public market are just a few of the 250 stores in the center. Cinemas, bowling lanes, a golf driving range, community and special events, and a food court are next door. 2002 Park Royal St. (at foot of Lion's Gate Bridge), West Vancouver. ✆ **604/ 925-9576.** www.shopparkroyal.com.

Sinclair Centre   The Sinclair Centre incorporates four Vancouver landmarks: the Post Office (1910), Winch Building (1911), Customs Examining Warehouse (1913), and Federal Building (1937). Now restored, they house elite shops like Armani and Leone, as well as smaller boutiques, art galleries, and a food court. 757 W. Hastings St. ✆ **604/ 659-1009.** www.sinclaircentre.com.

Vancouver Centre   Here you'll find the Bay, restaurants, a food fair, a pair of Famous Players cinemas showing first-run movies, and more than 115 specialty stores (including high-fashion hair salon Suki's and the electronics and pharmacy outlet London Drugs). The complex is connected underground to the adjoining Pacific Centre Mall (see above). 650 W. Georgia St. (at Granville). ✆ **604/684-7537.**

MARKETS

Chinatown Night Market *Value*   Across Asia, prime shopping time comes only after the sun has gone down and the temperature has dropped to something bearable. Friday and Saturday nights May through September, merchants in Chinatown bring the tradition to Canada by closing 2 separate blocks to traffic and covering them with booths, tables, and food stalls offering all manner of things, useful and otherwise. Come down, grab a juicy satay skewer, sip the juice from a freshly cracked coconut, and see what's up. 200 Keefer St. and 200 E. Pender St. Phone the Vancouver Tourism Info Centre at ✆ **604/683-2000** for dates, times.

Granville Island Public Market ✮✮✮   This 4,645-sq.-m (49,998-sq.-ft.) public market features produce, meats, fish, wines, cheeses, arts and crafts, and lots of fast-food counters offering a little of everything. The market is open daily 9am to 6pm. From mid-June to September, the Farmers' Truck Market operates here Thursday from 9am to 6pm. 1669 Johnston St. ✆ **604/666-6477.** www.granvilleisland.com.

Lonsdale Quay Market *(Kids)*   Located at the SeaBus terminal, this public market is filled with produce, meats, fish, specialty fashions, gift shops, food counters, coffee bars, a hotel, and Kids' Alley (a section dedicated to children's shops and a play area). The upper floor houses a variety of fashion stores, bookstores, and gift shops. 123 Carrie Cates Court, North Vancouver. ℂ **604/985-6261.** www.lonsdalequay.com.

New Westminster Quay Public Market   A smaller version of Granville Island, it is located 25 minutes away by SkyTrain from downtown Vancouver. The market has a variety of gift shops, specialty stores, a food court, a delicatessen, and produce stands. Once finished browsing the market, make sure to have a gander at the neighboring Fraser River. A walkway extends along the river and allows great views of the waterfront, the busy boat traffic, and the occasional seal or sea lion. 810 Quayside, New Westminster. ℂ **604/520-3881.**

Vancouver Flea Market *(Value)*   Near the train/bus terminal, Vancouver's largest flea market boasts more than 350 stalls. A lot of cheap T-shirts, linens, used tools, and such, but it's still possible to discover some real finds. Go early or the savvy shoppers will have already cleaned out the gems. Open weekends and holidays 9am to 5pm. 703 Terminal Ave. ℂ **604/685-0666.**

MUSIC

The Magic Flute   Located in the heart of Kitsilano's 4th Avenue shopping area, the Magic Flute carries a large selection of classical music, including recordings of local choirs and orchestras. The collection also includes jazz, world music, and soundtracks. Listening stations allow you to "browse" before you buy. 2203 W. 4th Ave. ℂ **604/736-2727.** www.magicflute.com.

OnDeck   This is a small shop with an impressive collection of vintage vinyl (plus T-shirts). 416 W. Georgia St. ℂ **604/662-7723.** www.ondeckrecords.com.

Virgin Megastore   With over 150,000 titles housed in a three-story, 3,902-sq.-m (42,001-sq.-ft.) space, this is Canada's largest music and entertainment store. 788 Burrard St. at Robson St. ℂ **604/669-2289.** www.virginmega.com.

Zulu Records *(Finds)*   A few blocks east of the Magic Flute, Zulu Records specializes in alternative music, local and import, new and used. You will also find a good selection of vinyl and magazines. The staff is happy to make recommendations and bring you up to speed on what's hot in the local music scene. 1972 W. 4th Ave. ℂ **604/738-3232.** www.zulurecords.com.

SHOES

David Gordon   Vancouver's oldest Western boot, hat, and accessories store is far from stodgy. Boots include an extensive selection of Tony Lama, Boulet, Durango, HH Brown, and Dan Post. You'll also find Vans, Doc Martens, and a lineup of other funky footwear that attracts skateboarders and club kids. 822 Granville St. ℂ **604/685-3784.**

John Fluevog Boots & Shoes Ltd.   This native Vancouverite has a growing international cult following of designers and models clamoring for his under-C$200 (US$150) urban and funky creations. You'll find outrageous platforms and clogs, Angelic Sole work boots, and a few bizarre experiments for the daring footwear fetishist. 837 Granville St. ℂ **604/688-2828.** www.fluevog.com.

SPECIALTY

Lush   Lush has the look of an old-fashioned deli with big wheels of cheese, slabs of sweets, and vats of dips and sauces, but all those displays are really soaps (custom-cut from a block), shampoos, skin treatments, massage oils, and bath bombs made from all natural ingredients. 1025 Robson St. ℂ **604/687-5874**. www.lushcanada.com.

The Market Kitchen Store   This store has everything you'd like to have (or could even imagine) on your kitchen counters or in your kitchen drawers—gourmet kitchen accessories, baking utensils, gadgets, and the like. 2–1666 Johnston (Net Loft, Granville Island). ℂ **604/681-7399.**

Three Dog Bakery   Beagle Bagels, Scottie Biscotti, or Gracie's Rollovers. Canines will have a hard time deciding on a favorite treat from this gone-to-the-dogs bakery. The store also has leashes, collars, greeting cards, and other dog paraphernalia. 2186 W. 4th Ave. ℂ **604/737-3647.** www.threedog.com.

SPORTING GOODS

A 2-block area near the Mountain Equipment Co-op (see below) has become Outdoor Central, with at least a half-dozen stores such as **Altus Mountain Gear** (137 W. Broadway; ℂ **604/876-2525**); **Great Outdoors Equipment** (222 W. Broadway; ℂ **604/872-8872**); and **AJ Brooks** (147 W. Broadway; ℂ **604/874-1117**). Just a block north on 8th Avenue, you'll find **Taiga** (380 W. 8th Ave.; ℂ **604/875-8388**) for inexpensive fleece and other quality outdoor gear.

In the past few years, the corner of 4th Avenue and Burrard Street has become the spot for high-quality snow/skate/surfboard gear as well as the spot to see top-level boarders and their groupies hanging out. Shops here include **Pacific Boarder** (1793 W. 4th Ave.; ℂ **604/734-7245**), **Thriller** (1710 W. 4th Ave.; ℂ **604/736-5651**), and the particularly noteworthy **West Beach** (1766 W. 4th Ave.; ℂ **604/731-6449**), which sometimes hosts pro-skate demos on the half-pipe at the back of the store.

Comor Sports   "Go play outside" is Comor's motto, and they certainly have the goods to get you out there. Pick up some skateboard garb, swimwear, or hiking shoes, in-line skates, skis, boards, and snow toys. 1090 W. Georgia St. ℂ **604/899-2111**. www.comor sports.com.

Mountain Equipment Co-op   A true West Coast institution and an outdoors lover's dream come true, this block-long store houses the best selection of top-quality outdoor gear: rain gear, clothing, hiking shoes, climbing gear, backpacks, sleeping bags, tents, and more. Memorize the MEC label; you're sure to see it later—at the beach, the bar, or the concert hall. 130 W. Broadway (between Manitoba and Columbia). ℂ **604/872-7858.** www.mec.ca.

TOYS

The Games People (*Kids*)   The Games People carries a huge selection of board games, strategy games, role-playing games, puzzles, models, toys, hobby materials, and other amusements. It's difficult to walk past this store—whether you're an adult or a kid. 157 Water St. ℂ **604/685-5825.**

Kids Market (*Kids*)   Probably the only mall in North America dedicated to kids, the Kids Market on Granville Island features a Lilliputian entranceway; toy, craft, and book stores; play areas; and services for the younger set, including a "fun hairdresser." 1496 Cartwright St. (on Granville Island). ℂ **604/689-8447.** www.kidsmarket.ca.

Kites on Clouds *(Kids)*   This little Gastown shop has every type of kite. Prices range from C$10 to C$20 (US$7.50–US$15) for nylon or Mylar dragon kites to around C$200 (US$150) for more elaborate ghost clippers and nylon hang-glider kites. The Courtyard, 131 Water St. ℂ 604/669-5677.

WINE

British Columbia's **wines** are worth buying by the case, especially rich, honey-thick ice wines, such as Jackson-Triggs gold-medal-winning 1994 Johannesburg Riesling Ice wine, and bold reds, such as the Quail's Gate 1994 Limited Release Pinot Noir. Five years of restructuring, reblending, and careful tending by French and German master vintners have won the province's vineyards world recognition.

When buying B.C. wine, look for the VQA (Vintner Quality Alliance) seal on the label; it's a guarantee that all grapes used are grown in British Columbia and meet European standards for growing and processing.

Summerhill, Cedar Creek, Mission Hill, and **Okanagan Vineyards** are just a few of the more than 50 local estates producing hearty cabernet sauvignons, honey-rich ice wines, and oaky merlots. These wines can be found at any government-owned **LCB** liquor store, such as the one at 1716 Robson St. (ℂ **604/660-4576**) and at some privately owned wine stores.

Marquis Wine Cellars   The owner and staff of this West End wine shop are dedicated to educating their patrons about wines. They conduct evening wine tastings, featuring selections from their special purchases. They also publish monthly newsletters. In addition to carrying a full range of British Columbian wines, the shop also has a large international selection. 1034 Davie St. ℂ **604/684-0445**. www.marquis-wines.com.

The Okanagan Estate Wine Cellar   This department store annex, located in the Vancouver Centre mall Market Square, offers a great selection of British Columbian wines by the bottle and the case. The Bay, 674 Granville St. ℂ **604/681-6211**.

10

Vancouver After Dark

Vancouver is a fly-by-the-seat-of-the-pants kind of town. There's so much to see and do—and the outdoors always beckons—that Vancouverites wait till the day or the hour before a show to plunk their cash down for a ticket. It drives promoters crazy. Entertainment options run the gamut, from cutting-edge theater companies to a well-respected opera and symphony to folk and jazz festivals that draw people from up and down the coast. And then there are the bars and pubs and clubs and cafes—lots of them—for every taste, budget, and fetish; you just have to get out there and see. By the way, dining out at a fine restaurant is considered an evening's entertainment in and of itself; at a restaurant like C (reviewed in chapter 6), the presentation is theater-on-a-plate.

For the best overview of Vancouver's nightlife, pick up a copy of the weekly tabloid, the *Georgia Straight* (www. georgiastraight.com). The Thursday edition of the *Vancouver Sun* contains the weekly entertainment section *Queue.* The monthly *Vancouver Magazine* is filled with listings and strong views about what's

really hot in the city. Check out their website at www.vanmag.com. Or get a copy of *Xtra! West,* the free gay and lesbian biweekly tabloid, available in shops and restaurants throughout the West End.

The **Vancouver Cultural Alliance Arts Hot Line,** 100–938 Howe St. (© **604/ 684-2787** or 604/681-3535; www.alliance forarts.com), is a great information source for all performing arts, literary events, and art films. The office is open Monday through Friday from 9am to 5pm.

Ticketmaster (Vancouver Ticket Centre), 1304 Hornby St. (© **604/280-3311;** www.ticketmaster.ca), has 40 outlets in the Vancouver area.

Half-price tickets for same-day shows and events are available at the **Tickets Tonight** (www.ticketstonight.ca) kiosk (open Tuesday to Saturday 11am to 6pm) in the **Vancouver Tourist Info Centre,** 200 Burrard St. (© **604/683-2000**). The Info Centre is open from May to Labour Day daily from 8am to 6pm; the rest of the year, it's open Monday through Saturday from 8:30am to 5pm.

1 The Performing Arts

Three major theaters in Vancouver regularly host touring performances. The **Orpheum Theatre,** 801 Granville St. (© **604/665-3050;** www.city.vancouver.bc.ca/theatres/ orpheum/orpheum.html), is an elegant 1927 theater that originally hosted the Chicago-based Orpheum vaudeville circuit. The theater also hosts pop, rock, and variety shows. The Queen Elizabeth Theatre and the Vancouver Playhouse comprise the **Queen Elizabeth Complex,** 600 Hamilton St., between Georgia and Dunsmuir streets (© **604/ 665-3050;** www.city.vancouver.bc.ca). It hosts major national and touring musical and theater productions. It's also home to the Vancouver Opera and Ballet British Columbia. The 670-seat Vancouver Playhouse presents chamber-music performances and recitals.

Located in a converted turn-of-the-20th-century church, the **Vancouver East Cultural Centre** (the "Cultch" to locals), 1895 Venables St. (© **604/251-1363;** www.vecc.bc.ca), coordinates an impressive program that includes avant-garde theater productions, performances by international musical groups, festivals and cultural events, children's programs, and art exhibitions.

On the campus of UBC, the **Chan Centre for the Performing Arts,** 6265 Crescent Rd. (© **604/822-2697;** www.chancentre.com), showcases the work of the UBC music and acting students and also hosts a winter concert series. Designed by local architectural luminary, Bing Thom, the Chan Centre's crystal-clear acoustics are the best in town.

THEATER

Theater isn't just an indoor art here. There's an annual summertime Shakespeare series, **Bard on the Beach,** in Vanier Park (© **604/737-0625**). You can also bring a picnic dinner to Stanley Park and watch **Theatre Under the Stars** (see below), which features popular musicals and light comedies.

Arts Club Theatre Company   The 425-seat Granville Island Mainstage presents major dramas, comedies, and musicals, with post-performance entertainment in the Backstage Lounge. The Arts Club Revue Stage is an intimate, cabaret-style showcase for small productions, improvisation nights, and musical revues. The smaller Art Deco Stanley Theatre has recently undergone a glorious renovation and now plays host to longer running plays and musicals. The box office is open 9am to 7pm. Granville Island Stage, 1585 Johnston St., and The Stanley Theatre, 2750 Granville St. © 604/687-1644. www.artsclub.com. Tickets C$25–C$59 (US$20–US$47).

The Centre in Vancouver for Performing Arts   This theatre was hailed as Vancouver's newest prime entertainment venue when it opened in 1996, but then its owner went bankrupt and the theater sat empty until the spring of 2002. The new owners have given the venue new life and are once again bringing big productions to town. Check the calendar or contact Ticketmaster for an updated schedule. 777 Homer St. © 604/602-0616. www.centreinvancouver.com. Tickets C$25–C$70 (US$20–US$56).

Firehall Arts Centre   Housed in Vancouver's Firehouse No. 1, the Centre is home to the cutting-edge Firehall Theatre Company. Expect original and experimental plays. Dance events, arts festivals, and concerts are also staged here. The box office is open Monday through Friday 9:30am to 5pm and for 1 hour before the show begins. 280 E. Cordova St. © 604/689-0926. www.firehallartscentre.ca. Tickets C$8–C$18 (US$6.50–US$14).

Frederic Wood Theatre (Value   Forget that "student production" thing you've got in your head. Students at UBC are actors in training, and their productions are extremely high-caliber. For the price, they're a steal. Their presentations range from classic dramatic works to Broadway musicals to new plays by Canadian playwrights. The box

---

(Finds   **Art on the Edge**

For more original performance fare, don't miss **The Fringe—Vancouver's Theatre Festival** (© 604/257-0350; www.vancouverfringe.com). Centered on Granville Island, the Fringe Festival features more than 500 innovative and original shows each September, all costing under C$15 (US$12).

office is open Monday through Friday 10:30am to 3pm. All shows start at 7:30pm. There are no performances during the summer. Gate 4, University of British Columbia. 📞 604/ 822-2678. www.theatre.ubc.ca. Tickets C$16 (US$13) adults, C$10 (US$8) students and seniors.

Theatre Under the Stars   From mid-July to mid-August, old-time favorite musicals like *The King and I, West Side Story,* and *Grease* are performed outdoors by a mixed cast of amateur and professional actors. Bring a blanket (it gets cold once the sun sets) and a picnic dinner for a relaxing evening of summer entertainment. The box office is open Monday through Saturday 10am to 5pm and 7 to 8pm. Malkin Bowl, Stanley Park. 📞 604/257-0366 or 604/687-0174. www.tuts.bc.ca. Tickets C$30 (US$24) adults, C$25 (US$20) seniors and youth, C$20 (US$16) children 6–10, family (2 adults and 2 children) C$85 (US$68).

Vancouver Playhouse   Now in its third decade, the company at the Vancouver Playhouse presents a program of six plays each season, usually a mix of the internationally known, nationally recognized, and locally promising. The box office opens 30 minutes before show time. You can also buy tickets through **Ticketmaster** 📞 604/ 280-4444. 600 Hamilton, between Georgia and Hamilton sts. in the Queen Elizabeth complex. 📞 604/ 665-3050. www.city.vancouver.bc.ca/theatres. Tickets usually C$10–C$20 (US$8–US$16).

OPERA

Vancouver Opera 🎭🎭   In a kind of willful flirtation with death, the Vancouver Opera Company alternates between obscure or new (and Canadian!) works and older, more popular perennials, often sung by international stars. The formula seems to work, as the company is nearly 40 years old and still packing 'em in. The season runs October through May, with most performances in the Queen Elizabeth Theatre. The box office is open Monday through Friday 9am to 4pm. 500–845 Cambie St. 📞 604/683-0222. www. vanopera.bc.ca. Tickets usually C$30–C$125 (US$24–US$100).

CLASSICAL MUSIC

Fans of symphonic masterpieces, chamber music, baroque fugues, and popular show tunes will find world-class concert performances in Vancouver.

University of British Columbia School of Music   September through November and during January and March, UBC presents eight faculty and guest-artist concerts. They feature piano, piano and violin, opera, or quartets, plus occasional performances by acts like the Count Basie Orchestra. If the concert is in the Chan Centre, go. There are few halls in the world with such beautiful acoustics. Recital Hall, Gate 4, 6361 Memorial Rd. 📞 604/822-5574. www.music.ubc.ca. Tickets purchased at the door C$5–C$24 (US$4–US$19). Many concerts are free. The Wed noon hour series costs C$5 (US$4).

Vancouver Bach Choir 🎭   Vancouver's international, award-winning amateur choir, a 150-voice ensemble, presents five major concerts a year at the Orpheum Theatre. Specializing in symphonic choral music, the Choir's sing-along performance of Handel's *Messiah* during the Christmas season is a favorite. 805–235 Keith Rd., West Vancouver. 📞 604/921-8012. www.vancouverbachchoir.com. Tickets C$20–C$35 (US$16–US$28) depending on the performance. Tickets available through Ticketmaster at 📞 604/280-4444.

Vancouver Cantata Singers   This semiprofessional, 40-person choir specializes in early music. The company performs works by Bach, Brahms, Monteverdi, Stravinsky, and Handel, as well as Eastern European choral music. The season normally includes three programs: in October, December, and March at various locations. 5115 Keith Rd., West Vancouver. 📞 604/921-8588. www.cantata.org. Tickets C$20 (US$15) adults, C$16 (US$12) seniors and students. Tickets at Ticketmaster (📞 604/280-4444) or at the door.

Vancouver Chamber Choir 🧡 Western Canada's only professional choral ensemble presents an annual concert series at the Orpheum Theatre, the Chan Centre, and Ryerson United Church. Under conductor John Washburn, the choir has gained an international reputation. 1254 W. 7th Ave. ℂ 604/738-6822. www.vancouverchamberchoir.com. Tickets C$15–C$35 (US$12–US$28) adults, C$13–C$25 (US$10–US$20) seniors and students. Tickets through Ticketmaster at ℂ 604/280-4444.

Vancouver Symphony 🧡🧡 At its home in the Orpheum Theatre during the fall, winter, and spring, Vancouver's active orchestra presents the "Masterworks" series of great classical works; "Casual Classics," featuring light classics from a single area or composer and a casually dressed orchestra; "Tea & Trumpets," highlighting modern classics and ethnic works; "Symphony Pops," selections of popular and show tunes; and "Kid's Koncerts," a series geared toward school-age children. The box office is open Monday through Friday 1 to 5pm; on the day of the performance, the box office is open from 6pm until show time. 601 Smithe St. ℂ 604/876-3434 for ticket information. www.vancouversymphony.ca. Tickets C$22–C$60 (US$18–US$48).

DANCE

The new **Scotiabank Dance Centre** (677 Davie St.) provides a new focal point for the Vancouver dance community. Renovated by Arthur Erickson, the former bank building now offers studio and rehearsal space to more than 30 dance companies and is open to the general public for events, workshops, and classes. For more information, call ℂ **604/606-6400** or check www.vkool.com/dancentre.

For fans of modern and new dance, the time to be here is early July, when the **Dancing on the Edge Festival** (ℂ **604/689-0691;** www.dancingontheedge.org) presents 60 to 80 original pieces over a 10-day period. For more information about other festivals and dance companies around the city, call the **Dance Centre** at ℂ **604/ 606-6400.**

Ballet British Columbia 🧡 Just over 16 years old, this company strives to present innovative works, such as those by choreographers John Cranko and William Forsythe, along with more traditional fare, including productions by visiting companies, such as the American Ballet Theatre, the Royal Winnipeg Ballet, and the Moscow Classical Ballet. Performances are usually at the Queen Elizabeth Theatre, at 600 Hamilton St. 1101 W. Broadway. ℂ 604/732-5003. www.balletbc.com. Tickets C$25–C$50 (US$20–US$40) adults.

2 Laughter & Music

COMEDY CLUB/IMPROV SHOW

Vancouver TheatreSports League 🧡 Part comedy, part theater, and partly a take-no-prisoner's test of an actor's ability to think extemporaneously, TheatreSports involves actors taking suggestions from the audience and spinning them into short skits or full plays, often with hilarious results. Since moving to the Arts Club Stage, Vancouver's TheatreSports leaguers have had to rein in their normally raunchy instincts for the more family-friendly audience—except, that is, for Friday and Saturday at 11:45pm, when the Red-Hot Improv show takes the audience into the R-rated realm. Shows are Wednesday and Thursday at 7:30pm and Friday and Saturday at 8, 10, and 11:45pm. New Revue Stage, Granville Island. ℂ 604/687-1644. www.vtsl.com. Tickets C$10–C$17 (US$8–US$13).

STRICTLY LIVE

Besides the listings below, every June the **Vancouver International Jazz Festival** (© **604/872-5200;** www.jazzvancouver.com) takes over many venues and outdoor stages around town. The festival includes a number of free concerts.

The **Vancouver Folk Festival** (© **800/986-8363** or 604/602-9798; www.thefestival. bc.ca) is one of the big ones on the West Coast. Folks come from as far away as Portland and Prince George to take in the extended weekend of music. It takes place outdoors in July on the beach at Jericho Park.

The Brickyard   Once the city's most consistently innovative small venue for touring indie bands, the Brickyard has slipped a little in recent years but is now back to featuring cutting edge indie bands 4 nights a week (Wed–Sat). (**Note:** Pigeon Park—Vancouver's notorious open-air drug bazaar—is located but a half-block away. It's not pretty, but there's little danger of violence.) 315 Carrall St. © **604/685-3922.** Cover C$5–C$15 (US$4–US$12) depending on the band.

Cellar Restaurant and Jazz Club   Jazz has a loose definition on the West Coast. In this dark downstairs Kitsilano *boîte,* the live sounds stretch to include funk, fusion, jazz, and occasionally even hip-hop. Local jazz aficionados swear by this place. 3611 W. Broadway. © **604/738-1959.** www.cellarjazz.com. Cover C$10–C$20 (US$8–US$16).

The Commodore Ballroom ★   Every town should have one, but sadly very few do: a huge old-time dance hall, complete with a suspended hardwood dance floor that bounces gently up and down beneath your nimble or less-than-nimble toes. And though the room and floor date back to the jazz age, the lineup nowadays includes many of the best modern bands coming through town. In fact, the Commodore is one of the best places to catch a midsize band—and thanks to a recent renovation, the room looks better than ever. 868 Granville St. © **604/739-7469.** www.commodoreballroom.com. Tickets C$5–C$50 (US$4–US$40).

Piccadilly Pub   A downtown watering hole inhabited largely by lusting and inebriated university students, the Pic serves as a 7-nights-a-week live stage for the sort of bands drunken, libidinous college kids like to hear. 620 W. Pender St. © **604/682-3221.** Cover C$5–C$15 (US$4–US$12) depending on the band.

The Purple Onion   Some clubs DJ to survive, some have bands; the Onion serves up both, all for the same cover. The Club room is a dance floor pure and simple. Down the hall and round a left turn is the Lounge, where the house band squeals out funky danceable jazz for a slightly older crowd 3 nights a week. During the Jazz Festival, this place hops. 15 Water St. © **604/602-9442.** Cover C$5–C$10 (US$4–US$8).

The Roxy   Live bands play every day of the week in this casual club, which also features show-off bartenders with Tom Cruise *Cocktail*-style moves. The house bands Joe's Garage and Dr. Strangelove keep the Roxy packed, and on weekends, the lines are long. Theme parties (often with vacation giveaways), Extreme Karaoke, Canadian content, '80s only, and other events add to the entertainment. 932 Granville St. © **604/ 684-7699.** www.roxyvan.com. Cover C$5–C$15 (US$4–US$12).

The WISE Club *Finds*   Folk, folk, and more folk. In the far-off reaches of East Vancouver (okay, Commercial Dr. area), the WISE Club was unplugged long before MTV ever thought of reaching for the power cord. Bands are local and international, and the room's a lot of fun—like a church basement or community center with alcohol. 1882 Adanac St. © **604/254-5858.** Cover depends on show; C$15 (US$12) for most bands.

Yale Hotel This century-old tavern on the far south end of Granville is Vancouver's one and only home of the blues. Visiting heavyweights have included Koko Taylor, Stevie Ray Vaughan, Junior Wells, and Jeff Healey. The pictures in the entryway are a who's who of the blues. When outside talent's not available, the Yale makes do with what's homegrown, including Long John Baldry and local bluesman Jim Byrne. There are shows Monday through Saturday at 9:30pm. On Saturday and Sunday, there is an open-stage blues jam from 3 to 7pm. 1300 Granville St. ✆ **604/681-9253.** www.theyale.ca. Cover Thurs–Sat C$5–C$15 (US$4–US$12).

3 Bars, Pubs & Other Watering Holes

Vancouver has loosened up a great deal in the last few years. Until pretty recently, patrons in a restaurant could drink only if they were eating or *had the intention of eating*. Nowadays, Vancouver drinkers can stand tall and order that beer, with no fear of being forced to purchase a token cookie or French fry. Even better, bars can now regularly stay open till 2am, and as late as 4am in peak summer months.

That said, officialdom in the city still doesn't love the late-night crowd. They seem to look on drinkers and revelers as an unfortunate by-product of urbanism, and bars as a necessary evil. City policy has been to concentrate the city's pubs and clubs and discos into two ghettos—er, *entertainment zones*—one along Granville Street and the other along Water and Pender streets in Gastown. There are pubs and clubs in other places to be sure, and many are listed below, but if you just want to wander out for a serendipitous pub crawl, the Granville or Water street strips make fine destinations. Speaking generally, Granville Street tends more to Top-40 discos and upscale lounges, while down in Gastown, it's dark cellars spinning hip-hop and house. Yaletown is the newest late-night entertainment/drinking area, a place where martinis reign and some of the restaurants turn into cocktail lounges at 11pm.

BARS MASQUERADING AS RESTAURANTS

One holdover from the bad old days of the liquor license drought is the relatively large number of restaurants that look suspiciously like pubs. You can order food in these places. Indeed, it used to be a condition of drinking (wink, wink). But most patrons stick to a liquid diet.

The Alibi Room Higher-end, trendy restaurant/bar brought to you at least in part by *X-Files'* Gillian Anderson, the Alibi Room offers upstairs diners modern cuisine and a chance to flip through shelves full of old film scripts. Monthly script readings provide a venue for ever-hopeful wannabe screenwriters (call for details). Downstairs there's a DJ and dance floor. Located on the eastern edge of Gastown. 157 Alexander St. ✆ **604/623-3383.** www.alibiroom.com.

The Atlantic Trap and Gill Regulars in this sea shanty of a pub know the words to every song sung by the Irish and East Coast bands that appear onstage most every night. Guinness and Keith's are the brews of choice, and don't worry too much about ordering food. As the song goes: *"I'se the bye that orders the pint, I'se the bye that drinks her, keep your menus up in sight, and the government's none the wiser."* Or something like that. 612 Davie St. ✆ **604/806-6393.**

The Jupiter Cafe *Finds* Located just off busy Davie Street in the West End, the Jupiter Cafe combines a post-apocalyptic industrial look with lounge chic. Black ceilings, exposed pipes, and roof struts mix surprisingly well with chandeliers, velvet curtains, and plush chairs. More important, the Jupiter is open late (till 4am some nights). True, it can be a challenge to flag down your waiter, but that gives you more time to scope out the crowd: gay and straight, funky and preppy, casual and dressed to kill. A huge outdoor patio provides a pleasant refuge from the street, but on colder nights it's the exclusive domain of die-hard smokers. The menu—burgers, pastas, and pizzas—is largely decorative. 1216 Bute St. ℂ **604/609-6665.**

Monsoon Restaurant   What this slim little bistro in the otherwise sleepy section of Main and Broadway does really well is beer and fusion-induced tapas, accompanied by a buzzing atmosphere generated by interesting and sometimes beautiful people. Kitchen open noon until 11pm on weekdays, later on weekends. 2526 Main St. ℂ **604/879-4001.**

Urban Well   The taut and tanned from nearby Kits Beach drop into the Well as the sun goes down, and often don't emerge until the next day. Monday and Tuesday there's comedy; DJs keep things groovy the rest of the week. Regulars line up on the patio counter to people-watch, while inside there's a tiny dance floor for demonstrating once again that you can get down in beach sandals. The second, downtown Well (888 Nelson; ℂ **604/638-6070**) entertains a much similar jock(ette) crowd, but with a large dance floor and disco ball. 1516 Yew St. ℂ **604/737-7770.** www.urbanwell.com.

ACTUAL BARS
The Arts Club Backstage Lounge   The Arts Club Lounge has a fabulous location under the Granville Bridge by the water on the edge of False Creek. The crowd is a mix of tourists and art school students from neighboring Emily Carr College. Friday and Saturday, there's a live band in the evenings. Most other times, if the sun's out, the waterfront patio is packed. 1585 Johnston St., Granville Island. ℂ **604/687-1354.**

The Irish Heather   A bright, pleasant Irish pub in the dark heart of Gastown, the Heather boasts numerous nooks and crannies, some of the best beer in town, and a menu that does a lot with the traditional Emerald Isle spud. The clientele is from all over the map, including artsy types from the local gallery scene, urban pioneers from the new Gastown condos, and kids from Kitsilano looking for some safe but authentic grunge. 217 Carrall St. ℂ **604/688-9779.**

The Lennox Pub   Part of the renewal of Granville Street, this new pub fills a big void in the neighborhood; it's a comfortable spot for a drink without having to deal with lines or ordering food. The beer list is extensive, containing such hard-to-find favorites as Belgian Kriek, Hoegaarden, and Leffe. There is a great selection of single-malt scotches, too. The pub has a turn-of-the-20th-century feel with lots of brass, wood paneling, and a long bar. The menu covers all the pub-food basics. 800 Granville St. ℂ **604/408-0881.**

SPORTS BAR
The Shark Club Bar and Grill   The city's premier sports bar, the Shark Club—in the Sandman Inn—features lots of wood and brass, TVs everywhere, and on weekend evenings, lots of young women who don't look terribly interested in sports. Despite this—or because of it—weekend patrons often score. 180 W. Georgia St. ℂ **604/687-4275.** C$4–C$6 (US$3.20–US$4.80) Fri–Sat.

BARS WITH VIEWS
If you're in Vancouver, odds are you're aware that this is a city renowned for its "views." The entire population could go make more money living in a dull flat place

like Toronto, but stay here because they're addicted to the scenery. As long as that's your raison d'être, you may as well drink in style at one of the places below. Also check out the view at Lift, the new restaurant (p. 96); it's in the same Coal Harbour vicinity as Cardero's (see next review).

Cardero's Marine Pub   On the water at the foot of Cardero Street, this Coal Harbour pub and restaurant offers a great view of Stanley Park, the harbor, and the North Shore. Overhead heaters take away the chill when the sun goes down. 1583 Coal Harbour Quay. ℂ 604/669-7666.

Cloud Nine   View junkies will think they're in heaven. As this sleek hotel-top lounge rotates 6 degrees a minute, your vantage point circles from volcanic Mount Baker to the Fraser estuary to English Bay around Stanley Park to the towers of downtown, the harbor, and East Vancouver. And who knew you could get such a good martini in heaven? 1400 Robson St. (42nd floor of the Empire Landmark Hotel). ℂ 604/662-8328. Cover C$5 (US$3.75) Fri–Sat after 8:30pm.

The Dockside Brewing Company   The best waterside pub in the city, the Dockside is located in the Granville Island Hotel (reviewed in chapter 5) and looks out across False Creek to Yaletown and Burnaby Mountain far in the distance. The grub's not up to much, but the beer is among the best in town—brewed-on-the-premises lagers, ales, and porters. There are overhead gas heaters for chillier evenings, but even so, it's a good idea not to arrive too late: An hour or two after the sun goes down, the mostly 30-something patrons remember that now they have homes to go to. 1253 Johnson St. ℂ 604/685-7070.

The Flying Beaver Bar *Finds*   A West Coast tradition: Beaver and Cessna pilots pull up to the floating docks and step ashore to down a few in the floatplane pub. Located beneath the flyway of Vancouver International, the Beaver offers nonflyers great views of incoming jets, along with mountains, bush planes, river craft, and truly fine beer. 4760 Inglis Rd., Richmond. ℂ 604/273-0278.

LOUNGES

Afterglow   Intimate couches and a soft soundtrack (which gets cranked up as the evening wears on) make for candle-lit foreplay to a meal at Glowbal Grill (p. 92); you can also stay in the low-slung loveseats for a long evening's cuddle. 350 Davie St. ℂ 604/642-0577.

Bacchus Lounge ✺   Step into Bacchus and bask in the low light cast by the fireplace and tealights. This luxuriously comfy hot-spot in the tony Wedgewood Hotel (p. 70) stages a powerhouse cocktail hour for mostly well-to-do professionals, then becomes an irony-free piano bar. The pianist in the corner pounds out Neil Diamond, and the crowd of boomers and their children hum along. In the Wedgewood Hotel, 845 Hornby St. ℂ 604/608-5319. www.wedgewoodhotel.com.

Balthazar   A funky Spanish Revival building with a seedy past as a bordello, Balthazar's offers martinis, wine, and tapas till the wee hours (2am), plus two small dance floors each with its own DJ. One spins house, the other roams all over. The crowd in this West End lounge is a little older and dresses the part. 1215 Bidwell St. (at Davie St.). ℂ 604/689-8822.

Elixir ✺   Super-trendy Ian Schrager-ish decor—the designer apparently wanted to include a chair design from every historical period—has helped the Elixir lounge in the cool Opus Hotel (p. 68) become the Yaletown hotspot for a pre-dinner martini or an extended evening schmooze. In the Opus Hotel, 50 Davie St. ℂ **604/642-0577**. www.elixir-opusbar.com.

Ginger Sixty-Two   The once trendy, then slummy, and now yuppifying Granville Street has recently seen some great new places open. Ginger Sixty-Two is one of the most successful newcomers. A mix of lounge, restaurant, and club, it's the new darling of the fashion industry trendsetters who love to be spotted here. The room is funky warehouse-chic-meets-adult-rec-room, decorated in happening red, orange, and gold tones. Comfy crash pads are strategically placed throughout the room and plenty of pillows help prop up those less-than-young in the joints. 1219 Granville St. ℂ **604/688-5494**.

Gotham Cocktail Bar   A clear case of the law of unintended consequences: The lounge adjoining this new steakhouse was designed for a male clientele—thick leather benches and a mural of sensuous women in Jazz Age fashions. Men certainly did show up—well-off suits in their 30s and 40s particularly—but they were soon a tiny minority midst the great gaggles of women, all seemingly sharing Ally McBeal's age, romantic aspirations, and hem length. 615 Seymour St. ℂ **604/605-8282**.

BREWPUBS

In this category don't forget **The Dockside Brewing Company** (1253 Johnson St.; ℂ **604/685-7070**), in the Granville Island Hotel: It's listed under "Bars with Views," above.

Steamworks Pub & Brewery   Winding your way from room to room in this Gastown brewery is almost as much fun as drinking. Upstairs, by the doors, it's a London city pub where stockbrokers ogle every new female entrant. Farther in by the staircase, it's a refined old-world club, with wood paneling, leather chairs, and great glass windows overlooking the harbor. Down in the basement, it's a Bavarian drinking hall with long lines of benches, set up parallel to the enormous copper vats. Fortunately, the beer's good. Choose from a dozen in-house beers. 375 Water St. ℂ **604/689-2739**. www.steamworks.com.

Yaletown Brewing Company   Remember, if it's raining at 11:30am on a Thursday, all pints of brewed-on-the-premises beer are C$3.75 (US$3) for the rest of the day. The excellent beer is complemented by an extremely cozy room, a great summertime patio, and a good appetizer menu. Resist the urge to stay for supper, however: Snacks are the true forte. Sunday, all pizzas are half price. 1111 Mainland St. ℂ **604/681-2739**.

4 Dance Clubs

Generally clubs are open until 2am every day but Sunday, when they close at midnight. In the summer months (mid-June through Labour Day), opening hours are extended to 4am. The city's clubs and discos are concentrated around two "entertainment zones," one downtown around Granville Street and the other along Water and Pender streets in Gastown.

Au Bar   An address is unnecessary for Au Bar; the long Seymour Street line of those not-quite-beautiful-enough for expedited entry immediately gives it away. Inside, this newest of downtown bars is packed with beautiful people milling from bar to dance floor to bar (there are two) and back again. Observing them is like watching a nature documentary on the Discovery Channel: Doe-like women prance and jiggle while predatory men roam in packs, flexing pecs and biceps. To maintain some form of natural order, black-clad bouncers scan the room like game wardens, searching the horizon for trouble in paradise. 674 Seymour St. ✆ **604/648-2227.** www.aubarnightclub.com. Cover C$5–C$8 (US$4–US$6.50).

The Caprice Upstairs, it's The Lounge, with dark wood, a fireplace, a big-screen TV showing old Audrey Hepburn movies, and roll-top doors opening on a Granville Street patio. Downstairs, it's The Nightclub—a large room with a funky semi-circular glowing blue bar, big comfy wall banquettes, a secluded circular passion pit in one corner, and a medium-size dance floor. Earlier in the week the DJ spins house, but on weekends, when the older, richer 25-and-overs come out to play, the cover goes up and the DJ retreats to the safety of Top 40. 965 Granville St. ✆ **604/685-3189.** Cover Tues–Thurs C$6 (US$4.80); Fri–Sat C$10 (US$8).

The Cellar The Cellar inhabits that netherworld between dance club, bar, meat market, and personals listing. Dance club characteristics include a cover charge, small-ish dance floor, and a DJ, who mostly spins Top 40. But Cellar patrons are far less interested in groovin' than they are in meetin' other Cellar dwellers, a process facili-tated by a wall length message board upon which pick-up lines are posted. When not angsting over pickup notes, Cellar dwellers drink. 1006 Granville St. ✆ **604/605-4350.** Cover C$5–C$8 (US$4–US$6.40).

Crush Wine snobs will feel right at home at the Crush Champagne Lounge; unique for a dance club, this venue has a professional sommelier on staff to help you make your wine selection. The drink list also includes a large selection of sexy champagne cocktails and by-the-glass bubblies. The lounge has a small dance floor and the music is mellow R&B, soul, classic lounge, and jazz. Now it may just be the fancy drinks, but this crowd likes to dress up for the occasion; no fleece or Gore-Tex in sight. 1180 Granville St. ✆ **604/684-0355.** Cover C$5 (US$4).

The Drink This is a vast basement warren with two bars, numerous intimate cubby holes, and a DJ that does progressive house and hip-hop. And if that weren't enough, there's also a pool. 398 Richards St. ✆ **604/687-1307.** Cover C$5 (US$4) weeknights; C$10 week-ends (US$8).

Loft Six Newcomer Loft Six is a curious mix of contradictions. The upstairs space has open windows with a great view of Gastown's Maple Tree Square, but inside, the 20- to 30-something crowd is mostly interested in each other. Here, tattoos are more common than underwear, yet piercings are next to nonexistent. Denim is not only allowed but also seemingly *de rigueur*. And music is a kind of house-inflected world beat (think Hindi with heavy bass) but patrons are by and large lily white. 6 Powell St. ✆ **604/688-6440.** Cover C$5–C$10 (US$4–US$8).

The Plaza Cabaret This former movie theater makes a great nightclub with its high ceilings and spacious dance floor. Lineups start early at this popular club. Wednesday night is Alternative Night; Thursday is Best of British with all British tunes; and Friday nights are the DJ's domain, spinning Top-40 tunes. 881 Granville St. ✆ **604/646-0064.** Cover C$6–C$8 (US$4.80–US$6.50).

Richard's on Richards Dick's on Dicks has been packing 'em in longer than you'd care to know. What's the attraction? For years, the club was a notorious pickup spot. Things have mellowed since then, but as the line of limos out front on busy nights attests, Dick's is still hot. Inside there are two floors, four bars, a laser light system, and lots of DJ'ed dance tunes and concerts. Live music acts have included the likes of Junior

Wells, James Brown, 2 Live Crew, and Jack Soul. 1036 Richards St. ℂ **604/687-6794**. www.richardsonrichards.com. Cover Fri–Sat C$8 (US$6.50) for the club; concerts C$10–C$30 (US$8–US$24).

Shine   This downstairs cellar in Gastown plays house and hip-hop, with occasional forays into far-out stuff like reggae. 364 Water St. ℂ **604/408-4321**. www.shinenightclub.com. C$5–C$10 (US$4–US$8).

Sonar   Loud bass. Flashing lights. The endlessly thrumming rhythms of house. It's a combination that really works best with the aid of psychedelic substances with four-letter initials. Of course, the Sonar crowd of ravers-on-holiday already know that. 66 Water St. ℂ **604/683-6695**. www.sonar.bc.ca. Cover varies C$5–C$10 (US$4–US$8) and up to C$20 (US$16) for special events.

The Stone Temple   Here, frat boys from America are tickled pink that the drinking age in B.C. is only 19. And dude! The beer's so cheap! 1082 Granville St. ℂ **604/488-1333**. Cover C$5 (US$4) weeknights; C$10 (US$8) weekends.

Tonic   Squeeze past the well-endowed door bunnies and you're in a narrow room with a soaring ceiling, oversize paintings of hard liquor bottles, and an impressive-looking disco ball. The crowd is post-university but as yet unmated. Music is Latin, Brazilian, and Top-40 mix on weekends. On nights when it's packed, the sweat evaporates from dancers and rises high into the vast ceiling where it falls as smoke-machine fog. Or that's one theory anyway. 919 Granville St. ℂ **604/669-0469**. Cover C$6–C$10 (US$4.80–US$8).

Voda Nightclub   Voda has quickly made a name for itself, attracting folks young, old, and in-between, with the only real common denominator being cash. The intriguing interior boasts a mix of waterfalls, rocks, and raw concrete—like a beautiful piece of 1950s Modernism. The small dance floor basks in the warm light from the hundreds of candles everywhere. Monday night is old-fashioned R&B and funk, Tuesday is reserved for bands playing Latin or reggae, Thursday nights are martini-elegant and a mix of DJs, and bands fill out the rest of the week with lots of hip-hop and R&B. In the Westin Grand Hotel, 783 Homer St. ℂ **604/684-3003**. Cover C$5–C$8 (US$4–US$6.50).

5 Gay & Lesbian Bars

B.C.'s enlightened attitude—it's one of three Canadian provinces where same-sex couples can wed—has had a curious effect on Vancouver's queer dance club scene—it's so laid-back and attitude-free that it's often hard to tell straight from gay, male go-go dancers and naked men in showers notwithstanding. The "Gay Village" is in the West End, particularly on Davie and Denman streets. Many clubs feature theme nights and dance parties, drag shows are ever popular, and every year in early August, as Gay Pride nears, the scene goes into overdrive. The **Gay Lesbian Transgendered Bisexual Community Centre,** 2–1170 Bute St. (ℂ **604/684-5307;** www.lgtbcentrevancouver. com), has information on the current hot spots, but it's probably easier just to pick up a free copy of *Xtra West!,* available in most downtown cafes.

The Dufferin Pub   Buff at the Duff is a city institution; other drag shows might be raunchier, but none have quite the style. Shows are Monday through Thursday. Friday and Sunday, the go-go boys strut their stuff (and yes, they do take it all off). The rest of the time—and before, during, and after many of the shows—the DJs keep you grooving. 900 Seymour St. ℂ **604/683-4251**.

The Fountain Head Pub   Where do you go when you've run rings round the bath-house and the disco ball no longer beckons? Reflecting the graying and—gasp!—mellowing of Vancouver's boomer-age gay crowd, the hottest new hangout for gays is, well, a pub, the Fountain Head, located in the heart of the city's gay ghetto on Davie Street. The Head offers excellent microbrewed draught, good pub munchies, and a pleasant humming atmosphere till the morning's wee hours. Cruising has been known to happen, but more often customers come with friends and have things other than intimacy in mind: Most of the bragging at the Head involves the size of people's portfolios. 1025 Davie St. ✆ 604/687-2222.

Heritage House Hotel   Once among the most disreputable of Gastown gay bars, this aging beauty of a downtown hotel was given a total face-lift. It's now home to three separate bars and lounges, all with a largely gay clientele. Downstairs, the Lotus Lounge is one of the hottest house music venues in town, particularly on Straight Up Fridays when the all-female DJ team spins sexy funky house. On Saturdays, clubbers gather for the deep underground house also referred to as West Coast house. On the main floor, the Milk Lounge has a popular gay following; men flock to Friday's Cream night and on Saturdays, it's Ladies Only. The third venue on the main floor is Honey, a comfortable lounge where a mixed crowd gathers for cocktails or beers. On most nights, the DJs keep the music on a mellow, conversational level. However, on Saturdays, decibels go up significantly when the Queen Bee review, a New York–style cabaret drag show, fills the house. 455 Abbott St. ✆ 604/685-7777. Cover Milk and Lotus C$5–C$12 (US$4–US$10) some nights, Honey only on Sat C$7 (US$5.50).

Numbers Cabaret   A multilevel dance club and bar, Numbers has been around for over 20 years and hasn't changed a bit. Extroverts hog the dance floor while admirers look on from the bar above. On the second floor, carpets, wood paneling, pool tables, darts, and a lower volume of music give it a neighborhood pub feel. 1042 Davie St. ✆ 604/685-4077. Cover Fri–Sat C$3 (US$2.50).

The Odyssey   Odyssey is the hottest and hippest gay/mixed dance bar in town (alley entrance is for men; women go in by the front door). The medium-size dance space is packed. Up above, a mirrored catwalk is reserved for those who can keep the beat. Shows vary depending on the night. Monday it's Sissy Boy, Saturday it's Fallen Angel go-go dancers, and Sunday it's the Feather Boa drag show. And on Thursday, it's "Shower Power"—yes, that is a pair of naked men in the shower above the dance floor. 1251 Howe St. ✆ 604/689-5256. www.theodysseynightclub.com. Cover C$3–C$5 (US$2.40–US$4). Wed no cover.

6 Other Diversions

CINEMA

Thanks to the number of resident moviemakers (both studio and independent), Vancouver is becoming quite a film town. First-run theaters show the same Hollywood junk seen everywhere in the world (on Tuesday at a discount rate), but for those with something more adventurous in mind, there are lots of options.

Attendance at the **Vancouver International Film Festival** (✆ 604/685-0260; www.viff.org) reaches over 100,000, not including the celebs who regularly drop in. At this highly respected October event, over 250 new films are shown, representing filmmakers from 40 countries. Asian films are particularly well represented.

ART HOUSE & REPERTORY THEATERS

Since 1972, the **Pacific Cinematheque,** 1131 Howe St. (© **604/688-FILM;** www. cinematheque.bc.ca), has featured classic and contemporary films from around the world. Screenings are organized into themes, such as "Jean Luc Godard's Early Efforts," film noir, or the "Hong Kong Action Flick: A Retrospective." Schedules are available in hipper cafes, record shops, and video stores around town. Admission is C$8.50 (US$7) for adults, C$7 (US$5.75) for seniors and students; double features cost C$2 (US$1.60) extra. Annual membership, required to purchase tickets, is C$3 (US$2.40).

SPECIALTY THEATERS

At the **CN IMAX,** Canada Place (© **604/682-IMAX**), a gargantuan screen features large-format flicks about denizens of the animal kingdom (sharks, wolves, elephants, X-treme athletes). A similar large screen at the **Alcan OMNIMAX,** Science World (© **604/443-7443**), features flicks about empty, wide-open spaces, colorful coral reefs, and the like.

Way off in the strip-mall lands of farthest Kingsway stands the **Raja,** 3215 Kingsway (© **604/436-1545**), a modest single-screen movie house dedicated to bringing in the best flicks from Bombay, the world's moviemaking capital. For those unfamiliar with the Indian masala genre, expect raw violence mixed with big production numbers—think *Mary Poppins* does *Die Hard.* Sometimes there are English subtitles, though strictly speaking they're not necessary. If Kingsway is too far off, there's another Raja on 639 Commercial Dr. (© **604/253-0402**).

CASINOS

Well, it ain't Vegas—there's no alcohol and no floor shows, betting limits are in force, so you can't lose too much, and half of the proceeds go to charity, so it's all for a good cause.

To try your luck, head over to the **Great Canadian Casino Downtown,** 1133 W. Hastings St. (© **604/682-8415**), open daily from noon to 4am. For blackjack, roulette, pai gow poker, and mini-baccarat, you can also try the **Royal Diamond Casino,** 750 Pacific Blvd., in the Plaza of Nations (© **604/899-1061**). Here you can play high roller from noon to 4am daily.

11

Getting to Know Victoria

To realize Victoria, you must take all that the eye admires most in Bournemouth, Torquay, the Isle of Wight, the Happy Valley at Hong Kong, the Doon, Sorrento and Camps Bay; add reminisces of the Thousand Islands, and arrange the whole round the Bay of Naples, with some Himalayas in the background.

—Rudyard Kipling, after visiting the city around 1908

Okay, so he was a writer, and prone to a bit of exaggeration. But he wasn't too far off the mark.

If you want to experience something of Victoria as Kipling saw it, head over to the Bengal Lounge in the Fairmont Empress Hotel, sink into a leather armchair, and order a drink. Overhead, the old ceiling fans gently waft colonial-era breezes while the light from the roaring fire sparkles off the glass eyeballs of the poor Bengal tiger mounted above the mantelpiece. In this time-warped atmosphere you might think you're in colonial India or some outpost of the Empire on the edge of a barbarous wasteland. . . . Except that your drink might be a fluorescent blue martini, the music wafting from the sound system mellow jazz, and the coats piled up on a nearby armchair made of Gore-Tex and fleece instead of wool or oilskin.

And that's Victoria, or at least one part of it: a little patch of the former British Empire wading into the shoals of a highly internationalized 21st century, and doing it with a kind of appealing vitality that tweaks nostalgia for the past with a thoroughly modern sensibility.

It's a very polite city. As in Vancouver, you'll be amazed at how nice the people are. Of course, you'd be nice, too, if you lived in such a pleasant place surrounded by such generous doses of natural beauty. Victoria, after all, with a population of about 325,000, occupies just a tiny corner of an island about one-fifth the size as England but far more wild—so wild, in fact, that in parts of it there are still no roads and the only way to get around is by boat or on foot.

Speaking of boats: They are an essential ingredient in Victoria's generous allotment of maritime charm, and they partially help to explain why the people who live and work here are so nice and the pace so leisurely. The modern anxiety that comes from clogged traffic arteries and bumper-to-bumper commutes simply does not exist in Victoria. Instead of road rage, Victoria residents have "ferry stress." In order to get on or off their island, they have to take a ferry (or a floatplane). And gliding through the waters of the Pacific Northwest, with mountains gleaming and orcas (maybe) splashing, is not the same as driving along a monotonous freeway at 70mph. Getting to Victoria is half the fun, especially if you take one of the ferries that wind through the beautiful Gulf Islands. There's something magical and majestic about arriving by boat, and hearing the deep blasts of the ship's horn as the vessel glides into the Inner Harbour. During your stay in Victoria you'll be pleasantly aware of all kinds of marine activity. In the summer, of course, Victoria is a major port of call for cruise ships.

Even though they're in *British* Columbia, some people traveling here don't "get" the British part. Just what is this tie that Victoria has to England?

First of all, the entire region was once claimed by the British (among others), and came under British rule in the mid-19th century, when the Strait of Juan de Fuca became one of the new dividing lines between the U.S. and Canada. Victoria really was a British colony. That's why there's a statue of Queen Victoria, the city's namesake, standing in all her dumpy imperial glory in front of the Provincial Legislature building (which some still insist on calling "Parliament"). With colonyhood (and a big gold rush) came colonists, who imported many British customs and brought a kind of domesticating Old World sensibility to their wild, New World home. They thought they were bringing civilization, but that wasn't how the First Nations tribes that had been in the area for at least 8,000 years saw it.

British patriotism and customs might have faded away altogether except that, in the 1920s, Victoria's population began to drop as business shifted over to Vancouver. Local merchants panicked. And it was then that San Francisco–born George Warren of the Victoria Publicity Bureau put forward his proposal: Sell the Olde England angle.

Warren had never been to England and had no idea what it looked like. But to him, Victoria seemed English. To the city's merchants, Warren's scheme seemed like just the thing. And for three-plus generations it served the city well. While other places (including Vancouver) were leveling their "old" downtowns in the name of urban renewal, Victoria nurtured and preserved its heritage buildings, adding gardens and lavish city parks. Eventually it possessed that rarest of commodities for a North American city, a gorgeous, walkable, historic city center.

True, the "let's pretend we're in England" mindset meant ignoring certain details. Whales sometimes swam into the Inner Harbour; snowcapped mountain peaks loomed just across the water from Ross Bay; and trees in the surrounding forests towered far higher than Big Ben. So be it. It worked, and it didn't turn into Disneyland in the process.

The city is one thing, its location something else. Only in the past decade or so has Victoria finally begun to understand just what it has and make use of its stunning physical surroundings. Whale-watching is now a major industry. Kayak tours are becoming ever more popular. Mountain bikes have taken to competing for road space with the bright-red double-decker tour buses. Ecotourism is big, and "outdoor adventures" are available in just about every form you can think of. Your trip will be even more memorable if you move a bit beyond Tourist Central (the Inner Harbour area) and put yourself in touch with Mother Nature.

Afterwards, you can sip a lovely cream tea or a fluorescent blue martini.

1 Orientation

Victoria is on the southeastern tip of Vancouver Island, across the Strait of Juan de Fuca from Washington State's snowcapped Olympic peninsula. It's 72km (45 miles) south of the 49th Parallel, the border between most of Canada and the contiguous United States.

Once you've arrived, head for the Inner Harbour where lovingly restored vintage sailboats are berthed side by side with modern watercraft in the snug harbor, right in the heart of the city. A waterfront causeway runs along it in front of The Fairmont Empress hotel, one of Victoria's most picturesque spots. Just a few steps away are the Royal British Columbia Museum, Undersea World, Thunderbird Park's totem poles, Chinatown, downtown and Old Town's shopping streets and restaurants, and Beacon Hill Park.

ARRIVING
BY PLANE   The **Victoria International Airport** (© 250/953-7500; www.victoria airport.com) is near the Sidney ferry terminal, 26km (16 miles) north of Victoria off the Patricia Bay Highway (Hwy. 17). Highway 17 heads south to Victoria, becoming Douglas Street as you enter downtown.

The **Akal Airporter shuttle bus** (© 250/386-2525; wwwvictoriaairporter.com) makes the trip into town in about half an hour. Buses leave every 30 minutes daily from 4:30am to midnight; the fare is C$15 (US$12) one-way. Drop-offs are made at most hotels and bed-and-breakfasts, and pickups can be arranged as well. A limited number of hotel courtesy buses also serve the airport. A cab ride into downtown Victoria costs about C$45 (US$34) plus tip. **Empress Cabs** and **Blue Bird Cabs** (see "Getting Around," below) make airport runs.

Several **car-rental firms** have desks at the airport, including **Avis** (© 800/879-2847 or 250/656-6033; www.avis.com), **Budget** (© 800/668-9833 or 250/953-5300; www.budgetvictoria.com), **Hertz** (© 800/654-3131 or 250/656-2312; www.hertz.com), and **National** (© 800/227-7368 or 250/656-2541; www.nationalcar.com).

BY TRAIN, BUS & FERRY   VIA Rail Canada trains (© 888/842-7245; www.viarail.ca) arrive at Victoria's **E&N Station,** 450 Pandora Ave., near the Johnson Street Bridge (© 250/383-4324).

The **Victoria Bus Depot** is at 700 Douglas St., behind The Fairmont Empress hotel. **Pacific Coach Lines** (© 800/661-1725 U.S. and Canada, or 604/662-7575 from Vancouver; www.pacificcoach.com) offers daily service to and from Vancouver. **Island Coach Lines** (© 250/385-4411; www.victoriatours.com) has daily scheduled runs on Vancouver Island to Nanaimo, Port Alberni, Campbell River, and Port Hardy.

For information on arriving by **ferry,** see "Getting to Victoria," in chapter 2. Exiting the Swartz Bay ferry terminal by **car,** you'll be on Highway 17 (there is no other option), which leads directly into downtown Victoria where it becomes Blanshard Street, 3 blocks from the Inner Harbour.

VISITOR INFORMATION
TOURIST OFFICES & MAGAZINES   **Tourism Victoria Visitor Info Centre,** 812 Wharf St. (© 250/953-2033; www.tourismvictoria.com), is located on the Inner Harbour, across from The Fairmont Empress hotel. If you didn't reserve a room before you arrived, you can go to this office or call its **reservations hot line** (© 800/663-3883) for last-minute bookings at hotels, inns, and B&Bs. The center is open daily September 1 to June 15 from 9am to 5pm and June 16 to August 31 from 8:30am to 7:30pm.

If you want to explore the rest of 459km-long (285-mile) Vancouver Island, this office will help put you on the right track; you'll find a list of all the **regional tourism offices** on Vancouver Island at **www.islands.bc.ca**.

For details on the after-dark scene, pick up a copy of *Monday* magazine (www.mondaymag.com/monday), available free in cafes around the city. *Monday* not only is an excellent guide to Victoria's nightlife but also has driven at least one mayor from office with its award-winning muckraking journalism. The online version has detailed entertainment listings.

WEBSITES   See "The Best Websites for Vancouver & Victoria," on p. 15.

CITY LAYOUT

Victoria was born at the edge of the Inner Harbour in the 1840s and spread outward from there. The areas of most interest to visitors, including **downtown** and **Old Town,** lie along the eastern edge of the **Inner Harbour.** (North of the Johnson St. Bridge is the **Upper Harbour,** which is largely industrial but taking on new life as old buildings are redeveloped.) A little farther east, the **Ross Bay** and **Oak Bay** residential areas around Dallas Road and Beach Drive reach the beaches along the open waters of the Strait of Juan de Fuca.

Victoria's central landmark is **The Fairmont Empress** hotel on Government Street, right across from the Inner Harbour wharf. If you turn your back to the hotel, downtown and Old Town are on your right, while the provincial **Legislative Buildings** and the **Royal B.C. Museum** are on your immediate left. Next to them is the dock for the **Seattle–Port Angeles ferries** and beyond that the residential community of **James Bay,** the first neighborhood in the city to be developed.

MAIN ARTERIES & STREETS   Three main **north–south arteries** intersect just about every destination you may want to reach in Victoria.

Government Street goes through Victoria's main downtown shopping-and-dining district. Wharf Street, edging the harbor, merges with Government Street at The Fairmont Empress hotel. **Douglas Street,** running parallel to Government Street, is the main business thoroughfare as well as the road to Nanaimo and the rest of the island. It's also Trans-Canada Highway 1. The "Mile 0" marker sits at the corner of Douglas and Dallas Road. Also running parallel to Government and Douglas streets is **Blanshard Street** (Hwy. 17), the route to the Saanich Peninsula, including the Sidney–Vancouver ferry terminal, and Butchart Gardens.

Important **east–west streets** include the following: **Johnson Street** lies at the northern end of downtown and the Old Town, where the small E&N Station sits opposite Swans Hotel at the corner of Wharf Street. The Johnson Street Bridge is the demarcation line between the Upper Harbour and the Inner Harbour. **Belleville Street** is the Inner Harbour's southern edge. The Legislative Buildings and the ferry terminal are here. Belleville Street loops around westward toward Victoria Harbour before heading south, becoming Dallas Road. **Dallas Road** follows the water's edge past residential areas and beaches before it winds northward up to Oak Bay.

FINDING AN ADDRESS   Victoria addresses are written like those in Vancouver: The suite or room number precedes the building number. For instance, 100–1250 Government St. refers to suite 100 at 1250 Government St.

Victoria's streets are numbered from the city's southwest corner and increase in increments of 100 per block as you go north and east. (1000 Douglas St., for example, is 2 blocks north of 800 Douglas St.) Addresses for all the east–west streets (Fort, Yates, Johnson, and so on) in the downtown area start at 500 at Wharf Street; thus, all buildings between Wharf and Government streets fall between 500 and 599, while all buildings between Government and Douglas streets fall between 600 and 699, and so on.

STREET MAPS   Detailed street maps are available free at the **Tourism Victoria Visitor Info Centre** (see "Visitor Information," above). The best map of the surrounding area is the **B.C. Provincial Parks** map of Vancouver Island, also available at the Info Centre.

NEIGHBORHOODS IN BRIEF

Downtown & Old Town These areas have been the city's social and commercial focal points since the mid-1800s, when settlers first arrived by ship. This is also the area of the city most popular with visitors, filled with shops, museums, heritage buildings, and lots of restaurants. The area's fascinating Barbary Coast history—which includes rum smuggling, opium manufacturing, gold prospecting, whaling, fur trading, and shipping—is reflected in the hundreds of heritage buildings, once home to chandleries, warehouses, factories, whorehouses, and gambling dens.

The two neighborhoods are usually listed together because it's difficult to say where one leaves off and the other begins. The Old Town consists of the pre-1900 commercial sections of the city that grew up around the original Fort Victoria at View and Government streets. Roughly speaking, it extends from Fort Street north to Pandora and from Wharf Street east to Douglas. Downtown is everything outside of that, from the Inner Harbour to Quadra Street in the east and from Belleville Street in the south up to Herald Street at the northern edge of downtown.

Chinatown Victoria's Chinatown is tiny—only 2 square blocks—but venerable. In fact, it's the oldest Chinese community in North America. Its many interesting historic sites include Fan Tan Alley, Canada's narrowest commercial street, where legal opium manufacturing took place in the hidden courtyard buildings flanking the 1.2m-wide (3.9-ft.) way. (If you saw the movie *Bird on a Wire,* you may remember Mel Gibson riding through Fan Tan Alley in a great motorcycle chase scene.)

James Bay, Ross Bay & Oak Bay When Victoria was a busy port and trading post, the local aristocracy—merchant princes and their merchant princess daughters, for the most part—would retire to homes in these neighborhoods to escape the hustle-bustle in the city center below. Today, they remain beautiful residential communities. Houses perch on hills overlooking the straits or nestle amid lushly landscaped gardens. Golf courses, marinas, and a few cozy inns edge the waters, where you can stroll the beaches or go for a dip if you don't mind a chill.

2 Getting Around

Strolling along the Inner Harbour's pedestrian walkways and streets is very pleasant. The terrain is predominantly flat, and, with few exceptions, Victoria's main points of interest are accessible in less than 30 minutes on foot.

BY PUBLIC TRANSPORTATION

BY BUS   The **Victoria Regional Transit System (B.C. Transit)** (✆ **250/382-6161;** www.bctransit.com) operates 40 bus routes through greater Victoria as well as the nearby towns of Sooke and Sidney. Buses run to both the Butchart Gardens and the Vancouver Ferry Terminal at Sidney. Regular service on the main routes runs daily from 6am to just past midnight.

Schedules and route maps are available at the Tourism Victoria Visitor Info Centre (see "Visitor Information," above), where you can pick up a copy of the *Victoria*

The Ferry Ballet

Starting at 9:45am every Sunday during summer, the ferries gather in front of The Fairmont Empress to perform a **ferry "ballet"**—it looks much like the hippo dance in Disney's *Fantasia*.

Rider's Guide or *Discover Vancouver on Transit: Including Victoria.* Popular Victoria bus routes include **no. 2** (Oak Bay), **no. 5** (downtown, James Bay, Beacon Hill Park), **no. 14** (Victoria Art Gallery, Craigdarroch Castle, University of Victoria), **no. 61** (Sooke), **no. 70** (Sidney, Swartz Bay), and **no. 75** (Butchart Gardens).

Fares are calculated on a per-zone basis. One-way single-zone fares are C$2 (US$1.60) for adults and students, and C$1.25 (US$1) for seniors and children 5 to 13; two zones cost C$2.75 (US$2.20) and C$2 (US$1.60), respectively. Transfers are good for travel in one direction only, with no stopovers. A **DayPass,** C$6 (US$4.80) for adults and students, and C$4 (US$3.20) for seniors and children 5 to 13, covers unlimited travel throughout the day. You can buy passes at the Tourism Victoria Visitor Info Centre (see "Visitor Information," above), convenience stores, and ticket outlets throughout Victoria displaying the FAREDEALER sign.

BY FERRY   Crossing the Inner, Upper, and Victoria harbours by one of the blue 12-passenger **Victoria Harbour Ferries** (© **250/708-0201;** www.victoriaharbourferry.com) is cheap and fun. Identical to Vancouver's False Creek Ferries, these boats have big windows all the way around and look like they're straight out of a cartoon. Fortunately, the harbor is smooth sailing. May through September, the ferries to The Fairmont Empress hotel, Coast Harbourside Hotel, and Ocean Pointe Resort hotel run about every 15 minutes daily from 9am to 9pm. In March, April, and October, ferry service runs daily 11am to 5pm. November through February, the ferries run only on sunny weekends 11am to 5pm. The cost per hop is C$3.50 (US$2.80) for adults and C$1.50 (US$1.20) for children.

Instead of just taking the ferry for a short hop across, try the 45-minute **Harbour tour** ⚓ for C$14 (US$11) adults, C$12 (US$10) seniors, and C$7 (US$5.60) children under 12, or the 55-minute **Gorge tour** ⚓ for C$16 (US$13) adults, C$14 (US$11) seniors, and C$8 (US$6.40) children under 12.

BY CAR

You can easily explore the downtown area of Victoria by foot. If you're planning out-of-town activities, you can rent a car in town or bring your own on one of the car-passenger ferries from Vancouver. Traffic is light in Victoria by U.S. standards, largely because the downtown core is so walkable and there's no point in using a car. Gas is sold by the liter, averaging around C$1 (US80¢). That may seem inexpensive until you consider that a gallon of gas costs about C$3.80 (US$3). Speeds and distances are posted in kilometers. See the front cover of this guide for conversion tables.

RENTALS   Car-rental agencies in Victoria include the following: **Avis,** 1001 Douglas St. (© **800/879-2847** or 250/386-8468; www.avis.com; bus no. 5 to Broughton St.); **Budget,** 757 Douglas St. (© **800/668-9833** or 250/953-5300; www.budgetvictoria.com); **Hertz,** 655 Douglas St., in the Queen Victoria Inn (© **800/654-3131** or 250/360-2822; www.hertz.com); and **National,** 767 Douglas St. (© **800/227-7368** or 250/386-1213; www.nationalvictoria.com). These latter three can be reached on the no. 5 bus to the Convention Centre.

PARKING   Metered **street parking** is available in the downtown area, but be sure to feed the meter because rules are strictly enforced. Unmetered parking on side streets is rare. All major downtown hotels have guest parking, with rates from free to C$20 (US$16) per day. There are parking lots at **View Street** between Douglas and Blanshard streets, **Johnson Street** off Blanshard Street, **Yates Street** north of Bastion Square, and **the Bay** on Fisgard at Blanshard Street.

DRIVING RULES   Canadian driving rules are similar to regulations in the United States. Seat belts must be worn, children under 5 must be in child restraints, and motorcyclists must wear helmets. It's legal to turn right on a red light after you've come to a full stop. Unlike the U.S., daytime headlights are mandatory. Some of the best places on Vancouver Island can be reached only via gravel logging roads, on which logging trucks have absolute right-of-way. If you're on a logging road and see a logging truck coming from either direction, pull over to the side of the road and stop to let it pass.

AUTO CLUB   Members of the **American Automobile Association (AAA)** can get emergency assistance from the **British Columbia Automobile Association (BCAA)** by calling ✆ **800/222-4357.**

BY BIKE

Biking is the easiest way to get around the downtown and beach areas. There are bike lanes throughout the city and paved paths along parks and beaches. Helmets are mandatory, and riding on sidewalks is illegal, except where bike paths are indicated. You can rent bikes starting at C$5 (US$4) per hour and C$15 (US$12) per day (lock and helmet included) from **Cycle B.C.,** 747 Douglas St. (✆ **866/380-2453** or 250/885-2453; www.cyclebc.ca).

BY TAXI

Within the downtown area, you can expect to travel for less than C$6 (US$4.80), plus tip. It's best to call for a cab; drivers don't always stop on city streets for flag-downs, especially when it's raining. Call for a pickup from **Empress Cabs** (✆ **250/381-2222**) or **Blue Bird Cabs** (✆ **250/382-4235**).

BY PEDDLE-CAB

You get to sit while an avid bicyclist with thighs of steel peddles you anywhere you want to go for C$1 (US80¢) per minute (C$2/US$1.60 per minute if there are four of you). You'll see these two- and four-seater bike cabs along the Inner Harbour at the base of Bastion Square, or you can call **Kabuki Kabs** (✆ **250/385-4243;** www.kabukikabs.com) for 24-hour service.

FAST FACTS: Victoria

American Express   The office is at 1213 Douglas St. (✆ **250/385-8731**) and is open Monday through Friday 8:30am to 4:30pm and Saturday 10am to 4pm. Get there on bus no. 5 to Yates St.

Area Code   The telephone area code for all of Vancouver Island, including Victoria and most of British Columbia, is **250.** For the greater Vancouver area, including Squamish and Whistler, it's **604.**

Business Hours Victoria **banks** are open Monday through Thursday 10am to 3pm and Friday 10am to 6pm. **Stores** are generally open Monday through Saturday 10am to 6pm. Some establishments are open later, as well as on Sundays, in summer. Last call at the city's **bars** and **cocktail lounges** is 2am.

Consulates See "Fast Facts: Vancouver," in chapter 4.

Currency Exchange The best exchange rates in town can be found at banks and by using ATMs. **Royal Bank,** 1079 Douglas St. at Fort Street, is in the heart of downtown. Take bus no. 5 to Fort Street.

Dentist Most major hotels have a dentist on call. **Cresta Dental Centre,** 3170 Tillicum Rd., at Burnside Street in the Tillicum Mall (✆ **250/384-7711**; bus no. 10), is open Monday through Friday 8am to 9pm, Saturday 9am to 5:30pm, and Sunday 11am to 5pm.

Doctor Hotels usually have doctors on call. The **Tillicum Mall Medical Clinic,** 3170 Tillicum at Burnside Street (✆ **250/381-8112**; bus no. 10 to Tillicum Mall), accepts walk-in patients daily 9am to 9pm.

Electricity The same 110 volts AC (60 cycles) as in the United States.

Emergencies Dial ✆ **911** for fire, police, ambulance, and poison control. This is a free call.

Hospitals Local hospitals include the **Royal Jubilee Hospital,** 1900 Fort St. (✆ **250/370-8000**; emergency 250/370-8212) and the **Victoria General Hospital,** 1 Hospital Way (✆ **250/727-4212**; emergency 250/727-4181). You can get to both hospitals on bus no. 14.

Hotlines Emergency numbers include: **Royal Canadian Mounted Police** (✆ 250/ 380-6261), **Emotional Crisis Centre** (✆ 250/386-6323), **Sexual Assault Centre** (✆ 250/383-3232), **Poison Control Centre** (✆ 800/567-8911), and **Help Line for Children** (dial ✆ 0 and ask for Zenith 1234).

Internet Access Open late in the heart of the old town is **Stain Internet Café,** 609 Yates St. (✆ **250/382-3352**). Closer to the Legislature, try **James Bay Coffee and Books,** 143 Menzies St. (✆ **250/386-4700**). Most hotels also have Internet access, as does the Victoria Public Library; see below.

Library The **Greater Victoria Public Library** (✆ **250/382-7241**; bus no. 5 to Broughton St.) is at 735 Broughton St., near the corner of Fort and Douglas streets.

Luggage Storage & Lockers Most hotels will store bags for guests who are about to check in or who have just checked out. Otherwise, coin lockers for C$1 (US80¢) are available outside the bus station (behind The Fairmont Empress hotel). Take bus no. 5 to the Convention Centre.

Newspapers The morning *Times Colonist* comes out daily. The weekly entertainment paper *Monday* magazine comes out, strangely enough, on Thursday.

Pharmacies **Shopper's Drug Mart,** 1222 Douglas St. (✆ **250/381-4321**; bus no. 5 to View St.), is open Monday through Friday 7am to 8pm, Saturday 9am to 7pm, and Sunday 9am to 6pm.

Police Dial ✆ **911.** This is a free call. The **Victoria City Police** can also be reached by calling ✆ **250/995-7654.**

Post Office   The **main post office** is at 714 Yates St. (☎ **250/953-1352,** bus no. 5 to Yates St.). There are also postal outlets in **Shopper's Drug Mart** (see "Pharmacies," above) and in other stores displaying the CANADA POST postal outlet sign. Supermarkets and many souvenir and gift shops also sell stamps.

Radio   **CBC Radio One,** a public news and information broadcaster akin to National Public Radio or the BBC, is located at 690 AM in Vancouver, 90.5 FM in Victoria, 100.1 FM in Whistler, and 91.5 FM in Tofino.

Safety   Crime rates are quite low in Victoria, but transients panhandle throughout the downtown and Old Town areas. The most common crimes are property crimes, which are usually preventable with a few extra common-sense precautions.

Weather   Check the forecasts at www.weather.com.

12

Where to Stay in Victoria

Victoria has been welcoming visitors for over a century, so it knows how to do it with style. You'll find a wide choice of fine accommodations in all price ranges, most in the Old Town, in downtown, or around the Inner Harbour and within easy walking distance of the city's main attractions (except for Butchart Gardens). A 20-minute or half-hour drive north, east, or west takes you to Brentwood Bay, Sooke, and Malahat—wonderful hideaways offering more solitude.

Spas are now an almost essential part of big hotels in Victoria—so much so that the Inner Harbour has been dubbed Spa Harbour, with major spas at the Delta Ocean Pointe, the Fairmont Empress, and the Hotel Grand Pacific. You can get fine spa treatments at all three, and the hotels all offer special spa/accommodations packages on their websites.

Speaking of websites, it's always a good idea to check them out because you'll usually find much cheaper promotional rates or seasonal rates than the rack rates I list here.

You'll save big-time if you schedule your holiday from October to May. When the high summer season starts in June, rates tend to skyrocket, especially at the finer resort hotels.

Reservations are essential in Victoria June through September. If you arrive without a reservation and have trouble finding a room, **Tourism Victoria** (② **800/663-3883** or 250/953-2022) can make reservations for you at hotels, inns, and B&Bs. It deals only with establishments that pay a fee to list with them; fortunately, most do.

Prices quoted here don't include the **10% provincial accommodations tax** or the **7% goods-and-services tax (GST).** Non-Canadians can get a GST rebate on short-stay accommodations by filling out the Tax Refund Application (see "Taxes," under "Fast Facts: Vancouver," in chapter 4).

1 Best Victoria Hotel Bets

For a quick overview of the best splurge and moderately priced hotels in Victoria, see chapter 1, p. 11.

- **Best Historic Hotel:** Architect Francis Rattenbury's masterpiece, The **Fairmont Empress,** 721 Government St. (② **800/441-1414** or 250/384-8111), has charmed princes (and their princesses), potentates, movie stars, and the likes of you and me since 1908. See p. 195.
- **Best for Business Travelers:** With its central location, large desks and dataports, secretarial services, elegant lobby, small meeting rooms, dining rooms, and understated luxury at a reasonable price, **The Magnolia,** 623 Courtney St. (② **877/624-6654** or 250/381-0999), is Victoria's best spot for business. See p. 203.
- **Best Place to Pretend You Died & Went to Bel Air: The Aerie,** 600 Ebedora Lane, Malahat (② **800/518-1933** or 250/743-7115), a red-tiled villa high atop

Mount Malahat, features hand-carved king-size beds, massive wood-burning fireplaces, chandeliered Jacuzzis, and faux marble finish by the gross ton. See p. 206.

- **Best Hotel Lobby:** The two-story plate glass demi-lune in the lobby of the **Delta Victoria Ocean Pointe Resort and Spa,** 45 Songhees Rd. (© **800/667-4677** or 250/360-2999), provides the best vantage in Victoria for watching the lights on the legislature switch on. There are also comfy chairs and fireplaces to sit and get warm. See p. 195.

- **Best for Families:** The **Royal Scot Suite Hotel,** 425 Quebec St. (© **800/663-7515** or 250/388-5463), is a converted apartment building with spacious suites that'll make your family feel at home. They come with fully equipped kitchens, VCRs, and a video arcade and playroom in the basement. See p. 201.

- **Best B&B:** With rooms double the size of those in other B&Bs and every possible need taken care of, the friendly innkeepers at **The Haterleigh Heritage Inn,** 243 Kingston St. (© **866/234-2244** or 250/384-9995), do themselves proud. See p. 198.

- **Best Small Hotel:** The tastefully indulgent **Abigail's Hotel,** 906 McClure St. (© **866/347-5054** or 250/388-5363), has sumptuous sleeping chambers and warm, welcoming hosts. See p. 202.

- **Best Moderately Priced Hotel:** On the edge of the Inner Harbour, the **Admiral Inn,** 257 Belleville St. (© **888/823-6472** or ©/fax 250/388-6267), provides friendly service, free bikes, and the most reasonably priced harbor view around. See p. 199.

- **Best Inexpensive Hotel:** While the rooms in the main hotel are just okay, the next-door suites and cottage operated by **The James Bay Inn,** 270 Government St. (© **800/836-2649** or 250/384-7151), are a veritable steal. See p. 201.

- **Most Romantic Hotel:** Brand-new **Brentwood Bay Lodge & Spa,** 849 Verdier Ave. (© **888/544-2079** or 250/544-2079) is a small luxury resort overlooking a pristine fjord. Every detail in the rooms and bathrooms is perfect, from fabrics to fireplace; the finest Italian linens are on the beds, and there's a fabulous spa where you can get treatments for two. See p. 207.

- **Best Alternative Accommodations: The Boathouse,** 746 Sea Dr. (© **866/654-9370** or 250/652-9370), is a real (converted) boathouse, with a private dock and a rowing dinghy. Built in a secluded cove, the one-room cottage is a perfect spot for those seeking privacy. See p. 208.

- **Best Location:** Not only is **Swans Suite Hotel,** 506 Pandora Ave. (© **800/668-7926** or 250/361-3310), in the heart of the old town and just a block from the harbor, it's also right above **Swans Pub,** one of the most pleasant restaurant/brewpubs in the entire city. See p. 205.

- **Best Spas:** There are two in the city and one about a 20-minute drive from downtown. **Delta Victoria Ocean Pointe Resort and Spa,** 45 Songhees Rd. (© **800/667-4677** or 250/360-2999), is a calm, contemporary, Zen-like facility. More traditional, and completely luxurious, is the Willow Stream spa at the **Fairmont Empress,** 721 Government St. (© **800/441-1414** or 250/384-8111). The new Essence of Life spa at **Brentwood Bay Lodge & Spa,** 849 Verdier Ave. (© **888/544-2079** or 250/544-2079), has the most impressive hydro-bath in British Columbia. All three spas offer complete skin and body treatments, aesthetics, and aromatherapy treatments to pamper the body and spirit.

- **Best Fitness Center and Pool:** The fitness center at the **Hotel Grand Pacific,** 463 Belleville St. (*C* **800/663-7550** or 250/386-0450), offers aerobics classes, a 25m (82-ft.) ozonated indoor pool, a separate kids' pool, and a weight room; the hotel's sauna, whirlpool, and massage therapist can help ease the pain from all that exercise. See p. 198.
- **Best Views:** With panoramic harbor views in an elegant, Japanese-influenced decor, the **Laurel Point Inn,** 680 Montreal St. (*C* **800/663-7667** or 250/386-8721), is the place for view junkies. Outside of town, **The Aerie,** 600 Ebedora Lane, Malahat (*C* **800/518-1933** or 250/743-7115), offers private terraces with views across tree-clad mountains to a long blue coastal fjord. See p. 199 and 206, respectively.
- **Best Oceanside Inn:** In the little town of Sooke, just west of Victoria, the **Sooke Harbour House,** 1528 Whiffen Spit Rd., Sooke (*C* **800/889-9688** or 250/642-3421), offers quiet West Coast elegance and an exceptional restaurant. See p. 208.

2 The Inner Harbour & Nearby

VERY EXPENSIVE

Delta Victoria Ocean Pointe Resort and Spa 🖝🖝 *(Kids)*   You can always rely on a Delta hotel to provide top-quality service. The "OPR," located across the Johnson Street Bridge on the Inner Harbour's north shore, is a big, bright, modern hotel with commanding views of downtown, the legislature, the Fairmont Empress, and the busy harbor itself, full of boats and floatplanes. You'll see this view as you enter the grand lobby with its two-story-tall windows. The rooms here are nice and big, and so are the bathrooms. The decor, like the hotel itself, is a blend of contemporary and traditional; the beds, with duvets and fine linens, are really comfortable. The prime view rooms face the Inner Harbour; rooms with a "working harbor" view look out over a less interesting industrial mixed-use scene. A few extra dollars buys a few extra perks, like breakfast and evening hors d'oeuvres in the third-floor Signature Lounge. All guests have use of the big indoor pool, a really good whirlpool, and a fully equipped gym with racquetball and tennis courts. Lots of guests come for the new spa, one of the best in Victoria: It's a tranquil, Zen-like space. The hotel features accommodations/spa packages, so check the website for specials. Like all the Delta hotels, OPR is very kid-friendly. Kids receive a free welcome kit, and they'll love the pool.

45 Songhees Rd., Victoria, B.C. V9A 6T3. *C* 800/667-4677 or 250/360-2999. Fax 250/360-1041. www.delta hotels.com. 250 units. C$129–C$399 (US$103–US$319) double, C$350–$1299 (US$280–US$1039) suite. Children under 17 stay free in parent's room. AE, DC, MC, V. Underground valet parking C$12 (US$10). Bus: 24 to Colville. **Amenities:** 2 restaurants; bar; indoor pool; outdoor tennis courts; health club; full-service spa; Jacuzzi; sauna; concierge; 24-hr. business center; 24-hr. room service; in-room massage; babysitting; same-day dry cleaning; non-smoking rooms; executive-level rooms; rooms for those w/limited mobility. *In room:* A/C, TV/VCR w/pay movies, Internet, minibar, coffeemaker, hair dryer, iron, safe, bathrobes, complimentary newspaper.

The Fairmont Empress 🖝🖝   Francis Rattenbury's 1908 harborside creation is the most famous landmark on the Victoria waterfront. When you see it, you'll instantly think that you'd love to stay there. Think twice, however, before throwing down the plastic. The hotel's 256 standard rooms (called Fairmont rooms) cost more and offer less than you can find elsewhere in the city. They're small rooms with smaller bathrooms and little in the way of view. For some, the hotel's fabulous location and the

Where to Stay in Victoria

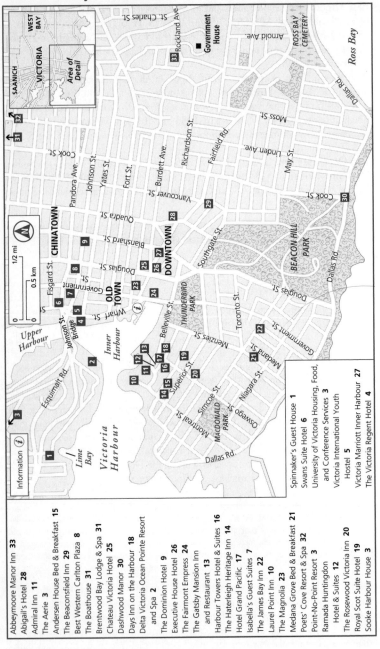

Abbeymoore Manor Inn **33**
Abigail's Hotel **28**
Admiral Inn **11**
The Aerie **3**
Andersen House Bed & Breakfast **15**
The Beaconsfield Inn **29**
Best Western Carlton Plaza **8**
The Boathouse **31**
Brentwood Bay Lodge & Spa **31**
Chateau Victoria Hotel **25**
Dashwood Manor **30**
Days Inn on the Harbour **18**
Delta Victoria Ocean Pointe Resort and Spa **2**
The Dominion Hotel **9**
Executive House Hotel **26**
The Fairmont Empress **24**
The Gatsby Mansion Inn and Restaurant **13**
Harbour Towers Hotel & Suites **16**
The Haterleigh Heritage Inn **14**
Hotel Grand Pacific **17**
Isabella's Guest Suites **7**
The James Bay Inn **22**
Laurel Point Inn **10**
The Magnolia **23**
Medana Grove Bed & Breakfast **21**
Poets' Cove Resort & Spa **32**
Point-No-Point Resort **3**
Ramada Huntingdon Hotel & Suites **12**
The Rosewood Victoria Inn **20**
Royal Scot Suite Hotel **19**
Sooke Harbour House **3**
Spinnaker's Guest House **1**
Swans Suite Hotel **6**
University of Victoria Housing, Food, and Conference Services **3**
Victoria International Youth Hostel **5**
Victoria Marriott Inner Harbour **27**
The Victoria Regent Hotel **4**

building itself as well as its first-class amenities—its large pool, good weight room, luxurious Willow Stream spa, lounge, restaurant, tea lobby, and so on—or just the aura of being in the Empress makes up for this lack of personal space. The 80 Deluxe rooms are bigger, with high ceilings and—for 60 of them anyway—a view of the harbor. They come with a small sitting area, a writing desk, and the same small, functional bathroom. The 12 Signature rooms are corner rooms with big desks, queen bed, and small seating area, and yes, the same small, functional bathroom. At the top of the heap are the Fairmont Gold rooms with high arched ceilings, wide windows, king beds, a big desk, CD player, and—finally—bathrooms with a (one-person) soaker tub and shower. If you can afford a Fairmont Gold or a Signature room—go for it. If you can't, it may be better to admire the Empress from afar. Or just come here for afternoon tea (see "Taking Afternoon Tea," in chapter 13).

721 Government St., Victoria, B.C. V8W 1W5. *C* **800/441-1414** or 250/384-8111. Fax 250/381-4334. www.fairmont.com/empress. 477 units. C$179–C$569 (US$143–US$455) double, C$279–C$1300 (US$223–US$1040) suite. AE, DC, DISC, MC, V. Underground valet parking C$19 (US$15). Bus: 5. **Amenities:** 2 restaurants; bar/lounge; tearoom (p. 216); indoor pool; high-quality health club; spa; Jacuzzi; sauna; concierge; business center; shopping arcade; limited room service; in-room massage; babysitting; laundry service; same-day dry cleaning service; nonsmoking rooms; executive-level room; rooms for those w/limited mobility. *In room:* TV w/pay movies, Internet, hair dryer, iron.

EXPENSIVE

Andersen House Bed & Breakfast *R*   The art and furnishings in Andersen House are drawn from the whole of the old British Empire and a good section of the modern world beyond. The 1891 house has the high ceilings, stained-glass windows, and ornate fireplaces typical of the Queen Anne style, but the art and decorations are far more eclectic. Each room has a unique style: The sun-drenched Casablanca room on the top floor, for example, boasts Persian rugs, a four-poster queen bed, and a boxed window seat. All rooms have private entrances and come with books, CD players and CDs, and complimentary high-speed wireless Internet access; all feature soaker tubs or two-person Jacuzzis. The Andersens have also recently opened **Baybreeze Manor** (3930 Telegraph Bay Rd.; *C* **250/721-3930;** www.baybreezemanor.com), a restored 1885 farmhouse that's a 15-minute drive from downtown. The two farmhouse units

---

The Best Bed & Breakfast Registries

If you prefer to stay at a B&B other than those listed in this chapter, the following agencies specialize in matching guests to the B&Bs that best suit their needs:

- **Born Free Bed & Breakfast of B.C.,** 4390 Frances St., Burnaby, B.C. V5C 2R3 (*C* **604/298-8815;** www.vancouverbandb.bc.ca).
- **Canada-West Accommodations Bed & Breakfast Registry,** P.O. Box 86607, North Vancouver, B.C. V7L 4L2 (*C* **800/561-3223** or 604/990-6730; www.b-b.com).
- **Town and Country Bed & Breakfast,** P.O. Box 74542, 2803 W. 4th Ave., Vancouver, B.C. V6K IK2 (*C*/fax **604/731-5942;** www.townandcountrybedandbreakfast.com).

feature hardwood floors, fireplaces, queen beds, and Jacuzzi tubs, as well as free bicycle, canoe, and kayak usage and easy access to Cadboro Beach.

301 Kingston St., Victoria, B.C. V8V 1V5. ℭ 877/264-9988 or 250/388-4565. Fax 250/721-3938. www.andersenhouse. com. 4 B&B units, 2 Manor units. C$95–C$275 (US$76–US$220) B&B double; C$135–C$235 (US$108–US$188) Manor double. Rates include breakfast. MC, V. Free off-street parking. Bus: 30 to Superior and Oswego Sts. Children under 12 not accepted. **Amenities:** Jacuzzi; nonsmoking rooms. *In room:* TV/VCR, wi-fi, coffeemaker, hair dryer, iron.

Harbour Towers Hotel & Suites ⭐ 🄺🄸🄳🄼 Though there are a few standard rooms in this 12-story tower by the Inner Harbour, the one- and two-bedroom suites with fully equipped kitchens are a better value. In recent years the hotel has added some great features, such as an impressively upscale lobby, a day spa, and an improved fitness center with indoor pool. The rooms also received a complete overhaul, though the traditional-looking decor, though comfy, is fairly uninspired and plastic plants look decidedly weird in verdant Victoria. Most units feature floor-to-ceiling windows opening onto private balconies; some of the suites are bi-level. The harbor views are quite spectacular and worth reserving. The best rooms are the 12th-floor deluxe penthouse suites with enormous bathrooms, Jacuzzi tubs, and fireplaces. The larger suites are great for families, and there's a glass-walled kids' play area in the gym, so you can keep your eyes on the little ones while working out.

345 Quebec St., Victoria, B.C. V8V 1W4. ℭ 800/663-5896 or 250/385-2405. Fax 250/360-2313. www.harbourtowers. com. 195 units. C$122–C$239 (US$98–US$191) double, C$142–C$289 (US$114–US$231) suite, C$300–C$600 (US$240–US$488) penthouse suite. Children 16 and under stay free in parent's room. Extra adult C$15 (US$12). AE, DC, MC, V. Underground parking C$5 (US$4). Bus: 30 or 31 to Superior and Oswego Sts. **Amenities:** Restaurant; bar; indoor pool; health club; spa; Jacuzzi; sauna; business center; limited room service; babysitting; laundry service; same-day dry cleaning. *In room:* TV w/pay movies, Internet, coffeemaker, hair dryer, iron.

The Haterleigh Heritage Inn ⭐ Haterleigh innkeeper Paul Kelly is a font of information, on Victoria in general and on this lovingly restored 1901 home in particular. With his wife, Elizabeth, he runs this exceptional B&B that captures the essence of Victoria's romance with a combination of antique furniture, original stained-glass windows, and attentive personal service. The rooms feature high arched ceilings, large windows, sitting areas, and large bathrooms, some with hand-painted tiles and Jacuzzi tubs. On the top floor, the cozy Angel's Reach room features a big four-poster bed. The second-floor Secret Garden room has a small balcony with views of the Olympic mountain range. The Day Dreams room downstairs is the dedicated honeymoon suite. A full gourmet breakfast with organic produce is served family style at 8:30am. There's also complimentary sherry in the drawing room each evening. Rates vary according to season.

243 Kingston St., Victoria, B.C. V8V 1V5. ℭ 866/234-2244 or 250/384-9995. Fax 250/384-1935. www.haterleigh. com. 7 units. C$135–C$355 (US$108–US$284) double. Rates include full breakfast. MC, V. Free parking. Bus: 30 to Superior and Montreal sts. **Amenities:** Jacuzzi; Internet. *In room:* Hair dryer, bathrobes.

Hotel Grand Pacific ⭐⭐⭐ On Victoria's bustling Inner Harbour, directly across the street from the Port Angeles–Victoria ferry dock, the Grand Pacific is more luxurious than the Delta Ocean Pointe and has rooms that are generally more spacious than those at the Fairmont Empress. Like those other two hotels on the Inner Harbour, the Grand Pacific has its own spa; its health club is better than the others, and features a huge ozonated indoor pool. All rooms have balconies and are attractively and comfortably furnished. Standard rooms face the Olympic Mountains and Ogden Point or, for a bit more money, the Inner Harbour; bathrooms are on the small side. Suites provide the best views, overlooking the harbor and the Empress. The fabulous luxury suites feature huge bathrooms, fireplaces, and several balconies. Fine dining options include the informal Pacific Restaurant and The Mark (reviewed in chapter 13).

463 Belleville St., Victoria, B.C. V8V 1X3. ℂ 800/663-7550 or 250/386-0450. Fax 250/380-4473. www.hotel grandpacific.com. 304 units. C$152–C$286 (US$122–US$229) double; C$212–C$320 (US$170–US$256) suite. Extra person C$30 (US$24). AE, DC, DISC, MC, V. Free self-parking; valet parking C$10 (US$8). Bus: 30 to Superior and Oswego sts. **Amenities:** 2 restaurants; cafe; bar; indoor pool; superior health club; full-service spa; Jacuzzi; concierge; tour desk; business center; 24-hr. room service; massage; babysitting; laundry service; same-day dry cleaning; squash courts; nonsmoking rooms. *In room:* A/C, TV w/pay movies, Internet, minibar, coffeemaker, hair dryer, iron, safe, bathrobes.

Laurel Point Inn 🏵🏵🏵   This art-filled, resort-style hotel occupies a prettily land-scaped promontory jutting out into the Inner Harbour, and consists of the original north wing and a newer and quite beautiful south wing designed by noted Vancouver architect Arthur Erickson in 1989. The lobby and overall design reflects the elegant simplicity of Japanese artistic principals and is a refreshing change from the chintz and florals found in so many Victoria hotels. In both wings the price is greater for rooms facing the Inner Harbour, though the Outer Harbour views are actually just as good. Rooms in the older north wing are nice enough—with king beds, pocket balconies, and nice bathrooms—but the south wing is where you want to be: All the rooms here are suites featuring blond wood with black marble accents, shoji-style sliding doors, Asian artworks, and spacious bathrooms with deep soaker tubs and floor-to-ceiling glassed-in showers. It's stylish and good value.

680 Montreal St., Victoria, B.C. V8V 1Z8. ℂ 800/663-7667 or 250/386-8721. Fax 250/386-9547. www.laurelpoint. com. 200 units. C$114–C$279 (US$91–US$223) double, C$169–C$329 (US$135–US$263) suite. Children under 18 stay free in parent's room. Additional person C$15 (US$12). AE, DC, DISC, MC, V. Free valet parking. Bus: 30 to Montreal and Superior sts. Small dogs accepted for C$25 (US$20). **Amenities:** Restaurant; bar; indoor pool; complimentary access to YMCA facilities; Jacuzzi; concierge; business center; 24-hr. room service; massage; babysitting; same-day dry cleaning; rooms for those w/limited mobility. *In room:* A/C, TV, Internet, coffeemaker, hair dryer, iron, safe.

MODERATE
Admiral Inn (*Value*) (*Kids*)   The family-operated Admiral is in a three-story building on the Inner Harbour, near the Washington-bound ferry terminal and close to restaurants and shopping. The combination of comfortable, immaculately clean rooms and rea-sonable rates attracts young couples, families, seniors, and other travelers in search of a harbor view at a price that doesn't break the bank. The rooms are pleasant and com-fortably furnished, a bit motel-like, with small bathrooms and balconies or terraces. The more expensive rooms come with a kitchenette with small fridge and stove. The suites come with full kitchens. Some units can sleep up to six (on two double beds and a double sofa bed). The owners provide sightseeing advice as well as extras like free bicycles, free local calls, and an Internet terminal in the lobby.

257 Belleville St., Victoria, B.C. V8V 1X1. ℂ 888/823-6472 or ℂ/fax 250/388-6267. www.admiral.bc.ca. 29 units. C$99–C$219 (US$79–US$175) double, C$129–C$249 (US$103–C$199) suite. Extra person C$10 (US$8). Children under 12 stay free in parent's room. Rates include continental breakfast. AE, DC, MC, V. Free parking. Bus: 5 to Belleville and Government sts. **Amenities:** Complimentary bikes; coin laundry; dry cleaning; nonsmoking rooms; complimentary Internet access. *In room:* A/C, TV, kitchen/kitchenette (in some units), fridge, coffeemaker, hair dryer, iron.

Days Inn on the Harbour   This hotel across from the MV *Coho* ferry terminal on the Inner Harbour has small, motel-like rooms that aren't very distinguished but at least put you in a great location. Half the rooms face the Inner Harbour; the other half have views of the nearby residential area. View rooms cost a little more. The rooms come with queen, king, or two double beds and are outfitted with standard furnishings and step-up bathtubs. Eighteen rooms are equipped with kitchenettes. There's a small outdoor pool in back and a patio overlooking the harbor in front.

427 Belleville St., Victoria, B.C. V8V 1X3. (*)* 800/665-3024 or (*)*/fax 250/386-3451. www.daysinnvictoria.com. 71 units. C$69–C$183 (US$55–US$146) double. Extra person C$10 (US$8). Children under 12 stay free in parent's room. AE, DC, MC, V. Free parking. Bus: 5 to Belleville and Government sts. **Amenities:** Restaurant; bar; seasonal heated outdoor pool; Jacuzzi; laundry service; nonsmoking floors. *In room:* TV, some units with kitchenettes, coffeemaker, hair dryer, safe.

The Gatsby Mansion Inn and Restaurant   Built in 1897, this white clapboard Victorian across from the Seattle–Port Angeles ferry terminal has been faithfully restored and now serves as a B&B-style inn. With its hand-painted ceramic-tiled fireplace, rich wood paneling, stained-glass windows, frescoed ceilings, and crystal chandeliers, it evokes a turn-of-the-last-century elegance. The spacious rooms feature down duvets, fine linen, and lots of Victorian antiques. Some rooms have views of the Inner Harbour, while others have private parlors. It's a pretty property, but because it's part of the larger Ramada hotel complex (see next listing), it lacks that owner-operated B&B feel. There's now an on-site spa.

309 Belleville St., Victoria, B.C. V8V 1X2. (*)* 800/563-9656 or 250/388-9191. Fax 250/382-7666. www.bellevillepark. com. 20 units. C$159–C$319 (US$119–US$239) double. Rates include breakfast. AE, DC, MC, V. Free parking. Bus: 30 or 31 to Belleville and Government sts. **Amenities:** Restaurant; spa; Jacuzzi; sauna; bike rental; limited room service; massage; laundry service. *In room:* TV w/pay movies, coffeemaker, hair dryer.

Ramada Huntingdon Hotel & Suites *Value* *Kids*   Set within a stone's throw of the Inner Harbour, the Ramada and the adjacent Gatsby Mansion Inn (owned by the same company) are set on a prettily landscaped block with a courtyard, cafes, and shops. Built in 1981, the three-story Ramada is a pleasant low-key hotel that's particularly good if you're traveling with children. It's a bit faded and would benefit from a complete refurb, but the standard rooms are fairly large, and all rooms come equipped with fridges. The prime rooms are the split-level gallery rooms or lofts on the third floor, which have a sitting room with TV and pullout double bed on the ground floor and a master bedroom (and second TV) upstairs; all sleep four comfortably; some even accommodate six. Some units have fully equipped kitchens, but there's an additional C$10 (US$7.50) charge to use them.

330 Quebec St., Victoria, B.C. V8V 1W3. (*)* 800/663-7557 or 250/381-3456. Fax 250/382-7666. www.bellevillepark. com. 116 units. C$89–C$189 (US$71–US$151) double, C$109–C$249 (US$87–US$199) suite. AE, DC, MC, V. Parking C$5 (US$4). Bus: 5, 28, or 30. **Amenities:** Restaurant; bar; Jacuzzi; sauna; limited room service; laundry; dry cleaning; nonsmoking rooms. *In room:* A/C (3rd-floor gallery suites only), TV, Internet, kitchen (in some units), fridge, coffeemaker, hair dryer, iron.

The Rosewood Victoria Inn   What was once one of Victoria's finest inns is now a timeshare property. This means that it's now possible to enjoy the inn's many fine rooms for less—provided you're good at saying no. You see, Aviawest, the Rosewood's new owners, are still selling bits and pieces of vacation property around B.C., and they use the Rosewood as sales bait to lure in customers for the full-on timeshare spiel. The price you're charged depends on which group of salesmen you make contact with. If you go through the Rosewood front desk you'll be charged the full rack rate, though first-time visitors can get a 20% discount from the rack rates by booking online. **Aviawest** (*)* 866/986-2222; www.aviawest.com) offers rooms starting at US$99; these are called "special promotions." In terms of actual accommodations, the Rosewood provides all the amenities and comfort of a modern B&B in a classy and romantic

setting. All rooms are tastefully decorated, each done in a unique style. Some have wood-burning or gas fireplaces, others balconies or large soaker tubs. A very good breakfast is served in the conservatory. After that, straight-arm the sales guy, step outside, and you're a block from the Legislature and Royal B.C. Museum and just a 5-minute walk to the Inner Harbour.

595 Michigan St., Victoria, B.C. V8V 1S7. *℗* **866/986-2222** or 250/384-6644. Fax 250/384-6117. www.rosewood victoria.com. 17 units. C$125–C$275 (US$100–US$220) double. Extra person C$35 (US$28). Rates include full breakfast. AE, MC, V. Free parking. Bus: 5 to Superior and Government sts. Children under 10 not accepted. **Amenities:** Rooms for those w/limited mobility. *In room:* TV, coffeemaker, hair dryer.

Royal Scot Suite Hotel *Value Kids*   A block from the Inner Harbour, the Royal Scot provides friendly service and good value, particularly if you opt for a studio or one-bedroom suite. It was constructed as an apartment building, so the rooms are larger than average. Each studio suite has a divider separating the bedroom from the living room. One-bedroom suites have separate bedrooms with king, queen, or twin beds. All suites have lots of closet space, fully equipped kitchens, complimentary refreshments, and sofa beds in the living rooms. The decor is comfortable but uninspired and bathrooms tend to be on the small side. In summer, the Royal Scot fills up with families. Kids make heavy use of the pool, game room, and the video arcade, which is tucked away out of earshot of other guests. In winter, the hotel is favored by retirees from the prairie provinces escaping subzero weather.

425 Quebec St., Victoria, B.C. V8V 1W7. *℗* **800/663-7515** or 250/388-5463. Fax 250/388-5452. www.royalscot.com. 176 units. C$155–C$229 (US$124–US$183) double; C$185–C$415 (US$148–US$332) suite. AE, DC, MC, V. Free parking. Bus: 5 to Belleville and Government sts. **Amenities:** Restaurant; indoor pool; exercise room; Jacuzzi; sauna; game room; shuttle service to downtown; limited room service; laundry service; nonsmoking rooms. *In room:* TV, Internet, kitchen, coffeemaker, hair dryer, iron.

Spinnaker's Guest House *Value*   This bed-and-breakfast–style guesthouse offers good accommodations at a moderate price. There are two separate buildings, owned and operated by the same local entrepreneur who runs Spinnaker's Brewpub. The 1884 heritage building on Catherine Street is the more luxurious. Rooms here feature queen beds, lovely furnishings, in-room Jacuzzis (except for no. 4 on the top floor, which only has a shower), fireplaces, high ceilings, and lots of natural light. There are also decks, but as they face onto an asphalt parking lot, they add very little. The three units on Mary Street are really self-contained apartments, with separate bedrooms and full kitchens, perfect for a longer stay or for families. Guests at both buildings get breakfast at Spinnaker's Brewpub, which is a 2-minute walk away. The drawbacks are the lack of personal service and the location, a 10- to 20-minute walk from downtown through the bland waterfront area of Songhees Point.

308 Catherine St., Victoria, B.C. V9A 3S3. *℗* **877/838-2739** or 250/384-2739. Fax 250/384-3246. www.spinnakers. com. 10 units. C$129–C$249 (US$103–US$199) double. Rates include full breakfast at Spinnaker's restaurant. AE, DC, MC, V. Free parking. Bus: 24 to Catherine St. **Amenities:** Nonsmoking rooms. *In room:* Kitchen (some units), fireplace (some units), Jacuzzi.

INEXPENSIVE

The James Bay Inn *Value*   The Inner Harbour/James Bay area isn't especially blessed with cheap digs, but this Edwardian manor on the edge of Beacon Hill Park is one of the few. Built in 1907, it still offers one of the best accommodations deals in downtown. The standard rooms in the main building of this four-story walk-up are somewhat small and very simply furnished. The real bargains: the adjacent cottage and four suites located next door in a renovated heritage property. The two studios are on the

small side but come with a separate full-size kitchen; the larger one-bedroom suites also feature a full kitchen, a bedroom with queen bed, and a separate living-room area. Furnishings and decorations are comfortable and almost elegant. The cottage is a fully furnished, two-bedroom house cater-corner to the James Bay Inn. With space for eight people and a peak-season price of C$237 (US$190), it's a steal.

270 Government St., Victoria, B.C. V8V 2L2. © 800/836-2649 or 250/384-7151. Fax 250/385-2311. www.jamesbayinn. bc.ca. 45 units. C$56–C$151 (US$45–US$121) double, C$87–C$217 (US$70–US$174) suite, C$127–C$237 (US$102–US$190) cottage. AE, MC, V. Free limited parking. Bus: 5 or 30 to Niagara St. **Amenities:** Restaurant; bar; tour desk; nonsmoking rooms. *In room:* TV, dataport, hair dryer, iron.

Medana Grove Bed & Breakfast   Just a few blocks from the Inner Harbour, this 1908 home is tucked away on a quiet residential street in the James Bay district. The front parlor and dining room on the main floor of this small and cheerfully unpretentious bed-and-breakfast are nicely restored with stained-glass windows, a fireplace, and hardwood floors. The three guest rooms are plainly furnished but provide comfortable accommodations. The smallest bedroom, with a queen-size bed, is located on the ground floor, across from the parlor. The other two rooms are on the second floor, up a steep and very narrow staircase. The one overlooking the front of the house accommodates three people with one double and one single bed. The other, with a king-size bed, looks out toward the garden. Smoking and pets aren't permitted, though the innkeepers themselves have two charming and very friendly Samoyeds.

162 Medana St., Victoria, B.C. V8V 2H5. © 800/269-1188 or 250/389-0437. Fax 250/389-0425. www.medanagrove. com. 3 units. C$80–C$135 (US$64–US$108) double. Rates include full breakfast. MC, V. Street parking. Bus: 11 to Simcoe at Menzies.

3 Downtown & Old Town

EXPENSIVE

Abigail's Hotel ✿   In a Tudor-style mansion in a residential neighborhood just east of downtown, Abigail's began life in the 1920s as a luxury apartment house before being converted to a boutique hotel. If you like small, personalized, bed-and-breakfast hotels, you'll enjoy this impeccably maintained property. Everything is done well here, and the quality is high throughout. Not all rooms come with all the frills, but pampering is always an objective. In the original building, some of the 16 rooms are bright and sunny and beautifully furnished, with pedestal sinks and goose-down comforters. Others feature soaker tubs and double-sided fireplaces, so you can relax in the tub by the light of the fire. The six Celebration Suites in the Coach House addition are done in a Mission style, have TVs (the other rooms don't), and four-poster beds. Abigail's chef prepares a multicourse gourmet breakfast served in the sunny breakfast room, on the patio, or in your room.

906 McClure St., Victoria, B.C. V8V 3E7. © 866/347-5054 or 250/388-5363. Fax 250/388-7787. www.abigails hotel.com. 23 units. C$149–C$475 (US$119–US$380) double. Rates include full breakfast. AE, MC, V. Free parking. Bus: 1 to Cook and McClure sts. Children under 10 not accepted. **Amenities:** Concierge; dry cleaning; complimentary afternoon tea. *In room:* TV (in some rooms), hair dryer, iron, bathrobes, Jacuzzi (in some rooms).

The Beaconsfield Inn ✿   Built in 1905, this elegantly restored Edwardian mansion is located just a few blocks from Beacon Hill park and the Inner Harbour. Commissioned by local industrial baron R. P. Rithet as a wedding gift for his daughter Gertrude, it seems only fitting that it survives today as a charming retreat favored by newlyweds and other incurable romantics. The lovely inn features fir paneling, mahogany floors, antique furnishings, and delicate stained glass windows. The nine guest rooms are lavishly decorated and filled with fresh flowers from the garden. Some suites also have fireplaces or skylights and French doors that open onto the garden. For couples who want to get away from it all, book the cozy Beaconsfield Suite. Located on the third floor, this attic room has a four-poster canopy bed, an elegant sitting area in front of the wood-burning fireplace, a jetted tub, and a window seat. A full hot breakfast is served in the sunroom or the dining room, and afternoon tea is served in the library. Children, pets, and smoking are not permitted.

998 Humboldt St., Victoria, B.C. V8V 2Z8. (℅ **888/884-4044** or 250/384-4044. Fax 250/384-4052. www.beaconsfield inn.com. 9 units. C$129–C$359 (US$103–US$287) double. Full breakfast, afternoon tea, and sherry hour included. AE, MC, V. Free parking. Bus: 1 or 2 to Humboldt and Quadra sts. Children 12 and over permitted. **Amenities:** Access to nearby health club; Jacuzzi. *In room:* Hair dryer, no phone.

The Magnolia A boutique hotel in the center of Victoria, the Magnolia was completed in 1999 and offers a taste of luxury at a reasonable price. The small lobby, with a fireplace, chandelier, and overstuffed chairs, has a clubby Edwardian look. The room decor manages to be classic without feeling frumpy, with high-quality linen, down duvets, and quality furnishings. The spacious marble bathrooms are perhaps the best in Victoria, with walk-in showers and deep soaker tubs. The windows extend floor to ceiling, letting in lots of light, but there are really no great views in this hotel. The needs of business travelers are kept in mind: Work desks are large and well lit with dataports and complimentary local calls and high-speed Internet access. The Diamond Suites on the sixth and seventh floors feature a sitting room with fireplace. The hotel has a good restaurant, a fine microbrewery, and a full-service Aveda day spa. If you want a small downtown hotel with personalized service and fine finishes, this is a good choice.

623 Courtney St., Victoria, B.C. V8W 1B8. (℅ **877/624-6654** or 250/381-0999. Fax 250/381-0988. www.magnolia hotel.com. 63 units. C$169–C$329 (US$135–US$263) double, C$289–C$499 (US$231–US$399) suite. Rates include continental breakfast. AE, DC, MC, V. Valet parking C$10 (US$8). Bus: 5 to Courtney St. **Amenities:** Restaurant; bar; access to nearby health club; spa; concierge; salon; limited room service; massage; laundry service; same-day dry cleaning; executive-level rooms. *In room:* A/C, TV w/pay movies, Internet, minibar, fridge, coffeemaker, hair dryer, iron, bathrobes, complimentary newspaper.

The Victoria Regent Hotel An outside upgrade freshened the exterior of this hotel, which sits right on the Inner Harbour, closer to the water than any other hotel in Victoria. On the inside, the Regent is dated and rather lackluster. Rooms are fairly large and comfortable, though the decor lacks charm. The 10 large one-bedroom suites feature king-size beds, good views and small balconies, and standard serviceable bathrooms. The 36 two-bedroom suites have larger bathrooms and great views of the harbor (you're right on it). All the suites have full kitchens, so it's popular with visiting snowbirds in winter and families year-round.

1234 Wharf St., Victoria, B.C. V8W 3H9. (℅ **800/663-7472** or 250/386-2211. Fax 250/386-2622. www.victoriaregent. com. 48 units. C$139–C$209 (US$111–US$167) double, C$209–C$599 (US$167–US$479) suite. Rates include continental breakfast. Additional person C$20 (US$16). Children under 16 stay free in parent's room. AE, DC, DISC, MC, V. Free underground parking. Bus: 6, 24, or 25 to Wharf St. **Amenities:** Restaurant; access to nearby health club; concierge; babysitting; laundry service; same-day dry cleaning; rooms for those w/limited mobility. *In room:* TV/VCR, Internet, minibar, coffeemaker, hair dryer, iron, CD player.

MODERATE
Best Western Carlton Plaza In the heart of Victoria's shopping and entertainment district, The Best Western Carlton is ideally located for those who like to

step right into the hustle and bustle of downtown. Rooms are comfortably furnished. Almost half the units come with a fully equipped kitchen, and even the standard rooms are pretty large. Perfect for families traveling together, the junior suites have two double beds, a sitting area with a pullout couch, a dining room table, and full kitchen. One-bedroom suites are also available; a number of these are wheelchair accessible. The Best Western prides itself on being a child-friendly hotel, and young guests are greeted with a goody bag, treats and toys, and a special room service delivery of milk and cookies. Even the family dog is welcome and receives a bag of home-baked biscuits upon arrival. Be sure to check the website for special low rates.

642 Johnson St., Victoria, B.C. V8W 1M6. ⓒ 800/663-7241 or 250/388-5513. Fax 250/388-5343. www.bestwestern carltonplazahotel.com. 103 units. C$79–C$190 (US$63–US$152) double; C$260 (US$208) suite. Children 17 and under stay free in parent's room. Extra person C$20 (US$16). AE, MC, V. Free parking. Bus: 5 to Douglas and Johnson sts. **Amenities:** Restaurant; exercise room; children's programs; concierge; salon; limited room service; laundry service; coin laundry; nonsmoking rooms; rooms for those w/limited mobility. *In room:* A/C, TV w/pay movies, coffeemaker, hair dryer, iron, complimentary newspaper.

Chateau Victoria Hotel *Value*   This 18-story hotel was built in 1975 as a high-rise apartment building, so the hotel's rooms and one-bedroom suites are unusually spacious; many suites have kitchenettes, and all have balconies. Everything's been renovated but don't expect luxury (the decor almost verges on tacky), just good value for your money (including free local phone calls and complimentary high-speed Internet access). Prices are higher for the 5th through 15th floors, where the views are better; if you can, get one of the corner 09 rooms with windows on two sides. The Chateau Victoria and the Executive House (see below) across the street are remarkably similar in age and quality of room. In fact, there's so little to distinguish one from the other that you should take a room in whichever offers the best price. On the 18th floor, the Vista 18 Rooftop Lounge offers one of the best views of downtown Victoria.

740 Burdett Ave., Victoria, B.C. V8W 1B2. ⓒ 800/663-5891 or 250/382-4221. Fax 250/380-1950. www.chateau victoria.com. 177 units. C$88–C$149 (US$70–US$119) double; C$95–C$199 (US$76–US$159) suite. Children under 18 stay free in parent's room. AE, DC, DISC, MC, V. Free parking. Bus: 2 to Burdett Ave. **Amenities:** Rooftop restaurant; bar; indoor pool; small exercise room; Jacuzzi; concierge; limited room service; babysitting; laundry service; same-day dry cleaning; nonsmoking rooms. *In room:* TV w/pay movies, Internet, coffeemaker, hair dryer, iron.

Executive House Hotel *Kids*   You can't miss the Executive House, a concrete high-rise looming above The Fairmont Empress on Old Town's east side. Inside, the rooms are of better than average size, and—as in the adjacent and very similar Chateau Victoria (see above)—some intelligent thought has gone into their layout. A recent renovation freshened up the decor and furnishings. Bathrooms are small and functional. Each penthouse-level suite has a Jacuzzi in its own little atrium, a fireplace, a garden terrace with a panoramic view, a dining table, and a fully equipped kitchen.

777 Douglas St., Victoria, B.C. V8W 2B5. ⓒ 800/663-7001 or 250/388-5111. Fax 250/385-1323. www.executivehouse. com. 181 units. C$195 (US$156) double; C$215–C$325 (US$172–US$260) suite; C$395–C$895 (US$316–US$716) penthouse rooms and suites. Extra person C$15 (US$12). Children under 16 stay free in parent's room. AE, DC, DISC, MC, V. Parking C$3 (US$2.40) per night. Bus: 2 to the Convention Center. **Amenities:** 2 restaurants; 3 bars; exercise room; spa; concierge; limited room service; babysitting; same-day laundry service; same-day dry cleaning; nonsmoking rooms; executive-level rooms. *In room:* TV w/pay movies, dataport, fridge, coffeemaker, hair dryer, iron, safe.

Isabella's Guest Suites *Kids* *Finds*   Two suites located above Willy's bakery provide affordable, fun, and surprisingly stylish accommodations in the heart of the city. The front suite is a large, elegantly furnished studio with a bed/sitting room that opens into a dining room and full kitchen. Bright colors and cheerful accents, upscale rustic furniture, high ceilings, large windows, and plenty of space make this a great home base for exploring Victoria. The second unit, a one-bedroom suite, overlooks the alley and patio of Il Terrazzo restaurant (reviewed in chapter 13). The living room is painted in bright red, which goes surprisingly well with the wood floors and funky furniture; the bedroom (with a king-size bed) is done in softer tones. The bathroom has a lovely claw-foot tub, breakfast is included and served at the bakery, parking is free, and you have your own front door. Not bad at all for C$150 (US$120) a night in high season.

537 Johnson St., Victoria, B.C. V8W 1M2. ✆ 250/595-3815. Fax 250/381-8415. www.isabellasbb.com. 2 units. C$130–C$150 (US$104–US$120) double. Rates include continental breakfast. Free parking. Bus: 5. *In room:* TV, full kitchen, hair dryer, iron.

Swans Suite Hotel 🌟🌟 *(Kids)*   This heritage building was abandoned for years until 1988, when it was turned it into a hotel, restaurant, brewpub, and nightclub all in one. Just by the Johnson Street Bridge, it's now one of Old Town's best-loved buildings. Like any great inn, Swans is small, friendly, and charming. The suites are large, with the quirky layouts you'd expect in a heritage renovation. Many are split level, featuring open lofts and huge exposed beams. All come with fully equipped kitchens, dining areas, living rooms, and queen-size beds. The two-bedroom suites are like little town houses; they're great for families, accommodating up to six comfortably. Want a room with your own totem pole? The 279-sq.-m (3,003-sq.-ft.) penthouse suite comes with fabulous original Pacific Northwest artwork and is the perfect spot for a special occasion. A split-level loft, the penthouse suite has a state-of-the-art kitchen, dining room, and a spacious bedroom with a queen-size sleigh bed. The deck offers city and harbor views, best appreciated from the rooftop hot tub.

506 Pandora St., Victoria, B.C. V8W 1N6. ✆ 800/668-7926 or 250/361-3310. Fax 250/361-3491. www.swanshotel. com. 30 units. C$185–C$205 (US$148–US$164) studio, C$225–C$369 (US$180–US$295) suite. Children under 12 stay free in parent's room. AE, DC, DISC, MC, V. Parking C$12 (US$9.50). Bus: 23 or 24 to Pandora Ave. **Amenities:** Restaurant; brewpub; limited room service; laundry service; same-day dry cleaning. *In room:* TV, Internet, kitchen, coffeemaker, hair dryer, iron.

Victoria Marriott Inner Harbour   Victoria's newest downtown hotel opened in April 2004. The Marriott is a high-rise hotel behind the old Crystal Gardens. Inside, you'll find lots of marble in the lobby, and all the usual Marriott amenities, including an added-price concierge level that offers a pleasant lounge with breakfast and evening hors d'oeuvres. What you won't find is a whole lot of personality. The rooms are nice enough, especially the concierge-level suites on the 16th floor, but they're decorated in an indefinable style that's meant to look traditional but doesn't convey much beyond a cookie-cutter corporate aesthetic. The hotel has a good workout room and a nice big indoor pool. If you're a fan of Marriotts, you'll find it all to your liking. If not, I'd suggest you look for a hotel with a bit more individuality.

728 Humboldt St., Victoria, B.C. V8W 3Z5. ✆ 877/333-8338 or 250/480-3800. Fax 250/480-3838. www.victoria marriott.com. 236 units. C$169–C$339 (US$135–US$271) double. AE, DC, MC, V. Valet or self-parking C$12 (US$10) per day. Bus: 2 to the Convention Center. **Amenities:** Restaurant; lounge; indoor pool; health club; Jacuzzi; 24-hr. room service; babysitting; laundry service; same-day dry cleaning; nonsmoking rooms; executive-level rooms; concierge-level rooms. *In room:* A/C, TV, Internet, minibar, coffeemaker, hair dryer, iron, safe, bathrobes.

INEXPENSIVE

The Dominion Hotel *(Value)*   Victoria's oldest hotel (built in 1876) is a bit of a Jekyll and Hyde. Half the rooms have been nicely restored, with new beds, rich woods and marble floors, brass trim, and red velvet upholstery on antique chairs. The small bathrooms have a couple of nice touches, such as high-pressure shower nozzles. The seven

fireplace rooms face into the interior courtyard and feature small wrought-iron balconies, as well as DVD players and large TVs. The unrenovated half is frankly a bit of a dump, and I don't recommend that you stay there, though the rooms are cheap at C$59 to C$129 (US$47–US$103). Rates below are for "boutique" (renovated) rooms and include dinner; the rates drop by as much as 50% in the winter.

759 Yates St., Victoria, B.C. V8W 1L6. ℂ 800/663-6101 or 250/384-4136. Fax 250/382-6416. www.dominion-hotel. com. 101 units. Boutique rooms C$149–C$199 (US$114–US$159) double; C$249 (US$199) suite. Extra person C$30 (US$24). Children under 16 stay free in parent's room. AE, MC, V. Parking C$5–C$10 (US$4–US$8). Bus: 10, 11, or 14 to Yates St. **Amenities:** 3 restaurants; access to nearby health club (YMCA); limited room service; babysitting; laundry service; dry-cleaning service; nonsmoking rooms. *In room:* TV, coffeemaker, hair dryer.

Victoria International Youth Hostel   The location is perfect—right in the heart of Old Town. In addition, this hostel has all the usual accouterments, including two kitchens (stocked with utensils), a dining room, a TV lounge with VCR, a game room, a common room, a library, laundry facilities, an indoor bicycle lockup, 24-hour security, and hot showers. The dorms are on the large side (16 to a room), showers are shared and segregated by gender, and a couple of family rooms are available (one of which has a private toilet). There's an extensive ride board, and the collection of outfitter and tour information rivals that of the tourism office. The front door is locked at 2:30am, but you can make arrangements to get in later.

516 Yates St., Victoria, B.C. V8W 1K8. ℂ 888/883-0099 or 250/385-4511. Fax 250/385-3232. www.hihostels.ca. 104 beds. International Youth Hostel members C$20 (US$16), nonmembers C$21 (US$17). Wheelchair-accessible unit available. MC, V. Parking on street. Bus: 70 from Swartz Bay ferry terminal. **Amenities:** Game room; kitchens; lounge; laundry facilities.

4 Outside the Central Area

EXPENSIVE

Abbeymoore Manor Inn *Finds*   This impressive 1912 mansion is in Rockland, an area of "Old Victoria" where grand homes were built by Victoria's elite. It's one of the best B&Bs you'll find, with large, attractive rooms, lots of period antiques and finishes, and an overall charm that's hard to beat. All the rooms have private bathrooms; all rooms are individually decorated, and the beds are fitted with fine linens. Two ground-floor garden suites have separate entrances and fully equipped kitchens. There's also a penthouse suite with views of the ocean. A delicious gourmet breakfast is served, and complimentary beverages are available throughout the day.

1470 Rockland Ave., Victoria, B.C. V8S 1W2. ℂ 888/801-1811 or 250/370-1470. Fax 250/370-1470. www.abbey moore.com. 7 units. C$109–C$195 (US$87–US$156) double; C$129–C$235 (US$103–US$188) suite. Extra person C$20 (US$16). Rates include full breakfast. MC, V. Free street parking. **Amenities:** Wi-fi. *In room:* TV, CD player.

The Aerie   On a forested mountain slope by a fjord about half an hour from town, this Mediterranean-inspired villa is just plain spectacular. A member of the prestigious Relais & Châteaux, The Aerie is one of the most elegantly luxurious retreats you'll find anywhere on Vancouver Island. In particular, the view over Finlayson Inlet—seen from your room, the indoor pool, the outdoor whirlpool, or the dining room—is stunning. Inside, the Aerie offers six room configurations: All include big comfortable beds with top-quality linen, and all but the standard rooms include a soaker tub for two. As you move into the master and residence suites, you get private decks and fireplaces. Full-service spa treatments are available. Dining is an integral part of the experience, and the Aerie restaurant (p. 220) is among the best on the island.

600 Ebedora Lane (P.O. Box 108), Malahat, B.C. V0R 2L0. (C) 800/518-1933 or 250/743-7115. Fax 250/743-4766. www.aerie.bc.ca. 29 units. C$195–C$345 (US$166–US$276) double, C$375–C$725 (US$300–US$580) suite. Rates include full breakfast. AE, DC, MC, V. Free parking. Take Hwy. 1 north, turn left at the Spectacle Lake turnoff; take the first right and follow the winding driveway. **Amenities:** 2 restaurants; bar; indoor pool; tennis courts; small weight room; full spa; indoor and outdoor Jacuzzis; concierge; 24-hr. room service; massage; laundry; dry cleaning; all non-smoking rooms. *In room:* A/C, TV, dataport, minibar, coffeemaker, hair dryer, iron.

Brentwood Bay Lodge & Spa ☆☆☆ *(Finds)*   Located on a pristine inlet about 20 minutes north of downtown Victoria, just minutes from Butchart Gardens, this contemporary timber-and-glass lodge opened in May 2004 and offers the best of everything, including a fabulous spa, boat shuttle to Butchart Gardens, and all manner of eco-adventures, including kayaking, scuba diving, fishing, and walks through the old-growth forest that surrounds it. One of only three Canadian hotels awarded membership in the prestigious Small Luxury Hotels of the World, this is a place where every detail has been carefully considered and beautifully rendered. The rooms are gorgeous, with handcrafted furnishings, fireplaces, luxurious bathrooms with soaker tubs and body massage showers, balconies, and king beds fitted with the highest quality Italian linen. Arbutus Grille and Wine Bar, the fine dining room, offers seasonal menus focusing on foraged and organic local ingredients, plus a wine-tasting bar with a selection of fine wines from the resort's award-winning Cellar. You can also dine in the casual Marine Pub. The hotel has its own marina and is a licensed PADI dive center—the fjord on which it sits is considered one of the best diving spots in the world. The Essence of Life spa offers fresh Pacific seaweed, herb, ocean salt, and other treatments in a tranquil environment.

849 Verdier Ave. on Brentwood Bay, Victoria, B.C. V8M 1C5. (C) 888/544-2079 or 250/544-2079. Fax 250/544-2069. www.brentwoodbaylodge.com. 33 units. C$295–C$495 (US$236–US$396) double, C$345–C$845 (US$276–US$676) suite. Rates include breakfast. AE, DC, MC, V. Free parking. Take Pat Bay Hwy. north to Keating Crossroads, turn left (west) to Saanich Rd., turn right (south) to Verdier Ave. **Amenities:** Restaurant; pub; cafe; heated outdoor pool; full-service spa; Jacuzzi; concierge; 24-hr. room service; laundry; dry cleaning. *In room:* A/C, TV/DVD, Internet, minibar, coffeemaker, hair dryer, iron, entertainment system, bathrobes, slippers, fireplaces, hot tubs (in suites), complimentary newspaper.

Dashwood Manor   This lovely old mock-Tudor manor sits in a great location: on the edge of Beacon Hill Park, just across Dallas Road from the beach and the Strait of Juan de Fuca. For years, the Dashwood seemed to be doing its own imitation of the British Empire and slowly going to seed. Recently, though, the place has been upgraded into an all-suites hotel. The rooms here were always large and bright, with period furniture and wood-paneled walls. Now stodgy old bathrooms have been updated with new tile and fixtures, including deep-jetted tubs. Several of the rooms have large Jacuzzis. Every suite has a kitchen. Overall, the decor in the Dashwood doesn't show the same consistent high level of taste you'll find in marginally more expensive properties like the Haterleigh or the Andersen House. On the plus side, most of the rooms offer excellent views; some have balconies. Kitchens come well stocked for do-it-yourself breakfast. Complimentary sherry, port, and wine are laid out in the lobby in the evenings.

1 Cook St., Victoria, B.C. V8V 3W6. (C) 800/667-5517 or 250/385-5517. Fax 250/383-1760. www.dashwoodmanor. com. 14 units. C$145–C$325 (US$116–US$260) suite. Extra person C$45 (US$36). AE, DC, MC, V. Free parking. Bus: 5 to Dallas Rd. and Cook St. **Amenities:** Nonsmoking rooms. *In room:* TV, kitchen, fridge, coffeemaker, hair dryer, iron.

Poets' Cove Resort & Spa ☆☆   To reach Pender Island, one of the Gulf Islands between the mainland and Vancouver Island, you have to take a ferry or water taxi

from Sidney, north of Victoria. It's worth the trip, because staying at Poet's Cove, the most luxurious resort and spa in the Gulf Islands, makes for a great romantic getaway. Overlooking Bedwell Harbour, it opened in 2004 and has its own marina. The resort, with a 22-room lodge and a cluster of seaside cottages and villas, was built with a contemporary Pacific Northwest look and ambience. All the accommodations feature ocean or forest-and-water views, fireplaces, big bathtubs for soaking, and all the amenities of an upscale resort. Cottages and villas have 2 or 3 bedrooms, gourmet kitchens, and usually come with a patio or outdoor hot tub. You can dine on fresh Pacific Northwest cuisine at the Aurora Restaurant in the lodge, or enjoy snacks and comfort food in the lounge. Sussurus Spa offers a full complement of relaxation and esthetic treatments, including spa treatments for couples.

9801 Spalding Rd., Pender Island, B.C. V0N 2M3. ⓒ 888/512-7638 or 250/629-2100. www.poetscove.com. 22 lodge units, 15 cottages, 9 villas. C$199–C$279 (US$159–US$223) double in lodge; C$299–C$579 (US$239–US$465) villa; C$349–C$649 (US$279–US$519) cottage. AE, DC, MC, V. Free parking. Take Island Hwy. **Amenities:** Restaurant; lounge; heated outdoor pool and hot tub (seasonal); fitness center; spa; concierge; complimentary shuttle service; laundry. *In room:* TV/DVD/CD entertainment systems, coffeemaker, hair dryer, iron, fireplace. *In cottages and villas:* Kitchen, patio (most units), outdoor hot tub (some units).

Sooke Harbour House ❀❀❀   This little inn/restaurant, located right on the ocean at the end of a sand spit about 30km (19 miles) west of Victoria, has earned an international reputation (voted second-best Country Inn *in the world* by *Gourmet Magazine* in 2000) thanks to the care lavished on the guests and rooms by owners Frederique and Sinclair Philip. Frederique looks after the sumptuous rooms, furnishing and decorating each according to a particular Northwest theme. The Herb Garden room, looking out over a garden of fragrant herbs and edible flowers, is done in pale shades of mint and parsley. The large split-level Thunderbird room is a celebration of First Nations culture, with books, carvings, totems, and masks. Thanks to some clever architecture, all the rooms are awash in natural light and have fabulous ocean views. In addition, all have wood-burning fireplaces and sitting areas, all but one have sun decks, and most have Jacuzzis or soaker tubs. The other half of the Harbour House's reputation comes from the outstanding cooking of Sinclair Philip (see p. 221 for more on the restaurant).

1528 Whiffen Spit Rd., Sooke, B.C. V0S 1N0. ⓒ 800/889-9688 or 250/642-3421. Fax 250/642-6988. www.sooke harbourhouse.com. 28 units. C$335–C$575 (US$268–US$460) double. Rates include full breakfast and picnic lunch (no picnic lunch weekdays Nov–Apr). MC, V. Free parking. Take the Island Hwy. (Hwy. 1) to the Sooke/Colwood turnoff (junction Hwy. 14); follow Hwy. 14 to Sooke; about 1.6km (1 mile) past the town's only traffic light, turn left onto Whiffen Spit Rd. **Amenities:** Restaurant; golf course; access to nearby health club; spa; limited room service; massage; babysitting; laundry service; nonsmoking rooms. *In room:* Dataport, fridge, coffeemaker, hair dryer, iron.

MODERATE

The Boathouse *(Finds)*   It's a short row (or a 25-min. walk) to Butchart Gardens from this secluded red cottage in Brentwood Bay, a converted boathouse set on pilings over Saanich Inlet. The only passersby you're likely to encounter are seals, bald eagles, otters, herons, and raccoons, plus the occasional floatplane flying in. The cottage is at the end of a very long flight of stairs behind the owner's home. Inside are a queen bed, a dining table, a kitchen area with a small refrigerator and toaster oven, an electric heater, and a reading alcove with a stunning view all the way up Finlayson Arm. Toilet and shower facilities are in a separate bathhouse, 17 steps back uphill. All the makings for a delicious continental breakfast are provided in the evening, plus free coffee and newspaper delivery. Just below the boathouse is a floating dock—which doubles as a great sun deck—moored to which is a small dinghy reserved for the exclusive use of guests. There can perhaps be nothing more stylish than pulling up to the Butchart Gardens dock in your own private watercraft. Open April through September.

746 Sea Dr., Brentwood Bay, Victoria, B.C. VM8 1B1. © **866/654-9370** or 250/652-9370. http://members.shaw.ca/ boathouse. 1 unit. C$215 (US$172) double with continental breakfast, C$195 (US$146) double without breakfast. 2-night minimum. AE, MC, V. Free parking. Closed Oct–Mar. Bus: 75 to Wallace Dr. and Benvenuto Ave. No children under 18. *In room:* Fridge, coffeemaker, hair dryer, iron.

INEXPENSIVE

Point-No-Point Resort *(Finds)*   Away from it all in your own little cabin, you'll have 40 acres of wilderness around you and a wide rugged beach in front of you, with nothing to do but laze away the day in your hot tub. Or walk the beach. Or the forest. Or look at an eagle. Since 1950, this oceanfront resort has been welcoming guests, first to a pair of tiny cabins, now to 25 units. Cabins vary depending on when they were built. All have fireplaces, full kitchens, and bathrooms; newer ones have hot tubs on their private decks. Lunch and afternoon tea are available daily in the small, sunny central dining room. Dinner is served Wednesday through Sunday. The dining-room tables are conveniently equipped with binoculars, so you won't miss a bald eagle as you eat.

1505 West Coast Hwy. (Hwy. 14), Sooke, B.C. V0S 1N0. © **250/646-2020**. Fax 250/646-2294. www.pointnopointresort. com. 25 units. C$110–C$250 (US$88–US$200) cabin. AE, MC, V. Free parking. No public transit. **Amenities:** Jacuzzi. *In room:* Kitchen, no phone.

University of Victoria Housing, Food, and Conference Services *(Value)*   One of the best deals going is found at the University of Victoria, when classes aren't in session and summer visitors are welcomed. All rooms have single or twin beds and basic furnishings, and there are bathrooms, pay phones, and TV lounges on every floor. Linens, towels, and soap are provided. The suites are an extremely good value—each has four bedrooms, a kitchen, a living room, and 1½ bathrooms. For C$5 (US$3.75) extra per day you can make use of the many on-campus athletic facilities. Each of the 28 buildings has a coin laundry. The disadvantage, of course, is that the U. Vic. campus is a painfully long way from everywhere—the city center is about a half-hour drive away.

P.O. Box 1700, Sinclair at Finerty Rd., Victoria, B.C. V8W 2Y2. © **250/721-8395**. Fax 250/721-8930. www.hfcs. uvic.ca. 898 units. MC, V. May–Aug C$45 (US$36) single, C$56 (US$45) twin, C$160 (US$128) suite (sleeps 4 people). Rates include full breakfast and taxes. Parking C$5 (US$4). Closed Sept–Apr. Bus: 4 or 14 to University of Victoria. **Amenities:** Indoor pool; access to athletic facilities; coin laundry; nonsmoking rooms.

13

Where to Dine in Victoria

Though early Victoria settlers were intent on re-creating a little patch of the Old Country on their wild western island, the one thing they were never tempted to import was British cooking. Thankfully. Instead, following the Canadian norm, each immigrant group imported its own cuisine, so that now Victoria is a cornucopia of culinary styles from around the world. With over 700 restaurants in the area, there's something for every taste and wallet.

Note that the touristy restaurants along Wharf Street serve up mediocre food for folks they know they'll never have to see again. The canny visitor knows to head inland (even a block is enough) where the proportion of tourists to locals drops sharply and the quality jumps by leaps and bounds.

The dining scene in Victoria isn't nearly as sophisticated as Vancouver's, but more and more attention is being paid to the glories of fresh local produce, foraged edibles such as mushrooms and berries, and seafood. Good wines are now produced in the Cowichan Valley, and cheesemakers on Salt Spring Island are producing some delicious cheeses. Though the city isn't as mad about multi-course "tasting menus" as its much larger neighbor, Vancouver, there's still plenty to taste.

The one aspect of English cuisine Victoria did import was the delicious custom of afternoon tea. American visitors in particular should give it a try. For the best places to try, see "Taking Afternoon Tea," later in this chapter.

Most restaurants close at 10pm, especially on weekdays. Reservations are strongly recommended for prime sunset seating during summer, especially on Friday and Saturday.

There's no provincial tax on restaurant meals in British Columbia, just the **7% federal goods and services tax (GST).**

Note: Because Victoria is so compact, most of the restaurants listed in this chapter are in Old Town and no more than a 10-minute walk from most hotels. Thus, in this chapter, we have listed public transit information only for those spots that are a bit farther out.

1 Best Victoria Dining Bets

For a quick overview of the city's top restaurants, see "The Most Unforgettable Dining Experiences: Victoria" in chapter 1, p. 13.

- **Best Spot for a Romantic Dinner: Camille's,** 45 Bastion Sq. (© **250/381-3433**), offers a quiet, intimate, candlelit room and a wine list with a bottle or glass for every occasion. See p. 215.
- **Best Chinese Cuisine:** A billion and a half people can't be wrong. Actually, all of China has yet to eat at **J&J Wonton Noodle House,** 1012 Fort St. (© **250/383-0680**), but if they had, they'd love it. See p. 218.

- **Best French Cuisine:** At **The Aerie,** 600 Ebedora Lane, Malahat (© **800/518-1933** or 250/743-7115), chef Christophe Letard's cooking is as unmistakably French as his accent. It's also quite wonderful. See p. 220.
- **Best Italian Cuisine: Il Terrazzo Ristorante,** 555 Johnson St., off Waddington Alley (© **250/361-0028**) features excellent northern-Italian cooking and extra points for the lovely patio. See p. 215.
- **Best Pacific Northwest:** The quality, freshness, inventiveness, and incredible attention to detail make the **Sooke Harbour House,** 1528 Whiffen Spit Rd., Sooke (© **800/889-9688** or 250/642-3421), the best in Victoria and the whole of Vancouver Island. It also wins for **best seafood** and **best wine list.** See p. 221.
- **Best Newcomer: Arbutus Grille and Winebar,** 849 Verdier Ave. (© **888/544-2079** or 250/544-5100), located 20 minutes north of Victoria in stunning Brentwood Bay Lodge and Spa, features a fresh Pacific Northwest menu full of daily surprises and wonderful tastes. See p. 221.
- **Best Brewpub Restaurant: Canoe,** 450 Swift St. (© **250/361-1940**), is casual but upscale, has great beer, good food, and the option of dining indoors or out. See p. 214.
- **Best Fish and Chips: Barb's Place,** 310 Erie St. (© **250/384-6515**), on Fisherman's Wharf, sells 'em freshly fried and extra delicious. See p. 214.
- **Best for Kids: rebar,** 50 Bastion Sq. (© **250/361-9223**), offers large portions, terrific quality, and a funky laid-back atmosphere. See p. 220.
- **Best Local Crowd: Pagliacci's,** 1011 Broad St. (© **250/386-1662**), noisy and crowded, is the place to be seen while you devour a plate of spaghetti Bolognese or a piping-hot sausage and mushroom pizza. See p. 217.
- **Best Burgers & Beer: Six Mile Pub,** 494 Island Hwy., View Royal (© **250/478-3121**), offers 10 house brews, juicy burgers (even veggie burgers), and loads of British pub–style atmosphere. See p. 221.
- **Best Afternoon or High Tea:** If you're doing the high tea thing only once, you may as well do it right and reserve a place at **The Fairmont Empress,** 721 Government St. (© **250/384-8111**), Victoria's crown jewel of a hotel. See p. 216.

2 Restaurants by Cuisine

BAKERY
Q V Bakery & Café (Downtown, $, p. 219)
Willy's (Old Town, $, p. 219)

BISTRO
Med Grill@Mosaic (Downtown, $, p. 219)

CARIBBEAN
The Reef (Downtown, $$, p. 218)

CHINESE
J&J Wonton Noodle House ⭐ (Downtown, $, p. 218)

DELI
Sam's Deli (Downtown, $, p. 220)

FISH & CHIPS
Barb's Place (Inner Harbour, $, p. 214)

FRENCH
The Aerie ⭐⭐⭐ (Greater Victoria, $$$$, p. 220)
Brasserie L'Ecole ⭐⭐⭐ (Old Town, $$$, p. 215)

INDIAN
Da Tandoor (Downtown, $$, p. 216)

Key to Abbreviations: $$$$ = Very Expensive $$$ = Expensive $$ = Moderate $ = Inexpensive

ITALIAN

Café Brio ☆ (Downtown, $$$, p. 215)
Il Terrazzo Ristorante ☆ (Downtown, $$$, p. 215)
Pagliacci's (Downtown, $$, p. 217)
Zambri's ☆ (Downtown, $$, p. 218)

PACIFIC NORTHWEST

Arbutus Grille & Winebar ☆☆ (Greater Victoria, $$$$, p. 221)
Café Brio ☆ (Downtown, $$$, p. 215)
Camille's ☆ (Downtown, $$$, p. 215)
Canoe ☆ (Inner Harbour, $$, p. 214)
Herald Street Caffe ☆ (Downtown, $$, p. 216)
The Mark ☆☆ (Inner Harbour, $$$, p. 212)
Sooke Harbour House ☆☆☆ (Greater Victoria, $$$$, p. 221)
Spinnakers Brewpub (Inner Harbour, $$, p. 214)

PUB GRUB

Canoe ☆ (Inner Harbour, $$, p. 214)
Six Mile Pub (Greater Victoria, $, p. 221)
Spinnakers Brewpub (Inner Harbour, $$, p. 214)

SEAFOOD

The Blue Crab Bar and Grill ☆ (Inner Harbour, $$$, p. 212)

TAPAS

The Tapa Bar (Old Town, $$, p. 218)
Med Grill@Mosaic (Downtown, $, p. 219)

TEA

Butchart Gardens Dining Room Restaurant ☆☆ (Greater Victoria, $$$, p. 217)
Fairmont Empress ☆☆ (Downtown, $$$$, p. 216)
Point Ellice House (Greater Victoria, $$, p. 217)
White Heather Tea Room (Greater Victoria, $, p. 217)

THAI

Siam Thai Restaurant (Downtown, $, p. 220)

VEGETARIAN

Green Cuisine (Downtown, $, p. 218)
rebar (Downtown, $, p. 220)

3 The Inner Harbour

EXPENSIVE

The Blue Crab Bar and Grill ☆ SEAFOOD   One of Victoria's best bets for seafood, the Blue Crab combines excellent fresh ingredients and straightforward preparation. It also has a killer view—floatplanes slip in and out while you're dining, little ferries chug across the harbor, and the sun sets slowly over the Sooke Hills. While other top-end restaurants in town have moved to sourcing all or nearly all ingredients locally, the Crab supplies itself from the world—scallops from Alaska, lamb from New Zealand, mahimahi from Hawaii, duck from the Fraser Valley, and halibut from B.C. For lunch you can find tasty offerings like seafood chowder, smoked salmon and crab sandwich, or seafood pasta. The award-winning wine list (*Wine Spectator* award of excellence in 2003 and 2004) features mid-range and top-end vintages, drawn mostly from B.C., Washington, and California. The service is deft and obliging.

146 Kingston St., in the Coast Hotel. © **250/480-1999**. Reservations recommended. Main courses C$24–C$35 (US$19–US$28). AE, DC, MC, V. Daily 6:30am–10:30pm (dinner from 5pm). Bus: 30 to Erie St. or harbor miniferry to Coast Hotel.

The Mark ☆☆ PACIFIC NORTHWEST   The Mark, the fine-dining room at the Hotel Grand Pacific, is a small, candlelit haven just off the larger Pacific Restaurant. Here you can enjoy highly personalized service, delicious food prepared with locally grown

Where to Dine in Victoria

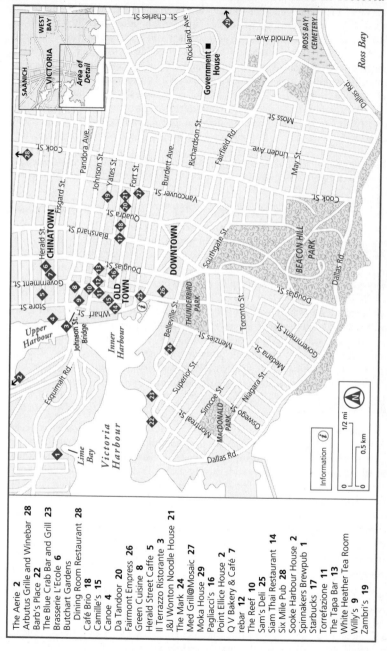

The Aerie **2**
Arbutus Grille and Winebar **28**
Barb's Place **22**
The Blue Crab Bar and Grill **23**
Brasserie L'Ecole **6**
Butchart Gardens
  Dining Room Restaurant **28**
Café Brio **18**
Camille's **15**
Canoe **4**
Da Tandoor **20**
Fairmont Empress **26**
Green Cuisine **8**
Herald Street Caffe **5**
Il Terrazzo Ristorante **3**
J&J Wonton Noodle House **21**
The Mark **24**
Med Grill@Mosaic **27**
Moka House **29**
Pagliacci's **16**
Point Ellice House **2**
Q V Bakery & Café **7**
rebar **12**
The Reef **10**
Sam's Deli **25**
Siam Thai Restaurant **14**
Six Mile Pub **28**
Sooke Harbour House **2**
Spinnakers Brewpub **1**
Starbucks **17**
Torrefazione **11**
The Tapa Bar **13**
White Heather Tea Room
Willy's **9**
Zambri's **19**

213

or harvested ingredients, and fine wines chosen by an astute sommelier. To sample the best of everything, try the 6-course seafood tasting menu, priced at C$70 (US$56), or C$105 (US$84) with wine pairings. The menu might start with a spot prawn "cappuccino" followed by hazelnut-crusted Alaska king scallop, a palate-cleansing pomegranate mandarin vodka ice, braised halibut, local Camembert with orange-fig marmalade, and three different kinds of chocolate. There's also an a la carte menu featuring rack of lamb, smoked tenderloin, roasted duck breast, and venison striploin. The hotel's casual Pacific Restaurant is also a good choice for lunch or dinner, with nicely done dishes such as West Coast seafood linguine, vegetarian pizzas, fresh local seafood, and high-quality steak and lamb. The Pacific has a great outdoor patio overlooking the harbor.

463 Belleville St., in the Hotel Grand Pacific. © 250/386-0450. www.themark.ca. Reservations required for The Mark, recommended for Pacific Restaurant. The Mark main courses C$26–C$48 (US$21–US$38); Pacific Restaurant main courses C$16–C$30 (US$13–US$24). AE, DC, MC, V. The Mark daily 5–9pm, Pacific Restaurant daily 6:30am–10pm.

MODERATE

Canoe ✦ PUB GRUB/PACIFIC NORTHWEST   What was once a Victorian power station is now one of the loveliest and liveliest brewpub restaurants in Victoria, with a fabulous outdoor patio overlooking the harbor toward the Johnson street bridge and an industrial-inspired interior with massive masonry walls and heavy timber crossbeams. Casual Canoe is popular because it basically has something for every taste and everything is very tasty. The kitchen offers intriguing variations on standard pub fare and bar snacks, including thin-crust pizzas (but with grilled lamb or chili prawns), classic burgers, and a Brewmaster's Plate with smoked oysters, chorizo sausage, and marinated grilled vegetables. But you also dine upstairs on finer fare, such as crisp skinned wild salmon, premium striploin steak, pennette pasta with wild forest mushrooms, or tagine, a North African stew served in an earthenware casserole. The ingredients for every dish are fresh and local, the beer is excellent, and there's also a small, select, award-winning wine list.

450 Swift St. © 250/361-1940. www.canoebrewpub.com. Reservations recommended for weekend dinner and Sun brunch. Main courses C$11–C$32 (US$9–US$26); pub fare and bar snacks C$4–C$15 (US$3.25–US$12). AE, MC, V. Daily 11am–midnight.

Spinnakers Brewpub PUB GRUB/PACIFIC NORTHWEST   Spinnakers beer has always been extraordinary—rich ales and stouts and lagers, craft-brewed on the premises. The cuisine, unfortunately, has been less consistent, with food quality rising and falling as different chefs try with varying success to deliver quality cooking from Spinnakers' cramped kitchen. The current menu offers above-average pub fare plus more adventurous fresh West Coast seafood, all served in a fun, bustling pub atmosphere. If you're feeling doubtful, test the waters first by ordering up a small plate of Fanny Bay oysters, prawn satay, or salmon cakes before diving into a main course.

308 Catherine St. © 250/384-2739. www.spinnakers.com. Main courses C$10–C$24 (US$8–US$19). AE, MC, V. Daily 7am–11pm.

INEXPENSIVE

Barb's Place (Kids) FISH & CHIPS   The best "chippie" in town, Barb serves lightly breaded halibut and hand-hewn chips, plus a good seafood chowder, seafood specialties, and burgers, from an outdoor stand at Fisherman's Wharf. There are picnic tables to sit on and boats, seagulls, and lots of other eye candy to amuse the kids. (There's also a kids' menu.) Barb's is a favorite among locals.

310 Erie St. © 250/384-6515. Reservations not accepted. Menu items C$5.50–C$17 (US$4.40–US$14). MC, V. Daily 10am–sunset.

4 Downtown & Old Town

EXPENSIVE

Brasserie L'Ecole *&&&* FRENCH   Top-end French in the middle of Chinatown may seem a bit of a stretch, but it all seems to make sense when you step inside this small, pleasant room and realize what's on offer is not high-end Parisian but simple country French cooking served at amazingly reasonable prices. The brainchild of long-time Victoria chef Sean Brenner, L'Ecole's menu changes daily, depending entirely on what comes in fresh from Victoria's hinterland farms. Preparation is simple, no big reductions or complicated *jus,* just shellfish, local fish, meats with red wine sauces, and fresh vegetables with vinaigrettes. Quality is excellent; L'Ecole has won a bevy of awards in its few short years on the scene. The wine list is smallish with no hugely expensive vintages but good straightforward wine to match the excellent but simple food.

1715 Government St. ✆ **250/475-6262.** www.lecole.ca. Reservations recommended. Main courses C$18 (US$14). AE, MC, V. Tues–Sat 5:30–11pm.

Café Brio *&* PACIFIC NORTHWEST/ITALIAN   Café Brio offers Tuscan-influenced cuisine that strongly reflects the seasons, fresh local produce, and Pacific seafood. The menu changes daily, but small plates may include carpaccio of albacore tuna or locally harvested mussels with bacon and smoked paprika, with entrees of sautéed spring salmon, grilled pork chop, or spaghettini alla puttanesca. The wine list is excellent, with an impressive selection of B.C. and international reds and whites. The service is deft and knowledgeable and the kitchen stays open as long as guests keep ordering. If the weather is fine, you can dine in the charming garden patio out front.

944 Fort St. ✆ **250/383-0009.** www.cafe-brio.com. Reservations recommended. Main courses C$14–C$29 (US$11–US$23). AE, MC, V. Daily 5:30pm–closing (usually 11pm).

Camille's *&* PACIFIC NORTHWEST   The most romantic of Victoria's restaurants, Camille's is tucked away in two rooms beneath the old Law Chambers. The decor contrasts white linen with century-old exposed brick, stained-glass lamps, and antique books. Chef and owner David Mincey uses only the freshest local ingredients; he was one of the founders of a Vancouver Island farm cooperative, which brings local farmers together with local restaurants. The ever-changing menu displays Mincey's love for cheeky invention: Think duck confit salad with slices of mandarin orange on a bed of baby greens or citrus and coffee-marinated pork tenderloin. A delicate roasted rack of lamb is also a perennial specialty. The reasonable and extensive wine list comes with liner notes that are amusing and informative.

45 Bastion Sq. ✆ **250/381-3433.** www.camillesrestaurant.com. Reservations recommended. Main courses C$22–C$34 (US$18–US$27). AE, MC, V. Daily 5:30–10pm.

Il Terrazzo Ristorante *&* ITALIAN   This charming spot in a converted heritage building off Waddington Alley is always a top contender for Victoria's best Italian restaurant. The food hails from northern Italy—wood-oven-roasted meats and pizzas as well as homemade pastas. But there's also an emphasis on fresh produce and local seafood, with appetizers such as thinly sliced smoked tuna over fresh arugula with horseradish dressing and entrees like spaghetti with clams in a spicy sauce of white wine, garlic, chiles, and tomatoes. The mood is bustling and upbeat; there's an atmospheric courtyard furnished with flowers, marble tables, wrought-iron chairs, and heaters. That, a good Chianti, and a piping hot *pizzetta* are enough to keep even the fiercest chill at bay.

555 Johnson St., off Waddington Alley. ℂ 250/361-0028. www.ilterrazzo.com. Reservations recommended. Main courses C$14–C$37 (US$11–US$30). AE, MC, V. Mon–Sat 11:30am–3pm (Oct–Apr no lunch on Sat); daily 5–10pm. Bus: 5.

MODERATE

Da Tandoor (Finds) INDIAN   The best of Victoria's several Indian restaurants, Da Tandoor hides itself behind an unprepossessing facade on the outer edge of Fort Street's antiques row, near Café Brio, Med Grill, and J&J Wonton Noodle House. The cuisine is well worth the 10-minute walk from downtown. Tandoori chicken, seafood, and lamb are the house specialties; but the extensive menu also includes masalas, vindaloos, goshts, and vegetarian dishes, as well as classic appetizers like vegetable and meat samosas, pakoras, and papadums. If you get inspired to try it at home, the restaurant sells a wide variety of spices and chutneys.

1010 Fort St. ℂ 250/384-6333. Reservations recommended. Main courses C$9–C$21 (US$7.20–US$17). MC, V. Sun–Thurs 5–9pm; Fri–Sat 5–10pm.

Herald Street Caffe ✿ PACIFIC NORTHWEST   An old converted warehouse on the far side of Chinatown, Herald Street Caffe is a large space with walls painted a warm red and covered with an ever-changing display of local art. The menu comes with a list of more than 20 martinis, and for oenophiles, the wine list offers French and Canadian labels, along with a good selection of B.C. reds and whites. The cuisine

---

(Moments) Taking Afternoon Tea

Okay, so it's expensive and touristy. Go anyway. Far from a simple cup of hot water with a Lipton's teabag beside it, a proper afternoon tea is both a meal and a ritual. The teapot is warmed before boiling hot water is poured over the tea leaves. The sweet and subtle flavor will almost certainly put you off the warm-water-and-tea-bag thing for life.

Any number of places in Victoria serves afternoon tea; some refer to it as high tea. Both come with sandwiches and berries and tarts, but high tea usually includes some more substantial savory fare such as a pasty meat-and-vegetable filled turnover. Though the caloric intake at a top-quality tea can be substantial, it's really more about the ritual than the potential weight gain. For that reason, you don't want to go to just any old teahouse. Note that in summer it's a good idea to book at least a week ahead, if not longer.

If you want the experience and can afford the price, you may as well do it right and go for the best. **The Fairmont Empress** ✿✿, 721 Government St. (ℂ 250/384-8111; bus no. 5 to the Convention Centre), serves tea in the Tea Lobby, a busy and beautifully ornate room at the front of the hotel. Price depends on the time and season, and runs from C$26 to C$52 (US$21–US$42). For that, you'll be pampered with fresh berries and cream; sandwiches of smoked salmon, cucumber, and carrot and ginger; scones, strawberry preserves, and thick Jersey cream. Even the tea is a special house blend. When you leave, you'll receive a canister of 10 bags to brew at home. There are four seatings a day: 12:30, 2, 2:30, and 5pm; reservations are essential in the summer.

is sophisticated without going too far over the top. Appetizers may include crab cakes with cilantro-lime pesto and roasted corn and tomato salsa. The entrees include many clever seafood dishes, as well as free-range chicken, duck, and lamb dishes, and several pastas. Portions are generous and the service is helpful, particularly when it comes to wine pairings. For dessert, don't miss the Boca Negra, a chocolate cake with rich chocolate bourbon sauce and fresh raspberries.

546 Herald St. ℂ 250/381-1441. Reservations required. Main courses C$17–C$39 (US$14–US$31). AE, DC, MC, V. Daily 5–10pm; Sat–Sun brunch 11am–3pm. Bus: 5.

Pagliacci's ITALIAN Victoria's night owls used to come here when Pagliacci's was one of the few places to offer late night dining. Though the city's evening scene has improved since expatriate New Yorker Howie Siegal opened the restaurant in 1979, Pagliacci's can still boast an un-Victoria kind of big city buzz and energy. Tables jostle against one another as guests ogle each other's food and eavesdrop on conversations. The menu is southern Italian—veal parmigiana, tortellini, and 19 or 20 other a la carte pastas, all fresh and made by hand, many quite inventive. Sunday through Wednesday there's live jazz, swing, blues, or Celtic music starting at 8:30pm. On Sunday, Howie hosts a very good brunch.

1011 Broad St. ℂ 250/386-1662. Reservations not accepted. Main courses C$12–C$24 (US$10–US$19). Sun brunch C$9.95–C$15 (US$8–US$12). AE, MC, V. Mon–Thurs 11:30am–10pm; Fri–Sat 11:30am–11pm; Sun 10am–10pm.

More affordable and just as historic is tea on the lawn of **Point Ellice House,** 2616 Pleasant St. (ℂ 250/380-6506), where the cream of Victoria society used to gather in the early 1900s. On the Gorge waterway, Point Ellice is just a 5-minute trip by ferry from the Inner Harbour, or take bus no. 14 to Pleasant Street. Afternoon tea costs C$17 (US$14) and includes a half-hour tour of the mansion and gardens, plus the opportunity to play a game of croquet. Open daily 10am to 4pm (tea served 11am–3pm) April 1 through Labour Day (the first Monday of September); phone ahead for Christmas hours.

With impeccably maintained gardens as a backdrop, "Afternoon Tea at the Gardens," at the **Butchart Gardens Dining Room Restaurant** ✻✻, 800 Benvenuto Ave. (ℂ 250/652-4422; bus no. 75), is a memorable experience. Sitting inside the Butchart mansion and looking out over the flowers, you can savor this fine tradition for C$22 to C$29 (US$18–US$23) per person. Tea is served daily noon to 5pm April 1 through Labour Day. Call ahead for winter hours.

What the **White Heather Tea Room,** 1885 Oak Bay Rd. (ℂ 250/595-8020) lacks in old-time atmosphere it more than makes up with the sheer quality and value of the tea and the charm of proprietress and tea mistress Agnes. What's more, there are numerous options on offer, all of them less expensive than a similar experience at the Empress. For those feeling not so peckish, there's the Wee Tea at C$8.25 (US$6.60). For those a little hungrier there's the Not So Wee Tea at C$13 (US$10). For the borderline starving there's the Big Muckle Great Tea for Two at C$32 (US$27).

The Reef CARIBBEAN   An outgrowth of the Vancouver restaurant (p. 108), this Island reef offers the same delectable menu, the centerpiece of which is jerk—a spicy marinade of bay leaves, scotch bonnets, allspice, garlic, soya, green onions, vinegar, and cloves. Slap it on a bird and the result is piquant, scrumptious chicken. The Reef serves up a number of jerk dishes, including their signature quarter jerk chicken breast. Other dishes are equally good, including a tropical salad of fresh mango, red onions, and tomatoes; shrimp with coconut milk and lime juice; and grilled blue marlin. In the evenings a DJ spins tunes and the Reef turns into its own little island lounge.

533 Yates St. ② 250/388-5375. www.thereefrestaurant.com. Main courses C$11–C$17 (US$9–US$14). MC, V. Daily 11am–midnight.

The Tapa Bar (Finds) TAPAS   The perfect meal for the commitment-shy, tapas are small and flavorful plates that you combine together to make a meal. Tapas to be sampled in this warm and welcoming spot include fried calamari, palm hearts, chicken chipotle, and grilled portobello mushrooms. Whatever else you order, however, don't pass up on the *gambas al ajillo*—shrimp in a rich broth of garlic. The martini list is likely longer than the list of wines, but between the two there's enough joy juice to keep the room buzzing till the witching hour.

620 Trounce Alley. ② 250/383-0013. Tapas plates C$7–C$15 (US$5.60–US$12). AE, MC, V. Mon–Thurs 11:30am–11pm; Fri–Sat 11:30am–midnight; Sun 11am–10pm.

Zambri's (★) (Finds) ITALIAN   This little deli-restaurant in a strip mall off Yates Street has earned numerous accolades for its honest and fresh Italian cuisine served in an unpretentious, no-nonsense style. The lunch menu, served cafeteria style, includes five daily pasta specials and a handful of entrees such as fresh rockfish or salmon. In the evenings, the atmosphere is slightly more formal with table service and a regularly changing a la carte menu. Menu items veer from penne with sausage and tomato to pasta with chicken liver pâté or peas and Gorgonzola. Many diners come for the three-course dinner (C$38/US$30).

110–911 Yates St. ② 250/360-1171. Reservations not accepted. Lunch C$6–C$15 (US$4.80–US$12); dinner C$10–C$25 (US$8–US$20). MC, V. Tues–Sat 11:30am–3pm and 5–9pm.

INEXPENSIVE

Green Cuisine (Value) VEGETARIAN   In addition to being undeniably healthy, Victoria's only fully vegan eatery offers remarkably tasty choices, with a self-serve salad bar, hot buffet, dessert bar, and full bakery. Available dishes range from Moroccan chickpea and vegetable soup to pasta primavera salad to pumpkin tofu cheesecake, not to mention a wide selection of freshly baked breads (made with natural sweeteners and fresh-ground organic flour). Green Cuisine also has a large selection of freshly squeezed organic juices, smoothies, and shakes as well as organic coffees and teas.

560 Johnson St., in Market Sq. ② 250/385-1809. www.greencuisine.com. Main courses C$4–C$10 (US$3.20–US$8). AE, MC, V. Daily 10am–8pm.

J&J Wonton Noodle House (★) (Finds) CHINESE   Real Chinese noodle houses are rare in North America, which is a shame, because the food is so good. This place doesn't go overboard on the atmosphere, but it's perfectly pleasant and you won't find better noodles anywhere in Victoria. The kitchen is glassed in so you can watch the chefs spinning out noodles and expertly whisking soups through woks into bowls. Lunch specials—which feature different fresh seafood every day—are good and cheap,

Finding High-Octane Coffee

Good coffee is one of the great joys of life. Fortunately, Victoria's tea-party Englishness hasn't stopped it from buzzing into the same coffee-cuckooness that's engulfed Vancouver and the rest of the Pacific Northwest. Some to savor:

- **Starbucks** has any number of outposts here. The one at the corner of Fort and Blanshard streets (© 250/383-6208) is fairly central, open 6am to 11pm Sunday through Thursday and 6am to midnight Friday and Saturday; bus no. 5 to Fort Street.
- Better for taste, and with interesting hand-painted Deruta ceramic mugs, is **Torrefazione**, 1234 Government St. (© 250/920-7203), open Monday through Friday 6:30am to 9pm, Saturday 7:30am to 10pm, and Sunday 8:30am to 7pm; bus no. 5 to View Street.
- Out in Cook Street Village, the **Moka House,** 345 Cook St. (© 250/388-7377), open daily 6am to midnight, also offers great desserts and snacks; bus no. 5 to Cook and Mary streets.
- On a sunny day, head for **Willy's,** 537 Johnson St. (© 250/381-8414). Order your brew of choice from the counter and take a seat on the patio. This bakery serves up excellent sweets and great hot breakfasts. It's open Monday to Friday 7am to 5pm, Saturday 8am to 5pm, and Sunday 8:30am to 4:30pm; bus no. 25.

so expect a line of locals at the door. If you miss the specials, noodle soups, chow mein, chow fun (wide noodles), and other dishes are also quick, delicious, and inexpensive. Dinner is pricier.

1012 Fort St. © 250/383-0680. Main courses C$11–C$16 (US$9–US$13); lunch specials C$6–C$13 (US$4.80–US$10). MC, V. Tues–Sat 11am–2pm and 4:30–8:30pm. Bus: 5.

Med Grill@Mosaic *(finds)* TAPAS/BISTRO   This tasty bistro and tapas bar is a welcome addition to Victoria's dining and nightlife scene. It's got a light, contemporary interior with lots of wood and huge windows, and on Friday and Saturday offers a late-night (10pm to midnight) happy hour with tasty bar treats (prosciutto-wrapped prawns, thin-crust pizzas, crab and shrimp cakes) that cost under C$8 (US$6.40). This is also a restaurant where you can get soup and salad and sandwiches, pasta, or an entree of fresh salmon, pork tenderloin, or oven-roasted chicken.

1063 Fort St. © 250/381-3417. Main courses C$10–C$12 (US$8–US$10); bar menu C$3–C$8 (US$2.40–US$6.40). AE, MC, V. Sun–Thurs 11am–10pm; Fri–Sat 11am–midnight. Bus: 5.

Q V Bakery & Café BAKERY   The main attraction of the simple food on offer at this spot on the edge of downtown isn't so much its quality—though the coffee, muffins, cookies, and light meals like lasagnas, quiches, and salads are all quite good—as is its availability. On weekends, Q V is open 24 hours, which in Victoria is enough to make it very special indeed.

1701 Government St. © 250/384-8831. Main courses C$4–C$10 (US$3.20–US$8). MC, V. Sun–Thurs 6am–3am; Fri–Sat 24 hr.

rebar *(Kids)* VEGETARIAN   Even if you're not hungry, it's worth dropping in here for a juice blend—say grapefruit, banana, melon, and pear with bee pollen or blue-green algae for added oomph. If you're hungry, then rejoice: rebar is the city's premier dispenser of vegetarian comfort food. Disturbingly wholesome as that may sound, rebar is not only tasty, but fun, and a great spot to take the kids for brunch or break-fast. The room—in the basement of an 1890s heritage building—is bright and funky, with loads of cake tins glued to the walls. The service is friendly and casual. The food tends toward the simple and wholesome, including quesadillas, omelets, and crisp sal-ads. Juices are still the crown jewels, with over 80 blends on the menu.

50 Bastion Sq. ℂ 250/361-9223. www.rebarmodernfood.com. Main courses C$7.50–C$16 (US$6–US$13). AE, MC, V. Mon–Thurs 8:30am–9pm; Fri–Sat 8:30am–10pm; Sun 8:30am–3:30pm. Reduced hours in the winter. Bus: 5.

Sam's Deli DELI   If you don't like lines, avoid the lunch hour, for Sam's is *the* lunchtime Victoria soup-and-sandwich spot. Sandwiches come in all tastes and sizes (mostly large), but the shrimp and avocado is the one to get. You can also get a ploughman's lunch (cheese, sourdough bread, apple, and other options) here. Sam's homemade soups are excellent, as is his chili. And Sam's is right across the street from the harbor, so it's unbeatably convenient.

805 Government St. ℂ 250/382-8424. Main courses C$4–C$10 (US$3.20–US$8). MC, V. Summer Mon–Fri 7:30am–10pm; Sat–Sun 8am–10pm; winter Mon–Fri 7:30am–5pm.

Siam Thai Restaurant *(Value)* THAI   There aren't many opportunities to satisfy your craving for Thai food in Victoria, but tucked away in a vintage building just half a block or so from the waterfront, this little local favorite offers good-quality Thai cook-ing done with varying levels of spiciness to suit every palate. Menu items are starred from mild to spicy (one to four peppers), so there's no risk of having your tongue scorched. The menu includes many signature Thai dishes such as coconut–lemon grass chicken or shrimp soup, pad Thai noodles, garlic and pepper pork, as well as a variety of curries (red, yellow, and green). Most items can be adapted to accommodate vegetarians. The lunch specials are a great deal.

512 Fort St. ℂ 250/383-9911. Main courses C$10–C$18 (US$8–US$14); lunch specials C$7–C$11 (US$5.60–US$9). MC, V. Mon–Fri 11:30am–2:30pm and 5–9:30pm; Sat noon–2pm and 5pm–closing; Sun noon–2pm and 4–8:30pm. Bus: 5.

5 Outside the Central Area

VERY EXPENSIVE

The Aerie *(✿✿✿)* FRENCH   The dining room of this red-tile villa/hotel (p. 206) over-looks Finlayson Inlet, the Strait of Georgia, and, on a clear day, the Olympic Mountains. The room itself is bright and decorated with a 14-carat gold-leaf ceiling, crystal chan-deliers, and a large open-hearth fireplace. Chef Christophe Letard's creations combine West Coast freshness with unmistakably French accents. Eating at this award-winning restaurant is a culinary event: You choose from one of several tasting menus or a la carte options. A recent Discovery Tasting menu started with a smoked salmon mousse, went on to anise-cured scallop rosette, lemon and saffron marinated lobster, smoked venison, veal tenderloin, and a roasted delicata and fromage frais cheesecake. Excellent wine pair-ings, featuring many local vintages, help to make meals here exciting and memorable.

600 Ebedora Lane, Malahat. ℂ 800/518-1933 or 250/743-7115. www.aerie.bc.ca. Reservations required. Main courses C$27–C$35 (US$22–US$28); tasting menus C$55-C$105 (US$44–US$84). AE, DC, MC, V. Daily noon–1:30pm and 6–9:30pm. Take Hwy. 1 to the Spectacle Lake turnoff; take the first right and follow the winding driveway.

Arbutus Grille and Winebar *☆☆* PACIFIC NORTHWEST   The dining room of beautiful Brentwood Bay Lodge (p. 207), about a 20-minute drive north of Victoria, is all warm wood with giant windows overlooking Saanich Inlet. The food prepared here is from the region, with a menu that changes daily according to what is fresh and in season. You might find loin of fallow deer with pickled bing cherries, a miso-glazed sablefish, or duck breast and confit with a white bean cassoulet. If everything looks good, try the 5- or 7-course tasting menu, a memorable experience that begins with an amuse bouche and continues through fish, pasta, meat, and dessert courses. The wine list is exemplary, and so is the service.

In Brentwood Bay Lodge and Spa, 849 Verdier Ave., Brentwood Bay. *©* **888/544-2079** or 250/544-5100. www.brentwoodbaylodge.com. Reservations recommended. Main courses C$29–C$44 (US$23–US$35); tasting menu C$78-C$98 (US$62–US$78). AE, DC, MC, V. Daily noon–2pm and 5:30–10pm. From Victoria, take Pat Bay Hwy. north to Keating Crossroads, turn left (west) to Saanich Rd., turn right (south) to Verdier Ave.

Sooke Harbour House *☆☆☆* PACIFIC NORTHWEST   On a bluff at the edge of the Pacific, the dining room of this small restaurant/hotel (p. 208) offers spectacular waterfront views, a relaxed atmosphere, and what could be the best food in all Canada. Chef/proprietor Sinclair Philip is both a talented innovator and a stickler for detail, which results in an ever-changing menu in which each of the dishes is prepared with care, imagination, and flair. The ingredients are resolutely local (many come from the inn's own organic herb garden or from the ocean at the Harbour House's doorstep). On any given night, dishes might include grilled sablefish with a leek, lavender, squash, ginger emulsion or split-pea crusted halibut. The presentation is always interesting, and the staff is knowledgeable and professional. The wine cellar is extensive (one of the best in Canada), and the pairings for Philips' culinary creations are particularly well chosen. There is a set menu from Sunday through Thursday, and an a la carte menu on Fridays and Saturdays.

1528 Whiffen Spit Rd., Sooke. *©* **800/889-9688** or 250/642-3421. www.sookeharbourhouse.com. Reservations required. Main courses C$27–C$37 (US$22–US$30); set menu C$70–$100 (US$56–US$80). MC, V. Daily 5:30–9pm. Take the Island Hwy. to the Sooke/Colwood turnoff (Junction Hwy. 14); continue on Hwy. 14 to Sooke; about a mile past the town's only traffic light, turn left onto Whiffen Spit Rd.

INEXPENSIVE

Six Mile Pub PUB GRUB   In an 1855 building, this pub has a rich history. Originally named the Parson's Bridge Hotel (after the man who built Parson's Bridge, which opened the Sooke area to vehicle traffic), it was filled with sailors when the Esquimalt Naval Base opened nearby in 1864. When Victoria elected to continue Prohibition until 1952, the Six Mile Pub became the hub for provincial bootleggers. Loyal locals still come for the atmosphere and the dinner specials. You can enjoy the warm ambience of the fireside room, or the beautiful scenery from the outdoor patio. Start with one of the 10 house brews on tap, then enjoy a hearty Cornish pasty (stringy mystery meat, peas, potatoes, and carrots in a pastry envelope), steak-and-mushroom pie, or juicy prime rib. If meat isn't part of your diet, try a tasty veggie burger. They've recently gone "international," too, and serve various tapas, pot stickers, and more adventuresome seafood dishes.

494 Island Hwy., View Royal. *©* **250/478-3121**. www.sixmilepub.com. Main courses C$7–C$14 (US$5.60–US$11). MC, V. Mon–Thurs 11am–11pm; Fri–Sat 11am–1am; Sun 10am–11pm. Must be over 19 to enter.

14

Exploring Victoria

Victoria's top draws are its waterfront—the beautiful viewscape created by the Fairmont Empress and the Parliament Buildings on the edge of the Inner Harbour—and its historic Old Town. So attractive are these that folks sometimes forget what a beautiful and wild part of the world the city is set in. If you have time, step out of town a little and see some nature: Sail out to see killer whales, beachcomb for crabs, kayak along the ocean shorelines, or hike into the hills for some fabulous views and scenery. Two world-class attractions are the Butchart Gardens, about a 20-minute drive from downtown, and the Royal B.C. Museum across from the Inner Harbour.

In chapter 3 you'll find a suggested 1-day itinerary for Victoria, including all the must-see sights, and in chapter 15 you'll find walking and bike tours that cover the best this waterfront city has to offer. If you want to fully experience this part of the Pacific Northwest, consider a visit to **Pacific Rim National Park** ✹✹✹, about a 4½-hour drive from Victoria. This old-growth temperate rainforest stretches along a rugged and pristine stretch of shoreline on the western side of Vancouver Island, and it's an unforgettable spot. You'll find it described in "Ucluelet, Tofino & Pacific Rim National Park," p. 285, in chapter 18.

1 Seeing the Sights

THE TOP ATTRACTIONS

Art Gallery of Greater Victoria   Housed in a combination of contemporary exhibition space and a historic 19th-century mansion called Gyppeswick, the Art Gallery of Greater Victoria features a permanent collection of over 15,000 objets d'art, drawn from Asia, Europe, and North America, though the gallery's primary emphasis is on Canada and Japan. The permanent **Emily Carr exhibit** ✹ integrates Carr's writings, works from the Gallery collection, and images from the British Columbia provincial archives to create a compelling portrait of this pre-eminent Victoria artist. Allow 1½ hours.

1040 Moss St. ⓒ 250/384-4101. www.aggv.bc.ca. Admission C$8 (US$6.40) adults, C$6 (US$4.80) students/seniors. Daily 10am–5pm (Thurs until 9pm). Closed Dec 24–25, Good Friday, Easter, Nov 11. Bus: 11, 14, or 22.

British Columbia Aviation Museum ✹   A must for plane buffs, or for anyone with an interest in the history of flight. Located adjacent to Victoria International Airport, this small hangar is crammed to bursting with a score of original, rebuilt, and replica airplanes. The collection ranges from the first Canadian-designed craft ever to fly (a bizarre kitelike contraption) to World War I–vintage Nieuports and Tiger Moths, to floatplanes and Spitfires and slightly more modern water bombers and helicopters. Thursdays you can watch the all-volunteer crew in the restoration hangar working to bring these old craft back to life. Allow 1 hour.

Victoria Attractions

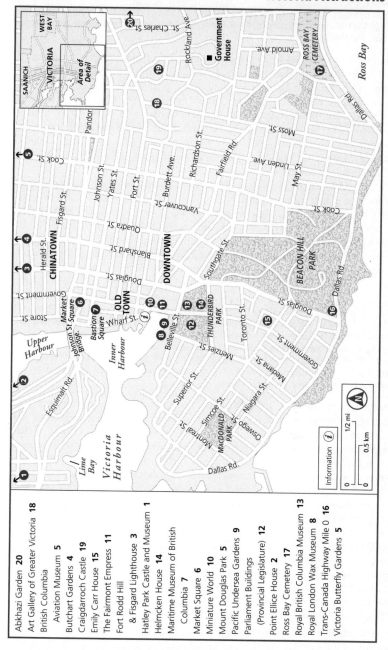

Abkhazi Garden **20**
Art Gallery of Greater Victoria **18**
British Columbia
  Aviation Museum **5**
Butchart Gardens **4**
Craigdarroch Castle **19**
Emily Carr House **15**
The Fairmont Empress **11**
Fort Rodd Hill
  & Fisgard Lighthouse **3**
Hatley Park Castle and Museum **1**
Helmcken House **14**
Maritime Museum of British
  Columbia **7**
Market Square **6**
Miniature World **10**
Mount Douglas Park **5**
Pacific Undersea Gardens **9**
Parliament Buildings
  (Provincial Legislature) **12**
Point Ellice House **2**
Ross Bay Cemetery **17**
Royal British Columbia Museum **13**
Royal London Wax Museum **8**
Trans-Canada Highway Mile 0 **16**
Victoria Butterfly Gardens **5**

223

1910 Norseman Rd., Sidney. ℂ 250/655-3300. www.bcam.net. Admission C$7 (US$5.60) adults, C$5 (US$4) seniors, C$3 (US$2.40) students, children under 12 free. Summer daily 10am–4pm; winter daily 11am–3pm. Closed Dec 25, Jan 1. Bus: Airport.

Butchart Gardens ⍟⍟⍟   These internationally acclaimed gardens were created after Robert Butchart exhausted the limestone quarry near his Tod Inlet home, about 22km (14 miles) from Victoria. His wife, Jenny, gradually landscaped the deserted eyesore into the resplendent **Sunken Garden,** opening it for public display in 1904. A **Rose Garden, Italian Garden,** and **Japanese Garden** were added. As the fame of the 20-hectare (49-acre) gardens grew, the Butcharts also transformed their house into an attraction. The gardens—still in the family—now display more than a million plants throughout the year. As impressive as the numbers is the sheer perfection of each garden—gardeners will be amazed.

Evenings in summer, the gardens are beautifully illuminated with a variety of softly colored lights. June through September, musical entertainment is provided free Monday through Saturday evenings. You can even watch fireworks displays on Saturdays in July and August. A very good lunch, dinner, and afternoon tea are offered in the Dining Room Restaurant in the historic residence; afternoon and high teas are also served in the Italian Garden (reservations strongly recommended). Allow 2 to 3 hours; in peak summer months you'll experience less congestion in the garden if you come very early or after 3pm.

800 Benvenuto Ave., Brentwood Bay. ℂ **866/652-4422** or 250/652-4422; dining reservations 250/652-8222. www.butchartgardens.com. Admission June 15–Sept C$22 (US$18) adults, C$11 (US$9) youths 13–17, C$2.50 (US$2) children 5–12, free for children under 5; admission price reduced in spring, fall, and winter. Gates open daily 9am–sundown (call for seasonal closing time); visitors can remain in gardens for 1 hr. after gate closes. Bus: 75 or the Gray Line shuttle from the Victoria Bus Station. C$4 (US$3.20) one-way. Shuttle departure times vary seasonally; call ℂ 250/388-5248 for exact times. Take Blanshard St. (Hwy. 17) north toward the ferry terminal in Saanich, then turn left on Keating Crossroads, which leads directly to the gardens—about 20 min. from downtown Victoria; it's impossible to miss if you follow the trail of billboards.

Craigdarroch Castle ⍟   What do you do when you're the richest man in British Columbia, when you've clawed, scraped, and bullied your way up from indentured servant to coal baron and merchant prince? You build a castle, of course, to show the other buggers what you're worth. Located in the highlands above Oak Bay, Robert Dunsmuir's home, built in the 1880s, is a stunner. The four-story, 39-room Highland-style castle is topped with stone turrets and chimneys and filled with the opulent Victorian splendor you'd expect from an arriviste who finally arrived—detailed woodwork, Persian carpets, stained-glass windows, paintings, and sculptures. The nonprofit society that runs Craigdarroch does an excellent job showcasing the castle. You're provided with a self-tour booklet and there are volunteer docents who are happy to provide further information. To tour the castle takes from 30 minutes to an hour. The castle also hosts many events throughout the year, including theater performances, concerts, and dinner tours.

1050 Joan Crescent (off Fort St.). ℂ 250/592-5323. www.craigdarrochcastle.com. Admission C$10 (US$8) adults, C$6.50 (US$5.20) students, C$3.50 (US$2.80) children 5–12, children under 5 free. June 15 to Labour Day daily 9am–7pm; Labour Day to June 14 daily 10am–4:30pm. Closed Dec 25, 26, and Jan 1. Bus: 11 to Joan Crescent. Take Fort St. out of downtown, just past Cook, and turn right on Joan Crescent.

Fort Rodd Hill & Fisgard Lighthouse National Historic Site   Perched on an outcrop of volcanic rock, the **Fisgard Lighthouse** has guided ships toward Victoria's sheltered harbor since 1873. The light no longer has a keeper (the beacon has long been automated), but the site itself has been restored to its 1873 appearance. Two floors of exhibits in the light keeper's house recount stories of the lighthouse, its keepers, and the terrible shipwrecks that gave this coastline its ominous moniker "the graveyard of the Pacific."

Adjoining the lighthouse, **Fort Rodd Hill** is a preserved 1890s coastal artillery fort that still sports camouflaged searchlights, underground magazines, and its original guns. Audiovisual exhibits bring the fort to life with the voices and faces of the men who served at the outpost. Displays of artifacts, room re-creations, and historic film footage add to the experience. Allow 1 to 2 hours.

603 Fort Rodd Hill Rd. ☏ 250/478-5849. www.parkscanada.ca/fortroddhill. Admission C$4 (US$3.20) adults, C$3 (US$2.40) seniors, C$2 (US$1.60) children 6–16, C$10 (US$8) families, children under 6 free. Mar–Oct daily 10am–5:30pm; Nov–Feb daily 9am–4:30pm. No public transit. Head north on Douglas St. until it turns into Hwy. 1; stay on Hwy. 1 for 5km (3 miles), then take the Colwood exit (exit 10); follow Hwy. 1A for 2km (1¼ miles), then turn left at the 3rd traffic light onto Ocean Blvd.; follow the signs to the site.

Maritime Museum of British Columbia

Housed in the former provincial courthouse, this museum is dedicated to recalling B.C.'s rich maritime heritage. The displays do a good job of illustrating maritime history, from the early explorers to the fur trading and whaling era to the days of grand ocean liners and military conflict. There's also an impressive collection of ship models and paraphernalia—uniforms, weapons, gear—along with photographs and journals. The museum also shows films in its Vice Admiralty Theatre. Allow 1 hour.

28 Bastion Sq. ☏ 250/385-4222. www.mmbc.bc.ca. Admission C$8 (US$6.40) adults, C$5 (US$4) seniors and students, C$3 (US$2.40) children 6–11, C$20 (US$16) families, children under 6 free. Daily 9:30am–4:30pm (June 15–Sept 15 until 5pm). Closed Dec 25. Bus: 5 to View St.

Miniature World *(Kids)*

It sounds cheesy—hundreds of dolls and miniatures and scenes from old fairy tales. And yet Miniature World—inside the Fairmont Empress hotel (the entrance is around the corner)—is actually kinda cool. You walk in and you're plunged into darkness, except for a moon, some planets, and a tiny spaceship flying up to rendezvous with an orbiting mother ship. This is the most up-to-date display. Farther in are re-creations of battle scenes, fancy 18th-century dress balls, a miniature Canadian Pacific railway running all the way across a miniature Canada, a three-ring circus and midway, and scenes from Mother Goose and Charles Dickens stories. Better yet, most of these displays do something: The train moves at the punch of a button and the circus rides whirl around and light up as simulated darkness falls. Allow 1 hour to see it all.

649 Humboldt St. ☏ 250/385-9731. www.miniatureworld.com. Admission C$9 (US$7.20) adults, C$8 (US$6.40) youths, C$7 (US$5.60) children 4–12, children under 4 free. Summer daily 8:30am–9pm; winter daily 9am–5pm. Bus: 5, 27, 28, or 30.

Pacific Undersea Gardens *(Kids)*

Locals aren't very keen on the sight of this conspicuous white structure floating in the Inner Harbor, but your kids might enjoy a visit. A gently sloping stairway leads down to this marine observatory's glass-enclosed viewing area, where you can observe the Inner Harbour's marine life up close. Some 5,000 creatures feed, play, hunt, and court in these protected waters. Sharks, wolf eels, poisonous stonefish, sea anemones, starfish, sturgeon, and salmon are just a few of the organisms that make their homes here. Every hour, on the hour, there's an underwater show in which a diver-naturalist catches and—thanks to a microphone hook-up—explains a variety of the undersea fauna. One of the star attractions is a remarkably photogenic huge octopus (reputedly the largest in captivity). Injured seals and orphaned seal pups are cared for in holding pens alongside the observatory as part of a provincial marine-mammal rescue program. Allow 1 hour.

490 Belleville St. ✆ **250/382-5717**. www.pacificunderseagardens.com. Admission C$8.50 (US$6.80) adults, C$7.50 (US$6) seniors, C$6 (US$4.80) youths 12–17, C$4.50 (US$3.60) children 5–11, free for children under 5. Sept–Apr daily 9:30am–5pm; May–June daily 9:30am–6pm; July–Sept daily 9am–8:30pm; Jan–Feb closed Tues–Wed. Bus: 5, 27, 28, or 30.

Parliament Buildings (Provincial Legislature) ☞

Designed by 25-year-old Francis Rattenbury and built between 1893 and 1898 at a cost of nearly C$1 million (US$750,000), the Parliament Buildings (also called the Legislature) are an architectural gem. The 40-minute tour comes across at times like an eighth-grade civics lesson, but it's worth it to see the fine mosaics, marble, woodwork, and stained glass. And if you see a harried-looking man surrounded by a pack of minicam crews, it's likely just another B.C. premier getting hounded out of office by the aggressive and hostile media: Politics is a blood sport in B.C.

501 Belleville St. ✆ **250/387-3046**. www.protocol.gov.bc.ca. Free admission. Late May to Labour Day daily 9am–5pm; Sept to late May Mon–Fri 9am–5pm. Tours offered every 20 min. in summer; in winter call ahead for the public tour schedules as times vary due to school group bookings; no tours noon–1pm. Bus: 5, 27, 28, or 30.

Royal British Columbia Museum ☞☞☞ *Kids*

One of the world's best regional museums, the Royal B.C. has a mandate to present the land and the people of coastal British Columbia. The second-floor **Natural History Gallery** showcases the coastal flora, fauna, and geography from the Ice Age to the present; it includes dioramas of a temperate rainforest, a seacoast, an underground ecology of giant insects, and (particularly appealing to kids) a live tidal pool with sea stars and anemones. The third-floor **Modern History Gallery** presents the recent past, including historically faithful recreations of Victoria's downtown and Chinatown. On the same floor, the **First Peoples Gallery** ☞☞☞ is an incredible showpiece of First Nations art and culture with rare artifacts used in day-to-day Native life, a full-size re-creation of a longhouse, and a hauntingly wonderful gallery with totem poles and masks. The museum also has an **IMAX theater** showing an ever-changing variety of large-screen movies. On the way out (or in), be sure to stop by **Thunderbird Park,** beside the museum, where a cedar longhouse (Mungo Martin House, named after a famous Kwakiutl artist) houses a workshop where Native carvers work on new totem poles. To see and experience everything takes 3 to 4 hours.

675 Belleville St. ✆ **888/447-7977** or 250/387-3701. www.royalbcmuseum.bc.ca. Admission C$13 (US$10) adults, C$8.70 (US$7) seniors/students/youths, C$34 (US$27) families, children under 6 free. Combination museum and Imax C$21 (US$17) adults, C$17 (US$14) seniors/youths, C$18 (US$15) students. Daily 9am–5pm; Imax daily 9am–8pm. Closed Dec 25 and Jan 1. Bus: 5, 28, or 30.

Royal London Wax Museum

I've never understood why one of Victoria's most beautiful classical buildings, right on the waterfront, had to be used for a wax museum. And a pretty cheesy wax museum at that, with figures that often look more like old store mannequins than the people they're based on. Inside, you can see the same dusty royal family you already get too much of on television and other insignificant royals from times past. But there are other figures, too—everyone from Buddha to Charlie Chaplin, Marilyn Monroe, and Goldie Hawn (the most recent addition). It's doubtful even your kids will much enjoy it, except, of course, for the gory Chamber of Horrors (which might put off some kids).

470 Belleville St. ✆ **877/929-3228** or 250/388-4461. www.waxmuseum.bc.ca. Admission C$10 (US$8) adults, C$9 (US$7.20) seniors, C$7 (US$5.60) students 13 and older, C$5 (US$4) children 6–12, children under 6 free. Tues–Sat 10am–5pm, Sun–Mon 11am–4pm. Bus: 5, 27, 28, or 30.

On the Lookout: Victoria's Best Views

In town, the best view of The Empress and the Parliament buildings (the Legislature) comes from walking along the pedestrian path in front of the **Delta Ocean Pointe Resort,** off the Johnson Street Bridge. In summer, there's a patio there where you can sit and enjoy a coffee or glass of wine with the view.

When the fishing fleets come in, head over to **Fisherman's Wharf** at St. Lawrence and Erie streets, to watch as the fishermen unload their catches. Later on, you can enjoy the sunset from the wharf along the eastern edge of the Inner Harbour or from the 18th floor of the **Vista 18 Restaurant,** 740 Burdett Ave. (© **250/382-9258**).

Just south of downtown, you can see across the Strait of Juan de Fuca and the San Juan Islands to the mountains of the Olympic Peninsula from the **Ogden Point** breakwater, from the top of the hill in **Beacon Hill Park,** or from the walking path above the beach along **Dallas Road.** Farther afield, **Fort Rodd Hill** and **Fisgard Lighthouse** offer equally good views of the mountains, as well as a view of the ships in Esquimalt Harbour.

Mount Douglas ✦, a 15-minute drive north of the city on Shelbourne Street, offers a panoramic view of the entire Saanich Peninsula, with a parking lot just a 2-minute walk from the summit. To the east, **Mount Work** offers an equally good view, but you have to walk up. It takes about 45 minutes. At the top of Little Saanich Mountain (about 16km/10 miles north of Victoria) stands the **Dominion Astrophysical Observatory,** 5071 W. Saanich Rd. (© **250/363-8262**) and its new **Centre of the Universe** interpretive center, which offers guided tours and activities for C$9 (U$7.20) adults, C$8 (US$6.40) seniors and students, C$5 (U$4) youths 6 to 18, and families C$23 (US$18). The interpretive centre is open Tuesday through Saturday from 10am to 4:30pm (Sat until 5:30pm) November through March. The observatory stays open later in the year, with evening prices:C$12 (US$9.60) adults, C$10 (US$8) seniors and students, C$7 (US$5.60).

Victoria Butterfly Gardens ✦ *(Kids)*   This is a great spot for kids, nature buffs, or anyone who just likes butterflies. Hundreds of exotic colorful butterflies flutter freely through this lush tropical greenhouse and you're provided with an ID chart and set free to roam around. Species range from the tiny Central American Julia (a brilliant orange butterfly about 3 in. across) to the Southeast Asian Giant Atlas Moth (mottled brown and red, with a wingspan approaching a foot). Other butterflies are brilliant blue, yellow, or a mix of colors and patterns. Naturalists are on hand to explain butterfly biology, and there's a display where you can see the beautiful creatures emerge from their cocoons. Allow 1 hour. *Note:* The Gardens are closed from November through February.

1461 Benvenuto Ave. (P.O. Box 190), Brentwood Bay. © 877/722-0272 or 250/652-3822. www.butterflygardens. com. Admission C$9.50 (US$7.60) adults, C$8.50 (US$6.80) students/seniors, C$5.50 (US$4.40) children 5–12, children under 5 free. Mar–May 13 and Oct daily 9:30am–4:30pm; May 14–Sept daily 9am–5:30pm. Closed Nov–Feb. Bus: 75.

Finds Emily Carr—Visionary from Victoria

Victoria was the birthplace of one of British Columbia's most distinguished early residents, the painter and writer Emily Carr (1871–1945). Though trained in the classical European tradition, Carr developed her own style in response to the powerful landscapes of the Canadian west coast. Eschewing both marriage and stability, she spent her life traveling the coast, capturing the landscapes and Native peoples in vivid and striking works. In addition to visiting the great collection of Carr's paintings at the Art Gallery of Greater Victoria (see above), you can visit the **Emily Carr House** ⨏, 207 Government St. (Ⓒ 250/383-5843; www.emilycarr.com), where she was born. The house has been restored to the condition it would have been in when Carr lived there. In addition, many of the rooms have been hung with reproductions of her art or quotations from her writings. From May 24 to September 6, the house is open daily 10am to 5pm; September 7 to October 9 it's open the same hours but closed Sunday and Monday. On Sundays from June through August, a local actress portrays Emily Carr and regales visitors with Carr family stories. Admission is C$5.35 (US$4.20) for adults, C$4.25 (US$3.40) for students/seniors, C$3.25 (US$2.60) for children 6 to 12, and free for children under 6. The Vancouver Art Gallery (see chapter 7, p. 119) also has a major collection of Carr's hauntingly evocative paintings.

ARCHITECTURAL HIGHLIGHTS & HISTORIC HOMES

First a trading post, then a gold-rush town, naval base, and sleepy provincial capital, Victoria bears architectural witness to all these eras. What Vancouver mostly demolished, Victoria saved, so you really do have a feast of heritage buildings to enjoy. The best of Victoria's buildings date to the pre–World War I years, when gold poured in from the Fraser and Klondike rivers, fueling a building boom responsible for most of downtown. For a good walking tour that shows off Victoria's heritage, see Walking Tour 2 ("Old Town and Chinatown") in chapter 15.

Perhaps the most intriguing downtown edifice isn't a building but a work of art. The walls of **Fort Victoria,** which once spanned much of downtown, have been demarcated in the sidewalk with bricks bearing the names of original settlers and traders. Look on the sidewalk on Government Street at the corner of Fort Street.

Most of the retail establishments in Victoria's Old Town area are housed in 19th-century shipping warehouses that have been carefully restored as part of a heritage-reclamation program. You can take a **self-guided tour** of the buildings, most of which were erected between the 1870s and 1890s; their history is recounted on easy-to-read outdoor plaques. The majority of the restored buildings are between Douglas and Government streets from Wharf Street to Johnson Street. The most impressive structure once housed a number of shipping offices and warehouses and is now the home of a 45-shop complex known as **Market Square** (560 Johnson St./255 Market Sq.; Ⓒ **250/386-2441**).

Some of the British immigrants who settled Vancouver Island during the 19th century built magnificent estates and mansions. In addition to architect Francis Ratten-bury's crowning turn-of-the-20th-century achievements—the provincial **Parliament Buildings,** 501 Belleville St. (completed in 1898), and the opulent **Fairmont Empress Hotel,** 721 Government St. (completed in 1908)—you'll find a number of other magnificent historic architectural sites.

Helmcken House, 610 Elliot St. Sq. (℡ **250/361-0021**), is the oldest house in B.C. on its original site. Dr. John Sebastian Helmcken, a surgeon with the Hudson's Bay Company, set up house here in 1852 when he married the daughter of Governor Sir James Douglas. Originally a three-room log cabin, the house was built by Helmcken and expanded as both the prosperity and size of the family grew. It still contains its original furnishings, imported from England. Helmcken went on to become a statesman and helped negotiate the entry of British Columbia as a province into Canada. From May through September, the house is open daily 10am to 5pm. Admission is C$5 (US$4) for adults, C$4 (US$3.20) for seniors and students, and C$3 (US$2.40) for children.

Craigdarroch Castle (p. 224) was built during the 1880s to serve as Scottish coal-mining magnate Robert Dunsmuir's home. Dunsmuir's son, James, built his own pala-tial home, **Hatley Castle.** The younger Dunsmuir reportedly commissioned architect Samuel Maclure with the words "Money doesn't matter, just build what I want." The bill, in 1908, came to over C$1 million (US$750,000). The grounds of the castle, now home to **Royal Roads University,** 2005 Sooke Rd. (℡ **250/391-2511**), feature exten-sive floral gardens and are open to the public free of charge. There's also a volunteer-run **Hatley Park Castle and Museum,** 2005 Sooke Rd. (℡ **250/391-2600,** ext. 4456), which offers tours of the grounds and the castle Monday through Friday 1 to 4pm. Admission is by donation. Call ahead—if no volunteers show up or if school events occupy the grounds, the museum doesn't open. Hatley Castle is off Highway 14 in Colwood. Take Government Street north for about 2km (1¼ miles). Turn left onto the Gorge Road (Hwy. 1A) and follow about 20km (12 miles). Note that after about 10km (6¼ miles), the road jogs to the south and becomes the Old Island Highway. Turn left onto Sooke Road (Hwy. 14) and look for the signs for Royal Roads University.

CEMETERIES

Ross Bay Cemetery, 1495 Fairfield St. at Dallas Rd., has to be one of the finest loca-tions in all creation to spend eternity. Luminaries interred here include the first gov-ernor of the island, James Douglas; frontier judge Matthew Begbie; and West Coast painter Emily Carr. *An Historic Guide to Ross Bay Cemetery,* available in Munro's Books (p. 254) as well as other bookstores, gives details on people buried here and directions to grave sites.

Pioneer Square, on the corner of Meares and Quadra Streets beside Christ Church, is one of British Columbia's oldest cemeteries. Hudson's Bay Company fur traders, ship captains, sailors, fishermen, and crew members from British Royal Navy vessels lie beneath the worn sandstone markers.

Contact the **Old Cemeteries Society** (℡ **250/598-8870;** www.oldcem.bc.ca) for more information on tours of both of these graveyards.

⟮*Tips* **Another Victoria Tea House**

On a promontory above the Gorge Waterway, the completely restored **Point Ellice House,** 2616 Pleasant St. (℡ **250/380-6506**), was the summer gathering place for much of Victoria's Victorian elite. From mid-May to mid-September, it's open for 30-minute guided tours daily noon to 5pm; admission is the same as for Carr House, above. Point Ellice is also one of the better spots for after-noon tea (p. 216). The easiest way to reach the house is by harbor ferry from in front of the Fairmont Empress, for C$4 (US$3.20) one-way.

Heading North to a Provincial Park, a Native Village & Some Wineries

A short and stunning drive north from Victoria along the Island Highway takes you to three spots well worth a visit: Goldstream Provincial Park, the Quw'utsun' (Cowichan) Cultural Centre, and the Cowichan Valley wineries. The drive—along the ocean, up over the Malahat mountains, and then through the beautiful Cowichan Valley—is short enough to complete in one fairly leisurely day.

GOLDSTREAM PROVINCIAL PARK   This quiet little valley overflowed with prospectors during the 1860s gold-rush days. Trails take you past abandoned mine shafts and tunnels as well as 600-year-old stands of towering Douglas fir, lodgepole pine, red cedar, indigenous yew, and arbutus trees. The **Gold Mine Trail** leads to Niagara Creek and the abandoned mine that was operated by Lt. Peter Leech, a Royal Engineer who discovered gold in the creek in 1858. **The Goldstream Trail** leads to the salmon spawning areas. (You might also catch sight of mink and river otters racing along this path.)

For general information on Goldstream Provincial Park and all other provincial parks on the South Island, contact **B.C. Parks** at ℂ 250/391-2300 or check www.bcparks.ca. Throughout the year, Goldstream Park's **Freeman King Visitor Centre** (ℂ 250/478-9414) offers guided walks, talks, displays, and programs geared toward kids but interesting for adults, too. Open daily 9am to 4pm. Take Highway 1 about 30 minutes north of Victoria. Note that B.C. government cutbacks have significantly reduced the number of events and services in most provincial parks. There is now a C$3 (US$2.40) day-use parking fee at Goldstream.

Three species of salmon (chum, chinook, and steelhead) make **annual salmon runs** up the Goldstream River during October, November, December, and February. You can easily observe this natural wonder along the riverbanks. Contact the park's **Visitor Centre** for details.

QUW'UTSUN' CULTURAL AND CONFERENCE CENTRE   The main reason for visiting the town of Duncan is to see the Quw'utsun' Cultural and Conference Centre, 200 Cowichan Way (ℂ **877/746-8119** or 250/746-8119; www.quwutsun.ca). Created by the Cowichan Indian Band, the center brings Native culture to visitors in a way that's commercially successful yet still respectful of Native traditions.

The longhouses built along the Cowichan River contain an impressive collection of cultural artifacts and presentations of life among the aboriginal tribes who have lived in the area for thousands of years. On Thursday, Friday, and Saturday, from July through September, there's a tour, ceremonial

NEIGHBORHOODS OF NOTE

From the time the Hudson's Bay Company settled here in the mid-1800s, the historic **Old Town** was the center of the city's bustling business in shipping, fur trading, and legal opium manufacturing. Market Square and the surrounding warehouses once brimmed dances, and salmon barbecue. Master and apprentice carvers create poles, masks, and feasting bowls in workshops open to the public. Two large gift shops in the complex sell some of those works as well as Native-made jewelry, clothing, silk-screened prints, and other items. The center and gift shops are open May through September daily 9am to 6pm; October through April daily 10am to 5pm. Admission is C$13 (US$10) for adults, C$10 (US$8) for seniors and youth 12 to 18, C$2 (US$1.60) for children 6 to 11, and C$30 (US$24) for families.

The **Duncan-Cowichan Visitor Info Centre** is at 381A Trans-Canada Hwy. (in the Overwaitea Mall), Duncan, B.C. V9L 3R5 (© **250/746-4636**). During July and August, it's open daily from 9am to 6pm; September through June, hours are Monday through Saturday 9am to 3pm.

THE COWICHAN VALLEY WINERIES   The Cowichan Valley is a gorgeous agricultural area a couple hours' drive from Victoria. Area wineries and the seaside town of Cowichan Bay are worth a stop.

The vintners of the Cowichan Valley have gained a solid reputation for producing fine wines. Several of the wineries have opened their doors and offer 1-hour tours that are a great introduction for novices. They usually include a tasting of the vintner's art as well as a chance to purchase bottles or cases of your favorites.

Cherry Point Vineyards, 840 Cherry Point Rd., Cowichan (© **250/743-1272;** www.cherrypointvineyards.com), looks like a slice of California's Napa Valley. The wine-tasting room and gift shop is open daily 10am to 5pm. **Blue Grouse Vineyards,** 4365 Blue Grouse Rd., Mill Bay (© **250/743-3834;** www.bluegrousevineyards.com), is a smaller winery that began as a hobby. April through September, it's open for tastings and on-site purchases Wednesday through Sunday 11am to 5pm (Wed–Sat the rest of the year). **Merridale Cidery,** located just south of Cowichan Bay at 1230 Merridale Rd. (© **800/998-9908** in B.C. only or 250/743-4293; www.merridalecider.com), is worth a stop to taste their ciders. Open daily 10:30am to 5:30pm (phone ahead to confirm open hours).

Cowichan Bay (off Hwy. 1, south of Duncan) is a pleasant half-hour drive from the wine country. Just southeast of Duncan, Cowichan Bay is a pretty little seaside town with a view of the ocean and a few attractions. The **Cowichan Bay Maritime Centre,** 1761 Cowichan Bay Rd., Cowichan Bay (© **250/746-4955**), is a unique museum where the boat-building and local history displays sit atop an old, picturesque pier that stretches out into the bay.

with exports like tinned salmon, furs, and timber bound for England and the United States. Now part of the downtown core, this is still a terrific place to find British, Scottish, and Irish imports (a surprising number of these shops date back to the early 1900s), souvenirs of all sorts, and even outdoor equipment for modern-day adventurers.

Just a block north on Fisgard Street is **Chinatown.** Founded in 1858, it's the old-est Chinatown in Canada. One of the more interesting structures is a three-story school built by the Chinese Benevolent Society in the early 1900s, when non-Cana-dian Chinese children were banned from public schools. Lined with Chinese restau-rants, bakeries, and specialty shops, Chinatown is a wonderful spot to stop for dim sum or for a full Hong Kong–style seafood dinner.

The **James Bay** area on the southern shores of the Inner Harbour is a quiet mid-dle-class residential community. As you walk through its tree-lined streets, you'll find many older private homes that have maintained their original Victorian flavor.

Beautiful residential communities such as **Ross Bay** and **Oak Bay** have a more modern West Coast appearance with houses perched on hills overlooking the beaches amid lush, landscaped gardens. Private marinas in these areas are filled with perfectly maintained sailing craft.

PARKS & GARDENS

In addition to the world-renowned **Butchart Gardens** ✿✿✿ (p. 224), several city parks attract strollers and picnickers whenever the weather is pleasant. The 61-hectare (151-acre) **Beacon Hill Park** ✿ stretches from Southgate Street to Dallas Road between Douglas and Cook streets. In 1882, the Hudson's Bay Company gave this property to the city. Stands of indigenous Garry oaks (found only on Vancouver, Hornby, and Salt Spring islands) and manicured lawns are interspersed with floral gar-dens and ponds. Hike up Beacon Hill to get a clear view of the Strait of Georgia, Haro Strait, and Washington's Olympic Mountains. The children's farm (see "Especially for Kids," below), aviary, tennis courts, lawn-bowling green, putting green, cricket pitch, wading pool, playground, and picnic area make this a wonderful place to spend a few hours with the family. The Trans-Canada Highway's "Mile 0" marker stands at the edge of the park on Dallas Road.

Abkhazi Garden ✿, 1964 Fairfield Rd. (✆ **250/598-8096;** www.conservancy. bc.ca), is one of the world's best and most unique small gardens. This one-acre jewel created by Prince and Princess Nicholas Abkhazi in the middle of the last century and now administered by The Land Conservancy takes full advantage of a dramatic site that contains quiet woodland, rocky slopes, and gorgeous vistas. The rhododendron woodland includes treelike plants over 100 years old. A charming tearoom and gift shop are located in the Abkhazi house. The gardens are open 1 to 5pm Wednesday through Sunday from April through September. Admission is C$7.50 (US$6) adults, C$5 (US$4) seniors and students, and C$15 (US$12) for a family.

Just outside downtown, **Mount Douglas Park** offers great views of the area, several hiking trails, and—down at the waterline—a picnic/play area with a trail leading to a good walking beach.

About 45 minutes southwest of town, **East Sooke Park** ✿ is a 1,400-hectare (3,459-acre) microcosm of the West Coast wilderness: jagged seacoast, Native petroglyphs,

---

(**Finds** **Strolling the Governor's Gardens**

Government House, the official residence of the lieutenant governor, is at 1401 Rockland Ave., in the Fairfield residential district. Around back, the hillside of Garry oaks is one of the last places to see what the area's natural fauna looked like before European settlers arrived. At the front, the rose garden is sumptuous.

and hiking trails up to a 270m (886-ft.) hilltop. Access is via the Old Island Highway and East Sooke Road.

2 Especially for Kids

Nature's the thing for kids in Victoria. The city offers unique opportunities for kids to view creatures from whales to goats to giant butterflies and flying insects to sea anemones and hermit crabs. The oldest of petting zoos is the **Beacon Hill Children's Farm,** Circle Drive, Beacon Hill Park (© 250/381-2532), where kids can ride ponies; pet goats, rabbits, and other barnyard animals; and cool off in the wading pool. From May to Labour Day, the farm is open daily 10am to 5pm (11am–4pm in the fall, 10am–4pm in the spring). Admission is by donation; most visitors give C$1 (US80¢) toward the park's upkeep.

To see and touch (or be touched by) even smaller creatures, visit the **Victoria Butterfly Gardens** (p. 227). Closer to town is the **Victoria Bug Zoo,** 631 Courtney St. (© 250/384-BUGS; www.bugzoo.bc.ca), home to praying mantises, stick insects, and giant African cockroaches. Knowledgeable guides bring the bugs out and let you or your kids touch them. Admission is C$7 (US$5.60) for adults, C$6 (US$4.80) students, C$5 (US$4) for seniors, and C$4.50 (US$3.60) for children 3 to 16, free for children under 3; open 9:30am to 5:30pm Monday through Saturday and 11am to 5:30pm on Sundays.

The **Pacific Undersea Gardens** (p. 225) is a face-to-face introduction to the sea creatures of the Pacific coast. In the underwater observatory, kids can meet a wolf eel eye-to-eye, view a giant octopus up close, and watch harbor seals cavort underwater with their pups. Better still, take the kids out to explore any of the tide pools on the coast. **Botanical Beach Provincial Park** ♔, near Port Renfrew, is excellent, though the 60km (37-mile) drive west along Highway 14 may make it a bit far for some. Closer to town, try **French Beach** ♔ or **China Beach** ♔ (also along Hwy. 14), or even the beach in **Mount Douglas Park.** The trick is to find a good spot, bend down over a tide pool, and look—or else pick up a rock to see crabs scuttle away. Remember to put the rocks back where you found them.

In **Goldstream Provincial Park** (p. 230), the Visitor Centre (© 250/478-9414) has nature programs and activities geared especially for children. The **Swan Lake Christmas Hill Nature Sanctuary,** 3873 Swan Lake Rd. (© 250/479-0211; www.swanlake.bc.ca), offers a number of nature-themed drop-in programs over the summer, including Insectmania and Reptile Day.

Back in the city, the **Royal British Columbia Museum** (p. 226) has many displays geared toward kids, including one simulating a dive to the bottom of the Pacific. Others illustrate the intriguing life and culture of the West Coast Native tribes, who've inhabited the province for more than 10,000 years, and show the majestic beauty of the province's temperate rainforests and coastlines.

Miniature World (p. 225), with its huge collection of dolls and dollhouses, model trains, and diminutive circus displays, is a favorite with kids of all ages.

Located in Elk and Beaver Lake Regional Park (p. 236), **Beaver Lake** is a great freshwater spot where kids can enjoy a day of water sports and swimming in safe, lifeguard-attended waters.

On truly hot days, head for the waterslides at the **All Fun Recreation Park,** 2207 Millstream Rd. (© 250/474-3184; www.allfun.bc.ca). From mid-June to Labour Day it's open daily 11am to 7pm. The cost is C$20 (US$16) for sliders 11 years and older and C$15 (US$12) for those 4 to 10 years old; it's free for children under 4. Cost for observers (which includes use of the hot tub, mini-golf, and beach volleyball courts) is C$6 (US$4.80). The park also has go-carts and batting cages.

3 Organized Tours

BUS TOURS

Gray Line of Victoria, 700 Douglas St. (© **800/440-3885** or 250/388-5248; www.grayline.ca), conducts a number of tours of Victoria and Butchart Gardens. The 1½-hour "Grand City Tour" costs C$19 (US$15) for adults and C$9.50 (US$7.60) for children ages 5 to 11. There are daily departures at noon and 2pm. For other tours check the website.

SPECIALTY TOURS

Victoria Harbour Ferries, 922 Old Esquimalt Rd. (© **250/708-0201**), offers a terrific 45-minute **Inner and Outer harbor tour** ⚓ for C$14 (US$11) for adults and C$7 (US$5.60) for children under 12. Harbor tours depart from seven stops around the Inner Harbour every 15 minutes daily 10am to 10pm. If you wish to stop for food or a stroll, you can get a token good for reboarding at any time during the same day. A 50-minute **Gorge Tour** ⚓ takes you to the gorge opposite the Johnson Street Bridge, where tidal falls reverse with each change of the tide. The Gorge Tour costs C$16 (US$13) for adults, C$14 (US$11) for seniors, and C$8 (US$6.40) for children. June through September, gorge tours depart from the dock in front of the Fairmont Empress every half-hour 9am to 8:15pm; at other times the tours operate less frequently, depending on the weather. The ferries are 12-person, fully enclosed boats, and every seat is a window seat.

Heritage Tours and Daimler Limousine Service, 713 Bexhill Rd. (© **250/474-4332**), guides you through the city, Butchart Gardens, and Craigdarroch Castle in a six-passenger British Daimler limousine. Rates start at C$65 (US$52) for the Daimler per hour per vehicle (not per person). Also available are stretch limos that seat 8 to 10 people, starting at C$70 (US$56) per hour per vehicle.

The bicycle-rickshaws operated by **Kabuki Kabs,** 613 Herald St. (© **250/385-4243;** www.kabukikabs.com), can usually be found on the causeway in front of The Fairmont Empress or hailed in the downtown area. Prices for a tour are C$1 (US80¢) per minute for a two-person cab and C$1.50 (US$1.20) per minute for a four-person cab.

Tallyho Horse-Drawn Tours, 2044 Milton St. (© **250/383-5067;** www.tallyhotours.com), has conducted tours of Victoria in horse-drawn carriages and trolleys since 1903. Horse-drawn trolley and carriage excursions start at the corner of Belleville and Menzies Streets. Fares for the trolley are C$15 (US$12) for adults, C$9 (US$7.20) for students, C$7 (US$5.60) for children 17 and under. Trolley tours operate daily every 30 minutes 9am to 3pm during summer. Private tours in carriages (maximum six people), available in the summer from 10am to 10pm, cost C$80 (US$64) for 30 minutes, or C$160 (US$128) for an hour.

To get a bird's-eye view of Victoria, take a 30-minute tour with **Harbour Air Seaplanes,** 1234 Wharf St. (© **800/665-0212** or 250/384-2215; www.harbour-air.com). Rates are C$99 (US$79) per person or C$79 (US$63) if there are four or more in your party; C$54 (US$43) for children under 12. Flights depart whenever there are three or more people ready. For a romantic evening, try the *Fly and Dine* to Butchart Gardens deal; C$205 (US$164) per person includes the flight to the gardens, admission,

Finds **Victoria's Cemetery Tours**

The **Old Cemetery Society of Victoria** (℗ 250/598-8870; www.oldcem.bc.ca) runs regular cemetery tours throughout the year. Particularly popular are the slightly eerie **Lantern Tours of the Old Burying Ground** ☝, which begin at the Cherry Bank Hotel, 845 Burdett St., at 9pm nightly in July and August. The tour lasts about 1 hour. On Sundays throughout the year, the Society offers historically focused tours of **Ross Bay Cemetery.** Tours depart at 2pm from Bagga Pasta, in the Fairfield Plaza, 1516 Fairfield Rd., across from the cemetery gate. Both tours are C$5 (US$4) per person.

dinner, and a limousine ride back to Victoria. The price drops to C$165 (US$132) per person if there are four or more people.

WALKING TOURS

See chapter 15 for two self-guided walking tours around Victoria. If you'd prefer to have a guide, **Victoria Bobby Walking Tours** (℗ 250/995-0233; www.walkvictoria. com) offers a leisurely story-filled walk around Old Town with a former English bobby as guide. Tours depart at 11am daily, May through September 15, from the Visitor Centre on the Inner Harbour; cost is C$15 (US$12) per person.

Discover the Past (℗ 250/384-6698; www.discoverthepast.com) organizes interesting year-round walks; in the summer, **Ghostly Walks** explores Victoria's haunted Old Town, Chinatown, and historic waterfront; tours depart from the front of the Visitor Info Centre on Friday and Saturday at 7:30pm, and nightly at 7:30 and 9:30pm from June through September. The cost is C$12 (US$9.60) adults, C$10 (US$8) seniors/students, C$8 (US$6.40) children 6 to 10, and C$30 (US$24) for families. Check the website for other walks.

The name says it all for **Walkabout Historical Tours** (℗ 250/592-9255; www. walkabouts.ca). Charming guides lead tours of the Fairmont Empress, Victoria's Chinatown, Antique Row, Old Town Victoria, or will even help you with your own private itinerary if you're interested. The Empress Tour costs C$9 (US$7.20) and begins at 10am daily in the Empress Tea Lobby. Other tours have different prices and starting points.

The **Victoria Heritage Foundation,** No. 1 Centennial Square (℗ 250/383-4546; vhf@pinc.com), offers the excellent free pamphlet *James Bay Heritage Walking Tour.* The well-researched pamphlet (available at the Visitor Info Centre or from the Victoria Heritage office) describes a self-guided walking tour through the historic James Bay neighborhood.

4 Outdoor Activities

Mountain biking, ecotouring, in-line skating, alpine and Nordic skiing, parasailing, sea kayaking, canoeing, tidal-water fishing, fly-fishing, diving, and hiking are popular in and around Victoria.

BEACHES

The most popular beach is Oak Bay's **Willows Beach,** at Beach and Dalhousie roads along the esplanade. The park, playground, and snack bar make it a great place to spend the day building a sand castle. **Gyro Beach Park,** Beach Road on Cadboro Bay, is another good spot for winding down. At the **Ross Bay Beaches,** below Beacon Hill Park, you can stroll or bike along the promenade at the water's edge.

For a taste of the wild and rocky west coast, hike the oceanside trails in beautiful **East Sooke Regional Park** ☘. Take Hwy. 14 west, turn south on Gillespie Road, and then take East Sooke Road.

Two inland lakes give you the option of swimming in fresh water. **Elk and Beaver Lake Regional Park,** on Patricia Bay Road, is 11km (6¾ miles) north of downtown Victoria; **Thetis Lake,** about 10km (6¼ miles) west, is where locals shed all their clothes but none of their civility.

BIKING

Biking is one of the best ways to get around Victoria. You can rent a bike for a few hours or a few days in the downtown area (p. 190). The 13km (8-mile) **Scenic Marine Drive bike path** ☘ begins at Dallas Road and Douglas Street, at the base of Beacon Hill Park. The paved path follows the walkway along the beaches before winding up through the residential district on Beach Drive. It eventually turns left and heads south toward downtown Victoria on Oak Bay Avenue. The **Inner Harbour pedestrian path** has a bike lane for cyclists who want to take a leisurely ride around the entire city seawall. The new **Galloping Goose Trail** (part of the Trans-Canada Trail) runs from Victoria west through Colwood and Sooke all the way up to Leechtown. If you don't want to bike the whole thing, there are numerous places to park along the way, as well as several places where the trail intersects with public transit. Call **B.C. Transit** at ✆ 250/382-6161 (www.bctransit.com) to find out which bus routes take bikes. Bikes and child trailers are available by the hour or day at **Cycle B.C. rentals,** 747 Douglas St. (year-round) or 950 Wharf St. (May–Oct; ✆ 250/885-2453; www.cyclebc.ca). Rentals run C$6 (US$4.80) per hour and C$20 (US$16) per day, helmets and locks included.

Also see "Biking Tour: Dallas Road," in chapter 15 for a self-guided trip.

BIRDING

For those wanting to hook up with the local birding subculture, the **Victoria Natural History Society** (www.vicnhs.bc.ca) runs regular weekend birding excursions. Their **event line** at ✆ 250/479-2054 lists upcoming outings and gives contact numbers. **Goldstream Provincial Park** (p. 230) and the village of **Malahat**—both off Highway 1 about 40 minutes north of Victoria—are filled with dozens of varieties of migratory and local birds, including eagles. **Elk and Beaver Lake Regional Park,** off Highway 17, has some rare species such as the rose-breasted grosbeak and Hutton's vireo. Ospreys also nest there. **Cowichan Bay,** off Highway 1, is the perfect place to observe ospreys, bald eagles, great egrets, and purple martins.

⌐Tips **Suiting Up for the Outdoors**

In the sections below, specialized rental outfitters are listed for each activity. **Sports Rent,** 611 Discovery St. (✆ 250/385-7368), is a great general equipment and watersports rental outlet. Its entire inventory, including rental rates, is online at **www.sportsrentbc.com**.

BOATING

Kayaks, canoes, rowboats, and powerboats are available from **Great Pacific Adventures,** 811 Wharf St. (℗ **877/733-6722** or 250/386-2277; www.greatpacificadventures.com).

CANOEING & KAYAKING

Ocean River Sports, 1437 Store St. (℗ **800/909-4233** or 250/381-4233; www.ocean river.com), can equip you with everything from single kayak, double kayak, and canoe rentals to life jackets, tents, and dry-storage camping gear. Rental costs for a single kayak range from C$14 (US$11) per hour to C$42 (US$34) per day. Multiday and weekly rates are also available. In addition, the company offers numerous **guided tours** ☞ of the Gulf Islands and the B.C. west coast. For beginners, there's the guided 3-hour Explore Tour of the coast around Victoria or Sooke, which costs C$59 (US$47). There's also a guided 3-day/2-night Expedition trip to explore the nearby Gulf Islands for C$479 (US$383).

    Blackfish Wilderness Expeditions (℗ **250/216-2389;** www.blackfishwilderness. com) helps you kayak the wild side on a number of interesting kayak-based tours such as the kayak/boat/hike combo where you get a head start by boat to the protected waters of the Discovery Islands. After you explore the coves and inlets and eat a picnic lunch, a naturalist takes you on a hike around one of the islands. Whale-watchers can combine a few hours of kayaking with a trip on a motorized boat to get a better look at the pods of resident killer whales that roam the waters around Victoria. Day tours start at C$69 (US$55) per person.

DIVING

The coastline of **Pacific Rim National Park** is known as "the graveyard of the Pacific." Submerged in the water are dozens of 19th- and 20th-century shipwrecks and the marine life that has taken up residence in them. Underwater interpretive trails help you identify what you see in the artificial reefs. If you want to take a look for yourself, contact **Ocean Sports,** 800 Cloverdale St. (℗ **800/414-2202** or 250/475-2202; www.oceansports.ca), or **The Ogden Point Dive Centre,** 199 Dallas Rd. (℗ **250/380-9119;** www.divevictoria.com). Through Ocean Sports, head-to-toe equipment rental costs about C$50 (US$40) for 2 days, and dive trips start at C$50 (US$40) for two dives plus lunch. The **Saanich Inlet,** about a 20-minute drive north of Victoria, is a pristine fjord considered one of the top diving areas in the world. Classes and underwater scuba adventures can be arranged through **Brentwood Bay Lodge & Spa** (p. 207), Canada's only luxury PADI dive resort.

FISHING

Saltwater fishing's the thing out here, and unless you know the area, it's probably best to take a guide. **Adam's Fishing Charters** (℗ **250/370-2326;** www.adamsfishing charters.com) and the **Marine Adventure Centre,** 950 Wharf St. (℗ **250/995-2211;** www.marine-adventures.com), are good places to start. Both are on the Inner Harbour down below the Visitor Info Centre. (See also "Boating," above.) Chartering a boat and guide starts around C$90 (US$72) per hour per boat, with a minimum of 3 or 4 hours.

    To fish, you need a nonresident saltwater fishing license. Licenses for saltwater fishing (including the salmon surcharge) cost C$14 (US$11) for 1 day for nonresidents and C$12 (US$10) for B.C. residents. Tackle shops sell licenses, have details on current restrictions, and often carry copies of the *B.C. Tidal Waters Sport Fishing Guide* and *B.C. Sport Fishing Regulations Synopsis for Non-Tidal Waters.* Independent anglers should also pick up a copy of the *B.C. Fishing Directory and Atlas.* **Robinson's Sporting Goods Ltd.,** 1307 Broad St. (𝄐 **250/385-3429**), is a reliable source for information, recommendations, lures, licenses, and gear. For the latest fishing hot spots and recommendations on tackle and lures, check out **www.sportfishingbc.com**.

GOLFING

Fortunately for golfers, Victoria's Scottish heritage didn't stop at the tartan shops. The greens here are as beautiful as those at St. Andrew's, yet the fees are reasonable. The **Cedar Hill Municipal Golf Course,** 1400 Derby Rd. (𝄐 **250/595-3103**), is an 18-hole public course 3km (1¾ miles) from downtown Victoria; daytime greens fees are C$38 (US$30) and twilight fees (after 3pm) are C$23 (US$18). Golf clubs can be rented for C$15 (US$12). The **Cordova Bay Golf Course,** 5333 Cordova Bay Rd. (𝄐 **250/658-4075;** www.cordovabaygolf.com), is northeast of the downtown area. Designed by Bill Robinson, the 18-hole course features 66 sand traps and some tight fairways. Greens fees are C$60 (US$48) Monday through Thursday and C$65 (US$52) on Friday, Saturday, Sunday, and holidays; the twilight fee is C$55 (US$44). The **Olympic View Golf Club,** 643 Latoria Rd. (𝄐 **250/474-3673;** www.olympicview. bc.ca), is one of the top 35 golf courses in Canada. Amid 12 lakes and a pair of waterfalls, this 18-hole, 6,414-yard course is open daily year-round. Daytime greens fees, depending on day and season, are C$65 to C$75 (US$52–US$60) and twilight fees are C$30 to C$40 (US$24–US$32). Power carts cost an additional C$30 (US$24). You can call **Last Minute Golf Hot Line** at 𝄐 **800/684-6344** for substantial discounts and short-notice tee times. **Island Links Hot Line** at 𝄐 **866/266-GOLF** acts as a booking agent for courses around Vancouver Island and will provide transportation from your hotel to the course.

HIKING

Goldstream Provincial Park (30 min. west of downtown along Hwy. 1; p. 230) is a tranquil site for a short hike through towering cedars and past clear, rushing waters. The hour-long hike up **Mount Work** provides excellent views of the Saanich Peninsula and a good view of Finlayson Arm. The trailhead is a 30- to 45-minute drive. Take Highway 17 north to Saanich, then take Highway 17A (the West Saanich Rd.) to Wallace Drive, turn right on Willis Point Drive, and right again on the Ross-Durrance Road, looking for the parking lot on the right. There are signs along the way. Equally good, though more of a scramble, is the hour-plus climb up **Mount Finlayson** in Gowland-Tod Provincial Park (take Hwy. 1 west, get off at the Millstream Rd. exit, and follow Millstream Rd. north to the very end). The very popular **Sooke Potholes** trail wanders up beside a river to an abandoned mountain lodge. Take Highway 1A west to Colwood, then Highway 14 (the Sooke Rd.). When you reach Sooke, turn north on the Sooke River Road, and follow it to the park.

For a taste of the wild and rocky west coast, hike the oceanside trails in beautiful **East Sooke Regional Park** 𝄐𝄐. Take Hwy. 14 west, turn south on Gillespie Road, and then take East Sooke Road.

For serious backpacking, go 104km (65 miles) west of Victoria on Highway 14 to Port Renfrew and **Pacific Rim National Park** 𝄐𝄐𝄐 (p. 285). The challenging **West Coast Trail,** extending 77km (48 miles) from Port Renfrew to Bamfield, was originally established as a lifesaving trail for shipwrecked sailors. Plan a 7-day trek if you want to cover the entire route; reservations are required, so call 𝄐 **604/663-6000.**

The trail is rugged and often wet, but the scenery changes from old-growth forest to magnificent secluded sand beaches, making it worth every step. You may even spot a few whales along the way. **Robinson's Sporting Goods Ltd.,** 1307 Broad St. (© **250/385-3429**), is a good place to gear up before you go. Ask at Robinson's about the newer, less challenging **Juan de Fuca Marine Trail,** connecting Port Renfrew and the Jordan River, about 48km (30 miles) long.

Island Adventure Tours (© **866/812-7103;** www.islandadventuretours.com) offers a number of options for folks wanting to get out into the outdoors. There are half-day guided **rainforest walks** for C$39 (US$31) or C$95 (US$76) for a full-day hike including transportation and lunch. For the deluxe Juan de Fuca experience, sign up for a 3-day fully catered backpacking trip along this rugged West Coast trail for C$499 (US$399).

For groups of 10 or more who want to learn more about the surrounding flora and fauna, book a naturalist-guided tour of the island's rainforests and seashore with **Coastal Connections Interpretive Nature Hikes,** 1027 Roslyn Rd. (© **250/480-9560**). A 6-hour rainforest hike, including a gourmet picnic lunch, provides a wonderful introduction to this unique ecosystem. The hike costs C$79 (US$63) per person. For something less strenuous but still scenic, try the **Swan Lake Christmas Hill Nature Sanctuary,** 3873 Swan Lake Rd. (© **250/479-0211;** www.swanlake.bc.ca). A floating boardwalk winds its way through this 40-hectare (99-acre) wetland past resident swans; the adjacent Nature House supplies feeding grain on request.

PARAGLIDING

Vancouver Island Paragliding (© **250/886-4165;** www.viparagliding.com) offers tandem paraglide flights. The pilot steers; you hang on and enjoy the adrenaline rush. Flights last around 25 minutes. They also offer 1-day training courses that allow you to take off on your own.

SAILING

One of the most peaceful ways to explore the Strait of Juan de Fuca is aboard the *Thane,* a 16.5m (54-ft.) wooden ketch that offers **3-hour sail tours of the Strait** ⏣ for C$60 (US$48) per person. The vessel is moored in front of the Empress Hotel. Daily summer sailings leave at 9am, 1, and 5pm. Guests are welcome to bring along a picnic. To contact them, call **SV** *Thane* at © **877/788-4263** or 250/885-2311, or surf over to www.eco-correct.com.

SKIING

Mount Washington Ski Resort, P.O. Box 3069, Courtenay, B.C. V9N 5N3 (© **888/231-1499** or 250/338-1380; 250/338-1515 snow report; www.mtwashington.bc.ca), in the Comox Valley, is British Columbia's third-largest ski area, a 5-hour drive from Victoria and open year-round (for hiking or skiing, depending on the season). A 480m (1,575-ft.) vertical drop and 50 groomed runs are serviced by four chairlifts and a beginners' tow. The terrain is very popular among snowboarders and well suited to intermediate skiers. For cross-country skiers, 31km (19 miles) of track-set Nordic trails connect to Strathcona Provincial Park. Full-day rates are C$49 (US$39) for adults, C$40 (US$32) for seniors and students, and C$26 (US$21) for kids 7 to 12; free for kids under 7. Equipment rentals are available at the resort. Take Highway 19 to Courtenay and then the Strathcona Parkway. It's 37km (23 miles) to Mount Washington.

WATERSPORTS

The **Crystal Pool & Fitness Centre,** 2275 Quadra St. (© **250/361-0732**), is Victoria's main aquatic facility. The 50m (164-ft.) lap pool; children's pool; diving pool; sauna; whirlpool; and steam, weight, and aerobics rooms are open Monday through Friday 5:30am to 10:30pm, Saturday 6am to 4pm, and Sunday 9am to 4pm. Drop-in admission is C$4.50 (US$3.60) for adults, C$3.50 (US$2.80) for seniors and students, and C$2.50 (US$2) for children 6 to 12; free for children under 6. **Beaver Lake** in Elk and Beaver Lake Regional Park (see "Birding," above) has lifeguards on duty as well as picnicking facilities along the shore.

Surfing has recently taken off on the island. The best surf is along the west coast at **China, French,** and **Mystic beaches** . To get there, take Blanshard Street north from downtown, turn left onto Highway 1 (Trans-Canada Hwy.), then after about 10km (6¼ miles), take the turnoff onto Highway 14 (Sooke Rd.). Follow Highway 14 north along the coast. The beaches are well signposted. You can rent boards and wet suits—along with almost any kind of watersports gear—at **Ocean Sports,** 800 Cloverdale St. (© **800/414-2202;** www.oceansports.ca).

Windsurfers skim along outside the Inner Harbour and on Elk Lake when the breezes are right. Though there are no specific facilities, French Beach, off Sooke Road on the way to Sooke Harbour, is a popular local windsurfing spot.

WHALE-WATCHING

The waters surrounding the southern tip of Vancouver Island teem with orcas (killer whales), as well as harbor seals, sea lions, bald eagles, and harbor and Dall porpoises. All whale-watching companies basically offer the same tour; the main difference comes in the equipment they use: Some use a 12-person Zodiac, where the jolting ride is almost as exciting as seeing the whales, whereas others take a larger, more leisurely craft. Both offer excellent platforms for seeing whales. In high season (June to Labour Day), most companies offer several trips a day.

Seafun Safaris Whale Watching, 950 Wharf St. (© **877/360-1233** or 250/360-1200; www.seafun.com), is just one of many outfits offering whale-watching tours in Zodiacs and covered boats. Adults and kids will learn a lot from the naturalist guides, who explain the behavior and nature of the orcas, gray whales, sea lions, porpoises, cormorants, eagles, and harbor seals encountered along the way. Fares are C$99 (US$79) for adults and C$69 (US$55) for children.

Oak Bay Beach Hotel and Marine Resort, Oak Bay Beach Hotel, 1175 Beach Dr. (© **800/668-7758** or 250/598-4556; www.oakbaybeachhotel.com), offers 3½-hour whale-watching charters daily on either a 13.5m (44-ft.) catamaran or an 8.4m (28-ft.) converted pleasure cruiser. Both have restroom facilities and bar service.

Other reputable companies are **Prince of Whales,** 812 Wharf St. (© **888/383-4884** or 250/383-4884; www.princeofwhales.com), just below the Visitor Info Centre, and **Orca Spirit Adventures** (© **888/672-ORCA** or 250/383-8411; www.orcaspirit.com), which departs from the Coast Harbourside Hotel dock.

Victoria Strolls & Biking Tour

Victoria has always been a transient's town, from miners and mariners to loggers and lounge-lizards, from hard-core hippies to retired but involved investment counselors. On three occasions I've packed up and moved from Victoria myself.

—Folk Singer Valdy

Victoria's ambience is made for the wanderer, its pavements picture-perfect for perambulation—Victoria, in short, is a great place to walk. Or bike. In-line skating is good, too. Scooters and skateboards are also gaining ground. The tours below work whatever your favored form of transportation.

WALKING TOUR 1   THE INNER HARBOUR

Start and Finish: The Tourist Info Centre (812 Wharf St.) on the Inner Harbour.

Time: 2 hours, not including shopping, museum, and pub breaks.

Best Time: Late afternoon, when the golden summer sunlight shines on The Fairmont Empress.

Worst Time: Late in the evening, when the shops close and the streets empty.

Victoria was born on the Inner Harbour. When the Hudson's Bay Company's West Coast head of operations, James Douglas, happened across this sheltered inlet in 1843 while searching for a new corporate HQ, it was love at first sight. "The place appears a perfect Eden," he wrote to a friend. High praise indeed, although as Douglas was pretty deep into local real estate, his words should be taken with a wee bit of salt. His confidence in the location certainly paid off, however, for less than 20 years after Douglas set foot onshore, the native stands of Garry oak had been supplanted by small farms, the town was choked with miners and mariners, and the harbor was full of ships, many of which had circumnavigated the globe. This trip doesn't go nearly as far, but it does circumnavigate the Inner Harbour, showing some of its lesser-known nooks and crannies, while providing an opportunity to enjoy the view as a Victorian sailor would have, quaffing a locally brewed pint from the deck of a stout Victoria pub.

We begin our tour at the:

❶ Victoria Tourist Info Centre

At 812 Wharf St., this is without a doubt one of the finest-looking tourist centers in the world—a masterful Art Deco pavilion topped with a shining white obelisk rising high above the Inner Harbour. It would be a tribute to the taste and vision of city tourism officials, except that it started out life as a gas station.

From the Info Centre, thread your way south through the jugglers and musicians on the causeway until you're opposite 721 Government St., where stands:

❷ The Fairmont Empress

"There is a view, when the morning mists peel off the harbor, where the steamers tie up, of the Houses of Parliament on one hand, and a huge hotel on the other, which is an example of cunningly fitted-in waterfronts and facades worth a very long journey." Thus spoke Rudyard Kipling during a visit to the city in 1908. If he'd come only 5 years earlier he would've been looking at a swamp, and a nasty garbage-choked one at that. The causeway was then a narrow bridge over the tidal inlet, and as Victorians made a habit of pitching their refuse over the rail, the bay was, not surprisingly, a stinking cesspit of slime. In 1900, the ever-shrewd Canadian Pacific Railway made an offer to the city—we'll build a causeway and fill in the stinky bay if you let us keep the land. The city jumped at the offer. Little was expected—the land was swamp after all. But taking their cue from the good folk in Amsterdam, the CPR drove long pilings down through the muck to provide a solid foundation. And on top of that, they built The Fairmont Empress. The architect was Francis Rattenbury, and his design was masterful, complementing his own Legislature Buildings to create the viewscape that has defined the city ever since.

Around the south side of The Fairmont Empress is a formal rose garden—well worth poking your nose in for a sniff. Cut through the garden and cross over Belleville Street and continue another half block east to the corner of Douglas Street, where you'll find:

❸ Thunderbird Park

The park is instantly recognizable by its forest of totem poles. Even if you've overdosed on the ubiquitous 6-inch souvenir totem, take a second look at these. The original poles on this site had been collected in the early 1900s from various villages up and down the coast. Some

decades later, when officials decided the severely weathered poles needed restoring, they discovered the art of Native carving had eroded even more than their collection of poles. From all the thousands of carvers on the coast, only one man still carried on the craft. In 1952, Kwakiutl artist Mungo Martin set up a carving shed on the park grounds and began the work of restoration. Martin replaced or repaired all the existing poles. At the same time, he taught his son and step-grandson-in-law to carve. Seeing them at work renewed public interest in the form. Other young artists came to learn and train. Eventually, this modest training ground led to a revival of totem carving and Native artistry among coastal Natives.

All poles have a purpose; most tell a story. The stories associated with the poles in Thunderbird Park have unfortunately been lost, but many of the figures are easily recognized, including Thunderbird (look for the outstretched wings and curly horns on the head), Raven, Bear, and Killer Whale.

On the edge of the park is the shed where Martin carved many of the poles. Feel free to poke your head in to take a look and ask the carvers what they're up to. The Native artists generally welcome questions and enjoy sharing their stories.

Further back in the park, at 610 Elliot St. Sq., stands the:

❹ Helmcken House

Dr. John Sebastian Helmcken, a surgeon with the Hudson's Bay Company, set up house here in 1852 when he married the daughter of Governor Sir James Douglas. Originally a three-room log house, the house was built by Helmcken and expanded as both the prosperity and size of the family grew. It's now the oldest house in B.C. on its original site. Helmcken went on to become a statesman and helped negotiate the entry of British

Walking Tour 1: The Inner Harbour

1 Victoria Tourist Info Centre
2 The Fairmont Empress
3 Thunderbird Park
4 Helmcken House
5 Parliament Buildings
6 Coast Hotel Docks
6a Fisherman's Wharf
7 West Bay
8 Songhees Point
9 Johnson Street Bridge
10 Bastion Square
11 Floatplane Docks

"Take a Break" stop

SAANICH
VICTORIA
WEST BAY
Area of Detail

0   1/4 mi
0   0.25 km

Columbia into Canada, as a province. From May through September, the house is open daily 10am to 5pm. Admission is C$5 (US$4) for adults, C$4 (US$3.20) for seniors and students, and C$3 (US$2.40) for children.

Walk west along Belleville past the modern-looking Carillon Tower (a gift from the Dutch people who settled in B.C.) and the not-to-be-missed Victoria Royal British Columbia Museum (p. 226) and cross Government Street. You're now standing in front of 501 Belleville St. at the:

❺ Parliament Buildings

In 1892, a 25-year-old Yorkshireman arrived on the West Coast just as an architectural competition for a new Legislature Building in Victoria was announced. Francis Mawson Rattenbury had no professional credentials but was blessed with both talent and vaulting ambition. He submitted a set of drawings and, to the surprise of all, beat out 65 other entries from around the continent. It made his career. For the next 30 years, nearly all official buildings in Victoria, and many around the province, would be Rattenbury creations.

The Parliament Buildings are open for tours 9am to 5pm. In summer, the 40-minute tours start every 20 minutes (p. 226).

Across the street, the Greek temple–style **Royal London Wax Museum** (p. 226) is another Rattenbury creation, built originally as the CPR's Steamship ticket office. From here, ocean liners once departed for San Francisco, Sydney, and Canton China.

From the Legislature lawn, make your way past the horse-drawn calèches parked on Menzies Street and walk west on Belleville Street for 2 blocks to Pendray Street. The road takes a sharp right, but follow the path leading down to a waterfront walkway as it curves around Laurel Point. This headland was long the site of a stinking, fuming paint factory, so residents were delighted when it finally shut down and the luxurious Laurel Point Inn was erected in its place. Around the back of the Laurel are a pleasant Japanese garden and a patio restaurant. Continuing around the pathway past the first few jetties takes you to the:

⑥ Coast Hotel Docks

Here is one of several ports of call for the **Victoria Harbour Ferry Company** (② 250/708-0201; p. 234). From here, the official Frommer's route is to take the ferry all the way across the harbor to West Bay (stop 7). Along the way, there'll be views of the Olympic Mountains to the south and possibly a seal or bald eagle for company. Alternatively, you can take a short hop out to **Fisherman's Wharf** (6A on the map on p. 227), where there are fresh-fish sales in season. Or you can go directly across to Spinnaker's Brewpub on the far shore. Or you can take the ferry across to Songhees Point (stop 8) or even directly to Canoe (see "Take a Break," after stop 9). You can even give up on your feet entirely and take the full Harbour Ferries tour.

If you stick with the program, however, the next stop is:

⑦ West Bay

A pleasant little residential neighborhood with a picturesque marina, West Bay isn't anything much to write home about. What is worthwhile is the waterfront walkway that wends its way from here back east toward the city. The trail twists and curves through several parks, and there are views south through the harbor out to the Strait of Juan de Fuca and the Olympic Mountains beyond. After about 20 minutes of walking, it may be time to:

TAKE A BREAK
Excellent beer brewed on the premises, combined with an above-average patio, make **Spinnaker's Brewpub**, 308 Catherine St. (② 250/386-BREW; p. 214), open daily 11am to 11pm, a dangerously time-consuming port of call. For those looking for more substantial fare, the pub grub's very good and the entrees are above average. The on-site bakery makes inspired beer bread, as well as a range of more delicate goods.

From the pub, continue along the shoreline until you see the totem pole standing at:

⑧ Songhees Point

The point is named after the Native band that once lived on the site. The Songhees had originally set up their village close to Fort Victoria, near the current site of Bastion Square, but relations with the Hudson's Bay Company were always strained. In 1844, a dispute over a pair of company oxen slaughtered by the Songhees was settled only after Commander Roderick Finlayson blew up the chief's house. A few years later, after a fire, started in the Native village, spread and nearly burned down the fort, Finlayson told the Songhees to relocate across the Inner Harbour. They refused at first, pointing out quite rightly that as it was their land, they could live wherever they liked. They assented to the move only after Finlayson agreed to help dismantle and transport the Songhees' longhouses.

The totem pole here is called the **Spirit of Lakwammen**, presented to the city to commemorate the 1994 Commonwealth Games.

Continue on the pathway around the corner. The patio of the Ocean Point Resort, on your right, provides a great view of The Fairmont Empress. In summer, they show silent movies after sunset. A little farther on is the:

❾ Johnson Street Bridge

Trivia question: Who designed San Francisco's Golden Gate Bridge? Answer: The same guy who designed Victoria's Johnson Street Bridge. Alas, while the soaring Golden Gate span is justly famous for its elegance, this misshapen lump of steel and concrete is something designer Joseph Strauss would likely wish forgotten. Fortunately for him, word of this effort seems not to have reached San Fran.

Cross the bridge and walk past the Esquimalt and Nanaimo (E&N) Railway station and turn left onto Store Street. Walk 1 block north to Swift Street, turn left, walk downhill to the end of the street, and:

TAKE A BREAK
Having a drink at **Canoe**, 450 Swift St. (℃ **250/361-1940**; p. 214), it's hard to know who to admire more: the 19th-century engineers who built everything with brick and beam and always twice as thick as it had to be; the restorers who took this old building (once the site of the City Light Company) and turned it into a sunlit cathedral of a room; the owner, who had the vision to pay the restorers; the chef, who made the delicious plate of appetizers now quickly disappearing from the huge wooden bench; or the brew master, whose copper cauldrons produce such a superior brew. Try the taster option—six small glasses of different brews for about the price of a pint—and toast them all. Canoe is open Saturday through Thursday 11am to midnight.

Salutations complete, wander back up Swift Street, turn right, and continue south down Store Street for 2 blocks, where Store Street becomes Wharf Street. Walk another 3 blocks until you reach:

❿ Bastion Square

This pleasant public space stands on the site of the Hudson's Bay Company's original Fort Victoria. The fort was demolished in 1863 and the land sold off for development. When the B.C. government bought and renovated the Rithet Building on the southwest corner of the square, workers uncovered Fort Victoria's original water well, complete with mechanical pump. It's now in the building's lobby.

Continue south on Wharf Street another 2 blocks until you come to the pinkish Dominion Customs House. Built in 1876, it was one of the first tangible signs of British Columbia's new status as a Canadian province. The Second Empire style was meant to impart a touch of European civilization in the midst of this raw wilderness town. Take the walkway by the Customs house down to the waterline and walk out on the:

⓫ Floatplane Docks

Early in the morning these docks buzz with activity as floatplanes fly in and out on their way to and from Seattle, Vancouver, and points north. The **Blackfish Cafe,** 950 Wharf St. (℃ **250/385-9996**), open 8am to 4pm, is a good spot to tuck into a big greasy-spoon breakfast and eavesdrop on some pilot gossip. The docks are also the place to come to arrange diving and whale-watching tours.

Back up on Wharf Street, you're just a hop, skip, and a jump from the Visitor Info tower, where the tour began.

WALKING TOUR 2   THE OLD TOWN & CHINATOWN

Start and Finish: The Fairmont Empress hotel, 321 Government St.

Time: 2 hours, not including shopping, sightseeing, and eating stops.

Best Time: Any day before 6pm.

Worst Time: Any day after 6pm, when the shops close.

This tour also begins at one of Victoria's most impressive landmarks. In front of you is:

❶ The Fairmont Empress

At 321 Government St., this architectural delight was designed by Francis Rattenbury (see "Architectural Highlights & Historic Homes," on p. 228).

Walking north up Government Street, you'll find a number of historic buildings. British Columbia's oldest brick structure, at 901 Government St., is the:

❷ Windsor Hotel building

Built in 1858 as the Victoria Hotel, the building's actually a perfect metaphor for the city. The original structure was a robust yet stylish piece of frontier architecture, with heavy red bricks formed into graceful Romanesque arches. Then, in the 1930s, when the city began pushing the "little bit of England" shtick, the original brick was covered over with stucco and fake Tudor half-timbering. Somewhere under the phony gentility, however, the robust frontier structure survives. (It's been through worse: In 1876, the hotel underwent major unexpected remodeling after the owner searched for a gas leak with a lit candle.)

On the next block, you'll find a brass sidewalk plaque at 1022 Government St., indicating the former site of:

❸ Fort Victoria

The fort was constructed in 1843 by the Hudson's Bay Company as the western headquarters of its fur-trading empire. Bound by Broughton and View streets, between Government and Wharf streets, the fort had two octagonal bastions on either side of its tall cedar picket walls. It was torn down during the 1860s gold boom to make room for more businesses. You can get an idea of its size and shape from the line of light-colored bricks—inscribed with the names of early settlers—in the sidewalk that delineates the boundaries of the original walls. The first school in British Columbia was built on this site in 1849. The spot now houses **The Spirit of Christmas** shop.

Continue north 2 more blocks, just past View Street, where a little byway cuts off on the right, running 1 block to Broad Street. It's known as:

❹ Trounce Alley

This is where miners and mariners spent their extra cash on the ladies. The alley is still lit by gas lamps, hung with heraldic crests, and ablaze with flower baskets and potted shrubs. You can stroll through shops selling jewelry, fashions, and crafts, or stop for a bite to eat. Trounce Alley ends abruptly at Broad Street.

Turn left on Broad Street, walk north 1 block, turn left on Yates Street, and walk west 1 block until you come to the:

❺ Starfish Glassworks

At 630 Yates St., this ex-bank building is one of the city's finest examples of the Moderne style, but what makes it especially worth a visit is the gallery and workshop inside (p. 256). Set up by a couple of glassblowing artists who couldn't get kiln time in Vancouver, the interior has been cleverly designed with the workshop on the ground floor and the gallery space on an open catwalk above. Step inside and watch the glassblowing, or wander around the gallery and admire the finished products. In summer (May 15–Sept 15), the building is open Monday through Saturday from 10am to 6pm and Sunday from noon to 6pm. From September 16 through May 14, the gallery is closed on Tuesday.

From here, go 1 more block west on Yates; between Government and Store streets on the north side of the block you'll find a collection of mid-19th-century brick storefronts, including at no. 564 Yates the former Majestic Theatre dating from 1860. From Yates, turn left on Langley Street, and go 1 block south. Turn right on View Street and you're in:

❻ Bastion Square

This square was a bustling area with waterfront hotels, saloons, and warehouses during the late 19th century. Earlier, it had been the site of one of Fort Victoria's octagonal gun bastions. In

Walking Tour 2: The Old Town & Chinatown

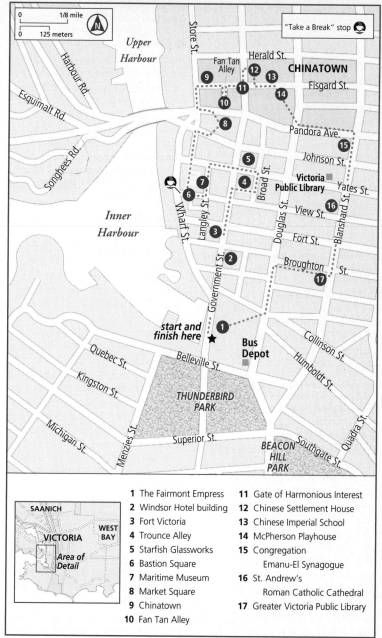

0   1/8 mile
0   125 meters

N

"Take a Break" stop

Upper Harbour

Store St.

Fan Tan Alley

Herald St.

CHINATOWN

Fisgard St.

9

12

13

11

14

10

8

Pandora Ave.

15

Johnson St.

5

Broad St.

Victoria Public Library

Yates St.

7

4

View St.

16

6

Wharf St.

Langley St.

Douglas St.

Blanshard St.

Inner Harbour

3

Fort St.

2

Broughton St.

17

Esquimalt Rd.

Harbour Rd.

Songhees Rd.

start and finish here

1

Bus Depot

Collinson St.

Quebec St.

Belleville St.

Humboldt St.

Kingston St.

THUNDERBIRD PARK

Quadra St.

Michigan St.

Menzies St.

Superior St.

BEACON HILL PARK

Southgate St.

SAANICH

WEST BAY

VICTORIA

Area of Detail

1 The Fairmont Empress
2 Windsor Hotel building
3 Fort Victoria
4 Trounce Alley
5 Starfish Glassworks
6 Bastion Square
7 Maritime Museum
8 Market Square
9 Chinatown
10 Fan Tan Alley

11 Gate of Harmonious Interest
12 Chinese Settlement House
13 Chinese Imperial School
14 McPherson Playhouse
15 Congregation
    Emanu-El Synagogue
16 St. Andrew's
    Roman Catholic Cathedral
17 Greater Victoria Public Library

1963, the area was restored as a heritage square. This is a good place to:

TAKE A BREAK
Even if you're not hungry, it's worth stopping at **rebar**, 64 Bastion Sq. (© **250/361-9223**; p. 220), for a juice—maybe a combination of grapefruit, banana, melon, and pear, with bee pollen to keep your energy up. If you're hungry, then rejoice: rebar has the city's best vegetarian comfort food. Disturbingly wholesome as that may sound, it's not only tasty, it's also fun, and a great spot to go with kids. It's open Monday through Thursday 8:30am to 9pm, Friday and Saturday 8:30am to 10pm, and Sunday 8:30am to 3:30pm.

The provincial courthouse and hangman's square were once located on Bastion Square, but now you'll find the:

❼ Maritime Museum

At 28 Bastion Sq. you can get a glimpse into Victoria's naval and shipping history (p. 225). The museum is housed in Victoria's original courthouse and jail, which opened in 1889.

Turn north up Commercial Alley. Cross Yates Street, and a few steps farther west, turn north again up Waddington Alley. On the other side of Johnson Street is:

❽ Market Square

This restored historic site was once a two-story complex of shipping offices and supply stores. It now contains more than 40 shops that sell everything from sports equipment to crafts, books, and toys. There are also seven restaurants in the square; some have outdoor seating in the large open-air court where musicians often perform in summer.

More than a century ago, Victoria's business was transacted in this area of winding alleys and walkways. Warehouses, mariner's hotels, and shipping offices have been carefully restored into shops, restaurants, and galleries. You'll occasionally find historic plaques explaining the function of each building before it was renovated.

Go north 1 block on Store Street and turn right (away from the harbor) onto Fisgard Street. You're now in North America's oldest:

❾ Chinatown

Established in 1858 when the first Chinese arrived as gold seekers and railroad workers, this 6-block district (roughly between Store and Blanshard sts. and Herald St. and Pandora Ave.) fell into decline after World War I (as did many West Coast Asian communities when the U.S. and Canadian governments restricted Asian immigration). What remains is a fascinating peek into a well-hidden and exotic heritage.

On your right, halfway up the block, you'll find:

❿ Fan Tan Alley

The world's narrowest street, it's no more than 1.2m (4 ft.) wide at either end and expands to a little over 1.8m (6 ft.) in the center. Through the maze of doorways (which still have their old Chinese signage), there are entries to small courtyards leading to more doorways.

During the late 1800s, this was the main entrance to "Little Canton," where the scent of legally manufactured opium wafted from the courtyards. Opium dens, gambling parlors, and brothels sprang up between the factories and bachelor rooms where male immigrants shared cramped quarters to save money.

Today, you won't find any sin for sale here—just a few little shops dealing in crafts and souvenirs. You can enter the **Chinatown Trading Company,** 551 Fisgard St., from Fisgard Street or via a back door facing onto Fan Tan Alley. Hidden in its back room are a couple of minimuseums cleverly displaying artifacts from old Chinatown, including the original equipment from a 19th-century Chinese gambling house.

When you're finished exploring the alley, return to Fisgard Street and continue heading east. At the corner of Government and Fisgard streets is the:

⓫ Gate of Harmonious Interest

This lavishly detailed dragon-headed, red-and-gold archway was built in 1981 to commemorate the completion—after years of deterioration—of Chinatown's revitalization by the city and the Chinese Consolidated Benevolent Association. The gate is guarded by a pair of hand-carved stone lions imported from Suzhou, China.

A half block up at 1715 Government St. is the former location of the:

⓬ Chinese Settlement House

Newly arrived Chinese families once lived upstairs in this balconied building and made use of social services here until they were able to secure work and living quarters. The original Chinese Buddhist temple has been moved from the storefront to the second floor, but it's still open to visitors. Although admission is free, hours vary. You will have to check with temple staff to see if you may enter.

A half block up from the Gate of Harmonious Interest at 36 Fisgard St. is the:

⓭ Chinese Imperial School (Zhonghua Xuetang)

This red-and-gold, pagoda-style building with a baked-tile roof and recessed balconies was built by the Chinese Benevolent Society. In 1907, the Victoria School Board banned non-Canadian Chinese children from attending public school, and in response, the society started its own community elementary school the following year. The school is open to the public during the week and still provides children and adults with instruction in Chinese reading and writing on weekends.

Just east of the school at 3 Centennial Sq. is the:

⓮ McPherson Playhouse

Formerly a vaudeville theater, this was the first of the vast Pantages Theatres chain (Alex Pantages went into showbiz after striking it rich in the Klondike gold fields). The building was restored in the 1960s and is now Victoria's main performing arts

center (☎ 250/386-6121). Although there are no formal tours of the theater, the center is usually open during the day; if you ask nicely, you may be allowed to take a peek inside at the ornate interior. You could also try to get tickets to a show there. (*Note:* City Hall and the police department are located in the office plaza surrounding the playhouse.)

When you get to the southeast corner of Centennial Square, walk east 1 more block on Pandora Avenue to Blanshard Street. At 1461 Blanshard St. (at Pandora Ave.), you'll find:

⓯ Congregation Emanu-El Synagogue

This is the oldest surviving Jewish temple on North America's west coast. Built in 1863, it has been proclaimed a national heritage site. The temple (which is not particularly impressive on the outside) is not open to the public.

Turn south on Blanshard Street and walk 3 blocks to 740 View St., where you'll see the impressive:

⓰ St. Andrew's Roman Catholic Cathedral

Built during the 1890s, this is Victorian High Gothic at its best. The facade is 23m (75 ft.) across, the spire 53m (174 ft.) tall, and no frill or flounce or architectural embellishment was left out of the design. Renovations in the 1980s incorporated the works of First Nations artists into the interior. Go inside and see the altar by Coast Salish carver Charles Elliot.

One block south at Fort Street is the beginning of Antique Row, which stretches 3 blocks east to Cook Street. Ignore that for the moment (or go explore and then come back) and continue 1 more block south on Blanshard. Walk across the plaza to 735 Broughton St., where you'll find the:

⓱ Greater Victoria Public Library

The attraction here is the huge skylit atrium, complete with George Norris's massive hanging artwork, *Dynamic Mobile Steel Sculpture.* Built in 1979, the library complex takes up most of the block. Library hours are Monday,

Wednesday, Friday, and Saturday 9am to 6pm and Tuesday and Thursday 9am to 9pm. The Library is closed on Sunday.

Duck out through the portal on Broughton Street and walk west to Douglas Street, then turn left and walk a block and a half south on Douglas until you see the entrance to the Victoria Convention Centre. Walk in and admire the indoor fountain and aviary. The Centre connects to The Fairmont Empress, which was our starting place.

BIKING TOUR   DALLAS ROAD

Start and Finish: The Fairmont Empress, 321 Government St.

Time: 2 hours, not including picnic stops, sightseeing, shopping, or food breaks.

Best Times: Clear days with the sun shining, when the Olympic Mountains are out in all their glory.

Worst Times: Gray, rainy days.

Victoria cries out to be biked. The hills are modest, the traffic light and very polite, and the views incredible. When touring around by bike, you rarely have time to stop and pull out a point-by-point guide, so the descriptions offered here are shorter than for walking tours. The route is designed to take you a bit beyond what would be possible on foot, without getting into an expedition-length tour.

This tour is about 15km (9⅓ miles) long and stays on bike paths through much of its length, although there is some driving on lightly trafficked streets in the second half of the tour. The ride from the Dallas Road shoreline to Craigdarroch Castle involves an elevation gain of about 150m (492 ft.).

Start at **Cycle B.C. Bike Rental,** 747 Douglas St. (© **250/380-2453**), behind **The Fairmont Empress** hotel. Ride south down Douglas Street to **Thunderbird Park** and have a look at the totem poles. Continue east along Belleville Street past the **Legislature** and the **Coho ferry terminal;** then go round the corner onto Kingston Street, and go left through the small park to **Fisherman's Wharf.** From here, go south along **Dallas Road,** past the helijet pad and the car-ferry docks, and stop at the entrance to the breakwater at **Ogden Point.** By this time, you should have a fabulous view of the Olympic Mountains. Park your bike and wander out along the breakwater or stop in at the **Ogden Point Cafe,** 204 Dallas Rd., for the same view without the wind.

Continue east along the seaside bike path or on Dallas Road. Stop here and there as the urge strikes and do some beachcombing. A little ways on, past Douglas Street, cross Dallas and cut north into **Beacon Hill Park** (p. 232). Stop at the petting zoo, look at the 38m-tall (125-ft.) totem pole, or just enjoy Victoria's favorite park. Exit the park by the northeast corner on Cook Street and cycle a few blocks north into **Cook Street Village.** This is a good spot to grab a coffee and dessert or to shop for picnic supplies at the local deli or supermarket. Head back south on Cook Street to Dallas Road; turn left and continue east a kilometer or so to **Clover Point,** a short peninsula sticking out into the Strait of Juan de Fuca. It makes a fine picnic spot. From here, head east to **Ross Bay Cemetery** (p. 229), Victoria's second oldest, where many local notables are buried, including former governor James Douglas and painter Emily Carr. From the north side of the cemetery, ride up the hill on **Stannard Street,** skirting the eastern edge of **Government**

House (p. 232), the official residence of the lieutenant governor.

When you reach **Rockland Avenue,** turn right and ride a few hundred meters past the many fine homes of this elite enclave to the main entrance to Government House. Though the residence itself is closed to the public, the formal gardens are open and well worth a wander. Round back, the hillside of Garry oaks is one of the last places to see what the area's natural fauna looked like before European settlers arrived. The rose garden in front is sumptuous. Just west of the gate on Rockland Avenue, turn right onto **Joan Crescent** and ride up the small hill to opulent **Craigdarroch Castle** (p. 224), built by coal magnate Robert Dunsmuir for his wife, Joan. The castle is open for self-guided tours. From here, continue up Joan Crescent to Fort Street, turn right and go a very short way east to Yates Street, turn left and go 1 block to Fernwood Street, turn right and go 1 block north to **Pandora Street,** then turn left again and ride west down the hill. Keep an eye out for the **Christian Science church** at 1205 Pandora St. (where the street widens to include a boulevard in its center). Another 6 blocks west and you're at **Pandora** and **Government streets,** with **Chinatown** (see stops 9–13 of Walking Tour 2, above) to your right and **Market Square** (see stop 8 of Walking Tour 2, above) to your left, and The Fairmont Empress and the bike-rental spot just a few blocks south.

Victoria Shopping

Victoria has dozens of little specialty shops that appeal to every taste and whim, and because the city is built on such a pedestrian scale, you can easily wander from place to place seeking out whatever treasure you're after. Nearly all of the areas listed below are within a short walk of The Fairmont Empress; for those shops located more than 6 blocks from The Fairmont Empress hotel, bus information is provided. Stores in Victoria are generally open Monday through Saturday from 10am to 6pm; some, but not many, are open on Sundays during the summer.

1 The Shopping Scene

Explorers beware: The brick-paved **Government Street promenade,** from the Inner Harbour 5 blocks north to Yates Street, is a jungle of cheap souvenir shops. There are gems in here, certainly—Irish linen, fine bone china, quality Native art, and Cowichan Indian sweaters thick enough to bivouac in—but to find these riches, you'll have to hack your way through tangled creepers of Taiwanese-made knickknacks and forbidding groves of maple-syrup bottles.

Farther north, the **Old Town district** and **Market Square** feature a fascinating blend of heritage buildings and up-to-date shops. Victoria's **Chinatown** is tiny and since most of the city's Chinese population has moved elsewhere, it lacks some of the authenticity and vitality of Chinatowns in Vancouver or San Francisco. The area has been charmingly preserved, however, and there are a number of gallery-quality art and ceramic shops, quirky back alleys (including Canada's thinnest commercial street, Fan Tan Alley), and at least one tourist trap that knows not to take itself too seriously.

On the eastern edge of downtown, **Antique Row** is justifiably renowned for its high-quality British collectibles. And if you're at all interested in the Native art of the Pacific Northwest, Victoria is a great place to look for pieces to add to your collection.

2 Shopping A to Z

ANTIQUES

Victoria has long had a deserved reputation for antiques—particularly those of British origin. Many of the best stores are in **Antique Row,** a 3-block stretch on Fort Street between Blanshard and Cook streets. In addition to those listed below, check out **Jeffries and Co. Silversmiths,** 1026 Fort St. (© **250/383-8315**); **Romanoff & Company Antiques,** 837 Fort St. (© **250/480-1543**); and for furniture fans, **Charles Baird Antiques,** 1044A Fort St. (© **250/384-8809**).

David Robinson Antiques   Here you'll find oriental rugs, silver, oil paintings, brass, porcelain, and period furniture. Though it's not as large as Faith Grant's shop (see below), Robinson's pieces—especially his furniture—are particularly well chosen. 1023 Fort St. © 250/384-6425. Bus: 10 to Blanshard or Cook St.

Faith Grant's Connoisseur Shop Ltd. *(Finds)* The farthest from downtown, this shop is also the best. The 16 rooms of this 1862 heritage building contain everything from Georgian writing desks to English flatware, not to mention fine ceramics, prints, and paintings. Furniture is especially strong here. 1156 Fort St. © 250/383-0121. Bus: 10 to Fort and Cook St.

Vanity Fair Antique Mall *(Value)* This large shop is fun to browse, with crystal, glassware, furniture, and lots more. If you're feeling flush, it's certainly possible to spend here, but there are also many items you can easily pick up without taking out a bank loan. 1044 Fort St. © 250/380-7274. Bus: 10 to Blanshard or Cook St.

ART
CONTEMPORARY

Fran Willis Gallery Soaring white walls and huge arched windows make this one of Victoria's most beautiful display spaces. The collection is strong on contemporary oils, mixed media, and bronzes, almost all by B.C. and Alberta artists. 1619 Store St. © 250/381-3422. www.franwillis.com. Bus: 5 to Douglas and Fisgard.

Open Space When does self-confidence start edging into pretension? This artist-run gallery and self-declared flag-bearer of the avant-garde has trod one side or the other of that line since 1972. Mostly, they get it right, so the gallery is usually worth a visit. Exhibits run the full gamut, from paintings and sculpture to literary and dance performances. 510 Fort St. © 250/383-8833. www.openspace.ca.

Winchester Galleries This slightly daring gallery features mostly contemporary oil paintings. Unlike elsewhere in town, very few wildlife paintings ever make it onto the walls. 1010 Broad St. © 250/386-2773. www.winchestergalleriesltd.com.

NATIVE

Alcheringa Gallery What began as a shop handling imports from the Antipodes has evolved into one of Victoria's truly great stores for aboriginal art connoisseurs. All the coastal tribes are represented in Alcheringa's collection, along with pieces from Papua New Guinea. The presentation is museum quality, with prices to match. 665 Fort St. © 250/383-8224. www.alcheringa-gallery.com.

Hill's Native Art Exquisite traditional Native art includes wooden masks and carvings, Haida argillite and silver jewelry, bentwood boxes, button blankets, drums and talking sticks, and carved wooden paddles. Hill's is the store for established artists from up and down the B.C. coast, which means the quality is high, and so are the prices. Of course, you don't stay in business for 50 years without pleasing all comers, so Hill's has its share of dream catchers and other knickknacks. 1008 Government St. © 250/385-3911. www.hillsnativeart.com.

BOOKS

Avalon Metaphysical Centre It's not the West Coast unless you've had a spiritual experience or brushed auras with someone who has. Avalon specializes in New Age books, angels, crystals, rune stones, body oils, and videotapes of gurus who've already trodden the path to enlightenment. 62–560 Johnson St. (in Market Sq.). © 250/380-1721.

Crown Publications Inc. In addition to dry, but informative, government publications, this store stocks an excellent selection of books covering the history, nature, and culture of the Victoria area. Keeping up with the times, digital maps are now available on CD-ROM. 521 Fort St. ℰ 250/386-4636. www.crownpub.bc.ca.

Munro's Books *(Finds*   All bookstores should look so good: a mile-high ceiling in a 1909 heritage building, complete with heavy brass lamps and murals on the walls (never mind that the building was originally a bank). The store stocks many well-chosen books—over 35,000 titles, including an excellent selection of books about Victoria and books by local authors. The staff is friendly and very good at unearthing obscure titles. The remainder tables have some incredible deals. 1108 Government St. ℰ 888/243-2464 or 250/382-2464. www.munrobooks.com.

Russell Books *(Value*   This shop offers two floors of used (and some new, remaindered) books for browsing. 734 Fort St. ℰ 250/361-4447.

CAMERAS
Lens and Shutter   Come here for all your camera needs—film, filters, lenses, cameras, or just advice. 615 Fort St. ℰ 250/383-7443.

CHINA & LINENS
Irish Linen Stores   Everything Irish since 1910: handkerchiefs, scarves, doilies, napkins, lace, and more. 1019 Government St. ℰ 250/383-6812.

Sydney Reynolds   This building opened as a saloon in 1908, became a bank in 1909, was converted into a shop in 1929, and now houses a wide array of fine porcelains, including tea sets and Victorian dolls. 801 Government St. ℰ 250/383-3931.

CHINESE ARTS & CRAFTS
Chinatown Trading Company *(Finds*   This unobtrusive storefront on Fisgard opens onto a veritable bazaar—three connected shops stocked with Chinese goods either useful or endearingly corny or both. Who wouldn't want kung fu shoes or a tin pecking chicken? There are also bamboo flutes, origami kits, useful and inexpensive Chinese kitchenware, and a few small museum displays of artifacts from Chinatown's past. Look for the sneaky back entrance off Fan Tan Alley. 551 Fisgard St. ℰ 250/381-5503. Bus: 5 to Douglas and Fisgard sts.

CHRISTMAS ORNAMENTS
The Spirit of Christmas *(Finds*   The thought of a shop selling Christmas ornaments year-round may send you reaching for lost bits of Dickensian invective, but before you start hurling "Bah humbugs," step inside and have a look. The store has everything from C$300 (US$225) woven vine wreaths to cotton nightshirts with caroling cows. 1022 Government St. ℰ 250/385-2501.

CIGARS & TOBACCO
E.A. Morris Tobacconist Ltd.   A century-old tradition of custom-blended pipe tobacco is maintained in this small shop. You'll also find an impressive selection of cigars, including Cubans. Cuban cigars can't be brought into the United States, but a few brands like Horvath Bances duck the blockade by importing the tobacco into Canada and rolling the cigars here. 1116 Government St. ℰ 250/382-4811.

DEPARTMENT STORE & A SHOPPING MALL
The Bay Centre   Formerly known as the Eaton Centre, the Bay Centre is named after its new anchor store, Hudson's Bay Company. Canada's oldest department store

sells everything from housewares to fashions to cosmetics and of course the classic (and expensive) Hudson's Bay woolen point blankets. The store also has a very large china and crystal department. The rest of the large complex houses a full shopping mall disguised as a block of heritage buildings. Between Government and Douglas sts., off Fort and View sts. For the Bay, call ✆ 250/385-1311. For the mall, call ✆ 250/389-2228.

FASHIONS
FOR WOMEN

Breeze   This high-energy fashion outlet carries a number of affordable and trendy lines such as Mexx, Powerline, and Mac+Jac. Shoes by Nine West and Steve Madden and other stylish accessories such as purses and jewelry complete the look. 1150 Government St. ✆ 250/383-8871.

Hughes Ltd.   This local favorite features designer fashions and trendy casual wear. 564 Yates St. ✆ 250/381-4405.

The Plum Clothing Co.   This local chain features quality dressy casuals designed with the baby-boomer in mind. 1298 Broad St. ✆ 250/381-5005.

FOR WOMEN & MEN

The Edinburgh Tartan Shop   If there's even a drop of Celtic blood in ye, this shop can set ye up in a kilt made from your family tartan. It also stocks sweaters, blankets, tartan by the yard, and kilt pins with authentic clan crests. 909 Government St. ✆ 250/953-7788.

Still Life   Originally known for its vintage clothes, Still Life has updated its collection and moved to a new contemporary style that includes fun and active street clothes for the young and the young at heart, from Diesel, Workwear, and Toronto designer Damzels-in-distress. 551 Johnson St. ✆ 250/386-5655.

W. & J. Wilson's Clothiers   Canada's oldest family-run clothing store, this shop has been owned/managed by the Wilsons since 1862. When you're in it for the long haul, you try not to get too far ahead of the pack. Look for sensible casuals or elegant cashmeres and leathers from British, Scottish, and other European designers. 1221 Government St. ✆ 250/383-7177.

FOR MEN

British Importers   Victoria may be laid-back, but a man still needs a power suit, and this is the place to get it. Designer labels include Calvin Klein and Hugo Boss. Ties and leather jackets are also for sale. 1125 Government St. ✆ 250/386-1496.

FOOD

Murchie's   It's worth coming here just to suck up the coffee smell or sniff the many specialty tea flavors, including the custom-made Empress blend, served at the Fairmont Empress hotel's afternoon tea. While you're imbibing the air, browse the collection of fine china, silver, and crystal. 1110 Government St. ✆ 250/383-3112. www.murchies.com.

Rogers' Chocolates   "Quite possibly the best chocolates in the world" is how Rogers' bills itself. For a more accurate (but litigation-proof) description, how about "quite possibly the best 98-year-old shrine to all things dark and sweet; still with original Tiffany glass and old-fashioned counters, and free samples, too." Rogers' has shops in Oak Bay and Whistler—quite possibly just as good. 913 Government St. ✆ 800/663-2220 or 250/384-7021. www.rogerschocolates.com.

Silk Road Aromatherapy and Tea Company *(Value)* Before setting up shop, the two Victoria women who run this store first trained to become tea masters in China and Taiwan. Their Victoria store on the edge of Chinatown sells a wide variety of teas, including premium loose blends and tea paraphernalia such as teapots, mugs, and kettles; they offer a full line of aromatherapy products as well. The latest addition is the spa, which offers a range of treatment services at very reasonable prices; their 2-hour full facial and full-body massage at C$99 (US$79) is a steal. 1624 Government St. ✆ 250/382-0006. www.silkroadtea.com. Bus: 5 to Douglas and Fisgard sts.

GARDENING
Better Gnomes and Gardens If looking at Victoria's picture-perfect gardens has given you a serious case of garden lust, a visit to Better Gnomes and Gardens may be the solution. Get inspired by the many flowers and plants, statues, and large selection of garden accessories and pick up some "inside" tips from the helpful staff. 3200 Quadra St. (at Tolmie). ✆ 250/386-9366.

Western Canada Wilderness Committee (WCWC) Committed to protecting Canada's endangered species and environment, the WCWC sells a variety of items to raise funds for the cause. Choose from beautiful gift cards, posters, and souvenir T-shirts or mugs. 651 Johnson St. ✆ 250/388-9292. www.wildernesscommittee.org.

GLASS
Starfish Glassworks *(Finds)* Who says artists don't have a head for business? The principals of this gallery-cum-workshop moved to Victoria when they couldn't get kiln time in Vancouver. They took over and renovated an ex-bank building, installing the kiln on the ground floor and the gallery on an open catwalk above, so potential customers could watch works in progress while browsing among the finished products. You can watch the artists blowing glass daily from noon to 6pm. Wannabe glass blowers can now take 1-day workshops; check their website for dates. Closed Tuesdays, September 16 through May 14. 630 Yates St. ✆ 250/388-7827. www.starfishglass.bc.ca.

JEWELRY
Jade Tree Here you'll find jewelry made from British Columbia jade, which is mined in northern Vancouver Island, then crafted in Victoria and in China into necklaces, bracelets, and other items. 606 Humboldt St. ✆ 250/388-4326.

MacDonald Jewelry Ian MacDonald designs and makes all his own jewelry: diamonds cut in squares and triangles and styles from the traditional to cutting edge. It's a great place to hunt for rings and pearls as well as precious gems like sapphires, rubies, and emeralds. 618 View St. ✆ 250/382-4113.

The Patch The Island's largest provider of body jewelry has studs and rings and other bright baubles for your nose, navel, or nipple, much of it quite creative and reasonably priced. They also carry funky youthful fashions. 719 Yates St. ✆ 250/384-7070.

NATIVE CRAFTS
Natives from the nearby Cowichan band are famous for their warm, durable sweaters, knitted with bold motifs from hand-spun raw wool. In addition to these beautiful knits, craftspeople create soft leather moccasins, moose-hide boots, ceremonial masks, sculptures carved from argillite or soapstone, intricate baskets, bearskin rugs, and jewelry.

Cowichan Trading Company   A downtown fixture for almost 50 years, Cowichan Trading follows the standard layout for its displays: junky T-shirts and gewgaws in front, Cowichan sweaters, masks, and fine silver jewelry farther in. 1328 Government St. © 250/383-0321.

Quw'utsun' Cultural and Conference Centre   Though a bit of a drive out of town, this store, owned/operated by the Cowichan, sells beautiful crafts and allows you to watch artisans at work. It also stocks an excellent selection of books and publications on First Nations history and lore. 200 Cowichan Way, Duncan. © 250/746-8119. www.quwutsun.ca. No public transit. Take Douglas St. north, which turns into Hwy. 1 (the Trans-Canada Hwy.); remain on the Trans-Canada for about 60km (37 miles) to Duncan, then turn right onto Cowichan Way.

OUTDOOR CLOTHES & EQUIPMENT
Ocean River Sports   This is the place to go to arrange a sea kayak tour—they'll be happy to rent (or sell) you a boat and all the gear. This is also a good spot for outdoor clothing and camping musts, such as solar-heated showers or espresso machines. 1824 Store St. © 250/381-4233. www.oceanriver.com.

Pacific Trekking   An excellent source of rain and hiking gear, this store is also good for information on local hiking trails. 1305 Government St. © 250/388-7088.

PAWNSHOPS
Universal Trading *(Value)*   So it's not where you normally shop. This isn't your usual down-at-the-heels pawnbroker, either, but rather a quirky little curio shop with a few pieces that wouldn't be out of place in Antique Row. 584 Johnson St. © 250/383-9512.

PUBLIC MARKETS
Market Square   Constructed from the original warehouses and shipping offices built here in the 1800s, this pleasant and innovative heritage reconstruction features small shops and restaurants surrounding a central courtyard, often the site of live performances in summer. 560 Johnson St. © 250/386-2441.

WINE
The Wine Barrel   This shop sells over 300 B.C. VQA (Vintner Quality Alliance) wines and wine accessories. It's known for carrying the largest selection of B.C. ice wines (a type of wine where grapes have to be picked when the temperature has been below 0°C/32°F for a certain amount of time) in Victoria. 644 Broughton St. © 250/388-0606. www.thewinebarrel.com.

17

Victoria After Dark

Victoria is God's waiting room. It's the only cemetery
in the entire world with street lighting.

—a visitor from Gotham, as quoted in *Monday* magazine

Ouch. That's harsh. More important, it's not exactly accurate. True, with retirees and civil servants making up a sizable segment of the population, Victoria is never going to set the world on fire. But taken together, the U. Vic. students, tourists, and a small but dedicated cadre of Victoria revelers form a critical mass large enough to keep a small but steady scene alive.

Monday magazine, a weekly tabloid published on Thursdays, is the place to start. Its listings section provides comprehensive coverage of what's happening in town and is particularly good for the club scene. If you can't find *Monday* in cafes or record shops, visit it on the Web at www.mondaymag.com.

For information on theater, concerts, and arts events, contact the **Tourism** **Victoria Visitor Info Centre,** 812 Wharf St. (© **800/663-3883** or 250/953-2033; www.tourismvictoria.com). You can also buy tickets for all of Victoria's venues from the Info Centre, but only in person.

Whatever you decide to do with your Victoria evenings, chances are that your destination will be close at hand: One of the great virtues of Victoria's size is that nearly all of its attractions—concert halls, pubs, dance clubs, and theaters—are no more than a 10-minute walk from the Fairmont Empress hotel, right in the heart of the city, and easily reached by taking bus no. 5 to the Empress Hotel/Convention Centre. For those few nightlife spots a little farther out, bus route information is provided throughout the chapter.

1 The Performing Arts

The **Royal Theatre,** 805 Broughton St., and the **McPherson Playhouse,** 3 Centennial Sq., share a common box office (© **888/717-6121** or 250/386-6121; www.rmts.bc.ca). The **Royal**—built in the early 1900s and renovated in the 1970s—hosts concerts by the Victoria Symphony and performances by the Pacific Opera Victoria, as well as touring dance and theater companies. The **McPherson**—built in 1914 as the first Pantages Vaudeville Theatre—is home to smaller stage plays and performances by the Victoria Operatic Society. The box office is open Monday through Saturday from 9:30am to 5:30pm and on performance days for 2 hours before showtime.

THEATER

Performing in an intimate playhouse that was once a church, the **Belfry Theatre Society,** 1291 Gladstone St. (© **250/385-6815;** www.belfry.bc.ca; bus no. 22 to Fernwood St.), is a nationally acclaimed theatrical group that stages four productions

October through April and a summer show in August, usually dramatic works by contemporary Canadian playwrights. Tickets are C$17 to C$31 (US$14–US$25). The box office is open Monday through Friday from 9:30am to 5pm, and an hour before showtime on performance days.

The **Intrepid Theatre Company,** 301–1205 Broad St. (© 888/FRINGE-2 or 250/383-2663; www.intrepidtheatre.com), runs two yearly theater festivals. In spring, it's the **Uno Festival of Solo Performance** ⚘, a unique event of strictly one-person performances with tickets at C$12 (US$10). Come summer, Intrepid puts on the **Victoria Fringe Festival** ⚘. Even if you're not a theater fan—*especially* if you're not—don't miss the Fringe. Unlike mainstream theater, fringe festivals are cheap (about C$8/US$6) and short (an hour or so), so you're not gambling much by stepping inside one of the six venues—and the rewards are often great. More than 50 performers or small companies come from around the world, and the plays they put on are often amazingly inventive. The festival runs from late August to mid-September, and performances go on at six downtown venues daily noon to midnight.

The **Theatre Inconnu** (© 250/360-0234) is mostly known for its annual production of Victoria's **Shakespeare Festival,** held in a restored theater in the historic St. Ann's Academy, 835 Humboldt St. The festival puts on two or three of the Bard's best for several weeks in July and August. The actors are local and often semiprofessional, but quality is excellent and tickets are an eminently affordable C$5 to C$14 (US$3.75–US$11). The Theatre Inconnu also stages a two-man adaptation of Charles Dickens's *A Christmas Carol* every year.

The **Langham Court Theatre,** 805 Langham Court (© 250/384-2142; www.langhamcourttheatre.bc.ca), performs works produced by the Victoria Theatre Guild, a local amateur society dedicated to presenting a wide range of dramatic and comedic works. From downtown take bus no. 14 or 11 to Fort and Moss Streets.

OPERA

The **Pacific Opera Victoria,** 1316B Government St. (© **250/385-0222;** box office 250/386-6121; www.pov.bc.ca), presents three productions annually during the October-to-April season. Performances are normally at the McPherson Playhouse and Royal Theatre. The repertoire covers the classical bases, from Mozart and Rossini to Verdi and even Wagner. Tickets cost C$24 to C$82 (US$19–US$66) and are available at the McPherson Playhouse box office or at the Opera box office during office hours.

The **Victoria Operatic Society,** 10–744 Fairview Rd. (© **250/381-1021;** www.vos.bc.ca), presents Broadway musicals and other popular fare at the McPherson Playhouse. Tickets cost C$18 to C$30 (US$14–US$24).

ORCHESTRAL & CHORAL MUSIC

The well-respected **Victoria Symphony Orchestra,** 846 Broughton St. (© **250/385-9771;** www.victoriasymphony.bc.ca), kicks off its season on the first Sunday of August with Symphony Splash, a free concert performed on a barge in the Inner Harbour. Regular performances begin in September and last through May. The Symphony Orchestra performs at the Royal Theatre or the University Farquhar Auditorium. Tickets are C$19 to C$56 (US$15–US$45) for most concerts.

DANCE

Dance recitals and full-scale performances by local and international dance troupes such as **Danceworks** and the **Scottish Dance Society** are scheduled throughout the year. Call the **Visitor Info Centre** at ℂ **250/953-2033** to find out who's performing when you're in town.

COMEDY & SPOKEN WORD

Mocambo, 1028 Blanshard (ℂ **250/384-4468**), a coffeehouse near the public library, hosts a range of spoken-word events through the week (multimedia fusion demos, philosopher's cafes, argument for the joy of it, slam poetry), then lets loose on Saturdays with improv comedy. There is no cover.

2 Music & Dance Clubs

MUSIC FESTIVALS

Folkfest ⓕ   A free multicultural celebration of song, performances, food, and crafts, Folkfest is sponsored by the International Cultural Association of greater Victoria. The largest outdoor event on Vancouver Island, it takes place late June through early July on Ship Point (the parking space below Wharf St. on the edge of the Inner Harbour). ℂ **250-388-4728.** www.icafolkfest.com.

Summer in the Square   From early July to late August, this festival in downtown's Centennial Square is popular because it offers free music outside every day. Each day features a different band and musical style: The Monday noon-hour concerts feature mostly jazz; Tuesdays offer a noon-hour selection of Big-Band golden oldies; Wednesday through Saturday is potluck (show up at noon and take your chances). The festival's showstoppers are the Concerts Under the Stars held each Sunday from 7 to 9:30pm; the series features some 15 local bands over the 6-week length of the festival. And if you can't make it down to the square, the concerts are also broadcast live over a local radio station, the Q (100.3 FM). Centennial Sq. ℂ **250-361-0388.**

Victoria Jazz Society/Jazz Fest International ⓕ   The Jazz Society is a good place to call any time of year to find out what's happening; it runs a hotline listing jazz events throughout the year. Its raison d'être, however, is the **Jazz Fest International,** held from late June to early July. The more progressive of Victoria's two summer jazz fests, this one offers a range of styles from Cuban and salsa and world beat to fusion and acid jazz. Many free concerts are given in the Market Square courtyard. Other concerts are in live-music venues around the city. This organization also puts on the excellent **Blues Bash** on Labour Day weekend on an outdoor stage in Victoria's Inner Harbour. ℂ **888/671-2112** or 250/388-4423. www.vicjazz.bc.ca.

LIVE MUSIC

Hermann's Jazz Club   There's a community center feel to this View Street venue, which is definitely and defiantly *not* chic. Still, there's good old-time jazz and Dixieland at a reasonable cover, usually open Friday through Sunday at 7pm, call for schedule. 753 View St. ℂ **250-388-9166.** C$4 (US$3.20) cover.

Legends ⓕ   This live-music venue is in the city within a city that's the Strathcona Hotel. At this pop-music palace you'll encounter some hopping international bands, covering the gamut from afro-pop to blues to R&B and zydeco. Legends is one of the best places to hear live music in Victoria. 919 Douglas St. ℂ **250-383-7137.** www.legends nightclub.com. C$6 (US$4.80) cover or more depending on the band Thurs–Sat.

Lucky Bar   This long, low, cavernous space has a pleasantly grungy feel to it. Owned and operated by the team in charge of next-door Süze, Lucky's DJs spin house and trance on the weekends, with bands often showing up earlier in the week. 517 Yates St. © 250/382-5825. www.luckybar.ca. Cover hovers around C$5 (US$4), bigger shows up to C$20 (US$16).

Steamers ⚜   One of the best places to catch live music on the cheap, Steamers features live music 7 nights a week. Once a grubby strip bar, this long, narrow downtown spot got a totally new interior and was reborn as the city's premium blues bar. "Blues" here isn't taken too literally, of course. Acts often stray into the far-off musical realms of zydeco, Celtic, and world beat. On Mondays, there's an open-stage acoustic jam (no cover). 570 Yates St. © 250/381-4340. Cover free–C$5 (US$4).

The Upstairs Lounge   Victoria's new hotspot for live music sits overtop of Darcy's Wharf Street Pub (see below) on the edge of Bastion Square. The Upstairs has space and good sightlines and a selection of pretty Victoria people who come for touring bands and when those aren't available for DJ'd house, Top 40, and groove. 15 Bastion Sq. © 250/385-5483. Cover about C$6 (US$4.80), bigger shows up to C$12 (US$10).

DANCE CLUBS

Most places are open Monday through Saturday until 2am and Sunday until midnight. Drinks run from C$4 to C$8 (US$3.20–US$6.40).

The One Lounge   Open Thursday to Saturday, this Top 40 club spins dance tracks for a late twenties to early thirties crowd. The format (1970s and 1980s retro) depends on the night of the week. 1318 Broad St. © 250/384-3557. C$5 (US$4) cover on weekends.

The Red Jacket   Victoria's newest dance club opened in 2004 and quickly became *the* hoppin' hot spot thanks to Caramel @ The Red Jacket, a Friday night bash featuring some of Victoria's finest urban DJ talent. 751 View St. © 250/384-2582.

Sugar   Groove the night away under an old-fashioned disco ball. Open Thursday through Saturday only; line-ups start at 10pm so come early. DJs spin mostly hip-hop, house, and Top-40 tunes. 858 Yates St. © 250/920-9950. C$3–C$6 (US$2.40–US$4.80) cover Fri–Sat.

3 Lounges, Bars & Pubs

LOUNGES

Bengal Lounge ⚜   A truly unique experience, the Bengal is one of the last outposts of the old empire—a Raffles or a Harry's Bar—except the martinis are ice cold and jazz plays in the background (and on weekends, live in the foreground). The couches are huge and covered in leather thick enough to stop an elephant gun. The cocktail list is extensive. The combination has lately attracted the young and elegant lounge-lizard crowd. 721 Government St., in The Fairmont Empress. © 250/384-8111.

Gambling

At the **Great Canadian Casino**, 1708 Old Island Hwy. (© **250/391-0311;** www.gcgaming.com), there are no floorshows, no alcohol, no dancing girls in glittering bikinis—just a casual and slightly genteel casino. Games include blackjack, roulette, sic bo, red dog (diamond dog), and Caribbean stud poker. It's open daily noon to 3am. Contact the casino for complimentary shuttle service from downtown Victoria.

Med Grill@Mosaic ✿   A bistro by day, this coolly contemporary space turns into a loungy martini 'n' tapas spot every Friday and Saturday night at 10pm, when DJs spin mellow sounds. Everything's reasonably priced and very pretty. 1063 Fort St. ℂ 250/381-3417.

The Reef   The Caribbean restaurant next door to Süze Lounge and Restaurant transforms into a funky reggae lounge when the sun has faded away. Features here include great martinis and good tunes, with a DJ thrown in now and again just to spice things up. 533 Yates St. ℂ 250/388-5375.

BARS & PUBS

Big Bad John's   Victoria's first, favorite, and only hillbilly bar is a low, dark warren of a place, with thick gunk on the walls, inches of discarded peanut shells on the plank floor, and a crowd of drunk and happy rowdies. 919 Douglas St., in the Strathcona Hotel. ℂ 250/383-7137.

Canoe ✿   If it's a nice night, head for the fabulous outdoor patio overlooking the Upper Harbour. The beer is brewed on the premises and is utterly superb (try the taster option—six small glasses of different brews for more or less the price of a pint), the century-old brick and beam building is a joy to look at, and the food is fun and hearty. 450 Swift St. ℂ 250/361-1940.

Darcy's Wharf Street Pub   Eating anywhere on Wharf Street would be a foolish newbie move, but drinking? That's another story. This large, bright, harborfront pub features a range of fine brews, pool tables, occasional live bands, and a lovely view of the sunset. The crowd is usually young and lively. 1127 Wharf St. ℂ 250/380-1322.

Spinnaker's Brewpub ✿   One of the best brewpubs in town, Spinnaker's did it first and did it well, setting standards other pubs had to match. Overlooking Victoria Harbour on the west side of the Songhees Point Development, Spinnaker's view of the harbor and Legislature is fabulous. On sunny days it's worth coming here for the view alone. At other times (all times in fact), the brewed-on-the-premises ales, lagers, and stouts are uniformly excellent. For those looking for more substantial fare, the pub grub is always good. An on-site bakery sells various beer breads. On the weekends there's often a band, or, if that doesn't suit you, there are also dartboards and pool tables. 308 Catherine St. ℂ 250/386-2739. www.spinnakers.com. Bus: 24 to Songhees Rd.

The Sticky Wicket   This is yet another pub in the Strathcona Hotel (see Big Bad John's, above)—but the Wicket is a standout. The beautiful wood interior—including dividers, glass, and a long teak bar—spent many years in Dublin before being shipped here to Victoria, making it about as original an Irish bar as you're likely to find. Elevators can whip you from deepest Dublin up three floors to the mini-Malibu on the outdoor patio balcony. 919 Douglas St., in the Strathcona Hotel. ℂ 250/383-7137.

Swans Pub ✿   There are few drinking spots anywhere more intriguing—or more enjoyable—than Swans. The enjoyment comes from the room itself, on the ground floor of a beautifully converted 1913 feed warehouse across from the Johnson Street Bridge. The intrigue comes from the founding owner's vast Pacific Northwest and First Nations art collection, portions of which are regularly rotated through the pub. The beer here is brewed on-site and is delicious. On weekends, usually starting around 8pm, Swans now sometimes offers bands. 506 Pandora Ave., in Swans Hotel. ℂ 250/361-3310.

4 Gay & Lesbian Bars

Victoria's entertainment options for the gay and lesbian community are few. A good resource for local contacts can be found online at **www.gayvictoria.ca**.

Electric Avenue   The grotto beneath Swans Hotel has tried just about everything—swing, Top 40, grunge, jazz—now it's gay cabaret and burlesque, leather and fetish nights, and support your homo-grown disco. The owners are trying hard, but call ahead (or check *Monday*) before heading here: By the time you descend the Avenue's staircase, it could be a country and western bar. Open Monday through Saturday from 2pm to 2am and Sundays from 2pm through midnight. 1601 Store St. Ⓒ **250/920-0018.** C$5 (US$3.75) cover on weekends.

Hush   This straight-friendly space (crowd is about 50/50) features top-end touring DJs spinning house, trance, and disco house. Open Wednesday to Sunday. 1325 Government St. Ⓒ **250/385-0566.** C$5 (US$4) cover on weekends.

Prism Lounge   Drag shows, techno, Top 40, and lots and lots of elbow room. The gay bar formerly known as BJs has grown ever more militant about its homo-only policy, and discovered that loneliness is often the price of purity, at least in a city as small as Victoria. 642 Johnson St. (entrance on Broad St.). Ⓒ **250/388-0505.**

18

Side Trips:
The Best of British Columbia

Set on the very edge of a great wilderness, southwestern British Columbia offers visitation rights to places and experiences you'll find nowhere else on earth. North and east of Vancouver/Victoria, the skiing and mountain-biking in Whistler are truly world class, and the place has become a year-round mecca for recreation that goes from X-treme to sublime. Alternatively, on the west coast of Vancouver Island, in Tofino, is an ocean resort town of phenomenal beauty, with crashing surf and the old-growth giants that make Pacific Rim National Park Reserve of Canada an ecotourist's dream come true.

1 Whistler: One of North America's Premier Ski Resorts ★★★

The premier ski resort in North America, according to *Ski* and *Snow Country* magazines, the **Whistler/Blackcomb complex** boasts more vertical runs, more lifts, and more varied ski terrain than any other ski resort on the continent. On this pair of mountains only 2 hours north of Vancouver and 80km (50 miles) from the Pacific Ocean, winter sports rule from December through April. Downhill, backcountry, cross-country, snowboarding, snowmobiling, heli-skiing, sledding, and sleigh riding are just some of the possibilities. In 2003, the International Olympic Committee recognized Whistler's superb winter-sports quality by granting it the right to host the skiing events in the 2010 Winter Games.

Whistler isn't just about downhill skiing, though. It has become a mecca for mountain biking, too, with a world-class mountain-bike park to match the world-class skiing. If you're not a fan of that sport, you can spend your summer days in Whistler rafting, hiking, golfing, and horseback riding.

The focus for all this action is **Whistler Village.** Sophisticated, international, and overwhelmingly youthful, this resort community is so new that at first it might strike you almost a bit like Disneyland. Back in the 1970s, a few visionary planners made a decision to build a resort town and set about creating a carefully planned infrastructure and aesthetic. The results are impressive—a compact resort town arranged around a strollable, ski-able, and completely carless village street lined with chalet-style buildings, upscale shopping, some great restaurants, and plenty of outdoor plazas and fountains. What was sacrificed in this drive to become the perfectly planned community was space for the odd, the funky, the quaint, and the nonconforming. It's just too new and too affluent. When word came that the 2010 Winter Olympics would be held here, real estate prices skyrocketed and more luxury hotels went up.

The resort is divided into Whistler Village (where you get the gondola for Whistler Mountain) and the Upper Village (where you get the gondola for Blackcomb Mountain);

Southwestern British Columbia

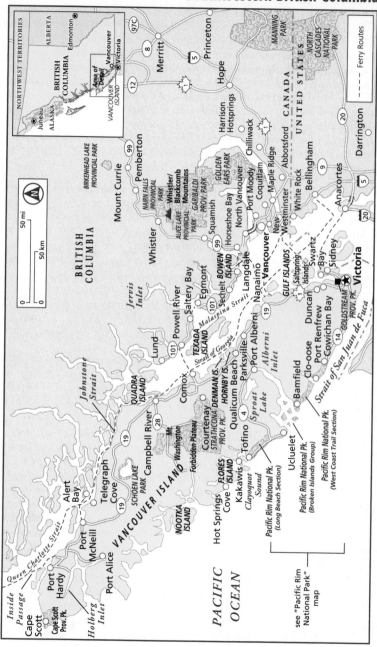

it takes about 5 minutes to walk between them. At some of the hotels you can ski from the front entrance directly to the gondolas. Prices for hotels jump considerably during the high season from December through April, and that is also—not surprisingly—when Whistler is at its most seductive, blanketed with snow and twinkling with lights. July, August, and September are the best months for summer recreation on the mountains. During the shoulder seasons, May and June and October and November, you can expect rain—the area is, after all, a coastal rainforest.

The towns north of Whistler, **Pemberton** and **Mount Currie,** are refreshment stops for touring cyclists and hikers and the gateway to the icy alpine waters of **Birkenhead Lake Provincial Park** (p. 275) and the majestic **Cayoosh Valley,** which winds through the glacier-topped mountains to the Cariboo town of Lillooet.

ESSENTIALS

GETTING THERE   By Car   Whistler is about a 2-hour drive from Vancouver along Highway 99, also called the **Sea-to-Sky Highway.** The drive is spectacular, winding first along the edge of Howe Sound before climbing through the mountains. Parking at the mountain is free for day skiers. For overnight visitors, most hotels charge about C$20 (US$16) for underground parking.

By Bus   The **Whistler Express,** 8695 Barnard St., Vancouver (© 877/317-7788 or 604/266-5386; www.perimeterbus.com), operates bus service from Vancouver International Airport to the Whistler Bus Loop, as well as drop-off service at many of the hotels. In summer, there are 7 daily departures; in winter, there are 11 departures daily. The trip takes about 2½ to 3 hours; one-way fares are C$65 (US$52) adults and C$45 (US$36) for children 5 to 11 years of age; children under 5 ride free. Reservations are required year-round.

Greyhound, Pacific Central Station, 1150 Station St., Vancouver (© 800/661-8747 or 604/662-8074), operates daily bus service (six trips a day between 5:30am and 5:30pm) from the Vancouver Bus Depot to the Whistler Bus Loop. The trip takes about 2½ hours; round-trip fares are C$35 (US$28) for adults and C$18 (US$14) for children 5 to 12; children under 5 ride free.

VISITOR INFORMATION   The **Whistler Visitor Info Centre,** 201–4230 Gateway Dr., Whistler, B.C. V0N 1B4 (© 604/932-5528; www.whistlerchamberof commerce.com), is open daily from 8:30am to 6:30pm (Friday and Saturday until 7:30pm). This center can help you with all Whistler-related questions, help you to locate a hotel and answer questions about restaurants. **Tourism Whistler Activity Centre** (© 877/991-9988 or 604/938-2769; www.tourismwhistler.com), located in front of the TELUS Conference Centre near the Whistler gondola, is open daily 9am to 5pm and can assist you with ski-lift and other activity tickets and information, and last-minute accommodations bookings. For **hotel reservations** call © 800/ **WHISTLER.** Another good website to check is **www.whistlerblackcomb.com.**

GETTING AROUND   Compact and pedestrian-oriented, Whistler Village has signed trails and pathways linking the shops and restaurants with the gondolas up to Whistler and Blackcomb mountains. If you're staying in the Village, you can park your car and leave it for the duration of your stay. The walk between Whistler Mountain (Whistler Village) and Blackcomb Mountain (Upper Village) resorts takes about 5 minutes.

By Bus   Whistler and Valley Express (WAVE; © 604/932-4020; www.busonline.ca), a year-round public transit service, operates from the Gondola Transit Exchange to the

Whistler Valley

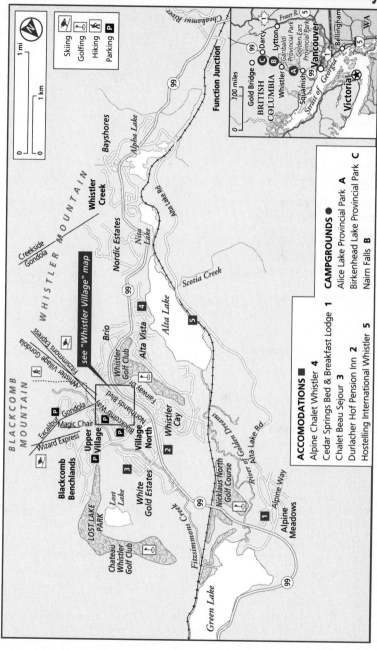

ACCOMODATIONS ■
Alpine Chalet Whistler **4**
Cedar Springs Bed & Breakfast Lodge **1**
Chalet Beau Séjour **3**
Durlacher Hof Pension Inn **2**
Hostelling International Whistler **5**

CAMPGROUNDS ●
Alice Lake Provincial Park **A**
Birkenhead Lake Provincial Park **C**
Nairn Falls **B**

Skiing | Golfing | Hiking | Parking P

see "Whistler Village" map

Whistler Village

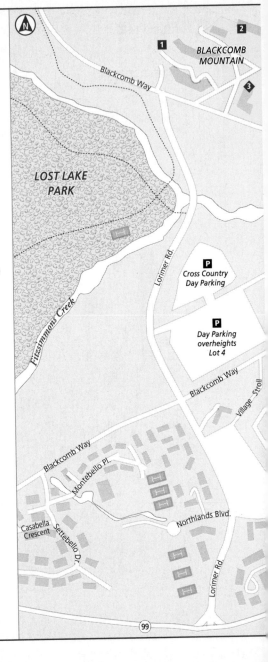

RESTAURANTS ◆
Araxi **11**
Bearfoot Bistro **16**
Caramba! Restaurant **8**
Chef Bernard's Chow Thyme Bistro
    and B.B.K.'s Pub **3**
Citta Bistro **13**
Dubh Linn Gate Irish Lounge/Pub **4**
Hy's Steakhouse **21**
Ingrid's Village Café **12**
Quattro **19**
Rimrock Cafe and Oyster Bar **23**
Whistler Brewhouse **24**

ACCOMMODATIONS ■
Delta Whistler Village Suites **20**
The Fairmont Chateau Whistler **2**
Four Seasons Resort Whistler **1**
Pan Pacific Whistler Mountainside **4**
Pan Pacific Whistler Village Centre **10**
Summit Lodge & Spa **17**
The Westin Resort & Spa Whistler **6**

NIGHTLIFE ▼
Buffalo Bills **14**
Dubh Linn Gate Irish Lounge/Pub **4**
Garfinkel's **9**
Maxx Fish **12**
Savage Beagle **11**
Tommy Africa's **11**

OTHER ATTRACTIONS ●
Maurice Young Millenium Place **7**
Whistler Conference Centre
    Tourism Whistler **15**
Whistler Golf Course **22**
Whistler Museum & Archives **18**
Whistler Village Gondola **5**

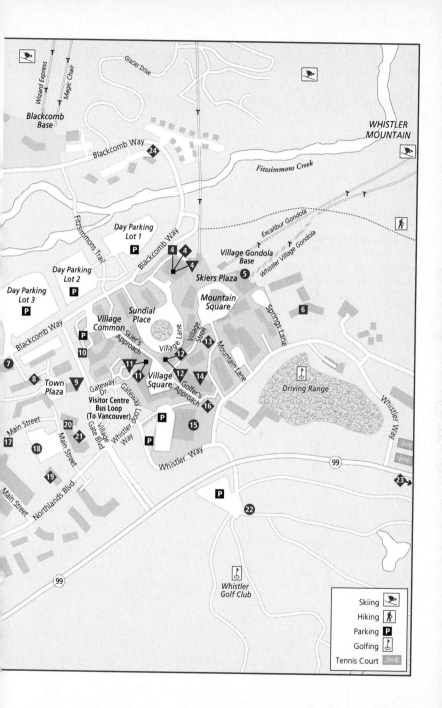

Glacier Drive

Wizard Express

Magic Chair

Blackcomb
Base

Blackcomb Way

24

Fitzsimmons Creek

WHISTLER
MOUNTAIN

Fitzsimmons Trail

Day Parking
Lot 1

P

Blackcomb Way

Excalibur Gondola

Village Gondola
Base

Whistler Village Gondola

Day Parking
Lot 2

P

4 **4**

4

Skiers Plaza

5

Day Parking
Lot 3

P

Blackcomb Way

Sundial
Place

Mountain
Square

6

Village
Common

Skier's
Approach

Springs Lane

P

Village Lane

Village
Stroll

13

10

Village Lane

12

Mountain Lane

7

11

11

Village
Square

12

14

Driving Range

Whistler Way

8

9

Gateway
Dr.

Golfer's
Approach

16

Town
Plaza

Gateway Loop

Visitor Centre
Bus Loop
(To Vancouver)

Village Gate Blvd.

Whistler Way

P

15

Main Street

20

P

17

21

Main Street

19

Northlands Blvd.

Whistler Way

99

23

Main Street

P

22

99

Whistler
Golf Club

Skiing		
Hiking		
Parking	**P**	
Golfing		
Tennis Court		

neighboring districts of Nester's Village, Alpine Meadows, and Emerald Estates. Bus service from the Village to Village North and Upper Village accommodations is free. For other routes, one-way fares are C$1.50 (US$1.20) for adults and C$1.25 (US$1) for seniors/students; children under 5 ride free.

By Cab   Sea-to-Sky Taxi (© 800/203-5322 or 604/932-3333) operates around the clock.

By Car   Rental cars are available from **Avis,** 4315 Northlands Blvd. (© **800/879-2847** or 604/932-1236), and **Budget,** 4005 Whistler Way (© **800/299-3199** or 604/493-4122).

SPECIAL EVENTS   Dozens of downhill **ski competitions** are held December through May; contact Tourism Whistler (see "Visitor Information," above) for event listings.

Mountain bikers compete in the **24 Hours of Adrenalin bike races** in September.

Cornucopia (© **604/932-3434;** www.whistlercornucopia.com) is Whistler's premier wine-and-food festival. Held in November, the opening gala showcases 50 top wineries from the Pacific region. Other events include a celebrity chef competition, food and wine seminars, and wine tastings.

WHERE TO STAY

The first and biggest decision to make is whether to stay in or out of Whistler Village. Staying in the Village, you can forget about your car for the duration of your visit and walk along cobblestone pathways from hotel to ski lift to restaurant to pub. Staying outside the Village, you'll have a short drive to the parking lots on the perimeter of Whistler Village (many hotels outside the Village offer shuttle service). Accommodations within the Village are top quality, while outside the Village there's a bit more variety, including some fine European-style inns.

Whether you decide to stay in or out of town, the best thing to do is simply decide on your price point and call one of the central booking agencies. Studios, condos, town houses, and chalets are available year-round. **Whistler Central Reservations** (© **800/944-7853;** www.tourismwhistler.com) can book a wide range of accommodations in the Whistler area, from B&Bs to hotel rooms or condos. They can also provide a customized package with lift tickets and air or ground transportation to and from Vancouver. Other booking agencies, including **Resort Quest** (© **888/898-9208** or 604/932-6699; www.resortquest.com) and **Rainbow Retreats Accommodations Ltd.** (© **866/932-2343** or 604/932-2343; www.rainbowretreats.com), have properties to suit every budget and group size.

Reservations for peak winter periods should be made by September at the latest. To get the best rates on the hotels listed below, check out the hotel's website to see if there are special packages or promotions going on. In some cases, you can nab incredible ski/hotel packages.

IN THE VILLAGE

Delta Whistler Village Suites 🛱🛱 (Kids)   Just minutes from all the major attractions in Whistler, the Delta offers a variety of comfortable, unpretentious, one- and two-bedroom suites with gas fireplaces, balconies, living rooms, fully equipped kitchens, and washer and dryer. They have standard double rooms as well. The beds are firm and comfortable, and the bathrooms are more than adequate. You will not find the fine finishes and furnishings of a luxury hotel, but you will get great service and the use of a large heated pool with three Jacuzzis. Hy's Steak House (reviewed later in this chapter) is in the same building. The hotel welcomes children and has special kids' programs for them.

4308 Main St., Whistler, B.C. V0N 1B4. (C) **888/299-3987** or 604/905-3987. Fax 604/938-6335. www.deltahotels. com. 207 units. May–Dec 15 C$151–C$227 (US$121–US$182) double, C$184–C$381 (US$147–US$305) suite; Dec 16– Apr C$359–C$596 (US$287–US$477) double, C$518–C$810 (US$414–US$648) suite. AE, MC, V. Underground valet parking C$20 (US$15). **Amenities:** Restaurant; heated outdoor pool; health club; spa; indoor and outdoor Jacuzzi; sauna; ski and bike rental; children's programs; concierge; business center; 24-hr. room service; babysitting; laundry service; same-day dry cleaning; executive-level rooms; rooms for those w/limited mobility. *In room:* A/C, TV w/pay movies, wi-fi, kitchen, minibar, coffeemaker, hair dryer, iron, safe, fireplace (in suites), robes, complimentary newspaper.

The Fairmont Chateau Whistler ⟨⟨ The Chateau Whistler in the Upper Village at the foot of Blackcomb Mountain is absolutely enormous, and before the Four Seasons (see below) opened, the Fairmont was considered Whistler's pre-eminent luxury hotel. It tries hard to have the look and feel of an elegant country retreat, utilizing massive wooden beams in the lobby and double-sided stone fireplaces, and every service imaginable, including a major on-site spa, is available. The hotel decor, however, looks oddly dowdy rather than sumptuous, and the overall style is something of a mystery: is it a French chateau or an English manor or both? The rooms and suites are quite large (the Mountain Suites, in fact, are huge), very quiet, and have good-size bathrooms with separate soaker tub and shower. Gold-service guests can have breakfast or relax après-ski in a private lounge. All guests can use the heated outdoor pool and Jacuzzis, which look out over the base of the ski hill. Wildflower is the hotel's fine-dining restaurant, Portobello is a place for more casual fare.

4599 Chateau Blvd., Whistler, B.C. V0N 1B4. (C) **800/257-7544** or 604/938-8000. Fax 604/938-2291. www.fairmont. com. 550 units. Spring–fall C$129–C$409 (US$103–US$327) double, C$269–C$1,189 (US$215–US$951) suite; winter C$249–C$1,099 (US$199–US$879) double, C$409–C$2,699 (US$327–US$2,159) suite. AE, MC, V. Underground valet parking C$28 (US$22). **Amenities:** 2 restaurants; bar; 2 heated outdoor pools; 3 tennis courts; health club; spa; Jacuzzi; children's programs; concierge; tour desk; business center; shopping arcade; 24-hr. room service; in-room massage; babysitting; coin laundry; laundry service; same-day dry cleaning; nonsmoking rooms; concierge-level rooms; rooms for those w/limited mobility. *In room:* A/C, TV w/pay movies, dataport w/high-speed Internet, minibar, coffeemaker, hair dryer, iron, safe, bathrobes.

Four Seasons Resort Whistler ⟨⟨⟨ Whistler's newest resort hotel opened in June, 2004, in the Upper Village, near the Fairmont Chateau, and immediately set a new standard for luxury and service. The guest rooms, suites, and town houses are the largest in Whistler. All feature beautifully detailed wood-trimmed interiors, gas-burning fireplaces, and views of the mountains, forest, valley, pool, or courtyard from private or step-out balconies. The decor is a kind of upscale rustic modern, an updated version of a 1920s grand mountain lodge look. The beds are fitted with Frette sheets. You won't find larger or more luxurious bathrooms anywhere in Whistler; each one has a deep soaker tub, a separate glass-enclosed shower, and two sinks. Every amenity you can think of is available here, including valet ski service. If you want the best, this is it.

4591 Blackcomb Way, Whistler, B.C. V0N 1B4. (C) **888/935-2460** or 604/935-3400. Fax 604/935-3455. www. fourseasons.com. 273 units. Summer–fall C$245–C$445 (US$196–US$356) double, C$590–C$2,400 (US$472– US$1,920) suite; winter C$495–C$665 (US$396–US$532) double, C$970–C$2,800 (US$776–US$2,240) suite. AE, DC, MC, V. Underground valet parking C$28 (US$22). **Amenities:** Restaurant; bar; heated outdoor pool; health club; spa; Jacuzzi; sauna; children's programs; concierge; tour desk; business center; 24-hr. room service; in-room massage; babysitting; laundry service; same-day dry cleaning; nonsmoking rooms; executive-level rooms; rooms for those w/limited mobility. *In room:* A/C, TV w/pay movies, dataport w/high-speed Internet, minibar, coffeemaker, hair dryer, iron, safe, robes, DVD/CD player, fireplace.

Pan Pacific Whistler Mountainside ✿✿✿   The Pan Pacific's furnishings and appointments are really attractive, and the location, overlooking the Whistler gondola and ski slopes, puts this hotel right in the center of the action. You can literally ski out the door and right to the gondola. The look here is contemporary lodge-style, nicely sophisticated, and very comfortable, with lots of warm wood in the rooms. Every suite has a fully equipped kitchenette and balcony. The studio suites with fold-down Murphy beds are the smallest units available, and there are also roomy 1- and 2-bedroom suites. One of the best features is the huge heated outdoor pool and Jacuzzi deck overlooking the snowy slopes. The hotel's Dubh Linn Gate Irish Lounge and Pub is a popular après-ski rendezvous point.

The new **Pan Pacific Whistler Village Centre,** 4299 Blackcomb Way, scheduled to open in 2005, is an all-suites, full-service boutique hotel with fine amenities and a village location. To book, use the same reservations numbers as the Pan Pacific Whistler Mountainside, below.

4320 Sundial Crescent, Whistler, B.C. V0N 1B4. ⓒ 888/905-9995 or 604/905-2999. Fax 604/905-2995. www.panpacific.com. 121 units. Spring–fall C$129–C$709 (US$103–US$567) studio, C$169–C$1,039 (US$135–US$831) suite; winter C$309–C$559 (US$247–US$447) studio, C$459–C$1,069 (US$367–US$855) suite. AE, MC, V. Underground valet parking C$20 (US$16). **Amenities:** Restaurant; pub; heated outdoor pool; fitness center; Jacuzzis; steam room; concierge; limited room service; laundry; rooms for those w/limited mobility. *In room:* A/C, TV, dataport, kitchen, minibar, fridge, coffeemaker, hair dryer, iron, safe.

Summit Lodge & Spa ✿✿   Peace and harmony reign at this classy boutique hotel located just a short stroll from the slopes and featuring a unique, full-service spa. Essence of bergamot and grapefruit wafts through the lobby, hallways, and rooms, all of which are suites with kitchenettes, fireplaces, and balconies. All the units showcase granite countertops, custom-designed cherry wood furnishings, original artwork, and oversized beds with down-filled duvets and pillows. The bathrooms are very nice. There's a complimentary yoga program, and portable Zen waterfalls and tranquillity rock/sand gardens you can borrow, as well as complimentary hot chocolate every evening. The hotel's on-site Taman Sari Royal Heritage Spa features traditional Javanese spa treatments as well as Swedish and French massage, herbal body masks, facials for men and women, aromatherapy foot and hand spa treatments, manicures, and pedicures. You'll be surprised at how tense you were!

4359 Main St., Whistler, B.C. V0N 1B4. ⓒ 888/913-8811 or 604/932-2778. Fax 604/932-2716. www.summitlodge.com. 81 units. C$199–C$420 (US$159–US$336) double, C$420–C$720 (US$336–US$576) suite. AE, MC, V. Underground valet parking C$18 (US$14). **Amenities:** Cafe; heated outdoor pool; full-service spa; Jacuzzi; concierge; ski shuttle; babysitting; wi-fi; laptop computer rental; rooms for those w/limited mobility. *In room:* A/C, TV, Internet, kitchenette, minibar, fridge, coffeemaker, hair dryer, iron, safe, bathrobes, microwave.

The Westin Resort & Spa Whistler ✿✿✿   Though a latecomer to the Whistler hotel scene, the Westin Resort managed to snap up the best piece of property in town and squeezed itself onto the mountainside below the main ski run into the village. The Whistler gondola is within a few hundred yards from its doorstep. Built in 2000, the hotel has the fine finishes and luxury service amenities Westin is known for. It's a very handsome property, with contemporary Western decor that includes lots of granite and cedar finishes. All 419 generously-sized suites include full and very elegant kitchens and most have balconies. Westin's signature *Heavenly Beds* are indeed divine, with down blankets, three layers of heavy cotton sheets, a down duvet, and the best pillows in the biz. To get you going in the morning, little luxuries include a ski valet service and a boot warming service. There's also a full-service spa, Avello, on the premises.

4090 Whistler Way, Whistler, B.C. V0N 1B4. © 888/634-5577 or 604/905-5000. Fax 604/905-5640. www.westin whistler.net. 419 units. Low season C$459 (US$367) junior suite, C$509 (US$407) 1-bedroom suite; high season C$899 (US$719) junior suite, C$1,099 (US$879) 1-bedroom suite. Children 17 and under stay free in parent's room. AE, DC, DISC, MC, V. Underground valet parking C$23 (US$18). **Amenities:** Restaurant; bar; indoor and outdoor pool; outstanding health club; spa; indoor and outdoor Jacuzzi; sauna; children's program; concierge; business center; shopping arcade; salon; 24-hr. room service; babysitting; laundry; dry cleaning. *In room:* TV w/pay movies, dataport w/high-speed Internet, kitchen, coffeemaker, hair dryer, iron, safe, bathrobes.

OUTSIDE THE VILLAGE

Alpine Chalet Whistler 🐾
This elegant newcomer was built to the exacting specifications of a Czech couple who have taken up a second career as innkeepers. The common room is a dream, with comfy chairs and a big fireplace. The adjoining dining area is flooded with natural light from the overhead skylights. Rooms are named after trees and come in essentially two configurations: Standard rooms are comfortable but not huge, and come with either two twins or a king bed, bathrooms with heated floors, and a functional shower/tub combo. Signature rooms are larger, with vaulted ceilings, and the same bed combinations but with Italian linen, as well as a gas fireplace and comfy leather armchairs. Several of these rooms also have pocket balconies, though with views of nothing much. Breakfasts are a top-quality feast.

3012 Alpine Crescent, Whistler, B.C. V0N 1B3. © 800/736-9967 or 604/935-3003. Fax 604/935-3008. www.alpinechalet whistler.com. 8 units. C$129–C$429 (US$103–US$343) double. Rates include full breakfast. MC, V. Free parking. Take Hwy. 99 about 2km (1¼ miles) past Whistler Creekside (before Whistler Village), turn left onto Hillcrest Dr., then a quick right onto Alpine Crescent; the chalet is on the left side about a block away. **Amenities:** Hot tub; small steam room; nonsmoking lodge; drying room; ski and bike storage. *In room:* TV, dataport w/high-speed Internet.

Cedar Springs Bed & Breakfast Lodge (Kids)
This is one of the few Whistler B&Bs that welcomes children. That's not to say it's overrun with rug-rats, but the option is there if you're planning a family skiing holiday. All guests at this charming lodge have a choice of king-, queen-, or twin-size beds in comfortably modern surroundings. The largest room (no. 4) features a fireplace and balcony, though the bathroom is shower only. Room 8 has space for a queen bed and two single futons plus a big soaker tub, while the shower-only Room 7 has space for two queens. The guest sitting room has a fireplace, TV, VCR, and video library, while a sauna and hot tub on the sun deck (overlooking the gardens) fill out the list of amenities. An excellent breakfast is served by the fireplace in the dining room, and guests are welcome to enjoy afternoon tea. All in all, the experience is not as pampered or luxurious as at the Durlacher Hof (see below), but in compensation, it's more casual and homey, and charming owners Joern and Jackie Rohde go out of their way to make guests feel comfortable. A complimentary shuttle service takes you to and from the ski lifts.

8106 Cedar Springs Rd., Whistler, B.C. V0N 1B8. © 800/727-7547 or 604/938-8007. Fax 604/938-8023. www. whistlerbb.com. 8 units, 6 with private bathroom (5 with shower only). Winter C$109–C$205 (US$87–US$164) double; summer C$89–C$129 (US$71–US$103) double. Rates include full breakfast. AE, MC, V. Take Hwy. 99 north toward Pemberton 4km (2½ miles) past Whistler Village; turn left onto Alpine Way, go a block to Rainbow Dr., and turn left; go a block to Camino St. and turn left; the lodge is a block down at the corner of Camino and Cedar Springs Rd. Free parking. **Amenities:** Jacuzzi; sauna; bike rental; game room; courtesy car to ski slopes; nonsmoking lodge. *In room:* Hair dryer, no phone.

Chalet Beau Sejour (Value)
The standout feature of the Beau Sejour is a large common room, with a fireplace and a fine view of Whistler Mountain and valley. The medium-size rooms are comfortable and clean, with two single beds that can be joined together to make a king. There's also a self-contained suite with a queen bed and its

own fireplace and full kitchen. All provide the best value you're likely to find in a Whistler B&B. There's a large hot tub on the back patio for the use of all guests. The B&B is on a public bus route, and located only about a 15-minute walk from the Village via pedestrian paths. Guests are provided with lockers at the base of Whistler for the duration of their stay, plus a shuttle to/from the Chalet on their first/last day (so you can drop off/pick up your ski gear).

7414 Ambassador Crescent, Whistler, B.C. V0N 1B0. ✆ 604/938-4966. Fax 604/938-6296. www.beausejourwhistler. com. 4 units, shower only. Summer C$95–C$105 (US$76–US$84) double; winter C$115–C$165 (US$92–US$132) double. Rates include full breakfast. AE, MC, V. No children under 12. Take Hwy. 99 north toward Pemberton about 2km (1¼ miles) past Whistler Village; turn right onto Nancy Green Dr., go over the creek then 3 blocks to Ambassador Crescent and turn right. Free parking. **Amenities:** Large hot tub; nonsmoking lodge. *In room:* No phone.

Durlacher Hof Pension Inn ★ *(Finds)*   This lovely inn has an Austrian feel and a wonderfully sociable atmosphere. Both are the result of the exceptional care and service shown by owners Peter and Erika Durlacher. The guest rooms in this two-story chalet-style property vary in size from comfortable to spacious and come with goosedown duvets and Ralph Lauren linens on extra long twin- or queen-size beds, private bathrooms (some with jetted tubs) with deluxe toiletries. There are incredible mountain views from the private balconies. Better still is the downstairs lounge, with a welcoming fireplace and complementary après-ski appetizers baked by Erika, who also provides a substantial gourmet breakfast.

7055 Nesters Rd., Whistler, B.C. V0N 1B7. ✆ 877/932-1924 or 604/932-1924. Fax 604/938-1980. www.durlacher hof.com. 8 units. Summer C$99–C$359 (US$79–US$281) double; winter C$129–C$499 (US$103–US$399) double. Extra person C$35 (US$28). Rates include full breakfast and afternoon tea. MC, V. Free parking. Take Hwy. 99 about .8km (½ mile) north of Whistler Village to Nester's Rd.; turn left and the inn is immediately on the right. **Amenities:** Jacuzzi; sauna; laundry service; dry cleaning; nonsmoking lodge; ski and bike storage; 1 room for those w/limited mobility. *In room:* Hair dryer, no phone.

Hostelling International Whistler *(Value)*   One of the few inexpensive spots in Whistler, this hostel also happens to have a great location on the south edge of Alta Lake, with a dining room, deck, and lawn looking over the lake to Whistler Mountain. Inside this pleasant hostel there's a lounge with a wood-burning stove, a common kitchen, a piano, Ping-Pong tables, and a sauna, as well as a drying room for ski gear and storage for bikes, boards, and skis. In the summer, guests have use of a barbecue, canoe, and rowboat. As with all hostels, most rooms and facilities are shared. Book by September at the latest for the winter ski season.

5678 Alta Lake Rd., Whistler, B.C. V0N 1B5. ✆ 604/932-5492. Fax 604/932-4687. www.hihostels.ca. 32 beds in 4- to 8-bed dorms. C$20–C$24 (US$16–US$19) IYHA members, C$24–C$28 (US$19–US$22) nonmembers; annual adult membership C$35 (US$28). MC, V. Free parking. The turnoff for Alta Lake Rd. is before the main village, to the left of Hwy. 99. **Amenities:** Sauna; watersports equipment; bike rental.

CAMPGROUNDS

You can reserve spots for the campgrounds listed here at **Discover Camping** (✆ 800/ 689-9025) or online at **www.discovercamping.ca**. South of Whistler on the Sea-to-Sky corridor is the very popular **Alice Lake Provincial Park.** Free hot showers, flush toilets, and a sani-station are among the available facilities. Hiking trails, picnic areas, sandy beaches, swimming areas, and fishing spots are also on the grounds. Campsites cost C$22 (US$18). Twenty-seven kilometers (17 miles) north of Whistler, the well-maintained campground at **Nairn Falls** on Highway 99 is more adult-oriented, with pit toilets, pumped well water, fire pits and firewood, but no showers. Its proximity to the roaring Green River and the town of Pemberton makes it appealing to many hikers, and the sound of the river is sweeter than any lullaby. Prices for the 88 campsites are C$14 (US$11) per night, on a first-come, first-served basis. The 85 campsites at **Birkenhead Lake Provincial Park,** off Portage Road, Birken, fill up quickly in summer. Boat launches, great fishing, and well-maintained tent and RV sites make the park an angler's paradise and one of the province's top 10 camping destinations. Facilities include fire pits, firewood, pumped well water, and pit toilets. Campsites are C$14 (US$11) per night. Please note that many provincial parks now charge a day-use parking fee of C$3 to C$5 (US$2.40–US$4) per vehicle; you may also encounter a C$2 (US$1.60) charge for using the sani-station.

WHERE TO DINE

Whistler literally overflows with dining choices. A stroll through the Village will take you past 25 or 30 restaurants. Some serve overpriced resort food but a number of them stand out for either atmosphere or the quality of their meals. For those willing to spend a bit more, Whistler has some outstanding fine dining options. See below for detailed reviews.

On the Village Square, **Ingrid's Village Cafe** (*C* **604/932-7000**), open daily 7:30am to 6pm, is a local favorite for quality and price. A large bowl of Ingrid's daily soup costs C$4.50 (US$3.60), a veggie burger, C$6.50 (US$5.20). Right across from Ingrid's, **Citta Bistro** (*C* **604/932-4177**), is a favorite dining and nightspot, open daily 9am to 1am. It serves thin-crust pizzas, gourmet burgers, and various appetizers. Besides having great food and good prices (main courses are C$7–C$15/US$5.60–US$12), it has umbrella tables on the terrace, the best people-watching corner in town.

For good beer and stick-to-your-ribs grub, try the family-friendly **Whistler Brewhouse,** 4355 Blackcomb Way (*C* **604/905-2739;** www.drinkfreshbeer.com), located just over the creek in Upper Village. It's open Sunday through Thursday from 11:30am to midnight and Friday and Saturday from 11:30am to 1am. Main courses in the less-expensive pub run from C$10 to C$18 (US$8–US$14), in the restaurant, where prime rib is a featured specialty, prices are C$18 to C$38 (US$14 to US$30). There's a special kids' menu, too. Equally fun indoor dining can be had at the **Dubh Linn Gate Irish Lounge/Pub** (*C* **604/905-4047**) in the Pan Pacific hotel. The Gate offers solid pub grub and the atmosphere of the Emerald Isle. Open Monday through Saturday 7am to 1am, Sundays 7am to midnight; main courses cost C$11 to C$18 (US$9–US$14).

Araxi ✦✦✦ PACIFIC NORTHWEST   The haute spot of Whistler cuisine, award-winning Araxi was voted "2005 Best Restaurant in Whistler" by Vancouver Magazine, an award it has won for 16 consecutive years. The menu is nominally Italian but with a Pacific Northwest bent that emphasizes fresh regional products. The seafood is extraordinary, with appetizers such as fresh-shucked B.C. oysters, lightly breaded B.C. albacore tuna, and a seafood tower stacked two tiers high with fresh-shucked oysters, Pacific prawns, smoked wild salmon, clams, mussels, jellyfish salad, and Dungeness crab rolls. For meat eaters, there are appetizers such as veal carpaccio or a superlative foie gras parfait that melts in the mouth. When it comes to main courses, Araxi offers a host of wonderful possibilities: a superb garlic-crusted halibut, a confit of Canadian lamb, sautéed calf's liver, roasted B.C. pork loin, risotto with heirloom tomatoes, or a Canadian Kobe rib-eye steak. Araxi's wine list inspires awe: 27 pages long, 12,000 bottles strong, with numerous exceptional vintages (many of them from B.C.) and—for those without unlimited wealth—one of the best selections of wines by the glass around. Dinner is served in a warm, woody, beautifully designed space that looks out on the main village street.

4222 Village Sq. ℂ 604/932-4540. www.araxi.com. Reservations recommended. Main courses C$20–C$40 (US$16–US$32). AE, MC, V. Mid-May to Oct daily 11am–11pm; during ski season daily 5–10pm.

Bearfoot Bistro 🏶🏶🏶 FRENCH In less than a decade this restaurant has gone from a fairly simple French bistro to one of the most lauded restaurants in Canada. The kitchen procures the finest wild and cultivated products and almost everything is prepared "a la minute," and in such a manner as to emphasize the quality of the ingredients without over-complication. Diners choose from a variety of tasting menus which change daily. For an appetizer you might choose honey-tamari-glazed quail or cauliflower and porcini cream soup with Dungeness crab and truffle oil. Your main course might be white cornmeal-crusted wild turbot with Dungeness crab and leek ravioli or wild Arctic caribou loin with potato chanterelle mushroom terrine. This is a place where you need to allot at least 2 hours to dine; with the Menu Gastronomique it might be more like 3 or 4. The wine list at Bearfoot Bistro is outstanding, and a sommelier can help you with wine pairings.

4121 Village Green. ℂ 604/932-3433. www.bearfootbistro.com. Reservations essential. Tasting menus C$90–C$225 (US$72–US$180). AE, MC, V. Daily 5–10pm.

Caramba! Restaurant MEDITERRANEAN The room is bright, the kitchen open, and the smells wafting out hint tantalizingly of fennel, artichoke, and pasta. Caramba! is casual dining, but its Mediterranean-influenced menu offers fresh ingredients, prepared with pizzazz. Try the pasta, free-range chicken, or roasted pork loin. If you're into sharing, order a pizza or two; a plate of grilled calamari; some hot spinach, cheese, and artichoke-and-shallot dip; and a plate of sliced prosciutto and bullfighter's toast (savory toasted Spanish bread with herbs).

12–4314 Main St., Town Plaza. ℂ 604/938-1879. Main courses C$11–C$18 (US$9–US$14). AE, MC, V. Daily 11:30am–10:30pm.

Chef Bernard's Chow Thyme Bistro and B.B.K.'s Pub 🏶 *Finds* *Kids* CASUAL/ PACIFIC NORTHWEST Bernard Casavant was the executive sous chef at the Fairmont Chateau until he left to start his own special little place, which quickly became a favorite with locals and a dream come true for visitors who want to eat well on a limited budget. The bistro is small and the lines can be long but the fresh, delicious food is worth any wait you may have. The bistro is a great spot for breakfast, lunch, or dinner, serving a menu that ranges from free-range egg omelets and French toast made with Tuscan bread to seared wild salmon, grilled steak salad, duck leg confit, braised beef ribs, and signature carrot and brie soup. There's a special kids' menu with grilled cheese sandwiches and pasta. At night, a few doors down, Chef Bernard serves dinner in his nonsmoking pub. The menu is the same in both bistro and pub.

4573 Chateau Blvd., Upper Village. ℂ 604/932-9795. Main courses C$11–C$23 (US$9–US$18). AE, DC, MC, V. Daily 8am–4pm and 6–10pm.

Hy's Steakhouse 🏶 NORTH AMERICAN This is the place to go if you're hungering for a big slab of roast beef with garlic mashed potatoes or a juicy steak. Hy's is famous for the quality of its beef, and it's the beef you should go for. There are other things on the menu, including seafood and even a vegetarian dish of grilled vegetables, but it's the meat that keeps 'em coming back.

4308 Main St., in the same building as Delta Whistler Village Suites Hotel. ⓒ **604/905-5555.** Main courses C$30–C$40 (US$24–US$32). AE, DC, MC, V. Daily 5–10pm (opens 5:30pm in summer).

Quattro 𝒢𝒢 ITALIAN   Quattro is in the Village, but it's a little off the beaten track. The room is warm and slightly quirky. The food is fairly simple (fresh ingredients in uncomplicated seasonings), but extremely well done. The three-course menu option (soup/salad, appetizer, main) offers fine dining at a very reasonable price (C$35/US$28 per person). Though menus change regularly, typical appetizers might include fresh minestrone with pesto or the signature grilled fresh mozzarella wrapped in prosciutto ham and radicchio in a cherry vinaigrette. Main courses include a variety of great pastas (if you can't decide, order the *combinazione* and sample all five), as well as daily specials such as saltimbocca (veal scaloppine with sage and prosciutto in a butter sauce). The wine list is extraordinary, with a few token vintages from B.C. and California, but a heart and soul residing in Italy.

4319 Main St. ⓒ **604/905-4844.** www.quattrorestaurants.com. Reservations recommended. Main courses C$12–C$35 (US$10–US$28). AE, MC, V. Daily 5:30–11pm. Closed Mon–Tues mid-Apr–June.

Rimrock Cafe and Oyster Bar 𝒢𝒢 SEAFOOD   Upstairs in a long narrow room with a high ceiling and a great stone fireplace at one end, Rimrock is like a Viking mead hall of old. It's not the atmosphere, however, that draws folks in; it's the food. The first order of business should be a plate of oysters. The chef serves them up half a dozen ways, from raw with champagne to cooked in hell (broiled with fresh chiles). The signature Rimrock oyster is broiled with béchamel sauce and smoked salmon. Entrees are seafood-oriented. Look for wild sockeye salmon with lobster mashed potatoes, and sea bass pan-fried in an almond-ginger crust. There's also a crispy duck breast with porcini cream, pancetta, and portobello mushrooms. The accompanying wine list has a number of fine vintages from B.C., California, New Zealand, and Australia.

2117 Whistler Rd. ⓒ **877/932-5589** or 604/932-5565. www.rimrockwhistler.com. Reservations recommended. Main courses C$24–C$40 (US$19–US$32). AE, MC, V. Daily 6–11:30pm, but call ahead in the low season (May–June and Sept–Nov) as hours may change.

THE OUTDOORS: WHISTLER'S RAISON D'ETRE

Whistler/Blackcomb Mountain 𝒢𝒢𝒢   Now that both mountain resorts are jointly operated by Intrawest, your pass gives you access to both ski areas. Locals have their preferences, but the truth is that both offer great skiing; Whistler is generally considered better for beginners and middle-range skiers, while steeper Blackcomb is more geared to the experienced. **Whistler Mountain** has 1,502m (4,928 ft.) of vertical and over 100 marked runs that are serviced by a high-speed gondola and eight high-speed chairlifts, plus four other lifts and tows. Helicopter service from the top of the mountain makes another 100-plus runs on nearby glaciers accessible. There are cafeterias and gift shops on the peak as well as a restaurant. **Blackcomb Mountain** has 1,584m (5,197 ft.) of vertical and over 100 marked runs that are serviced by nine high-speed chairlifts, plus three other lifts and tows. The cafeteria, restaurant, and gift shop aren't far from the peak. Both mountains also have bowls and glade skiing, with Blackcomb Mountain offering glacier skiing well into August.

4545 Blackcomb Way, Whistler, B.C. V0N 1B4. ⓒ **604/932-3434;** snow report 604/687-7507 in Vancouver, 604/932-4211 in Whistler. www.whistler-blackcomb.com. Winter lift tickets C$45–C$72 (US$36–US$58) adults, C$36–C$62 (US$29–US$50) youths 13–18 and seniors, C$22–C$38 (US$18–US$30) children 7–12 per day for both mountains, free for children 6 and under. A variety of multiday passes are also available. Lifts open daily 8:30am–3:30pm (until 4:30pm mid-Mar until end of season, depending on weather and conditions).

⸤Moments⸥ Après Ski

"Après ski" refers to that delicious hour after a hard day on the slopes, when you sit back with a cold or hot drink, nurse the sore spots in your muscles, and savor the glow that comes from a day well skied. On the Whistler side, the many loud and kicky beer bars will be in your face the moment your skis cease to schuss. On the Blackcomb side, **Merlin's Bar** (✆ 604/938-7735) is almost as obvious and equally young and lubricated. For those with just a tad more sophistication, however, there's something far better hidden away inside the Fairmont Chateau Whistler: the **Mallard Bar** ⚜ (✆ 604/938-8000), one of the most civilized après-ski bars on earth.

DIFFERENT SLOPES FOR DIFFERENT FOLKS: THE LOWDOWN ON SKIING IN WHISTLER

Whistler/Blackcomb mountain offers **ski lessons** and **ski guides** for all levels and interests. (For skiers looking to try snowboarding, a rental package and a half-day lesson are particularly attractive options.) Phone **Guest Relations** at ✆ 604/932-3434 for details.

You can **rent ski and snowboard gear** at the base of both Whistler and Blackcomb Villages, just prior to purchasing your lift pass. No appointment is necessary (or accepted) but the system is first-come, first-served. Arrive at 8am and you'll be on the gondola by 8:15. Arrive at 8:30am, and you won't be up until 9:15 at the earliest.

Summit Ski (✆ 604/932-6225; www.summitsport.com), at various locations, including the Delta Whistler Resort and Market Pavilion, rents high performance and regular skis, snowboards, telemark and cross-country skis, and snowshoes.

BACKCOUNTRY SKIING   The **Spearhead Traverse,** which starts at Whistler and finishes at Blackcomb, is a well-marked backcountry route that has become extremely popular in the past few years.

Garibaldi Provincial Park (✆ 604/898-3678) maintains marked backcountry trails at **Diamond Head, Singing Pass,** and **Cheakamus Lake.** These are ungroomed and unpatrolled rugged trails, and you have to be self-reliant—you should be at least an intermediate skier, bring appropriate clothing and avalanche gear, and know how to use it. There are several access points along Highway 99 between Squamish and Whistler. If you're not sure of yourself off-*piste,* hire a guide. The **Whistler Alpine Guides Bureau** (✆ 604/938-9242; www.whistlerguides.com) can hook you up with a licensed alpine guide for one or multiple days in the backcountry. **Whistler Cross Country Ski and Hike** (✆ 888/771-2382; www.whistlerski-hike.com) is another local guiding company.

CROSS-COUNTRY SKIING   Well-marked, fully groomed cross-country trails run throughout the area. The 30km (19 miles) of easy-to-very-difficult marked trails at **Lost Lake** start a block away from the Blackcomb Mountain parking lot. They're groomed for track skiing and ski-skating. They're also patrolled. Passes are C$10 (US$8) per day; a 1-hour cross-country lesson runs about C$45 (US$36) and can be booked at the same station where you buy your trail pass. For more information, check the website www.crosscountryconnection.bc.ca. The **Valley Trail System** in the village becomes a well-marked cross-country ski trail during winter.

HELI-SKIING   For intermediate and advanced skiers who can't get enough fresh powder or vertical on the regular slopes, there's always heli-skiing, where a helicopter whisks you and fellow skiers and boarders up to the pristine powder. **Whistler Heli-Skiing** (© 888/847-7669 or 604/932-4105; www.whistlerheliskiing.com) is a well-established operator. A three-run day, with 2,400 to 3,000m (8,000–10,000 ft.) of vertical helicopter lift, costs C$640 (US$512) per person. A four-run day for expert skiers and riders only, with 3,000 to 3,600m (10,000–12,000 ft.) of vertical helicopter lift, costs C$720 (US$576) per person, including a guide and lunch.

OTHER WINTER PURSUITS

SLEIGHING & DOG-SLEDDING   From mid-December through March, **Cougar Mountain Adventures** (© 888/297-2222; www.cougarmountain.ca) and **Whistler-Blackcomb** (© 888/403-4727; www.whistler-blackcomb.com) offer dog-sled rides. A musher and his team of Inuit sled dogs will take you for a backcountry dogsled tour at C$140 (US$112) per person, with a minimum of two people.

For a different kind of sleigh ride—with horses—contact **Blackcomb Horsedrawn Sleigh Rides,** 103–4338 Main St. (© 604/932-7631; www.blackcombsleighrides.com). In winter, tours go out every evening and cost C$45 (US$36) for adults and C$25 (US$20) for children under 12. The tour will take you up past the ski trails and into a wooded trail with a magnificent view of the lights of Whistler Village. A stop at a cabin for a mug of hot chocolate will warm you up for your ride home. There are also daylight sleigh rides.

SNOWMOBILING & ATVs   Year-round combination ATV and snowmobile tours of the Whistler Mountain trails are offered by **Canadian Snowmobile Adventures Ltd.,** Carleton Lodge, 4290 Mountain Sq., Whistler Village (© 604/938-1616; www.canadiansnowmobile.com). All tours are weather- and snow conditions–permitting. Exploring the Fitzsimmons Creek watershed, a 2-hour tour, costs C$119 (US$95) for a driver and C$89 (US$71) for a passenger. Drivers on both the snowmobile and ATV must have a valid driver's license. On Blackcomb Mountain, Snowmobile Adventures offers a popular 2-hour Mountain Safari that costs C$159 (US$127) for a driver and C$119 (US$95) for a passenger.

Blackcomb Snowmobile (© 604/932-8484; www.blackcombsnowmobile.com) offers a variety of guided snowmobile tours, including family tours on Blackcomb Mountain. A 2-hour tour costs C$119 (US$95) for one adult or C$178 (US$142) for two adults, and half-price for children.

SNOWSHOEING   Snowshoeing is the world's easiest form of snow-comotion; it requires none of the training and motor skills of skiing or boarding. You can wear your own shoes or boots, provided they're warm and waterproof, strap on your snowshoes, and off you go! Rentals are available at the ski-and-board rental companies listed above.

Outdoor Adventures@Whistler (© 604/932-0647; www.adventureswhistler.com), has guided snowshoe tours starting at C$69 (US$55) for 1½ hours to an evening snowshoe tour along the shores of Green Lake followed by a fondue dinner for C$109 (US$87) adults, C$49 ($39) for children under 12. **Cougar Mountain Adventures** (© 888/297-2222; www.cougarmountain.ca) has guided tours to the Cougar Mountain area at C$49 (US$39) for 2 hours, or try a snowshoe/snowmobile combination—a 3-hour trip into the backcountry for C$119 (US$95) per person, with a minimum of two people.

SUMMER PURSUITS

CANOEING & KAYAKING   The 3-hour River of Golden Dreams Kayak & Canoe Tour is a great way for novices, intermediates, and experts to get acquainted with a beautiful stretch of slow-moving glacial water running between Green Lake and Alta Lake behind the village of Whistler. Contact the **Whistler Activity and Information Centre** (© **877/991-9988**) for information. Packages begin at C$35 (US$28) per person, unguided, and include all gear and return transportation to the village center. The Whistler Activity and Information Centre also offers lessons and clinics as well as sailboat and windsurfing rentals.

FISHING   Spring runs of steelhead, rainbow trout, and Dolly Varden char; summer runs of cutthroat and salmon; and fall runs of coho salmon attract anglers from around the world to the area's many glacier-fed lakes and rivers and to **Birkenhead Lake Provincial Park,** 67km (42 miles) north of Pemberton.

   Whistler River Adventures (© **888/932-3532** or 604/932-3532; www.whistler river.com), offers half- and full-day catch-and-release fishing trips in the surrounding glacial rivers. Rates are C$150 to C$210 (US$120–US$168) per person, based on two people, which includes all fishing gear, round-trip transport to/from the Whistler Village Bus Loop, and a snack or lunch.

GOLFING   Robert Trent Jones, Jr.'s, **Chateau Whistler Golf Club,** at the base of Blackcomb Mountain (© **604/938-2092,** or pro shop 604/938-2095; www.whistler blackcomb.com), is an 18-hole, par-72 course. With an elevation gain of more than 120m (394 ft.), this course traverses mountain ledges and crosses cascading creeks. Midcourse, there's a panoramic view of the Coast Mountains. Greens fees range from C$125 to C$225 (US$100–US$180), which includes power-cart rental.

   A multiple-award-winning golf course, **Nicklaus North at Whistler** (© **604/938-9898;** www.golfwhistler.com) is a 5-minute drive north of the village on the shores of Green Lake. The par-71 course's mountain views are spectacular. It's only the second Canadian course designed by Nicklaus, and, of all the courses he's designed worldwide, the only one to bear his name. Greens fees are C$115 to C$210 (US$92–US$168).

   Whistler Golf Club (© **800/376-1777** or 604/932-4544; www.golfwhistler.com), designed by Arnold Palmer, features nine lakes, two creeks, and magnificent vistas. Recently having undergone a C$2-million renovation, this 18-hole, par-72 course offers a driving range, putting green, sand bunker, and pitching area. Greens fees are C$79 to C$159 (US$63–US$127).

   A-1 Last Minute Golf Hotline (© **800/684-6344** or 604/878-1833) can arrange a next-day tee time at Whistler golf courses and elsewhere in B.C. at over 30 courses. Savings can be as much as 40% on next-day, last-minute tee times. No membership is necessary. Call between 3 and 9pm for the next day or before noon for the same day. The hotline also arranges advanced bookings, as much as a year ahead, as well as group bookings.

HIKING   There are numerous easy hiking trails in and around Whistler. Besides taking a lift up to Whistler and Blackcomb mountains' high mountain trails (you can somewhat easily hike to the foot of a glacier) during summer, you have a number of other choices.

   Lost Lake Trail starts at the northern end of the Day Skier Parking Lot at Blackcomb Mountain. The lake is less than a mile from the entry. The 30km (19 miles) of marked trails that wind around creeks, beaver dams, blueberry patches, and lush cedar groves are ideal for biking, cross-country skiing, or just strolling and picnicking. The **Valley Trail System** is a well-marked paved trail that connects parts of Whistler. The trail starts on the west side of Highway 99 adjacent to the Whistler Golf Course and winds through quiet residential areas as well as golf courses and parks.

Garibaldi Provincial Park's **Singing Pass Trail** is a 4-hour hike of moderate difficulty. The fun way is to take the Whistler Mountain gondola to the top and walk down the well-marked path that ends in the village on an access road. Winding down from above the tree line, the trail takes you through stunted alpine forest into Fitzsimmons Valley. There are several access points into the park along Highway 99 between Squamish and Whistler.

Nairn Falls Provincial Park 𝄞𝄞 is about 33km (20 miles) north of Whistler on Highway 99. This provincial park features a mile-long trail that leads you to a stupendous view of the glacial Green River as it plunges 59m (194 ft.) over a rocky cliff into a narrow gorge on its way downstream. There's also an incredible view of Mount Currie peeking over the treetops.

On Highway 99 north of Mount Currie, **Joffre Lakes Provincial Park** has an intermediate-level hike that leads past several brilliant blue glacial lakes up to the very foot of a glacier. The **Ancient Cedars** area of Cougar Mountain is an awe-inspiring grove of towering cedars and Douglas firs. (Some of the trees are over 1,000 years old and measure 3m/9¾ ft. in diameter.)

Guided nature hikes provide an excellent opportunity to learn more about the ecology of the region, whether it's up in the alpine meadows or among the trees lower down. Black bear viewing trips are increasingly popular and are a safe way to get a close-up look at these magnificent animals. Contact the **Whistler Activity and Information Centre** (© 877/991-9988 or 604/938-2769; www.tourismwhistler.com) for guided hikes and interpretive tours. Two- to three-hour nature walks start at C$35 (US$28).

HORSEBACK RIDING   Whistler River Adventures (© 888/932-3532 or 604/ 932-3532; www.whistlerriver.com) offers 2-hour trail rides along the Green River, through the forest, and across the Pemberton Valley from its 4-hectare (10-acre) riverside facility in nearby Pemberton, a 35-minute drive north of Whistler. The 2-hour ride costs C$60 (US$48); longer rides can be arranged.

JET BOATING   Whistler River Adventures, Whistler Mountain Village Gondola Base (© 888/932-3532 or 604/932-3532; www.whistlerriver.com), takes guests up the Green River just below Nairn Falls, where moose, deer, and bear sightings are common in the canyon. Later in the season, tours go up the Lillooet River past ancient petroglyphs, fishing sites, and the tiny Native village of Skookumchuk. Tours range from C$120 to C$145 (US$96 to US$116).

MOUNTAIN BIKING   There's a rumor afloat that within 5 years mountain biking at Whistler will be bigger than skiing. It's certainly a recreational sport that's taken off big time, thanks in large part to **Whistler Mountain Bike Park** 𝄞𝄞𝄞 (© 866/218-9688; www.whistlerblackcomb.com/bike), which offers some of the best mountain-biking trails, skill centers, and jump parks in the world. When the snow melts and skiing is over, the slope is reconfigured for biking—there are 48km (30 miles) of marked trails, open daily mid-May to mid-October from 10am to 5pm (until 8pm Sat; additional late openings June and July). There are trails for almost all ages and experience levels. Single-day ticket prices with gondola are C$41 (US$33) for adults, C$36 (US$29) for youths 13–18 and seniors, and C$21 (US$17) for children 10 to 12.

Note: Children 12 and under are not permitted in the bike park unless accompanied by parents.

You can rent the best mountain bikes (C$69/US$55 for 4 hours) and body armor (C$20/US$16) right next to the bike park.

Cross Country Connection (© 604/905-0071; www.crosscountryconnection. bc.ca) offers bike rentals and guided tours for levels from beginner to expert.

RAFTING   Whistler River Adventures (© 888/932-3532 or 604/932-3532; www. whistlerriver.com) offers 2-hour, 4-hour, and full-day round-trip rafting runs down the Green, Birkenhead, Elaho, and Squamish rivers. They include equipment and ground transportation for C$69 to C$109 (US$55–US$87) for a 2- to 4-hour tour or C$154 (US$123) for a full day on the Elaho and Squamish rivers. Children and youths are welcome as long as they're able to hold on by themselves and weigh a minimum of 90 pounds. Novices are taken to the Green River, where small rapids and snowcapped mountain views highlight a half-day trip. Experts are transported to the Elaho River or Squamish River for full-day, Class IV excitement on runs with names like Aitons Alley and Steamroller. May through August, trips depart daily. The full-day trip includes a salmon barbecue lunch.

For first-timers, **Wedge Rafting,** Carleton Lodge, Whistler Village (© 604/932-7171; www.wedgerafting.com), offers a Green River, Birkenhead River, and Cheaka-mus River tour. For the Green River trip, about 2½ hours, the shuttle picks up rafters in Whistler and takes them to the wilderness launch area for briefing and equipping. It's an exciting hour or more on the icy rapids. After the run, rafters can relax at the outfitter's log lodge with a snack and soda before being shuttled back into town. Tours cost C$69 (US$55), with up to three daily departures. The Birkenhead River tour takes about 4 hours and costs C$87 (US$70). Discounts are available for youths 10 to 16; however, they must weigh at least 90 pounds.

Located in the gorgeous Squamish valley, **Sun Wolf Outdoor Centre** (© 877/806-8046; www.sunwolf.net) has summer rafting trips on the Elaho River and winter eagle viewing trips on the Cheakamus and Squamish rivers. Full-day summer rafting trips cost C$119 (US$95) per person, and the winter eagle trips cost C$99 (US$79) per person.

ROCK CLIMBING   The Great Wall (4340 Sundial Crescent; © 604/905-7625; www.greatwallclimbing.com) offers a year-round indoor climbing center and summer outdoor climbing wall, as well as guided climbs and instruction. The indoor center is in the lower level of the Sundial Boutique Hotel at the base of Whistler. The outdoor center is in the Blackcomb Upper Village near the Wizard Chair. A day-pass to the indoor wall is C$16 (US$13). On the outdoor wall, it's C$5 (US$4) per climb.

TENNIS   The Whistler Racquet & Golf Resort, 4500 Northland Blvd. (© 604/932-1991; www.whistlertennis.com), has three covered courts, seven outdoor courts, and a practice cage, all open to drop-in visitors. Indoor courts are C$32 (US$24) per hour and outdoor courts C$16 (US$12) per hour. Adult and junior tennis camps are offered in summer. Camp prices run C$295 to C$315 (US$236–US$252) for a 3-day adult camp. Kids' camps cost C$46 (US$37) per day drop-in, or C$149 (US$119) for a 3-day camp. Book early, as these camps fill up very quickly.

The **Mountain Spa & Tennis Club,** Delta Whistler Resort, Whistler Village (© 604/938-2044), and the **Chateau Whistler Resort,** Fairmont Chateau Whistler Hotel, Upper Village (© 604/938-8000), also offer courts to drop-in players. Prices

Zipping with Ziptrek

The Whistler/Blackcomb area is full of recreational opportunities. One of the newest and most exciting is offered by **Ziptrek Ecotours** (© 604/935-0001; www.ziptrek.com). On these guided 2½ hour tours you're taken through Whistler's ancient forests on a network of five zipline rides joined by canopy bridges, boardwalks, and trails. Along the way you're harnessed into a diaper-like safety contraption that lets you whiz out on cables suspended over deep river valleys. It sounds hair-raising, but it's completely safe for all ages and abilities, and you'll never forget the experience. Individual Ziptrekkers must be over 5 years old and weigh between 65 and 275 pounds; children under 5 and under 65 pounds can ride tandem with one of the guides. The sales desk is located in the Carleton Lodge right across from the Whistler Village Gondolas. The tour price is C$98 (US$78) for adults, C$78 (US$62) for seniors over 65 and children 14 and under.

run about C$20 (US$16) per hour per court; racquet rentals are available for C$5 (US$4) per hour.

There are **free public courts** (© 604/935-7529) at Myrtle Public School, Alpha Lake Park, Meadow Park, Millar's Pond, Brio, Blackcomb Benchlands, White Gold, and Emerald Park.

URBAN PURSUITS

A MUSEUM   To learn more about Whistler's heritage, flora, and fauna, visit the **Whistler Museum & Archives Society,** 4329 Main St., off Northlands Boulevard (© 604/932-2019; www.whistlermuseum.com). The museum exhibits reveal the life and culture of the Native Indian tribes that have lived in the lush Whistler and Pemberton valleys for thousands of years. There are also re-creations of the village's early settlement by British immigrants during the late 1800s and early 1900s. The museum is open daily from 10am to 4pm in July and August, and Thursday through Sunday 10am to 4pm September through June (Thurs until 8pm year-round). Admission is C$5 (US$4) for adults, C$4 (US$3.20 for seniors and students, C$3 (US$2.40) ages 7 to 18, and free for children 6 and under.

For **performing arts,** from classical to choral to folk and blues, check out the newly opened **Maurice Young Millennium Place (My Place)** (© 604/935-8414; www.whistlermillenniumpl.com).

SHOPPING   The **Whistler Marketplace** (in the center of Whistler Village) and the area surrounding the **Blackcomb Mountain lift** brim with clothing, jewelry, crafts, specialty, gift, and equipment shops that are generally open daily from 10am to 6pm. **Horstman Trading Company** (© 604/938-7725), beside the Fairmont Chateau Whistler at the base of Blackcomb, carries men's and women's casual wear, from swimwear and footwear to polar-fleece vests and nylon jacket shells. **Escape Route** (© 604/938-3228), at Whistler Marketplace and Crystal Lodge, has a great line of outdoor clothing and equipment.

For some of the finer things in life, visit the **Whistler Village Art Gallery** (© 604/938-3001) and **Adele Campbell Gallery** (© 604/938-0887). Their collections include fine art, sculpture, and glass. **Keir Fine Jewelry,** Village Gate House (© 604/ 932-2944), sells Italian gold, Swiss watches, and Canadian handmade jewelry. For a list and map of all the galleries in town, as well as information on events, contact the **Whistler Community Arts Council** (© 604/935-8419; www.whistlerartscouncil.com).

SPAS   That resort lifestyle can be hard on the body, so why not try some relaxation at one of Whistler's outstanding spas? The **Taman Sari Royal Heritage Spa** (© 888/ 913-8811; www.summitlodge.com/sumservices/spa.shtml), one of the newest in town, offers an unusual array of Javanese and European spa treatments. **Avello** (© 877/935-3444; www.whistlerspa.com), the spa in the Westin, has a variety of sig-nature treatments, including hot rock massage, Chinese massage, Satago massage, and acupuncture. The **Spa at Chateau Whistler Resort** (© 604/938-2086), open daily 8am to 9pm, provides massage therapy, aromatherapy, skin care, body wraps, steam baths, and makeup.

Whistler Body Wrap, 210 St. Andrews House (© 604/932-4710; www.whistler bodywrap.com), next to the Keg in the Village, can nurture you with an array of serv-ices, such as shiatsu massage, facials, pedicures or manicures, waxings, sun beds, and aromatherapy. If something didn't quite go right on the slopes or on the trails, **Whistler Physiotherapy** specializes in sports therapy. The therapists at this clinic treat many professional athletes and have experience with ski, board, and hiking injuries. There are two locations: 339–4370 Lorimer Rd., at Marketplace (© 604/932-4001; www.whistlerphysio.com), and 202–2011 Innsbruck Dr., next to Boston Pizza in Creekside (© 604/938-9001).

ESPECIALLY FOR KIDS

Near the base of the mountains, Whistler Village and the Upper Village sponsor daily activities tailor-made for active kids of all ages. There are mountain bike races; an in-line skating park; trapeze, trampoline, and wall-climbing lessons; summer skiing; snowboarding; snowshoeing; and bungee jumping. There's even a first-run multiplex movie theater.

Based at Blackcomb Mountain, the **Dave Murray Summer Ski and Snowboard Camp** (© 604/932-5765; www.skiandsnowboard.com) is North America's longest-running summer ski camp. Junior programs cost C$1,995 (US$1,596) for 8 days or C$1,225 (US$980) for a 5-day package from mid-June to mid-July. The packages include food, lodging (day-camp packages without the hotel are also available), and lift passes, as well as tennis, trapeze, and mountain-biking options. Mornings and early afternoons are spent skiing, boarding, or free-riding on the excellent terrain parks and half-pipes. This ski-and-board camp accommodates a range of abilities from beginners to champion-level skiers and riders; the age group is 10 to 18 years. In the afternoons, the campers can choose from a wide range of other outdoor activities. The comprehensive instruction and adult supervision at this activity-oriented camp are excellent.

WHISTLER AFTER DARK

For a town of just 10,000, Whistler has a pretty good nightlife scene. Of course, it *is* considered the pre-eminent ski resort in North America, and attracts millions of year-round visitors. Bands touring through Vancouver regularly make the trip up the Sea-to-Sky Highway; some even make Whistler their Canadian debut. Concert listings can be found in the *Pique,* a free local paper available at cafes and food stores.

Tommy Africa's (© 604/932-6090), beneath the Pharmasave at the entrance to the Main Village, and the dark and cavernous **Maxx Fish** (© 604/932-1904), in the Village Square below the Amsterdam Cafe, cater to the 18- to-22-year-old crowd: lots of beat and not much light. The crowd at **Garfinkel's** (© 604/932-2323), at the entrance to Village North, is similar, though the cut-off age can reach as high as 27. The **Boot Pub** (© 604/932-3338), Nancy Green Drive, just off Highway 99, advertises itself as Whistler's living room and more than lives up to its billing: Throngs of young Australian ski-lift operators cram the room, bouncing to the band or deejay and spilling draft beer all over the floor. **Buffalo Bills** (© 604/932-6613), across from the Whistler Gondola, and the **Savage Beagle** (© 604/938-3337), in the Village, cater to the 30-something crowd. Bills is bigger, with a pool table and video ski machine, a smallish dance floor, and music straight from the 1980s. The Beagle has a fabulous selection of beer and bar drinks, with a pleasant little pub upstairs and a house-oriented dance floor below.

If all you want to do is savor a beer and swap ski stories, try the **Whistler Brew-House** (© 604/905-2739) in the Upper Village or the fun and very Irish **Dubh Linn Gate Irish Lounge/Pub** (© 604/905-4047) in the Pan Pacific Whistler Mountainside Hotel.

2 Ucluelet, Tofino & Pacific Rim National Park Reserve of Canada (Long Beach Section) ★★★

The West Coast of Vancouver Island is a magnificent area of old-growth forests, stunning fjords (called "sounds" in local parlance), rocky coastline, and long sandy beaches. And though **Pacific Rim National Park Reserve of Canada** ★★★ was established in 1971 as Canada's first marine park, it wasn't until 1991 that it really exploded into the consciousness of people outside the area. That was when thousands of environmentalists from across the province and around the world gathered to protest the clear-cutting of old-growth forests on Meares Island in Clayoquot Sound. When footage of the protests ran on the evening news, people who saw the unspoiled beauty of this coastal landscape for the first time were moved to come experience it firsthand. Tourism in the area has never looked back, and because of its importance as a pristine marine environment, Clayoquot Sound was designated a UNESCO Marine Biosphere Reserve in 2000.

The three main areas to visit are **Ucluelet, Tofino,** and the **Long Beach section** of Pacific Rim National Park. Tofino and Ucluelet are small towns on the northern and southern edges of a peninsula about halfway up the western shore of Vancouver Island, with the Long Beach section of the park between them. From Victoria, the trip by car—along a highway considered one of the top three scenic drives in Canada—takes about 4½ hours and includes such highlights as massive old-growth trees (Cathedral Grove), an enormous mountain lake (Kennedy Lake), snow-covered peaks, and stretches of oceanside highway.

Surfing has become a booming business in this part of the world, but most people come to enjoy the spectacular coastal scenery and to enjoy nature. Nesting bald eagles and migrating gray whales are a common but always thrilling sight.

The park as a whole receives about 1 million visitors a year, most of them in June, July, and August. In those high season summer months, traffic between Ucluelet and Tofino becomes an all-day jam, beaches are crammed with international vacationers, and every restaurant, hotel room and B&B is full. Thick fogs that don't burn off until mid-afternoon are typical in August. As locals will tell you, September and October are actually the best times to visit, and coming out for winter storm-watching is becoming increasingly popular.

The town of **Ucluelet** (pronounced "you-*clue*-let," meaning "safe harbor" in the local Nuu-chah-nulth dialect) sits on the southern end of the peninsula, on the edge of Barkley Sound. It's the first town you come to if you're driving across the island from Victoria. Back when fishing was the dominant local industry, Ucluelet was the primary town on the peninsula. When tourism began to take over, Tofino became more popular (it's the better developed). Ucluelet, gorgeously situated, has about 2,100 permanent year-round residents; in the summer, however, its population jumps tenfold. Like Tofino, it's a small coastal town with mostly newish houses and businesses, so don't expect a quaint old fishing village.

At the far northern tip of the peninsula, about a 25-minute drive from Ucluelet, **Tofino** (pop. 1,800) sits on beautiful Clayoquot Sound and is the center of the West Coast growing ecotourism business. Hikers and beachcombers come to Tofino simply for the scenery—few landscapes in the Pacific Northwest are more majestically diverse, with the Island Mountains rising to the east of island-studded Clayoquot (pronounced *clay*-oh-quot) Sound, and the thundering-surf beaches of the Pacific just to the west. The town, with its eco-tour and fishing outfitters, a growing number of restaurants, and new beachfront lodges, provides all the ingredients necessary for a memorable getaway. Meares Island, where you can walk among giant old-growth trees, is a 10-minute boat ride from Tofino.

Long Beach, part of the Pacific Rim National Park group, stretches between Tofino and Ucluelet. The beach is more than 30km (19 miles) long, broken here and there by rocky headlands and bordered by groves of cedar and Sitka spruce. The rocky, fish-rich coastline is popular with countless species of birds and marine life—bald eagles routinely nest in the vicinity, and between March and May as many as 20,000 Pacific gray whales pass close to the shore as they migrate north to their summer feeding grounds in the Arctic Circle. Tofino has also become a mecca for wet-suited surfers and surf-kayakers. In the end, though, it's the gargantuan presence of the sea, with its thundering surf and salty breath, that casts a spell over Tofino.

ESSENTIALS

GETTING THERE   By Car   To get to Vancouver Island, where the park is located, see "Getting to Victoria" in chapter 2 (p. 34). Once you are on Vancouver Island, the same scenic, easy-to-follow route takes you to Ucluelet, Long Beach, and Tofino. Considered one of the top three scenic drives in Canada, the route is paved the entire way, mostly two lanes, gets twisty towards the end, and takes about 4 to 4½ hours from Victoria. From Victoria, take Hwy.1 north along the Saanich Peninsula to Nanaimo, where you take the Island Highway (Hwy. 19) north for 52km (32 miles). Just before the town of Parksville, turn west on Hwy. 4, which leads past Cathedral Grove—worth a stop to see the old-growth inland forest—to the mid-island town of Port Alberni (about 38km/24 miles west). Hwy. 4 continues west, past giant Kennedy Lake, and reaches the Pacific Ocean just north of the coastal town of Ucluelet (103km/64 miles west of Port Alberni). Hwy. 4, also called Pacific Rim Highway, then turns north, passing through the Long Beach section of Pacific Rim National Park, to Tofino (34km/21 miles north of Ucluelet). You can arrive by ferry and rent a car on

Pacific Rim National Park Reserve

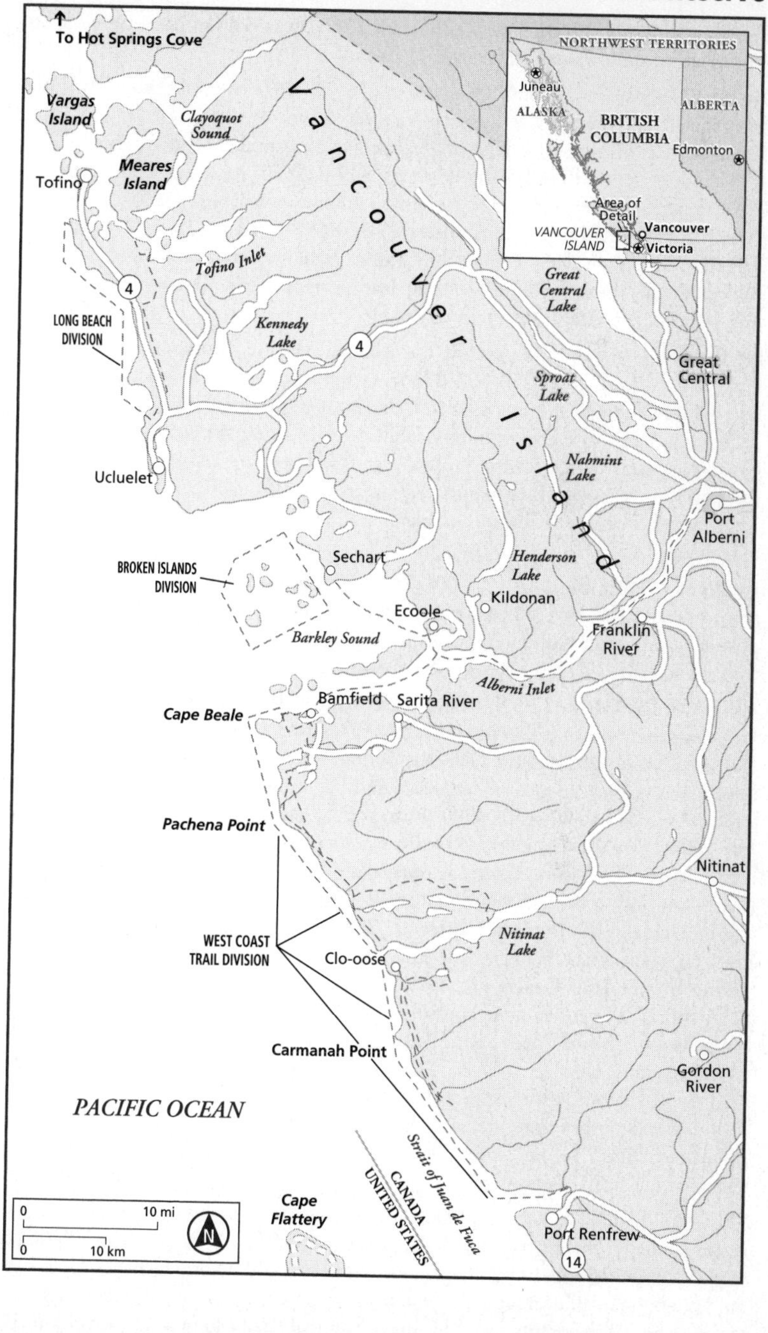
To Hot Springs Cove
Vargas Island
Clayoquot Sound
Meares Island
Tofino
Tofino Inlet
Vancouver Island
Kennedy Lake
LONG BEACH DIVISION
4
Ucluelet
Great Central Lake
Great Central
Sproat Lake
Nahmint Lake
Port Alberni
Sechart
BROKEN ISLANDS DIVISION
Henderson Lake
Kildonan
Ecoole
Franklin River
Barkley Sound
Alberni Inlet
Bamfield
Sarita River
Cape Beale
Pachena Point
Nitinat
WEST COAST TRAIL DIVISION
Nitinat Lake
Clo-oose
Carmanah Point
Gordon River
PACIFIC OCEAN
Strait of Juan de Fuca
CANADA
UNITED STATES
Cape Flattery
Port Renfrew
14
0
10 mi
0
10 km
N
NORTHWEST TERRITORIES
Juneau
ALASKA
BRITISH COLUMBIA
ALBERTA
Edmonton
Area of Detail
VANCOUVER ISLAND
Vancouver
Victoria

Vancouver Island from **Budget** (© 888/368-7368), which offers customer pick-up at all the ferry terminals in Victoria and Nanaimo.

By Bus   **Tofino Bus** (© 866/986-3466 or 250/725-2871; www.tofinobus.com) operates regular daily bus service between Victoria, Nanaimo, Port Alberni, and Tofino/Ucluelet. The 5½-hour trip, departing Victoria at 8:30am daily and arriving in Tofino at 1:55pm, costs C$50 (US$40) one-way, C$95 (US$76) round-trip. There are additional departures from Victoria at 2:45pm in the summer. More expensive but quicker (5 hr.) is **Pacific Rim 5-Star Shuttle** (© 800/697-1114 or 250/954-8702; www.prshuttle.ca), which does pickups in Victoria, Nanaimo, or Comox and then drops you off at your door in Tofino/Ucluelet. Transportation is in a luxury SUV, and costs C$75 (US$60) per hour for up to six people.

By Ferry   A 4½-hour ride aboard the **Alberni Marine Transportation** passenger ferry MV *Lady Rose* (© 250/723-8313; www.ladyrosemarine.com) takes you from Port Alberni through Alberni Inlet to Ucluelet. It makes brief stops along the way to deliver mail and packages to solitary cabin dwellers along the coast and to let off or pick up kayakers bound for the Broken Islands Group. The *Lady Rose* departs at 8am three times per week (Tues, Thurs, Sat) year-round from Alberni Harbour Quay's Angle Street. The fare to Tofino/Ucluelet is C$28 (US$22) one-way or C$55 (US$44) round-trip.

By Plane   **Sonic Blue Air** (© 800/228-6608 or 604/278-1608; www.sonicblueair. com) operates daily scheduled services between Vancouver and Seattle to Tofino airport at Long Beach Golf Course. Round-trip fares from Seattle are US$350; to and from Vancouver, C$268–C$342 (US$214–US$274).

VISITOR INFORMATION   The **Pacific Rim Visitor Centre** (© 250/725-4600; www.pacificrimvisitor.ca), at the Junction of Highway 4 and Ucluelet, serves as a general information gateway for Ucluelet, Tofino, Port Alberni, and Banfield; you can book a room, pick up area information, and buy a **day-use park pass** (C$10/US$8 per day), which you'll need if you want to park at any of Pacific Rim's official parking lots (passes can also be purchased from machines at the parking lots, using cash or credit card). The Visitor Centre is open daily May through October, 9am to 5pm (8am–8pm July and Aug); winter hours are Thursday through Sunday 10am to 4pm.

The **Ucluelet Visitor Info Centre** (© 250/726-4600; www.uclueletinfo.com), in town on Main Street, is open daily June through September from 9am to 4pm. The **Tofino Visitor Info Centre** (© 250/725-3414; www.tofinobc.org), 380 Campbell St. in Tofino, is open the same hours. For information on the park itself, stop in at the **Long Beach Unit of Pacific Rim National Park Reserve of Canada** (© 250/726-4212), north of Ucluelet (take the Wickaninnish Interpretive Centre exit from Hwy. 4). This park office, with a spectacular location above Wickaninnish Beach, is home to the Wickaninnish Interpretive Centre and a scenically stunning restaurant (see "Where to Dine," Tofino, below). The center is open daily from mid-March through mid-October from 10am to 6pm. A good all-purpose website is **www.gotofino.com**.

SPECIAL EVENTS   About 20,000 whales migrate past this section of Vancouver Island annually. During the third and last week of March, the **Pacific Rim Whale Festival** (© 250/726-4641 or 250/726-7742) is held in Tofino and Ucluelet. Crab races, the Gumboot Golf Tournament, guided whale-watching hikes, and a Native festival are just a few of the events that celebrate the annual Pacific gray whale migration. The Edge to Edge Marathon in June is a distance run between Tofino and Ucluelet through Pacific Rim National Park; contact Ucluelet Chamber of Commerce for details (© 250/726-4641). July and August bring the Pacific Rim Summer Festival (www.pacificrimsummerfestival.ca), two weeks of chamber music and multi-cultural concerts featuring national and international performers at venues in Ucluelet, Tofino, and the national park.

UCLUELET

Ucluelet boasts a beautiful location and a growing number of fine B&Bs and cabin accommodations, but it has yet to develop the same range of restaurants and activities as Tofino. The **Wild Pacific Trail** 𝕲𝕲𝕲, a spectacular and easy to walk seaside hiking path begins in Ucluelet.

WHERE TO STAY

If you're backpacking and want budget hostel accommodations or a place to pitch a tent, try **Ucluelet Hostel**, 2081 Peninsula Road, Ucluelet, B.C. V0R 3A0 (© **888/ 434-6060** or 250/726-7416; www.cnnbackpackers.com). The hostel, on its own private beach, provides free linen, use of a kitchen and lounge, Internet, and kayak and bike rentals. Rates are C$55 (US$44) for a private room, C$20 (US$16) for a single dorm bed, or C$20 (US$16) for a 2-person tent. Campers seeking a family-friendly campground close to the park can reserve a spot at **Ucluelet Campground** (© **250/ 726-4355**; www.uclueletcampground.com), located at the edge of the village. There are 125 campsites, ranging from no service to full service; prices range from C$20 to C$32 (US$16 to US$26).

Ocean's Edge B&B 𝕲   This remarkable B&B sits on its own tiny peninsula jutting out into the Pacific, with only a thicket of old-growth cedar and spruce trees sheltering it from the wind and the surf of the ocean, which roars up surge channels on either side. The rooms here are pleasant and spotless, without being opulent, with sliding glass doors that provide private entrances and look out through the trees to the ocean. The real attractions are the scenery and the wildlife. Owners Bill and Susan McIntyre installed a skylight in the kitchen so breakfasting guests could keep an eye on the pair of bald eagles and their chicks nesting in a 200-year-old Sitka spruce in the driveway. The former chief naturalist of Pacific Rim National Parks, host Bill McIntyre is a font of information and specializes in storm-watching tours and various hikes around the region (see "Activities" below and "Guided Nature Hikes," under "Tofino," later in this chapter). The new Wild Pacific Trail, skirting the spectacularly rugged coast, starts almost from the McIntyres' front door.

855 Barkley Crescent, Box 557, Ucluelet, B.C. V0R 3A0. © **250/726-7099**. Fax 250/726-7090. www.oceansedge. bc.ca. 3 units. C$130 (US$109) double. Breakfast included. MC, V. 2-night minimum on holiday weekends and high season. No children under 12 permitted.

WHERE TO DINE

Matterson Teahouse and Garden ECLECTIC/PACIFIC NORTHWEST
Located on Ucluelet's main street, this is a good spot for lunch; sandwiches, salads, and a great seafood chowder are served in the two front rooms of a small frame house. On a nice summer day, you have the option of sitting on the shady porch or the sunny back deck, listening to the surfers plan their next ride. The Teahouse also serves dinner, with seafood always on the menu along with other eclectic offerings.

1682 Peninsula Rd. © **250/725-2200**. Reservations recommended for dinner in summer. Soup and sandwiches C$5–C$8 (US$4–US$6.50), lunch and dinners C$17–C$25 (US$14–US$20). MC, V. Daily summer 7:30am–8pm; winter weekends only 7:30am–7:30pm.

ACTIVITIES

Fishing is still the big outdoor activity in Ucluelet, and salmon is still the most sought-after catch. Charter companies in Ucluelet that can take you out in search of salmon, halibut, and other fish include **Island West Resort** (© 250/726-1515; www. islandwestresort.com), **Castaway Charters** (© 250/720-7970; www.castawaycharter. com), and **Long Beach Charters** (© 877/726-2878 or 250/726-3474; www.long beachcharters.com).

The newly completed **Wild Pacific Trail** ⟲⟲⟲ skirts the rugged coastline with fabulous views of the Pacific and the Broken Islands; bald eagles nest along parts of the trail. For an easy and fabulously **scenic walk**, take the 2.7km/1.75-mile) stretch from Peninsula Road in Ucluelet to the lighthouse. On this 30- to 45-minute **hike** along a gravel-paved trail, the path winds as close as possible to the ocean's edge, passing surge channels and huge rock formations. Viewpoints and benches are found all along the trail. Check out **www.wildpacifictrail.com** for more information on walks and access points.

For **kayaking** in the Ucluelet area, contact **Majestic Ocean Kayaking** (© 800/889-7644; www.oceankayaking.com). The company runs half-day harbor trips, full-day paddles in Barkley Sound or the Broken Islands, and week-long adventures in Clayoquot Sound.

Long Beach Nature Tours ⟲ (© 250/726-7099; www.oceansedge.bc.ca), run by retired Pacific Rim Park chief naturalist Bill McIntyre, does **guided beach, rainforest, and storm walks** that explain the ecology and wildlife of the area. His walks will take you to the most interesting trails, beaches, and wildlife-viewing spots.

TOFINO

The center of the environmental protest against industrial logging—and the center of the ecotourism business ever since—**Tofino** was and to some extent remains a schizophrenic kind of town. Until very recently, about half of the town was composed of ecotourism outfitters, nature lovers, and activists, while the other half was loggers and fishermen. Conflict was common in the early years, but gradually the two sides have learned how to get along—more important than ever, now that a million visitors a year come to experience the area's natural wonders. Recently, the balance has definitely swung over in favor of the eco-preservationists, who seek to manage growth and preserve the diverse habitats in a sustainable manner.

WHERE TO STAY

Tofino sits at the tip of Long Beach peninsula. One paved road—Highway 4—runs down the spine of the peninsula through Pacific Rim National Park to Tofino. The big resort hotels are all located on their own private roads, each of which has a name and each of which connects to Highway 4 and only to Highway 4. There are big signs on Highway 4 advising drivers of the location of these private access roads, which will help you find your way to your hotel. If you're traveling with a tent, see "Campgrounds" below.

Brimar Bed and Breakfast ⟲   The location, right on Chesterman Beach, is what makes this place special. From your room, you can step out onto the sand and start exploring the wild Pacific. All three rooms have antique furnishings and lots of natural light. The upstairs Loft room features a queen bed, bathroom with claw-foot tub and separate shower, and a bay window with a seat—and a view of the ocean. The cozy (that is, smallish) Moonrise room has a queen-size sleigh bed and its own private bathroom, located across the hall. The larger, brighter Sunset room has a king bed and bathroom with shower. Pleasant breakfast and common areas look out over the ocean.

1375 Thornberg Crescent, Tofino, B.C. V0R 2Z0. ℂ 800/714-9373 or 250/725-3410. Fax 250/725-3410. www.brimarbb.com. 3 units. C$110–C$200 (US$88–US$160) double. Rates include breakfast. AE, MC, V. No pets. No children under 12. Remain on Hwy. 4 going north through Pacific Rim National Park until you pass the turnoff for the Pacific Sands Resort; take the next left on Chesterman Beach Rd.; proceed to the fork in the road and take Thornburg Crescent (the left fork) and follow it to the end. *In room:* TV, no phone.

The Inn at Tough City

Right in town, overlooking Clayoquot Sound, this is Tofino's nicest and quirkiest small inn. Built in 1996 from salvaged and recycled material, it's filled with antiques, stained glass, and bric-a-brac. Several of the spacious rooms feature soaker tubs, fireplaces, or both. Rooms at the back boast views over the Sound and Tofino harbor. Three rooms on the main floor are wheelchair accessible. The sushi restaurant on the Inn's main floor is open for dinner only.

350 Main St., P.O. Box 8, Tofino, B.C. V0R 2Z0. ℂ 877/725-2021 or 250/725-2021. Fax 250/725-2088. www.tough city.com. 8 units. C$90–C$165 (US$72–US$132). MC, V. Drive into town and you'll see it—it's impossible to miss. **Amenities:** Restaurant; laundry service; nonsmoking rooms; 3 rooms for those w/limited mobility. *In room:* TV.

Long Beach Lodge Resort 🎯🎯

Opened in 2003, this luxurious beachfront resort perched on the edge of Cox Bay, a couple miles south of Tofino, is a more relaxed alternative to the Wickaninnish Inn (see below). Built to resemble a grand West Coast–style home, the lodge has a cedar board-and-shingle exterior and a central great room (with bar and restaurant) with a massive granite fireplace and stunning ocean views—of all the oceanfront resorts, this is the one closest to the beach. The guest rooms in the lodge are luxuriously comfortable, some with fireplaces, balconies, and soaker tubs; all have marvelous beds and fine linens. Each of the 20 two-bedroom cottages, located in the forest and without ocean views, features a ground-floor master bedroom and bathroom with soaker tub and separate shower, a sitting area with gas fireplace, dining area, fully equipped kitchen, private hot tub, and a second bedroom and bathroom upstairs. The dining room serves fresh regional cuisine with a hint of Asian influence.

1441 Pacific Rim Hwy., P.O. Box 897, Tofino, B.C. V0R 2Z0. ℂ 877/844-7873 or 250/725-2442. Fax 250/725-2402. www.longbeachlodgeresort.com. 61 units. C$229–C$429 (US$183–US$393) double; C$379–C$529 (US$303–US$423) suite, C$259–C$429 (US$207–US$343) cottage. Rates include continental breakfast. AE, DC, MC, V. At the Pacific Rim Hwy. junction, turn right (north), and travel through Pacific Rim National Park; watch for lodge sign on the left after you exit the park. **Amenities:** Restaurant; lounge. *In room:* TV, dataport w/high-speed Internet access, fridge, coffeemaker, hair dryer, iron, fireplace (in some rooms), Jacuzzis (in some rooms), bathrobes, DVD/CD player.

Middle Beach Lodge 🎯🎯 *(Kids)*

This beautiful resort complex is on a headland overlooking the Pacific and features Middle Beach Lodge at the Beach, for adult guests only, and Middle Beach Lodge at the Headlands, a lodge and cabins suitable for families. The centerpiece of the first and smaller of the lodges is a large but rustically cozy common room with big windows that look out over crashing waves. Accommodations here are simple lodge rooms (26 of them) with private bathrooms and balconies but no phone or TV. The 38 rooms and suites in the second lodge have more of the standard amenities, and nearby are 19 cabins designed for 1 to 6 people, with decks, kitchenettes, and wood-burning fireplaces, some with soaker tubs or outside Jacuzzis. This is a very comfortable, unpretentious place with a good restaurant, lots of nooks and crannies, and wonderful outlooks.

P.O. Box 100, Tofino, B.C. V0R 2Z0. ℂ 866/725-2900 or 250/725-2900. Fax 250/725-2901. www.middlebeach.com. 64 units, 19 cabins. Lodge rooms C$105–C$325 (US$84–US$260) double; C$245–C$350 (US$196–US$280) cabin.

Rates include continental breakfast. AE, MC, V. **Amenities:** Exercise room; laundry service. *In room:* TV/VCR, kitchenette, coffeemaker, no phone/TV in one lodge.

The Wickaninnish Inn 𝒢𝒢𝒢   A five-star Relais & Chateau property, the Wickaninnish sets the standard for all high-end accommodations in the area; it's the most beautifully designed and built of all the Long Beach resorts, and the place to stay if you're looking for the best of everything. There are two buildings, and no matter which room you book you'll wake to a magnificent view of the untamed Pacific. The inn sits on a rocky promontory, surrounded by an old-growth spruce and cedar rainforest and the sands of Chesterman Beach. All rooms in the original cedar, stone, and glass lodge feature handcrafted furniture, richly printed textiles, and local artwork, as well as a fireplace, soaker tub, and private balcony. The Wic's new wing features deluxe rooms or suites with more space, more light, and a higher price. The Pointe Restaurant (see "Where to Dine," below) and On-the-Rocks Bar serve three meals daily with an oceanfront view. The staff can arrange whale-watching, golfing, fishing, and diving packages, and there's an on-site Aveda spa.

Osprey Lane at Chesterman Beach, P.O. Box 250, Tofino, B.C. V0R 2Z0. ⓒ 800/333-4604 or 250/725-3100. Fax 250/725-3110. www.wickinn.com. 75 units. C$220–C$780 (US$176–US$624) double. AE, DC, MC, V. Drive 5km (3 miles) south of Tofino toward Chesterman Beach to Osprey Lane. **Amenities:** Restaurant; bar; spa; concierge; in-room massage; babysitting; rooms for those w/limited mobility. *In room:* TV, dataport w/high-speed Internet, minibar, coffeemaker, hair dryer, iron.

CAMPGROUNDS

The 94 campsites on the bluff at **Green Point** 𝒢𝒢 are maintained by Pacific Rim National Park. Reservations are required in high season as the grounds are full every day in July and August, and the average wait for a site is 1 to 2 days. To make a reservation, call ⓒ **800/689-9025** or go online at www.discovercamping.ca. The cost is C$14 to C$20 (US$11–US$15) per night. You're rewarded with a magnificent ocean view, pit toilets, fire pits, pumped well water, and free firewood, but no showers or hookups. The campground is closed October through March.

Bella Pacifica Resort & Campground (ⓒ **250/725-3400;** www.bellapacifica.com), 3km (1¾ miles) south of Tofino on the Pacific Rim Highway (P.O. Box 413, Tofino, B.C. V0R 2Z0), is privately owned. March through November, it has 165 campsites from which you can walk to Mackenzie Beach or take the resort's private nature trails to Templar Beach. Flush toilets, hot showers, water, laundry, ice, fire pits, firewood, and full and partial hookups are available. Rates are C$20 to C$41 (US$16–US$33) per two-person campsite. Reserve at least a month in advance for a spot on a summer weekend.

WHERE TO DINE

Tofino is gaining a reputation for fine dining, with new restaurants opening every year, but it's also a laid-back place where you can grab a bite with the locals. If you're just looking for a cup of coffee and a snack, it's hard to beat the **Coffee Pod,** 151 4th St. (ⓒ **250/725-4246**), located at the entrance to town. Open daily from 7am to 9pm, the Pod also does an excellent breakfast and a good lunch, with main courses running C$7 to C$9 (US$5.50–US$7.25). The **Common Loaf Bakeshop,** 180 1st St. (ⓒ **250/725-3915**), open 8am to 9pm, is locally famous as a gathering place for the community. Located at the "far" end of town, the Loaf does baked goods really well and serves a healthy lunch or dinner for C$4 to C$8 (US$3.20–US$6.50). You can get herbal teas, coffee, juices, wine, and beer. And to find out what's the latest *cause célèbre*, just have a look at the Loaf's bulletin board. For the best handmade chocolates and gelato on the west coast, visit **Chocolate Tofino**, 1180 Pacific Rim Hwy. (© **250/725-2526**; www.chocolatetofino.com), about 3.25km (2 miles) south of town at the Live to Surf location next to Groovy Movies.

The Pointe Restaurant ☆☆☆ PACIFIC NORTHWEST   Perched on the water's edge at Chesterman Beach, with a 280-degree view of the roaring Pacific, The Point offers a dining experience that is pure Pacific Northwest. A very talented kitchen applies its know-how to an array of top West Coast ingredients, including Dungeness crab, spotted prawns, halibut, salmon, quail, lamb, duck, and rabbit. The Pointe is one of those places where you may as well go all out, or don't go at all. Put yourself in the hands of the chef and order the daily tasting menu: a progression of four courses priced at C$75 (US$60), C$120 (US$96) with wine pairings. The menu changes daily, but a recent offering started with seared rock scallops, went on to roast caribou loin, had a cheese course of warm Qualicum brie, and finished with a vanilla crème brulee. The wine list is drawn from the best B.C. has to offer.

The Wickaninnish Inn, Osprey Lane at Chesterman Beach. © **250/725-3100**. Reservations required. Main courses C$25–C$40 (US$20–US$32). MC, V. Daily 8am–2:30pm, 2–5pm (snacks), and 5–9:30pm.

The RainCoast Cafe ☆☆ FUSION/PACIFIC NORTHWEST   This tiny restaurant has developed a deserved reputation for some of the best—and best value—meals in town. The decor is calm and simple, the atmosphere cozy and casually romantic, the service professional. Mainstays include fresh seafood (including a delicious hot and sour seafood soup), duck, lamb, and beef courses, and Asian-style noodle dishes, such as the salmon, mussels, and stir-fried vegetables served on soba noodles and pad Thai noodles with shrimp. There are fresh daily specials and vegetarian choices as well.

120 4th St. © **250/725-2215**. Main courses C$17–C$35 (US$14–US$28). AE, MC, V. Reservations recommended. Daily 5–10pm (9pm in winter), weekend brunch (winter only) 10am–2pm.

Sobo ☆☆ ECLECTIC PACIFIC NORTHWEST   Located in Tofino Botanical Gardens, Sobo started life as a food truck and became so popular that it expanded into a sit-down restaurant. But the truck is still there, and once you taste the famous fish tacos made with wild salmon and halibut topped with fresh fruit salsa, you'll know why locals line up here every day. Sobo is short for "sophisticated bohemian," which is how chef Lisa Ahier describes her cooking: She's interested in street food and tastes from all over the world. You can enjoy your meal at picnic tables next to the truck or take it into the restaurant, where dinner is served five nights a week. The dinner menu includes seafood tapas, soups, salads, and complete meals with offerings such as pan-roasted pancetta-and-sage-crusted pork loin and anise-and-garlic-roasted chicken.

1184 Pacific Rim Highway (Tofino Botanical Gardens turnoff). © **250/725-4265**. Truck lunch and snacks C$3.75–C$6.50 (US$3–US$5.25), restaurant complete dinners C$18 (US$14). MC, V. Truck daily 11am–5pm, restaurant dinner Thurs–Mon 5–11pm. Closed last 2 weeks of Dec.

Wickaninnish Restaurant ☆ PACIFIC NORTHWEST   Located in the Wickaninnish Interpretive Centre, this restaurant is notable for the incredible ocean views from its wall of glass windows. It's a good lunch spot, with lots of fresh seafood on the menu, plus soups, salads, and sandwiches in addition to fresh daily specials and vegetarian choices. Main courses include fisherman's stew, roasted chicken, sirloin steak, and baked salmon.

In the Wickaninnish Interpretive Centre, north of Ucluelet off Hwy. 4 (take Wickaninnish Centre exit). © 250/726-7706. Main courses C$18–C$29 (US$14–US$23). MC, V. Reservations recommended in summer. Daily May–mid-Oct 11am–9pm.

WHAT TO SEE & DO

For a good, overall introduction to the unique ecology of this area, stop by the **Raincoast Interpretive Center,** 451 Main St. (© **250/725-2560;** www.tofinores.com). Open daily in summer from noon to 5pm, this new center features exhibits on local flora, fauna, and history, and often has guest speakers and slide shows relating to the area; off-season hours vary, so call ahead. Another good place to visit, as much for its stunning views over Wickaninnish Beach as for its exhibits on coastal life, is the **Wickaninnish Interpretive Center**, described under "Visitor Information," earlier.

BIRDING   The Tofino/Ucluelet area is directly in the path of the Pacific Flyway and attracts tens of thousands of birds and wildfowl, and it's also home to bald eagles. The area celebrates its rich birdlife with the annual **Flying Geese & Shorebird Festival** every April and May. During those months, large flocks of migrating birds fill the skies and estuaries along Barkley Sound and Clayoquot Sound. Avid aviophiles should contact **Just Birding** (© **250/725-8018;** www.justbirding.com), a company run by keen birders who can show you the best bird spots on shore (very early in the morning) or on the open ocean.

FIRST NATIONS TOURISM   Clayoquot Sound is the traditional home of the Nuu-chah-nulth peoples, some of whom have recently gone into the cultural and eco-tourism business. **Tla-ook Cultural Adventures** 🐾🐾 (© **250/725-2656;** www.tlaook.com) run three different tours: a daylong Cluptl-Chas **(canoeing and salmon barbecue)** Adventure (C$140/US$112) in which participants paddle ancient fishing grounds and clam beds, explore the rainforest, hear traditional stories, and feast on fresh local salmon; a 2½ hour **Sunset Paddle** (C$44/US$35), in which participants paddle and serenade the dying sun with a traditional song; and a 4-hour **Cultural Mystery Tour** (C$58/US$46), which explores the ancient rainforest on Meares Island. All tours are lead by Native guides and use traditional-style Nuu-chah-nulth canoes (often made of fiberglass because it's a lot lighter to paddle).

FISHING   Sport fishing for salmon, steelhead, rainbow trout, Dolly Varden char, halibut, cod, and snapper is excellent off the West Coast of Vancouver Island. Long Beach is also great for bottom fishing. To fish here, you need a nonresident saltwater or freshwater license. Tackle shops sell licenses, have information on current restrictions, and often carry copies of *B.C. Tidal Waters Sport Fishing Guide* and *B.C. Sport Fishing Regulations Synopsis for Non-tidal Waters.* Independent anglers should also pick up a copy of the *B.C. Fishing Directory and Atlas.*

Chinook Charters, 450 Campbell St., Tofino (© **250/725-3431;** www.chinookcharters.com), organizes fishing charters throughout the Clayoquot Sound area. Fishing starts in March and goes until December. The company supplies all the gear, a guide, and a boat. Prices start at C$95 (US$76) per hour, with a minimum of 6 hours. A full-day, 10-hour fishing trip for four people, on a 7.5m (25-ft.) boat, costs C$850 (US$680).

GOLF   Year-round golfing is available at **Long Beach Golf Course** (© **250/725-3332;** www.longbeachgolfcourse.com), one of the most challenging—and scenically situated—9-hole champion courses in British Columbia; guest rate is C$23 (US$18).

GUIDED NATURE HIKES   Owned and operated by Bill McIntyre, former chief naturalist of Pacific Rim National Park, **Long Beach Nature Tours** ⚲ (© 250/726-7099; www.oceansedge.bc.ca), offers guided beach walks, storm-watching, land-based whale-watching, and rainforest tours, customized to suit your needs. **Raincoast Interpretive Center,** 451 Main St. (© 250/725-2560; www.tofinores.com) offers guided 1-hour and longer rainforest and shore walks for a suggested donation of C$5 (US$4). This is a great way to enhance your knowledge of the local flora and fauna and the ecology of this unique rainforest.

HIKING   The 11km (6.75-mile) stretch of rocky headlands, sand, and surf along the **Long Beach Headlands Trail** is the most accessible section of the Pacific Rim National Park system, which incorporates Long Beach, the West Coast Trail, and the Broken Islands Group. No matter where you go in this area, you're bound to meet whale-watchers in spring, surfers and anglers in summer, hearty hikers during the colder months, and kayakers year-round.

In and around **Long Beach,** numerous marked trails .8km to 3.3km (.5–2 miles) long take you through the thick, temperate rainforest edging the shore. The 3.3km (2-mile) **Gold Mine Trail** near Florencia Bay still has a few artifacts from the days when a gold-mining operation flourished amid the trees. And the partially board-walked **South Beach Trail** (less than 1.6km/1mile) leads through the moss-draped rainforest onto small quiet coves like Lismer Beach and South Beach, where you can see abundant life in the rocky tidal pools.

For a truly memorable walk, take the 3.3km (2-mile) **Big Cedar Trail** ⚲⚲⚲ on Meares Island in Clayoquot Sound. You can canoe or kayak to the island, or the **Big Tree Water Taxi** (© 250/726-7827) can drop you off and pick you up for C$20 (US$16) round-trip per person. Built in 1993 to protect the old-growth temperate rainforest, the boardwalked trail is maintained by the Tla-o-qui-aht First Nations band, it has a long staircase leading up to the Hanging Garden Tree, the province's fourth-largest western red cedar.

HOT SPRINGS COVE   A rare, natural, coastal hot springs about 67km (42 miles) north of Tofino, this cove is accessible only by water and makes a wonderful day trip from Tofino. Take the **Hot Springs Water Taxi** (© 888/781-9977; www.tourismhot springs.com), sail, canoe, or kayak up Clayoquot Sound to enjoy swimming in the steaming pools and bracing waterfalls. A number of kayak outfitters and boat charters offer trips to the springs (see "Whale-Watching & Bear-Watching," below).

KAYAKING   Perhaps the quintessential Clayoquot experience, and certainly one of the most fun, is to slip into a kayak and paddle out into the calm waters of the sound. For beginners, half-day tours to Meares Island (usually with the chance to do a little hiking) are an especially good bet. For rentals, lessons, and tours, try **Pacific Kayak,** 606 Campbell St., at **Jamie's Adventure Centre** (© 250/725-3232; www.jamies.com); the **Tofino Sea Kayaking Company,** 320 Main St. (© 800/863-4664 or 250/725-4222; www.tofino-kayaking.com); or **Remote Passages Sea Kayaking,** 71 Wharf St. (© 800/666-9833 or 250/725-3330; www.remotepassages.com). Kayaking packages range from 4-hour paddles around Meares Island (from C$64/US$51 per person) to weeklong paddling and camping expeditions. Instruction by experienced guides makes even your first kayaking experience a comfortable, safe, and enjoyable one. Single kayak rental averages around C$40 (US$32) per day.

Moments Two Trips of a Lifetime

These two trips are within striking distance of Vancouver or Victoria and can't be done anywhere else on earth.

SAILING THE GREAT BEAR RAINFOREST 🐻🐻   If you look at a map of British Columbia, about halfway up the West Coast you'll see an incredibly convoluted region of mountains, fjords, bays, channels, rivers, and inlets. There are next to no roads in this area—the area is only accessible by boat. Thanks to that isolation, this is one of the last places in the world where grizzly bears are still found in large numbers, not to mention salmon, old-growth trees, killer whales, otters, and porpoises.

With 3 decades of sailing experience in the region, Tom Ellison and his wife Jen run **Ocean Light 2 Adventures** (© 604/328-5339; www.oceanlight2.bc.ca), which has a number of trips to this magic part of the world on a 21.3m (70-ft.) sailboat. Skipper Tom Ellison is extremely knowledgeable and takes great delight in exploring the waters and coastline, looking for whales, dolphins, and grizzlies. Covering territory from the midcoast to the Queen Charlotte Islands (Haida Gwaii) to the coasts of Alaska, the trips vary in duration from 4 to 10 days and in price from C$1,500 to C$3,075 (US$1,125–US$2,306). All include excellent home cooked meals and comfortable but not luxurious accommodations aboard the Ocean Light.

HORSE TREKKING THE CHILCOTIN PLATEAU 🐻🐻   The high plateau country of the B.C. interior has some of the most impressive scenery around. Soaring peaks rise above deep valleys, and mountain meadows are alive with flowers that bloom for just a few weeks in high summer. In British Columbia, one guide company is granted exclusive rights to run tours through particular sections of wilderness. The territories are typically 5,000 sq. km (1,930 sq. miles) of high-country wilderness, where you won't meet another horse team. One of the guide-outfitters closest to Vancouver is **Chilcotin Holidays Guest Ranch,** Gun Creek Road, Gold Bridge (© 250/238-2274; www.chilcotinholidays.com), in the Chilcotin Mountains north of Whistler. Their trips, running from 4 to 7 days and costing C$600 to C$900 (US$450–US$675), involve encounters with wildflowers, bighorn sheep, grizzly bears, and wolves.

STORM-WATCHING   Watching the winter storms behind big glass windows has become very popular in Tofino. For a slight twist on this, try the outdoor storm-watching tours offered by the **Long Beach Nature Tour Co.** (© 250/726-7099; www.oceansedge.bc.ca). Owner Bill McIntyre used to be chief naturalist of Pacific Rim National Park. He can explain how storms work and where to stand so you can get close without getting swept away.

SURFING   More and more people make the trip out to Tofino for one reason only: to surf. The wild Pacific coast is known as one of the best surfing destinations in Canada, and most surfers work in the tourism industry around Tofino, spending all their free time in the water. To try this exciting and exhilarating sport, call **Live to**

Surf, 1180 Pacific Rim Hwy. (© **250/725-4464;** www.livetosurf.com). Lessons start at C$55 (US$44) without gear. Live to Surf also rents boards at C$25 (US$20) and wet suits (don't even think about going without one) at C$20 (US$16). Another option is **Pacific Surf School,** 444 Campbell St. (© **888/777-9961;** www.pacific surfschool.com). There's also an all-girl surfing school, **Surf Sister** (© **877/724-7873;** www.surfsister.com).

URBAN PURSUITS   Though the outdoors is Tofino's focus, there are other less strenuous pursuits as well. Browse the excellent selection of books at **Wildside Book-sellers,** 320 Main St. (© **250/725-4222**), located in the same building as the Tofino Sea Kayaking Company. Or tour the **galleries.** There are more than 20 in the Tofino area. The Tourist Info Centre has a pamphlet with a map and contact info for all of them. Standouts include **Sandstone Jewellery and Gifts,** at the corner of Campbell and 2nd streets (© **250/725-4482**), and the **Reflecting Spirit Gallery,** 411 Campbell St. at 3rd Street. (© **250/725-2472**).

Just outside of town, the 5-hectare (12-acre) **Tofino Botanical Gardens** ๔, 1084 Pacific Rim Hwy. (© **250/725-1220;** www.tofinobotanicalgardens.com), features a landscaped walking garden with native and exotic plants from rainforests of the world, as well as outdoor sculptures and small pavilions for sitting and contemplating the surroundings. It's open daily from 9am to dusk; admission is C$10 (US$8). You can combine a trip to the gardens with a fabulous fish taco from Sobo's food truck (see "Where to Dine," above).

WHALE-WATCHING & BEAR-WATCHING   A number of outfitters conduct tours through this region, which is inhabited by gray whales, bald eagles, black bears, porpoises, orcas, seals, and sea lions. One of the oldest, **Jamie's Whaling Station,** 606 Campbell St. (© **800/667-9913** or 250/725-3919; www.jamies.com), uses a glass-bottomed 19.5m (64-ft.) power cruiser as well as a fleet of Zodiacs for tours to watch the gray whales March through October. A combined Hot Springs Cove and whale-watching trip aboard a 9.6m (31-ft.) cruiser is offered year-round. Three-hour bear-watching trips are normally scheduled around low tides when the bruins are out foraging for seafood on the mudflats. Fares (for this and other companies) generally start at around C$65 (US$52) per person; customized trips can run as high as C$200 (US$160) per person for a full day. For an interesting combination, try the Sea-to-Sky tour, a 5-hour trip with a boat ride, a hike through the rainforest, and a return to Tofino by floatplane, at the cost of C$149 (US$119) for adults.

Remote Passages, Meares Landing, 71 Wharf St. (© **800/666-9833** or 250/725-3330; www.remotepassages.com), runs 2½-hour-long whale-watching tours in Clay-oquot Sound on Zodiac boats, daily March through November. Fares are C$69 (US$55) for adults and C$55 (US$44) for children under 12. The company also conducts a 7-hour combination whale-watching and hot springs trip at C$110 (US$88) for adults and C$79 (US$63) for children under 12. Reservations are recommended.

Index

See also Accommodations and Restaurant indexes, below.

FROMMER'S® COMPLETE TRAVEL GUIDES

Alaska
Alaska Cruises & Ports of Call
American Southwest
Amsterdam
Argentina & Chile
Arizona
Atlanta
Australia
Austria
Bahamas
Barcelona
Beijing
Belgium, Holland & Luxembourg
Bermuda
Boston
Brazil
British Columbia & the Canadian
  Rockies
Brussels & Bruges
Budapest & the Best of Hungary
Calgary
California
Canada
Cancún, Cozumel & the Yucatán
Cape Cod, Nantucket & Martha's
  Vineyard
Caribbean
Caribbean Ports of Call
Carolinas & Georgia
Chicago
China
Colorado
Costa Rica
Cruises & Ports of Call
Cuba
Denmark
Denver, Boulder & Colorado Springs
Edinburgh & Glasgow
England
Europe
Europe by Rail
European Cruises & Ports of Call
Florence, Tuscany & Umbria

Florida
France
Germany
Great Britain
Greece
Greek Islands
Halifax
Hawaii
Hong Kong
Honolulu, Waikiki & Oahu
India
Ireland
Italy
Jamaica
Japan
Kauai
Las Vegas
London
Los Angeles
Madrid
Maine Coast
Maryland & Delaware
Maui
Mexico
Montana & Wyoming
Montréal & Québec City
Munich & the Bavarian Alps
Nashville & Memphis
New England
Newfoundland & Labrador
New Mexico
New Orleans
New York City
New York State
New Zealand
Northern Italy
Norway
Nova Scotia, New Brunswick &
  Prince Edward Island
Oregon
Ottawa
Paris
Peru

Philadelphia & the Amish Country
Portugal
Prague & the Best of the Czech
  Republic
Provence & the Riviera
Puerto Rico
Rome
San Antonio & Austin
San Diego
San Francisco
Santa Fe, Taos & Albuquerque
Scandinavia
Scotland
Seattle
Seville, Granada & the Best of
  Andalusia
Shanghai
Sicily
Singapore & Malaysia
South Africa
South America
South Florida
South Pacific
Southeast Asia
Spain
Sweden
Switzerland
Texas
Thailand
Tokyo
Toronto
Turkey
USA
Utah
Vancouver & Victoria
Vermont, New Hampshire & Maine
Vienna & the Danube Valley
Virgin Islands
Virginia
Walt Disney World® & Orlando
Washington, D.C.
Washington State

FROMMER'S® DOLLAR-A-DAY GUIDES

Australia from $50 a Day
California from $70 a Day
England from $75 a Day
Europe from $85 a Day
Florida from $70 a Day
Hawaii from $80 a Day

Ireland from $80 a Day
Italy from $70 a Day
London from $90 a Day
New York City from $90 a Day
Paris from $90 a Day
San Francisco from $70 a Day

Washington, D.C. from $80 a Day
Portable London from $90 a Day
Portable New York City from $90
  a Day
Portable Paris from $90 a Day

FROMMER'S® PORTABLE GUIDES

Acapulco, Ixtapa & Zihuatanejo
Amsterdam
Aruba
Australia's Great Barrier Reef
Bahamas
Berlin
Big Island of Hawaii
Boston
California Wine Country
Cancún
Cayman Islands
Charleston
Chicago
Disneyland®
Dominican Republic

Dublin
Florence
Frankfurt
Hong Kong
Las Vegas
Las Vegas for Non-Gamblers
London
Los Angeles
Los Cabos & Baja
Maui
Miami
Nantucket & Martha's Vineyard
New Orleans
New York City
Paris

Phoenix & Scottsdale
Portland
Puerto Rico
Puerto Vallarta, Manzanillo &
  Guadalajara
Rio de Janeiro
San Diego
San Francisco
Savannah
Vancouver Island
Venice
Virgin Islands
Washington, D.C.
Whistler

FROMMER'S® NATIONAL PARK GUIDES

Algonquin Provincial Park
Banff & Jasper
Family Vacations in the National
  Parks

Grand Canyon
National Parks of the American West
Rocky Mountain

Yellowstone & Grand Teton
Yosemite & Sequoia/Kings Canyon
Zion & Bryce Canyon

FROMMER'S® MEMORABLE WALKS

Chicago
London

New York
Paris

San Francisco

FROMMER'S® WITH KIDS GUIDES

Chicago
Hawaii
Las Vegas
New York City

Ottawa
San Francisco
Toronto

Vancouver
Walt Disney World® & Orlando
Washington, D.C.

SUZY GERSHMAN'S BORN TO SHOP GUIDES

Born to Shop: France
Born to Shop: Hong Kong, Shanghai
  & Beijing

Born to Shop: Italy
Born to Shop: London

Born to Shop: New York
Born to Shop: Paris

FROMMER'S® IRREVERENT GUIDES

Amsterdam
Boston
Chicago
Las Vegas
London

Los Angeles
Manhattan
New Orleans
Paris
Rome

San Francisco
Seattle & Portland
Vancouver
Walt Disney World®
Washington, D.C.

FROMMER'S® BEST-LOVED DRIVING TOURS

Austria
Britain
California
France

Germany
Ireland
Italy
New England

Northern Italy
Scotland
Spain
Tuscany & Umbria

THE UNOFFICIAL GUIDES®

Beyond Disney
California with Kids
Central Italy
Chicago
Cruises
Disneyland®
England
Florida
Florida with Kids
Inside Disney

Hawaii
Las Vegas
London
Maui
Mexico's Best Beach Resorts
Mini Las Vegas
Mini Mickey
New Orleans
New York City
Paris

San Francisco
Skiing & Snowboarding in the West
South Florida including Miami &
  the Keys
Walt Disney World®
Walt Disney World® for
  Grown-ups
Walt Disney World® with Kids
Washington, D.C.

SPECIAL-INTEREST TITLES

Athens Past & Present
Cities Ranked & Rated
Frommer's Best Day Trips from London
Frommer's Best RV & Tent Campgrounds
  in the U.S.A.
Frommer's Caribbean Hideaways
Frommer's China: The 50 Most Memorable Trips
Frommer's Exploring America by RV
Frommer's Gay & Lesbian Europe

Frommer's NYC Free & Dirt Cheap
Frommer's Road Atlas Europe
Frommer's Road Atlas France
Frommer's Road Atlas Ireland
Frommer's Wonderful Weekends from
  New York City
Retirement Places Rated
Rome Past & Present

THE NEW TRAVELOCITY GUARANTEE

EVERYTHING YOU BOOK WILL BE RIGHT, OR WE'LL WORK WITH OUR TRAVEL PARTNERS TO MAKE IT RIGHT, RIGHT AWAY.

To drive home the point, we're going to use the word "right" in every single sentence.

Let's get right to it. Right to the meat! Only Travelocity guarantees everything about your booking will be right, or we'll work with our travel partners to make it right, right away. Right on!

Here's a picture taken smack dab right in the middle of Antigua, where the guarantee also covers you.

The guarantee covers all but one of the items pictured to the right.

For example, what if the ocean view you booked actually looks out at a downright ugly parking lot? You'd be right to call – we're there for you. And no one in their right mind would be pleased to learn the rental car place has closed and left them stranded. Call Travelocity and we'll help get you back on the right track.

Now, you may be thinking, "Yeah, right, I'm so sure." That's OK; you have the right to remain skeptical. That is until we mention help is always right around the corner. Call us right off the bat, knowing that our customer service reps are there for you 24/7. Righting wrongs. Left and right.

Now if you're guessing there are some things we can't control, like the weather, well you're right. But we can help you with most things – to get all the details in righting,* visit **travelocity.com/guarantee**.

*Sorry, spelling things right is one of the few things not covered under the guarantee.

I'd give my right arm for a guarantee like this, although I'm glad I don't have to.

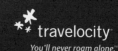

travelocity
You'll never roam alone.

IF YOU BOOK IT, IT SHOULD BE THERE.

Only Travelocity guarantees it will be, or we'll work with our travel partners to make it right, right away. So if you're missing a balcony or anything else you booked, just call us 24/7 **1-888-TRAVELOCITY**

✶✶ travelocity

You'll never roam alone